Champion Hill

Decisive Battle
for Vicksburg

Also by Timothy B. Smith

This Great Battlefield of Shiloh: History, Memory, and the Establishment of a Civil War National Military Park

Timothy B. Smith

Champion Hill

Decisive Battle
for Vicksburg

Savas Beatie

SB

ISBN 1-932714-00-6

SB

Published by
Savas Beatie LLC
521 Fifth Avenue, Suite 3400
New York, NY 10175
Phone: 610-853-9131

To my mother and father

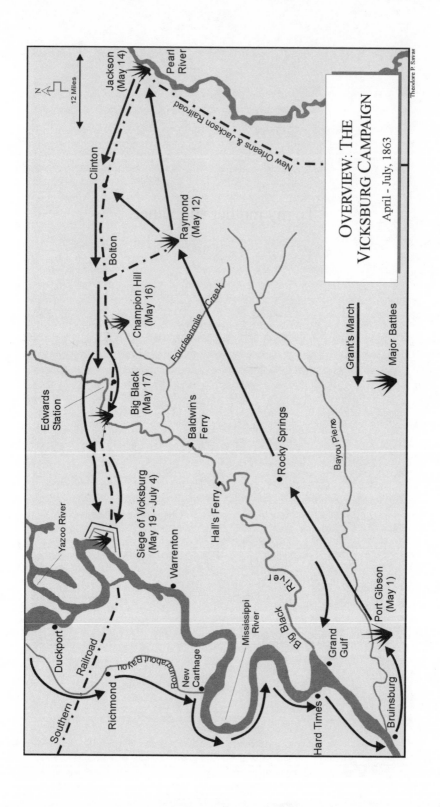

OVERVIEW: THE
VICKSBURG CAMPAIGN
April - July, 1863

Theodore P. Savas

N
12 Miles

Jackson
(May 14)

Pearl
River

New Orleans & Jackson Railroad

Clinton

Bolton

Raymond
(May 12)

Champion Hill
(May 16)

Fourteenmile Creek

Edwards
Station

Big Black
(May 17)

Baldwin's
Ferry

Rocky Springs

Bayou Pierre

Yazoo River

Siege of Vicksburg
(May 19 - July 4)

Warrenton

Hall's Ferry

Big Black River

Port Gibson
(May 1)

Grant's March

Major Battles

Southern Railroad

Duckport

Richmond

Roundabout Bayou

New Carthage

Mississippi River

Grand Gulf

Hard Times

Bruinsburg

Contents

Contents (continued)

Maps and Photographs

Maps and photographs are located throughout for the convenience of the reader. A gallery of modern photographs begins on page 462.

Foreword

ON MAY 16, 1863, JOHN A. LEAVY, A CONFEDERATE SURGEON IN THE Army of Vicksburg, took pen in hand to write in the pages of his diary critical observations of Lt. Gen. John C. Pemberton and the battle of Champion Hill. "To-day proved to the nation the value of a general," he began. "Pemberton is either a traitor, or the most incompetent officer in the Confederacy. Indecision, Indecision, Indecision." He lamented, "We have been badly defeated where we might have given the enemy a severe repulse. We have been defeated in detail, and have lost, O God! how many brave and gallant soldiers." Leavy's sentiments were echoed by hundreds of soldiers clad in butternut and gray who on that day and into the next streamed toward the Confederate Gibraltar on the Mississippi River cursing their commanding general stating, "It's all Pem's fault."

News of Confederate defeat spread as wildfire throughout the city. Mrs. Emma Balfour, a Vicksburg socialite, wrote with trembling hand, "My pen almost refuses to tell of our terrible disaster of yesterday. . . . <u>We are defeated</u>—our army in confusion and the carnage, awful! Whole batteries and brigades taken prisoners—awful! Awful!"

Details of the engagement at Champion Hill were slowly pieced together by the shocked citizenry of Vicksburg. To those who listened to the woeful details of battle, one fact became apparent. The incisive Mrs. Balfour, sensitive of the discontentment with General Pemberton being freely expressed by soldiers and officers alike, recorded the essence of failure with these words: "I knew from all I saw and heard that it was want of confidence in the General commanding that was the cause of our disaster." Late that night, overcome by emotion, she confided her fears to the pages of her diary as she wrote, "What is to become of all the living things in this place . . . shut up as in a trap . . . God only knows." Mrs. Balfour's perception of affairs proved both accurate and ominous, for less than two months later, the Stars and Bars atop the courthouse in Vicksburg was replaced by the Stars and Stripes.

The momentous events that transpired in Mississippi in the late spring and early summer of 1863 were largely ignored by the Northern press. Overshadowed by the bloodier, but less significant actions in the Eastern Theater at Chancellorsville and Gettysburg, the campaign for control of the Mississippi River failed to gain the national attention merited by such a large scale and complex operation. A century would pass before British military historian J. F. C. Fuller, in writing of the Vicksburg campaign, declared, "The drums of Champion's Hill sounded the doom of Richmond."

Despite General Fuller's observation, only a few stalwart historians, most notable of whom are Edwin C. Bearss (author of the monumental three-volume work *The Vicksburg Campaign*) and Warren Grabau (whose work *Ninety-eight Days: A Geographer's View of the Vicksburg Campaign* stands as the most analytical volume on the military operations that focused on Vicksburg) have ventured to analyze the impact of Champion Hill on the Vicksburg campaign and the fate of the Confederate nation. Perhaps more significant than any larger or bloodier action of the Civil War, the Battle of Champion Hill was the decisive action of the campaign for Vicksburg, led directly to the fall of the Confederate bastion on the Mississippi River and, truly, sealed the fate of Richmond. Thus the battle that raged on the heights of Champion Hill on May 16, 1863, warrants further investigation.

Tim Smith has risen to the challenge to help fill this void in the vast field of literature on the Civil War and adds a desperately needed volume to the scholarly works available on the Vicksburg campaign. With a talented pen, he has produced the first ever full-length study on the Battle of Champion Hill. Tapping on scores of previously untouched sources, the author has woven a tapestry worthy of this action, and the delightful mix of detail and human interest will thrill the general reader and intrigue the serious student of the Civil War.

This volume appears at an important point in time as attention to the battlefield is at its height from competing interests. Long undisturbed, the pastoral setting of Champion Hill is now being dotted with residential development that threatens this hallowed ground and will serve to deprive future generations of a site where events crucial to the history of this nation occurred. The level of development now threatening Champion Hill has led to its listing among the Ten Most Endangered Battlefields by the Civil War Preservation Trust and a similar listing among state-wide endangered historic sites by the Mississippi Heritage Trust.

Thankfully, that same development has ignited efforts to preserve the field of action that have thus far achieved significant results. The Conservation Fund, utilizing a generous grant from the Richard King Mellon Foundation, has secured more than 800 acres of the battlefield. This acreage has been generously given to the Mississippi Department of Archives and History, and could someday become the nucleus of a national military park. The Jackson Civil War Round Table, which expended its limited financial resources to save the Coker House (one of only two historic structures on the battlefield today), has turned the once-proud home over to the state of Mississippi. And the legislature in Jackson has appropriated sizeable funds for restoration of the Coker House and for battlefield preservation efforts statewide. Thus the preservation community is now locked in a struggle with developers, the outcome of which is of equal importance to posterity as the bloody conflict that was waged by Americans in blue and gray almost a century and a half ago.

Dr. Smith's work, which places Champion Hill within the broader and complex context of the Vicksburg campaign, serves to deepen our understanding of the significance of the battle and will enhance public awareness of our nation's rich Civil War heritage. May it also fuel preservation initiatives and help crown those efforts with success, so that Americans for generations ahead are "heart-drawn to see where and by whom great things were suffered and done for them, shall come to this deathless field, to ponder and dream."

Terrence J. Winschel
May 2004

Preface

FEW HISTORIANS DISPUTE THE PREMISE THAT THE VICKSBURG campaign was one of the most important operations of the Civil War. Ulysses S. Grant's victory opened the Mississippi River for the Union, captured an entire enemy army, propelled Grant and several of his top subordinates into national prominence, led Grant to his victories at Chattanooga and eventually east against Robert E. Lee, and devastated Southern morale. During the researching and writing phase of this book, several people asked me why I was not writing about the entire campaign instead of a detailed battle history of its largest and most important engagement. The answer is a simple one. Many more qualified historians than I have spent entire careers exploring and writing on the campaign. Chief among them are Edwin Bearss, Terrence Winschel, Warren Grabau, and Michael Ballard.

Ed Bearss served as Vicksburg's park historian for many years and thereafter as National Park Service's chief historian. Ed has probably studied the campaign more deeply and longer than anyone else, and has written extensively about it. Indeed, his crowning achievement is *The Vicksburg Campaign*, a massive three-volume work published by Morningside in 1985-1986. Terry Winschel serves as the current Vicksburg park historian. Terry has made a career of Vicksburg and has produced fine monographs on the subject, including *Triumph & Defeat: The Vicksburg Campaign* (Savas Publishing, 1999, reissued in paper in 2004), and *Vicksburg is the Key: The Struggle for the Mississippi River*, with William Shea (University of Nebraska Press, 2003). Many more fine studies await Terry's pen. Warren Grabau's *Ninety-Eight Days: A Geographer's View of the Vicksburg Campaign* (University of Tennessee Press, 2000) is a definitive geographical study of the campaign. Mike's outstanding treatment of the Confederate commander in *Pemberton: A Biography* (University Press of Mississippi, 1991), is available, and he is nearing completion of what may become the campaign's definitive single volume account. The Vicksburg campaign is in good hands, and I am not in a position to improve upon any of this work.

However, the important battles that made up this complex and important campaign have not yet found their way into print. And at the top of that list is Champion Hill. Without a thorough understanding of the marching and fighting that led the respective armies to Champion Hill, together with an appreciation of the tactical aspects of what transpired on May 16, 1863, it is impossible to fully understand the campaign itself. Champion Hill was the key to the entire operation, and as such it deserves a book of its own. My objective was to evaluate the original sources, walk the ground, and write the history of the battle. As one might expect, many of my conclusions agree with what others have written in broader studies about the Champion Hill combat; some of my interpretations and conclusions, however, differ from what others have written.

As noted above, many fine historians have written about the Vicksburg campaign and have placed it in its proper military, political, economic, and social context. Anyone searching for social, economic, or political history in this volume will, for the most part, be disappointed. I am in general agreement with the new wave of historiography that stresses factors other than purely military movements and actions, but I support them on a case-by-case basis. When there is need for such studies, they should be written. When there is a need for focused military history, that need should be filled. Fine historians such as Gordon Rhea in *Cold Harbor* and Earl Hess in *Pickett's Charge* have recently written tremendously helpful works without incorporating copious amounts of social, political, and economic history. *Champion Hill: Decisive Battle for Vicksburg* is a history of a battle that, on its own, had very little impact on social and political events. Seven sizeable battles were fought within twenty-two days. Collectively, the Vicksburg campaign's battles had a tremendous effect on the nation, but as individual combats they did not. Therefore, the individual effect of each of these battles on American society, politics, and economics cannot be weighed. But it is a simple task to select the campaign's single engagement that, more than all the others combined, was the key to the entire operation. Therefore, what you are about to read is a battle study molded out of the old school.

My first recollection of anything having to do with Champion Hill was from family lore about my great-great-great grandfather. Private James Franklin Pierce, Company D, 3rd Mississippi Infantry, Featherston's Brigade, fought in and survived the battle of Bakers Creek. The stories about his service were fascinating. I grew up and became seriously interested in Civil War history and traveled to many battlefields, but Champion Hill was not on the top of my list to visit. This had more to do with the fact that the field is largely inaccessible and unmarked than with its importance to the course of the war. During my formative years our family drove past the battlefield on Interstate 20 many times on the way to Vicksburg National Military Park. As we passed by, someone would inevitably mention Grandfather Pierce, but we never stopped to visit Mississippi's most important battlefield.

Eventually, however, when my passion for the Civil War began to nudge aside other interests, the combat at Champion Hill attracted my attention. But the idea of writing a book about the battle did not occur to me until I met one of my mentors in the history profession. Dr. David Sansing's passion for the serious study of history led me into this profession. I was a dawdling sophomore at Ole Miss when I took his course on the Old South—his last offering, as it turned out, before he retired. His lectures captivated me. I remember thinking at the time, "I want to do what he does for the rest of my life." I declared my major, took the requisite courses, and graduated two years later with a degree in

American history. My path carried me into graduate school and I received a Master's Degree in history from Ole Miss. Although Dr. Sansing had retired, the department head allowed him to oversee special topics classes for me. I wrote papers on several Civil War subjects for him and he served on my thesis committee. Something during this time must have impressed him, because he approached me about working on Champion Hill. He had contemplated writing a book about the battle, but for one reason or another had never gotten around to doing it. Because he was then actively engaged in researching and writing what would become his monumental history of the University of Mississippi, Professor Sansing asked if I would like to write the history of Champion Hill.

I jumped at the chance and began digging through manuscript material, but the demands of daily life slowed the project to a crawl for years. I transferred to Mississippi State University, earned a Ph.D., and began working for the National Park Service. In the interim I published a history of Shiloh National Military Park. Still, the Champion Hill story was never far from my mind and I continued working on the battle.

Several years ago historian Terrence Winschel and I spoke at a conference in Louisiana. He convinced me it was time to make Champion Hill a priority and *finish* it! After many years of work and manuscript revisions (many brought about by Terry's helpful prodding), I sought out a publisher. Terry recommended Theodore P. Savas, an independent publisher, editor, and all around good guy, who had published Terry's *Triumph & Defeat: The Vicksburg Campaign.* I knew Ted and had conversed with him on other issues. He expressed immediate interest in the project. The result of our collaboration is what you are now holding in your hands.

As I quickly learned, authors do not write books by themselves. Each must of necessity lean on many other people for help and encouragement along the way. Thankfully, I learned how to keep a list of all those who have helped me. It is a long list, and I cannot mention everyone, and will probably forget to mention someone who really deserves public thanks. I cannot begin to repay their kindness. Errors of judgment, fact, or analysis that ended up in this study are, of course, strictly of my own making.

David Sansing deserves special thanks for handing the topic off to a young and inexperienced historian. He has built an unmatched reputation in Mississippi, and almost everyone I spoke with knew Champion Hill was *his* project. When I explained he had passed the topic on to me, I was welcomed into the fold simply because they knew I had his backing. Without his guidance and help, this book would not have been possible.

Terry Winschel also deserves more thanks than I can provide. Edwin C. Bearss will always be "Mr. Vicksburg," but Terry is every bit as knowledgeable, friendly, and helpful. Terry has become the "new" Ed Bearss around Vicksburg, and many now mention both men in the same breath when referring to the campaign. He has been supportive throughout the entire process. He read the manuscript not once, not twice, but three times, and was gracious enough to pen the Foreword. He facilitated my research at the park and spent time with me touring the battlefield. He always made time to answer my endless questions and guide me in the right direction. Terry is one of the nicest people in the world and is absolutely a class act. His insight and help made this a much better book.

Theodore P. "Ted" Savas also deserves special mention. His interest in the book propelled me forward, and his abundant editorial skills made the book much better than it otherwise would have been. I am sure at times he wanted to kill me as he plowed through the manuscript. I am probably still alive only because I live in Tennessee and he lives in northern California. He often peppered me with questions when he saw a need for additional material in this or that place, and his keen eye caught many potentially embarrassing errors. We enjoyed many late night conversations about the ebb and flow of this confusing battle. Ted also produced the great maps that grace this book, and I truly appreciate them.

Many others deserve special mention. Several read parts or all of the manuscript and offered valuable advice. John Marszalek, Michael Ballard, Kenneth Noe, and Benjamin Cooling offered helpful comments, as did my brother Danny Smith; Ed Bearss cleared up several matters of varying import, and we are all in his debt for the years of work he put into writing his monumental history of the campaign; Ben Wynne at Florida State helped clarify the role played by the 15th Mississippi at Champion Hill; Bob Jenkins of Dalton, Georgia, pointed me toward important material on the 31st Mississippi; Jim Martin, Kevin Lindsey, and Craig Dunn all generously helped make this a better book. So did many others, too numerous to mention: you know who you are, and I thank you.

I have been privileged to spend many hours on the battlefield with numerous historians, gaining insight and familiarity with the area. In addition to Terry Winschel, I also walked the battlefield with Parker Hills and Ron Graves, both of whom are very knowledgeable about the battle.

Jim Woodrick of the Mississippi Department of Archives and History spent a day on the field with me, as did Sid Champion V, who still owns much of the land upon which the combat raged. The Champion family's assistance and encouragement has been very helpful. Sid was kind enough to show me family mementoes such as letters, photos, and even a bloodstained table from the Champion house. He and his late father were also kind enough to allow me to wander their property on many occasions. The family is understandably protective of their land and work hard to preserve it from relic hunters, many of whom do not ask permission before digging up their land. Some even sneak onto the land after permission has been denied. The elder Champion, Sid IV, once shot the head off a relic hunter's metal detector after he discovered the man trespassing on his land—which was after he had denied the fellow permission to relic hunt.

My family has been extremely supportive of my work, not just with Champion Hill but with my entire history career. My parents deserve special mention for raising me to love history and honor those who came before us, and for supporting me in my chosen field (not to mention their monetary, emotional, and parental support through all the years). My dad is my best friend and deserves special mention. A lover of history himself, he often went with me on research trips and to the battlefield. In fact, he has spent just about as much time on the Champion Hill battlefield as I have. It is for all their love and help that I dedicate this book to my parents.

My princess, Kelly, came into my life on the tail end of this effort, but she has supported my odd fascination and livelihood with history without question and supports, loves, and encourages me in everything I do.

Finally, I must thank the men who fought at Champion Hill and all the other places during our Civil War. They settled issues in our country's history that could have doomed us as a nation. Their efforts long before any of us were born secured for future generations of Americans an incredibly strong nation and a haven of freedom and democracy for the world. The soldiers of Champion Hill were some of the best the nation had to offer. It is my sincere wish that this book will serve as a memorial to those brave men of blue and gray who fought the decisive battle of the Vicksburg campaign—and perhaps the Civil War.

Timothy B. Smith
Pittsburg Landing, Tennessee

Chapter 1

Trial and Error

"The great Battle of Vicksburg has commenced."
— Confederate Soldier

VICKSBURG, MISSISSIPPI, IS DEFINED BY ITS PAST. LIKE A QUEEN surveying her realm, she sits atop tall bluffs overlooking a great bend in the Mississippi River. The land beneath and surrounding it was once called Walnut Hills, after the tall trees of the same name and beautiful rolling and lush landscape. High and mighty, the proud river city has served for centuries as a crossroads for trade and political discourse. Its colorful history also includes more than its share of bloodshed.

For all the obvious reasons, Indians utilized the strong defensive position, as did the Europeans who arrived in the area in the 16th, 17th, and 18th centuries. The flags of England, France, and Spain have all flown over Walnut Hills. The Spaniards were the first to seriously fortify the site with the erection of Fort Nogales, a foreshadowing what was to come at Vicksburg.[1]

By the late 18th century a new flag rippled over the bluffs in the stiff river breezes. The Spanish moved out and abandoned Fort Nogales, which fell into decay. The recently established United States now owned Walnut Hills. American explorers and entrepreneurs moved into the area, intent on making homes and fortunes. A large swath of land was carved out of the wilderness, designated Mississippi, and organized as a territory in 1798.[2]

The newcomers to the region included the Rev. Newet Vick and his family, who moved to the northern part of what would become Warren County in 1814. Most of the sprawling settlements had taken hold south and southeast of Walnut Hills. The northern region was as agriculturally desirable as the south, but adjacent to the Choctaw Indians and bounded on the east and north by what was called the great Indian Wilderness. Vick and others cleared land about seven miles from where Vicksburg would eventually take root. Others followed over the ensuing years, and the town of Vicksburg was born. The new town was chartered in 1825, eight years after Mississippi was admitted as the country's 20th state. The development of the steamboat and railroad connected the fledgling river town with other centers of population and trade.

By the late 1830s, Vicksburg was a bustling commercial center boasting banks, newspapers, churches, stores of all kinds, and industry. A steady influx of farmers, laborers, and merchants arrived to help turn the rich Mississippi soil surrounding Vicksburg into land capable of producing cash crops. Everyone in that part of the state, from the smallest of farmers to the largest of plantation owners, sold their crops in Vicksburg. Cotton and grain had become the lifeblood of the city.[3]

Vicksburg's position of prominence as the state's most important logistical hub was inextricably linked with the Mississippi River. Unfortunately, its connection to and dependence upon that waterway gave her a new-found importance when the United States began breaking apart in 1860. Vicksburg's leading citizens knew that if war came, control of the river would be essential to both sides. They also appreciated that Vicksburg was the key to the river's unfettered navigation. A war would be disastrous to the city and the economic prosperity enjoyed by its nearly 5,000 citizens. Pro-Union delegates attended Mississippi's secession convention on the city's behalf.[4] Vicksburg's efforts to sway other delegates notwithstanding, Mississippi left the Union on January 9, 1861. A fifth national flag fluttered over the Walnut Hills area. Vicksburg was now one of the salient points of the new Confederacy.

Other than two small foundries that cast cannon and munitions for the Confederacy, the city held little of military value. Nor was Vicksburg a major rail hub. The only line that served the city was a small though important railroad running east to the state capital at Jackson and points beyond. A ferry was required to haul supplies across the river to a railroad west of the Mississippi. These logistical lines, however, did not make Vicksburg any more of a key connection to the vast Trans-Mississippi Theater than many other points along the wide river, including Columbus, Kentucky, Memphis, Tennessee, and the Louisiana cities of Baton Rouge and New Orleans. What made Vicksburg so important was its defensibility. Sitting as it did high above the great elbow of the river on 200-foot high bluffs, the city was well positioned as a citadel and dominated the control of the Mississippi.

As soon as war began, the Confederacy erected earthen fortifications at several points along the river, including Vicksburg. The Mississippi city was roughly midway between New Orleans and Memphis, which meant the latter cities would almost certainly be targets before any major Federal offensive locked on Vicksburg as an objective.

Vicksburg also boasted a defensible river front. Powerful artillery mounted on the bluffs could shell any Union gunboat or transport on the river below with a plunging fire. Even the vaunted enemy ironclads would be susceptible from above with their wooden decks and grated skylights, unable to elevate their guns high enough to return fire. Other guns were positioned on the river bank itself. The geography of the Mississippi also aided the defenders. After running generally south and southeast for several miles, the river made a sharp turn northeast, followed by a sudden and narrowing twist almost 180 degrees to the southwest past the city. Negotiating the tight loop was tricky enough in peace time; doing so under deadly plunging cannon fire would make it doubly difficult.

The land approaches to the city were also easily defensible. There was no good way to approach Vicksburg. A river assault up the steep bluffs from the west was out of the question. Like a shield, the vast Mississippi Delta, a morass choked with streams, bayous, swamps, snakes, and vermin of all types, covered the city's northern approaches. The Delta would not fully prevent any serious large-scale movements against the city from that direction, but it would hinder them significantly. An approach from the east posed other thorny issues in addition to difficult terrain. In order to get around the Delta, an army would have to move southward from northern Mississippi and capture the state's capital at Jackson. Only then would a movement against the fortified river city be possible. Making a deep and successful penetration to Jackson, however, would be very difficult. As the capital of Mississippi and an important rail center, it was bound to be vigorously defended (though no fortifications of note had been constructed, and no sizeable garrison was posted there). Geography also favored the Southerners on this front. Several broad rivers cut across the northern and central parts of the state. These would provide the Confederates with several good defensive lines—and the invader with vexing obstructions. An invading army could count on meeting stiff resistance during any move south, and would require a long and vulnerable supply line that would siphon off thousands of troops for its defense.

The best avenue to reach Vicksburg (something not readily discernable from a map) was from the south, where rolling hills and several passable roads allowed for an advance. However, the Federals would have to figure out how to bypass the Vicksburg batteries in order to effect a crossing of the wide Mississippi River before moving deep into Confederate territory, where a single battlefield reverse could result in the loss of an entire field army. Every approach posed its own unique problems. Even if the city could be reached—and that was a big if—enormous fortifications had been thrown up around it during the fall of 1862. The Confederates had an ideal defensive position on the most important river in North America, and this was recognized by both Presidents Abraham Lincoln and Jefferson Davis. Capturing Vicksburg would be a difficult, lengthy, and costly effort under the best of circumstances.

General Winfield Scott, the commander of the Union armies at the outbreak of the war, developed an early strategy for victory that hinged on the opening of the river. His "Anaconda Plan" called for wrapping the North's military coils around the Southern Confederacy and constricting it, squeezing off supplies and choking off everything it needed to wage war. At the heart of the ambitious scheme was control of the Mississippi River, which would cut the Confederacy in half. But this could only come about if Vicksburg and her sister strongholds fell.[5]

Although most politicians and soldiers scoffed at Scott's plan, the war implemented by the Union eventually achieved much of what the hero of the Mexican War proposed. A blockade initiated at the beginning of the war, though at first ineffective, slowly but steadily made it more difficult to shuttle goods in and out of Southern ports. Land and sea operations closed these ports one by one. The initial fighting in Virginia focused on capturing Richmond while a drive down the Mississippi River governed early movements in the Western Theater. Using the Mississippi River valley and its contiguous river systems, the Federals effectively drove the Confederates from one position after another. The twin Union victories at Forts Henry and Donelson (which included the capture of Fort Heiman across the Tennessee River from Henry) flanked the stronghold at Columbus, Kentucky, which fell in early 1862. With it crumbled Gen. Albert S. Johnston's tissue-thin Southern line across the Blue Grass State. The victorious Union army, led by a little-known general named Ulysses S. Grant, moved south intent on capturing Corinth, a vital railroad crossroads in northern Mississippi just below the Tennessee line. A Southern surprise attack at Shiloh against Grant's scattered army on April 6, followed by a second day of fighting on the 7th, killed Johnston, drove away a crippled Confederate army, and sealed the fate of Corinth. The city fell the following month under a Federal force led by Maj. Gen. Henry W. Halleck, who had superceded Grant after the near-disaster at Shiloh.[6]

While these major operations were underway, smaller Federal armies took key positions on the Mississippi River. New Madrid and Island No. 10 fell in March and April, respectively. Horrified Confederate authorities in Richmond read the gloomy reports pouring in from beyond the Appalachian range as Fort Pillow, Memphis, and several smaller fortifications fell in early June, outflanked by the Confederate loss of Corinth and Union naval victories along the sprawling river system.[7]

While Federal armies pushed to open the Mississippi from the north, other forces moved against the opposite end of the river. On April 24, Forts Jackson and St. Philip, two massive bastions protecting the mouths to the river below New Orleans, were unable to stop David Farragut's fleet. The next day the South's largest city and most important seaport was in Union hands. Baton Rouge, Louisiana, another important river town, fell without a fight in early May. By early August 1862, following the Battle of Baton Rouge, the Confederacy's grip on the Mississippi River had been reduced to the narrow stretch of water running from Vicksburg south to Port Hudson, Louisiana. Vicksburg was now the only real impediment to controlling the river.[8]

After taking Corinth in north Mississippi, Halleck's Federals were poised to make a move south against Vicksburg. As early as June 1862, messages concerning operations against the river city ticked off telegraphs. Instead of making a concentrated push against the river citadel, however, Halleck set his sights on lesser objectives and divided the forces under his command hither and yon. His decision killed the momentum for an immediate Union advance.[9]

Ulysses Grant believed Halleck's decision was a mistake. When Halleck was called to Washington in July so President Lincoln could tap his administrative abilities, Grant resumed command of the armies in north Mississippi and prepared to move south. Before he could advance, however, the Confederates struck again. At Iuka in September and Corinth in October, the Southerners sought to regain control of north Mississippi and even carry the war back into Tennessee and Kentucky. A Confederate victory followed by a drive north would quell any threats against Vicksburg or other important points in the Deep South.[10]

Unfortunately for the Southerners, the twin battlefield failures at Iuka and Corinth erased these dreams and the battered forces withdrew to Holly Springs, Mississippi. Unperturbed by the attacks, Grant reorganized and supplied his army and prepared to follow them. By November of 1862, Vicksburg had again become the chief target of Union efforts in the Mississippi valley.[11]

The relentless campaigns Grant and his officers launched against Vicksburg were later described by a Confederate soldier as "the storm . . . in the West." It was an apt description. The months-long tempest would eventually draw in tens of thousands of men from all points of the compass and trigger dozens of engagements large and small. The titanic effort was a necessary step in the quest for final victory. Grant realized fully what both Lincoln and Davis had seen from the beginning—that Vicksburg was the key to unlocking the river and splitting the South in two. It was not a closely-held secret. Many, even in the rank and file, grasped for some time that the fighting must inevitably focus on the river city. When Grant's target became clear, one Southern soldier wrote his relative, "the great Battle of Vicksburg has commenced." No one thought the endeavor would be easy. "It is the best fortified place I ever saw," wrote home one Confederate. Six months later Grant believed the same thing. His six different efforts encompassing millions of acres across several states had each ended in failure. The Confederates had a fortress surrounded by near-perfect defensible geography. Little wonder the city became known as the "Gibraltar of the Confederacy."[12]

Grant's first effort, undertaken in the late fall of 1862, consisted of a movement down the Mississippi Central Railroad from La Grange, Tennessee, through Holly Springs and Oxford, toward Grenada, Mississippi. It was an obvious overland approach. Grant believed a movement south to Jackson could isolate Vicksburg from the rest of the South. Between Holly Springs and Jackson, however, lay two hundred miles of country swarming with state troops, unfriendly citizens—and the main Confederate army commanded by Lt. Gen. John C. Pemberton. The Mississippi army had taken up a position along the Tallahatchie River in north Mississippi to block Grant's advance. Grant knew dislodging Pemberton and keeping his own army supplied at the same time would be a very difficult proposition.

Grant set out in several columns from La Grange, Germantown, and across The Delta. The advance covered a wide swath of the state, but Grant quickly discovered its downside: every step south required the detachment of troops to guard his ever-lengthening line of supply. Consequently, he decided to simply draw Confederate forces responsible for the defense of the Vicksburg-Jackson enclave into north Mississippi and keep them pinned there. William T. Sherman's men were sent back to Memphis, where his command would board transports and, by taking advantage of Union naval superiority on the inland waters, scoot around Pemberton's left flank, race to Vicksburg, and capture a lightly defended city. Flanking opportunities created by converging columns, coupled with a raid from Arkansas toward Grenada, levered Pemberton from his Tallahatchie River line. The Federals followed and took the university town of Oxford ten miles farther south in early December. Pemberton fell back some 25 miles to a position below the Yalobusha River just north of Grenada, where he awaited Grant's next move.[13]

Federal units cautiously followed the Southern withdrawal, triggering skirmishes at Water Valley and Coffeeville. When they reached the Yalobusha, the Federals discovered a strong line of Confederate fortifications spread out along the river protecting Grenada (where Confederate President Davis happened to be visiting during his trip to Mississippi to confer with Gen. Joseph E. Johnston). Most of Grant's army did not pass below Oxford, however, and those units that did soon withdrew. It was not Pemberton's army that directly forced

Grant's evacuation, however, but a pair of brilliantly conceived and executed cavalry raids. The first was carried out by Brig. Gen. Nathan Bedford Forrest, who struck Grant's thin supply lines in western Tennessee during the latter half of December 1862. Major General Earl Van Dorn, who had been transferred to the mounted arm following his defeat at Corinth in October, led the other raid against Grant's advance supply base at Holly Springs. Van Dorn entered the town at the head of 3,500 cavalry on December 20 and destroyed Grant's advance supply depot. With Forrest tearing up track on the Mobile & Ohio Railroad in Tennessee (which fed supplies to the Federals from Paducah, Kentucky) and his logistics base at Holly Springs smoldering, Grant reported, "Farther advance by this route is perfectly impracticable." His first attempt at Vicksburg had reached an anti-climactic finish.[14]

Grant was already mulling other options. This time he would employ naval power to outflank the Confederates. His plan was to dispossess Maj. Gen. John A. McClernand of thousands of troops he was recruiting with Lincoln's blessing in the Midwest and have William Sherman use them for the effort against Vicksburg by way of the Yazoo River and an overland attack. Though very successful in his effort to raise troops, McClernand did not move to Memphis quickly. He decided to get married instead, which allowed Sherman time to assume command of McClernand's men in Memphis while the political general was tending to his personal affairs. When he had enough soldiers and transports, Sherman left Memphis on December 20 in conjunction with Rear Adm. David D. Porter's gunboats. Counting the contingents he gathered along the way, Sherman ultimately amassed some 32,000 men. The transports entered the Yazoo River a few miles above Vicksburg on December 26 and the troops disembarked at Johnson's plantation, intent on moving up the bluffs forming the southern border of the Delta. At the southern end of the bluffs was Vicksburg. The idea was for Sherman to thrust hard and fast, occupy the high dry ground, and either capture the town directly or at least establish a foothold for attacking Vicksburg.[15]

The Confederates had been alerted to the effort. Soldiers under the command of Brig. Gen. Stephen Dill Lee (including reinforcements from Pemberton's army from northern Mississippi) poured into rifle pits and entrenchments covering the approaches to Walnut Hills. Sherman faced an important choice. With his way clearly blocked, he could withdraw without a fight and concede a bloodless defeat or attack up the steep slopes and suffer it in actuality. Unwilling to endure the psychological trouncing a trip back upriver would inflict, Sherman went over to the offensive.

Between December 27 and 29, he ordered several assaults against the Confederate infantry, which was entrenched at the base of the ridges with supporting artillery deployed at the top. Federal artillery was ineffective, as the infantry discovered to their dismay when they assaulted and found the approaches swept by Confederate guns. The flooded and muddy terrain constricted Federal assaults into small areas, against which the Confederates concentrated their fire. By the evening of December 29, Sherman realized the assaults were useless and ordered his men to fall back. The rebuff had been sharp and, at more than 1,700 casualties, bloody. Southern losses were approximately 200. The fiasco at Chickasaw Bayou ignited a firestorm of bad press for Sherman, with many Northern papers reviving the issue of his alleged insanity.[16]

To his credit Sherman did not shirk from his responsibility: "I reached Vicksburg at the time appointed, landed, assaulted, and failed. Re-embarked my command unopposed." He and his men left the Yazoo on January 2, 1863. The second of Grant's attempts at Vicksburg was over, but this time it ended in a dramatic battlefield reverse. It was time to devise another way to reach the Gibraltar of the Confederacy.[17]

During January, Grant organized his army into four corps: XIII under McClernand; XV under Sherman; XVI under Maj. Gen. Stephen Hurlbut; and XVII under Maj. Gen. James B. McPherson. His new objective was to isolate Vicksburg from the capital at Jackson—its sole rail link to the outside world. The question was how to accomplish this feat. Advancing south using railroad communications was untenable, so Grant decided to substitute the Mississippi River as his line of operations. Porter's gunboats protected the waterway from attack. Good terrain for army operations was south and east of Vicksburg, but the only way to get there was to expose his boats and transports to the powerful river batteries, an option even the audacious Grant did not favor. Beginning in early February, the general put into motion several simultaneous and unorthodox maneuvers. Whether he actually had much faith in these efforts is debatable; in all likelihood he intended to keep his army busy and its morale up and the enemy guessing as to his objectives until the winter months passed. If he was wagering any bets on his bayou operations, however, he was soon to be sorely disappointed.

Grant moved three of his corps (XIII, XV, and XVII) southward along the river. One of his early ideas to bypass the Vicksburg artillery was to utilize a small and little known pass from the Mississippi River opposite Helena, Arkansas, to the Coldwater River in the Mississippi Delta. Grant sent an engineer to look into blowing the levee across Yazoo Pass to flood the passage and allow access into the Coldwater. From there the Federals could move southward into the Tallahatchie River, which combined with the Yalobusha at Greenwood to form the Yazoo. If successful, Grant's army could steam down the Yazoo and arrive north of Vicksburg above the point where Sherman had failed in December at Chickasaw Bayou. Confederate river batteries had stopped his transports during the earlier effort, but nothing would stop the Federals if they managed to arrive from the north by this means.[18]

Engineer and Lt. Col. James Harrison Wilson cut the levee 325 miles north of Vicksburg. By February 24, Union workers had cleared Yazoo Pass of felled trees and stumps, assuring Federal access to the Coldwater. Brigadier General Leonard F. Ross led his division southward aboard transports through the narrow, winding, and complex waterways. One Union soldier described this path as "a kind of overland steamboat, mud paddle route unheard of but in the philosophy of modern warfare." When his transport left Moon Lake, another soldier simply lamented, "went into the woods again." Ross steamed south for several days but stalled before Fort Pemberton. The Confederate fortification was erected near Greenwood by Maj. Gen. William W. Loring, who had been dispatched by General Pemberton with his division to interrupt the expedition. Loring threw up the fort 90 miles north of Vicksburg on a narrow neck of land between the Tallahatchie and a bend in the Yazoo River. It was well sited and effectively blocked movement south. For days the belligerents eyed one another. Minor skirmishing between Rebel land batteries and Union gunboats sent to protect the transports did nothing to alter the balance of power. The Federals could not figure out a means of reducing the fort, which was defended almost entirely by flooded or swampy ground. Ross gave up and began withdrawing only to discover reinforcements moving toward him. Brigadier General Issac F. Quinby assumed command and the expedition tried again to capture or silence the fort, with similar results. Fort Pemberton controlled this water route. Grant's third attempt to reach Vicksburg was over.[19]

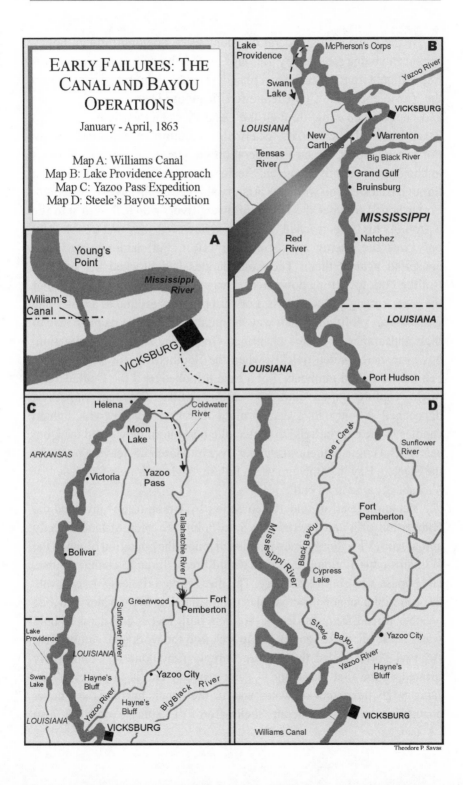

EARLY FAILURES: THE CANAL AND BAYOU OPERATIONS

January - April, 1863

Map A: Williams Canal
Map B: Lake Providence Approach
Map C: Yazoo Pass Expedition
Map D: Steele's Bayou Expedition

Theodore P. Savas

While some of his Federal divisions were slogging through boggy terrain and being rebuffed by a strong Confederate fort in the Yazoo Pass Expedition, Grant was offered a plan devised by Admiral Porter to reach the Yazoo above the Confederate fortifications. There was a dangerous and complicated route through the Delta that emerged into the Yazoo River south of Yazoo City. Sherman's infantry, in cooperation with Porter's gunboats, began the operation on March 14. Five of Porter's gunboats successfully navigated Steele's Bayou and reached Deer Creek through Black Bayou while the infantry slogged along as best they could. Porter hoped to enter the Big Sunflower River, which flowed into the Yazoo. As his boats reached Deer Creek, however, they met trouble. Not only was the enemy aware of their effort, but nature herself also conspired against them. The Confederates had blocked the route at Rolling Fork by cutting down trees. Large willows growing in the bed of the creek entangled the vessels. Forward progress ground to a halt. "The gunboats . . . plo[u]ghed their way through without other damage than to their appearance," wrote a chagrined Grant. The maddening situation, however, deteriorated quickly when the Southerners cut down timber behind the stalled gunboats. For a time it looked as if the Confederates might capture Porter and his entire flotilla. Sherman, however, dispatched infantry in a daring night march (complete with lighted candles in the rifle barrels) to protect the boats until they could back out safely. The entire pathetic affair was over by March 25, leaving no doubt the Steele's Bayou campaign was a failure. And so Grant's fourth stab at Vicksburg came to an end.[20]

Yet another effort undertaken earlier by Union troops involved the completion of a canal across De Soto Point, the neck of land directly across from Vicksburg. Grant decided to renew the operation (dubbed the Williams canal) hoping the river would break through, change course, and bypass Vicksburg's artillery. The men worked tirelessly to excavate the mile-long channel across the peninsula, but high water and bad weather forced frequent delays. Soldiers built levees and dams to hold water back, but these soon began to leak into the work site. Acting Rear Admiral Porter called the venture "simply ridiculous . . . improperly located, in the first place, and . . . not properly cut, in the second." By January 26 three feet of water was in the canal, but the river never changed course. Confederate shells from Vicksburg's defenses also hampered the effort. In late March Grant ordered the work stopped. The fifth effort to get at Vicksburg was now history.[21]

Before the end of the canal fiasco Grant looked into another canal venture, or what Sherman called "the Lake Providence scheme." The large lake was formed by an earlier change in the river's course. Several bayous meandered into and out of the lake, and some of them connected with the Black, Tensas, and Red rivers well below Vicksburg. The determined Grant intended to dig a canal large enough to allow transports into Lake Providence and send his men and vessels down river, bypassing Vicksburg's batteries. If successful, he would finally be in a position to land his army on the high (and dry) ground south of Vicksburg.[22]

It was not successful. Once again high water and difficult terrain hampered operations from the outset. After tampering with the river system, water even flowed in reverse through the canal, seriously confounding Grant's plans. The Federals finally tried to cut the Mississippi River levee to allow the canal and bayous to flood, but this produced no appreciable results. By the end of March Grant deemed this option "wholly impracticable." His sixth attempt to reach Vicksburg had failed.[23]

For the six months of November 1862 through April 1863, Grant had relentlessly tried to reach Vicksburg. Six attempts went forward, each with its own bit of ingenuity and recklessness. Pemberton and his Confederates, with no little help from Mother Nature, successfully repelled each effort. The campaign had degenerated into a stalemate, with the two forces warily watching one another across the river, battling "body bugs" and the "itch" more often than each other. Disillusioned but still determined, Grant refused to give up. His efforts eventually led him to yet another plan—one he had hoped to avoid. The new strategy involved a direct confrontation with the Confederate water batteries at Vicksburg. By late March, however, he had no other viable choice. If he was going to put his army below Vicksburg, he would have to test the effectiveness of Pemberton's river batteries.[24]

While it was clear to Grant he could not reach Vicksburg from the west, east, or north, the approach from the south also presented enormous problems. First, Grant would have to pass the big guns trained on the waterway. That meant risking Porter's ironclads and the army's transports in a bold move directly past the batteries. If Porter reached safety south of Vicksburg, Grant could march his infantry down the west side of the river and cross below the city to the eastern shore—and Mississippi. The Confederates, however, held the river south of Vicksburg at select points all the way to Port Hudson, Louisiana. If Pemberton's earlier defensive efforts were an indication of what he could expect, any crossing to the eastern side where the Confederates were present would be vigorously contested. But if Grant could somehow land by force or surprise, the Union army would be on dry land on the same side of the river as his objective, a feat he had unsuccessfully attempted for months on end. The entire plan hinged on Porter being able to slip past Vicksburg.

David Dixon Porter had been at sea since the age of ten. He served as an officer in the Mexican Navy, was held prisoner for a time by the Spanish, and had been a member of the United States Navy since 1829. His firm hand had commanded the mortar flotilla during the bombardment of Forts Jackson and St. Philip, and as acting rear admiral his boats had helped capture Arkansas Post in January 1863. Never one to shy away from a challenge—indeed he actually sought them out—Porter moved south with a dozen boats on the moonless night of April 16 in an

effort to slip past the guns. His effort was greeted with barrels of tar, cotton soaked in turpentine, and buildings on De Soto Point set ablaze to back light the river

Rear Admiral
David Dixon Porter

National Archives

so Confederate gunners on the opposite side could take aim at the brightly silhouetted gunboats. One Union veteran described the bombardment as "disagreeable music." To everyone's surprise the event itself was almost anti-climactic. The Southerners poured everything they had at the vessels, all but one of which arrived south of Vicksburg. Some boats drifted helplessly out of control, but the strong river current saved most of them as they bobbed out of range down the river. The Federal high command was elated at the success and what it meant. Six days later on April 22, an emboldened Grant sent another fleet past the batteries. This supply flotilla was composed of barges and transports loaded with provisions and ammunition. Fewer of these unarmed vessels made the successful trip past the Confederate cannon fire, which was more effective the second time around. Still, the paltry losses mattered not at all. After a few days of repairs, the gunboats and transports were back in service and ready to ferry Grant's army to the soil of Mississippi. The vaunted water batteries were vaunted no more.[25]

By the end of April, Grant and the Army of the Tennessee were poised for an operation of enormous import. If the army was turned away in yet another failed effort to reach Vicksburg, Grant's career—as well as the careers of several other high ranking officers in his army—would probably end. He had readily risked portions of his army in a wide variety of attempts to reach Vicksburg. This move was different because it gambled his entire force on the effort. A successful retreat following a battlefield loss south of Vicksburg would be nearly impossible. It was as close to an all-or-nothing gamble as any Union commander would ever make during the entire war. But the fruits of any success would be substantial. Victory would open the river all the way to the Gulf of Mexico (plans were underway elsewhere to similarly besiege Port Hudson with the Army of the Gulf under Maj. Gen. Nathaniel P. Banks), split the South in two, inflict heavy losses on what Grant hoped would be a trapped enemy field army, and expose a large swath of the South to invasion.

Never one to back down from a fight, the decisive Grant pondered these and other issues. His mind made up, he ordered his army onto the road that would eventually lead it into the heart of Confederate Mississippi.

Chapter 2

Port Gibson

"[We] found our troops falling back at all points, pressed by greatly superior numbers."
—Brig. Gen. William Baldwin, CSA

JOHN PEMBERTON SAT CONFIDENTLY IN MISSISSIPPI'S CAPITAL AT Jackson, justifiably pleased with himself. He had successfully deflected several Federal attempts to reach Vicksburg. Grant had tried every way he could think of to capture the river bastion, from the obvious overland route to a variety of bayou approaches, all to no avail. The Union general would continue trying, of that Pemberton was convinced. He was equally sure, however, he would find a way to meet and drive him back. Vicksburg was, after all, virtually impregnable.

Pemberton's self-confidence was shattered, however, when some of the worst news imaginable reached him: the Federal navy had passed the city's river defenses. He knew exactly what that meant. The powerful Union navy could threaten Port Hudson, Vicksburg, or worse yet, ferry Grant's army across the Mississippi River below the city. The threat was immediate and significant, and Pemberton knew he would have to act decisively to counter it. One of the first things he did was cancel orders for troop movements out of his department, and he begged that those already departed be returned forthwith. Now that Grant knew the navy could safely pass the enemy batteries, what would his next move be? It seemed logical he would cross the river and try to get at the city from the south, but where would he attempt to ferry his men to the east bank? Pemberton had deployed his divisions in the areas he believed most likely to be threatened, from Grand Gulf in the south to Walnut Hills in the north. The sheer size of the area now directly threatened by the enemy was almost overwhelming. There were too many points to defend. He could not possibly defend them all. How could he choose? Ironically, Pemberton's dilemma at Vicksburg paralleled much of his life.[1]

John Clifford Pemberton was born a Pennsylvanian on August 10, 1814. He learned the classical languages from tutors and, his Quaker lineage notwithstanding, entered West Point in 1833. Four years later he graduated in the middle of his class (27th of 50) with his best marks in mathematics and horsemanship. It was at the Academy that Pemberton

met and developed many longstanding relationships with Southern students, largely because he supported the idea of states rights. After receiving his commission as a brevet 2d lieutenant in the artillery, he was shipped south to fight Seminoles in Florida, went on to serve along the Canadian border,

Lieutenant General
John C. Pemberton

National Archives

and as a 1st lieutenant was posted on the tip of Virginia's peninsula at Fort Monroe. There he met and fell in love with Norfolk native Martha "Pattie" Thompson. Their plans to marry were interrupted by the Mexican War. Pemberton served as an aide-de-camp for Maj. Gen. William Worth and saw action in most of the major battles, winning two brevets and suffering two minor wounds in the process. The Pennsylvania-born veteran finally married his Virginia belle in 1848, a union that would link him forever with the Southern states.[2]

In 1858, the 44-year old captain joined Albert S. Johnston's campaign against the Mormons in Utah before spending the next three years in the Northwest. Throughout the 1850s, the looming sectional conflict highlighted the divisions plaguing Pemberton from within. As a Northerner and officer in the United States Army, he was pulled toward allegiance to the Union. His marriage into a strong Southern family and belief in the doctrine of states rights, however, bound him emotionally and philosophically to the South. The decision weighed heavily and at times seemed more than a man could bear. None of his options were palatable. The choices confronting him foreshadowed other and even more momentous decisions he would be forced to make in Mississippi.

Two of his brothers enlisted in the Union army, but Pemberton opted to cast his lot with the South. Even the offer of a colonel's commission from Maj. Gen. Winfield Scott did not change his mind. He submitted his resignation in April 1861, and began his Southern career as a lieutenant colonel organizing Virginia cavalry in Richmond, but climbed the ladder of promotion quickly. By the middle of June he was a brigadier general in the Confederate Provisional Army training artillery units in Norfolk. Before the end of the year he was in Charleston, South Carolina, serving under Gen. Robert E. Lee. It was there Pemberton gained his first experience in the field and developed strategic ideas that he would one day carry with him to Vicksburg.

On the first day of 1862, Pemberton's men fought and won a small but sharp engagement on the Coosaw River in what is known as Port Royal Ferry. The following month he was promoted to major general and when Lee was recalled to Richmond, he assumed command of the Department of South Carolina, Georgia, and Florida. His promotion raised eyebrows and tempers because his field experience was limited and his native state was Pennsylvania. Still, Pemberton worked hard preparing coastal defenses and strengthening existing fortifications.

Only one action of significance—the June 16, 1862, fighting at Secessionville—transpired within his department, but he had little to do with the repulse of the enemy there. Pemberton's outspoken personality and passive strategy for defending the coastline, coupled with his Northern lineage, alienated him from many of South Carolina's leading citizens. His short temper under stressful circumstances did not ease the situation. A months-long drumbeat for his removal eventually pressured President Davis to assign Gen. P. G. T. Beauregard in his place. The Creole and hero of First Manassas officially assumed command in South Carolina on September 24, 1862.

Pemberton promptly requested an assignment elsewhere, and took a train with his wife to Richmond. Shortly after his arrival, Special Orders No. 73 was issued: "The State of Mississippi and that part of Louisiana east of the Mississippi River is constituted a separate military district, the command of which is assigned to Maj. Gen. John C. Pemberton." While he had turned in a workman-like job under difficult conditions in the Charleston theater, Pemberton was a bureaucrat and not a field general. His forte was organization, not leading men. Before he left Richmond, the president and Secretary of War George Randolph made it plain to him that he should "consider the successful defense of [his district] as the first and chief object of your command." The secretary also ordered him to attempt the capture of New Orleans, if possible. A final sentence in an official directive dated September 30 read as follows: "Until further orders you will report directly to this [War] Department." Pemberton's biographer aptly noted that this unfortunate directive, which was never rescinded, "created a mind-set that was to cause major command problems in the Confederate western theater."[3]

Pemberton arrived in Mississippi on October 9 and discovered he was outranked by the district's two senior major generals, Earl Van Dorn and Mansfield Lovell. Richmond solved this potentially embarrassing problem by promoting Pemberton to lieutenant general to date from October 13, 1862. The Pennsylvanian's meteoric rise through the ranks from lieutenant colonel to lieutenant general in only 18 months was nothing short of astounding.[4]

The assignment to Mississippi introduced Pemberton to the city with which he would forever be associated. Regrettably, the department that boasted Vicksburg as its crown jewel was poorly organized and desperately in need of a leader with the ability to defend it against a determined enemy. The sprawling region was laced with rivers, streams, and bayous—geographic features that had thus far in the war been successfully exploited by the Union's powerful inland navy. How to defend this vast expanse of invasion avenues would have perplexed the best of field commanders. As historian Michael Ballard concluded, "All in all, there was probably not a more difficult, complex command in the entire Confederacy than the one John Pemberton assumed in October 1862."[5]

His limitations notwithstanding, Pemberton had thus far effectively parried Grant's attempts to reach Vicksburg. He had formulated (after a suggestion by a subordinate) Van Dorn's raid against Holly Springs that destroyed Grant's supply base and stalled his overland campaign through north Mississippi, and then confidently rushed reinforcements to and from threatened sites including Fort Pemberton, Steele's Bayou, and Walnut Hills. But Pemberton's situation suddenly took a turn for the worse with the Federal navy's passing of Vicksburg. The bureaucrat within him began to weigh numbers and doubt his ability to rise to the situation. He dispatched alarming messages predicting the fall of Vicksburg and recalled troops he had only recently sent to other departments. To date Pemberton had carved out a reasonably successful record in Mississippi, but Admiral Porter's passage of the batteries on the night of April 16 shook the man to his foundation. His response to the new threat would not only determine victory or defeat at Vicksburg, but also perhaps for the Confederacy as well.

The army upon which Pemberton depended for the defense of Vicksburg included roughly five divisions. The men who commanded them varied significantly in their abilities and experience, though most were reasonably skilled and capable officers.

Like Pemberton, Maj. Gen. Martin Luther Smith was a native Northerner. Born on September 9, 1819, in New York, Smith graduated from West Point near the top of the celebrated class of 1842, which included such luminaries as James Longstreet and William Rosecrans. He entered the engineers and spent most of his antebellum career in the South, where he became associated with Southern ideas and married a Southern woman. After service as an engineer during the Mexican War (during which he received a brevet for gallantry), Smith spent the remaining years before the Civil War on surveying duty in the South. When the war began, he resigned from the army resolving not to fight against the South. He entered the Confederacy as a major and served as Mansfield Lovell's chief engineer and ordnance officer, erecting fortifications at New Orleans before becoming colonel of the 21st Louisiana. A promotion to brigadier general in April 1862 was closely followed by the loss of the Crescent City and new orders for Smith to take command at Vicksburg. Once there, Smith began doing what he did best, which was mounting guns and digging entrenchments. He retained command of the city during the first serious Union effort to take it during the summer of 1862, even though his superiors Lovell and Van Dorn were both present. That June, Smith's area of authority was designated the 2nd District of the Department of South Mississippi and East Louisiana. When Pemberton arrived three months later, Smith retained command of Vicksburg. A promotion to major general arrived in November, and he earned the extra pay the following month when his troop dispositions and orders repulsed Sherman's assault at Chickasaw Bayou.

When Pemberton reorganized the army, he handed Smith command of a division, ordered him to retain control of the immediate area around Vicksburg, and placed him in charge of construction of defensive works. Obviously the New Yorker had the complete faith of his superior.[6]

When Grant's next attempt began in earnest with the running of the river batteries, Smith's division contained three brigades led by Brig. Gens. William E. Baldwin, Francis A. Shoup, and John C. Vaughn, together with a motley assortment of Mississippi State Troops brigaded under Mississippi brigadier Jeptha V. Harris. Batteries of artillery were attached to some of the brigades, and the division itself had an artillery battalion consisting of eighteen guns. In all, Smith's command numbered only about 3,500 effectives, primarily Mississippians, Louisianans, and Tennesseans.[7]

Major General John H. Forney led another of Pemberton's divisions. The native North Carolinian was born on August 12, 1829. He entered West Point and graduated in 1852, after which he held several posts on the frontier and in 1860 taught infantry tactics at West Point. The outbreak of war convinced him to resign and return home to his adopted state of Alabama, where he raised the 10th Alabama Infantry and became its colonel. He fought at First Manassas and was severely wounded later in the year at Dranesville. Forney was promoted to brigadier in March of 1862 and, though his resume did not boast of any spectacular exploits, was ordered to assume command of the Department of Alabama and West Florida (later the District of the Gulf). Still suffering from his wound and in weak health, Forney was promoted to major general on October 27, 1862. A leave of command soon followed so he could recuperate. When he finally returned to duty in March of 1863, Richmond ordered Forney to take command of a division in Pemberton's department. His brigades covered Vicksburg's northern approaches near Chickasaw Bayou and Snyder's Bluff.[8] Forney's division, made up of men mostly from Louisiana, Mississippi, and Alabama, was comprised of two brigades led by Brig. Gens. Louis Hebert and John C. Moore. Each contained several batteries. In all, the division numbered around 5,500 troops.[9]

Brigadier General John S. Bowen was Pemberton's finest field subordinate and the commander of a third division. The Georgia native was born on October 30, 1830, graduated from West Point in 1853, and remained in the army for three years. Like so many others, he resigned when promotions came slowly and duty in the peacetime army meant little more than long stretches of boredom. An engineering job in St. Louis occupied his time until war erupted. After his early capture and parole at Camp Jackson in Missouri, Bowen organized what would become the famous 1st Missouri Infantry and served as its

Brigadier General
John S. Bowen

National Archives

colonel. As a brigadier, Bowen led a brigade well at Shiloh, where he had two horses shot from beneath him and was seriously wounded. Solid service was again his trademark at Corinth. When Pemberton's army fell back overland toward Vicksburg, Bowen's Brigade was posted at Big Black River Bridge before being marched to Grand Gulf below the city on the Mississippi River. A soldier of the old school and viewed by many as a martinet, Bowen turned Grand Gulf (effectively Pemberton's far left flank) into a stronghold and gained a division in the process.[10]

Bowen's division contained two brigades led by Col. Francis M. Cockrell and Brig. Gen. Martin E. Green. Both had artillery attached to them. The Missourians and Arkansans of Bowen's Division numbered 4,500.[11]

Leading another of Pemberton's divisions was an old line officer who had risen steadily through the ranks of the pre-war army. William W. Loring was born on December 4, 1818, in North Carolina. Unlike so many other general officers in the Confederate army, Loring did not attend West Point. He secured an education in Florida and entered law and politics, serving in the state legislature for several years. In 1846 he received a commission as captain in the Regulars. His pair of brevets in Mexico cost him an arm at Chapultapec. After the war Loring was promoted to colonel of his regiment. Unwilling to fight against the South, he resigned his commission and entered Confederate service. Loring's service in Virginia's Shenandoah Valley was marred by a quarrel with Thomas "Stonewall" Jackson. Loring bypassed proper channels and communicated directly with Richmond, a personality trait that did not endear him to Old Jack, who threatened to resign over the incident. President Davis resolved the issue by promoting Loring to major general in February 1862 and sending him into western Virginia. Before the end of the year he was transferred again, this time to Pemberton's command in Mississippi. His solid service in the defense of Vicksburg included his notable performance in the erection of Fort Pemberton and stalwart defense against Grant's Yazoo Pass Expedition.[12]

When Grant crossed his army to the east bank below Vicksburg, Loring worked overtime collecting his scattered three brigades into a unified divisional command. They had been dispersed to watch various approaches to Vicksburg and chase down a raid led by Benjamin Grierson and his cavalry. Loring's infantry subordinates included Brig. Gens. Lloyd Tilghman, Abraham Buford, and Winfield S. Featherston.

Artillery units were assigned to each brigade. Volunteering mostly from Mississippi and Alabama, Loring's command numbered a respectable 7,800.[13]

Major General Carter L. Stevenson's 12,000-man division was by far the largest in Pemberton's army. Stevenson's troops were mostly veterans from the Army of Tennessee and hailed primarily from Georgia, Alabama, and Tennessee. Their commander was born in Virginia on September 21, 1817, graduated near the bottom of his West Point class in 1838 (42 out of 45), and served in the 5th Infantry on the frontier. He turned in commendable service during the Mexican War and spent his remaining pre-war years working railroad expeditions, fighting Indians, and participating in the Mormon Expedition. When civil war broke out, Stevenson resigned and entered Confederate service.

Stevenson had the unfortunate luck of missing virtually every major action during the first two years of service—and yet steadily climbed the ladder of seniority. He served briefly in the east as colonel of the 53rd Virginia before being promoted to brigadier general and transferred to the Department of East Tennessee. He was flanked out of Cumberland Gap, given command of a division, and arrived with it in Kentucky too late to participate in the bloody tactical stalemate known as Perryville. Shortly thereafter he was promoted to major general and given a division in the Army of Tennessee under Braxton Bragg. Just a few weeks before the heavy fighting at Murfreesboro, however, Stevenson was ordered with his division to Vicksburg, where he arrived one day too late to join in the repulse of Sherman's troops at Chickasaw Bayou. Because of his seniority, he assumed command north of the city. And so, when Grant crossed the river and moved northeast toward the railroad connecting Vicksburg with Jackson, Pemberton's largest division was in the hands of a thoroughly untested field commander. How he would respond to the crisis was anyone's guess.[14]

Carter Stevenson's Division contained four large brigades and several batteries of artillery. Three brigades were led by Brig. Gens. Seth Barton, Alfred Cumming, and Edward D. Tracy. The last was in the hands of Col. Alexander Reynolds.[15]

Pemberton had one other unit under his command at Vicksburg. Colonel Edward Higgins was in charge of the river defenses along Vicksburg's water front. His force was composed primarily of artillery units positioned to defend the water routes to Vicksburg. Numerous batteries sporting guns of varying type and caliber, mostly worked by men from Louisiana, Tennessee, and Mississippi, covered the river along Vicksburg's western edge. A handful of other miscellaneous units not organized as brigades also fell under Pemberton's charge. Taken as a whole, the army upon which the Pennsylvania lieutenant general depended to cover Vicksburg and its surrounding environment numbered only slightly more than 32,000 troops.[16]

Other units scattered across Mississippi and Louisiana were also under Pemberton's command, including the major conglomerations at Jackson and Port Hudson, as well as those routinely shuttled into and out of the state. Taken all together, the Confederate commander outnumbered his Federal opponent. In order for his numbers to have a bearing on the developing campaign, however, Pemberton would have to find a way to quickly concentrate them and be prepared to strike a decisive blow when the opportunity arose.

*   *   *

Pemberton was not the only general shaken by Grant's decision to cross the Mississippi River below Vicksburg. When he heard of the plan, William Sherman paid his chief a visit and wrote a long letter in an effort to persuade Grant to take a more careful route. Unlike Grant, the corps commander could not foresee how the new strategy could end in success. Marching the army south along the west side of the Mississippi was one thing. Shuttling the army to the eastern shore in the face of what would almost certainly be a vigorous defense, and then moving unsupported inland and without a safe supply line seemed a fool's errand. The sticking point for Sherman was the crossing itself. How could Grant get his entire force quickly enough across the river to take the Southerners by surprise? Any delay—and military operations almost always fall behind schedule—would leave the first troops to make the far side in great danger of being cut off and destroyed. Moreover, if the Confederates divined Grant's intentions and concentrated their forces, they would outnumber the entire army Grant intended to ferry over to their side of the river.[17]

Despite his trusted lieutenant's pessimistic outlook, Grant considered his seventh and perhaps most difficult attempt at Vicksburg a necessity. Prior expeditions had proven Vicksburg virtually impregnable from above and from naval forces along the Mississippi. The defiant city's continued existence under the Southern banner served as a daily reminder of Federal failure. Political considerations, too, crept into the decision-making process. The stinging defeats suffered during the second half of 1862 at Second Bull Run, Fredericksburg, and at Chickasaw Bayou, coupled with the bloody stalemate at Antietam and inconclusive fighting along Stones River, had left the Lincoln Administration badly in need of an unambiguous battlefield success to keep up the morale and hope of both the soldiers and citizens. Other failures large and small, including Grant's setbacks in northern Mississippi and the calls for his removal in the press only added to the strain. When encouraged by others to replace the Illinois general, Lincoln replied, "I can't spare this man, he fights. I'll try him a little longer." The president's instincts were correct—the man would fight. A decisive victory could only be gained by a general willing to engage the enemy relentlessly on his own terms. Grant fully appreciated this. A bold stroke into the heart of Mississippi from an unexpected direction, followed up with the defeat of Pemberton's field army and the capture of Vicksburg, could turn the tide of the war. Few generals had the courage to attempt such an audacious and possibly career-ending stratagem. Despite Sherman's (and others' misgivings), Grant ordered his columns to prepare for the arduous campaign.

While still flirting with canals and roundabout routes away from Vicksburg, Grant began sliding his army slowly south on March 31, 1863. The column snaked its way several miles inland following the general course of Roundaway Bayou on the way to the river town of New Carthage. From that point the Federals marched south along the west bank of the river, following its muddy twists and turns to Hard Times, opposite Confederate-held Grand Gulf. The march was not an easy one. Considerable time was expended preparing soggy roads for passage and skirmishing with curious enemy cavalry. When Porter's fleet passed Vicksburg's river defenses on April 16 and 22, Grant had the means in place to ferry his army across the river. By the end of April his leading corps was ready to cross, with another directly behind and waiting its turn. Other parts of the army, detailed on other assignments, would follow.

Grant originally intended to cross the Mississippi at Grand Gulf, twenty-five miles south of Vicksburg. John Bowen's strong Confederate fortifications and water batteries, however, ended that possibility when

Porter shelled them for hours with but little success. When he reported to Grant he could not take the stronghold, the commander continued southward in search of another crossing point.[18]

As was so often the case during the Civil War, Grant was operating without the benefit of accurate maps. Using scouts and cavalry, he learned of a suitable crossing opposite Bruinsburg, Mississippi, ten miles below Grand Gulf. An Illinois regiment there had ferried a battalion across the river and forcefully abducted a slave. The captive provided Grant with the information he needed to make a decision: a good road led from Bruinsburg inland several miles to Port Gibson. This information, Grant remembered, "determined me to land there." The news, explained one historian, was exactly what the general needed to hear, and "nothing better could be desired."[19]

Grant was well aware the Confederates had a general idea his army had marched south along the western levee and was probably seeking a place to cross. Because Pemberton had proven astute at moving troops and repelling his expeditions, Grant decided an immediate attempt to force a major landing in Mississippi was not wise. A distraction was needed to throw Pemberton off guard and call into doubt Grant's intentions. Two feints under trusted lieutenants were already underway, but it was another raid ordered by Grant that paid dividends many times over.

One operation that had been planned for some time and fortuitously assisted Grant in his effort to cross the Mississippi without major fighting took place in far away Tennessee, Alabama, and finally, Georgia. Between April 10 and May 3, Col. Abel D. Streight mounted his 2,000 infantry and took them on what has been called the "Mule March." The long raid, the brainchild of Maj. Gen. William S. Rosecrans, was designed to strike at Southern railroads. Problems with the mules and other troubles hampered the effort from the beginning. Streight's Raid, however, drew after it important Confederate cavalry units—most notably Nathan Bedford Forrest and his veteran horsemen. Forrest's earlier effort in west Tennessee (combined with Van Dorn's Holly Springs victory) had helped drive Grant out of Mississippi in December. His pursuit of Streight led him out of the range of possible assistance during one of the campaign's most critical moments.[20]

Another foray that had a more direct impact on the campaign in Mississippi took place between April 2 and 25. Major General Frederick

Steele, a division commander in Sherman's corps, headed an expedition across the river to Greenville, Mississippi, and drove inland some distance. The thrust struck at the heart of Pemberton's commissary supply area and replanted in Confederate minds the idea of a move through the Delta to Vicksburg. Carter Stevenson dispatched a sizeable force to deal with the threat, but Steele adeptly withdrew to Milliken's Bend. The raid distracted Pemberton and sidetracked Stevenson, who paid little attention to information flowing from across the river that a large Union force was moving south through Louisiana.[21]

Other activity in west central Mississippi also worked to stretch Pemberton's nerves. From April 29 through May 1, portions of Sherman corps revisited the site of their earlier thrashing on the Yazoo River. The feint centered on Snyder's Bluff, the Southern position that blocked the Yazoo to Union traffic. Grant ordered his lieutenant to "make all the show possible." Sherman never contemplated a serious assault and would hasten to join Grant when he received word of the crossing at Bruinsburg. Although Sherman's ruse did not seriously affect Confederate troop dispositions (one Southerner later wrote that Sherman "did not accomplish anything"), his feint continued the Federal game of showing the flag in as many places as possible, which served to further muddle the strategic situation as viewed through Confederate eyes.[22]

While each of these distractions worked to one degree or another, it was Col. Benjamin H. Grierson's rush through the heart of Mississippi that thoroughly befuddled Pemberton. All these efforts, however, were related. Historian Edwin C. Bearss noted the infantry and mounted operations were "part of a well orchestrated combined operation." On Grant's orders, Grierson led his 1,700 men out of La Grange, Tennessee, on April 17. They rode hard and fast, striking deep into the Mississippi countryside. Pemberton's crippled communications network and scattered forces made it nearly impossible for him to track the various Union efforts taking place at several compass points simultaneously. Indeed, he did not even learn of Grierson's thrust until three days after it began. Two days later the Southern commander wired Gen. Joseph E. Johnston, the head of the Western Theater, with a plea for cavalry support. William Loring's Division of infantry, meanwhile, was sent tramping to Meridian in a futile effort to cut off the Federals. By April 24 Grierson was in Newton, severing the vital Southern Railroad of Mississippi that connected Jackson and Vicksburg with points elsewhere in the Confederacy. With enemy units closing in from his rear, Grierson galloped southward. The effect of Streight's Raid now came into play. One major reason Grierson was able to strike deeply into Mississippi was because effective opposition was busy chasing Streight's mule-mounted Union infantry. The result of these raids led Pemberton to follow events on the east side of the river more closely than he followed events unfolding on the west side, where the real danger lurked.[23]

Grierson reached safety on May 2 in Union-held Baton Rouge, Louisiana. Contrary to contemporary newspaper claims that the raid was "a success without opposition," Confederate cavalry and infantry had doggedly trailed Grierson, but it was too little too late.[24]

While Steele and Sherman probed and Grierson ripped through Mississippi like a tornado, Grant waited patiently on the western side of the river opposite Bruinsburg. Although the strategic situation was finally tilting in his favor, he was no Union favorite. The authorities in Washington had high hopes for William Rosecrans in Tennessee, Joseph Hooker in Virginia, and Nathaniel Banks in Louisiana. Like Grant, each was beginning or would soon commence an advance of his own. Grant, however, had lost much of his political and public relations capital by attempting and failing to capture the river bastion; the result of his latest stab at Vicksburg would almost certainly determine his future in the war and beyond.

Grant's earlier triumphs in the field were balanced by reverses and near-disasters. A surprise Confederate counterattack at Fort Donelson almost sprung the trapped Confederates, though in the end the enemy surrendered to him. He was surprised and nearly routed from the field at Shiloh on April 6, 1862. He stubbornly held his ground until reinforcements came up and took the fight to the enemy the next day, driving the Southerners from Tennessee. His efforts to capture Vicksburg were nothing more than a string of failures, one after the other without respite. The shadow that hung over this mixed resume was Grant's reputation for the bottle. The press often accused him of binging on duty, though real evidence of drunkenness in the field is thin. Drunkard or not, Lincoln backed his general publicly and privately. Given the man's precarious past, it was quite an executive gamble.[25]

The general waiting on the west bank at the end of April 1863 was born in the last week of April 1822, in Point Pleasant, Ohio. He entered the United States Military Academy at West Point in 1839 and graduated four years later with little in the way of notoriety except the ability to ride a horse. He had learned the equestrian art as a boy and excelled in it at the Academy. Without the grades to enter the elite Corps of Engineers, Grant gained an infantry commission as a second lieutenant. He performed well under Zachary Taylor with the 4th Infantry in Mexico before being transferred to Winfield Scott's army at Vera Cruz. There, his duties changed to regimental quartermaster, and he once again capably discharged his responsibilities. Combat service at Molino del Rey and Chapultepec earned him two brevets to captain. His record was one of competence, but it was not exceptional. After the war he was assigned to the Pacific Northwest, where rumors of drunkenness were first raised. A sharp reprimand by Grant's superior triggered his eventual resignation in 1854.[26]

The next several years of Grant's life were both personally and financially difficult. He moved back to Missouri and tried his hand at several odd jobs, including tilling the ground, selling real estate, and working as a customs clerk. Desperate for success, Grant ran for political office. He lost. By the time the Civil War erupted, he had fallen to a clerkship in his family's small leather goods store back in Galena, Illinois.[27]

The hand of war plucked Ulysses S. Grant from obscurity. With an academy degree and military

Major General
Ulysses S. Grant

National Archives

experience—and the backing of a watchful congressman who would soon look out for his well-being—Grant was made colonel of the 21st Illinois. Thanks to Congressman Elihu Washburne, a powerful member of the Illinois Congressional delegation who would become Grant's guardian in Washington, Grant was promoted to brigadier general to date from May 15, 1861. After a brisk but inconclusive fight at Belmont, Missouri, that November, Grant set about breaking the Confederate line in West Tennessee. His combined operations against Forts Heiman, Henry, and Donelson in early 1862 resulted in the surrender of an entire Confederate army and the opening of a large swath of territory to invasion via the Tennessee and Cumberland rivers—a stunning victory that electrified the nation. The press fed on the public relations coup and the sobriquet "Unconditional Surrender" Grant (after the terms he gave the Confederate commander—unconditional surrender) stuck fast. A commission as major general of volunteers was the result.[28]

Grant's rise to prominence met resistance from both the enemy in his front and his own comrades in his rear. After the Donelson victory and promotion, his jealous superior Henry Halleck looked upon him as an unworthy rival. Certainly he did not trust him. Halleck wrote to General-in-Chief George B. McClellan in an effort to rid himself of Grant and smear his name at the same time. "His army seems to be as much demoralized by the victory of Fort Donelson as was that of the Potomac by the defeat of Bull Run," exaggerated Halleck. After mischaracterizing a trip Grant took to Nashville, which though beyond his sphere of command was shaded by Halleck as an abandonment of his responsibilities, Halleck concluded, "I am worn out and tired with this neglect and inefficiency." On March 4 Halleck removed his competitor from field command. Threatened with arrest and the undoing of his military career, Grant asked to be relieved. Only Lincoln's intervention with a demand for specifics from Halleck saved the Illinois general's career. Halleck relented; Grant resumed command of the Army of the Tennessee.[29]

The battle of Shiloh almost ended his career again. The sudden massive attack by Albert Sidney Johnston's Corinth-based Confederates hit Grant's divided army like a tidal wave on April 6. Driven back to the Tennessee River, Grant's army was saved only by desperate fighting and darkness. Demonstrating his ability to remain calm and focused on victory, Grant gathered his disorganized units, absorbed reinforcements coming onto the field, and counterattacked the following day. His focused effort drove the enemy in headlong retreat into Mississippi. Steadfast courage in the face of pending annihilation, coupled with determination to see his way through a difficult situation, offered a clear picture of Grant the soldier. He won the battle decisively, but reports of the surprise, his supposed drunkenness, and even dereliction of duty cut away at him personally and professionally. Halleck assumed command for the pending Corinth operation, leaving Grant as his second in command. The victor of Donelson and Shiloh spoke quietly again of resignation.[30]

As he had so many times throughout his life, Grant stuck it out—and his fortunes began to turn. After Halleck was called to Washington, Grant assumed command of the armies operating in northern Mississippi. He set his sights on his next objective: Vicksburg. Six failures and months of effort were the result. The goal of defeating Pemberton and taking the stronghold, however, boxed Grant into a ticklish corner while politicians and the press wondered aloud about his ability to prevail. There was no doubt about it. Grant (and Lincoln) needed a victory in Mississippi. Not only was his army floundering about in the Deep South, but so too was his reputation.[31]

*   *   *

Accompanied by his twelve-year-old son Fred (who regularly donned his father's sword and sash), Grant set out on April 30, 1863, for what he hoped would be the final operation to capture Vicksburg. Most of his infantry was concentrated at Hard Times, Louisiana. Porter's fleet was ready to transport the army across the river. The cavalry and infantry feints had all but run their course. It was time to move. Grant ordered his first units to cross to the eastern shore. Once safely over, he intended to continue advancing and fighting until Vicksburg was in Union hands. The honor of establishing the daring eastern bridgehead was given to Maj. Gen. John A. McClernand and his XIII Corps.[32]

McClernand was a unique character in an army brimming with unusual personalities. He could boast of no more than a handful of months of experience as a private before the war, and yet managed to rise to a high rank as a result of his political connections. Those same connections have obscured his abilities, for McClernand was more able

Major General
John A. McClernand

National Archives

as a combat officer than most historians give him credit. For political reasons, President Lincoln appointed the Democratic congressman as a brigadier general, hoping in return to gain the support of war Democrats from the southern counties of Illinois. McClernand proved a thorn in Grant's side, and often bypassed his commander to converse directly with the president.[33]

Born on May 30, 1812, near Hardinsburg, Kentucky, McClernand grew up in and is associated with Illinois. He educated himself, read for the bar, and saw service during the Black Hawk War. After serving as an Assemblyman, McClernand was elected to several terms in Congress. When war broke out he was one of the first politicians to join the army, though he did not resign his seat for several months. Combat came early and often for McClernand, who fought at Belmont, Fort Donelson, and Shiloh under Grant. In early January 1863, he organized and led a combined operation with Admiral Porter's gunboats up the Arkansas River against Arkansas Post, a strong Southern fort obstructing river navigation. Grant frowned upon the effort as a waste of time, but it netted some 5,000 prisoners and was generally well conducted. It also gave the Union a sorely needed battlefield victory. Now with the XIII Corps and under Grant's watchful eye (and thumb), the political general found himself that April in charge of the most important assignment in Grant's latest effort to capture Vicksburg. As it turned out, establishing a firm foothold in Mississippi proved a much easier task than anyone could have guessed.[34]

McClernand's XIII Corps of four divisions crossed the Mississippi without incident and formed a defensive line a short distance inland to hold the bridgehead while other units arrived behind it. Ready to fight their way ashore, the uncontested landing took nearly everyone by surprise. McClernand smartly reacted by probing inland. When he did not encounter the enemy in any strength, he selected a road and marched his troops east toward Port Gibson.

The divisions making up XIII Corps tramped toward their first battle of the new campaign led by Brig. Gens. Peter J. Osterhaus, Andrew J. Smith, Alvin P. Hovey, and Eugene A. Carr. Each consisted of two brigades, with artillery batteries attached to each division. The entire corps, made up of men primarily from Indiana, Ohio, Illinois, and Iowa, numbered more than 17,000 men. Its commander had Grant's confidence, but not his affection.[35]

One man who had both was the leader of XVII Corps, Maj. Gen. James Birdseye McPherson. His soldiers comprised the next segment of Grant's army to cross the river. Their commander was a young and vibrant officer bound for fame. Like McClernand, he had risen quickly to high command. Unlike the politician, however, the platform upon which he built his career was not as broad or richly connected to a network rich with political power. McPherson was born in Ohio on November 28, 1828. He worked at a store to support his family as a youngster

Major General
James B. McPherson

National Archives

when his father was declared incompetent. The owner took a liking to the young man and saw to it he received an education at Norwalk Academy in Ohio. An appointment to West Point followed. The scholastically brilliant student graduated first in his class in 1853 and entered the elite Corps of Engineers. Duty eventually sent him to both coasts, where he worked on harbor defenses and supervised construction on Alcatraz Island in San Francisco Bay. He was still a 1st lieutenant when war swept across the land.[36]

McPherson spent most of his early Civil War career as an aide to Halleck and as Grant's chief engineer at Forts Henry and Donelson, Shiloh, and during the snail-like advance upon Corinth. A brief posting during the occupation of west Tennessee overseeing railroads followed. Both Halleck and Grant recommend McPherson for promotion and in August 1862, he was commissioned brigadier general. He led a hastily formed division but arrived too late to see action in the Corinth fight that October. His pursuit of the defeated Southern army did not result in any significant fighting. Still, McPherson's star was rising, and a promotion to major general followed. When the Federal XVII Corps took form, McPherson was tapped in January 1863 to lead it. Like everyone else, he endured the frustration and setbacks experienced during the long months of failure in the Mississippi and Louisiana swamps. When Grant's order for the seventh attempt against Vicksburg arrived, McPherson ordered his corps southward through Louisiana and crossed the Mississippi River without incident behind McClernand.[37]

McPherson's corps consisted of three divisions led by Maj. Gen. John A. Logan and Brig. Gens. Marcellus M. Crocker and John McArthur. The entire corps, comprised mostly of soldiers from Illinois, Ohio, and Iowa, totaled eight brigades. Artillery was assigned to each division. McPherson's command numbered almost 16,000 men when it floated across the Mississippi. Unlike McClernand, however, the brilliant McPherson was one of Grant's favorite subordinates. He had Grant's guarded confidence, but he was also inexperienced for he had yet to lead large numbers of men in any serious fighting.[38]

The XV Corps, Grant's last to make the river crossing, was led by his favorite subordinate and friend. Grant and Sherman had been through much together and each held the other in high esteem. The two were such close friends that Grant withheld Sherman's gloomy note regarding the dangerous offensive in an effort to shield him from future criticism.[39]

William T. Sherman was born on February 20, 1820, at Lancaster, Ohio. His father died when he was nine, and the youngster ended up under the roof of Thomas Ewing, a prominent United States senator who took him under wing as his own son and gave him the name William. Ewing's influence delivered Sherman to West Point, where he graduated a respectable sixth in his 1840 class. Perhaps Grant and Sherman got along so well because their pre-war experiences were so similar. "Cump's"—short for Tecumseh—military career had been, like so many of his fellow officers, a run-of-the-mill existence. He spent the Mexican War years in California, itching for action while many of his peers experienced combat south of the Rio Grande. Fed up with army boredom, he resigned in 1853 and tried his hand at banking in San Francisco. The bank soon failed, and his subsequent foray into law in Kansas was only moderately more successful. A steady living came his way in 1859, when he accepted a position as superintendent of the Louisiana State Seminary of Learning and Military Academy (now Louisiana State University at Baton Rouge). When Louisiana left the Union, Sherman left the state, unwilling to fight for the Confederacy against the United States. He ended up in St. Louis running a street car company, but in May 1861 was

commissioned as a colonel of the newly authorized 13th U. S. Infantry.[40]

His first entry into combat came quickly at the head of a large brigade at Bull Run, where he fought his infantry well. A

Major General
William T. Sherman

National Archives

commission as brigadier general of volunteers in August (to date from May 17) made him the seventh ranking officer at that level—eleven rungs ahead of U. S. Grant. In that capacity, he was transferred to Kentucky and assumed command there when his superior fell ill. With little more than mobs of volunteers to hold the important state, and believing the war would be long and bloody, Sherman's intemperate tongue got the best of him. Stories filled the newspapers that the commander was unstable and even crazy. The rumors of insanity resulted in his replacement. He left in shame for Missouri and reported to Henry Halleck, where he assumed command of the District of Cairo. Sherman rebounded when he assumed command of a division under Grant and led it at Shiloh, where he was lightly wounded. He was surprised on the morning of April 6, but worked overtime to rectify his mistake and played a significant role in the final outcome of the battle. A promotion to major general followed, as did the Corinth campaign, during which Sherman continued at the head of his division.[41]

When Grant took over command of the Western armies in July, Sherman was in Memphis establishing its defense and suppressing guerrillas. It was there he organized the new soldiers funneled from points north by McClernand for the speedy thrust that was bloodily repulsed at Chickasaw Bayou. The failed effort brought painful new accusations of insanity. Sherman, like his old friend Grant, craved a major victory to show the press, politicians, and the public at large he could fight and knew what he was doing in the field. His chance arrived during the spring of 1863. After his feint, Sherman effected a brisk march down the Louisiana shore in preparation for a crossing to join Grant and the other two corps of the army.[42]

Sherman's XV Corps consisted of three divisions of three brigades each. Major Generals Frederick Steele and Frank Blair led two, with the third under Brig. Gen. James M. Tuttle. Each division was accompanied by artillery batteries. Men of Missouri, Iowa, Ohio, and Illinois made up the majority of this corps, which numbered just shy of 17,000 men.[43]

* * *

Grant's plan had met with only minor difficulties thus far. Damage inflicted on the army's transports during the passing of Vicksburg's batteries meant only small numbers of men could be ferried across the river at a time. This could have endangered the initial landing on April 30. The 24th and 46th Indiana regiments formed the tip of the spear and were the first regiments to reach Mississippi soil. Ferried by the gunboat *Benton*, the Hoosiers must have felt some concern for their safety, but other units eventually poured ashore without incident. Two vessels collided on the night of April 30 during the transportation process; one went to the bottom with some of the 2nd Illinois Artillery's equipment. Trouble also developed with rations and a train to haul ammunition. Grant ordered every rolling vehicle in the neighborhood confiscated to carry the much-needed projectiles and ammunition. The caravan that moved inland, remembered Grant, was "a motley train."[44]

With roughly two-thirds of his troops safely ashore on the eastern bank below Vicksburg, Grant ordered them to move inland far enough to safely protect the bridgehead and clear enough room for Sherman's corps, which everyone hoped would soon arrive. Mixed feelings pervaded the Union camps as the army prepared for its campaign into the interior of the Magnolia state. The troops knew they would meet the enemy, and many were confident of ultimate success. One private wrote home, "Remember me in your prayers for we will need help from every source in our undertaking. I think err you get this we will have been in deathly conflict with the enemy and if victorious will be camped in Vicksburg." His request for divine intervention notwithstanding, the soldier felt certain of victory. "It seems to me after all I have seen of Rebel soldiers, that we have enough men here to whip the entire south," he concluded. The sight of Confederates barely bothered him. Out of 5,000 Confederates, he reported, "I could see no two alike. . . . They were all lousy and ragged." Perhaps Grant summed up the confident but careful feelings best many years later when he observed, "When this was effected I felt a degree of relief scarcely ever equaled since. Vicksburg was not yet taken . . . nor were its defenders demoralized by any of our previous moves. I was now in enemy territory, with a vast river and the stronghold of Vicksburg between me and my base of supplies. But I was on dry ground on the same side of the river with the enemy. All the campaigns, labors, hardships, and exposures of December previous to this time that had been made and endured, were for the accomplishment of this one object."[45]

Grant's first objective was the occupation of Port Gibson, a small village ten miles inland with an important hub of roads leading to

Vicksburg, Grand Gulf, and inland to Jackson. There were also vital bridges in the area Grant would need to move north across Bayou Pierre. After landing enough men east of the river to secure their toehold, the Federals pushed forward. McClernand's corps took the lead and marched away from Bruinsburg around 4:00 p.m. on April 30. "[We] started back into the country," one of his soldiers wrote home. His adventure was only beginning.[46]

McClernand's men marched throughout the late afternoon hours of April 30. After taking paltry rations on the roadside, they received orders from the corps leader to continue advancing. Grant wanted Port Gibson occupied before the Confederates had a chance to destroy the vital bridges over Bayou Pierre or reinforce the position. Accordingly, the long column of blue infantry, some 17,000 men strong, marched into the night toward its objective. McClernand covered seven miles before minor skirmishing brought the advance to a halt. The enemy was finally making an appearance.[47]

* * *

"Six gunboats, averaging ten guns, have been bombarding my batteries terrifically," John Bowen messaged Pemberton from Grand Gulf on April 29. "They pass and repass the batteries at the closest ranges. . . . Six transports in sight, loaded with troops, but stationary." Pemberton studied the message from the general who was about to become his most trusted subordinate. What did all this mean?[48]

Pemberton had been justifiably worried when Admiral Porter's gunboats ran the river batteries on April 16 at Vicksburg. Information of simultaneous advances and cavalry raids across Mississippi only heightened his stress. Now Grand Gulf was under serious bombardment. Was Grant planning a direct assault or was it merely another feint? If the latter, where would the real blow fall? Thankfully, Bowen had held off Porter's attack throughout the nearly seven-hour barrage of 3,000 shells. For a time things looked a bit shaky for the defenders when Fort Wade was silenced by the enemy guns. In the end, however, Porter withdrew and Bowen counted his losses: three killed and 15 wounded. A grateful Pemberton thanked him profusely for his conduct and informed the division commander, "Yesterday I warmly recommended you for a major-generalcy. I shall renew it."

Bowen suspected the naval assault signaled a massive operation was in the offing somewhere south of Vicksburg. His suspicions were confirmed when Porter gave up at Grand Gulf and slipped below on the night of April 29. Reinforcements in the form of brigades under Brig. Gens. Ed Tracy and William Baldwin from the Vicksburg garrison had been sent to Grand Gulf, but they had not yet arrived. Bowen faced down a difficult decision. In order to adequately defend against a river crossing below Bayou Pierre, he would have to strip his own defenses at Grand Gulf and subject them to a river-based assault. If Grant managed to land in strength at Bruinsburg or elsewhere, Bowen would not have sufficient strength to knock him back into the river. He compromised. While waiting for reinforcements, he ordered Brig. Gen. Martin E. Green to pull together some 500 Arkansas troops and march them south to patrol the roads leading inland from Port Gibson. His brigade would follow. Bowen had to hold the enemy below Bayou Pierre or his position at Grand Gulf would be outflanked and he would be forced to withdraw.[49]

The worst fears of the Southern high command assumed concrete form early on May 1 when word reached Pemberton that a large portion of Grant's army had crossed at Bruinsburg and was moving inland. The bits and pieces of reconnaissance from the far bank about Union troops marching south through Louisiana began to make sense. The puzzle pieces were beginning to fit together. The picture they formed was a grim one. A short time later Bowen reported the enemy was "still landing," as if appalled at the magnitude of the operation. Without cavalry to probe and conduct proper reconnaissance—Pemberton had sent most of it after Grierson—it was difficult for Bowen to sift rumor from fact. The division commander decided to act on the information he had and send more units to Port Gibson. A few hours later he followed them there.[50]

By this time it was all but too late for Pemberton to salvage the quickly deteriorating situation. Hindsight is always clear, but the signs of Grant's developing campaign had been plentiful. Report after report of a southward Federal movement in Louisiana had reached him. Indeed, Grant had been moving south since the last day of March. Pemberton could have shifted more troops to the Port Gibson-Grand Gulf region, but did not do so. Instead he retained a large force north of Vicksburg, wary of Sherman's infantry, and thousands of foot soldiers and cavalrymen had been sent to intercept Benjamin Grierson's raiders. The U.S. Navy was also a threat, for it could easily move Grant's infantry quickly north toward Vicksburg. Had Pemberton retained his cavalry instead of sending it off to chase Grierson, it would have been available to Bowen to picket the riverbank and road network and provide timely and accurate reports. A vigorous delaying action near the river might have allowed Pemberton to move his divisions south, where they would have been in a position to meet Grant with equal and perhaps superior numbers. By May 1, the best chance to confront the enemy and defeat him in the field was passing. Pemberton had allowed Grant to not only land unopposed, but also march inland some seven miles before a Confederate skirmish line met Union advance pickets during the night of April 30 and the early morning hours of May 1.[51]

*   *   *

By dawn of May 1, McClernand had made good progress toward Port Gibson, despite the natural obstacles he faced. The route from the river was steep and lined with thick undergrowth, few clearings, and deep hollows and gullies, all of which played havoc with his organization and slowed his march. One Federal dreaded combat under these conditions, calling the area "an awful place to fight," while another described the ground as "the roughest country God made." McClernand's journey inland was immediately complicated by the discovery of two roads leading to Port Gibson. Without good maps it was difficult to know which to take. The area of operations was roughly triangular, with the river forming the base and the two roads to Port Gibson forming the sides. The Bruinsburg Road (the northern route below Bayou Pierre) and the Rodney Road (the southern route) began at the river several miles apart at the base of the triangle. The distance between the roads steadily narrowed until they came together west of Port Gibson. Using intelligence gleaned from local black men, McClernand decided to shift his corps a short distance to the southwest and march inland northeast toward Port Gibson along the Rodney Road.[52]

The undulating terrain and narrow roads were unpleasant for McClernand's troops, and the nighttime humidity, though not as bad as it would become in a few weeks, made the march that much more exhausting. The monotony was lessened somewhat whenever they passed one of the few plantations that dotted their route of march.

Women, curious but not overly friendly, rushed outdoors to watch the enemy tramp past. The column snaked its way forward through the night as April 30 passed and May 1 arrived. Shortly after midnight McClernand's advance pickets from Brig. Gen. Eugene Asa Carr's division, at the head of the corps column, ran into enemy skirmishers. Carr deployed his two brigades quickly, one on each side of the road, and held his position. A brisk firefight, soon joined by Federal artillery, erupted in the Mississippi darkness. Wary of developing a serious night action in difficult terrain deep in enemy country, Carr wisely decided to wait for daylight before feeding more men into the action. An uneasy silence ensued, punctuated here and there by a skirmisher's musket. The Southerners had finally been found a few miles west of Port Gibson.[53]

The Battle of Port Gibson

The skirmishers that McClernand's advance brushed up against had been waiting impatiently for several hours for the enemy to arrive. Unlike the approaching Federals, the Confederates knew the roads and terrain leading inland fairly well and had formulated a good plan to delay the invading army. The commander at Port Gibson was Brig. Gen. Martin Green, who had been sent with an advance force by Bowen to block the roads while his brigade followed. Green reached Port Gibson about daylight on April 30 and decided to form his main defensive line near Magnolia Church on the Rodney Road. The aggressive and competent veteran was a native of Virginia who moved to Missouri before the war and opened a sawmill with his family. When war broke out, he raised a company of cavalry and served with Sterling Price in the Missouri State Guard, taking part in the fight at Lexington. He assumed command of a Confederate infantry brigade when commissioned brigadier general in July 1862, and led his men well at Corinth and Hatchie Bridge. Green's dilemma at Port Gibson was how to stop or even slow down the massive Federal incursions with only about 1,000 men.[54]

Before darkness fell on the last day of April, Green established his regiments on high ground perpendicular to the Rodney Road and 200 yards east of Magnolia Church, with the 6th Mississippi on the right, the 12th Arkansas Sharpshooter Battalion in the center, and the 15th and 21st Arkansas regiments extending the line to the left (south) into the Widows

Brigadier General
Martin E. Green

National Archives

Creek bottomland. Green deployed a four-gun battery of artillery north of the roadway and a strong picket line trotted up and spread out near the church itself. Another small group of men advanced still farther and took up position near the Shaifer house. It would have been difficult to find better ground upon which to wage a delaying action. This section of Mississippi was crisscrossed with cleared flat-topped ridges and steep gullies filled with just about every form of growth imaginable, making movement off the few roads in the area extremely difficult. From the top of the ridges, however, visibility was good and the high ground provided the Southerners with a platform to watch for the approaching Federals.

Green's predicament lessened slightly with the arrival of Edward Dorr Tracy's brigade of Alabamans. They appeared about 10:00 p.m. on April 30 after a fatiguing hike of almost 40 miles in slightly more than 24 hours. The soldiers, Bowen later reported, were "completed jaded and broken down with continuous marching." The approximately 1,400 Alabama infantrymen formed the right of a very divided Confederate line of defense. Originally they faced generally west, perpendicular to the Bruinsburg Road less than one mile northwest of Green's position. When the battle between Carr and Green woke them that morning, Tracy readjusted his lines to face generally south, or parallel to the road facing Green. The 29-year-old Georgia brigadier and pre-war lawyer could boast of no military experience before the war. He fought at First Manassas with an Alabama regiment because he had moved to that state in 1855 and raised a company there in Madison County. As a lieutenant

Brigadier General
Edward D. Tracy

National Archives

colonel with the 19th Alabama, he endured the terrible field at Shiloh and had his horse shot out from under him. His calm composure during the metal maelstrom impressed his superiors and subordinates alike. A brigadier general's commission dating from August 1862 and brigade command followed. Tracy's service in Mississippi had been spent in and around Vicksburg as part of Carter Stevenson's Division. The pressing situation at Bruinsburg and Grand Gulf had resulted in his division scurrying to reinforce Bowen. The Alabama regiments under the command of this lawyer- turned-soldier were deployed from right to left as follows: 20th, 30th, 31st, and 23rd. His right flank was secured on a piece of high ground overlooking Bayou Pierre. Between the Tracy-Green wings, however, was a large gap full of thick growth and the deep and nearly impassable gully formed by Centers Creek. Direct communication was impossible except via a four-mile roundabout route. The Confederates were as ready to meet McClernand as they would ever be.[55]

* * *

McClernand was ready to restart his advance shortly after daybreak on May 1. The Federals were near the Shaifer house skirmish site and formed to move east toward Magnolia Church and Martin Green's waiting line of Confederate infantry stretched across the Rodney Road. Carr was determined his two-brigade division would knock Green back and seize the high ground around the church. Carr led the way, but this was McClernand's battle. From the Shaifer property the political general could clearly see another Confederate line of battle (Tracy's) off to the north about one mile distant blocking the Bruinsburg Road. The left flank of XIII Corps was thus vulnerable to attack. McClernand dispatched Brig. Gen. Peter Osterhaus's division along a lateral plantation road leading to the Bruinsburg Road to confront the waiting enemy and protect his advance along the Rodney Road.[56]

On the first day of May 1863, New Yorker Eugene Asa Carr was still in the "early" years of what would be a very long and distinguished military career that would not end until 1891. The 1850 West Point graduate was a soldier's soldier, a veteran of Indian frontier warfare and the pre-war 1st U.S. Cavalry. He began the war with the mounted arm but led an infantry division at Pea Ridge, suffered a trio of wounds, and was awarded the Medal of Honor for his efforts. If anyone could brush aside Green's defenders, Carr was the man for the job. With Col. William M. Stone's brigade on the left of the road, Brig. Gen. William P. Benton's brigade on the right, and supported by a dozen guns, Carr advanced about 6:30 a.m. His heavy musket and artillery fire, coupled with the steady pressure of his firm lines, knocked Green's men rearward a few hundred yards east of Magnolia Church. "Having driving the stubborn enemy at the point of the bayonet several hundred yards from one ravine to

another, and completely turned his left flank," Benton later reported, "I ordered a change of front forward . . . which was accomplished most handsomely, at a double-quick, over the most difficult ground." The entire

Brigadier General
Eugene Asa Carr

Library of Congress

movement, remembered Benton, was conducted "under a galling fire of shell and musketry." The Southerners had been knocked back on their heels, and Carr kept up the pressure.[57]

It was only about 7:00 a.m. and Green's defensive effort was on the verge of collapsing. The heavy cane and undergrowth south of the road had done surprisingly little to stop the advancing enemy. When his artillery ran low of ammunition, he dispatched a courier to gallop several miles to Tracy pleading for reinforcements. Without them, Green explained, he could not hold another fifteen minutes. Because he was not yet under attack Tracy reluctantly complied, sending a regiment and section of guns (two pieces) to aid Green. The troops were barely out of site when Federal shells from Osterhaus's artillery began raining down on Tracy's position. His own artillery answered, and for the better part of an hour a severe gunnery duel seesawed back and forth. To Tracy's dismay, the Union guns began to gain the upper hand.

Peter Osterhaus calmly surveyed the situation before him and deployed his men accordingly. The Prussian-born officer, one year shy of 40 and with a military education tagged on his resume, had participated in the revolutions that swept much of Europe in 1848. In an attempt to avoid prison or worse, he fled to the United States and settled in St. Louis, where the sizeable German population warmly welcomed him. He vigorously supported the Union cause and fought in the disaster at Wilson's Creek as a major. Thereafter he rose to colonel and led the 12th Missouri Infantry. A series of circumstances tossed him up into command of a division at Pea Ridge. His commission as brigadier general arrived in June 1862. On the morning of May 1, his division consisted of two brigades, which he deployed across the plantation road facing north toward Tracy's partially visible line of battle. Brigadier General Theophilus Garrard's men tramped off the road and formed on the west or left side, while Col. Lionel Sheldon's men took up their position on the east side of the dirt road. With a shout the lines surged forward through the heavy undergrowth and maddening tangle of ravines, which tore apart organization and swallowed hundreds of men at a time.[58]

Much of the fighting for possession of the Bruinsburg Road took place near a large bend of Bayou Pierre around a former Presbyterian church, where Osterhaus discovered he had more on his hands than he had perhaps anticipated. The Alabamans stood their ground and refused to give an inch, their skirmishers well to the front absorbing much of the first shock of the attack. The Federal division ground to a halt after only a few hundred yards, unable to push through the galling fire laid down by the lone Southern brigade. Some of Osterhaus's initial difficulty was also the result of the nearly impenetrable terrain. Negotiating the confusing concave system of ravines while maintaining something approaching unit cohesion was more than challenging. Large gaps permeated his line. Some Union regiments were so confused by the foreign environment they fired blindly into one another.[59]

Osterhaus adjusted his lines and sent forward sharpshooters to probe Tracy's line and develop weaknesses that could be exploited.

Brigadier General
Peter Osterhaus

Missouri Historical Society

The skirmishers began to pick off Confederate artillerymen and with steady pressure from the rest of the division, which moved forward in another attack, the battle erupted with renewed fury. Tracy, who was near the front at this time, met his end. Various accounts exist as to how the brigadier was killed. Artilleryman Sgt. Francis G. Obenchain was speaking with Tracy when "a ball struck him on the back of the neck passing through. He fell with great force and in falling cried, 'Oh Lord!'" Colonel Isham W. Garrott of the 20th Alabama assumed command of the brigade after Tracy was killed. Unlike Obenchain, Garrott was not present when Tracy fell.

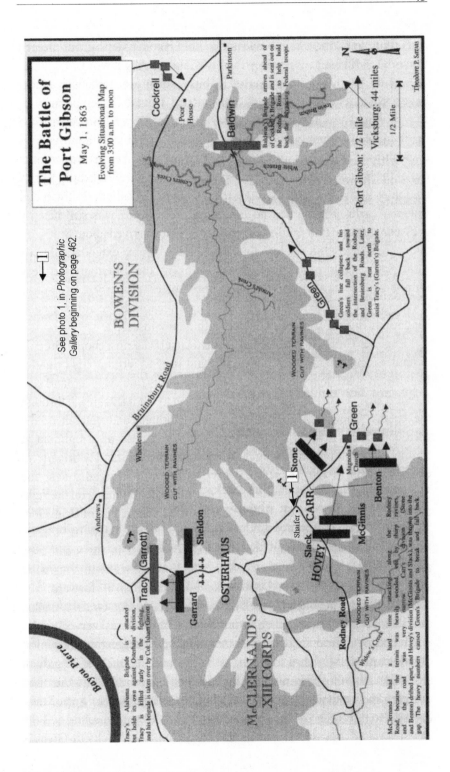

The Battle of
Port Gibson

May 1, 1863

Evolving Situational Map
from 3:00 a.m. to noon

See photo 1, in *Photographic
Gallery* beginning on page 462.

BOWEN'S
DIVISION

McCLERNAND'S
XIII CORPS

OSTERHAUS

HOVEY

CARR

Cockrell

Baldwin

Parkinson

Poor
House

Green

Stone

Shaifer

Slack

McGinnis

Benton

Sheldon

Garrard

Tracy (Garrott)

Wheeless

Andrews

Magnolia
Church

Bayou Pierre

Bruinsburg Road

Rodney Road

WOODED TERRAIN
CUT WITH RAVINES

WOODED TERRAIN
CUT WITH RAVINES

WOODED TERRAIN
CUT WITH RAVINES

Centers Creek

White Branch

Irwin Branch

Arnold's Creek

Widow's Creek

Port Gibson: 1/2 mile

Vicksburg: 44 miles

1/2 Mile

N

Theodore P. Savas

Tracy's Alabama Brigade is attacked
but holds its own against Osterhaus' division.
Tracy is killed early in the fighting,
and his brigade is taken over by Col. Isham Garrott.

Baldwin's Brigade arrives ahead of
Cockrell's Brigade and is sent out on
the Rodney Road to help hold
back the retreating Federal troops.

Green's line collapses and his
soldiers fall back toward
the intersection of the Rodney
and Bruinsburg Roads. Later,
Green is sent north to
assist Tracy's (Garrott's) Brigade.

McClernand had a hard time attacking along the
Road, because the terrain was heavily wooded, left by sharp
and the road was very narrow Carr's division
and Benton) drifted apart, and Hovey's division (McGinnis and Slack) was the
gap. The heavy numbers caused Green's Brigade to break and fall back.

the Rodney ravines.
(Stone the into
and back.

According to Garrott, "our brave and gallant commander . . . was pierced through the breast and instantly died without uttering a word."[60]

While Tracy's Alabamans were busy stifling Osterhaus's attack, Green's Confederates on the Rodney Road front had, temporarily at least, stymied McClernand's two-brigade thrust. General Bowen arrived behind Green's embattled line about 7:30 a.m. He quickly approved his dispositions. There was little doubt now Grant's main effort was coming out of the Bruinsburg area. Bowen sent couriers to wire Vicksburg from a station at Port Gibson and request the brigades of William Baldwin and Francis Cockrell hot-foot it to the battle area. Green was still heavily pressed when the thin reinforcements from Tracy arrived about 8:30 a.m. and were quickly thrown into line. The 23rd Alabama extended Green's right flank while a pair of Virginia guns of the Botetourt Artillery unlimbered east of the church on the Foster property. A reactive counterattack, led personally by Bowen to recapture the ridge around Magnolia Church, was thrown back with heavy losses.[61]

Eugene Carr's attack finally spent itself against both Green's defenders and the heavy undergrowth and rugged terrain. His brigades had drifted apart, leaving a gap in the center of his line. McClernand sent forward Brig. Gen. Alvin P. Hovey's division to fill it and smash through the enemy front. A 42-year-old native of Indiana and veteran of the Mexican War, Hovey's fine performance at the head of a regiment at Shiloh earned him a brigadier general's commission and a brigade in Grant's Army of the Tennessee. Hovey formed his brigades near the Shaifer house on the road, with Brig. Gen. George McGinnis on the right and Col. James R. Slack on the left. Yet a third division, that of Brig. Gen. Andrew J. Smith, formed behind Hovey in reserve. By 10:00 a.m. McClernand had two front line divisions deployed in the small area astride the road. Because of crowded conditions, some regiments were stacked three and four deep. McClernand ordered them all forward.[62]

The Union line extended well beyond both of Martin Green's flanks, and that became painfully obvious to the Confederates very quickly. After a bloody piecemeal attack by two of Hovey's regiments, the Union divisions moved forward together with a shout. The thick undergrowth shielded them until they climbed the last slope and broke into the open ground. The Federals rushed out and smothered the pair of guns Tracy had sent to reinforce Green. The loaded pieces were spun around and the canister rounds inside the barrels discharged into the backs of Green's

Brigadier General
William Baldwin

Library of Congress

fleeing Rebels. Green's line crumbled under the overwhelming pressure and fell back along the Rodney Road.

A short time earlier, Bowen had sent couriers to hunt up any approaching reinforcements and speed them to the field. William Baldwin's Brigade from Vicksburg was found a few miles away approaching Port Gibson. The former Mississippi store owner and militia officer hurried his men forward through the town at the double-quick. Baldwin's conduct as a colonel at the head of an ad-hoc brigade in the attack designed to break out of Fort Donelson had earmarked him for higher command. Here, at Port Gibson, was the first large-scale opportunity to validate the trust others had placed on his shoulders. When his brigade pushed well west of Port Gibson, reported Baldwin, "[we] found our troops [Green] falling back at all points, pressed by greatly superior numbers." At Bowen's direction Baldwin established a new defensive position about one and one-half miles behind Green's original line in the thicket-filled low land between two meandering branches of Willow Creek. The brigade was deployed with one regiment north of the road and his remaining two below it. A small salient following the topography was studded with artillery. Baldwin's fourth regiment was placed several hundred yards behind the bulge as a reserve. Deploying in the low ground made sense because fighting exposed on the top of ridges had not proven effective. Additional reinforcements were on the road and heading in their direction. Bowen, therefore, ordered Green to gather his beaten soldiers behind Baldwin and when organized, march with haste around to the Bruinsburg Road and help Tracy (Garrott) hold back Osterhaus. If either wing was defeated, the other was likewise doomed. Green had fought well at Magnolia Church but was chagrined by the collapse of his line. When describing the retreat in his report, he simply noted, "My men were exhausted, and being outflanked at both flanks, were compelled to fall back."[63]

*   *   *

The flight of Green's men at Magnolia Church exhilarated the Federals. "The bayonets of the Twelfth Division were glittering in the sun," Hovey later reported. "A wild shout, a shout of triumph, reverberated through the hills. The enemy was beaten back, between 200 and 300 taken prisoners, and 1 stand of colors, 2 12-pounder howitzers, 3 caissons, and 3 six mule teams, loaded with ammunition, was the reward of this chivalric action." In a less expressive report, Carr simply noted, "[T]he enemy retreated about 2 miles, and took up a new position." The first, though small, victory had been achieved east of the Mississippi River and Grant was there to savor it. He looked over the field with McClernand and the pair planned their next move. By about noon the Federal divisions had been reformed and the lines began moving slowly forward, probing east down the Rodney Road toward Baldwin's new position.[64]

*   *   *

While the Confederate left flank under Green was being subjected to McClernand's crippling assault, Tracy's men under Colonel Garrott were doing their best to hold the line along the Bruinsburg Road against Osterhaus. The colonel had no idea of Tracy's overall plan. The courier he dispatched to Green returned with no more information other than he was to hold his position to the last. By mid-morning, Osterhaus's two brigades were finally gaining an advantage. The line surged forward on the left, swinging as if on a giant hinge from left to right. The 120th Ohio Infantry on the extreme left, part of Theophilus Garrard's brigade, crossed the Bruinsburg Road beyond Garrott's right flank and pushed it away from Bayou Pierre. Garrott adroitly pulled his line back and reformed it essentially perpendicular to his former front, with the Bruinsburg Road bisecting the new line's left center. Unfortunately for the Southerners, the heavy exchanges of artillery fire had crippled their own guns and their small arms ammunition was running low. Garrott summed up his situation after the battle when he remembered, "At 11 o'clock heavy columns of the enemy could be distinctly seen, and it appeared evident that if they could be brought up to make a charge that our slender force would be overwhelmed by vastly superior numbers."[65]

To Garrott's relief, Osterhaus slowed his advance to a methodical crawl. The terrain and heavy opposing fire had made him cautious, but he continued to press here and probe there with an eye to slipping beyond and turning the Alabamian's exposed right flank. Light but steady firing continued. Shortly after 2:00 p.m. Martin Green's tired men (augmented by the 6th Missouri Infantry from Francis Cockrell's Brigade) arrived after their circuitous tramp from the Rodney Road battle front. Green moved to Garrott's unengaged left flank overlooking Centers Creek and deployed there, replacing one of the Alabama regiments which moved to the embattled right. Green did not check with Garrott to determine where his men were most needed. His despondent statements on the field about the hopelessness of holding the position, uttered after he arrived there, suggest the man was simply mentally exhausted.[66]

By the middle of the afternoon Osterhaus was ready to make a decisive push in his sector and end the matter. McClernand had dispatched a brigade from John Logan's division under Brig. Gen. John E. Smith to assist Osterhaus. Smith moved north to Osterhaus's left in an attempt to envelop Garrott's right flank. The effort made slow but steady progress, and by 5:00 p.m. another of Logan's brigades under Brig. Gen. Elias Dennis was sent up the plantation road. The final wave about to crash against the Confederate position, however, slapped against a largely empty line. An order from Bowen reached Garrott at this time to withdraw. Green pulled out first, sending his men northeast toward Bayou Pierre along the Andrews farm road. Garrott's survivors followed. The Southerners crossed the bridge over Bayou Pierre as darkness closed over them. Losses in the Bruinsburg Road fighting had been heavy. Garrott reported 18 killed, 112 wounded, and 142 missing, for a total of 272. Colonel Eugene Erwin of the 6th Missouri, which was engaged for only a short period of time, reported four killed, 32 wounded, and 46 missing out of 400. Osterhaus's losses were reported as 41 killed, 205 wounded, and three missing. The tide of battle at Port Gibson had irrevocably turned.[67]

The afternoon hours along the Rodney Road about one-half mile to the southeast had also not gone well for the Confederates. At 1:20 p.m., Bowen telegraphed Pemberton at Jackson to notify him of the "furious battle," heavy losses, Tracy's death, and the precarious ammunition supply situation. "They outnumber us trebly," Bowen wired. "There are three divisions against us. My whole force is engaged. . . . The odds are overpowering." Pemberton wired Bowen that two of Loring's brigades were on the road from Jackson and urged him to hold until they arrived. His last words were sobering: "You had better whip them before he [Loring] reaches you." Bowen knew what his superior meant: Jackson was a long way off and Loring was not going to arrive in time to help him before the end of the day.[68]

Bowen was pondering how to hold his line with Baldwin when Francis Cockrell's Brigade appeared. The three regiments of Missourians trotted up the road after a fast march of several hours from Grand Gulf. Colonel Erwin's 6th Missouri was dispatched to follow Martin Green, who was on his way to reinforce Garrott on the Bruinsburg Road. The remaining pair of Missouri regiments took up a position behind Baldwin's left flank.

* * *

While Bowen was pleading for help and positioning his paltry reinforcements, McClernand's juggernaut ground slowly forward through the wooded and undergrowth-strewn terrain. The advance was led by Carr and Hovey, whose divisions were deployed in a double line of battle. Behind them and in column was Andrew Smith's division. McClernand stopped only when Baldwin's new line in the Widows Creek bottomland was discovered. "We found them again, ready to show fight," recalled a member of the 24th Indiana, McGinnis's brigade, Hovey's division. McClernand's vision was impaired by terrain that could be hiding Southern soldiers, and a ridge that should have been occupied—but was not. Puzzled and more than a little wary, he stopped and called up Smith's column. Brigadier General Stephen Burbridge's and Col. William J. Landram's brigades were uncoiled into line, as was one of John Logan's brigades under Brig. Gen. John D. Stevenson. A brisk artillery fire covered the movement. By the time McClernand was again ready to move forward, the left of his front line brushed against Centers Creek and the far right was some 2,000 yards to the south. Put another way, a third of the Federal line was north of the Rodney Road and two-thirds was below it. The first line was composed of four brigades, with three more in a second reserve line. It was an overpowering force, and it was about to be unleashed against Bowen's lean group of defenders.[69]

*   *   *

It was now about 3:00 p.m. Bowen wired Pemberton with a renewed sense of urgency: "We have fought 20,000 men since dawn. . . . They are pressing me hard on the right. My center is firm; left is weak. When can Loring get here?" The answer, of course, was not soon enough, as the erupting engagement clearly communicated. McClernand's assault splashed through White Branch and up the rising ground beyond, where it came face to face with Baldwin's line. Southern muskets and artillery exploded, driving the Federals back into the low ground. The heavy pressure, however, pinned Baldwin's men firmly in place. As the two sides exchanged an intense fire, McClernand shifted regiments into this center determined to bull his way through the enemy line.[70]

Another concern crept into Bowen's mind. Just 1,200 yards to the south beyond the Federal right flank was the Natchez Road, another artery feeding into Port Gibson. If the enemy found it and moved troops along it, Bowen's position would be untenable. The increase in enemy troops to his front convinced him to launch a flank attack to roll up or at least push the Federal right away from the vicinity of the Natchez Road. The only troops available belonged to Francis Cockrell. Bowen ordered him to march his two regiments behind a knoll on the far side of Irwin's Branch and attack. Cockrell's movement, however, was spotted almost immediately by Hovey, who shifted two dozen guns and the equivalent of some two brigades to his threatened right overlooking White's Branch. Cockrell's effort was doomed almost before it began.

The Confederate attack column was formed deep, with the 5th Missouri in front and the 3rd Missouri in its immediate rear. Despite having been seen, Cockrell's attackers still managed to fall upon the flank of Colonel Slack's brigade and roll it up, beginning with the 56th Ohio and continuing with the 47th Indiana. Slack tried to explain how

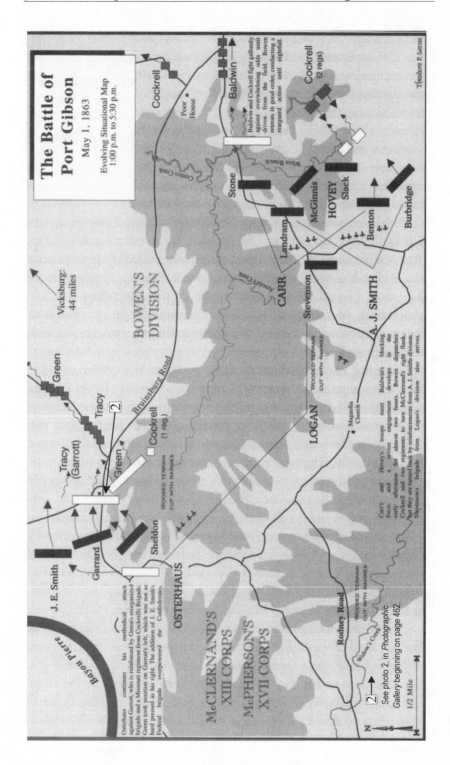

The Battle of Port Gibson

May 1, 1863

Evolving Situational Map
1:00 p.m. to 5:30 p.m.

Theodore P. Savas

Vicksburg:
44 miles

Bayou Pierre

J. E. Smith

Green

Tracy

Tracy (Garrott)

Green

Garrard

Sheldon

OSTERHAUS

McCLERNAND'S XIII CORPS

McPHERSON'S XVII CORPS

Rodney Road

WOODED TERRAIN CUT WITH RAVINES

Widow's Creek

Cockrell (1 reg)

WOODED TERRAIN CUT WITH RAVINES

Bruinsburg Road

BOWEN'S DIVISION

Centers Creek

Cockrell

Poor House

Baldwin

Stone

White Branch

Landram

CARR

Stevenson

Arnold Creek

LOGAN

Magnolia Church

WOODED TERRAIN CUT WITH RAVINES

McGinnis

HOVEY

Slack

Benton

A. J. SMITH

Burbridge

Cockrell (2 regs)

Baldwin and Cockrell fight gallantly against overwhelming odds until driven from the field. Bowen retreats in good order, conducting a rearguard action until nightfall.

Osterhaus continues his methodical attack against Garrott, who is reinforced by Green's reorganized brigade and a Missouri regiment from Cockrell's Brigade. Green took position on Garrott's left, which was not as hard pressed as his right. The addition of J. E. Smith's Federal brigade overpowered the Confederate.

Carr's and Hovey's troops meet Baldwin blocking in the dispatches road, and a severe engagement develops in the early afternoon for almost two hours. Bowen Cockrell and two regiments to turn McClernand's right flank, but they are turned back by reinforcements from A. J. Smith's division. Stevenson's brigade from Logan's division also arrives.

See photo 2, in *Photographic Gallery* beginning on page 462.

1/2 Mile

N

that happened in his report, noting his lines had barely formed before the storm broke upon them. The Southerners assaulted "with terrific yells, and could not be seen, because of the very thick growth of cane, until they reached a point within 30 yards of my line." Cockrell remembered that the "enemy immediately began to change their lines to meet our troops." The Missouri regiments reformed side-by-side and a bitter firefight erupted for some forty minutes at rock throwing range. Cockrell had stirred up a hornet's nest. "As often as one line was driven back, another of fresh troops was thrown in our front," he wrote. "When it became manifest that a continuance of the engagement could result in no advantage to us, these two regiments fell back and took their original position on the extreme left, having inflicted on the enemy a heavy blow which deterred him from attempting to pursue." Cockrell's bloodied regiments fell back east and reformed on the left of Baldwin's 4th Mississippi while Bowen rode amongst the men offering words of encouragement.[71]

Following Cockrell's repulse, Bowen ordered Baldwin to move his regiments forward in a heavy probing attack to ascertain Federal intentions. The violent response and heavy concentrations of enemy troops convinced both officers further effort was futile. Baldwin flatly noted as much in his report, observing that a continuation of the attack "would result in the destruction of the entire command without accomplishing the object." Bowen knew he could no longer remain at Port Gibson. He wired Pemberton the bad news shortly after 5:00 p.m.: "I still hold my position. I will have to retire under cover of night to the other side of Bayou Pierre and await re-enforcements." Waiting until nightfall proved difficult. McClernand had been continually pressing Bowen's lines, moving up artillery pieces and driving back the Southerners one step at a time. By 5:30 p.m. the line was manifesting signs of breaking. Bowen had held out as long as possible; it was now time to save his command. He ordered his brigade commanders to fall back and make for the Bayou Pierre crossing via the Andrews farm road. Another wire was sent to Jackson advising Pemberton of the retreat across the bayou: "I will endeavor to hold that position [Bayou Pierre] until re-enforcements arrive . . . The men did nobly, holding out the whole day against overwhelming odds."[72]

Three of Bowen's four brigades withdrew via the Andrews farm road, but Baldwin's men were forced to withdraw east through Port

Gibson. The Confederates crossed Little Bayou Pierre about 9:00 p.m. and burned the bridge in their wake. They marched all that night, crossed Big Bayou Pierre at Grindstone Ford about midnight, and burned that bridge as well. They finally reached camp at 9:00 a.m. the next morning. Bowen's brigades had suffered significant losses. On the Rodney Road, Martin Green's well-traveled brigade left 13 killed, 71 wounded and 76 missing on the field. This estimate did not include his 6th Mississippi; its casualties went unreported. Baldwin's losses were somewhat lighter at 12 killed, 48 wounded, and 27 missing. Losses in Cockrell's Brigade—excluding the 6th Missouri, which had fought with Tracy— were nine killed, 65 wounded, and 50 missing.[73]

McClernand's steady and aggressive tactics, coupled with his considerable advantage in numbers, had finally wrested the field from the stubborn enemy. Pursuit was almost impossible because the men were worn out by the river crossing, march inland, and twelve hours of fighting. The cost of victory was not light. Excluding Osterhaus's losses (reported above), McClernand's Rodney Road action cost 90 killed, 514 wounded, and 22 missing. These figures include the units from McPherson's Corps that had been fed into the action. These losses notwithstanding, John Logan described the fight in paradoxical terms to his wife: "a hard battle[;] we won it easy."[74]

General Grant had been in the vicinity almost all day and ordered a resumption of the fighting at first light, but there was no enemy within reach when the sun rose on May 2. Pemberton was now fully aware of where Grant's army was and that his advance inland to capture Port Gibson's crossroads and the crossings over Little Bayou Pierre had been slowed considerably. Nevertheless, good news abounded for Grant. The battle had solidified his bold strategic crossing of the Mississippi River. With orders to keep stragglers to a minimum, McClernand took possession of Port Gibson soon after dawn on May 2. With the vital road hub in his hands, Grant later remarked, "I was delighted . . . that the enemy had not stopped."[75]

In Jackson, Pemberton fretted over the heavy fighting and what to do about it. He had a good sense about its importance, as evidenced by a telegraph he sent to President Davis that afternoon: "A furious battle has been going on since daylight just below Port Gibson. . . . Large reinforcements should be sent to me from other departments. Enemy's movement threatens Jackson and, if successful, cuts off Vicksburg and

Port Hudson from the east." His last sentence summed up the strategic nature of Grant's successful crossing: "Enemy's success in passing our batteries has completely changed character of defense." The Southern commander realized the strategic outlook had "changed," and yet squandered the little time he had left to act decisively to snatch success from the jaws of pending defeat. Bowen's sharply fought holding action south of Bayou Pierre had purchased Pemberton time to concentrate his army and move every available soldier south to meet the obvious crisis and bring on a decisive battle near the Mississippi River. He had two-and-one-half divisions at or near Hankinson's Ferry south of Vicksburg, about 6,000 men in and around Jackson, and another two divisions in the vicinity of Vicksburg. Other than dribble a few brigade-size units forward, however, he did next to nothing of substance. By not acting decisively, Pemberton allowed Grant (whom he outnumbered) the foothold he needed to launch his inland campaign against Vicksburg. And matters were about to yet take another turn for the worse.[76]

John Bowen's intent to hold the Bayou Pierre line was predicated upon strong reinforcements reaching him in time to strengthen and extend his southern-facing left flank. When he learned to his dismay only small pieces from Loring's Division has been dispatched to aid him, and a brigade from Carter Stevenson's Division had not yet arrived, he "determined to abandon the position." Bowen also ordered the evacuation of the outflanked stronghold of Grand Gulf he had done so much to create and hold. William Loring arrived on the scene and, since he outranked Bowen, assumed command of the retreat north across the Big Black River.[77]

Without an enemy to confront the crossing, Grant had little difficulty rebuilding the bridges and slipping north over Little Bayou Pierre and then Bayou Pierre at Grindstone Ford. By May 4 all of Grant's men were above the waterway. The evacuation of Grand Gulf was another major victory for Grant, who could now claim the strategic river location he had desired as his original crossing point. Writing about the abandoned bastion, a Federal soldier observed, "they evacuated Grand Gulf blew up their magazines left nine large siege peaces and run away." Grant took advantage of Bowen's evacuation order to change his base from Bruinsburg north to Grand Gulf while he pondered his next move.[78]

With pressure from President Davis to hold Vicksburg at all costs, Pemberton gathered his forces behind the Big Black River, concentrating in the city's safe zone; he would not leave the city defenseless. Instead of marching to intercept Grant, he decided to stay primarily behind the Big Black River, defend its crossings, and shift his position to keep his army between Grant and the city. His habit of holding fortified points, first developed in South Carolina, made it difficult for him to think in terms of fluid and aggressive field movement.

The Natchez *Weekly Courier* loudly proclaimed on May 6 that Vicksburg was under siege. It was not true, but only decisive action by Pemberton and his key subordinates would prevent the premature report from becoming reality.[79]

Chapter 3

Raymond

"It was absolutely necessary for me to await their coming, or to fall back without knowing whether the force of the enemy was superior or inferior to mine."

— Brig. Gen. John Gregg, CSA

"SOLDIERS OF THE ARMY OF THE TENNESSEE!," WAS HOW GRANT kicked off his congratulatory order thanking his troops for their hard work and victory at Port Gibson, which he called "one of the most important of the war." More hard work lay before them: "A few days' continuance of the same zeal and constancy will secure to this army the crowning victory over the rebellion. More difficulties and privations are before us. Let us endure them manfully. Other battles are to be fought. Let us fight them bravely. A grateful country will rejoice at our success, and history will record it with immortal honor." Chests swelled with pride as the Army of the Tennessee prepared for its march on Vicksburg in search of a decisive victory.[1]

By the fourth day of May Grant was still in a rather precarious position, not unlike a man straddling an uncomfortably tall barbed wire fence. Two corps, his XIII and XVII, were east of the Mississippi River. However his third corps, the XV under Sherman, was still on the west side. When Sherman received word of the successful Bruinsburg crossing, he gave up his feint at Snyder's Bluff and made his way south with speed through Louisiana. By the time his divisions were ready to cross the river on May 7, the stronghold of Grand Gulf had been abandoned by the Confederates. Sherman's legions boarded transports opposite the deserted fortifications and shipped east for Mississippi. While Sherman rushed to join them, the other two corps of the Army of the Tennessee bided their time, waiting for their sister corps before resuming the advance on Vicksburg.[2]

Grant, meanwhile, made three key decisions: what his next move would be, the troops he would employ, and how he would keep his forces supplied. He had intended to remain for some time in the Grand Gulf area, solidifying his position while McClernand's XIII Corps tramped south to cooperate with Nathaniel Banks' move against Port Hudson, the only other remaining Confederate Mississippi River bastion. Washington authorities were counting on this corps-level cooperation. Once Port Hudson fell, Banks and his army (plus McClernand) would move north to join Grant for the final campaign against Pemberton for the possession of Vicksburg. When Grant learned Banks was not in position before Port Hudson, however, he used the delay to keep his army intact and strike out on his own. McClernand would stay with him.

Logistics often determine success in the field. Capable generals always pay close attention to how their armies are fed and equipped. This particularly complex issue gnawed away at Grant. His army required a steady and dependable stream of supplies for what promised to be a very difficult campaign. The only land route was south through Louisiana on bad roads routinely bisected by enemy cavalry and Southern partisans. The water route south past Vicksburg's guns was viable, but the passage could only get more dangerous and costly as the level of surprise diminished and Confederate gunnery skills improved. Port Hudson's guns were still commanding the river below Vicksburg, so shipping supplies north from New Orleans would at best be unreliable. Grant never considered retreating; hunkering down near the river while the element of strategic surprise slipped through his fingers was almost as unpalatable. Melding the finesse of his combined operation at Forts Henry and Donelson with the bulldog tenacity that enabled him to walk off the field at Shiloh a victor, Grant audaciously decided he must move inland in force. He would do so by carrying everything he could on the backs of his men and in wagons without a secure line of supply in his wake. He would live as he could off the countryside, and arrange for a slow-moving supply train to (hopefully) rumble after him on a daily basis from Grand Gulf. Sherman questioned his friend about the wisdom of moving without a sure line of supply, "unless you intend to live on the country." Grant replied forthrightly: "I do not calculate upon the possibility of supplying the army with full rations from Grand Gulf. I know it will be impossible without constructing additional roads. What I do expect, however, is to get what rations of hard bread, coffee, and salt we can, and make the country furnish us the balance."[3]

The last major issue Grant confronted was how best to capture Vicksburg and defeat Pemberton. The obvious move was to march across the Big Black River directly against Vicksburg from the south. Union patrols, however, had developed Confederate concentrations at Warrenton, eight miles below Vicksburg, and the Big Black River Bridge, ten miles east of Vicksburg. Pemberton was wisely planning for the obvious and was concentrating on the west side of the waterway. Grant could move directly against the city and Pemberton from the east, but he did not want to ignore the line of communications running between Vicksburg and the state capital at Jackson. Pemberton could be isolated by cutting the railroad between the two Mississippi cities and inserting the Army of the Tennessee between Pemberton and Jackson (and thus the rest of the Confederacy). Vicksburg's only major line of communications and supply would be cut.[4]

Convinced of the efficacy of his plan, Grant prepared to march his army northeast on the east side of the Big Black River. A march on the river's west side would place his army within striking distance of Pemberton's divisions and confine his own men inside a narrow triangular box running southwest to northeast bordered by two large waterways (the Mississippi and Big Black). Perhaps Grant remembered the near-disaster at Shiloh, where Confederates trapped his army inside a narrowing swath of land between the Tennessee River and Owl Creek. He would not make that mistake again. He would march along the watershed of the river east of the main channel with the objective of striking and cutting the railroad somewhere between Bolton and Edwards Station.[5]

Thinking Sherman had crossed the Mississippi River on May 6, Grant put his two other corps in motion the next day. Although Sherman had not yet crossed, he did so that night and the following day, making

May 7 the first day Grant had all three infantry corps on the east side of the river. Marching orders called for a movement inland northeast between the Big Black River and Bayou Pierre. The route posed few natural hindrances and was well suited for marching, but care had to be taken to protect his left flank from an attack across the Big Black. Grant had intended Sherman would lead the move inland, but the XV Corps was not yet up. The vanguard honor instead fell to McClernand's XIII Corps, which was ordered to march northeast about ten miles from Rocky Springs to Old Auburn. Sherman's divisions would follow and pass around and ahead of McClernand in the middle of the march somewhere around Cayuga. These two corps comprised the left or western-most column closest to the Big Black. McPherson's XVII Corps, meanwhile, would move more directly east to Utica, roughly paralleling Bayou Pierre, and then northeast another fifteen miles to Raymond, a small road junction and the end point of a small rail spur jutting south from Bolton. McPherson formed the right or eastern-most wing of the Army of the Tennessee. Once the entire army was in place in a line stretching from Old Auburn through Raymond, Grant would move quickly northward and sever the railroad. McPherson's men would only be about six miles south of the critical lifeline.[6]

Before the sun set on May 7, McPherson's divisions had reached Rocky Springs; McClernand's corps encamped three miles ahead. Once on the east side of the river, Sherman's corps moved quickly in their wake. As planned, his troops marched ahead of McClernand's near Cayuga a few miles southwest of Old Auburn. Once there the corps diverged. McClernand moved north along the Telegraph Road toward Edwards Station while Sherman marched a few miles east to Dillon's plantation. McPherson, meanwhile, had swung east to Utica and was marching northeast toward his objective at Raymond. The inland march unfolded without interruption.

"We are having schumishes every day," an Indiana infantryman wrote home, but no major fighting had taken place on the march from Port Gibson. As the Federals quickly discovered, this part of Mississippi was still untouched by war. One soldier reported that peaches were plentiful, as were berries. Apples were few, he said, but the soldiers made up for them with "chickens and mutton." By the afternoon of May 12 two of Grant's three corps, supplied by daily foraging and caravans from Grand Gulf, had crossed north of Fourteenmile Creek. His army was facing north stretching from near Raymond on the right to the Big Black River on the left. Although portions of each corps remained behind the line, Grant had almost his entire army, connected by lateral roads to ensure mutual support, concentrated and ready for the final push north against the Southern Railroad of Mississippi.[7]

*   *   *

Grant's improved strategic situation stood in stark contrast to John Pemberton's deteriorating state of affairs. Betraying his growing tendency to defend Vicksburg at all costs, he had moved his headquarters from Jackson to Vicksburg on May 1. Once Grant stood victorious at Port Gibson, Pemberton saw just as clearly as anyone the likely course of action the Federal general would pursue, and warned Mississippi government officials accordingly: Jackson was in jeopardy. On May 2 he wired Governor John J. Pettus, "I think it would be well to remove the State archives from Jackson. The enemy has or is crossing nearly his whole force. It is likely he will move on Jackson." Pemberton also saw to the removal of army records to a safer locale and ordered machinery and other valuable equipment shipped away to Alabama. Panic gripped many in the capital city, where rumors coursed through the streets of advancing Union columns. The growing fear caused at least one train derailment near Jackson, which only made the situation worse for its citizenry. Major Samuel Lockett, Pemberton's chief engineer, summed up the situation rather succinctly in a letter to his wife, "Things are once more looking very squarely."[8]

In the midst of this chaos Pemberton made several decisions, the most sound of which was the concentration of his available troops. As he later noted in his official report, the defeat at Port Gibson "rendered it necessary that I should as rapidly as possible concentrate my whole force for the defense of Vicksburg." With Bowen's withdrawal north across Bayou Pierre, four of Pemberton's divisions were in or near Vicksburg; only William Loring's was still dispersed after its futile effort to block Grierson's troopers. Pemberton had ordered Loring and several smaller commands from Meridian, Jackson, Grenada, and Port Hudson to unite with him so he could meet Grant in the field with as many men as possible. The orders to Loring and others, however, were vague and garbled, which only served to complicate the effort to reinforce Bowen at

Port Gibson. They also served to infuriate everyone involved. Pemberton also hoped for help from west of the river, pleading with Lt. Gen. Kirby Smith, the commander of the vast trans-Mississippi Department, to strike the Union forces in his department opposite Vicksburg. Communication problems exacerbated Smith's intrinsic tendency to thwart joint efforts. Relief would have to be found in Pemberton's own department.[9]

Confusion was found instead. The lack of cavalry transfixed Pemberton. Van Dorn's troopers had been dispatched to aid Braxton Bragg in Tennessee. Although he had other mounted troops, most of them were fanned out across northern Mississippi guarding a host of approaches and wide swaths of territory. Had he pulled in his cavalry and enveloped the van of Grant's army with mounted troops, he could have slowed his enemy's march and shadowed his movements. Pemberton was not about to strip the country bare—regardless of the serious threat approaching from Port Gibson. Doing so would have potentially exposed Vicksburg from above and required the adoption of an aggressive strategy rather than a more passive geographic defense. Pemberton was unwilling to adopt either course. With Loring and Bowen on the west side of the Big Black River, the defensive-minded general informed President Davis that he would concentrate on the same side with them and guard the eastern approaches to Vicksburg from behind the Big Black. Troops dribbled in for days; the enemy tramped deeper inland by the hour, unopposed. Pemberton's chief engineer was not fully convinced his superior had a firm grasp on the situation. "I think he knows what he is doing," was all the trust Lockett could muster when he wrote his wife at the end of the first week of May.[10]

In the days following Port Gibson, meanwhile, Pemberton remained between the Federals and Vicksburg as Grant moved his columns up the east side of the Big Black River. Unwilling to uncover any approach to the city, the Confederate leader kept each ford and bridge carefully cloaked to prevent a surprise Union thrust toward Vicksburg. It was a difficult task because a plethora of crossings (including Thompson's, Hankinson's, Horner's, Baldwin's, and Hall's Ferry, plus the railroad line west of Edwards Station), punctured the waterway. Grant took advantage of these fords and ferry points by feinting here and thrusting there, especially at Hankinson's Ferry. The diversions kept the Confederate leader off balance. Doing his best to mirror his opponent and divine his intentions, Pemberton eased his legions slowly northward as

Grant's men narrowed the distance to the critical rail line connecting Vicksburg and Jackson. All the while Pemberton was careful to keep his divisions within supporting distance of one another. By the time the fitful northward creep ended around the railroad bridge over the Big Black and at Edwards Station, however, Pemberton's army had drifted apart. He fixed Carter Stevenson's large division at Warrenton to watch Vicksburg's southern approaches, unsure whether Grant's nibbles toward the river crossings were feints or preludes to a serious passage. Other troops were shifted first one way and then a few miles in another direction, seemingly without purpose. Bits and pieces of various units were left watching the ferries and fords. Pemberton guessed correctly Grant's intention was to sever the rail line, but he was unable to gather the force of will necessary to issue the orders required to counter it. He understood his objective to be the defense of a place—Vicksburg—rather than the defeat of the Union army.[11]

The pugnacious William Loring had other ideas. Pemberton's division commander saw in the movement of Grant northeast toward Jackson an opportunity to attack the Union flank and rear. A memorandum was drafted on May 9 and submitted for consideration. Loring saw the situation clearly, and outlined why he believed the time and occasion for an attack had arrived. He suggested Bowen's Division move out behind Fourteenmile Creek opposite the center-left of the enemy advance. While these troops held the Federals in place, his own division and that under Carter Stevenson would cross the Big Black at Baldwin's and Halls ferries and strike Grant's exposed left flank and rear, rolling it up away from Grand Gulf and into Confederate strength. It was a bold but viable plan. Pemberton rejected it. He did, however, implement a fraction of the Loring memorandum by ordering a single brigade under Brig. Gen. John Gregg to move forward from Jackson to Raymond to watch for a Union advance in that direction. That was all Pemberton was willing to gamble. The seemingly innocuous move would have telling consequences.[12]

Pemberton's deportment seems to have firmed somewhat by May 11. Reports flowing into headquarters that day convinced him that Grant's movement toward the railroad between Edwards and Raymond was a prelude to a left-wheel against the Big Black railroad bridge, and thus his movement in the direction of Jackson was but a feint. Pemberton ordered Loring and Stevenson to march for the rail span. He informed his commissary officer in Jackson by wire that if Grant moved in that direction, "I will advance to meet him." As his biographer keenly noted, "This was the first aggressive statement Pemberton had made since Grant's crossing." The following day he shifted his headquarters closer to the front to Bovina, a small community just west of the railroad crossing. Bowen was ordered east of the river, a move that pleased the aggressive Loring, who sensed an attack lingering in the air. By this time Pemberton had with him almost 22,000 men. Most were deployed facing south by southeast along a line near the railroad and the Jackson Road, with Bowen on the left, Loring in the center, and Stevenson on the right. Scouts were sent forward to find and probe Grant's location. The army built "some slight field-works" south of Edwards, primarily overlooking Fourteenmile Creek, and remained stationary for two days "in line of battle . . . without tents and on short rations," remembered S. M. Thornton of the 31st Mississippi Infantry. Portions of McClernand's XIII Corps were so close Thornton and his comrades could hear their beating drums. Union soldiers experienced something similar. A member of the 24th Indiana of McClernand's corps recalled how he and his fellow soldiers "lay on our arms all night our pickets in sight of each other." The Confederates outnumbered McClernand's distant corps, but Pemberton was miles to the rear and Loring, who commanded in his absence, was not about to move forward and launch an attack on his own authority. The Confederates passed up another opportunity to fall upon one segment of Grant's army and defeat it in detail.[13]

Although he had five divisions at his call, Pemberton left two in and around Vicksburg to guard approaches to the city left uncovered by the eastward march of his other three to Edwards Station. The divisions under Maj. Gens. Martin Smith and John Forney were spread thin watching the area from up north at Snyder's Bluff on the Yazoo all the way south through Vicksburg to Warrenton. By this time, however, except for the Federal Navy no serious threat existed along Vicksburg's waterfront or the hills north of the city. The enemy's water-arm might have ferried troops against Vicksburg itself, but Southern artillery and unbrigaded units deployed there were probably adequate to deal with any such threat. The actual hazard remained Grant, and he was east of the Big Black River. Pemberton could have consolidated his entire army, more than 30,000 men, in and around Edwards Station. But when he needed every man he could get his hands on, the Pennsylvanian implemented halfway measures. His decision to cross the Big Black with only three divisions would prove a costly mistake.[14]

The Battle of Raymond

The march from Port Gibson east through Utica and northeast toward Raymond was conducted by James McPherson and his XVII Corps. Moving well to the southeast of the remaining two-thirds of the army, McPherson's column formed Grant's right wing and directly threatened the capital of Mississippi. With cavalry in the van, his divisions tramped forward on the warm dirt roads of Mississippi. Many in the ranks were without shoes, which had worn out weeks ago and had not yet been replaced. Utica was reached on May 10. The van of the corps took the Utica (or Raymond) Road and camped that night a few miles beyond Utica on the Weeks' plantation. On the following day, with Logan's division in the lead, XVII Corps eased forward another five miles to Roach's plantation, where it halted for the day about eleven miles below Raymond. Grant, who was riding with Sherman, dispatched an important order to his young protégé: "Move your command to-night to the next cross-roads if there is water, and to-morrow with all activity into Raymond. At the latter point you will use all your exertions to secure all the subsistence stores that may be there, as well as in the vicinity."[15]

McPherson issued the appropriate orders and the men were roused early and on the road hours before the sun rose over the horizon. Huge dust clouds marked the route of march. Led by Elias S. Dennis's brigade and followed by J. E. Smith's and John D. Stevenson's, Logan's division pressed onward toward the valley of Fourteenmile Creek, with Isaac Quinby's division (under Marcellus Crocker) tramping behind. One of Crocker's brigade commanders was Massachusetts native George B. Boomer. Though not a military man by training, he had the common sense and historical training to appreciate its art when masterfully executed. "Since General Grant commenced to move his columns he has displayed great tact and skill, together with immense energy and nerve," he penned his wife in one of his regular letters to her. "The passage of this army over the Mississippi River and up to this point is one of the most masterly movements known in the history of any warfare, and it is a success."[16]

The warm morning would only grow warmer, and the commanding general turned his thoughts to water. Most of the creeks were dry or thin ribbons of muddy ground, but Fourteenmile Creek below Raymond still flowed freely. His men could fill their canteens there. Captain John S. Foster's Provisional Cavalry Battalion screened Brig. Gen. Elias Dennis's sleepy Ohio and Illinois infantry brigade at the head of the column. The march had barely begun when skirmishing erupted out of the darkness. The fitful firing did not interrupt the steady pace of the march. One artilleryman from the Badger State scribbled in his diary the march "led through the best country we have seen since leaving the Mississippi. . . . It is heavily timbered—beautiful magnolias occasionally being seen in full bloom." The firing intensified about dawn and this time did not fall away so quickly. Progress slowed to a crawl.

By mid-morning McPherson wisely ordered Foster's cavalry to part to the sides of the road and advanced in its place a line of infantry. Two Ohio regiments, one on either side of the Utica Road, their skirmishers well forward, advanced cautiously down sloping terrain that fell away into the meandering line of timber that marked Fourteenmile Creek. The enemy cavalry had vanished. An eerie solitude had fallen over the Mississippi landscape. Other than scattered voice commands and the steady tramp of shoes in tall weeds, there was little to hear. The Yankees closed on the tree line. Without warning a pattering of infantry fire rippled through the skirmish line. A few seconds later a trio of artillery shells whizzed through the air and detonated above Dennis's forward regiments. Marching directly into Raymond on May 12 was not going to be as easy as Grant and McPherson had hoped.[17]

*   *   *

John Gregg was destined to be a well traveled man before a bullet would cut short his promising life in an attack along the Darbytown Road in Virginia in late 1864. He began his journey in Alabama in 1828, and as a young man moved with his family to Tennessee, and attended school and read law in Tuscumbia, Alabama. In 1852, he migrated west to the challenging frontier town of Fairfield, Texas. Little is known of his early years there other than he rose to prominence in the law and was elected to a judgeship two years before he turned thirty. His countenance befitted a frontier judge and must have been impressive from atop a judicial bench.

Brigadier General
John Gregg

National Archives

His high forehead, strong nose, and pronounced cheek-bones were elongated by a thick canopy of swept-back dark hair on top and a full and long beard on the lower end. His abilities must have matched his looks, for they landed him in a delegate's chair to the state convention in 1861, where he voted in favor of secession. Gregg sat for a time in the Confederate Provisional Congress in his home state of Alabama, and later in Richmond, but left his seat after First Manassas to answer his new calling as a leader of men in the field. Jumping a train to Texas, he raised the 7th Texas and was elected to serve as its colonel. Before long he found himself back in Tennessee and caught up in the early 1862 debacle at Fort Donelson. Gregg led a bloody attack to break free of the Union siege lines there, but in the end surrender mooted his worthy effort. Six months of captivity followed, first in Ohio and then in Massachusetts, before he and his men were released and returned to Grenada, Mississippi.[18]

That September Gregg was made a brigadier general. His brigade consisted of his Texans, five Tennessee regiments (two of which were consolidated into one), an infantry battalion, and a battery of artillery. His men were shuttled first to Vicksburg, where they played a minor role in the repulse of William Sherman at Chickasaw Bayou, and then south to Port Hudson, Louisiana, where the brigade remained until recalled to defend Vicksburg after Grant crossed the river at Bruinsburg. Pemberton dispatched Gregg's 3,000-man brigade from Jackson to Raymond, at least partially as a result of Loring's aggressive memorandum suggesting offensive action. Gregg's orders from Pemberton were rather vague and allowed wide discretion: he was to hold his regiments well in hand and hit the enemy in the flank as soon as Grant moved toward the Big Black railroad bridge. A second brigade was ordered out of the Jackson gathering to aid Gregg, whose lonely command was far in advance of any supporting units.

Gregg's infantry marched most of May 11 and reached Raymond late that afternoon. He discovered there a populace fearful of the pending approach of the enemy. To his dismay he also learned that Col. Wirt Adams's cavalry, which was to have screened his movements and position, was no where to be found. An ambiguous order from Pemberton had left the Southern horsemen miles away at Edwards Station; only about 40 troopers, "mostly youths from the neighborhood," was how Gregg later described them, were available. Because of this lack of cavalry, continued Gregg, "I was unable to ascertain anything concerning the strength of the enemy." The Southern commander also discovered that he had too few men to effectively cover the vicinity's spidery network of major roads. The Utica Road ran south from Raymond, a second road bisected the Utica artery about one-half mile behind Gregg's position and ran southwest to Port Gibson, and yet a third dirt thoroughfare angled off the main road to the southeast toward Gallatin. This layout forced Gregg to dismember his brigade and stretch it paper thin to cover the three major roads in some semblance of strength. Between the roads were thick belts of timber interspersed with patches of open fields, deep ravines, sloping hillsides, muddy creeks that once flowed full, and heavy underbrush. Across his front twisted knee-deep Fourteenmile Creek, a wide timber-lined and steeply banked waterway separating him from his enemies.

It was still dark early on the morning of May 12 when mounted couriers informed Gregg "the enemy was advancing rapidly by the road from Utica." Gregg was not overly concerned because he had inferred from Pemberton's orders "the force in front of me was a brigade on a marauding excursion." Scouts seemed to confirm this impression, telling Gregg the Federals numbered "2,500 or 3,000." News of a more unpleasant variety was about to find John Gregg: the enemy was in corps strength, and it was about to slap up against his thinly-held front.

Light picket fire echoed in the distant darkness as Gregg's various regiments moved to take up new positions. Captain Hiram Bledsoe's

Captain
Hiram Bledsoe

Confederate Veteran

veteran three-gun Missouri battery was ordered to select the most commanding positions he could find near the junction of the Utica and Port Gibson roads. The 1st Tennessee Battalion and 7th Texas were ordered up to support it and cover the road intersection. The 50th Tennessee, supported by the 10th-30th Tennessee consolidated regiments, moved to the left to cover the Gallatin Road. The 3rd Tennessee was ordered to move south from the town's graveyard about one-half mile, where it took up a position between the Raymond and Gallatin roads, while the 41st Tennessee moved to cover the position vacated by the 3rd. Even when fully deployed, large gaps punctured the Southern front. "It was absolutely necessary for me to await their coming," Gregg later explained, "or to fall back without knowing whether the force of the enemy was superior or inferior to mine."[19]

Whether Northern or Southern arms escalated the engagement beyond a smattering of skirmish fire is up for debate. Gregg claims the enemy moved up quickly "and commenced an artillery fire upon my picket post at 10 o'clock." Federal sources give Bledsoe's Southern artillery the same honor. What is not in question is the intense level of fighting that erupted just two miles below Raymond.

James McPherson's first glimpse of the field of battle gave him some pause. Distant 1,300 yards atop a ridge were three Southern guns. Bits and pieces of gray lines of battle were seen through the trees on both sides of the road. He later estimated his enemy at 4,000 to 5,000 strong (his

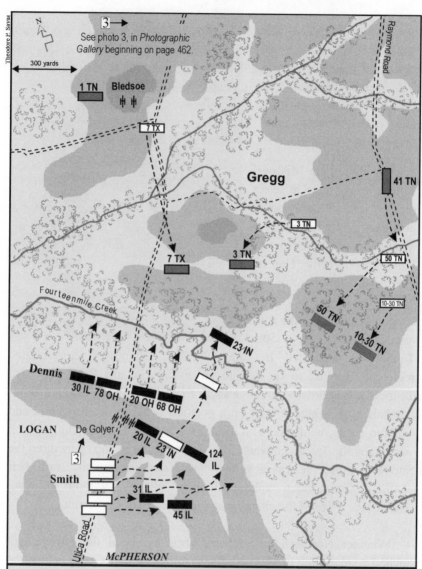

See photo 3, in *Photographic Gallery* beginning on page 462.

BATTLE OF RAYMOND

Deploy and Engage
10:30 a.m.-12:30 p.m., May 12, 1863

Told the enemy was in brigade strength on the Utica Road, Gregg deploys his regiments to stop them. His artillery fire and skirmishers bring the vanguard of McPherson's corps (Logan's division) to a halt. Logan deploys Dennis and Smith and moves into the bottomland around Fourteenmile Creek. The wooded terrain, creased by ravines filled with brush, makes maneuvering and reconnaissance difficult for both sides.

initial report claimed 6,000) with two batteries of artillery, "judiciously posted . . . to sweep the road and a bridge over which it was necessary to pass." He later learned he was wrong on both counts. Additional infantry was called forward. A 6-gun Michigan battery under Capt. Samuel De Golyer galloped up the Utica Road, unlimbered on both sides, and opened a counter-battery fire. While the noisy duel continued, Elias Dennis deployed his entire brigade, four regiments divided equally on either side of the Utica Road. The regiments threw out skirmishers and moved briskly forward to the belt of timber hugging shallow Fourteenmile Creek, chasing ahead of them enemy skirmishers hiding there. Other brigades from

Major General
John A. Logan

National Archives

the division of Maj. Gen. John A. Logan tramped up the roadway behind Dennis toward the sound of the guns. The battle that would spin the campaign in a different direction was about to get underway in earnest.[20]

The Civil War tossed up a host of political generals. John Alexander Logan was one of the finest. Born in southern Illinois on February 9, 1826, Logan soon made a name for himself through his exploits in fields ranging from law to service in the Mexican War to the state legislature. His growing popularity, along with his animated oratory, won for him a seat in Congress as a southern Illinois Democrat, which made him a very desirable political commodity. President Lincoln needed support in those Ohio River counties of Illinois, Indiana, and Ohio, where ties were closer to slavery than free labor. Logan was strongly pro-Union and accepted a commission from the president. Like John McClernand, Logan was able to raise support for the war in Illinois's southern counties.

Unlike so many political generals, however, Logan proved to be a capable combat leader. He also looked the part. Tall and well proportioned, his thick black hair worn long over the ears, sweeping mustache, and iron swarthy complexion combined to provide handsome qualities in a dashing sort of way. "Black Jack," as he was affectionately called, saw action early as a volunteer with a Michigan regiment at Bull Run before traveling home to raise the 31st Illinois. As its colonel, he led his men at Belmont, where his horse was shot from beneath him. The enemy aimed a bit higher in the Fort Donelson fighting and he fell wounded, missing completely the bloodbath that followed at Shiloh. In the interim Logan was promoted to brigadier general. Service at the head of first a brigade and then a division in Grant's Army of the Tennessee during the sloth-like Corinth campaign followed. At the head of the 3rd Division in McPherson's XVII Corps, Logan participated in the multiple failed attempts to get at Vicksburg. By March of 1863, he was doing so as a major general, to rank from the previous November. He had one most unusual personality quirk: once engaged in battle he always convinced himself the day was lost-no matter the outcome. With a gamble as large as the crossing of the Mississippi River and inland thrust into the heart of Mississippi, Grant would need capable and hard-fighting generals like Logan.[21]

Logan watched while his 2nd Brigade under Dennis was swallowed whole in the timber lining the creek. Several minutes passed before the next brigade made its appearance. The column's fitful march was the result of the narrow roadway and thick choking dust. The powdery grit scuffed up by each tramping unit triggered frequent halts to enable those unfortunate enough to be stuck in the middle and rear of the long column to see and breathe. Brigadier General John Smith's brigade of Indiana and Illinois troops followed Dennis's brigade. The third in line was a mixed brigade of Ohio, Missouri, and Illinois infantry under Brig. Gen. John D. Stevenson, though it was still some distance from the field. While Dennis's men were engaged in light skirmish fire with a largely unseen enemy, Logan shuttled Smith to the right of the roadway. Smith deployed his men well behind and beyond Dennis's right flank before heading into the heavy terrain for Fourteenmile Creek. The decision to deploy Smith east of the Utica Road seems as fortuitous as it would prove lucky.[22]

While Black Jack Logan rode behind his lines deploying his men, the aggressive-minded John Gregg was juggling the command decision of his career. "Finding that I would necessarily be driven into town by his artillery unless I moved up nearer, and believing from the evidence I had that his force was a single brigade, I made my dispositions to capture it." By now it was obvious the Federals were in strength on the Utica Road and no where else. About noon, Gregg began pulling together the far-flung pieces of his brigade to strike with all the power he could muster. The Texans moved forward and, together with the 3rd Tennessee, were ordered to advance south on the east side of the Utica Road toward the creek and pin the enemy. The Tennesseans of the 50th and 10th-30th regiments, meanwhile, would move away from the Gallatin Road in a southwesterly direction toward what Gregg believed was the exposed Federal right. The attack would be taken up first by the Texans on the far right, and continue down the line *en echelon* (one unit after another) until the enemy was pinned and then turned and the battery captured. When all was ready Col. Hiram Granbury's 306 men of the 7th Texas, followed a few minutes later by Col. Calvin Walker's slightly larger 3rd Tennessee, "rushed forward with a shout" toward Fourteenmile Creek, falling against the right half of Dennis's brigade and a fragment of Smith's brigade.[23]

Like his division commander, Elias Dennis was an untrained yet excellent combat leader. The native of New York and resident of Illinois married the widow of a congressman and entered the bare-knuckle politics of Illinois, where he was elected to the state house and senate. Tired of the verbal political wrangling, Dennis moved to the Kansas territory and served as a U.S. marshal, but returned when the war began and mustered into service as a lieutenant colonel with the 30th Illinois Infantry. The long-haired and thickly bearded New Yorker turned in solid service at Fort Donelson and was applauded for his efforts by his superiors. Promotions to colonel and later in the year to brigadier general followed. On May 12 he had no way of knowing Raymond would be the high point of his career east of the river in the Vicksburg campaign.[24]

The Utica Road bisected Dennis's brigade, the 20th and 68th Ohio regiments deployed east of the road and the 30th Illinois and 78th Ohio on the west side. When the Southern storm broke loose upon them, the

Brigadier General
Elias Dennis

National Archives

20th lowered their heads and raised their muskets in the naturally strong steep-banked bottomland along the creek, laying down a heavy fire into the right wing of the advancing Texans, slowing them to a standstill. A leaden slug fest followed. The 20th's sister regiment on its right remained in place but a short time after the Texans made their appearance. The 68th Ohio fired perhaps one volley and made for the rear. Little more than hot Mississippi air and a thin handful of skirmishers stood between the left companies of the 7th Texas and the vital Utica Road, where De Golyer's six guns were firing for all they were worth.

With screaming Texans in their front and threatening to envelop their exposed right, panic began to course through the men of the 20th Ohio. Much of it ebbed when General Logan himself trotted up and held them to their duty, "riding up and down the line, firing the men with his own enthusiasm," recalled one eyewitness. Logan echoed these observations in his after-action report, adding, "The engagement raged with great fury for at least two hours.[25]

A short distance to the east, the fighting was equally bumpy for some of Smith's Federals. A native of Switzerland and the son of a Napoleonic officer, John Eugene Smith emigrated to America as a child. Trained as a jeweler and goldsmith, he moved again, this time to Galena, Illinois. His close association with Governor Richard Yates and his suggestion to use U.S. Grant to raise Union troops, notes one historian, "may have been instrumental in rescuing Grant from obscurity." Smith raised the 45th Illinois Infantry, served at Fort Donelson and Shiloh, and was promoted

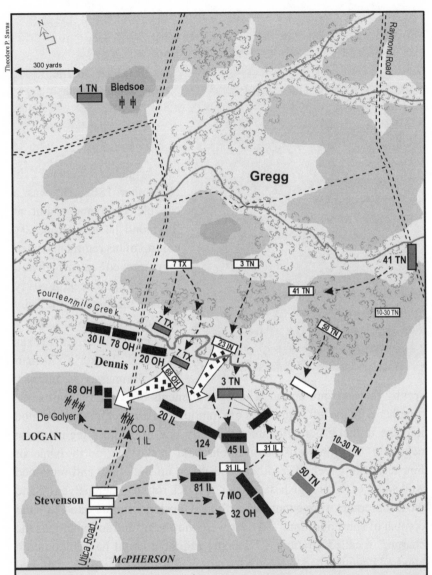

BATTLE OF RAYMOND

John Gregg's Attack
12:30 p.m. - 1:00 p.m., May 12, 1863

Gregg's attack takes McPherson by surprise and routs the 68th Ohio of Dennis's brigade and 23rd Indiana of Smith's brigade. With the enemy pinned in front, Gregg decides to turn their right, not realizing the heavy woods and ravines hold several enemy brigades with more reinforcements on the way. When the enemy keeps reinforcing with fresh troops, Gregg finally realizes he is heavily outnumbered.

Brigadier General
John E. Smith

National Archives

to brigadier general in November 1862. He was a capable commander, but at Raymond he lost temporary control of his regiments when they moved north toward Fourteenmile Creek, a costly mistake that brought the army within a whisker of disaster.[26]

Once the 7th Texas advanced, Walker's 550-man 3rd Tennessee Infantry sprung forward into action. The right elements of Walker's regiments, together with the left companies of Granbury's Texas regiment, slammed into the unlucky 23rd Indiana—the only one of Smith's regiments to negotiate the jungle-like conditions and make the north bank of Fourteenmile Creek. The others had given up the effort and remained well south of the sluggish waterway. A quick round of defensive fire and the Southerners were entangled with the Hoosiers in a rare hand-to-hand combat of short duration. "So near were the enemy and so impetuous the charge," recalled Granbury, "that my regiment could have bloodied a hundred bayonets had the men been supplied with that weapon." Clubbed muskets would have to do, and they did just fine. Back fled the 23rd Indiana across the creek. Thinned by the fallen and captured, the Hoosiers finally stopped and reformed on the right of Smith's 20th Illinois regiment. The Texans on the left of Granbury's line jumped into the natural trench of the creek bed and engaged their enemies across the waterway. The Tennesseans, meanwhile, continued forward with a shout, angling slightly southeast against another of Smith's regiments, the 45th Illinois. Waiting in the woods on Smith's far right and facing generally northwest, however, was the awkwardly aligned 31st Illinois. "Unperceived by the enemy," Smith wrote in his report, the 31st "opened fire upon them with such effect that they were driven from the right." The left of Smith's line squared off against the 3rd Tennessee and pieces of the 7th Texas while Dennis's Ohioans fought gamely against the balance of Granbury's Texans "under a galling fire nearly two hours." The repulse of the Tennesseans perplexed Gregg, who would later note in his report, "the enemy continued to re-enforce with fresh troops."[27]

Pieces of two of McPherson's brigades were in action by the time John Stevenson's four Federal regiments prepared to enter the Raymond maelstrom. The native Virginian-turned-Missourian was a Mexican War veteran, veteran politician, and an indefatigable grumbler, perhaps in part because of his low wartime rank compared to what he had held in the antebellum army as a volunteer. He had entered the war as a colonel of the 7th Missouri and saw service at Shiloh and Corinth. March of 1863 brought the officer with the walrus mustache a brigadier general's commission, to date from November 1862. Stevenson placed his men in position to the rear of the other two brigades, with his right withdrawn to protect the open flank of the division. It was shortly after 1:00 p.m. and Stevenson had barely formed near the Utica Road when the roar of battle washed across the front. Couriers soon arrived with disturbing news: a sizable body of rebels—the 50th and 10-30th Tennessee regiments—was approaching from the northeast, heading toward Smith's vulnerable

Brigadier General
John D. Stevenson

National Archives

right flank. Gregg's bold envelopment had been spotted. Stevenson wasted no time driving his men east through the largely open woods. His brigade was destined to fight in segments, however. Two of his regiments were quickly peeled off in succession by Logan to support Dennis's collapsed right and Smith's punctured line. Stevenson's remaining pair formed on the right of the 31st Illinois, extending McPherson's line to the east in a wide semi-circle roughly following the course of the creek as it bowed away to the east and south. Stevenson's hasty but sure-footed deployment ruined Gregg's audacious plan, for now there was no flank left to strike.[28]

Gregg, however, was still riding the high of his initial success. The Texans and Tennesseans had easily pushed through and across the creek, where the fighting was heavy, the enemy appearing to be in brigade strength and pinned in place for the *coup de grace*. Unfortunately for Southern arms, the dust, smoke, and heavy timber and brush hid from Gregg the true state of affairs. As historian Edwin Bearss has noted, "How was Gregg to know that the troops the Texans and Tennesseans had overthrown . . . consisted of isolated regiments of three brigades, rather than one? Thus far, by a peculiar combination of circumstances, the Confederates had made direct contact with only two regiments, although there were now 13 on the field." Of course the opposite was true as well, for the same factors that hindered Gregg's attack kept McPherson in the dark as to Gregg's paltry numbers and precarious disposition.[29]

Once the 7th Texas and 3rd Tennessee were fully engaged, Col. Thomas Beaumont's 50th Tennessee moved forward in double line of battle. Beaumont crossed the creek without opposition and sidled some distance to his left, unknowingly moving in the path of the 10th-30th Tennessee. The cautious Beaumont stopped his men and crept to the front to reconnoiter. His mouth must have fallen open when his eyes realized what lay before him. "A line of infantry . . . extended as far as I could see toward our right. . . . On our left another body of troops was seen, but their strength could not be estimated, as they were hidden from view, with the exception of one regiment." The enemy brigade he was attacking had suddenly grown to something closer to a division—or more. "I was satisfied that an attack would be uninviting," he added with delicious understatement. Beaumont dispatched a staffer to inform General Gregg of the bad news, but the officer returned without success. Meanwhile,

Colonel Randall MacGavock of the 10th-30th regiment itched to move forward. His orders were to await the sounds of Beaumont's battle before engaging. When the fight did not spread to that sector, MacGavock refused to budge. Gregg's attack had stalled.[30]

The tide of battle—and the inevitability of numbers—was about to turn decisively in McPherson's favor. Those left companies of Granbury's 7th Texas that had crossed the creek were driven back to the creek bed by Smith's 20th Illinois. General Logan was on the scene, pressing his men into the attack. "Lieutenant-Colonel Richards . . . while gallantly leading his men forward, was killed by a musket shot through the left breast," he recorded in his report. The 3rd Tennessee battled a hundred yards east of the 7th Texas. With his men well in hand, Walker advanced anew but was knocked back a second time by another deadly volley fired by the protruding and well sheltered 31st Illinois. Sensing the time had come for a counterpunch, Logan ordered the front line regiments (including the 81st Illinois from Stevenson's brigade) to attack Walker's isolated regiment. The fighting seesawed back and forth for about one hour before the Tennesseans finally broke and fled across the creek. A few well placed volleys by Col. Robert Farquharson's recently-arrived 41st Tennessee, which had been ordered up by Gregg to jumpstart his sluggish left hook, ended the tepid Federal pursuit. A four-gun Illinois battery sporting 24-lb. howitzers galloped up and deployed astride the road behind Dennis's embattled brigade, displacing De Golyer's pieces, which moved and dropped trail west of the roadway. Ten pieces were now defending the left front of McPherson's corps. The guns, Logan later claimed, "did some most splendid execution."[31]

What had begun with such promise for Gregg and his men was unraveling like a ball of yarn dropped down a staircase. The regiments that chased back Walker turned and struck Granbury's Texans, who fought tenaciously for a short time and then fell back in utter disarray. "My command pressed the enemy back under a most galling fire, and crossed the creek over which we have been fighting by wading it," wrote Logan. "The enemy were soon in total rout." The colonel of the 20th Ohio remembered how the 7th Texas was "slaughtered and driven" at Raymond. "Twenty-three dead were found in half an acre in front of the line of the Twentieth Ohio," he wrote. Seven more were discovered "behind a log, which was pierced by seventy-two balls." Granbury rallied his men north of the road junction, where they sought the protection of

Bledsoe's Missouri artillery and Maj. Stephen H. Colms's 1st Tennessee Battalion, which dressed ranks and marched south to intervene between the Texans and the advancing enemy.[32]

John Gregg's problems were only beginning. While the Texans were being assailed, the head of Isaac Quinby's Third Division, on this day under Brig. Gen. Marcellus Crocker, reached the field. The veteran officer had taken charge of the division when Quinby fell ill in early May. Crocker would demonstrate soon enough he had what it took to handle a division-sized command in the field. On the afternoon of May 12, his chief concern was getting his brigades to the front in time to turn the tide of battle.[33]

McPherson was pleased Crocker was up but anxious for his quiescent left flank, which thus far had not been threatened. He determined to extend it a bit in the hope of making contact with Sherman's corps, whose arrival he had been expecting. Crocker's leading brigade under Col. John Sanborn was thus ordered to move west (or left) of the road and form on Elias Dennis's left flank. Sanborn's three regiments "hurried into position," Crocker reported matter-of-factly, while a pair of other regiments headed east to support Stevenson. "Soon after making this disposition of troops," he wrote, "the enemy's whole line broke and fled in confusion."[34]

Gregg's right had collapsed and his left was about to suffer the same fate. The confused nature of the Raymond fighting is brought to light by the situation encountered by Colonel Beaumont and his 50th Tennessee. After discovering that strong infantry supported the battery he was to have flanked and captured, Beaumont (pursuant to earlier orders) edged his command eastward to make sure the entire Confederate line was not outflanked. He was surprised a second time that day when he discovered MacGavock's 10th-30th Tennessee Infantry during the movement. "I had supposed until then that he was farther toward the right," explained Beaumont. When he learned from MacGavock that Gregg still desired an attack, "I placed myself under Colonel MacGavock's order to insure concert of action, which I considered of the greatest importance to the success of the attack." After aligning his men, Beaumont sent word to MacGavock he was ready, but was told to wait for further orders. They never arrived. Instead, the 10th-30th Tennessee drifted off to the right "and I lost sight of him," wrote the frustrated Beaumont. "Our regiment was left entirely alone."[35]

A few minutes later a "rapid and continuous firing, indicating a hot engagement" between MacGavock's command and the Federals erupted. Scouts informed Beaumont that MacGavock was being driven and that heavy bodies of the enemy were about to strike his own 50th Tennessee. A barrage of fire swept through the regiment from the right, and Walker's men were pushed back step-by-step "in tolerable order" into a wide bend of the creek, where it fought for a time before spilling back over the meandering waterway and then east and north to the Gallatin Road. The Tennesseans reformed in the same area they had earlier used as a staging area. It was about this time when Beaumont was struck in the head by a musket ball. The wound "bled profusely," he later reported, "but did not disable me."[36]

Just as Beaumont had done, so too would Colonel MacGavock's 10th-30th Tennessee fight largely on its own hook. Whether driven back as Beaumont implies or ordered back by Gregg, MacGavock sidled several hundred yards to the right to block Smith's Union counterattack against Walker's 3rd Tennessee. MacGavock eventually formed near the top of a hill close to the left flank of Farquharson's recently arrived 41st Tennessee. There, Federal artillery found them and unloaded shell on his position. Stevenson's 7th Missouri soon caught up with them as well. Falling back was not an option for MacGavock, who instead ordered an attack. A bullet cut him down quickly, but his largely unbloodied 10th-30th Tennessee drove back the Missourians in confusion. Leaderless and perhaps aware of their exposed position, the Tennesseans, in turn, retreated back up the hill and laid down just behind the crest. Pressed by the same Missouri troops they had just chased away, they stood and exchanged fire, driving them back a second time.[37]

Gregg had realized for some time now that he had stirred up a hornet's nest larger than a brigade. When he wrongly perceived a threat to his far left, he ordered Farquharson to pull his 41st Tennessee out of line and march east. His thin right was now in shambles and a good punch up the Utica Road would rip it wide open and possibly cut off his retreat. Gregg proved himself a masterful tactician, plugging holes and patching his line in the midst of chaos that would have paralyzed many other leaders. When Sanborn's troops, Crocker's division, extended the Federal left and threatened to attack, Gregg ordered Major Stephen H. Colms's 1st Tennessee Battalion to posture strongly on the west side of the road to delay an enemy advance. "I immediately moved my command

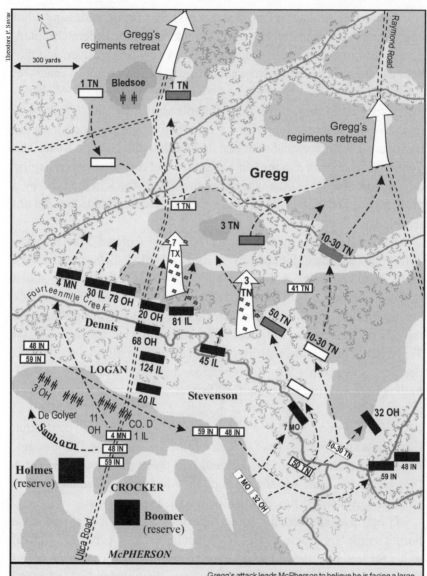

BATTLE OF RAYMOND

Repulse & Counterattack
1:30 p.m. - 4:00 p.m., May 12, 1863

Gregg's attack leads McPherson to believe he is facing a large opponent. Logan uncoils his division and once deployed, moves forward and sweeps back Gregg's fragmented brigade. Crocker's division arrives behind Logan; one brigade (Sanborn) joins the action. With a masterful tactical touch, Gregg pulls back his bloodied regiments and withdraws from the field. McPherson does not vigorously pursue.

forward and took position in the field south of the Port Gibson Road, under the fire of the enemy's batteries, and on his extreme left," observed Colms. The enemy, which Colms correctly assessed as two regiments, saw his movement and, perhaps believing it a prelude to attack, pulled back into the woods and disappeared. Not wasting a moment, Gregg ordered Colms to slide back east of the road to cover both it and the shattered Texans during a general withdrawal to Raymond.[38]

More fighting and confused maneuvering continued, but the battle was effectively lost for the Confederates. Beaumont's 50th Tennessee ended up several hundred yards to the west astride the Utica Road, falling back while protecting that vital artery during the retreat. The 3rd Kentucky (Confederate) Mounted Infantry arrived from Jackson and joined them on the road, too late and too weak to change the course of the battle. Gregg skillfully pulled his men back through Raymond and beyond Snake Creek, where they camped for the night five miles from the scene of battle. Federal pursuit was half-hearted and ineffective, largely because of the confusing terrain, dust, smoke, and fog of war, which conspired to make a vigorous chase difficult. Exhausted but elated, McPherson was satisfied to end the fight with his corps intact and without a defeat carved onto his resume. A Federal soldier felt much the same way when he wrote home that the corps "came very near getting whipped."[39]

The tired but victorious Federal infantrymen trudged up the Utica Road to Raymond. The Confederate retreat had been so hasty that food prepared by the ladies of Raymond went uneaten. The men found the treat much to their liking, prompting one to proclaim the village a "splendid little town." McPherson arrived a short time later and established his headquarters north of the town square.[40]

The Battle of Raymond is little more than a footnote in Civil War literature, but for several thousands of men it was the experience of a lifetime. Losses were moderate by Civil War standards. McPherson sat down later that evening and wrote out a brief report to Grant. He was still unaware he had fought only a single Confederate brigade. "We met the enemy, about 6,000 strong, commanded by Brigadier-General Gregg. After a sharp and severe contest of about three hours' duration . . . the enemy was driven back and retreated precipitately, passing out of this town on the Jackson road, Edwards Depot road, and Gallatin road." Perhaps in an attempt to ward off potential criticism, he added, "The heavy terrain prevented anything like the effective use of artillery or a very rapid pursuit." Federal casualties were eventually tabulated at 446 men—68 killed, 341 wounded, and 37 missing.

McPherson did not earn high marks for the handling of his corps at Raymond. He lost the initiative from the outset of the engagement and never regained it until his enemy was exhausted and ready to leave the field. He outnumbered his enemy by several factors (and by seven to one in artillery) and yet failed to bring these numbers to bear, fighting instead piecemeal at the regimental level. The fighting was not "about three hours duration," as McPherson wrote in his report, but nearly six hours (from 10:00 a.m. until about 4:00 p.m.). Yet, he was able to muster only one coordinated attack, and that composed of only a few regiments. When his enemy finally collapsed and melted away as fast as they could withdraw, McPherson was caught without plans for a pursuit even though he had ample reserves in hand and plenty of daylight left to launch one. Raymond was not James McPherson's best day, but it did offer a demonstration of his tactical abilities.[41]

John Gregg, on the other hand, demonstrated real ability in tactical planning, the judicious use of discretion, and the capacity for inspiring his men. He began the day on the defensive, developed a daring plan, implemented it, and held the initiative and the field for hours. Even though he believed initially the Federals were about equal in strength, most commanders would have remained in place and surrendered the initiative to the enemy. "Our aggregate engaged was 2,500," he wrote, with losses (which were later updated slightly) as 73 killed, 252 wounded, and 190 missing, or 515. His losses may have been even heavier. McPherson later reported his men buried 103 Rebels and captured 720, including some 80 wounded left on the field. If correct, Gregg suffered perhaps 300 more casualties than he reported. The simple fact is that we will probably never know for sure how many men were lost at Raymond.[42]

The importance of the meeting engagement at Raymond rests not with the numbers lost but in its strategic consequences. The fighting spun the entire inland campaign in a different direction. Grant had spent the day with Sherman's corps many miles southwest of Raymond and learned of the battle early that evening. True strategist that he was, Grant immediately grasped the significance of the combat on several levels. First, there were more Confederates on the Jackson front than he initially believed. For some time he had been receiving intelligence that enemy reinforcements had been collecting at Jackson, and Gen. Joseph E. Johnston was slated to lead them. While McPherson was battling Gregg, McClernand's corps had skirmished with elements of Pemberton's men who now seemed to be in force on the east side of the Big Black River. Grant's plan to move northwest and cut the railroad at Edwards Station and slide across the Big Black at that point had to be scrapped. He could not risk being bogged down against Pemberton with a capable general and sizeable field army directly in his rear. But a move against Johnston would endanger him from the west in the same manner.

Grant pondered the issue a short time and reached a decision: he would move northeast against Jackson, capture the important railroad and logistical center, defeat the enemy there or at least severely disrupt the Confederate concentration effort, and then turn quickly and move against Pemberton. As Grant later put it, "I will make sure of that place [Jackson] and leave no enemy in my rear." The capture of Mississippi's capital would also produce what one Confederate called "the *hallelujah* effect," or a boost in Northern morale. With Jackson subdued, Grant could then turn his full attention to Pemberton and Vicksburg. He would make the move with almost his entire army to ensure success. McPherson would move northeast toward Clinton, a small town on the rail line a few miles west of Jackson, and then drive dead east into the city; Sherman's XV Corps would approach from the southwest; McClernand would move with three of his four divisions to Raymond and be within supporting distance of the move, facing west to act as a shield against Pemberton. His last division would wait near Old Auburn for the arrival of Sherman's remaining division, which was moving inland with the supply trains from Grand Gulf.[43]

The audacious move to secure and exploit interior lines between two enemy armies demonstrated "the daring of Napoleon," exclaimed one Federal. Another, a member of the 33rd Illinois, described the situation as "extremely critical . . . and for any other general [it] would have been desperate." But for U. S Grant the plan was anything but desperate. It was a well calculated effort that took into consideration many factors— including the probability that a passive response would be the only reaction from John C. Pemberton and Joseph E. Johnston.[44]

Chapter 4

Jackson

"The advance was made in the most gallant and satisfactory manner."
— Brig. Gen. Marcellus Crocker, USA

WHEN CIVIL WAR ERUPTED IN EARLY 1861, THE QUARTERMASTER general of the United States was widely considered one of the most promising officers in the entire army. Because he was a native of Farmville, Virginia, it surprised no one that Joseph Eggleston Johnston "went South" on April 22, resigning his commission to follow his home state into the Confederacy. Like his good friend and academy classmate Robert E. Lee, Joe Johnston was born into a family with deep roots in American military lore (his father had a distinguished career in the Revolutionary War). He entered West Point in 1825 and graduated four years later thirteenth of forty-six cadets with a commission as second lieutenant in the artillery. Except for about one year in the late 1830s, his entire prewar career was in the service of the United States Army.

After several years in the artillery, Johnston transferred to the engineers, was promoted to captain in 1846, and lieutenant colonel of voltigeurs two years later. The man had a habit of attracting wounds, whether fighting Indians in Florida or Mexicans in the Mexican War. That troublesome tradition would continue after 1861. His rise through

General
Joseph E. Johnston

National Archives

the ranks would continue as well. In 1855, Johnston was bumped up to lieutenant colonel in the prestigious 1st United States Cavalry Regiment. Five years later he was elevated to Quartermaster General of the army with a staff rank of brigadier general. His highest line rank, however, was lieutenant colonel. The distinction was more important than anyone could have realized at the time, and would cause much angst after he shed his blue uniform for a coat of gray.[1]

Johnston began his Confederate career with much promise. The distinguished looking officer, "below middle height," about 5'8" tall, and all of 140 pounds when dripping wet, entered the service of Virginia as a major general for a short time before being reduced to a brigadier when it was decided too many held the higher rank in state service. On May 14, 1861, he was appointed brigadier general in the Provisional Confederate Army, the highest grade allowed by law. As the ranking officer on the field, the stunning July victory at Manassas was Johnston's to savor but P. G. T. Beauregard's to popularize. Three weeks later the Confederate Congress established the rank of full general. The law sought to place each officer at the relative rank and seniority he enjoyed while in the service of the United States. Using Johnston's line rank of lieutenant colonel, President Davis ranked him fourth—below Samuel Cooper, Albert S. Johnston, and Robert E. Lee. Often quick to perceive a slight, Johnson took his standing as a slap and opened a running feud on the matter with Davis that would fester until their deaths. The classification would also infect the course of military events in Mississippi in May 1863.[2]

Joe Johnston's record in the field is one of perplexing mediocrity. Although a master of logistics and organization, waging vigorous combat to further the objectives of the Davis administration was anathema to him. Davis waged a fixed defensive perimeter war designed to hold geography; Johnston favored maneuvering and trading space for time. These philosophies mixed like oil and water. At the head of the Virginia army he withdrew up the peninsula to the gates of Richmond, all the while refusing to discuss in detail his plans for stopping the enemy. With his back to the capital, Johnston launched a bungled offensive effort at Seven Pines that cost him his command at the end of May 1862, when Federal lead and metal knocked him from his saddle. The army ended up with Robert E. Lee, who led it into the pantheon of Confederate history. Johnston, meanwhile, recovered and was shipped west in November 1862 to assume command of the mammoth Department of the West. He professed but little faith in Davis's plans and privately seethed at his exile from Virginia and the circumstances of his rank. By the time the Vicksburg campaign was well underway, Johnston and Davis were barely on speaking terms.[3]

As a department commander, Johnson exercised little authority over his subordinates but was responsible for their actions. The two primary armies operating under his command were led by Braxton Bragg in Tennessee and John C. Pemberton in Mississippi. He realized by April 1863 that Mississippi was seriously threatened by Grant's army, but Johnston seemed unwilling to undertake anything of substance to alter the course of events. He was also ill much of that spring, which made it that much more difficult for him to act. On May 9, three days before the battle of Raymond but nine days after Grant crossed the river, Davis ordered Johnston to travel from Tullahoma to Mississippi: "[T]ake command of the forces there, giving to those in the field, as far as practicable, the encouragement and benefit of your personal direction."

He detrained in Jackson on the evening of May 13 with only a few additional troops in tow and without a clear idea of the situation. Inserting Johnston directly into the Mississippi maelstrom only worsened matters. Johnston had no intention of taking personal command of the army, and his presence increased the likelihood contradictory orders would be sent to Pemberton (some from Johnston, others from

Richmond). The situation was grave and worsening by the hour. When he learned from General Gregg of the fight at Raymond and the presence of Federals astride the railroad leading to Vicksburg ten miles west of Jackson at Clinton, Johnston threw up his hands in despair. He wired Pemberton shortly before 9:00 that night. "It is important to re-establish communications that you may be re-enforced. If practicable, come up on his rear at once. . . . The troops here could co-operate. All the strength you can quickly assemble should be brought. Time is all important." He also wired Richmond to inform Davis and the war department of the strategic situation, adding ominously, "I am too late."[4]

*   *   *

If Johnston was late, General Grant was ahead of schedule. Refusing to waste an hour, he had his men up early on May 13 in preparation for a giant strategic sweep eastward to knock Jackson out of the contest. McPherson's XVII Corps marched northeast from Raymond for Clinton. His was the intervening column that divided Pemberton from Jackson and prompted Johnston's hand-wringing telegraph to President Davis. Sherman's XV Corps, meanwhile, moved on the army's right, marching generally eastward to approach Mississippi's capital city from the southwest. After a feint toward Edwards Station and a skirmish with Pemberton's men, McClernand's XIII Corps also turned east toward Raymond. The noose on Jackson was closing quickly.[5]

McPherson reached Clinton and the vital Southern Railroad of Mississippi without opposition on the evening of May 13. The rain did little to dampen the spirits of the men, who realized the importance of their accomplishment. After cutting the telegraph and railroad, ending direct communication between Pemberton and the Confederate force gathering in Jackson, McPherson turned east toward the rail hub. Sherman, too, was heading toward the capital. His two-division advance brushed up against reconnaissance patrols sent out by John Gregg, who believed Sherman's men were moving north to join the two divisions already astride the railroad at Clinton. Believing the south and southwest approaches were not threatened, Gregg fell back into Jackson to prepare to meet an advance against the city from the west. It was a critical error that left the route up the Raymond Road open for Sherman. By 5:00 a.m. on May 14, both McPherson and Sherman were inching toward the outskirts of the capital. Skirmishing broke out. Confederate resistance was stiffening.[6]

*   *   *

Johnston wired Richmond he was too late to turn the tide in Mississippi, but in fact several options were still available to the Confederates. One opportunity had been slipping through Pemberton's fingers for two days. While McPherson and Sherman were moving toward Raymond, three divisions from John McClernand's XIII Corps had moved up to Fourteenmile Creek and established a bridgehead above it. From there, McClernand postured in the direction of Edwards Station. The presence of the Federals so close to the railroad extracted Bowen's Division (and later William Loring and Carter Stevenson) eastward to Edwards Station, where Bowen began entrenching on the hills to the south. Pemberton had some 22,000 men available against McClernand's 13,000. McClernand's heavy feint, however, was conducted with boldness and skill. Even as the Confederates were focusing attention on the head of his movement, McClernand was gone, moving with the balance of his corps east across Bakers Creek in the direction of Raymond. Just as Grant had done earlier in the campaign and was doing again in his march to Jackson, McClernand stole a march on Pemberton. Pemberton had for too long dallied at Bovina west of the Big Black River when his presence was urgently required in the field with his men. "Instead of using Fourteenmile Creek as an anvil and his army as a hammer with McClernand trapped between them," wrote one historian of the Confederate high command, "Pemberton did nothing at all." Another opportunity to engage a segment of Grant's army was missed.[7]

Johnston, meanwhile, had to make the decision whether to mount a vigorous defense of the important rail center or abandon it to the Federals. He had but little to work with in Jackson—at least initially. By the night of May 13 there were only some 6,000 Southerners under arms there. These included Gregg's Brigade, two recently arrived brigades under W. H. T. Walker and States Right Gist (the latter led by Col. Peyton Colquitt), and several miscellaneous organizations. Other regiments were riding the rails on their way to Jackson. By the next afternoon another 4,000 soldiers were slated to arrive, and that number would swell by another 3,000 late on May 16 with the addition of Matthew Ector's and Evander McNair's brigades, due to arrive from the Army of Tennessee. Johnston had other problems besides numbers. There were few entrenchments protecting the city, and those that existed were inadequate and improperly located. An aggressive enemy lurked in the countryside, though exactly which Union corps was where was not clear. Johnston evaluated his chances, spoke with General Gregg, and made a decision: evacuation was the best option. The order was issued at 3:00 a.m., just a handful of hours after his arrival. Valuable property that could be hauled away to safety was prepared for shipment. Jackson already belonged to the Union and there was not a Union soldier in sight.[8]

Given the critical importance of Jackson to the defense of Vicksburg and the potential survival of Pemberton's army, it is difficult to condone Johnston's decision to desert the city without attempting to mount a serious defense. Edwin C. Bearss, the former chief historian at Vicksburg, rebuked Johnston for not fighting for the capital. The basis of Bearss's assessment is grounded in convincing evidence Johnston ordered the withdrawal hours before the advance upon the city began, and before he learned Sherman's corps was close by at Mississippi Springs with Jackson as its destination. As historian Bearss puts it:

> The fight [at Jackson] is not a battle to be remembered because of great casualties, numbers engaged, or brilliant tactics. . . . . The Jackson engagement, however, was of major significance to Grant and his campaign east of the Mississippi. . . . Grant, by capturing Jackson scattered what within another 24 hours would have become a formidable force. Such an army in possession of Jackson and with the railroads passing through the city facilitating its reinforcement, and being commanded by the popular Johnston, could have constituted a terrible threat to Grant's army, dependent as it was for reinforcements of men and military hardware on a dirt road linking it to the Grand Gulf enclave.[9]

The Battle of Jackson

John Gregg was given tactical command of the defenses of Jackson. The situation was anything but enviable. His orders were to wage a delaying action to cover the evacuation of the city. The bold general of

Raymond set about his difficult task before dawn that same morning. Under a steady rain the 900 men comprising Gist's Brigade under Colonel Colquitt trudged through the mud a few miles west out the Clinton Road to the high ground of the Wright farm. They deployed astride the road with a battery of artillery and awaited the approach of the enemy. General Walker was ordered "to move his brigade to within easy supporting distance . . . and remain until it became necessary to render his assistance in order to prevent Colonel Colquitt's from being forced back." Gregg's own brigade, under the 41st Tennessee's Col. Robert Farquharson, followed Colquitt's men out of town and was ordered to sidle by the right flank (north) "across the open field . . . and whenever within sight of the enemy make such demonstrations as might impress him with the idea that it was our intention to fall upon his left flank." The 1st Georgia Sharpshooter Battalion, a Georgia battery from Walker's Brigade, and the 3rd Kentucky Mounted Infantry, all under Col. Albert P. Thompson, would later be dispatched out the Raymond Road to the southwest when Gregg learned Federals were approaching from that direction. Ringing the western and southern approaches in light field works behind these men were seventeen artillery pieces, most served by local troops and armed citizens.[10]

The Southerners looked to the east. Dawn was almost upon them.

*   *   *

The rain hampered Union efforts to get at Jackson. Wagon wheels churned the roads into mud. Soaked soldiers cursed their lot as they leaned tired shoulders into the caissons and wagons. From the west, McPherson's two divisions faced the city, Crocker's brigades in the lead followed by Logan's men. Foster's cavalry screened the front. Sherman's men, accompanied by General Grant and his staff, were also on the move southwest below Jackson. Brigadier General James M. Tuttle's division of three brigades was in front, slogging along the Raymond Road. Major General Frederick Steele's division trudged some distance behind. Iowa cavalry screened Sherman's route. "We communicated during the night," explained Sherman, "so as to arrive at Jackson about the same hour." It was a difficult converging operation, and a rare event during the Civil War. The fields were ankle-deep with water, the ground rough, and the going slow. Throughout the early morning hours, skirmishers of both armies traded shots as the twin blue hosts eased their butternut counterparts rearward toward the doomed state capital.[11]

Grant and his corps leaders expected a large-scale fight at Jackson. Joe Johnston's arrival had worried McPherson, who learned of his presence almost before the Southern leader got off the train and so notified Sherman. The heavy combat, however, failed to materialize. Early that morning, however, the promise of a stand-up fight loomed large on the eastern horizon. The opening shots of the engagement were launched by the artillery battery attached to Gist's Brigade. The guns were deployed below the Clinton Road with a South Carolina regiment on its left, and two regiments, the 14th Mississippi and 46th Georgia, extending the line north of the road. Crocker pushed out Colonel Boomer's brigade to the left above the road, most of Colonel Holmes's brigade below the road, and kept Colonel Sanborn's brigade in support. A Federal Missouri battery was brought up to engage the Confederate artillery. Gregg later credited Colquitt's vigorous skirmish and artillery fire and the appearance of his own brigade on the Confederate right for the "cautious and slow" enemy advance. In reality McPherson's guarded approach had more to do with the weather. The sun was well up but a sudden increase in the rain concerned McPherson. Worried the water would ruin his ammunition, he delayed his assault hoping the skies would clear.[12]

Southwest of the city a motley Confederate force had arrayed itself in the open ground near the bridge across the now unfordable Lynch Creek. Sherman was unimpressed. He ordered Tuttle to deploy his division into line on the high ground fronting the waterway about one and one-half miles outside the city. The civilian-turned-soldier had labored in a wide variety of fields before entering service with the 2nd Iowa as a lieutenant colonel. His keen mind and a willingness to mix politics with rank helped push him quickly up the command ladder, and his ability in the field was clearly evident at Fort Donelson and Shiloh. The Ohioan called Iowa home and was even then preparing to run for governor of the Hawkeye state. He would lose, as he would in a subsequent election in 1864. A cloud of graff and corruption would settle above his head before the war ended, and his resignation would be accepted by the war department in 1864. But on May 14, 1863, the pending battle for Jackson occupied his complete attention. Tuttle directed his brigades into a configuration similar to that employed by McPherson: one brigade on either side of the

Brigadier General
James M. Tuttle

Generals in Blue

road and a third behind in support. Up until that time the weather had been unrelenting. "[It was] the most drenching rain, which poured down on our men and flooded the roads," one Federal remembered. It was about one hour shy of noon when the rain suddenly stopped, only to be replaced by the iron shells of a Georgia artillery battery. Union batteries were called up to answer and the weight of the metal quickly took control of the situation, driving the defenders back to a distant fringe of woods. The narrow bridge slowed the Federal advance to a trickle, but the advance continued nonetheless.[13]

Sherman kept up the pressure. Tuttle's three brigades were each led by a brigadier general. They reformed north of the bridge. Charles Matthies's men took up position on the left of the road, Joseph Mower's on the right, and Ralph Buckland's regiments behind Mower. Buckland remembered Mower's men charged forward with a shout, and the outnumbered enemy turned tail and retreated again, this time back into the entrenchments ringing Jackson. When Sherman approached within artillery range, the batteries stationed in the earthworks opened fire. He stopped to assess the situation. It was about noon.[14]

North of Sherman's temporarily stalled effort, McPherson was enjoying success, folding the Confederate defenders back on Jackson in a powerful thrust that Gregg found impossible to resist. While the artillery duel was ongoing, Gregg's Brigade under Farquharson moved north across flooded Town Creek as previously ordered and threatened

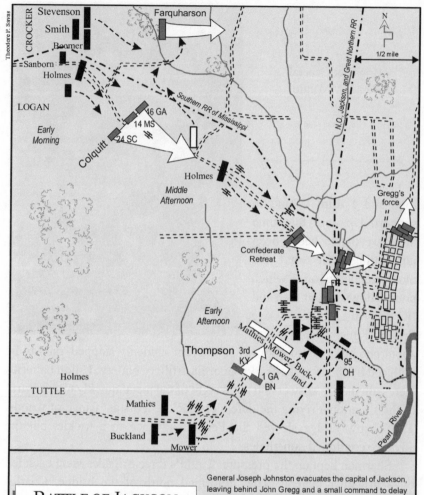

BATTLE OF JACKSON

Grant Captures the Capital
9:00 a.m. - 4:00 p.m., May 14, 1863

General Joseph Johnston evacuates the capital of Jackson, leaving behind John Gregg and a small command to delay Grant's entry into the city. After a brief but sharp fight northwest of town, the divisions of John Logan and Marcellus Crocker drive in the Rebels, who fall back and retreat northward out of the city. Sherman approaches from below and penetrates the city's southwestern defenses.

McPherson's left flank from behind the flooded waterway. Without missing a beat, McPherson ordered General Logan to deploy his division on Crocker's left to meet it. Stevenson's brigade trotted up and formed north of Boomer, while Smith's brigade formed a few hundred yards to the rear. Dennis's brigade remained in the rear with the baggage trains. When the rain stopped about 11:00 a.m. McPherson ordered his men forward.[15]

Gregg's situation now took on the appearance of the second half of the Raymond fight. He did not have enough men to effectively cover his front, no reinforcements could be expected, and the enemy now held the initiative. His Tennesseans and Texans under Farquharson could not effectively re-cross the swollen creek to engage McPherson's advancing left—although he might not have anyway because he was only under orders to threaten and not attack—leaving Colonel Colquitt's lone brigade to stop Crocker's division. Under a heavy fire, the Federals reached a ravine 500 yards from the Southern line. There they reformed and, according to Colonel Sanborn, were ordered by Crocker to fix bayonets and charge. "The advance was made in the most gallant and satisfactory manner," Crocker later reported. A savage hand-to-hand combat ensued. Crocker later wrote of driving the enemy "at point of the bayonet." Colquitt's outnumbered Confederates fought well but grudgingly gave ground yard-by-yard as they fell back to the Jackson fortifications. Knots of battling survivors fighting in buildings and other defensive positions eventually surrendered. Walker's elements could do nothing to help Colquitt and also fell back into the city's works. Farquharson pulled back his Tennesseans and Texans across the open country north of Jackson toward the Canton Road. A Federal artilleryman remembered the dead and wounded men who "lay over the whole field, the loss on both sides being very heavy."[16]

After reorganizing, McPherson ordered the pursuit to continue. It was about 3:00 p.m. Confederate artillery fire cracked in the air above the advancing lines. Federal batteries galloped into position, dropped trail, and responded in kind. Infantry fire joined the guns, rippling through the ranks. After a few minutes it slowly died away and the earthworks fell silent. Perplexed, the Federals formed a strike force composed of men from the 17th Iowa of Holmes's brigade that eased forward to probe the field works for weak points. Instead of fighting their way forward, they walked in without opposition. The Confederates were gone. "Our skirmishers and line steadily advanced into their works and into the town without further resistance," a relieved Crocker reported. Four guns stood silently guarding the earthworks. John Gregg had done his job. About 2:00 p.m. the Southern general received word the army's supply wagons had safely left Jackson and were well on their way north to Canton. Satisfied additional sacrifice was unnecessary, he ordered the works abandoned except for skeleton gun crews and a few miscellaneous troops to mask the evacuation for as long as possible. The Confederates withdrew on the Canton Road behind the supply trains.[17]

A short time before McPherson's men entered Jackson, Sherman's division under Tuttle moved toward the works on the southwest side of town. The Ohioan did not like what he saw. "As we emerged from the woods," he reported later with obvious apprehension, "to our front and as far to the left as we could see, appeared a line of entrenchments, and the enemy kept up a pretty brisk fire with artillery." When apprized of a flanking opportunity, Sherman sent the 95th Ohio on a right hook around the Confederate defenders, whom he later learned consisted of ten guns manned by state troops. The Ohioans gained the enemy's rear and captured the guns and Mississippians left behind to man them. Within a short time the flag of the 59th Indiana fluttered above Mississippi's domed capitol building. The Federals pursued Gregg's men north for a few hours, "but without further damage to him," wrote Grant in his report. The city cost the general, who would soon sleep in the bed occupied the night before by Joe Johnston, 42 killed, 251 wounded, and seven missing. Confederate casualties were not fully reported. Gist's (Colquitt's) Brigade, which shouldered the lion's share of the fighting, suffered 17 dead, 64 wounded, and 118 missing.[18]

It is difficult to overestimate the importance of Grant's capture of Jackson. Not only was the Confederate transportation center lost to the South, but more important was the scattering of Joe Johnston's small army (which after the battle became known as the Army of Relief). The force upon which so much hung in the balance was no longer a viable threat, at least in the short term. With Jackson's fall, Grant achieved one of his primary goals—destroying or removing one enemy wing from active operations. He was now free to deal with the other wing under Pemberton. With his army squarely on Pemberton's line of supply, Grant's own perilous position suddenly looked brighter. He was still deep in enemy territory with but a tenuous line of supply, but for the moment there was no viable threat against his rear. Vicksburg, the object of his attention for so many long and difficult months, now seemed within his grasp.[19]

That evening McPherson told Grant of a dispatch he had received at his headquarters. A Union spy, disguised as a Confederate and expelled from Memphis by its Federal commanding general, had gained access into the Confederate command system. He was one of three couriers entrusted with carrying messages between Confederate generals. One message outlined Confederate plans for a concentration of forces and an attack on Grant's rear at Clinton. With this news Grant had ample warning of the next likely Confederate move. On the night of May 14 the Federal commander issued orders for his army to make a complete turnaround. The three corps formed a rough line stretching from Clinton southwest to Raymond, with units stacked up around Jackson. Grant decided he had to remain between Johnston's forces (even though spread thin) and Pemberton's sizeable field army hovering some miles west around Bolton or Edwards Depot. As he crept west he would draw ever closer to Vicksburg. In order to avoid garrisoning Jackson, Grant ordered its railroads ripped up, its machine shops and industries burned, and telegraph lines cut.[20]

*　*　*

The Confederate situation in Mississippi worsened considerably with the evacuation and loss of Jackson on the late afternoon of May 14. It would take some hours before Pemberton learned of its fall. While McPherson was moving east toward Jackson that morning and Sherman northeast toward the same objective, Pemberton was pondering the wisdom of a move of his own east along the railroad toward Clinton. The possible move was prompted by Johnston's instructions to him of the previous night to "come up on his rear at once." Johnston had even promised Pemberton his forces in Jackson "could co-operate." Some 22,000 soldiers were readily available to Pemberton—not counting the pair of divisions under Smith and Forney left behind around Vicksburg. The rest of his men were deployed in relatively useless defensive positions to protect against threats that no longer existed. To Johnston's suggestion, Pemberton had wired back, "I move at once with whole available force (about 16,000 men) from Edwards Depot." He wrote those words believing the city on the Mississippi River would be left dangerously exposed by such a maneuver.

Striking out for a direct confrontation with the enemy seemed somehow out of character for Pemberton, and indeed it proved to be so. He immediately had second thoughts regarding the wisdom of Johnston's quasi-order, and reached the conclusion that if he advanced east against the enemy at Clinton, the Union corps he let escape unpunished the previous day (McClernand's) would be closer to Vicksburg than his own army. He also feared a move against his right flank by McClernand as his own army moved east. An attack by McClernand could pin him in place and prevent him from withdrawing in time to save Vicksburg. Pemberton suspended the marching orders and convened a council of war.[21]

The generals in attendance deliberated the prudence of Johnston's suggestion to move against McPherson. Pemberton told the men of his predicament, his orders, and his options, "placing the subject before them (including General Johnston's dispatch) in every view in which it appeared to me." He asked for their advice. Recollections of what transpired next vary with the telling. Some say the officers tossed the question back and forth, but could reach no consensus. One brigade commander recalled "the division of sentiment [that was] manifested." Certainly there was discord, and it had a less than calming effect on the group. A majority of the officers apparently favored the advance as planned, but Pemberton adamantly opposed it. His duty, he declared, was to defend Vicksburg. He spoke "at great length . . . and with great force," recalled one participant. After canvassing the generals, "not a voice in favor of moving on Clinton [was heard]." Perhaps. What we know for sure is that Pemberton preferred holding the Big Black River line. With Grant so far inland and now apparently reducing Jackson, moving back west of the river was a reasonable idea.[22]

William Loring, Carter Stevenson, and others, however, urged moving east and south against Grant's supply line from Grand Gulf to the Jackson area. Although Grant did not leave detachments to guard the route, he did have a line of communications stretching to the river that supplied him with ammunition and other provisions. Wagon trains frequently rolled out of Grand Gulf. Units of brigade strength or larger guarded these movements. The advance, these generals posited, would sever the line his wagons traveled (and, with luck, catch and destroy the lone division under Frank Blair marching with McClernand's corps near

New Auburn). If successful, Grant would not be able to linger long around Jackson; he would have to either retreat to Grand Gulf or meet Pemberton in battle on terrain of Pemberton's own choosing.[23]

Pemberton felt the heavy weight of what he judged to be a presidential directive to protect Vicksburg, and knew blame for losing the city, if the enemy marched in while he was away, would fall primarily on his shoulders. He tried to sway his subordinates to his side but soon realized the futility of such an attempt. Few if any of the generals supported him. As he later wrote, "I did not see fit to put my own judgment and opinions so far in opposition as to prevent a movement altogether." In this, Pemberton betrayed a serious lack of confidence in himself, and the lack of willpower to proceed with what he deemed as the best course of action.[24]

A large part of the confusion swirling in Pemberton's mind was the result of a series of communications he had been engaged in with Johnston and President Davis—both of whom were his superiors. This private triangular correspondence was contradictory, vague, and often outdated and unrealistic. Johnston had been lecturing Pemberton for weeks about the need to concentrate his forces (something the Pennsylvania native obviously needed to learn how to do). All during the critical stages of Grant's crossing and movement inland, messages flew from Johnston's headquarters urging Pemberton to bring together the troops at his disposal and fight. "If Grant's army lands on this side of the river," Johnston had written, "the safety of Mississippi depends on beating it. For that object you should unite your whole force." Another message in a similar vein read, "If Grant's army crosses, unite all your forces to beat it. Success will give you back what was abandoned [i.e., Vicksburg] to win it." Johnston favored concentration and maneuver. To his way of thinking, keeping the army free to move would prevent it from being trapped inside Vicksburg's extensive entrenchments. An aggressive early thrust was the only hope of beating Grant. And then Johnston arrived in Jackson and urged a strike toward Clinton.[25]

Much of Pemberton's hesitation—and why he called a council of war—was the result of Jefferson Davis. The Confederate president insisted on direct communication with Pemberton rather than going through Johnston as Pemberton's immediate superior and theater commander. (Worse still, occasionally these communications were in the form of orders.) Davis wrote Pemberton a week after Port Gibson, "To hold Vicksburg and Port Hudson is necessary to a connection with Trans-Mississippi." His orders sending him to Mississippi in the first place required him to "report directly to this [War] Department," so communication directly with Richmond and bypassing Johnston had been specifically authorized. Pemberton read Davis's missive as a directive: he was to defend Vicksburg at all costs.[26]

Conversely, Pemberton felt a need to comply with direct orders from his superior in Jackson. Johnston called for a movement east from Vicksburg and an attack on the enemy at Clinton. He was, in effect, asking Pemberton for assistance. Johnston was just a handful of miles away; Davis and Seddon were several states away. The quandary paralyzed Pemberton. What to do?[27]

The defender of Vicksburg finally reached a decision, the council broke up, and he wired Johnston at 5:40 p.m. on May 14: "I shall move as early as to-morrow morning as practicable with a column of 17,000 men to Dillon's, situated on the main road leading from Raymond to Port Gibson, 7 ½ miles below Raymond and 9 ½ miles from Edwards Depot." The intent of the movement, explained Pemberton, "is to cut [the] enemy's communications and to force him to attack me, as I do not consider my force sufficient to justify an attack on enemy in position or to attempt to cut my way to Jackson." Pemberton also noted his desire to "join my re-enforcements," but how he could bring that about by moving away from Johnston and Jackson is not clear.[28]

The main objectives were either Grant at Jackson or Vicksburg. Instead, Pemberton decided to march south—away from both. It was an unfortunate choice with ramifications that would ripple across the Confederacy.[29]

* * *

To study the generalship of Pemberton and Grant is to study contrasts. Grant's campaign, from his decision to cross the Mississippi River below Vicksburg through the capture of Jackson, was brilliantly planned and executed. The inland campaign was audacious from the start. Though outnumbered in the Port Gibson-Jackson-Vicksburg triangle 50,000 to 40,000, he led his troops into the heart of the Confederate defensive perimeter. By maneuver, feint, and guile he managed to outnumber his opponent at Port Gibson, Raymond, and

Jackson. Fast and decisive marching, driven on by bold leadership, placed his concentrated army between Pemberton and Johnston. One of Grant's brigade commanders summed the march up best when he wrote home, "Grant is making glorious progress and with all manner of obstacles to surmount."[30]

The Confederate response to Grant's brilliant campaign from Bruinsburg to Jackson was one of bungling incompetence. Grant acted quickly, decisively, and with strength; Pemberton reacted weakly and lethargically. The passing of the Vicksburg batteries in mid-April failed to alert Pemberton to the likely location of the next blow, precious troops were dispatched hither and yon chasing shadows they had little chance of catching, and division-size organizations were left garrisoning posts of little interest to the enemy when they could have been used to hammer the Federals early and often. Grant read Pemberton well. Indeed, he understood his opponent in a way Pemberton never comprehended him.

But Grant had not yet succeeded in gaining his objective. Vicksburg was still miles away and a potent army stood between him and the city. The coming days would determine how history would judge his actions.

Chapter 5

Prelude

"We turn our faces toward Vicksburg."
— Lt. William T. Rigby, 24th Iowa

GENERAL GRANT HAD THE UNIQUE ABILITY, MARVELED A Confederate soldier in the 22nd Mississippi, to concentrate his army "without our being permitted to fire a gun or to let our presence become known." Though wide of the mark, this observation demonstrates how some within the Confederate army viewed the developing campaign. Grant had certainly outgeneraled his opponent at every turn. Though it should not have, his crossing of the Mississippi River had caught Pemberton flatfooted. After Bowen's valiant effort at Port Gibson, Grant had marched inland quickly and confronted John Gregg's lone brigade at Raymond with a vastly superior force. Thereafter he stole a march and shooed Joe Johnston away from Jackson, Vicksburg's logistical hub and the Mississippi state capital. A stroke of good luck in the form of a Union spy doubling as a Confederate courier had deposited a copy of Johnston's May 13 dispatch to Pemberton in Grant's lap. Johnston was urging his subordinate to move toward Clinton and attack Grant in the rear. With his army fully concentrated, Grant issued orders for a movement to confront and destroy Pemberton's Confederates somewhere east of Big Black River before they could link up with Johnston's relief force.[1]

The corps closest to the enemy protecting Vicksburg belonged to John McClernand, and to him fell the honor of making contact with the Vickburg defenders. By the night of May 14, the Illinois general had three of his four divisions in a rough line running south from Clinton to Raymond. On the right was Alvin Hovey's division, camped for the night near Clinton. Peter Osterhaus's division spent the night in Raymond, with Eugene Carr's brigades nearby in Mississippi Springs. Only A. J. Smith's division was absent, marching on the road to Raymond guarding the trains with Frank Blair's division of Sherman's corps. (It was Blair's division Pemberton hoped to trap at Dillon's with his southeasterly thrust from Edwards. The Federals, however, would safely arrive in Raymond on the evening of May 15.) With McClernand's corps well situated, Grant ordered him, together with Blair's division, to "face their troops toward Bolton, with a view toward reaching Edwards, marching on different roads converging on Bolton." A Iowa Federal with the 24th regiment explained the move more simply: "We turn our faces toward Vicksburg."[2]

McClernand began his march early on May 15. With orders to take Bolton, he marched Osterhaus and Hovey west toward the railroad village. Both expected stout Confederate resistance. Osterhaus's men broke camp at 4:00 a.m. and arrived first. The 3rd Illinois Cavalry under Capt. John L. Campbell screened the advance and entered the town at 8:00 a.m. Several prisoners from the 20th Mississippi were captured and the rest were dispersed over the countryside. Once the town was free of Rebels, the horse soldiers commenced destroying vital bridges on both the railroad and road leading out of Bolton. The infantry arrived soon thereafter to tighten McClernand's grip on the small hamlet. Still, the situation was tense. "All reports and information obtained here confirmed the fact that large bodies of rebel forces were within a few miles of us and prepared to give us battle," wrote Osterhaus. By 9:30 a.m. Hovey's division tramped into view, prompting one of Osterhaus's men to remark, "We felt a little easier but not much." Both divisions were deployed to meet any attack Pemberton might launch against them.[3]

With Bolton secured and his divisions defensively deployed, McClernand spilled his cavalry west on both sides of the railroad to reconnoiter toward Edwards. It did not take long to find the enemy picket line. Light skirmishing occupied much of the middle of the day. Federal horsemen picked and probed at Confederate lines, "and at some points beyond," McClernand reported. His troopers made "every effort . . . to acquire familiar knowledge of the ground and roads for 7 miles west to Edwards Station." As he quickly discovered, a complicated system of roads fed into the Confederate concentration at Edwards, and the enemy seemed to be defending every one. At varying intervals, three good roads were found branching off the main Bolton-Raymond route, which McClernand tagged the "Northern, Middle, and Southern roads." Hovey's men were lucky; they remained guarding the northern approach along the Jackson Road at Bolton. Osterhaus's troops, however, drew the short straw and were directed to march back toward Raymond to block the Middle Road.[4]

Curses and profanity rang through the hills. The men from Indiana, Kentucky, and Ohio knew little and cared less about why the countermarch was necessary. What they did know was they had been up early and believed their marching was done for the day. At least the afternoon tramp was not too demanding. They stepped into the well traveled Raymond-Bolton road and paced off about three miles before Osterhaus ordered them to turn onto the Middle Road, where they "bivouacked on the same ground which the enemy's cavalry had just left." Osterhaus promptly threw out "cavalry vedettes and patrols [which] developed the enemy in the immediate vicinity." The Federals drove the Confederate pickets up the road only to uncover "a large body of mounted infantry." The enemy, wrote Osterhaus, "pressed into the line of my infantry pickets." Not knowing exactly what he had stumbled into, Osterhaus called up the 42nd Ohio, part of Col. Lionel Sheldon's brigade (which would soon be led by Col. Daniel W. Lindsey). The Buckeyes advanced to support the pickets, and "a lively engagement" ensued. "The enemy's forces retired and left us without further annoyance for that evening," reported Osterhaus. The Middle Road was not the only place to experience earnest skirmishing on May 15. The Confederates were well aware of the advancing Union fingers slipping up the road network toward Edwards. Unlike the enemy advance from Port Gibson to Raymond (which had been poorly screened), this time the Rebels smothered the creeping vanguards with skirmish fire as if to warn Grant that this time Pemberton was ready for him. The Confederates skirmished on May 15 "until they knew our force pretty well," remembered Pvt. Thomas Hawley.[5]

As Hovey and Osterhaus took up their positions, McClernand's other pair of divisions marched toward the rapidly developing front. Eugene Carr left his Mississippi Springs encampment and countermarched through Raymond, advancing up the Bolton Road and then onto the Raymond Road leading to Edwards Station. He camped for the night three miles northwest of Raymond at the Hawkins plantation. A. J. Smith's division was also on the move, following Blair's division on a vigorous march that carried it into Raymond about 9:00 p.m. Although Blair arrived ahead of Smith's two brigades, his men camped behind them.[6]

McClernand now had his entire corps up—four divisions of two brigades each. Each division controlled one of the three primary roads leading to Edwards, and one of Sherman's divisions (Blair) was bivouacked immediately in his rear at Raymond. Rumors of a pending Confederate attack coursed through the ranks much of the day. When officers refused to discount that possibility, the gossip fanned hotter and spread from camp to camp. Patrols fanned out on the roads and into the fields and woods flanking them. Clearly trouble was brewing close by.[7]

While McClernand's corps was uncovering the enemy, McPherson's corps moved up within supporting distance. After spending the night in and around Jackson, his men retraced their steps toward Clinton. John Logan's division led the way. The men broke camp two miles west of the smoldering Mississippi capital early on May 15 and were well on the road by 5:00 a.m. A steady cadence pulsed through the tramping column until the sun peaked high enough over the horizon to reveal the macabre aftermath of their recent work. Burial details were gathering the dead to get them underground before the hot Mississippi sun ripened the corpses beyond recognition or toleration. The sound of spades turning over fresh Mississippi mud filled their ears. Mutilated dead men were lying in all forms of repose. One was spotted firmly clutching his family bible. The men naturally quickened their step to put some distance between them and their unfortunate comrades. Within a short time, Logan's men reached Clinton, where the inhabitants seemed surprised to see the Federals again so soon. "They fully expected to hear of our being defeated and driven back [at Jackson]," wrote Osborn H. Oldroyd, a member of the 20th Ohio. Logan's men marched about seven miles that morning, stopping only when they reached the rear of Hovey's stationary division. Hovey briefed Logan on the situation and the latter deployed his division on Hovey's left. Heavy lines of skirmishers were thrown out "to avoid any flank movement of the enemy."[8]

Marcellus Crocker's division trailed Logan. One of his soldiers recalled eating "chicken and some cornbread" for breakfast that morning; others dined on bacon and meal, most of which had been discovered from stores captured at the Jackson penitentiary. Once their meager fare had been downed, the division was on the road by 7:00 a.m. John Sanborn's brigade took the vanguard with George Boomer's regiments next in the line of march. Samuel Holmes's men clomped through the deep (and by now well-churned) mud at the rear of the column, their only saving grace being a shorter march. The two leading brigades moved through Clinton and halted several miles behind Logan and went into bivouac there after a march of some fourteen miles. Holmes's men remained in Clinton four miles behind them.[9]

Sherman's corps, minus Blair's division, remained in Jackson. It was his responsibility to hold Joe Johnston's remnants at bay and destroy the capital as a center of communication and transportation. While McPherson and McClernand moved westward, Sherman set about to neutralize Jackson. He quickly issued orders for both the destruction and defense of the capital. His intent was to destroy what he termed military and public property beneficial to the Confederacy.[10] Brigadier General Joseph A. Mower was installed as Jackson's military governor and his brigade was tapped to serve as provost guards. Two other divisions under James Tuttle and Frederick Steele were dispatched into the city with orders to destroy. Tuttle's infantry fanned out into the northern and western areas of the capital while Steele's men tramped into the eastern and southern reaches of the city. The 31st Iowa camped in the Senate Chamber of the Mississippi State Capitol. Most units, however, were not so fortunate and had to camp outdoors. A soldier in the 30th Illinois wrote home that his regiment camped in the "Public Square at Jackson Miss." Working together, the pair of divisions effectively destroyed Jackson's railroads, bridges, Confederate warehouses, and factories.[11]

The railroads were of prime importance. Grant could not move freely against Vicksburg unless his rear areas were fully secure. Smashing the rail lines in and around Jackson would make it much harder for Johnston or the Davis administration to easily move troops and supplies into the region and gather a force sufficient to threaten Grant from the east. To effect the destruction, Sherman turned loose entire Union regiments, which lined the tracks, tore whole sections off the bed, burned the ties, and bent the rails beyond use. Using regiments en masse allowed Sherman to destroy the railroads in a very short amount of time.

Other troops, meanwhile, turned their attention to the military facilities. The railroad bridge across the Pearl River, just east of Jackson, was tarred and burned to destruction. Flames incinerated hundreds of feet of the region's trestles, which snapped and plunged into the waters below them, leaving nothing behind but a steaming mass of charred beams and metal. The Federals also burned factories. Sherman himself visited one of the textile facilities and found it full of female workers. It had continued producing cloth bolts stamped C.S.A. until he ordered the women to leave. The workers were allowed to remove all the cloth they could carry; the rest was destroyed. The soldiers also burned an arsenal, foundry, carriage factory, stables, and paint and carpenter shops. Enough limbers and caissons to equip two full artillery batteries were put to the torch.[12]

Arguments of the owners notwithstanding, Sherman felt fully justified in destroying Jackson's military establishments. "The arsenal buildings, the Government foundry, the gun-carriage establishment, including the carriages for two complete six-gun batteries, stable carpenter and paint shops were completely destroyed," he penned in his after-action report. He did not, however, condone the destruction of private property. Nor did he work overtime to prevent it. Drunken soldiers, a lack of guards, strong winds, and even perturbed residents contributed to the loss of non-military possessions. Before the Southerners had completely evacuated the place, someone opened the door to the local penitentiary, which "was burned, I think, by some convicts who had been set free." Sherman brushed aside a plea by the owner of a cotton factory to spare his establishment. Other buildings, too, burned to the ground, including a Catholic church and the Confederate Hotel—"the former resulting from accidental circumstances and the latter from malice." The "malice" Sherman referred to was manifested when prior prisoners of war in Jackson avenged a snub that had occurred earlier in the war. The hotel owner who had once stood and insulted the prisoners now watched in dismay while his frame building fell in a cloud of fire and smoke.[13]

Joe Mower's brigade tried to keep order in the town, but the task proved impossible. During our short stay in Jackson, a candid Sherman later admitted, "many acts of pillage occurred that I regret, arising from the effect of some bad rum found concealed in the stores of the town."[14] Sherman's corps had presided over the destruction of one of Mississippi's finest cities. Little of significance remained except for the tall state capitol, governor's mansion, and city hall. Not a single rail car would enter or leave the capital for months.[15]

While Sherman put the torch and crowbar to Mississippi's capital, Grant picked his way westward from Jackson with his staff along the line of the railroad. When he arrived in Clinton about 4:45 p.m. the Union general established his headquarters and shuffled through reports, pondering his next move. The Illinois general's way seemed clear: he would ease his way up the three main roads and try to bring Pemberton to battle on favorable terms. "I ordered McClernand to move his command early the next morning toward Edwards Depot," he would officially report, "marching so as to feel the enemy if he encountered him, but not to bring on a general engagement unless he was confident he was able to defeat him." Blair's division "would move with him [McClernand]."[16]

The directive to move out the next morning rippled down McClernand's chain of command. Hovey's two brigades were directed to follow the Jackson Road while Osterhaus's troops marched along the Middle Road, backstopped by Carr's division, which would move from the Raymond Road to the Middle Road and trail Osterhaus. A. J. Smith's division, meanwhile, followed by Blair's division of Sherman's corps, was ordered to march on the Raymond Road. McPherson's pair of divisions under Logan and Crocker received instructions to follow Hovey on the Jackson Road, reinforcing Grant's right flank.[17]

Grant had 32,000 men in seven divisions gathered about him by the time his campfires illuminated the evening sky on May 15. His army was in excellent shape. Not a man had walked more than fifteen miles that day. Indeed, few had endured a grueling march for a week or more. Perhaps most important was the early start his divisions had enjoyed that morning. Most of the men were in camp by nightfall. A good night's sleep, or the opportunity to get one, was their reward. His men were *ready* for battle. Although rations in many units were slim, the men freely foraged for anything they needed. One reported that his colonel told them to "jahawk all we could." Several Union soldiers described the results.

"My, how the boys are rolling into camp with chickens, bacon, sugar, molasses, drugs, clothing, etc! They get dishes of all kinds to bring off the plunder—which is usually something to eat—and then leave them on the ground." Another remembered he gathered "two old hens and 50 lbs. of sugar." As one lieutenant in Carr's division put it, "the boys is in good spirits and are ready for a fight when it comes."[18]

Once again, Grant's careful planning—coupled with a compliant enemy—had worked to his advantage. He now had a well-rested army within striking distance of Pemberton. A Federal fist closed tight holding seven divisions was ready to spring forward the next morning, confident that if Pemberton would stay put around Edwards, he would be defeated there. The rumors circulating through Union ranks were right after all: a large attack was indeed in the wind, but it would not be of Confederate origin.

* * *

The coherent operational plan and precise control Grant wielded over his legions was not in evidence in the ranks of his opponent just a handful of miles to the west. Unlike the Federals, John Pemberton's unlucky Vicksburg defenders had spent a long and miserable day on the road. And it did not end when the sun dropped below the hilly tree-lined horizon.

Ostensibly, Pemberton planned the movement of his army carefully (although the marching order of his divisions had been dictated by their prior alignment). The general's marching orders reveal his micro-managing and bureaucratic tendencies, and perhaps imply that he harbored doubts about the ability of some of his subordinates. His army was directed to "move in the direction of Raymond on the military road." And these movements were spelled out *to the letter*. Colonel Wirt Adams' Mississippi cavalry would screen the advance toward Dillon's, "keeping at least 1 mile in advance of the head of the column, throwing out one company in front of his column and a small detachment in its advance, besides the flankers upon his column, when practicable." William Loring's Division constituted "the right and the advance in the line of march." The army commander's orders to the one-armed division commander were similarly exhaustive—down to the number of yards (200) a regiment of infantry and section of artillery would advance in front of his column. Tacked on the end of the order was this admonition: "a company of infantry at least 75 yards in its advance with the necessary detachments and flankers" would lead the array. One wonders whether John Bowen would have received similarly precise direction if his division had formed the column's vanguard that morning.

The center and rear positions of the Confederate march were taken up by the divisions of Bowen and Carter Stevenson, respectively. The artillery assigned to each brigade followed its parent unit, as did division ambulances. The entire army's wagon train trailed Stevenson. One company of Adams's cavalry screened the rear of the column. Pemberton finished his orders by condemning those inclined to slip out of the ranks during a march. "Straggling, always disgraceful to an army, is particularly forbidden," he admonished his subordinates. "Stringent orders will be issued by the division commanders to prevent this evil."[19]

"It was a fine army," exclaimed Lt. William Drennan, an officer on Brig. Gen. Winfield Featherston's staff. "Bowen's men were veterans—every man had been in more than one battle—while the greater portion of Loring's Div. was in as good fighting trim as could be wished for." About the third and largest division in Pemberton's army, however, the young lieutenant harbored serious reservations. As he would later write his wife, "Stephenson's [sic] Div. had never been under fire, and was composed of the last regts. from Georgia and Alabama—very ignorant men—far away from their homes, and had been marched heavily for the past few days."

And then Drennan turned pensive:

> Everything being considered, we had nothing to look for but victory—and although I could assign no reasonable ground for my fears—yet I had them—and they weighed heavily. That superstition had something to do with my fears, I am candid enough to admit—yet even when I would shake off that feeling—and leave myself free to reason I had an innate feeling that all was not going to turn out well—and unfortunately my fears proved to be anything but groundless.[20]

Pemberton planned his march down to the last detail. Reality intervened. As he painfully discovered early that May 15 morning, even the best laid plans can go awry. His timetable crumbled almost immediately when his army did not break camp at 8:00 a.m. as he intended. Sloppy staff and commissary work, coupled with exhaustion, had seen to that. The weary veterans had spent the last thirty-six hours in line of battle at Edwards, on edge and on guard, alternating between preparing to move toward the enemy, skirmishing, and organizing to resist an attack. To their dismay, no one discovered until the morning of the march that there was not enough food and ammunition stockpiled at Edwards to supply the army. Because of this flagrant logistical oversight, a train had to be shuttled to Vicksburg to pick up what was needed and make the return trip. The army marked time for five hours. The hands on the army's pocket watches approached and passed 1:00 p.m. before Adams's cavalry finally trotted forward along Raymond Road, followed by Loring's annoyed infantrymen, who trudged through the thin sludge whipped up by the horses clomping ahead of them. Despite the delay, many in the ranks were confident of victory. "We will whip them or make them think we can," wrote a determined S. M. Thornton of the 31st Mississippi to his wife. "Monday or Tuesday next the ball will open."[21]

"An army in motion is a grand sight," Lieutenant Drennan marveled, "with its long lines of bayonets glistening in the sun—the rumbling of the artillery and the noise of the trains—all conspire to throw over one a feeling of the greatness and magnificence of War." The young lieutenant was writing from a ringside seat, mounted on his horse "George" and looking on with pride as Loring's Division tramped past. "I had a fine view of the troops . . . having to wait until the whole Div. filed by me before I could put my train in motion." Cognizant of the formality of rank, Drennan paid special attention to the division's marching order: "Tilghman's Brig. as he was Gen. Brig. had the right—and of course went in advance—Beafort [Buford] to save time, although not entitled to the place, followed, and Featherston brought up the rear—then came Bowen's Div. and next Stevenson." The morale in the ranks was good. "I . . . had never seen the Brig. Present a better appearance," remembered Drennan, "with fewer stragglers and every man appeared as if determined to do his duty. It was a bright, fine day—the rain of the previous evening had placed the roads in fine order for marching and so far as outward appearances had any weight, we were going out to victory." Another soldier, Almon Phillips of the 42nd Georgia, wrote his brother about the confidence that coursed through the army, the fine health among the troops, and the pending arrival of reinforcements.[22]

"But where were we going?"

It was a question that haunted Lieutenant Drennan throughout that Friday. "[F]rom all that I could gather, those in power knew very little of the movements of the Enemy. I saw no evidences of an organized system of information—no couriers passing to and from H'quarters, no signal corps in operation—nothing that led me to believe that Gen'l Pemberton knew either the number, intentions either real or probable of the Enemy, and more than that—not even his exact whereabouts."

If the speed and efficiency of the march provided any clues, the answer to Drennan's primary question was "not far." The center of the column had barely gotten underway before the long-delayed march ground to a disquieting halt. The troopers had only covered two miles when they discovered what Pemberton and his staff should have already known: the ford across Bakers Creek was too deep and swift because of the same heavy rain that only yesterday had stalled to a crawl the Federal advance against Jackson. Bakers Creek swirled and slopped over its banks. There was no way infantry, artillery, and wagons would cross there anytime soon. "A continuous and heavy rain had made Baker's Creek impassable by the ordinary ford, where the country bridge had been washed away [earlier in the year] by previous freshets," Pemberton later explained. What he failed to note was that he had spent the last two days within two miles of the bridge and had not seen fit to check the creek's condition. Unsure of how to proceed, Pemberton compounded his problems by ordering his army to stop and wait for the flood waters to subside. For two hours the Confederates stood idle. Why he did not immediately redirect his column across the creek via the Jackson Road bridge is unknown, and may simply be yet another indicator of his reluctance to seek out and engage the enemy. Certainly it was indicative of his lack of field experience. Whatever the reason, critical time was lost and another layer of the fighting edge peeled away from his army.[23]

After several hours, Pemberton finally acted on a recommendation made by Loring. About 4:00 p.m. he ordered the move he should have made hours earlier. Stymied at the crossing, Pemberton directed his divisions to tramp up the west bank of the flooded creek. When they arrived at the Jackson Road, he turned the head of the column east. He had been informed of a crossroads ahead where a plantation road angled in a southwesterly direction that would once again deposit the Confederates back onto the Raymond Road. The army lurched forward once more.

It was early evening by the time the head of Loring's column reached the crossroads. The Jackson Road, upon which his troops had been marching, took a hard left to the north and climbed over a commanding piece of high ground known as Champion Hill. Directly ahead was the Middle Road, which carved out a path to Raymond. As ordered, Loring turned his leading brigade right, guiding his division southwest down a narrow plantation lane known locally as Ratliff Road. Despite faulty maps and some question regarding the identify of the road, Loring pressed on. Darkness was fast approaching by the time his infantry finally swung east once more onto the Raymond Road. It has taken the army nearly eight hours to cover what was supposed to be a four-mile hike. One can only wonder what passed through Loring's mind as he pondered Pemberton's meticulous morning marching orders.[24]

Although most of the men tramping through the mud of a Mississippi May probably had little reason to believe otherwise, all was not well within the army. Indeed, only its façade was healthy. Beneath it creaked a rickety arrangement known as the Army of Vicksburg's command structure. And it was in a shambles. Quarrels washed away at the efficiency of Pemberton's army just as surely as Bakers Creek was eroding its banks, and the poorly planned march was sapping the army's strength. Envy ate away at Lloyd Tilghman, a brigade commander in Loring's Division and an officer who would soon play a prominent role in the unfolding drama. Tilghman was troubled that John Bowen, his junior, commanded a division while he was still in charge of a brigade. Perhaps he made his feelings known and they triggered Pemberton's ire. More likely it was Tilghman's handling of the march, for it was his brigade that led both Loring's Division and the army on May 15. Whatever the reason, at some point during the fitful advance "Tilghman had the misfortune to incur the displeasure of General Pemberton," explained F. W. Merrin in an article written three decades after the war. He was relieved and placed under arrest. Tilghman assigned Col. Robert Lowry of the 6th Mississippi to command the brigade in his absence, but the transition never fully transpired. In a letter Tilghman wrote later that same day to Col. Jacob Thompson, he claimed Loring (who was also feuding with Pemberton), boldly told the army commander that if he denied Tilghman his brigade, he could just as well do without Loring's services. Pemberton, continued the disgruntled brigadier, immediately wrote a revocation of his order on the pummel of his saddle.[25]

Whether the story is completely true or not it has the ring of authenticity—especially when read and compared against Lieutenant Drennan's recollections, penned just two weeks after Champion Hill. "There is quite a feud existing between Loring and Pemberton—so far as Loring is concerned I heard several expressions of disrespect at Greenwood—and also at Laniers and then at Edwards," explained Drennan. "In fact it amounted to that degree of hatred on the part of Loring that Capt. Barksdale and myself agreed that Loring would be willing for Pemberton to lose a battle provided that he [Pemberton] would be displaced."[26]

Matters were also deteriorating among those who shouldered fewer responsibilities. Any goodwill that had been coursing through the lower echelons earlier in the day was now but a distant memory. Night had arrived but only Loring's men were nearing the end of the line; the rest would continue marching. The parched infantrymen had been walking or standing all day and now could barely see the road in front of them. The vanguard of Loring's Division reached the Sarah Ellison plantation on the Raymond Road when Pemberton finally called a halt. "I expected— and so did every one up to Gen'l Loring, that we would go near Raymond that night," a disappointed Lieutenant Drennan observed, but the men were "assigned a camping ground . . . about seven miles from Edwards." It was not an ideal location. Despite recent rains, explained Loring, his division found "a great scarcity of water. This information was at once communicated to General Pemberton, so that he might make some other disposition of the forces which were following." Loring's men fell out along both sides of the road. Water was eventually found two miles west at the Raymond Road ford—the same flooded crossing point that had blocked the army's progress earlier that afternoon. Pemberton guided his mount to the Ellison place, where he set up headquarters. The Confederates had trekked perhaps twice as far as the crow flew, the entire day spent in formation to get almost nowhere. Ironically, the fiasco that was Pemberton's march of May 15 may have been a blessing in disguise, though one that would not become evident until the following day.[27]

Loring's concern about sufficient water was unnecessary because most of Pemberton's men were still hugging the flooded creek. The numerous delays had cracked open wide gaps in the marching order. Martin Green's Arkansans formed the spearhead of Bowen's Division. They stumbled along until after 10:00 p.m., when they finally fell out for the night near where the Ratliff Road intersected the Raymond Road. The tail of the division stretched back northeast along the roadway almost to the Roberts house. As the tired soldiers broke ranks and made camp, some in orchards along the road, they caught sight of "a number of lights" spreading away to the east in the direction of Clinton. Almost certainly they were enemy campfires, a discovery that caused significant discussion among the anxious soldiers. Thus alerted, Bowen ordered his column to bivouac in line of battle and pushed out a heavy line of skirmishers. One member of Bowen's Division later remembered he could "hear them [the enemy] moving into line of battle all night."[28]

Carter Stevenson's brigades did not even leave Edwards until 5:00 p.m.—four hours after Loring's men took their first step. The head of Stevenson's column had barely turned onto the Ratliff Road when it stumbled against the camped soldiers representing the tail end of Bowen's Division. Stevenson's men dropped to the ground. It was 3:00 a.m. They were so tired the officers did not even form a line of battle. Our organization was so exhausted and confused, recalled brigade commander Alfred Cumming, "it might be described [as] a huddle." Cumming's men were exhausted, but Stevenson's last brigade under Col. Alexander W. Reynolds's suffered the most that long and trying May 15-16. His Tennessee infantry and Maryland artillerists had marked time all day before finally taking up the rear guard position about midnight—just behind the army's trains. The worn out men toiled throughout the night through ankle-deep muddy slush until finally brought to a halt near the crossroads at daylight on May 16. "March much confused," a disgruntled member of Pemberton's staff scribbled into his diary.[29]

Going into camp did not mean an end of the day for everyone. "Upon this road the enemy was in large force within a few miles of my camp," explained Loring. Staff members sent forward to scout the front returned with reports that the enemy was close by, prompting Loring to deploy "very large picket forces . . . in my front, rear, and right flank." To their dismay, the men of the 35th Alabama (Buford's Brigade) and 22nd Mississippi (Featherston's Brigade) regiments were ordered to move forward into the black-as-pitch night and take up an advanced position near the Davis plantation. "I received an order . . . to report with my command to the headquarters of Major-General Loring," wrote Col. Edward Goodwin, the 35th's commander. The Alabaman was ordered to move his command about one mile "in advance of his quarters, and to picket the road at the point which his engineer should select." When he reached his position, the careful Goodwin wisely threw an entire company out in front of his own line, and vedettes beyond that point. The Mississippians supported his command. The lonely vigil was punctuated "by an occasional gun . . . fired by the cavalry pickets of both armies." Once his dispositions were complete, Loring met with General Pemberton, "to whom information of the near proximity of the enemy in large force was given." Additional information was soon gleaned, explained Loring, "establishing the fact that [Grant] was in our immediate front."[30]

Some of his army was bedded down for the night and some was still on the move when Pemberton reined in his mount and made camp himself. He had several important decisions to make. The army's late arrival and especially tiring day convinced him that an early start the next morning would be unwise. After meeting with Loring and discussing the proximity of the enemy, he sent for his cavalry commander, Col. Wirt Adams. "[I] gave him the necessary instructions for picketing all approaches in my front," reported Pemberton, "and directed him to send out scouting parties to discover the enemy's whereabouts." Efforts described by Pemberton as "strenuous" to learn similar information from local citizens, however, "were without success."

There were leaders with obvious deficiencies in Pemberton's army, but William Wirt Adams was not one of them. The 44-year old Kentuckian picketing Pemberton's advance beyond Bakers Creek had enjoyed a string of successes in his life. As a child he moved with his family to the Magnolia State in 1825, where he enlisted as a private fourteen years later in a regiment bound for service in the Army of the Republic of Texas. He fought Indians for a time before returning home to try his hand at planting. By the 1850s he was a prosperous sugar and cotton planter and banker in the Vicksburg-Jackson region, and in 1858 was elected to the state legislature. Adams was an ardent secessionist. As a commissioner to Louisiana, he helped secure the withdrawal of that state from the Union. Thereafter he rebuffed Jefferson Davis's offer of Postmaster General to instead raise the 1st Mississippi Cavalry (officially redesignated "Wirt Adams Regiment of Cavalry.") Adams proved as adept in the saddle as he was managing his business affairs. He served in a wide variety of capacities in many of the early actions in the Western

Colonel
William Wirt Adams

National Archives

Theater, including Shiloh and Iuka. His bold tactics at the Hatchie Bridge, notes one biographer, "probably saved Major General Earl Van Dorn's only line of retreat, which he desperately needed and used the following day." Adams performed valuable reconnaissance duties as well as he fought. His intelligence-gathering patrols during the early and middle stages of the months-long campaign to capture Vicksburg played no small role in confounding Grant's initial efforts to reach Vicksburg. His efforts would also earn Adams a wreath to wrap around his collar stars. Pemberton could count on him to screen his advance and convey timely and accurate information.[31]

Adams and his troopers had slipped across Bakers Creek ford earlier that day and spent hours surveying the Raymond Road while the infantry detoured around the flooded stream. Now, with the sun just a few hours below the horizon, Adams readjusted his cavalry to scout the countryside anew. Minor skirmishing occasionally broke the black stillness of the night, and a handful of prisoners were netted. The enemy was near, but in what strength and disposition he was still unsure. Pemberton's report for May 15 ended with these six words: "Nothing unusual occurred during the night." In fact, extraordinary events were unfolding within his earshot. The smattering crackle of Adams' gunfire was a message he was unable to fully heed: the inaugural shots of what would escalate into the decisive struggle for Vicksburg were already being fired.[32]

*   *   *

Many miles to the east another Confederate general was also contemplating his options. After abandoning Jackson on May 14, Joe Johnston had retreated with his army northward toward Canton. Sherman, whose men had filled the void left by Johnston's withdrawal, ordered his troops to fortify the roads in and out of town—especially those leading north. Sherman knew Grant had the resources to deal with Pemberton; Johnston and his growing force was the only foreseeable threat that could derail the campaign.

That first day "Ole Joe" retreated north and east six miles up the Canton road. He did nothing to disrupt Sherman's odious task in Jackson, choosing instead to march another ten miles the following day to Calhoun Station, leaving Sherman free to wreak havoc in Mississippi's capital. Johnston did so without any pressure being exerted against him; indeed, there had been no pursuit worthy of the name. The savior of Vicksburg—the general who urged his befuddled subordinate to concentrate in the face of the enemy—was marching away from the river fortress and its defending army, increasing the distance with each voluntary step.

Before he evacuated the Mississippi capital city, Joe Johnston dispatched orders that incoming reinforcements establish positions well away from the city. Those arriving from the south stopped at Brookhaven, 50 miles below the smoldering capital, while those coming from Meridian ended their rail journey at Forest, 35 miles east of Jackson. If Johnston had been an offensive-minded commander, he might have seen an opportunity in Jackson's fortuitous three-sided encirclement. Instead he saw nothing but obstacles to success. Virginia historian Clifford Dowdey once noted that Johnston "directed his army as if engaged in a contest without stakes." His handling of the army that Mississippi spring offers an outstanding example of that observation in action. [33]

Johnston failed to provide Pemberton with any substantive help during this period, but he did offer advice that would arrive too late to benefit Vicksburg's field army. (It will be recalled Pemberton had left his position at Edwards on the afternoon of May 15 in response to Johnston's May 13 message to move against Grant's rear from the west and Johnston would "cooperate" from the direction of Jackson. Pemberton then held his council of war, acknowledged he would advance, and marched across Bakers Creek to attack Grant's line of supply.) When he was free of having to defend Jackson and camped seven miles north of that city, Johnston penned a rambling message to his subordinate on the evening of May 14. The note advised Pemberton of the evacuation and inquired how Grant might be defeated. Johnston counseled Pemberton to join up with the reinforcements arriving from points east, but did not elaborate how that could be done with Grant's three corps blocking the way.

That evening, Johnston received Pemberton's response to his earlier May 13 letter advocating a cooperative pincer movement—the same message that had drawn Pemberton out of Edwards and east of Bakers Creek. Johnston was enough of a strategist to be mildly aghast at what the exchange of messages and evacuation of Jackson had wrought: Pemberton was sticking his head into a hornet's nest expecting help that would never arrive. A response was hurriedly penned at 8:30 a.m. on May 15: "Our being compelled to leave Jackson makes your plan impracticable," Johnston began. Improbably, the general advocated concentration—"The only mode by which we can unite is by moving directly to Clinton"—while he himself was in the process of moving another ten miles northeast *away* from Clinton. A gathering of his dispersed elements and a move *northwest* would have at least put Johnston in Pemberton's vicinity and his own small force on Grant's northern flank—which Grant could not then have ignored. As Pemberton's biographer trenchantly observed, "Johnston was increasing the time it would take to affect a junction with Pemberton. Grant's task would be made easier because he was facing two generals with poor senses of direction."[34]

Chapter 6

Commencement

"That there was no harmony—no unity of action, no clear understanding of the aims
and designs of our army was clearly apparent—and instead of there existing
mutual confidence on the part of the Commanding General and his
subordinates—there was just the opposite—and it amounted to
what in an ordinary matter would have been called distrust."

— Lieutenant William P. Drennan, CSA

TODAY, THE AREA SURROUNDING CHAMPION HILL IS A QUIET region, much as it was in May of 1863. There is little of interest to the outside world within the western end of Hinds County. A few small crossroad hamlets mark intersections of note, and most of the few residents who reside there live on farms or estates that have been in the family for generations. The terrain is rugged—hilly, brushy, wooded, cut by old farm lanes, ravines, and small creeks. Other than one tablet in Bolton and two small stone monuments, there is little to remind visitors and residents alike of what happened there.[1]

When the war began, no one who lived near Edwards Station dreamed their beloved central Mississippi region would bear witness to titanic armed struggles that would impact the war's outcome. By May 1863, the reality of war had reached their doorsteps. The enemy had crossed the Mississippi and pushed back the state's defenders. The capital at Jackson was in flames. Grant was poised to march directly west through Hinds County. Pemberton's army had moved east to Edwards. The armies were but a few miles apart.

The battle of Champion Hill was waged just south of the Southern Railroad and a few miles east of Edwards Station. The terrain over which it was fought (including the preliminary movements and withdrawal) is perhaps best thought of as a large acute triangle tipped over 90 degrees counterclockwise, with the tip pointing west—with the tip representing Edwards Station. The top (or northern) leg was formed by the railroad, which at this point in its course angled southwest into Edwards. The bottom (or southern) leg was etched by the Raymond Road, which carved its crooked path northwest across Bakers Creek into Edwards. The acreage between the railroad and the Raymond Road, therefore, shrinks as one moves west toward Edwards. The eastern leg of the triangle might then be a line running south from the railroad near Bolton behind Chapel Hill Church to its intersection with the Raymond Road.

Bakers Creek, by which the battle would also be called, sliced across the western quarter of this region and backstopped the fighting, most of which took place east of the waterway in the wider part of the triangle. Depending on one's vantage point, the waterway's twists and turns made the creek appear to flow in every direction. Its generally north-south axis angled away slightly to the southwest as it approached the Raymond Road. Closer to the railroad, however, the creek course turned eastward in a rough crescent around Champion Hill. Deep and muddy, especially at flood stage, Bakers Creek represented a formidable obstruction with banks separated by as much as 50 feet of fast flowing water. The other principal waterway inside this fighting triangle was Jackson Creek, which flowed in a generally north and south direction about two miles east of Bakers Creek.[2]

The village representing the tip of the battlefield triangle was established in 1827 by R. D. Edwards (who also founded Edwards House in Jackson). It was a small hamlet of fewer than 500 inhabitants, and was otherwise unremarkable except for the Southern Railroad and an outstanding road network that made the place an important stop between Vicksburg, Jackson, and other points north and south. An intricate network of smaller roads, much like veins on the back of a hand, cut spider-like through the hills and valleys of the surrounding countryside.[3]

Champion Hill, taken from near the summit looking north. This could be a wartime image, though it first appeared in print in 1911. Note the series of ravines and folds in the land as the hill falls away. *Miller's Photographic History*

As one might expect, the battle was dictated by its major land feature. Situated below the railroad and astride the Jackson Road, Champion Hill dominated the northern reaches of the field. Rising more than 100 feet above the surrounding terrain, its partially wooded slopes and bald crest offered whoever occupied it a powerful defensive position. A shorter timber-studded ridge ran from Champion Hill south to the Raymond Road and beyond, dividing the battlefield equidistant between Bakers Creek to the west and Jackson Creek to the east. Although not as high or commanding as Champion Hill, the ridge presented good defensible terrain. Another similar ridge ran westward from Champion Hill between two small creeks. Both ridges and the base of Champion Hill were

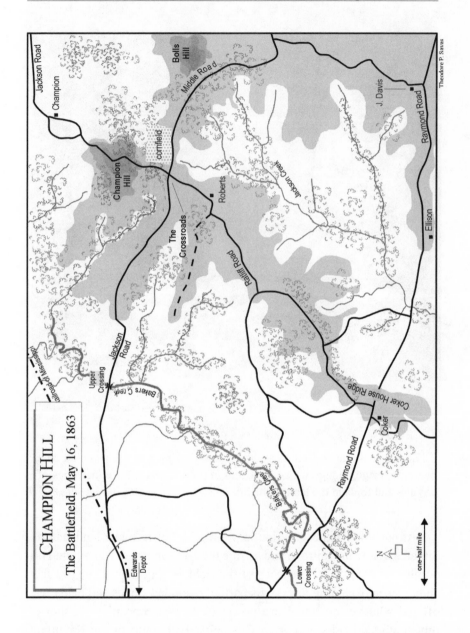

CHAMPION HILL
The Battlefield, May 16, 1863

Theodore P. Savas

one-half mile

hugged by large cultivated plantation fields. Another rising piece of ground was Bolls Hill, about 1,500 yards southeast of the larger height that would give the battle its name. The entire area was cut by small creeks that fed the much larger Bakers Creek. Taken together, these hills, ridges, hollows, creeks, lowlands, and stands of timber offered a variety of terrain features both sides would use to advantage.[4]

Through this jumbled geography ran three main roads (and one important lateral plantation road or lane). Except for the plantation route, each of these roads ran in a westerly direction toward Edwards Station from the Federal positions near Jackson and Raymond. The northernmost or Jackson Road was by far the best of the trio. It paralleled the Southern Railroad until it reached a point north of Champion Hill, where it turned sharply south in the vicinity of the Sidney S. Champion house. The road climbed over the hill of the same name for another 1,000 yards until it met the second major road, known as Middle Road. This critical junction (known more commonly as "the crossroads") split in three directions. The Jackson Road continued on, making a 90-degree turn to the west and running 3,000 yards along one of the lower east-west ridges until it crossed Bakers Creek. Once over the creek, the Jackson Road angled northwest toward the railroad, where together they made their way into Edwards.

The Middle Road began at the same crossroads and ran in the opposite direction, snaking its way east over Bolls Hill to a point between Bolton and Raymond. The last leg of the intersection south of Champion Hill was known as Ratliff or Plantation Road. This dirt lane began at the crossroads and ran south by southwest roughly parallel with Bakers Creek for some 4,000 yards along the ridge line until it intersected with the Raymond Road, the last of the three major roads running through the battlefield. Various dirt lanes branching off the main Ratliff Road at different points fed into the Raymond Road. Ratliff would serve as an important lateral artery linking the southern half of the field with the northern portion. The crossroads formed by the Jackson, Middle and Ratliff roads fashioned an important junction for shuttling troops back and forth across the battlefield. Its possession would play a critical role in the forthcoming battle.

Hugging what would become the southern rim of the Champion Hill battlefield was the Raymond Road, which originated in the town with the same name and ran northwest to Edwards, crossing Bakers Creek two miles southeast of where the Jackson Road spanned the waterway. These two main roads (Raymond and Jackson) formed a large V, with Edwards resting near the apex.

Champion Hill and most of the land around it was owned by Sidney S. Champion and his wife Matilda. The couple had four children and numerous slaves to work the large plantation. Sidney, however, was a school teacher and never styled himself a planter (the plantation was a gift from his father-in-law when Sidney married Matilda). He was also a soldier who had fought beside Jefferson Davis in the Mexican War. In May 1863 he was again in uniform, this time as a captain with Company I, 28th Mississippi Cavalry. Champion's unit was operating in the area.[5]

His winsome Champion property and homestead was about to host the largest field engagement of the Vicksburg campaign.

*   *   *

May 16, 1863, dawned cool and clear. "Not a cloud could be seen," remembered a Missouri Confederate. Emma Balfour, a citizen of Vicksburg, recalled the helpless feeling of uncertainty that plagued her. "No news from any quarter—not a word from our army," she scribbled in her diary. "It is terrible when we know that events, so fraught with deep interest to us, are transpiring."[6]

It is doubtful whether Mrs. Balfour's nerves would have been calmed had she known the opposing armies bedded down the night before less than five miles apart. The men on both sides woke with the dawn and went about their normal morning routines—gathering wood for fires, cooking breakfast, checking equipment, and waiting for orders while stretching out stiff muscles and sore backs. "We rolled out of bed this morning early, and had our breakfast of slapjacks," remembered Osborn Oldroyd of the 20th Ohio, part of Mortimer Leggett's brigade. The pancakes were "made of flour, salt and water, which lie on a man's stomach like cakes of lead—for we are out of all rations but flour and salt, though we hope soon for some variety." Many men woke up scratching. One Federal later described the area as a place with "lots of alligators and no end of mosquitoes." A comrade agreed, complaining "the mosquitoes are very annoying here so that we can hardly sleep." Within a short time no one would be paying attention to the buzzing insects.[7]

One hopeful Iowan had written home after the skirmish at Jackson saying he did not think there would be "any more fighting to do to take Vicksburg than we had at this place," but by the morning of May 16 most realized such observations were wishful thinking. The occasional shots exchanged between the armies during the pre-dawn darkness, together with the sounds that carried in the dark, convinced many veterans on both sides a battle was imminent. "Everything betokens an early collision with the enemy," penciled a private in his journal. Despite a lack of water, coffee, and food, explained another Federal, "every man felt jubilant, for it seemed that something great was about to happen."[8]

Men from Illinois and Indiana in A. J. Smith's division woke up strung out along the Raymond Road and prepared for whatever the day held for them. Just a few miles up the road the men of Loring's Confederate division did the same. Several miles to the north, Federals along the Jackson Road lighted their fires to heat up coffee about the same time Col. Alexander Reynolds' Tennesseans stumbled to a halt behind the Confederate wagon train after putting in a 24-hour day. It was a "bright May morning," one soldier remembered, but Matilda Champion probably took no such notice. Inside her large frame house she and her four children scurried about in a state of anxiety. Her property was sitting squarely between the two armies and she had been up since dawn, gathering goods and family heirlooms together to evacuate to a safer location.[9]

*   *   *

Ulysses S. Grant was closing in on Edwards. While Johnston fiddled north and east of Jackson penning unrealistic suggestions for a subordinate unskilled in the art of field command, the general from Illinois relentlessly pressed forward to come to grips with Vicksburg's defending field army. Pemberton and his men had slogged through much of the night while Grant slept in Clinton. Reliable information reached him there at dawn on May 16 that his Confederate opponent was on the move to strike in his rear. Two employees of the Southern Railroad, ushered into the commanding general's presence, claimed they had passed through Pemberton's army just that night. The railroaders reported he had 80 regiments and 10 batteries of artillery, a total of some 25,000 men. (In actuality he had 49 regiments and 15 batteries, totaling

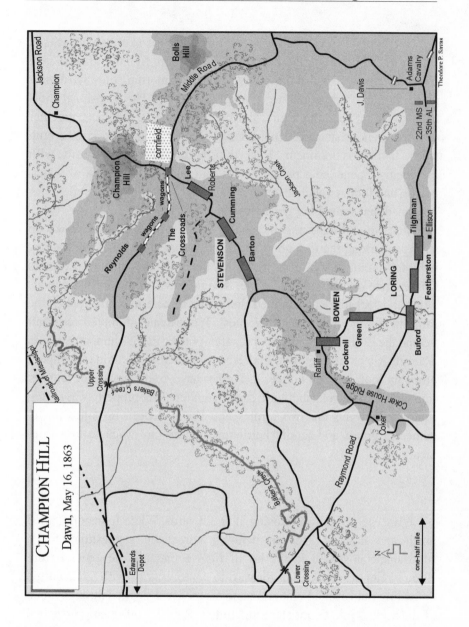

CHAMPION HILL
Dawn, May 16, 1863

about 23,000—but it still represented a remarkably precise field estimate.)[10]

Other information quickly arrived. The first colors of dawn were streaking the eastern horizon when Capt. Andrew P. Gallagher's Company C, 4th Indiana Cavalry, probed westward down the Raymond Road as far as the Davis plantation. They found there a thin veneer of enemy, skirmished for a time, and captured several, including a lieutenant from the 20th Mississippi Mounted Infantry and "a number of mules and negroes." Grant assessed this useful information. All of it painted a recognizable picture: the enemy was gathered in his front and avenues to reach him were plentiful. It was time to move.[11]

Grant dictated orders and dispatched them to his three corps leaders. McClernand's corps was well situated for a converging attack toward Edwards, and upon it would fall both the honor and responsibility of leading the way. He was ordered to press forward immediately. On the Union left were the divisions of A. J. Smith and Frank Blair (the latter belonged to Sherman's XV Corps but was attached to McClernand for the Champion Hill operation). They would strike west up the Raymond Road against what was believed to be the Confederate right flank. In the Union center were two of McClernand's other divisions under Peter Osterhaus and Eugene Carr. Both would move in the same direction up the Middle Road against the enemy center and the important crossroads. McClernand's last division under Alvin Hovey had spent the night along the railroad and so was well positioned on the Union right to march along the Jackson Road in the direction of Edwards. McPherson's two divisions under John Logan and Marcellus Crocker were behind Hovey on the Jackson Road. Grant ordered McPherson to clear his wagons off the road and tightly trail Hovey into action. The McClernand and McPherson combination down the Jackson Road, if properly carried out, would resemble a heavy right hook. Grant cautioned his generals to move ahead carefully with skirmishers fully deployed. He did not want to risk having any of his columns caught and destroyed piecemeal.[12]

Grant's orders to Sherman were simple: he was to send one of his two divisions (Steele's) west down the rail line to Bolton from Jackson and follow with his other division (Tuttle) as soon as the capital city had been neutralized. "It is important that the greatest celerity should be shown in carrying out this movement," pressed Grant, "as I have evidence that the entire force of the enemy was at Edwards Depot at 7 p.m. last night, and was still advancing. The fight may, therefore, be brought on at any moment. We should have every man in the field."[13]

McClernand's three-pronged advance along a very wide and confusing front was skillfully undertaken. He ordered his divisions to move at varying intervals "in consequence of the difference in the distances they had to march and was designed to secure a parallel advance of the different columns." The political general from Illinois had taken into consideration an important factor many others with professional educations habitually ignored. McClernand also admonished each of his division leaders to "keep up communication with that or those next to it." Once the advance was underway, he rode north to McPherson's headquarters two miles below Bolton at the William S. Jones plantation. McClernand wanted to make sure he would have that general's close support on the Union right flank along the Jackson Road. McClernand demonstrated a keen understanding of the relative disposition of the opposing armies by staggering his advance and telling McPherson his own corps, if pressed forward vigorously, might be in a position to "fall upon [Pemberton's left] flank and rear." They would prove prescient words of suggestion. Pleased with the result of the conference, he returned to the center. "Assurances altogether satisfactory were given by the general and I felt confident of our superiority on the right," was how McClernand later phrased it. Once back on the Middle Road, he met with his favorite division commander, Peter Osterhaus, whose brigades were easing their way cautiously forward, screened by the 3rd Illinois Cavalry.[14]

The Raymond Road

The first contact with the enemy was made on Andrew Jackson Smith's front on the Raymond Road about 6:30 a.m. A screen of dismounted and concealed Rebel troopers fanned out to meet them was discovered near the Gillespie plantation, about one and one half miles east of where the Ratliff Road intersected the Raymond Road. Someone whose name history did not record lifted a gun. A shot was fired. Another quickly followed. Several more at uneven intervals chased them. To Smith, the sound of sputtering carbines was music to live by. The Pennsylvanian was far from home but doing what he was born to do: lead

Brigadier General
Andrew J. Smith

Generals in Blue

troops in battle. Combat ran through his veins just as it had in his father's, who had freely bloodied the British in two wars. The younger Smith graduated from West Point at age 23, was commissioned into the 1st Dragoons, and went on to serve at posts across the country for another 23 years. He began the war as a colonel of the 2nd California Cavalry but resigned a few months later to serve as Henry Halleck's chief of cavalry. Early the following year, Smith was promoted to brigadier general and given a division. He was lightly engaged at Chickasaw Bayou at the end of 1862 and opened the new year with a prominent victory in the capture of Arkansas Post. His bald head and thick white beard aged him beyond his 48 years. There was much left for Smith to accomplish, both during the Vicksburg campaign and on other fields yet unnamed.[15]

Smith's column was screened by Gallagher's Indiana cavalry, and trailing the troopers was a line of skirmishers drawn from Smith's vanguard brigade under Brig. Gen. Stephen G. Burbridge. The Hoosiers had exposed one of Col. Wirt Adams' Confederate patrols. Smith was at the front when the scattered skirmish fire took on a more ominous, heavy character. An opportunity beckoned. Smith ordered Burbridge to shift from column into battle line and slowly press ahead.

The 31-year-old Kentucky native leading Smith's division that morning had no military experience before the Civil War. Burbridge had attended Georgetown College and the Kentucky Military Institute, apparently without graduating from either. Farming and the practice of law occupied him until he garnered a commission as a colonel in the 26th Kentucky (Union) Infantry in August 1861. Although the unit fought at Shiloh, Burbridge appears not to have been with it, though he was promoted to brigadier general two months later and given command of his own brigade. His first action as a general involved the reduction of Arkansas Post, where his command acted as a magnet for enemy metal and suffered heavily. A. J. Smith heaped Burbridge with "great praise" for his handling of the brigade, and once the attack was over handed him an American flag with instructions that he should be the first to plant it in the fort, which he did. At Port Gibson, Burbridge's mixed brigade of Midwestern regiments had joined in the late fighting that swept Bowen's defenders away from their Rodney Road position. Actions in Kentucky during the war's final year would one day result in his removal from command and financial and social ruin, but his future that morning along the Raymond Road looked as bright as A. J. Smith's.[16]

"Our line was quickly formed with heavy skirmishing parties in front," wrote Burbridge of his preliminary operations along the Raymond Road against Loring's Confederates. Men from the 23rd Wisconsin were

dispatched to form the picket line, which was taken under fire immediately. The Badger State infantry picked and prodded their way forward, feeling above and below the road for the enemy flanks. After carefully surveying the situation, Burbridge decided to test the mettle of the defenders. He ordered up

Brigadier General
Stephen G. Burbridge

National Archives

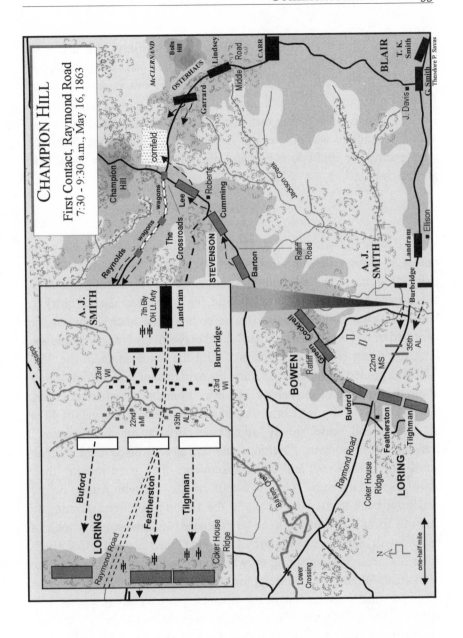

CHAMPION HILL
First Contact, Raymond Road
7:30 - 9:30 a.m., May 16, 1863

Capt. A. A. Blount's 17th Battery, Ohio Light Artillery. The artillerists deployed on a high piece of ground near the road, where their six 10-pound Parrott rifles opened with shell. The orders were to press forward cautiously, and Smith intended to follow his orders. He advised Burbridge to avoid anything rash because his second brigade under Col. William Landram was not yet up. Arkansas Post had taught Burbridge what enemy fire could do to human formations. He would proceed with all due caution.[17]

*   *   *

It is doubtful whether Col. Edward Goodwin of the 35th Alabama managed even two good hours of sleep after the previous day's exhausting march and all-night picket duty on the Raymond Road. If he was hoping for a more relaxing morning, his hopes were dashed quickly. Not long after sunrise, picket firing commenced anew between the mounted troops occupying no-man's land between the armies. Before too long the firing became "very brisk," and the commander of the 35th Alabama guided his mount east along the road to confer with Wirt Adams about the strength of the enemy. His eyes alone answered his question. "The Federal cavalry were drawn up in an open field, at intervals of 40 or 50 yards, and were slowly advancing, driving in our vedettes," remembered Goodwin. "Behind this cavalry I discovered a long battle-line of infantry, and I also discovered they were moving their skirmishers to the right." Goodwin conferred briefly with Adams before galloping back to his Alabamans at the Davis plantation, shouting to them to form a line of battle as he "prepared to contest every inch of ground with them back to our army." Behind Goodwin was Lt. Col. Hugh J. Reid's 22nd Mississippi, upon which Goodwin could call should the need arise. Adams, meanwhile, spurred his horse to find Pemberton so he could personally advise him of the advancing enemy threat.

The Alabamans move out quickly, carrying with them a distinct hand-painted flag. A member of the 35th had killed a Yellow Hammer, and his comrades commemorated the act by capturing the bird's likeness on their flag. Goodwin's men had barely formed when shells began bursting "over and about my command in every direction, yet they stood firm, ready to meet the advancing foe." The Federal artillery fire was long and split the air above the Mississippians, who took the brunt of the early shelling. "Between daylight and sunrise we were suddenly aroused [by artillery]," remembered Isaac Hirsh, a member of Company G, Black Hawk Rifles. Another described the barrage as a "new kind of 'long roll.'" The novel "long roll" left a pair of unlucky Mississippians severely wounded.[18]

The sudden burst of artillery also triggered a mini-stampede when the Mississippians fled precipitously westward. "Before the second [shots] could be fired at us, we had enough of the hillside between us to protect us," Hirsh later admitted. The Mississippians were not the only ones to run. Loring's command post was within fifty yards of the regiment, as was a unit of medical officers. "We were accompanied on the retreat by General Loring, Staff and the Medical Officers," recollected Hirsh with perhaps some embellishment. "[Officers] galloped around furiously delivering orders, and after innumerable maneuvers," steadied themselves behind the Alabamans once again, who had not retreated a step.[19] Many Confederates later described the short-lived yet panicked retirement. J. P. Cannon of the 27th Alabama, Buford's Brigade, recalled how he and his messmates were "breakfasting on the remnants of our scanty rations" when the enemy artillery opened. The big guns, coupled with the steady skirmishing, carried several of Wirt Adams's horsemen west through an amused line of infantry. One cavalryman bellowed out his excuse as he rode past one of Tilghman's men, shouting, "I can't hold my horse!" Another, who had managed to remain in position a bit longer, raised himself in his stirrups and yelled, "Boys, I will give $1,000 for one of them horses you can't hold." A nervous chuckle rumbled through the infantry line. Their turn would come soon enough.[20]

After catching little more than a catnap, John Pemberton rose early to tend to the pressing matters crying out for his attention. Any solitude he enjoyed that morning was cut short by the arrival of his cavalry commander on a lathered horse. As the general later recalled, Colonel Adams rode up to his headquarters at the Ellison house on the Raymond Road to report "his pickets were skirmishing with the enemy . . . some distance in our front." The patter of gunfire was clearly audible as the pair discussed the significance of the Federal movement. At that moment a courier reined in his sweaty mount and handed Pemberton a dispatch from General Johnston. The letter had been written almost twenty-four hours earlier and it was not good news: Jackson had been evacuated, Johnston had retreated north, and a unification of the two armies near Clinton was proposed.[21]

Word of Jackson's fall spread quickly through the army while a rocked Pemberton tried to figure out what impact the news would have on the present field operations. Lieutenant Drennan made his way to General Featherston's headquarters just after daylight, where he found "all in low spirits—the news of the capture of Jackson by the Enemy having just reached there—and many were the curses loud and deep that men in all positions poured on Lt. Gen'l Pemberton's devoted head." What he heard did not sit well with Drennan. "Some said he was a traitor—others that he meant well—but lacked the capacity to control so large a Dept." The staffer disagreed. "I have always thought Pemberton did well—having as he has had the most important Dept. to defend in the Confederacy—and from the topographical situation of the Country the most <u>difficult</u> <u>one</u> to defend."[22]

Drennan's quiet support notwithstanding, Pemberton faced a serious dilemma. Johnston suggested in his message that Pemberton move around Grant's army and march northeast to Clinton. It was time to make another important decision—and quickly. His options were limited: he could continue with his original plans and make for Dillon's, remain in place and await developments, or attempt to unite with Johnston. This time Pemberton acted with celerity. "I immediately directed a countermarch, or rather a retrograde movement, by reversing the column as it then stood, for the purpose of returning toward Edwards Depot . . . and thence to proceed toward Clinton by a route north of the railroad," explained Pemberton. The army, he reasoned, could march toward Brownsville, north of Edwards, and thence to Clinton. Why he acted so quickly, which was wholly out of character, is open to speculation, though it was probably because now the blame for any resultant disaster could be placed on someone else's shoulders. Pemberton realized that with Jackson (and Johnston) removed from the equation, the aggressive Grant would be free to focus his entire attention against his army. Too, the Confederates would have to remain in the Edwards area if Pemberton wanted to continue covering the approach to Vicksburg, and he could use the railroad hamlet as a springboard for linking up with Johnston—or falling back west behind the Big Black River. If the lengthy delay during the previous day's march had not transpired, Pemberton would have moved his army several miles farther—directly into the advancing enemy. The postponed and fitful meandering march of May 15 was perhaps proving to be a blessing in disguise, and would now make it easier for him to withdraw safely. Pemberton scribbled out a reply to Johnston, notifying him of his decision and the route he would take. A portentous nine words ended the missive: "Heavy skirmishing is now going on in my front." The response, he later recalled, was "dispatched in haste, and without allowing myself sufficient time to take a copy."[23]

His decision made, Pemberton called a brief meeting with his division commanders to apprise them of developments. Carter Stevenson recalled being summoned "at sunrise . . . to appear at headquarters, where I was informed" about the change of plans and that his men would lead the army and escort the wagons back the way they had come. The divisions would essentially slide northward up the Ratliff Road and take turns covering the vital crossroads as the army slipped back over Bakers Creek and made for Edwards. The alignment of Stevenson's brigades dictated that Alexander Reynolds' exhausted soldiers (who had not bedded down until dawn) would guide the march.[24] Pemberton knew he could not move his army rapidly with 400 wagons leading his column, so he instructed Stevenson to move the trains well behind the creek toward Edwards, where they were to be "arranged to the right and left of the road in such a manner as would afford an uninterrupted passage to the infantry and artillery." What Pemberton did not yet realize was that it was already too late to affect a withdrawal.[25]

Once Stevenson rode off to begin leading the army toward Edwards, Pemberton set about moving his headquarters to the Ratliff Road and the Isaac Roberts place, a "double log house" about 600 yards south of the crossroads. It was a wise move. Once the army's vanguard, Loring's Division now formed the rear of the army, which was no place for the commanding general to situate himself with the enemy in close proximity. Pemberton also dispatched his chief engineer, Maj. Samuel H. Lockett, to bridge Bakers Creek at the Raymond Road crossing—the same place the army was unable to cross the previous day. The creek had fallen to a manageable state, but if the enemy broke through along the Raymond Road front, the Confederates would need a bridge in order to rapidly make the western bank.[26]

While the army moved quickly to begin the counter- march (which was described by one of Stevenson's brigadiers as "a hustle to extricate

Major
Samuel H. Lockett

National Archives

ourselves from the predicament"), Lockett saw to the lower bridge over Bakers Creek. He placed a capable sergeant in charge of the operation and acquired a "pioneer company" from Cumming's Brigade to assist in the construction. The skirmish fire accompanying their labors, meanwhile, grew heavier by the minute.[27]

Lieutenant Drennan was still arguing the merits of Pemberton's abilities with his comrades—or as he put it, "each man was brooding over his own gloomy thoughts"—when the light staccato of rifle fire was suddenly washed out by the rolling thunder of artillery. "A report was . . . [circulated] that the Enemy's Cavalry were upon us—and in a moment more our Division was ordered to be formed." The deep hollow brass boom of artillery fire brought Pemberton up short. "The reverse movement [had just] commenced," he later explained, "[when] the enemy drove in Adams's cavalry pickets, and opened with artillery at long range." Adams had repeatedly warned of the enemy's presence, but Pemberton had not counted on a serious engagement that day and had no plan for battle. He was in good company. "No one felt a battle was near at hand," explained the always insightful Lieutenant Drennan. "In fact, I do not think that the Generals apprehended any contest to be dignified by the name of a battle." Drennan may have been echoing his superior's thoughts, for Featherston wrote the same thing in a postwar report: "no one suspected the enemy [so] near our lines." A member of the 15th Mississippi, part of Lloyd Tilghman's Brigade, later remarked, "I do not

believe that General Pemberton knew where [the Federals] were."
Perhaps Alabaman J. P. Cannon put it best when he observed, there was
"a failure somewhere to realize the situation as it was."[28]

Not knowing for certain whether the scuffle on the Raymond Road
was a serious threat or merely an armed reconnaissance, "and being
anxious to obey the instructions of General Johnston," Pemberton
"directed the continuance of the movement." Given the reports he had in
hand of the enemy's presence and the situation before him, the order was
breathtaking in its disregard of reality. Loring advised Pemberton
otherwise, telling him "that the sooner he formed a line of battle the
better, as the enemy would very soon be upon us." It was prudent advice.
The "brisk cannonade," as Loring described the bombardment, was now
serious enough that even Pemberton could no longer ignore it. Orders
were sent to his division commanders to form a line of battle and
especially cover the crossroads where the Jackson, Middle, and Ratliff
roads intersected. The army was being sucked into what was beginning to
look like the early stages of a general engagement—and Grant wholly
owned the initiative.

Ready or not the Confederates deployed for action. Initially
Pemberton ordered Loring to straddle Lloyd Tilghman's Brigade across
the Raymond Road near the Ellison house. The Mississippians were
attempting to do just that when Pemberton changed his mind. The
brigade was too far east and the position would soon be subject to
artillery fire. He ordered Loring to have Tilghman's regiments take up a
different position on a ridge about three-quarters of a mile to the west
overlooking Jackson Creek. "This line was almost immediately changed
for a ridge still farther back," explained Loring in his report. After but a
short time behind the waterway, the men moved west yet again. The new
position was atop the timbered Coker house ridge, a slightly lower piece
of ground 600 yards farther west that offered better protection and the
opportunity to cover the junction with the Ratliff Road. Loring went to
work in this third position and deployed his division. As he would later
claim, it was good terrain for defensive work. His infantry was generally
covered by a line of timber and his artillery "was advantageously posted
on both sides of the road, the field to the front being entirely open as far as
Mrs. Ellison's house."[29]

Abraham Buford agreed with Loring's assessment of the position's
natural strength. The Kentucky native and Mexican War veteran ushered

into place some 3,000 men—by far the largest brigade in Loring's outfit. Loring's Division, as he put it in his report, "formed the right wing of the army, my brigade being the left of the right wing." Buford formed his mixed brigade of Alabamans, Arkansans, and Kentuckians north of the road as fast as possible "on the ground on which I had bivouacked, it being a covered position, approached through an open field, and quite defensible." Buford's right flank rested on the Raymond Road, with his left extending across an open field to the Ratliff Road, which angled back to the northeast behind his location.[30]

General Featherston, with Lieutenant Drennan by his side, was scouting the terrain when Pemberton drew in his mount before them.

"Where is your brigade?" he inquired anxiously.

"I have just been ordered to form it on the right of the road," replied Featherston, "and am locating the ground for the line."

"Do so quickly," shot back the commanding general.

Featherston turned to Drennan and urged the staffer to "bring [up] the troops rapidly."

Drennan rode of to get the brigade, "and . . . heard no more of the conversation." The exchange left the lieutenant with an uneasy feeling. "Gen'l Pemberton looked as if he was confused—and he gave orders in a very uncertain manner that implied to me that he had no matured plans for the coming battle."[31]

"The line was quickly formed [and the] the artillery [put] in position," remembered Drennan. Tilghman's regiments arrived about the same time to extend the front farther south into the bottomland fed by the creek. With all three of his brigades in place (Buford's north of the road and Featherston's and Tilghman's below it) Loring had nothing to do but wait. His orders from Pemberton were to hold the position and not attack unless the enemy attempted to outflank him. "After waiting some time, no Enemy developed himself," recalled Drennan. "The impression was universal that the Enemy's force consisted of perhaps a small body of cavalry, not to attack—but only annoy us." They had no way of knowing that A. J. Smith's orders were to advance cautiously and merely develop the Confederate front. Featherston and Drennan, meanwhile, rode over and joined Pemberton, Loring, and Tilghman. The men were discussing the change of plans and withdrawal to Edwards. It was a telling conversation and one Drennan would remember for the rest of his life.

"We will move in the direction of Canton [Clinton] and there join Johnston. Stevenson will move out at once, Bowen will move up and occupy Stevenson's ground and your division," continued Pemberton, nodding toward Loring, "will move up by the left flank and take Bowen's position. We will move in this manner until we cross Bakers Creek and reach Edwards." The general added something else Drennan was unable to hear.

Loring shot back a reply, "I thought rather testily," recalled a stunned Drennan: "General Pemberton you did not tell me this last night!"

An equally irritated Pemberton retorted, "Yes, Loring, you know I did!" The army's two senior commanders were seriously bickering in the face of an enemy showing signs of aggression.

Drennan recorded his thoughts to his wife two weeks later: "Their manner was warm—and no good feeling was evinced by either party. There was ill-will and that too displayed in a manner that was to the credit of neither party. That there was no harmony—no unity of action, no clear understanding of the aims and designs of our army was clearly apparent—and instead of there existing mutual confidence on the part of the Commanding General and his subordinates—there was just the opposite—and it amounted to what in an ordinary matter would have been called distrust."[32]

*   *   *

John McClernand had hoped to find and draw the Confederates into an engagement simultaneously on each of the three primary roads of advance. Pemberton's heavy presence well down the Raymond Road, however, spun the Federal timetable off its axis. McClernand had no way yet of knowing the majority of the enemy army was concentrated opposite his center and left (from the crossroads south along the Ratliff road to the Raymond Road). When that fact became obvious, McClernand feared for a time Pemberton was gathering to outflank him on the south, but attacking the enemy was the last thing Pemberton had in mind.[33]

*   *   *

"Our regiment was the first that was fired [upon]," a proud member of Reid's 22nd Mississippi scrawled to his cousin. Reid's men, many of whom had earlier skedaddled when artillery shells erupted above their heads, were in support of Goodwin's 35th Alabama. The two regiments were the last organized infantry east of Jackson Creek, and the distance between them and Loring's Division had grown substantially when the battle line was repeatedly pulled westward until finally ensconced on the Coker house ridge. The Alabamans and Mississippians were standing tall, doing their best to implement Goodwin's boast about contesting "every inch of ground." Their belligerent bearing was not lost on either A. J. Smith or Burbridge, who already had orders to take it slowly.

Artillery and small arms fire had already wounded a handful of Confederates and the pressure against them was mounting. Skirmishers were in the process of turning Goodwin's right flank when orders from Loring finally reached him to retire. He pulled both regiments back slowly across the creek and destroyed the bridge. Goodwin guided his men north of the road and rejoined Buford's Brigade while Reid marched his Mississippi infantry south of the road and reported to Featherston. "After marching around for an hour or two we were at last put in line of battle," was how one disgruntled Mississippi Confederate remembered it. However it is remembered, Goodwin performed his difficult task east of Jackson Creek flawlessly. Adams's cavalry also withdrew from the front at this time and made for the deep rear along Bakers Creek, collecting stragglers and covering the various crossings. Loring's men were in a good defensible position, and the enemy opposite them had every reason to be wary.[34]

"We skirmished along gradually," was how General Burbridge wrote it up in his after-action report, "driving the enemy before us, while our main force followed along the road until we reached a water-course, across which the bridge had been broken down by the retreating enemy." While it may have seemed so to Burbridge, in reality there was more repositioning than driving taking place. Burbridge had mistaken the withdrawal of Tilghman's advance brigade to the new division line west of Jackson Creek, and then another extraction farther west as a forced retreat. The early morning rifle and artillery fire served to quicken the steps of the men marching in Col. William Landram's brigade, which was still some distance east of Burbridge. Frank Blair's division, which marched behind Landram, also picked up the pace. "I heard the report of General Smith's guns," reported Blair, "[and] immediately pressed forward to his support." As Blair's division wound its way forward, Burbridge ordered up additional guns, including the Chicago Mercantile Battery, which unlimbered and joined the Ohio artillerists in a slow-paced duel with the guns deployed in front of Loring's Division. Soon, four Federal brigades would be stacked up on the east side of Jackson Creek and ready to strike.[35]

*   *   *

While Loring was fitfully forming his three brigades into a stout line of battle astride the Raymond Road, elsewhere on the field Pemberton's other two divisions were busy doing the same thing. The order to form for battle reached John Bowen a short distance up the Ratliff Road, where his brigades had ended the day's previous march on Loring's left flank. Martin Green's Brigade was on the division's right flank south of the Ratliff homestead. Colonel Francis Cockrell's Missourians were a few hundred yards up the road holding Bowen's left. The small division formed the center of Pemberton's attenuated front atop the strong ridge running south from Champion Hill.[36]

Green's men were sprawled some distance east of the road when Bowen directed their commander to form up. The command probably surprised few men, for Green's pickets had been lightly engaged with Hoosier cavalry for some time. Battle was in the air and these veterans were all too familiar with its unique scent. The Arkansans and Missourians moved "back about 200 yards to the crest of the hill, and there form[ed] line of battle," Col. Thomas Dockery of the 18th Arkansas Infantry would write almost ten weeks later. General Green would survive May 16 and many other difficult days only to fall during the siege of Vicksburg, and so the responsibility of reporting the brigade's actions thereafter rested with Dockery. These same men had given a good account of themselves at Port Gibson, where overwhelming numbers and unfavorable terrain had conspired against them. The position east of the plantation lane—with troops securing their flanks and an open killing range falling away before them—was more to their liking. When his dispositions were complete, Green's right flank, held by Col. Elijah

Gates's 1st Missouri Cavalry (dismounted), extended south and east but was some distance ahead of Abraham Buford's left.[37]

Bowen's all-Missouri brigade under Francis Cockrell extended the division line northward. The terrain before Cockrell was also clear and fell away to the soggy bottomland fed by Jacksons Creek. A stand of timber several hundred yards to his left front blocked his view in that direction. As his men moved into place, Cockrell scanned the fields to the east, watching and listening while Adams's cavalry engaged the enemy about one mile distant. Within the hour many of those same riders "slowly retired to the rear through my line," wrote Cockrell. Bowen saw to it that the division's artillery was unlimbered along the high ground to support the Ratliff Road line.[38]

One of the men in Cockrell's line that morning was Cpl. Ephraim McDowell Anderson, a 21-year old native Tennessean who had moved to Missouri with his parents to farm. When war called, he enlisted in the Missouri State Guard, and when Confederate Missouri declared for the South he was discharged and enlisted in Company G, 2nd Missouri Infantry. He was already a hardened veteran, his belt notched with service marks for Pea Ridge, Iuka, Corinth, and a variety of operations across northern Mississippi. Anderson would one day put down his rifled musket for a pen and compose one of the finest regimental memoirs ever written. "[We] formed behind a gentle eminence, crowned with artillery," he later wrote. "It commanded a wide scope of cleared land, gradually but slightly sloping, and which extended for a mile in our immediate front." Anderson and his comrades watched with pride while "Colonel Cockrell rode up and down [and] spoke cheerfully and encouragingly to the men, and told them that he expected the brigade to give a good account of itself during the day. The men were in fine spirits," he concluded, "animated, gay and buoyant, and in good condition for the field."[39]

The crackle and pop of musket fire offered a more sobering backdrop, against which Cockrell selected Anderson's company and two others from the 1st Missouri to strike out across the open fields and fight a delaying action—should one become necessary. Cockrell handpicked Lt. Col. Finley L. Hubbell of the 3rd Missouri Infantry to lead the patrol. The "battalion of skirmishers" had moved well forward when a line of enemy troops made an appearance about 1,200 yards distant. Two of Cockrell's batteries—Landis's under Lt. John Langan and Wade's under Lt.

Richard Walsh—"opened on them and drove them" to cover. The initial success of the Southern long-arm, if indeed it was so, was short-lived. Anderson's skirmishers had "proceeded about four hundred yards in advance of the lines, when a Federal battery appeared in sight in the field below." Hubbell made a quick assessment and ordered the men to fall back "to the cover of a gully just in front of our guns," remembered Anderson.[40]

The enemy troops belonged to Burbridge's brigade, and the guns were the 17th Battery, Ohio Light Artillery, which had dropped trail north of the Raymond Road behind Jackson Creek. Cockrell's men were observing the same Federals Loring's men were confronting. The Ohio gunners quickly trained their pieces against Landis and Wade. At 1,200 yards, the Confederate guns were almost certainly ineffective, but the well-handled longer-ranged Parrott rifles opened up a killing fire. One of the shots disabled one of Landis's 12-pounders. Another exploded nearby and killed four men. "Very soon afterward [another shell] disabled the other 12-pounder gun," Cockrell later reported.

The artillery battle left a lasting impression on Corporal Anderson. The exchange took place over his head "with a tremendous crash. . . . The most splendid artillery duel followed that I have ever witnessed in open fields, when both parties were in full view." According to Anderson, the unfair exchange lasted about half an hour, "during which time the guns on both sides were handled in the most skillful and scientific manner." Although many of the shells passed well overhead, "many of them fell in and around the battery, while others struck the ground in our front, and, ricocheting, burst over our heads or beyond, near the guns; the fragments scattered and fell in every direction." William Sparks, a comrade in Anderson's company, "had his head shot off" during this exchange. In addition to Sparks and the four dead artillerists were many other injured men, "but not many of the wounds were dangerous." From Anderson's perspective the Southern guns "proved too heavy for the enemy," and caused "great execution," but this was wishful thinking on his part. The Ohio battery did not lose a single man killed or wounded during the entire battle.

Events might have come to a head sooner along the Raymond Road if the 19th Arkansas's Colonel Dockery had had his way. Dockery always worked overtime to find his way into a fight. The batteries were shelling one another, but without any infantry to engage, Dockery grew impatient.

Colonel
Thomas Dockery

Generals in Gray

"It was one of Colonel Dockery's hobbies to volunteer to take some battery or storm some difficult stronghold with his legion, as he often called the old 19th Regiment," recalled Pvt. A. H. Reynolds. Dockery asked Green if his men could make an attempt to capture the battery. Green wisely declined the offer.[41]

The perspective from across the field echoed Anderson's account in one crucial respect: it was indeed an intense bombardment. The Missouri guns "poured in a most terrific fire of shot, shell, grape, and canister, but my men were well protected by the crest of the hill, and my sharpshooters kept the enemy so much annoyed they had to abandon some of their guns," boasted Burbridge with some pride.[42]

*   *   *

While Cockrell was deploying his Missourians along the Ratliff Road, Carter Stevenson was implementing his new orders for the day. The May 15 march had carried his large four-brigade division part way down the Ratliff Road below the Roberts farm, where the Georgians under Seth Barton, who were leading the column, had dropped for the night. Bunched up behind Barton were the brigades of Alfred Cumming and Stephen D. Lee, the latter encamped near the crossroads. Alexander Reynolds' Tennesseans, as mentioned earlier, tramped onto the field with the wagons about dawn. The morning had not gone well for Stevenson. The heavy burden of command weighed on his shoulders during what must have been a long ride up the Ratliff Road after his meeting with

Pemberton. The general was now responsible for acting as the army's vanguard and covering the wagon train during its withdrawal. The close proximity of the enemy would only make it more difficult to hold the army's left flank and the vital crossroads near Champion Hill during the evacuation. Coupled with whatever comfort he took knowing he led the largest division in the army was the unease Stevenson surely felt at knowing his major generalcy had come without the battle honors that usually accompany such lofty rank. Simply put, Stevenson had never directly led so much as a regiment in combat. Now he found himself holding the field's most important acreage at the head of the army's largest division. His day had indeed begun badly. It would soon take a dramatic turn for the worse.[43]

The first thing Stevenson did after reining in near the crossroads early that morning was order the trains "to move to the rear as rapidly as possible." This unwelcome bit of news reached Reynolds perhaps an hour after his enervated soldiers had slumped to the ground after their previous day's march. Stevenson's order was very precise: move the wagons about three miles and then clear the road "in such a manner as would afford an uninterrupted passage to the infantry and artillery." One regiment would lead the wagons while the remainder of the brigade formed "in line of battle, covering the Clinton and Raymond Roads, there to remain until relieved by the next brigade in [your] rear." Stevenson would defend both routes feeding into the crossroads (Jackson and Middle Roads) "by the brigades as they successively arrived until the entire army could be [withdrawn]." Stevenson dispatched staff officers Howell Webb and Joseph W. Anderson to superintend the movement and make sure Reynolds fully understood the importance of the order.[44]

While the trains were being turned around, Reynolds moved his brigade east in a blocking position on "the Clinton road fronting the road leading in the direction of Raymond." He undertook his task in a workman-like and professional manner befitting a man of his background. The 47-year old Virginia native graduated from West Point in 1838, 35th out of 45. After serving on the frontier, he performed a long stint of quartermaster duties that stretched into the Mexican War and through his tenure in Indian Territory. Reynolds was dismissed from the service when money was discovered missing from his accounts and he was unable to explain the discrepancy. Reinstatement with rank and seniority intact arrived in 1858, but the stain of discharge remained.

Colonel
Alexander W. Reynolds

Generals in Gray

When Virginia left the Union, Reynolds left his post in Texas to travel home, where he accepted a colonel's commission and raised the 50th Virginia. He quickly saw service at Carnifax Ferry, and the following spring transferred to eastern Tennessee to take command of a brigade of Georgia regiments. That July he was pulled into Carter Stevenson's Division, extracted to join Kirby Smith in Kentucky, switched his Georgians for a brigade of four Tennessee regiments, and was transferred back to Stevenson in time to miss the fighting above Vicksburg at Chickasaw Bayou. Not unlike his division commander, Reynolds had seen much of the South but almost no battle action. For reasons unexplained, he remained a colonel.[45]

From his position around the crossroads, Reynolds could hear the dim crackle of sporadic musketry as it filtered its way through the wooded terrain that blocked his view to the east. Some mounted Mississippians were picketing the Middle Road, although it is not known whether Reynolds had been informed of this fact. He shook out a heavy line of skirmishers and pushed them east across the broken ground along both sides of the Middle Road. They picked their way forward until they reached the eastern edge of a thick skirt of woods some 800 yards from the crossroads and there took up a strong position. Advancing cautiously toward them over a patch of open ground was a line of Federal pickets. Behind them was an enemy force of uncertain strength. The Tennesseans raised their weapons and fired. The enemy answered in kind and the fight was on. The Tennesseans grimly held their ground, backing up slowly when the Federals fed more men into the skirmish line and pressed them ahead. Reynolds's stiffened his roadblock as both sides blazed away at the other, neither inflicting any significant damage. The Tennesseans had been holding the enemy in check for perhaps one hour when Stephen Lee slid his regiments into position around 8:00 or 8:30 a.m. to free Reynolds' men so they could oversee the critical withdrawal of the wagons. The exchange was done under a brisk fire, but was accomplished without mishap.[46]

"I immediately moved rapidly to the rear, overtook the train, and disposed . . . my troops," Reynolds later reported. A "detachment" was placed to lead the wagons, a regiment posted on its right flank, and the remainder of the brigade and the six guns of the 3rd Maryland Artillery deployed behind the trains. The colonel guided the trains back across Bakers Creek without incident and reached "the point designated at 11:00 a.m., when I parked the train and formed my line of battle, facing toward the enemy. . . . My battery was placed in position to protect my front and flanks." And there Reynolds waited, believing the army would soon follow in his footsteps.[47]

* * *

The line of Federals exchanging shots with Reynolds' Tennesseans east of the crossroads represented the vanguard of Peter Osterhaus's command. His 2,700-man division had broken camp that morning and moved up the Middle Road "precisely at 6 o'clock, with all those safeguards in front and flank which the enemy's vicinity rendered indispensable." Beneath Osterhaus's genial and pleasant nature was a conscientious soldier whose division was well known for its combat readiness. Colonel Theophilus Garrard's brigade led his column with Col. Daniel Lindsey's brigade immediately behind it. Eugene Carr's division, comprised of brigades led by Brig. Gens. William P. Benton and Michael K. Lawler, brought up the rear. A 90-man detachment from Capt. John Campbell's 3rd Illinois Cavalry "pushed vigorously forward," screening Osterhaus's advance. Ninety minutes passed without incident as the column snaked its way slowly forward before "the report of cannon on my left was heard." Cavalry soon confirmed for Osterhaus what his ears already told him: A. J. Smith's division had met the enemy on the Raymond Road. A short time later, light firing ahead of his own column signaled that Campbell had made contact with enemy vedettes. The shots also served notice to the Confederates that the Federals were approaching along the Middle Road. Cognizant of McClernand's desire to avoid a piecemeal engagement but to advance carefully, Osterhaus quickened his division's pace to coordinate his attack with Smith's.

His men strode rapidly past the Chapel Hill church and a cane field before entering "a very broken section of timbered land, behind which the enemy was formed, apparently in strong numbers," Osterhaus wrote. Though wrong about the enemy strength, his description of the ground he was now passing through was exactly correct. The terrain was not to his liking—"one of the most difficult . . . for the passage of troops which can be imagined. A chaos of ravines and narrow hills, sloping very abruptly into sink-hole-like valleys, diverge in all directions." Hugging much of the Middle Road was thick timber, and the road itself "winds its track in bizarre curves, and follows the hills and valleys, without permitting at any point an open view of more than 50 or 100 yards." Osterhaus, who concluded the area was "utterly impracticable for any military movements," welcomed the arrival of some 50 men from the pioneer corps to help him navigate the broken landscape.[48]

As he pushed and cut his way up the Middle Road, Osterhaus's Illinois skirmishers pushed and shot their way through the opposition. The first enemy encountered was a detachment from Lt. Col. William Brown's 20th Mississippi Mounted Infantry, a traditional infantry regiment thrown on horseback in late April to chase down Grierson's raiders. In this heavy country it was no longer feasible to remain mounted, and contact with the Confederates served as a good excuse for Captain Campbell to dismount his men and advance on foot. The troopers folded back the Mississippians with some difficulty, "driving them over 1 mile along the back brow of Champion Hill." The Confederates "yielded their ground with great reluctance, contesting every inch of it." They continued falling back, remembered Osterhaus, until they assumed a strong position inside the eastern edge of a stand of timber.[49]

With the enemy ahead, Osterhaus took a moment to carefully survey exactly what he was getting himself into. The only troops he could call upon were behind him, and the narrow road and nearly impassable brush and timber along it meant any help he would need would be slow in coming. The army's right flank on the Jackson Road (led by Alvin Hovey's division) was more than a mile distant as the crow flew, separated by land Osterhaus described as "utterly impracticable for any military movements, except in a loosely connected line of skirmishers." The army's left flank on the Raymond Road was about three and one-half miles away as the crow flew, separated from the Middle Road by alternating stands of timber and open fields falling away south to A. J. Smith's position. Much of this ground was cut by watery fingers angling off Jackson Creek. From what Osterhaus could determine, any serious enemy threat would have to come from either in front or from his left. He therefore ordered both of his brigades to form in an undulating field just south of the Middle Road, Garrard's in front and Colonel Lindsey's behind it. The former was ordered to deploy his regiments and advance, taking with it one section of the 7th Michigan Battery, "as there was hardly any prospect for artillery to be used on the ground before us."[50]

The former Kentucky state legislator and Mexican War veteran calling his men into the forward line of battle was three weeks shy of 51. Theophilus Toulmin Garrard had enlisted early in the war and was appointed colonel of the 7th Kentucky Infantry. One month later he guided his men in the skirmish at Wild Cat Mountain, the first gunfire exchanged between enemy troops on Kentucky soil, and again the following year during the 1862 Kentucky Campaign. After a short stretch as a staff officer for Gen. Samuel Carter, Garrard was attached to John McClernand's XIII Corps at the head of a brigade consisting of his former 7th Kentucky and the 118th Illinois, 120th Ohio, and 49th and 69th Indiana regiments.

Brigadier General
Theophilus T. Garrard

National Archives

Garrard's only opportunity to demonstrate his ability at the head of a brigade had come in the confused fighting at Port Gibson, where he had led his men in the attack through the congested terrain along the Bruinsburg Road. The broken landscape along the Middle Road may well have reminded him of that earlier fight.[51]

As three of his regiments were forming, Garrard ordered his fourth, his former 7th Kentucky, to advance to the front and support Campbell's embattled dismounted troopers. When he was ready, Osterhaus sent Garrard forward. Colonel Lindsey's brigade remained behind "on an open and commanding ridge," protecting the division's exposed left and ready to move to Garrard's assistance if necessary. Two sections of the 7th Michigan Battery and the 1st Wisconsin Battery reinforced Lindsey's line. McClernand, who was riding near the rear of the column, ordered General Carr to hold his division in reserve and await developments. "We advanced into the timber and against the enemy," remembered Osterhaus, "who had again selected one of his favorite positions in the brush to give us battle." The long delayed advance was accompanied by the steady patter of small arms fire. The heavy lifting was about to begin and the tight front, coupled with the exceedingly rough terrain, was no place for cavalry. Osterhaus recalled the troopers, whom he sent to his left to open a connection with General Smith and scout his flank. Osterhaus praised Captain Campbell in his report, writing, "I have derived a great deal of good from the captain's zeal."[52]

Shepherding his line forward, Garrard pushed ahead with the 7th Kentucky, 49th Indiana, and artillery. He had little trouble driving "the enemy's skirmishers from one ravine to another" for nearly one mile beyond where Osterhaus's division had formed for his advance. There, Osterhaus discovered a clearing suitable for the deployment of his field pieces. He ordered the pair of 10-pound Rodman rifles unlimbered, supported by two companies of infantry. Thinking ahead "in readiness for any emergency, the pieces were loaded with canister, in order to secure a rallying point in case my advancing infantry had to fall back."

The advance continued with the Kentuckians on the right side of the road and the Hoosiers on the left. A skirmish line picked its way west well ahead of the main line. Opposition remained surprisingly light, with the few Mississippians remaining in their front firing and melting away into the wooded terrain like gray ghosts without substance. Garrard moved forward covering what Osterhaus later estimated to be one mile of ground beyond where the Federal artillery had unlimbered. There, without warning, the regular tapping of scattered musketry steadily escalated until it reached a sustained rate of fire. The character of the Confederate resistance had changed. The Federal skirmish line had lapped up against what was probably the detachment of Alexander Reynolds' Tennesseans formed as a blockade across the road. Garrard called a halt and fed the 69th Indiana and 118th Illinois south of the road, strengthening and extending his front. The maneuver was not easily performed due to the nature of the terrain and narrow roadway.

Firing had also broken out off to the right: Hovey was engaged on the Jackson Road! Before long enemy artillery began to find the range and skim across the ravine tops and slice branches from the trees. Orders were issued for Lindsey's brigade to hasten to the front. Osterhaus had reached the advanced line of Confederates defending the vital crossroads.[53]

*   *   *

Carter Stevenson needed some good news, and it arrived about 9:30 a.m. in a message from Reynolds: "the road was open, the trains having been placed as ordered, and free for the passage of the troops." Stevenson later "immediately communicated [this news] to the lieutenant-general commanding." But the larger and more immediate problem remained: how to withdraw his remaining three brigades and keep the crossroads protected? A potentially serious engagement was developing on the Middle Road and for two hours the sound of gunfire and artillery had been drifting north from Loring's front on the Raymond Road. The situation was becoming increasingly precarious. Loring enjoyed one tactical luxury Stevenson did not: he could fall slowly back and give up ground without seriously compromising the army's position. The situation on the Middle Road was different: even a shallow withdrawal there would mean the loss of the crossroads, the Union possession of which would block the escape route for the rest of the army—especially with the lower bridge unfinished and the ford still too deep to cross. Stevenson had no choice: he had to hold firm and repulse the advancing enemy if the army had any hope of escaping west across Bakers Creek.[54]

Union columns approaching on the Jackson Road would soon extinguish that hope.

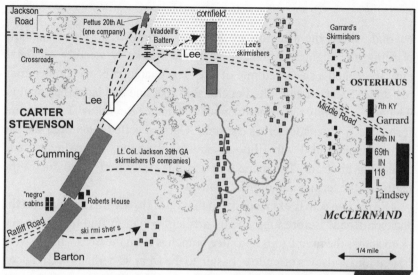

Jackson Road

Pettus 20th AL
(one company)

cornfield

Waddell's
Battery

The
Crossroads

Lee

Lee's
skirmishers

Garrard's
Skirmishers

OSTERHAUS

Lee

7th KY

Garrard

CARTER
STEVENSON

Cumming

Middle Road

49th IN

69th
IN

118
IL

Lt. Col. Jackson 39th GA
skirmishers (9 companies)

Lindsey

"negro
cabins"

Roberts House

McCLERNAND

Ratliff Road

ski rmi sher s

Barton

1/4 mile

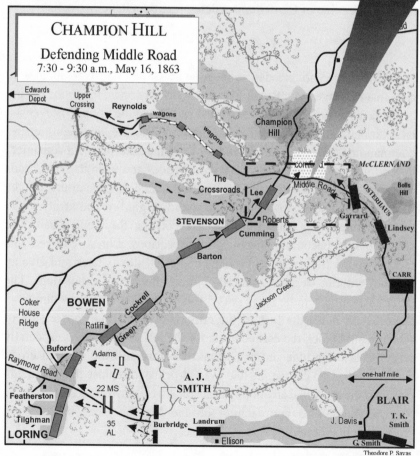

CHAMPION HILL

Defending Middle Road
7:30 - 9:30 a.m., May 16, 1863

Edwards
Depot

Upper
Crossing

Reynolds

wagons

Champion
Hill

McCLERNAND

The
Crossroads

Lee

Middle Road

OSTERHAUS

Bolls
Hill

STEVENSON

Roberts

Garrard

Lindsey

Cumming

Barton

CARR

Jackson Creek

Coker
House
Ridge

BOWEN

Cockrell

Ratliff

Green

Buford

Adams

Raymond Road

N

one-half mile

22 MS

A. J.
SMITH

BLAIR

Featherston

T. K.
Smith

Tilghman

35
AL

Burbridge

Landrum

J. Davis

LORING

Ellison

G. Smith

Theodore P. Savas

Chapter 7

Trapped

"No one felt a battle was near at hand. In fact, I do not think that the Generals
apprehended any contest to be dignified by the name of a battle."

— Lieutenant William P. Drennan, CSA

JOHN PEMBERTON'S WITHDRAWAL IN THE FACE OF THE ENEMY
appeared to be going smoothly. By 9:00 a.m. that morning his line of
battle, while thinly stretched, was deployed on good high ground from
the Raymond Road north all the way to the crossroads. His precious
wagon train—his greatest cause of concern that morning—was even then
passing across Bakers Creek and moving out of harm's way. To the
south, the enemy advance along the Raymond Road had initially looked
serious. Loring's three brigades on Coker house ridge, however, checked
those Federals, who now seemed content to lob a few shells and present a
menacing front without advancing. The probing enemy moving west
along the Middle Road was perhaps the most serious midmorning threat,
but their momentum had been stopped well east of the crossroads. The
army now had only to sidle north and pull back west down the Jackson
Road, cross Bakers Creek, and make for Edwards Depot.

*   *   *

Alvin Hovey's Twelfth Division made steady, if cautious, progress that morning tramping westward down the Jackson Road just below the Southern Railroad. Midwesterners all, his two brigades had spent the previous night camped around Bolton just a few miles to the east. Roused early, they were on the road heading toward Edwards by 6:00 a.m. "All were in good spirits," remembered Lt. Thomas J. Williams of the 56th Ohio Infantry, "the bloody reception so near being mercifully veiled from sight." Brigadier General George F. McGinnis's large brigade of 2,371 effectives led the march, followed closely by Col. James R. Slack's brigade, which would soon go into battle with 1,809 bayonets. A company of Hoosier riders under Lt. James L. Carey of the 1st Indiana Cavalry screened Hovey's advance with instructions to "scour the country and report any appearance of the enemy." McGinnis was a careful soldier with orders to advance "rapidly but cautiously." He did so by throwing well forward three companies of skirmishers from the 24th Indiana and another two companies from the 46th Indiana, one on either side of the road, to act as flankers. When the deep-throated but soft boom of artillery fire echoed against the morning sky far to the south, several soldiers marching in tight ranks turned to their neighbors to inquire, "Did you hear that?"

Protected by horsemen, the column moved nearly five miles without incident. As far as Carey could tell the land had been swept clear of Southerners. The young lieutenant led his men on. A long curve in the road carried the troopers southward past the Champion house. Beyond rose imposing Champion Hill. The Hoosier cavalry began ascending the eminence when the terrain suddenly seemed much less empty. The hands of the clock were approaching 9:30 a.m. when Carey dispatched a messenger to find Hovey.[1]

The 43-year old division commander was riding between his brigades when word reached him that the enemy had been found. The son of poor pioneers from Posey County, Indiana, Alvin Peterson Hovey would have to make his own way in life. Orphaned by 15, he educated himself, read the law with books borrowed from a friend, and began a career in the law that would one day carry him into the Indiana governor's mansion. After failing to see combat in the Mexican War, Hovey returned home and was elected to the 1850 Indiana Constitutional Convention. Subsequent legal positions he held included judgeships on both the circuit court and Indiana Supreme Court, where he was the

Brigadier General
Alvin Peterson Hovey

National Archives

youngest ever to sit at that time.
Hovey also served as a United
States district attorney. Although
he lost a Republican bid for
Congress in 1858, his future
prospects brightened when war
darkened the land in 1861. As a
colonel he led the 24th Indiana into the fighting on Shiloh's second day,
emerging with a reputation for gallantry, ability, and a bump upward to
brigadier. Now he headed up a division of confident veterans who had
seen action at Port Gibson and were ready for whatever waited ahead of
them as they drew near Edwards. According to Indiana historian Jacob P.
Dunn, the tall and distinguished looking Hovey may have believed he
was Napoleon's reincarnation (and even honored the anniversary of that
dictator's death). As of May 16, 1863, it was still too early to tell.[2]

The real-life Hovey spurred his horse forward to view the
Confederate position. It was indeed a strong one. The road that for some
miles had run west now curved sharply to the south and climbed over
Champion Hill where enemy soldiers, wrote Hovey, could be seen
"posted on the crest . . . with a battery of four guns in the woods near the
road, and on the highest point for many miles around, so as to be ready for
an attack on either flank." In reality, only two guns from the Botetourt
(Virginia) Artillery were on the hill when Hovey observed it, but the
Confederates were only a mere 800 yards distant to the south. The
general was not sure whether they knew of his approach.[3]

With a potentially strong enemy in his front, Hovey sent off couriers
in search of Brig. Gen. Osterhaus, who was spearheading McClernand's
thrust up the Middle Road, to advise him of what he had encountered.
Unfortunately, explained Hovey, "my messengers, not knowing the

country nor his exact locality, were unable to find his division." Hovey's effort to keep McClernand directly informed, however, was more successful. One of his riders found the corps commander somewhere on the Middle Road shortly before 9:45 a.m. The enemy is "strongly posted in front," Hovey had scribbled. A further advance will meet "stiff resistance." His orders were to advance cautiously. Should he "bring on the impending battle?" McClernand, who was told General Grant was even then riding toward the Champion house, decided to defer the matter to him in a dispatch marked 9:45 a.m., and so advised Hovey. Grant, however, would not receive the message until noon—after the fighting was well underway.[4]

When McGinnis learned that the enemy had been located, he formed his three leading regiments into a line battle while his other pair of regiments remained in marching order. "My command was immediately halted," remembered McGinnis, lines were formed . . . and nothing happened. After some time passed "and seeing no signs of the enemy," McGinnis began to wonder whether a real enemy had been found. "I determined to satisfy myself by personal observation." McGinnis snagged Sgt. David Wilsey of the 1st Indiana Cavalry to point out the enemy battery. After riding 600 yards, the sergeant quietly pointed out a section of guns which, remembered McGinnis, could be "distinctly seen." Hoosier cavalrymen riding nearby informed the brigadier they had "fired several shots at the battery without exciting a reply." As he rode back toward his command, McGinnis may well have shaken his head in disbelief. Why would the cavalrymen give away their position by randomly firing at the enemy?[5]

* * *

The section of artillery spotted by McGinnis belonged to Capt. John William Johnston's Botetourt (Virginia) Artillery, or what one soldier jokingly referred to as "the faction from Virginia." The gunners had only recently taken up a position on the hill after experiencing quite a journey to reach the field. About midnight an order had caught up with them near Bovina to make haste and join the army. A pair of guns limbered up and moved along the Jackson Road. "As far as we knew we were alone; that is, no other troops were in sight or hearing," remembered Sgt. Francis G. Obenchain. "The night was dark and in many places the darkness was intensified by the overlapping trees." As morning neared the men took a road just beyond Edwards that angled off southeast, but soon thereafter found their way blocked by Pemberton's long supply train. The teamsters worked hard to open an off-road path for the battery to pass, and once beyond that point, the artillerists stopped to remove the bits from the horses' mouths in order to water and feed them. The brief rest was interrupted by rifle fire (probably the fighting on the Middle Road) and an order delivered personally by Maj. Joseph W. Anderson, Carter Stevenson's chief of artillery and the original commander of the battery. The major carried a message from Pemberton to hurry the guns forward and take up a position on the high ground north of the crossroads. Pemberton wanted the guns there to help shield his withdrawal from the field. Obenchain and his men spurred the horses and the guns rumbled on, bouncing up the Ratliff Road until they reached Champion Hill. Losses suffered at Port Gibson had whittled the six-gun battery down to two pieces, a 12- pounder and an all-but-worthless 6-pounder.[6]

Major Anderson pointed out where to unlimber the smoothbores and rode away, leaving behind him one unhappy set of Virginians. The men had fought well on bad terrain at Port Gibson and had lost four guns as a result. The wooded and choppy landscape now surrounding them brought back memories of that recent battle and offered the gunners few advantages. "From our position we could not get a view of, maybe, more than 75 feet to the west of us," grumbled Sergeant Obenchain, who was rightly concerned that any enemy attack or breakthrough in that direction would not be spotted in time to save his pieces. "To our rear we could not see across the ravine that lay south of us. We had a better and longer view on the east side, while, in front, toward the enemy, it was only by peering through the little open spaces that we could locate the enemy."[7]

There was another major problem with the Virginians' new position: "no where to be seen were any of our infantry near us," remembered Obenchain. "Other than ourselves, the first troops we saw was a body of cavalry which retreated from the front along the road near us and told us the enemy was advancing." According to Obenchain, the Southern troopers belonged to Wirt Adams's command. With the 6-pounder on the right and 12-pounder on the left, the veteran Virginia gunners marked time. They would not have long to wait.[8]

Stephen Dill Lee may have seen Captain Johnston's caissons galloping up the Ratliff Road. At that time the brigadier was riding his line listening to the skirmish fire to the east on the Middle Road and waiting for the order to pull out and continue the army's withdrawal west on the leg of the Jackson Road that crossed Bakers Creek. "At about 9:00 o'clock it was discovered that the enemy was massing troops on the left," Lee wrote in his official report, "evidently with the purpose of turning our left flank and getting between our army and Edwards Depot."[9]

The 29-year old South Carolinian received the news with some surprise, for apparently no one suspected the enemy would appear in force beyond the army's left flank. Prompt action was required, but what form should it take? The answer did not elude him for long. Lee was no stranger to military matters.

After spending his youthful years in a military boarding school, Lee upgraded to West Point, where he stood out in only two subjects: artillery and cavalry. Still, he graduated a respectable seventeenth out of a class of forty-six in 1854, with William Dorsey Pender, Oliver O. Howard, John Pegram, and James Ewell Brown Stuart among his classmates. Artillery duty followed in Florida, where Lee saw some action in the conflict with the Seminoles, as did service along the Kansas and Missouri borders. His forte was the ability to organize and administrate, which one biographer noted bound him to "paper-shuffling jobs." When his native state left the Union, Lee left with it, though one friend reported he was "never

sanguine of the success of the Southern movement for independence." When the guns opened on Fort Sumter, Lee was present as an aide-de-camp to Gen. P. G. T. Beauregard. Thereafter he led an artillery battalion in

Brigadier General
Stephen Dill Lee

National Archives

Virginia, where he distinguished himself at Second Manassas and Sharpsburg. Lee was promoted to brigadier general in November 1862, and was eventually transferred to the Western Theater to serve with Pemberton. He was given a brigade of Louisianans—the same men who had stopped William Sherman cold at Chickasaw Bayou on the last day of 1862. Courteous, competent, inspirational, and talented were the adjectives others used to describe Lee. He would eventually command a corps in the defense of Atlanta, and though only a brigadier in May of 1863, had substantially more experience handling men in action than his superior Carter Stevenson.[10]

Earlier that morning, Lee had relieved Alexander Reynolds's 2,500 Tennesseans on the Middle Road so they could escort the army's trains west across Bakers Creek. The switch meant Lee's Brigade now comprised the army's far left flank. He faced his men generally east to guard the crossroads in preparation for the retrograde movement. Fully aware of the awesome responsibilities resting on his shoulders, Lee unlimbered half a dozen guns under Capt. James F. Waddell to bolster his position. The battery, organized by plucking six men from each company of the reenlisting 6th Alabama Infantry in Virginia in early 1862, had experienced war in Tennessee and Kentucky, but had yet to experience serious combat. A skirmish team about company strength under Lt. Col. Edmund Pettus (the younger brother of Mississippi's sitting governor) from the 20th Alabama moved north up the Jackson Road to extend a watchful eye behind the army's left flank. Pettus took up a position in a line of trees south of the Champion homestead—the far side of the hill bearing the family's name. It was one of Pettus's couriers who alerted Lee that the army's left was about to be turned by a powerful enemy column moving south up the Jackson Road.[11]

Without much hesitation Lee ordered his regiments out of line and "at once for the purpose of checking the enemy" marched his brigade under fire by the left flank. It was a bold move. It was also one few officers would have undertaken without positive orders to do so, for it left the all-important crossroads only lightly defended. As his men were shuffling into marching order for Champion Hill, Lee dispatched a courier to fellow brigade commander Alfred Cumming, whose regiments were in line of battle along the Ratliff Road south of his position. The courier informed Cumming that the enemy has been spotted to the north, Lee was moving to oppose them, and he needed the Georgians to move

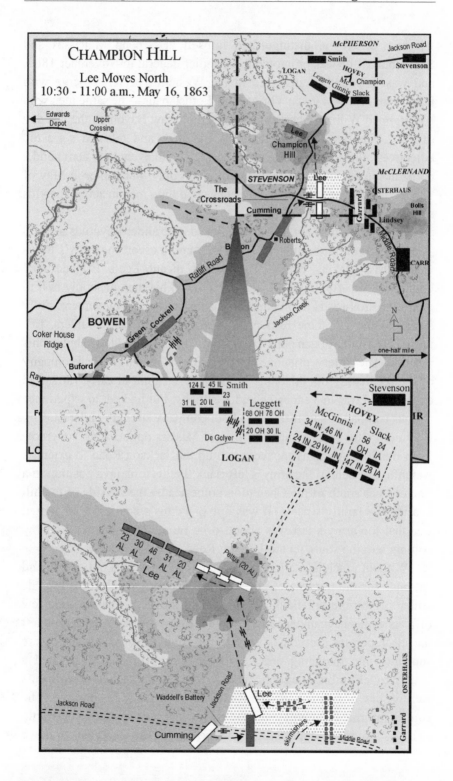

north and cover the intersection. Lee, meanwhile, set his spurs to his mount and rode ahead of his men in the direction of Champion Hill.[12]

Cumming's Georgians had dropped to sleep early that morning along the dirt road, only to learn of the retrograde order soon after rising. The brigade had marched perhaps one mile north when the enemy pressure against Loring's Division on the Raymond Road grew serious enough for Pemberton to halt the army in its tracks. When orders reached Cumming to stop and form line of battle, he was within 500 yards of the crossroads. "The brigade was established on a succession of slight ridges overlooking a clear field," remembered the Georgia brigadier. "Strong parties of skirmishers were at once thrown out beyond this field, with directions to penetrate the woods on the other side and engage and hold in check those of the enemy." The skirmishers comprised nine companies of the 39th Georgia under "the efficient management" of Lt. Col. J. F. B. Jackson. The Georgians spread out across the fields and trekked into the woods beyond, where they soon met the far left elements of McClernand's Federals moving up the Middle Road. Jackson's skirmishers had barely disappeared into the trees when word of the enemy turning movement from the north and Lee's request that Cumming cover his movement arrived. Fortunately, Carter Stevenson was with Cumming when word of the Lee's change of position reached him. The division leader approved the movement and Cumming went to work, sidling his brigade northward across the all-important Middle Road junction.[13]

*   *   *

Lieutenant Carey's Indiana cavalrymen were warily watching the enemy artillerists, barely visible atop Champion Hill, when Alvin Hovey guided his mount forward toward McGinnis's position around the Champion house. He was pleased the brigadier had a strong battle line ready, but ordered him to deploy his remaining two regiments behind it. McGinnis's first line of battle consisted of three regiments. On the east side of the Jackson Road he posted the 11th Indiana as his left flank regiment. The 29th Wisconsin and 24th Indiana deployed on the west or right side. McGinnis's 46th and 34th Indiana regiments took up a position behind them. The men were ordered to lie down and wait for orders.[14]

Colonel
James Richard Slack

National Archives

Hovey, meanwhile, sent a courier to have Colonel Slack hurry forward and extend McGinnis' left flank southeast of the Champion residence in a field of summer rye. James Richard Slack came into life on September 28, 1818, in Bucks County, Pennsylvania. At the end of his teen years he moved to Indiana, was admitted to the bar three years later, and served seven terms as a state senator. When civil war arrived, he was commissioned colonel of the 47th Indiana and capably led a brigade under John Pope at New Madrid and Island No. 10. He continued in brigade command with a colonel's rank, taking part in the White River expedition and Yazoo Pass affair. Slack's first major ground combat was experienced at Port Gibson, where Francis Cockrell's Missourians surprised and partially rolled up his front. Slack restored control and, together with assistance from other troops, realigned his ranks and threw the Confederates back. Though unschooled in the profession of military science, Slack would prove a quick study.

"I formed the Second Brigade in two lines to the left of the road, in the field of one Champion," wrote Slack, the front line composed of the 28th Iowa on the left and 47th Indiana on the right, with the 56th Ohio and 24th Iowa regiments in the rear line. A half-dozen small caliber 6-pounder pieces from Company A, 1st Missouri Light Artillery, unlimbered in front of the ranks in the rye field and opened a desultory fire against the hillside and into the distant woods. The men were ordered to lie down and wait for further orders.

Captain John Cook, commanding the 56th Ohio's Company K, had been too ill to march with his company but suddenly appeared at the front as his regiment awaited orders to attack. "He appeared very weak," recalled Lieutenant Williams, "and our captain urged him to retire to the rear." Cook would have none of it. "I am going in with the boys if it is the last thing I ever do," he answered. The Hawkeyes and Hoosiers waiting anxiously in Slack's front ranks would spend the next sixty minutes or more watching the unfolding drama. Six companies of skirmishers "covered the whole front of the line and advanced toward the enemy," reported Slack. "How earnestly we watched their every movement," remembered Williams when thinking of their advance. "Now entered the brush and are lost to our sight, many of them forever." Through the distant drifting wisps of powder smoke that curled up near the tree line, the Federals peered toward the uninviting landscape and imposing hill they knew they would soon be asked to traverse. "The little while we lay in this position facing the dark woods in front, with the pattering bullets falling thick and fast from an unseen foe," continued the lieutenant, "was a time of watchful foreboding on the part of all of us."[15]

Quartermaster Sergeant Charles A. Longley, Company C, 24th Iowa, recalled how the men passed the time that morning by horsing around and telling jokes. "But the jokes were not able-bodied nor the laughter natural," he wrote. Some men prayed and other made "mental promises of amendment." The praying might be expected—especially in the 24th, which was nicknamed the "temperance" or "Methodist" regiment because its commanding officer, Col. Eber C. Byam, was a clergyman of the Linn County Methodist Episcopal Church. Those who did not think prayer would save them scribbled small notes for comrades to carry back to loved ones—just in case. While the men occupied their time in the multitude of ways men do in advance of combat, "the imperturbable face of the great commander appear[ed]," recalled Longley. Seeing Grant was "a welcome though brief diversion." The general took a look around, asked a question Longley did not hear, and rode on. Alvin Hovey, meanwhile, wisely cautioned both of his brigade commanders "not to bring on the action until we were entirely ready." He had no idea what was in his front, and Hovey was not a man to be rushed into a fight.[16]

*   *   *

The Southern gunners atop the hill could not believe their eyes. Approaching from the north were thousands of soldiers and artillery batteries, and they were deploying on either side of the Jackson Road. These men, explained one artillerist, "were the next troops we saw . . . immediately in front of us. We opened on them with our two guns using only canister and shrapnel." The Virginians had been firing for a few minutes when Stephen Lee rode up to their position and spoke with Captain Johnston.

"I am moving my brigade up on this high ground to protect the army's left flank," explained the brigadier. His men would arrive within a few minutes.

"They can't get here fast enough, general," replied Johnston. "The enemy has a large force in line of battle at the bottom of the hill and they look like they are planning to march right up here."

"We are not strong on this flank, and your position is not a good one for artillery, Captain," answered Lee. "You are in danger of losing your guns if the enemy advances. I don't want to see that happen, especially after the losses your battery suffered at Port Gibson."

Sergeant Obenchain, who had been listening to the conversation between Lee and Johnston, pointed out the battery did not have any supporting infantry, and both the sergeant and the captain offered to show Lee "how close upon us the enemy was."

"I will see that your guns are supported," answered Lee, "Hold your position." With that he set his spurs and hurried his Alabamans forward.

Within a few minutes Lee's leading regiment arrived well to the rear of the gunners, followed by the balance of the brigade. His Alabama soldiers had marched about 400 yards from the intersection he had just abandoned. The heavy landscape was so cut by ridge spurs and ravines— one of which was directly in the rear of the parked caissons—that the Virginia gunners were convinced Lee had reneged on his promise, never realizing his brigade had deployed behind them.[17]

*   *   *

Surgeons were busy establishing a field hospital in anticipation of what was to come when General Grant arrived at the Champion residence about 10:00 a.m. He had left Clinton early that morning. His ride took him through Bolton, where McPherson's Corps had been marking time waiting for a bridge to be reconstructed over Bakers Creek. Finding the Champion house to his liking, Grant requisitioned the place as his headquarters and interviewed Hovey and McGinnis to learn as much as he could about the enemy blocking their advance and the surrounding terrain. McGinnis's reconnaissance helped him explain the situation to the commanding general. The enemy had a strong position on a narrow ridge with their right flank on the bald crest of the hill. The upper slopes of the hillside were thickly wooded, as was the terrain east of the road, which was also cut with ravines and dense underbrush. The ground west of the Jackson Road beyond McGinnis's right was mostly open cultivated fields, sprinkled with knots of woods. In his front the ground was rough and cut by ravines and clogged with underbrush and timber. Hovey was ready to go in and asked Grant whether he should move forward. The sounds of a static small arms fight could be heard coming from Osterhaus's Middle Road engagement, and artillery fire from the crest of Champion Hill was annoying but not overly disconcerting. Hovey "could have brought on an engagement at any moment," recalled Grant, who wisely demurred by telling his subordinate to be patient and wait for McPherson, who was just coming up the Jackson Road.[18]

Hovey would get his wish soon enough, for McPherson's XVII Corps was rapidly approaching the field. John Logan's division led the way, with Marcellus Crocker's division marching behind it. "The roads are very dusty and marching is very disagreeable," one soldier scrawled in his diary. Considering what they encountered that morning—dust, burning cotton bales on the road, and Hovey's slow-moving wagon train—McPherson's men made good time. Logan could put up with dust and smoke from burning cotton, but being stuffed behind stationary wagons was another matter entirely. War correspondent Sylvanus Cadwallader was riding with McPherson's column when he witnessed and recorded Logan's reaction to Hovey's constipated wagon advance. Logan filled "the air . . . blue with oaths, till speech was exhausted," wrote Cadwallader. The oaths failed to move even a single wagon. It took Grant himself, on his way to the front with his young son Fred at his side, to order the wagons over to the side of the road "jammed . . . against the trees," before McPherson's troops could pass. A few minutes before ordering the wagons off the road Grant had ridden past Col. John Sanborn's brigade (Crocker's division). The normally taciturn general, feeling confident about what the day would bring Federal arms, yelled out, "to-day we shall fight the battle for Vicksburg!" Cheers followed him into the distance.

Skirmishing ahead and to the south on the Middle Road was clearly audible and triggered the usual banter in the ranks. When a pair of shots rang out in rapid succession, a soldier in the 20th Ohio (Mortimer Leggett's brigade, Logan's division) declared, "Hello, somebody is shooting squirrels!" Three shots followed in response, prompting another veteran to answer, "The squirrels are shooting back!" Osborn Oldroyd, a Buckeye with choirboy good looks, scribbled simply, "We heard heavy firing."[19]

McPherson rode ahead to confer with Grant and others, and when his corps arrived about 10:00 a.m., he pointed out to Logan where to align his three brigades. First in line were the regiments under Brig. Gen. Mortimer Dormer Leggett. The 42-year-old native New Yorker had moved with his parents to Ohio where, at the age of 15, he helped his father carve out a farm from the wilderness. Self-educated, Leggett joined the Ohio bar and helped found the state's graded-school system and served as a superintendent while actively practicing law. His partner in the legal profession was Jacob D. Cox, another prominent Union general. Wholly without military experience, Leggett served as a civilian

on George B. McClellan's staff during the war's early months before being given a colonel's commission and the 78th Ohio to go with it. He missed serious fighting at Fort Donelson and Shiloh. Elias Dennis had been

Brigadier General
Mortimer D. Leggett

National Archives

commanding the brigade, which had been heavily engaged at Raymond. When Leggett returned from leave, Dennis was shuttled to other duty. Leggett's first serious contest lay immediately before him.

Leggett led the vanguard brigade west off the Jackson Road. He deployed his Ohioans and Illinoisans on McGinnis's right, with the 20th Ohio and 30th Illinois in the first line, and 68th and 78th Ohio regiments behind them. "We were drawn up in a line facing the woods through which ran the road we had just left," wrote Oldroyd of the 20th Ohio. "It was by this road the rebels came out of Vicksburg to whip us." Six guns from Battery A, 8th Battery Michigan Light Artillery under Capt. Samuel De Golyer, four James Rifles and two 12-pound Howitzers, unlimbered 200 yards behind Leggett's lines. Colonel Manning Force of the 20th Ohio remembered an exchange of words when someone in his regiment spotted the imposing John Logan riding by on horseback. "General," shouted the soldier, "shall we not unsling our knapsacks?" No one wanted to carry the heavy baggage into action. Logan did not miss a beat, snapping back, "No! Damn them, you can whip them with your knapsacks on!"[20]

Words were not the only thing being exchanged that morning on Logan's front. His two brigades were ready for action, but no orders had yet arrived to move forward and engage the enemy. Finally orders the men could appreciate arrived. "We had orders to lie down," recalled Osborn Oldroyd. "The command was obeyed with alacrity, for bullets were already whizzing over our heads." The Confederates on the ridge, complained Colonel Force of Leggett's 20th Ohio, "kept up a dropping fire," which made finding a safe spot next to impossible. "Every few minutes a soldier would rise, bleeding, and be ordered back to the hospital." The colonel and several of his officers took advantage of a stump near the front to seek some modicum of protection themselves. The small group presented quite an image, jumping from side to side depending upon the direction of the latest incoming shell. One of Force's skirmishers, Pvt. Mitchell Bryant, was well in advance of the main battle line, sheltered in a ditch with several comrades when he heard one of the Virginia gun crew yell out for his men to take aim. Mitchell yelled back, "Shoot away and be damned to you!"[21]

Brigadier General John E. Smith's brigade was the next to shuttle off the road and tramp through the woods into the fields behind Leggett. Logan ordered Smith to post his five regiments on Leggett's right, which

Smith later described as "the right and rear of De Golyer's battery." Smith's five regiments were aligned three in front—the 23rd Indiana and 20th and 31st Illinois—and the 45th and 124th Illinois behind them. Once deployed, Smith ordered the brigade forward until it took position on Leggett's right "near a ravine about 300 yards from the crest of the hill." Company D, 1st Illinois Light Artillery under Capt. H. A. Rogers unlimbered four 24-pound Howitzers on Smith's right a bit ahead on a small cleared rise in the ground. Farther west was a thick stand of woods, which Smith filled with skirmishers to protect his flank and give warning of any enemy turning movement. Logan's third brigade, under Brig. Gen. John D. Stevenson, took up a reserve position behind De Golyer's artillery, where Stevenson held his brigade "massed in column of battalions." Once the front elements were deployed, Logan divisional line angled toward the enemy. The entire Federal front naturally formed around the hill in an effort to overlap the far left (Stephen D. Lee's Brigade) of the Confederate line. When it finally moved forward it resembled a giant blue crescent with a very sharp edge.[22]

A few infantry skirmishers from the 24th Indiana, the right-front regiment in McGinnis's brigade, eased their way south into a wood lot and beyond to see what was waiting ahead of them. Two Southerners, probably from Lt. Col. Edmund Pettus's combat patrol, were spotted in a field beyond the trees. "We called them over and took them prisoners," one of the Federals remembered. The willing captives told the Hoosiers startling news: the Confederate line of battle was only one hundred yards away. The choppy and congested terrain had completely blocked their view. When the information was verified, the Federals quickly and silently fell back in search of better cover.[23]

*   *   *

The sudden arrival of thousands of Union and Confederate troops justifiably terrified Matilda Champion. It was all as she had feared it would be: the war for Vicksburg was unfolding in her front yard. Grant and his staff had seized her home as their headquarters, cannon was booming to the south, and thousands of boots were tramping through her fields, knocking down fences, trampling the rye, and preparing to do much worse. Anxious to get as far away as possible, she gathered together her four children in a carriage, stuffed her valuables and other

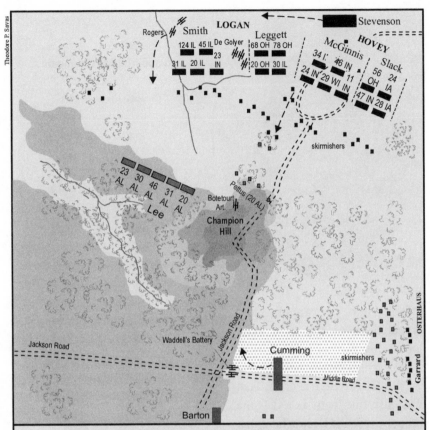

CHAMPION HILL

Federals Prepare on Jackson Road
10:45 - 11:15 a.m., May 16, 1863

Logan's division continues deploying west of the Jackson Road, stretching toward the Bakers Creek bottomland. Skirmishers from both Logan's and Hovey's divisions move forward to cover the front and a scattered light picket fire opens up. John Stevenson's brigade moves behind Leggett and takes up a position behind Smith, while a battery of four 24-pounders under Rogers rolls onto the field and unlimbers on a small rise. Alfred Cumming, meanwhile, begins his movement to help Lee.

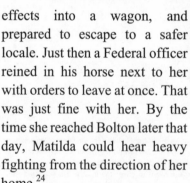

Sid and Matilda Champion

Champion Family Archives

effects into a wagon, and prepared to escape to a safer locale. Just then a Federal officer reined in his horse next to her with orders to leave at once. That was just fine with her. By the time she reached Bolton later that day, Matilda could hear heavy fighting from the direction of her home.[24]

Some distance behind Logan marched Marcellus Crocker's three brigades under Cols. John Sanborn, Samuel Holmes, and George Boomer. The men woke well before dawn and cooked their breakfasts, which "consisted of some poor wet flour [made into] little dough balls, and cooked at the ends of ramrods," remembered regimental adjutant Samuel Byers of the 5th Iowa, Boomer's brigade. Riding with Crocker was Brig. Gen. Isaac F. Quinby. The division belonged to Quinby, but Crocker had assumed command when Quinby left on a medical leave of absence. He had made a hard ride to rejoin the army in the field and reached it that morning, "just as it was about to perform its part in the battle of Champion's Hill," he explained. "It was deemed inexpedient to relieve [Crocker] . . . and assign me to command of the division at the moment it was engaging the enemy." There was also a more practical reason: Quinby was not yet physically fit to lead in the field. "My still feeble condition and the exhaustion consequent upon a ride of 16 miles before the ground was gained, incapacitated me for the command," was how he later described it. Marcellus Crocker would guide the brigades this day.[25]

Colonel Boomer's men were on the road early that morning when General Grant rode by, followed by his staff, on his way to the Champion Hill field. "He rode through the woods and field at the road side on a gallop, his horse leaping logs and whatever obstructions happened in his way," remembered Sam Byers. The general "was then a perfect picture of fresh strong manhood, and he sat his horse like a sportsman behind the hounds." Seeing Grant ride by encouraged the men and steadied their nerves, continued the Iowan, "but no one cheered."[26]

*   *   *

With Grant now at the front and with at least two divisions formed for action, the battle was about to begin in earnest. The extension of the Federal line of battle westward, however, had been matched by Lee's Confederates, who had taken up a line running roughly northwest along a ridge from the crest of Champion Hill. McPherson was impressed by what his eyes beheld. The high terrain gave "the enemy a commanding point for his artillery, and was really the key of the position." Their right flank was on the "bald" hill, "his center and left bearing off in the direction of Edwards Depot through a piece of woods and behind a rail fence on the crest of a ridge, with woods in his rear and open fields in his front." Federal artillery opened the action by taking the Southerners under fire. Grant's line wrapped around to the west and southwest, enabling De Golyer and Rogers to enfilade part of the Confederate position. It was the sounds of these guns that carried on the wind to Matilda Champion's ears.[27]

*   *   *

The sudden appearance of a large Federal force on the Jackson Road methodically unwinding into a line of battle stretching in the direction of Bakers Creek caused a flurry of activity atop the ridge spurs emanating from Champion Hill. After double-quicking his brigade north to the hill crest, Lee rode out to watch the grand pageantry unfold in the distance, first with dismay and then with alarm when he realized the extent of the enemy buildup and length of their front. Brigade after enemy brigade was marching off the road, extending Grant's line west toward the Bakers Creek bottomland, overlapping Lee's own left flank by a wide margin. If the enemy advanced, they would easily cut off the army from its only viable means of escape across Bakers Creek. Lee had little choice but to dangerously extend his own line in response.

Lee notified Stevenson of the dangerous situation and began shifting his Alabamans northwesterly along the hill's major ridge spur. He stopped two or three times along the way, but each time was forced anew to shift farther northwest to correspond his movements with those of the enemy. When Lee halted for the last time, he deployed his men behind a rail fence in the near edge of a stand of timber facing the enemy. His left was refused slightly to resist a turning movement. Open ground fell away toward the gathering Federal host. It was a good position. His Alabama regiments were aligned from left to right, as follows: 23rd, 30th, 46th, 31st, and 20th. My front, explained Lee after the war, "covered a line of nearly three-quarters of a mile in a single line of battle, with . . . no artillery. As early as 10 o'clock . . . it became evident that the enemy was in heavy force and determined on battle." Lee took notice that enemy skirmishers "were bold and aggressive, and several divisions of his troops were visible in front of our left." Although Lee overstated enemy numbers, he must have felt quite lonely watching these events unfold. He had not a man in reserve.[28]

Carter Stevenson was apprised of Lee's movements, although where he was when he learned Lee had moved northwest away from Champion Hill is not clear. Stevenson had available only three of his four brigades to prepare to receive what was shaping up to be a large scale attack. Alexander Reynolds, it will be recalled, had moved west of Bakers Creek with the army's wagon train. Once across, he had deployed his regiments and the 3rd Maryland Artillery to protect the wagons and the army's left rear. The trains could not be left unattended. Reynolds would have to stay put. Lee's Alabamans had sidled along the ridge holding the far left of the division, and his pickets were already exchanging shots with enemy skirmishers. Alfred Cumming's Georgia brigade held the center of Stevenson's divisional line. Cumming had shifted northward along

Ratliff Road to cover the intersection when Lee pulled his brigade out of line there to march to Champion Hill. Seth Barton's command, the fourth of Stevenson's brigades, held the division's far right, which extended south toward John Bowen's position well down Ratliff Road.[29]

As General Cumming recalled the moment, Stevenson notified him that Lee "had bent the left of his line toward the rear . . . and I was directed to accord my movements with his." In the space of a few minutes, the enormity of that directive sunk in. Stevenson may or may not have fully appreciated Cumming's dilemma, but the native of Augusta, Georgia, surely did. He was no stranger to combat, but he was a stranger to both Pemberton's army and the Georgians he now commanded. "I had been with it [the brigade] but three or four days—coming immediately from the Vicksburg R.R. Depot to join it in the field," he wrote Stephen Lee after the war. His field officers "were scarcely known to me by sight, or I to them." Cumming knew nothing of the abilities of either his subordinate commanders or the men in his ranks except that the brigade had not yet seen serious combat. As he explained to Lee, "Never before had it engaged in close action—if indeed it had ever before been under fire. It labored also under the disadvantage that between it and its commander there existed no acquaintance." The Augustan faced a difficult task indeed.[30]

After graduating from West Point in 1849, Alfred Cumming entered the 8th U.S. Infantry and served across the western territories, escorting wagons and fighting Indians. Like so many Civil War officers, he also participated in the Mormon Expedition with Albert

Brigadier General
Alfred Cumming

Generals in Gray

Sidney Johnston in the latter years of the 1850s. Cumming was a captain on leave with the 10th U.S. Infantry when Georgia left the Union. There was never any doubt about his allegiance to his state. He demonstrated his field abilities early and often in Confederate gray. As a lieutenant colonel, Cumming saw heavy action with the 10th Georgia on the Virginia Peninsula and was wounded by a shell fragment at Malvern Hill. He assumed temporary command of a brigade during the Maryland campaign and was wounded a second time while vigorously defending the Bloody Lane at Sharpsburg. While convalescing in Augusta, Cumming received a well deserved promotion to brigadier general and after a short time in the Gulf region was shuttled to Mississippi. Pemberton was pleased to receive the veteran combat leader into his army and assigned him to replace Kentuckian Thomas Taylor at the head of a Georgia brigade; the capable Taylor was moved to Pemberton's staff. Three days later the Augustan found himself standing a few hundred yards south of Champion Hill defending a vital crossroads and facing an important decision upon which the fate of Pemberton's army depended.[31]

Stephen Lee was moving north and west down the ridge line, and unless Cumming shifted his own Georgians north—and quickly—Champion Hill would be left undefended. But he could not adequately cover the hill and defend the vital crossroads without splitting his command and leaving a gap between the two halves. Cumming acted decisively within the best tradition of an officer schooled in the Army of Northern Virginia, where he was encouraged to use discretion and aggression in equal measure. He left the 56th and 57th Georgia regiments at the crossroads with Waddell's artillery to stabilize and hold the Middle Road sector. With his remaining three Georgia regiments, the 34th, 36th, and 39th, he moved by the left flank up the Jackson Road. Their skirmishers—three companies from each regiment were deployed well to the east opposing McClernand's cautious (as ordered) advance on the Middle Road—were ordered to correspond their movements with his own so as to keep the front covered well in advance of the line of battle. The march north, remembered Cumming, was through "a wood rather open for the first few hundred yards, but gradually becoming denser," until the crest of Champion Hill was reached.[32]

To Cumming's dismay, Lee—"whose brigade was concealed from my observation by the density of the wood"—was by this time hundreds

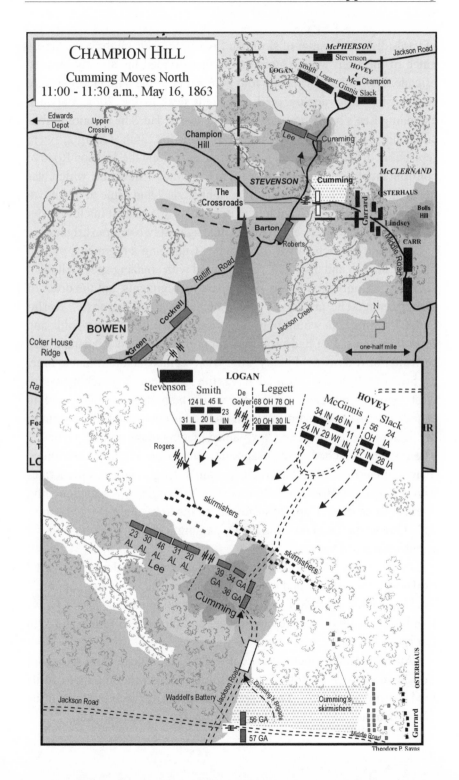

CHAMPION HILL

Cumming Moves North
11:00 - 11:30 a.m., May 16, 1863

Theodore P. Savas

of yards distant. A patter of skirmish fire rippled like a light wave across much of the front while Cumming further divided his already cleaved brigade. The 39th Georgia and four companies of the 34th Georgia were sent westward to deploy on Lee's right next to the 20th Alabama, extending Lee's battle line east to the Jackson Road. The remaining four companies from the 34th, together with the 36th Georgia, were repositioned, bent, and faced just south of east along the Jackson Road to confront any threat from that direction. Cumming's new line, which was not at all to his liking, "was nearly a right angle," and came to be known simply as "the angle." What he did not yet know was that his few under strength regiments were about to be pitted against two veteran brigades.[33]

Sergeant Obenchain was on hand as Cumming's regiments poured onto the hill top and distinctly remembered with amazing specificity and accuracy not only the identity of the passing regiments, but the order of their passing. The artillerists had waited "in great suspense," fearful Federal skirmishers would pour out of one of the hill's many folds and seize their guns. Lee had promised support, but not an Alabaman was seen after he rode away. Finally, after what seemed an interminable time, the head of a regiment appeared. It was the 39th Georgia marching east to west "between our caissons and the ravine behind us," remembered an elated Obenchain. Captain Johnston kicked his horse and rode in front of the head of the regiment and "explained matters to the comdg. Officer." The gunners watched with disappointment as the regiment continued marching west out of sight. To Obenchain's delight, more Confederates were spotted. "Soon another regiment (34th Georgia) was seen marching over the same route. Capt. Johnston asked me to try and get it to support us." Obenchain walked along the passing column seeking out its commanding officer.

"The enemy is forming in large numbers just down the hill," explained Obenchain, "and our guns do not have any infantry support."

"I am sorry, I would like to help you," explained Col. James A. W. Johnson, "but I have to obey my orders and they are to follow the 39th Georgia."[34]

An exasperated Obenchain kept walking until yet a third regiment, Col. Jesse A. Glenn's 36th Georgia, tramped past him on its way to its final position on the hill. The sergeant ran over and "stood in front of its line of march. Colonel Glenn called out for the regiment to halt.

"Colonel, I have tried to explain to the others passing by here. The enemy has formed by the thousands down the hill to the north," explained Obenchain yet again. "We were ordered to this position, our guns do not have any infantry support, and if they attack we will lose them. We need your help."

Colonel Glenn demurred. "No, sir, I cannot help you. My orders are to take a position further on."

With his voice rising in anger, Obenchain shot back, "We will not be responsible for the loss of our guns. And if this part of the line is broken, the battle will be lost to us!"

Moved by the artilleryman's passion and plight, Glenn relented. "Very well. I can give you one company—but no more than that."

That suited Obenchain just fine, even though the company numbered fewer than 50 men. Unfortunately, the artillerists could not lend a hand to help them because two-thirds of battery men were without both their artillery pieces and small arms.

Cumming had barely taken up position with his "two sides of the square faced outward" when he received word Lee was moving forward to engage the enemy. It was not true, but he had no way of knowing that. In an effort to avoid a piecemeal attack, Cumming "immediately advanced . . . with a view to keep abreast with the supposed movement." The Georgians had tramped "but a few paces" when Cumming learned Lee was in fact not moving anywhere. He bellowed out orders to halt, "and the line, somewhat disordered [by] the broken and wooded character of the ground traversed [was] rectified." Cumming's new line atop Champion Hill was drawn up on a succession of "ridges and knolls heavily timbered." Fifty yards beyond the ground fell away toward Grant's waiting army. As amazing as it sounds today, Cumming himself did not even see the Virginia artillery posted on Champion Hill. "At no time during that day was it immediately under my command or did it come under my observation," he later wrote Lee.[35]

A combination of factors, including terrain, timing, and poor planning, had contorted Pemberton's left flank into a large "L" shape, with the long shank representing Lee and part of Cumming's Brigade facing generally north, and the short shank facing south of east along the Jackson Road comprised of the balance of the Georgians who made the move to Champion Hill. A 300-yard gap existed between the Georgians left behind to defend the crossroads (56th and 57th regiments) and

Cumming's right flank along the Jackson Road. A gap several times that distance existed between Stephen Lee's left flank and the Bakers Creek crossing. There was more bad news, but Cumming would not learn of it until it was too late to do anything about it: the nine companies of skirmishers from his 34th, 36th, and 39th regiments had been unable to keep up with the move to the hill crest, and were not in the woods in front of his position. Adding to his woes was the absence of two additional companies, one each from the 34th and 36th Georgia, which were on bridge-building duty with Samuel Lockett, the army's engineer. (Yet another, at least according to Obenchain, had been dribbled out from the 36th Georgia to support the Virginia guns.) The luck of the draw had pulled Cumming northward that morning to hold what was obviously shaping up to be a critical position in Pemberton's line. The result offered the enemy a tantalizing right angle salient to assail, defended by a brigade 11 companies light.[36]

By this time, and probably much earlier, Carter Stevenson realized he was in serious trouble. When Lee initially notified him of the approach of Federals along the Jackson Road, Stevenson informed Pemberton of the threat. With each change of position, another courier galloped to the commanding general to "promptly [warn]" him of the build-up opposite the army's left. Stevenson's messages might well have read like his official report of the battle: "The enemy, in columns of division, moved steadily around out left, forcing it to change direction to correspond, and their movement was so rapid as to

Major General
Carter Littlepage Stevenson

Alabama Department of

Archives and History

keep my line (a single one) in constant motion by the left flank."
Stevenson realized the enemy front was heavier and broader than his
own, and that he did not have enough men to cope with the threat. The
enemy, explained the major general, "were about to concentrate on the
left with the larger part of their force, still moving a column to the flank."
And the sounds of battle beyond Champion Hill and on Lee's front
farther west were growing louder.[37]

*   *   *

The rising crescendo of gunfire troubling Carter Stevenson heralded
the opening of Grant's attempt to crush Pemberton at Champion Hill.

It is doubtful General Grant expected to find Pemberton's
Confederates deployed in line of battle this far east of Edwards. The wide
area over which the divisions were forced to march, coupled with the
rough terrain between the roads and lack of good lateral communication
routes, made coordinated action between the separated wings of the
Federal army difficult. John Myers, a private in the 28th Iowa Infantry,
wrote home to "Dear woman" and described the problem in his simple
homespun language: "[We] was met with a heavy forse of rebels . . . hat
our forses scattered over consiterable spase of country." Grant
appreciated this and did his best to bring the dispersed sections of his
army together to strike simultaneous blows against Pemberton's line. As
he later explained, even after McPherson's troops had taken up their
position, "I would not permit an attack to be commenced by our troops
until I could hear from McClernand, who was advancing with four
divisions, two of them on a road intersecting the Jackson Road about 1
mile from where [McPherson's] troops were placed, and about the center
of the enemy's line." When a staff officer sent by McClernand arrived
shortly thereafter with word of the situation on the Middle Road, Grant
discovered that, "by the nearest practicable route of communication
[McClernand] was 2 ½ miles distant [though only one mile as the crow
flies]." "Several successive messages" were sent urging his corps leader
to "push forward with all rapidity." Unbeknownst to Grant, it would take
much longer for the order to reach McClernand than he imagined. The
result would be a methodically slow and cautious advance by
McClernand up the Middle Road—exactly as ordered.

And with that Grant ordered McPherson, resplendent in his full uniform, to take tactical charge of the attack and open the engagement. Federal watches recorded the time as 10:30 a.m.[38]

Chapter 8

Collapse

"A halt is made and the Enfields of the 24th add their clamor to the hell of sound, and their missiles to the many that make the very air writhe."

— Sgt. Charles Longley, 24th Iowa Infantry

BY THE TIME GRANT WENT OVER TO THE ATTACK, FOUR UNION divisions had made contact with Pemberton's Confederates. Far to the south on Grant's left flank, A. J. Smith's division had pressed along the Raymond Road early that morning until confronted by William Loring's three-brigade line of battle posted strongly on the Coker house ridge. A temporary stalemate ensued there while both sides assessed the threat posed by the other. In the center, Peter Osterhaus's division marching on the Middle Road had come up against a vigorous, if thinly-held, Rebel defensive line opposite the all-important crossroads. The heavy terrain and orders to advance cautiously slowed down the Middle Road advance to a crawl. The Jackson Road front on the right flank of Grant's army offered more obvious possibilities—especially since Grant traveled with this part of his army. There, Hovey (McClernand's corps) and Logan (McPherson's corps) were aggressively moving forward to bring on what Grant hoped would be the decisive battle of the campaign. Three more divisions under Frank Blair (behind Smith), Eugene Carr (behind Osterhaus), and Marcellus Crocker (behind Logan and Hovey) were all within striking distance of Pemberton's extended line.

Grant's seven divisions, however, were on three different roads separated by almost impassable terrain. He had done a good job moving his army quickly and bringing it into contact with the enemy, and was generally well positioned to wage a major offensive battle. Pemberton's army, though also dispersed, enjoyed three advantages Grant's Federals did not: fighting on the defensive while protecting a road network at its confluence, better terrain, and interior lines of communication. How Pemberton would utilize his advantages remained to be seen. His more experienced opponent had seized the initiative and was now working to exploit it, leaving Pemberton flat-footed and reacting to circumstances as they developed with a largely impassable stream behind him.

As it was since early that morning when initial contact was made, Grant's most difficult dilemma remained command coordination. His scattered deployment left only three of the seven divisions under his (or a trusted subordinate's) immediate command. Grant was in contact with his center and left wings by courier, but the roads were congested with wagons, men, horses, and other associated baggage that trails in the wake of moving combat columns, and thus difficult to traverse. It took a long time to dispatch a rider from the Jackson Road sector to the center and back again. Communication with his distant southern wing was even more problematic. As Hovey and Logan rolled forward under Grant's watchful eye, more than one-half of the army was under someone else's tactical command—and that someone was John A. McClernand.

There was no love lost between Grant and McClernand. They treated one another with professional respect, but they were never on friendly terms. As far as Grant was concerned, McClernand was a grandstanding politician more concerned with his media image than taking care of and leading the men who served under him. The self-educated McClernand, distrustful of professionally-trained soldiers, thought little of Grant and his obvious favorites in the army—Sherman and McPherson. As the morning of May 16 was about to expire, the civilian-politician McClernand controlled the four divisions on the Middle and Raymond roads. Grant dispatched couriers urging McClernand to "push forward with all rapidity" and seemed convinced McClernand's twin punches (one on the Middle Road and the other on the Raymond Road), coupled with his own thrust south along the Jackson Road over and around Champion Hill, would win a decisive victory.[1]

Despite what Grant may have believed, McClernand's effective command and control—much like his own on the far right—did not extend beyond his immediate Middle Road front. The politician's communication with A. J. Smith's and Frank Blair's divisions on the Raymond Road was tenuous at best. Osterhaus's far left and Smith's far right stretched toward one another in an attempt to make and remain in contact, but direct communication over the rough and rolling creek-cut ground was extraordinarily challenging in a fluid battlefield environment. Major General Frank Blair, whose division trailed Smith's on the left flank, never took charge there. That meant Smith, a brigadier general leading the forward division with little information about what was transpiring elsewhere, controlled the ebb and flow of battle on the army's distant southern front. William Sherman, as we know, was still back at Jackson. With McPherson commanding the attack of the right wing, Grant could have ridden to the center or left flank to oversee McClernand or Smith, but he instead chose to remain on the Jackson Road. Why?

The answer will never be known for certain. Despite his dislike of McClernand, Grant probably considered him a better tactician and a more reliable field commander than McPherson. Despite what Grant later wrote, this conclusion seems evident in the tasks Grant assigned McClernand. The advance down the west side of the Mississippi River through Louisiana, arguably the most important assignment of all, had been given to McClernand. The honor of establishing the all-important bridgehead on the eastern side of the Mississippi, where heavy fighting was expected to take place, was given to McClernand and his XIII Corps. It was McClernand who was tasked with leading the march inland against an uncertain foe through difficult terrain. It was McClernand who competently waged the battle of Port Gibson and handled his corps well thereafter. In similar circumstances but facing a far weaker opponent at Raymond, McPherson had fed his men piecemeal into the action and was ill-prepared to follow up his expensive victory. To McClernand fell the task of finding Pemberton's army, and his divisions, on Grant's orders, led all three prongs of the advance on the morning of May 16. Grant could easily have left McPherson in command on the army's right that morning and ridden south to oversee McClernand. Instead, he chose to give his favored subordinate tactical control while he remained by his side.

* * *

John Pemberton was sifting through reports at his headquarters at the Isaac Roberts house when Grant went over to the offensive. The home was about 600 yards south of the crossroads, a good central location given the deployment of his army—except during a battle. Pemberton knew his left was seriously threatened and that its defense was in the hands of an inexperienced division commander. Yet he chose to remain on the Roberts property, dispatching couriers and managing his army like the bureaucrat he was. Grant was at the point of decision at the head of his army; Pemberton was at his headquarters.

"It was at this time the battle began in earnest along Stevenson's entire front about noon," admitted Pemberton in his report of the action. The thunder of artillery and small arms fire portending the breakout of a full-scale battle continued to mount on Carter Stevenson's front to the north well beyond the crossroads. The earlier withdrawal of Cumming's Brigade from the Ratliff Road front had seriously weakened Pemberton's center. Pemberton would soon learn by courier that Stevenson had ordered Seth Barton's Georgians away from the crossroads area running northwest to support the far left. That decision, Pemberton would later write, left "a gap between his [Stevenson's] and Bowen's divisions." Matters on the army's right would get even more complex for Pemberton.

Still, the events unfolding opposite the center and right wings were secondary to what was transpiring on the left (to the north) around the battlefield's dominant terrain feature. Stevenson's steady stream of messages alerting Pemberton to that fact, however, had yet to convince him that decisive action—and his presence—was required there. As the keen Stephen D. Lee would later write, "[Pemberton] did not realize his condition until it was too late."[2]

Hovey's Attack

Two divisions—four brigades comprising some 10,000 men—swept forward toward the enemy-held high ground. John Logan moved out on the right and Alvin Hovey on the left. The advance rooted out Confederate skirmishers who had taken up positions in the rough terrain, sending those still able scampering back to their parent organizations.

Alvin Hovey's wish for a prominent role in the upcoming battle was rapidly coming to fruition. For the better part of an hour or more, skirmishers from his pair of brigades had been engaged with their enemy counterparts. Artillery shells arced through the air over their heads, exploding in the trees and open fields with, thus far, but little effect. Now, the moment he had been waiting for had arrived. Described by newspaper editor and assistant secretary of war Charles Dana as someone who "makes it his business to learn the military profession just as if he expected to spend his life in it," the hard-hitting and glory-seeking Hovey jumped off to battle. Upon his shoulders fell the task of seizing imposing Champion Hill. The division leader "ordered General McGinnis and Colonel Slack to press their skirmishers forward up the hill, and follow them firmly with their respective brigades." Within a few minutes "the fire opened briskly along the whole line," he observed, "from my extreme left to the right of the forces engaged under Major-General McPherson." Hovey's pair of brigades slowly picked their way toward the crest of the hill some 600 yards to the front, the Jackson Road dividing the division almost in half. His line, he noted, "conformed to the shape and became crescent-like, with the concave toward the hill."[3]

On the right side of this "concave" line of battle was George McGinnis's brigade. The 37-year-old Bostonian's path to a brigadier generalcy in the Federal army was a circuitous

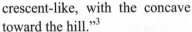

Brigadier General
George F. McGinnis

National Archives

one. Like his father, McGinnis was a haberdasher. After a move to Ohio and service in the Mexican War, he relocated in Indianapolis, Indiana, where he began manufacturing hats. Service below the Rio Grande in the 1840s seems to have whetted his appetite for war, and just days after Fort Sumter, McGinnis enlisted in April 1861 as a private in Lew Wallace's 11th Indiana, a three-month outfit. When these same Hoosiers mustered in for three years that August, McGinnis was sworn in as their colonel. He proved himself fit for field command at Fort Donelson, Shiloh, and during the Yazoo Pass expedition. He was about to do so once more.

The 11th Indiana held his left flank east of the Jackson Road, and the 29th Wisconsin and 24th Indiana stretched the line west on its right. The 46th and 34th Indiana regiments took up a position behind them. "The order to advance was given, and almost immediately a sharp and rapid firing was commenced between the skirmishers," he reported. The skirmishers moved faster than the heavier line of battle and eased their way forward several hundred yards before the artillery stationed atop Champion Hill opened fire. The distance was about 300 yards. The firing was fast and furious, recalled the brigadier, and consisted of "volley after volley of grape and canister." The confusing knoll-studded and partially wooded terrain made it difficult for McGinnis to determine the exact strength and position of the main Confederate line of battle. Clouds of powder smoke settled in the timber and low-lying ravines. The 46th Indiana had begun the advance strung out in front as skirmishers, but "owing to the unevenness of the ground . . . had been crowded clear out of its position and in rear of the line." Orders ran up and down McGinnis's battle line for the men to go to ground until a more accurate assessment could be achieved, and we could "inform ourselves more accurately in regard to the . . . nature of the ground over which we had to move."[4]

With McGinnis's main line prone, knots of skirmishers threaded their way through the smoky folds and rifts of Mississippi topography, steadily drawing nearer the main Confederate line. After a short halt McGinnis ordered his men up. "The whole line moved forward with bayonets fixed, slowly, cautiously, and in excellent order, and when within 75 yards of the battery every gun was opened upon us and every man went to the ground." McGinnis's battle line had emerged from the blind terrain and the Confederate artillerists once again had a target upon which to train their pieces. Lead and iron in the form of "grape and canister" whined through the air but "passed [harmlessly] over us." At that point, remembered the brigadier, he yelled an order up and down the line: charge![5]

On McGinnis's left were Colonel Slack's four regiments. On his left was the 28th Iowa, his right the 47th Indiana, and behind them a second line of battle with the 56th Ohio and 24th Iowa. "Attention! Forward!" came the order as Slack moved his lines forward. "We entered the dark brush in the footsteps of our skirmish line," remembered Lt. Thomas J. Williams of the 56th Ohio. The advance was simultaneously performed with McGinnis's brigade.[6]

Much like McGinnis, Slack experienced some difficulty moving forward, writing later that "the thick growth of underbrush and vines, ravines, and hills made it very difficult to advance." As it is in every battle, a man's place in line dictates what the fight looks like to him, and thus how he remembers it. The men who went in on Slack's right (the 47th Indiana in front and the 56th Ohio in the rear) had a tougher time of it because waiting for them at the top of the rough incline along the Jackson Road, perpendicular to their line of advance, was the right side of Cumming's Georgia-held angle. An advance of about 200 yards was followed, "like a flash . . . [with the] crash of thousands of muskets," recalled Lieutenant Williams. "The bullets made the dust fly as they fell all around us." As he discovered, the skirmishers directly in his front had not gotten far because "the enemy was there in force, and they gave us a heavy fire to start with." Tragedy struck quickly in the ranks of the 56th Ohio when this early fire killed two brothers "within a second of each other." The crash of musketry here was "tremendous and continual," remarked Williams.[7]

Slack's left regiments (the 28th Iowa and 24th Iowa) marched forward without encountering heavy early enemy fire. Southern artillery had deployed west of the road and was focusing on McGinnis's less fortunate infantry, Cumming's Jackson Road line was engaged with the right side of the brigade, and his Georgia skirmishers, mired in the rough terrain triangle formed by the intersection of the Jackson and Middle roads, had not yet taken position across his front.[8]

According to Hovey, "At 11 o'clock the battle opened hotly all along the line." The general hurled his division at the enemy "with his usual impetuosity," wrote one observer. Every man in his organization would experience something very similar—rough terrain sloping upward with an enemy waiting at the top to kill them.[9]

*   *   *

Shortly before Hovey unleashed McGinnis and Slack, two additional Napoleons from Capt. James F. Waddell's Alabama Battery arrived from the area of the crossroads and unlimbered next to Johnston's Virginia guns on Champion Hill. When the familiar rumble of artillery was heard behind them, a member of the Botetourt Battery yelled out, "more artillery is coming!" Another remembered the caissons bouncing toward them "at a furious race." Section leader Lt. T. Jeff Bates saluted the Virginians as his men unlimbered their pieces on the right of Johnston's guns. "I have the honor of relieving you," Bates announced. "Gen. Pemberton says you have suffered enough and wishes you to retire from the fight." Stephen Lee, it seems, had indeed kept his word to the Virginians.

Flat terrain suitable for use as a gun platform was hard to come by, and Bates was forced to drop his left piece "hardly more than eight or ten feet from my gun," remembered Obenchain. Bates "impressed me as being a very brave—a very Gallant man, but [more importantly] as a man who knew his business and determined to do his part to the fullest." With a desperate battle obviously about to begin in earnest, however, the Virginia red legs scoffed at the suggestion to withdraw. Still, orders were orders. Perhaps they were needed elsewhere. According to one of the Virginia artillerists, they limbered their pieces and retired a short distance when Hovey's storm broke forth in full fury. Johnston's gunners were promptly recalled and within a few minutes had their pieces unlimbered and firing for all they were worth.[10]

*   *   *

"The whole line went forward as one man," remembered McGinnis. Opposing him was what Alfred Cumming called "the second front," or those Georgians facing northward near the crest of Champion Hill. This slim handful of men included the 39th Georgia and four companies of the 34th Georgia at the Angle. "Favored by the broken and wooded character of the locality, the enemy advanced two very full regiments. . . . [E]ach of these regiments would seem to have been formed into a double column, occupying a half regimental front, and their whole line to have extended from the point of the angle to about the right of the Thirty-Ninth

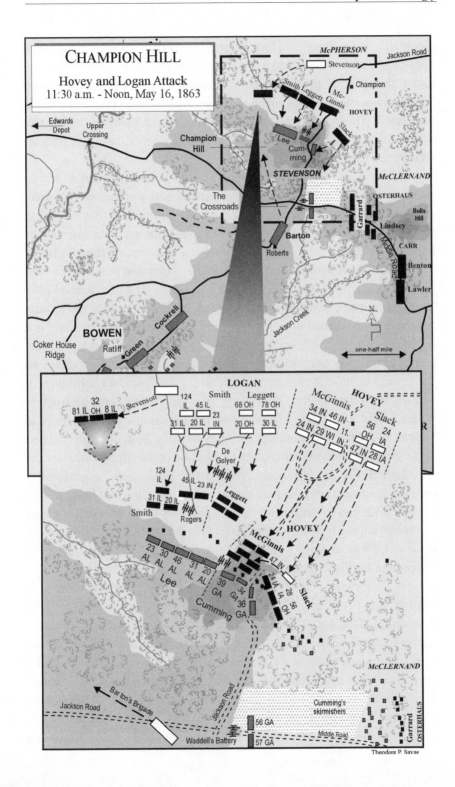

CHAMPION HILL

Hovey and Logan Attack
11:30 a.m. - Noon, May 16, 1863

Theodore P. Savas

Georgia." According to the Georgia brigadier, McGinnis's men approached unseen to within a distance of less than fifty yards. The ridge along this part of the front, he explained more fully after the war, "enabled the enemy to approach so nearly without our cognizance of his presence." The result was that "an attack broke upon us with great impetuosity and vehemence, in overwhelming force, and in a manner wholly unexpected and unlooked for."[11]

The sudden shock of seeing a heavy line of battle within rock-throwing distance momentarily stunned both opponents. "To meet an attack so sudden and unexpected in its precipitation, so overwhelming in its preponderance of force—the best dispositions which circumstances admitted of were made, and an effort made to retain the position," explained Cumming after the war. From their elevated position his men leveled their rifles and fired first. The cacophony of battle washed over every participant, remembered an Ohioan, and "like a flash, there came the crash of thousands of muskets." Firing accurately down a slope is a difficult feat to do well, and because of this most of the lead minie balls passed harmlessly overhead (McGinnis ordered his men to get down on the ground to make it even more difficult for the defenders to hit them.). The enemy returned fire, "pour[ing] in a very heavy and destructive volley," said Cumming. He was not exaggerating even a little. The Federal fire was much more devastating, and men from Georgia dropped to the ground in large numbers, their ranks and bodies ripped apart by the accurate rifle fire. Within seconds the fighting had became general across the Georgia front, with the men on both sides standing and firing at one another with just a handful of yards separating them. McGinnis's men continued edging forward, using the folds in the landscape for protection. Billows of smoke from small arms fire on both sides made it nearly impossible for the defenders to see the approaching enemy.[12]

To Cumming's consternation, heavy enemy columns were also bearing down on his "first front," which was comprised of four companies of the 34th Georgia and the 36th Georgia, perhaps 600 men, facing generally east in a line running south along the Jackson Road. "About the same moment the enemy appeared in front of [this line] and opened fire, but not so near and destructive as that on the second front." This new threat was Colonel Slack's advancing brigade. After a long tramp uphill, Slack "found the enemy in very heavy force about 200 yards in front of us and under cover of a wood beyond a field." From that moment the action quickly evolved from a skirmish into something much louder and deadlier. "The battle began with great fury, our troops advancing for the purpose of driving the enemy from the cover of the woods, which was done at double-quick and in a most gallant manner, the men loading and firing as they advanced," Slack wrote in his report of the action. Charles Longley of the 24th Iowa remembered how "the warming blood begins to be felt bounding through the veins and throbbing at the temples" while waiting to engage the enemy. Then, he continued, "for the first time [you] begin to hear the wicked *zipping* of the hostile lead. Soon it tells its errand—the first man falls." The Hawkeyes of Longley's regiment, as were all the Federals on the move that day, were now tramping into a more personal war:

> The more accustomed eye now detects here and there a gray-clad enemy marking their line at but a few rods distant. You note one, perhaps, striving to find shelter behind a slender tree—he is reloading, and hastily withdrawing his rammer, uncovers the upper part of his body—instantly you aim and fire, and when he falls backward, throwing the useless gun over his head, you forget that other bullets than your own have sped and scream aloud in the very frenzy of self congratulation.[13]

According to Slack—and his observation was certainly true for the men advancing on his right flank—his infantry "unfalteringly received a most deadly fire from the enemy; yet they pressed forward, as men only can do who are prompted by intelligent motives of patriotic devotion to a common country." Cumming, of course, received little or no advance notice of their arrival because his skirmishers had been unable to swing around from the Ratliff Road front with the balance of the brigade during his move to Champion Hill. My pickets, he later fumed to Lee, were not driven in upon us, and there "were no scattering shots" to give intimation of the presence of the enemy.[14]

Lieutenant Colonel John A. McLaughlin led the 47th Indiana into battle on the right front of Slack's advancing line. On his left were the Hawkeyes of the 28th regiment—the left regiment of Slack's two-regiment front. McLaughlin had earlier thrown forward C and G companies to act as skirmishers. The rough terrain, however, quickly separated the Hawkeyes from the Hoosiers as both regiments climbed toward the crest of the hill. "Word was received that the enemy were attempting to flank us on the left," recalled McLaughlin. The source of the threat is not certain, but it may have been Cumming's errant skirmish companies attempting to get into position well east of the Jackson Road. Lieutenant Joseph G. Strong, the 28th Iowa's adjutant who penned the after-action report for Col. John Connell, also noted that skirmishers from the 28th spotted Confederates in force on his front and left. So notified, McLaughlin changed his line of battle and threw his left three companies well out to the southeast to meet the threat, but after advancing a short distance the enemy was not found.[15]

Shortly after McLaughlin dispatched his defensive strike force, a courier reached him with orders to move his entire regiment to the support of the 11th and 46th Indiana regiments, both fighting with McGinnis's brigade on the far side of the Jackson Road. "I ordered in the companies that were out at the time, and immediately moved by the right flank in double-quick time." The Hoosiers crossed the road "under a galling fire" and their commander formed the regiment "on the crest of the hill, within 50 yards of the enemy." To McLaughlin's dismay, some of Cumming's Georgia troops had managed to find shelter "behind a dwelling house and out- buildings and heavy timber, which gave them decided advantage, and enabled them to pour a heavy fire upon us."

Holding his men to their task, McLaughlin returned fire.[16]

John Connell's 28th Iowa, meanwhile, drove rapidly forward deeper and faster than McLaughlin's 47th Indiana had on its right, though the Hawkeyes drifted

Colonel
John A. McLaughlin

Courtesy of Craig Dunn,
Civilwarindiana.com

southeast. The lay of the terrain and position of the enemy eventually served as a pivot that naturally swung Connell's regiment to the right until it was facing more west than south. Somehow, at least according to Connell, the 56th Ohio appeared on the left of his Iowans. In an effort to engulf Cumming's staunch defenders, Slack ordered Connell to slide his regiment farther by his own left. The uneven ground made it difficult to maintain unit cohesion, and bullets from Cumming's defenders were splattering through the underbrush and with increasing regularity biting into flesh and bone, but Connell complied. My regiment passed "to the left of the Fifty-Sixth Ohio (which placed us on the extreme left of the division), and engaged the enemy, our left resting on the north of the Raymond road." Connell's regiment was now at least partially in a field and within sight of the Middle Road, but his losses steadily mounted. Lieutenant John H. Legan of Company A was "gallantly leading his men on" when a bullet struck and killed him. A captain from Company I, Benjamin F. Kirby, also fell about this time and Lt. John Buchanan suffered a severe wound that would cost him an arm. The Hawkeyes were not suffering alone: the Ohioans on Connell's right were also having a hard time of it.[17]

As Slack's regiments pinned the right side of Cumming's susceptible "angle" and "first front" in place, McGinnis's brigade, with help from Slack's 24th Iowa (which had veered southwest during its advance before moving back southeast again) and McLaughlin's 47th Indiana began dismantling Cumming's position. The brigade made its last determined push over the crest, a move, reported McGinnis, apparently "unexpected to the rebels." The final push was not successful because it was "unexpected," but because it was delivered from a short distance against a line ill-prepared and under strength—and thus incapable of meeting it. "The portions of the regiments engaged held for a time their position against a greatly superior enemy," was how Cumming later described it. The bloody, grinding work of close-quarter firing gave way to hand-to-hand combat—one of the rare occasions where bayonets and musket butts were actually stabbed and clubbed against human enemies. The 39th's commander, Col. Joseph T. McConnell, "incited" the men to stand firm in the face of the swarming enemy. A former lieutenant of Georgia state troops, McConnell had been elected colonel just two months earlier. Champion Hill was his first opportunity to lead his men in action. Someone unnamed by history leveled his rifle and pulled the trigger, discharging a bullet that cut McConnell down at the height of the fighting with a severe wound in his thigh. He would survive only to be mortally wounded at Missionary Ridge six months later. A scant few yards east of McConnell was Col. James A. W. Johnson's embattled (and squared-off) 34th Georgia. The regiment had been raised a year earlier and Johnson had been with the men from the start, but until that morning none of them had performed more than skirmish work. Now Johnson was setting an "example," according to Cumming, struggling to keep his few hundred men in position while many times that number stormed his regiment's vulnerable apex or snaked their way around it on the eastern side. Heroic efforts notwithstanding, there was little Cumming or his Georgians could do to stem the storming tide that had splashed against and was now washing over Champion Hill.[18]

From his high perch but limited vantage point, Sergeant Obenchain of the Botetourt Artillery could see the "assaulting troops . . .form[ed] two sides of a square." Hovey's men had wrapped themselves around Cumming's irregular L-shaped configuration and were now overrunning its north front. At least two tightly stacked Federal regiments "bore down" and struck the joint where the 39th Georgia's right and 34th Georgia's left came together. Near this point were the guns from Johnston's and Waddell's batteries. The enemy was by this time "apprised now of the exact position occupied by [the guns]," explained Cumming, who was by now on foot after his horse was shot out from beneath him. The paltry few men from the 34th Georgia were "unable to withstand the charge of so overpowering a force, and it, together with the right [of the 39th Georgia], was compelled to give way." The color bearer for the 34th Georgia, remembered Joseph Bogle, a private in Company I, was shot down during the collapse of the line.[19]

Seeing his line crumble, Cumming strode into the midst of the maelstrom and desperately tried to get the men to stand fast, to no avail. "The opposing fire was too withering, the opposing force too preponderant in numbers, to admit of a long continuance of the unequal struggle," was how the brigadier explained it in a letter long after the war to Stephen Lee. "And the brigade gave way." When Cumming realized "it was not longer possible to hold the depleted ranks to the line," he rode with members of his staff "speedily to the rear" about halfway back to the crossroads. There, he recalled, he "sought to rally the fugitives, assisted

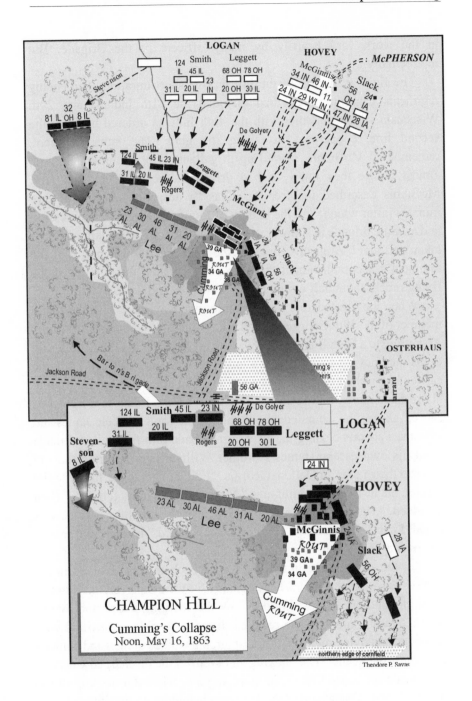

CHAMPION HILL

Cumming's Collapse
Noon, May 16, 1863

Theodore P. Savas

in the work very heartily by many officers of the Brigade. But ineffectually."[20]

The fight at the top of the hill was of short duration. The enemy regiments Cumming described included the 11th Indiana and 29th Wisconsin which, together with the 46th Indiana ordered up from the second line, cooperated in taking the guns. The latter regiment, remembered McGinnis, moved up in gallant style, double-quick, and, almost before they knew it, had driven the rebels from a battery. McGinnis described the free-for-all as "a desperate conflict of five minutes [after which] . . . the battery of four guns was in our possession and a whole brigade in support was fleeing before us, and a large number taken prisoner." Augustus Sinks of the 46th Indiana was proud of the regiment's accomplishment, and remembered how they "pursued the flying rebels about half a mile through the hills and woods."[21]

When the Confederate line began to give way, James Brotherton, a member of the 39th Georgia, yelled out for his comrades to stand strong. According to a friend, as he was "waving his Hat over his Head, hollering to his men never to give it up," a bullet pierced his chest. His comrade carried him a short distance to the rear and laid him down on the ground. "Lord have mercy on me and . . . tell [my] folks I died in a righteous cause," gasped the wounded man. Realizing he could not help James and with the Federals closing in, his comrade bade him farewell and made good his own escape. James's brother William later reported the sad news to their father in Dalton, Georgia. "I did not get to see him after he was hit, but he lived 2 or 3 minutes." More cheerless news followed when he added, "The Yankees are in possession of the ground where he was killed. I can't get his body." Father, he concluded, "he died as brave as any man ever did, which is some consolation."[22]

For the second time in two battles, Obenchain was involved in the rout of his battery. "Under a heavy charge we were run over, our infantry breaking, and our horses shot down by the charging troops and by our own retreating infantry," he recalled. It was a terrible sight filled with wounded and dying men and the ear-piercing whines of men and animals dying terrible deaths. The choking smoke from the discharged weapons only made the scene that much more surreal. "They did not kill all the horses," wrote Obenchain of the Hoosiers belonging to the 46th Indiana. "Some they shot and some they bayoneted." Fearing the hard-charging Federals would dispatch the wounded strewn in every direction, "I begged them not to murder the men." The surge of bluecoats continued driving uphill, and "very soon [crossed] the ravine to our rear in very broken order."[23]

With his guns lost and once again without infantry support, Captain Johnston and several other artillerists made their way on foot "through the canebrake" to find their horses. Johnston mounted his animal and noticed his hat had been lost at some point during the fighting and only one stirrup was left on his saddle. The men made their way rearward through the detritus of battle where they found Maj. Joseph W. Anderson, Carter Stevenson's chief of artillery and other artillerists. Together, the small group "[did] all we could to cheer our troops and . . . rally the broken infantry regiments." Obenchain experienced much the same thing. After pleading with some of the attackers to spare the wounded, he discovered the enemy "seemed to give me no special attention." Seizing the opportunity to avoid becoming a prisoner of war, he struck out for the rear to find his horse, which he had left tied to a tree near the ravine. "I got on him [and] slid down the ravine, but [it] was too steep on the south side." Using some thick underbrush to aid his escape, he turned westward and rode on, escaping the closing jaw of McGinnis's attack. Within only a few minutes, McGinnis' men had cracked the Confederate line wide open, captured four guns (two each from the Botetourt Artillery and Waddell's Battery), and driven back most of the men Cumming had aligned along the northern face of the Angle.[24]

Despite McGinnis's later claim that Cumming's entire brigade had broken, only the 39th and part of the 34th Georgia regiments had fled the front. Their sudden collapse allowed McGinnis's troops to continue pushing uphill and threaten to completely envelope the Georgians still fighting Slack's brigade along the eastern face of the angle. Colonel Glenn of the 36th Georgia was probably thinking the battle was going reasonably well when he suddenly discovered "the enemy had penetrated in his rear as far as his colors." The Badger and Hoosier troops had driven so deeply into the line that they had completely passed the four right companies of the 34th Georgia. When shots from the 11th Indiana began enfilading his line from the left and behind, Glenn yelled out orders to retreat. The 36th fell back in good order and rallied on a higher elevation and held that position for a short time against continued thrusts until, "threatened with being flanked on its right, it was again compelled to fall back," reported Cumming.[25]

The sweeping breakthrough action and collapse of Cumming's regiments uncovered the left flank of the eastward-facing 56th and 57th Georgia, the two regiments he had left behind on either side of the Middle Road to defend the vital crossroads. Bearing down on them from the north and east were Slack's four regiments. The 56th Georgia's colonel, Elisha Pinson Watkins, had been ill in Vicksburg for some time, but when Pemberton's army moved out of Edwards on May 15 he "left his sick-room," determined to rejoin his regiment. To the surprise of his men, "his tall and slender form appeared before his regiment," though he was barely able to stay mounted on his horse. Watkins and the rest of the Georgians, together with the remaining four guns of Waddell's Battery, watched with increasing horror as strong lines of Federals tore their way toward them through the undergrowth. Waddell's guns were spun 90 degrees and opened fire. Longley recalled suddenly seeing the enemy battery, "and at the same instant the horrid howling of grape and canister is about us." The Iowans of the 24th regiment halted, "and the Enfields of

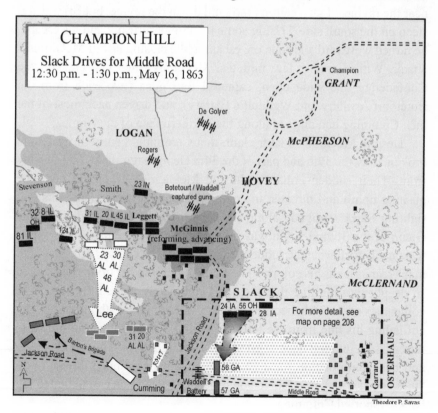

Theodore P. Savas

the 24th add[ed] their clamor to the hell of sound, and their missiles to the many that make the very air writhe. . . . Every human instinct is carried away by a torrent of passion, while kill, kill, kill, seems to fill your heart and be written over the face of all nature—at this instant you hear a command (it may have come from the clouds above, you know not), to 'Fix bayonets, forward, charge!' and away you go with a wild yell in which all mouths join."[26]

Colonel Watkins, meanwhile, ordered the two Georgia regiments to take up a new position perpendicular to the one they had held facing McClernand on the Middle Road. They could do so because McClernand was under orders to move slowly and not bring on a general engagement. The Georgians spun, faced north, and deployed behind a rail fence running along the road. The move left Colonel Jackson's nine companies of the 39th Georgia (the strong skirmish line Cumming had earlier dispatched to hold back McClernand's advance) as the only organized Confederate force standing between McClernand's two divisions under Osterhaus and Carr and the crossroads.[27]

Sensing a sweeping victory, Slack wasted little time attacking the new enemy line. Longley recalled the Middle Road as being "sunken," and from which rose "a line of gray." His men left the shelter of the timber and streamed into a long cornfield, where zipping Southern lead began to carve up the leading ranks, knocking soldiers to the ground with all forms of ghastly injuries. The Georgians leveled their rifles and "poured into us a deadly fire," recalled the 56th Ohio's Lieutenant Williams. "The first of our company, Henry Richards, fell, shot through the brain." Captain Cook, the ill commander of 56th Ohio's Company K who had earlier refused to go to the rear, fell mortally wounded and died six days later. After advancing a few more yards, the regiment "halted to give them a volley," continued the officer, and "my brother, John Williams, was shot through the heart." John had just taken aim at a Confederate when the bullet slammed into his chest. A macabre scene followed. "As he fell in death, he pitched his musket toward the enemy. It fell with the bayonet stuck in the ground, the stock standing up." The company's captain grabbed the musket and delivered the round while the lieutenant hovered over his brother's corpse. "He never moved. The fatal ball, like an electric flash, had blotted out his young life," grieved his surviving brother. The screams of the other men being torn to pieces by lead balls and shell fragments was almost too much to bear. A dazed

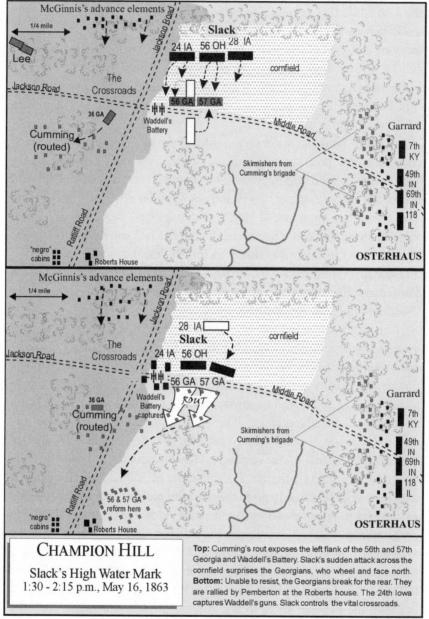

CHAMPION HILL

Slack's High Water Mark
1:30 - 2:15 p.m., May 16, 1863

Top: Cumming's rout exposes the left flank of the 56th and 57th Georgia and Waddell's Battery. Slack's sudden attack across the cornfield surprises the Georgians, who wheel and face north. **Bottom:** Unable to resist, the Georgians break for the rear. They are rallied by Pemberton at the Roberts house. The 24th Iowa captures Waddell's guns. Slack controls the vital crossroads.

Theodore P. Savas

Williams stood to gather his wits about him when a soldier on his left "had his arm shot off. Other comrades in the company were being hit, but there was no halt. Closing up ranks we pressed on."[28]

The heavily outnumbered Georgians did not stand a chance. They broke under the pressure and poured south across the Middle Road into the field and trees beyond. An Iowan was surprised when he realized he was seeing the backs of the enemy: "They fly—the lines becomes a crowd—you pause only to fire—from one end of the regiment to the other the leaden hail converge[d] upon that fated band." These Georgia regiments, lamented Alfred Cumming, "were compelled in succession, by the uncovering of their left and the pressure of the enemy on their front, to fall back, which they did, holding the enemy in check at various points, when they were able to make a stand." Cumming was being charitable, for the Georgians were unable to make a stand any where once they vacated their original position in an attempt to avoid Slack's juggernaut. The immediate consequence was that Waddell's men were abandoned, left to fight on their own hook.[29]

Captain Waddell knew he was in serious trouble as soon as Federals were seen moving out of the trees. He immediately ordered the horses forward to limber up the guns, but it was already too late. By the time the animals reached the front, the Federals were close enough to shoot them down. The 24th Iowa's Charles Longley remembered seeing "a full artillery team" and watching as its "leader and six horses almost stand on end as they go over and down in struggling confusion," riddled with Iowa lead. The determined Waddell next tried to pull his guns away by hand. This time it was his gunners who fell just as quickly. Those still alive and able to do so made their way rapidly to the rear in an effort to escape the catastrophe. In their wake were killed and wounded cannoneers, dead horses, the corpses of infantrymen, and Waddell's four guns, complete with limbers and caissons. As Slack later put it, "the ground [was] literally covered with dead and wounded rebels." Longley later gloated, "Now the battery itself is ours, and fairly won, and cheer follows cheer." Israel Ritter of the same regiment scrawled in his journal that he and his comrades "made a gallant charge, taking a battery of four guns. The Rebs ran like sheep. Our boys did nobly but paid dearly of the ground gained." Slack's attack decimated Cumming and disorganized his own ranks, which had also been thinned in the fighting. Though casualties had yet to be counted, some 300 Southerners were even now shuffling their way northward as prisoners of war.[30]

The first Federals to reach the abandoned position along the Middle Road were probably the Hawkeyes of the 24th Iowa. Their charge, observed Slack, "was most gallant [and fell] upon a rebel battery of five guns [Waddell's], and took it at the point of the bayonet." Screaming from anger and adrenaline, the Iowans splashed around and over the smoking artillery while other men from Slack's brigade, now congealed into one long mass, their organization torn apart by the uneven ground, fired into the fleeing Georgians. Once again on this field, hand-to-hand combat erupted among Rebel guns, this time with Iowans using their bayonets and gun butts to pry the gunners away from their precious cannon.[31]

It was a climactic moment for Northern arms. McGinnis's men were pushing Cumming's broken regiments down the south side of Champion Hill toward the crossroads while Slack's men were spilling across the Middle Road. The 56th Georgia's ill Colonel Watkins, a former quartermaster of the 9th Georgia Infantry and future Confederate senator, had risked all to be with his men, but accomplished nothing more than falling near the crossroads severely wounded by a Federal minie ball.[32]

Although the unfortunates from Cumming's Georgia brigade made an attempt to stem the enemy, the nature of the terrain and breadth and depth of Hovey's assault made the mounting of a serious stand impossible. Fortunately for the Confederates, Hovey's advance, as all advances inevitably must, began to lose steam. Cumming pieced together a patchwork line made up of the 39th, 36th, and 34th Georgia regiments near the Jackson Road west of the crossroads. The 56th and 57th Georgia, meanwhile fell back all the way to Pemberton's headquarters at the Roberts house, 600 yards south of their original position. The army commander himself yelled and cajoled in an effort to shepherd them into order. Alvin Hovey's division had bitten off 800 yards of terrain, swallowed whole eight guns, and captured the all-important crossroads.[33]

When a momentary lull settled over the field on the eastern side of the Jackson Road, Lieutenant Williams sought and received permission to return to the cornfield to locate his dead brother's body. "Thinking it would be my only chance," he explained, the young officer hopped between the slain and wounded men until he arrived at the spot where his brother had fallen. Williams reached down to remove his brother's gum blanket when he noticed "it was perforated through the several folds by the ball that took his life." He used the blanket to cover the corpse and returned to his regiment, which had taken up a position behind the abandoned fence.[34]

Slack's front was now stabilized, but enemy fire from across the road slowly increased as the minutes ticked past. Opposing him were the shattered elements of Cumming's Brigade, parts of which were still streaming off Champion Hill and retreating south down the Jackson Road, flooding into the intersection and beyond. Some of the Georgians took up positions in a ditch behind the Middle Road east of the intersection, and from there returned fire. Slack's own line was jumbled behind the heavy rail fence, and he set out to straighten it as best he could, though Sergeant Longley later recollected that the "scattered" lines "were not improved by even a company formation" during the short time they had before the battle renewed once more. Most of the sergeant's 24th Iowa was crowded on the right front of the brigade line, with the 56th Ohio extending the line east along the road. The 28th Iowa, however, had stopped in a swale near the center of the cornfield, and Lieutenant Williams was directed by Lt. Col. William H. Raynor to "bring [this] regiment up in line with the Fifty-sixth Ohio." The lieutenant did not relish this duty, and remembered moving "at a rapid gate" as the bullets flew thick around him. Longley of the 24th Iowa remembered thinking, "What next?" before realizing some of the regiment's key officers had been shot down. "[Lt. Col. John Q.] Wilds is wounded," he lamented, "and so is [Maj. Edward] Wright." Major Wright's story did end with his injury. The officer had taken a shot through the abdomen but somehow managed to keep his wits about him. The redoubtable wounded major captured "a stalwart rebel prisoner and made him carry him off the field," explained Slack, who deemed the event worthy of inclusion in his official report.[35]

Logan's Attack Begins

While Hovey's division was steamrolling through Cumming's line, John Logan's division on the right side of McPherson's attack was encountering more difficult going. Like the maze of ravines and ridges that plagued Hovey's men, Logan's soldiers faced similar difficult terrain. Hovey, however, had drawn the long straw and faced but three green regiments poorly deployed with an inviting apex to strike. Logan's short straw earned him the right to go up against two full brigades (Lee's and shortly, Barton's), one of which was well deployed on very defensible terrain and under capable leadership. As he quickly discovered as soon as contact was made, Logan would need his entire division to break down and defeat the enemy on his front.

William M. Beach, an assistant surgeon with the 78th Ohio, had just finished preparing the Champion house for use as a hospital when he experienced something that would linger with him for the rest of his life. "About this time I was fairly ready to receive the wounded," remembered Beach. "The steady roar of battle had rolled from Hovey's front by this time to that of Logan's, who was steadily advancing, and where the sound of the conflict was now simply *terrific*." While he was listening to the battle unfold, General Grant and his staff rode up from Hovey's position and the general dismounted at the front gate, "within twenty feet of where I was standing." Grant had barely climbed down when it became obvious to the doctor he now clearly heard the heavy thunder of the battle rolling in from the more distant right flank. "Leisurely taking his cigar from his mouth, he turned to one of his staff and said, 'Go down to Logan and tell him he is making history to-day.'"[36]

The fighting civilian general was indeed going to make history this day, but he had yet to do so. The manner in which his fight was unfolding, at least initially, seemed to hold but little promise. His forward brigades under Mortimer Leggett and John Smith, on the left and right, respectively, had been moving slowly south and west toward the creek bottomland for the better part of an hour before the signal to launch a serious attack was given. Logan's division-size attack, remembered Wilbur F. Crummer of the 45th Illinois, Smith's brigade, "was one of the finest charges of troops that I witnessed during the war, and I was in nine different battles."[37]

One Federal in the ranks vividly remembered the general's actions that morning were "quite silly for him," concluding Logan "must have found some whiskey." He was referring to a brief speech Logan gave to the 31st Illinois of Smith's brigade to fire them up for battle. "Thirty-onesters!" shouted the division commander, "remember the blood of your mammas. We must whip them here or all go under the sod together!"[38]

If the 20th Illinois's Cpl. George Freil heard any inspirational words that morning, they did little to prepare him for the difficult work ahead. The soldier from Loda, Illinois, standing in the middle of Smith's front line, felt the cold hand of death approaching. Convinced of his pending demise, Freil turned to his friend, Pvt. John Vennum, who was standing next to him in line. William Clemans, another nearby companion, looked on and listened while Friel explained his last wishes.

"Here," he said, handing Vennum his wallet and pocket watch. "I want you to send these to my father back home because I am going to be killed today."

"George, you are not going to be killed," replied a nervous Vennum. "Keep them yourself."

"No, I know it. I will be killed," insisted the corporal. "Take these things and please do as I say. Send them to my father."

Vennum and others tried their best to talk Friel out of his premonition, without success.[39]

With that the Midwesterners moved out, picking their way across a ravine choked with underbrush and across one of the thin branch fingers of Bakers Creek. Screened by skirmishers, they worked up the main ridge itself. Lee's Alabamans, however, spotted the early move and opened fire. "The enemy," wrote Logan, "were strongly posted in the outskirts of the timber, directly in my front, and were discovered in force behind the fence." The Alabama fire flew thick and fast for many minutes, the buzzing minie balls tearing through the Federal ranks, breaking limbs and knocking men to the ground. Logan's advance, at least temporarily, ground to a halt.

"I never hugged Dixie's soil as close as I have today," remembered the 20th Ohio's Oldroyd. "We crowded together as tight as we could, fairly plowing our faces into the ground. Occasionally a ball would pick its man in spite of precaution, and he would have to slip to the rear." From General Lee's vantage point, the enemy "advanced in force on my center and left but was handsomely repulsed." Lee's early success would prove fleeting.[40]

Logan's feeling out of the Confederate line revealed an interesting development: both flanks—his own and the enemy's—were "up in the air." The prudent move for Logan was to extend his line farther right so he could "prevent any flank movement of the enemy." By doing so, however, he would also be in a position to take the Confederates in flank, cut the Jackson Road, and drive them away from the bridge. If successful, Logan could sever the enemy from their base at Vicksburg. A courier was dispatched to the rear to order John Stevenson's brigade out of its reserve position. Stevenson remembered the moment: "As the line advanced, I was ordered to move my command to the right, and deploy my column so as to let my left rest on the right of General Smith's brigade." The brigadier moved up on the double and formed in a "skirt of timber," skirmishers extending "considerably beyond my right flank." When fully formed, the brigade was aligned with the 8th Illinois on the left and the 32nd Ohio and 81st Illinois extending the line westward. The 7th Missouri remained in the rear to guard the wagon train.[41]

Barton Marches for the Left Flank

While Logan's men were moving south, a column of Georgians was on the move behind the heavily-defended ridge Logan was desperate to capture. The 1,400 men were making for the Southern army's left flank at the double-quick, clutching their rattling accouterments as they trotted through brushy undergrowth, across pastures, and over fences. Grant's attack was the siren song that had put them in motion, which also alerted Carter Stevenson that his small piece of the world was about to collapse, and with serious consequences for the entire army. He had been watching the disconcerting movement around his left and escalating skirmish fire for some time now, and had kept Pemberton well informed. The escalation into full-scale battle, however, forced Stevenson into action. With a largely quiescent enemy east of the crossroads, he had little choice but to draw upon that sector of the line and hope the Federals did not push forward along the Middle Road. "As I had no reserve," he later explained, "I moved General Barton (my right brigade) by the rear to the extreme left." It was a gamble, but one Stevenson had to risk. Barton regiments were in position just south of the vital intersection, and comprised the last brigade Stevenson could call upon to defend the Middle Road front. Barton also linked Stevenson's right with John Bowen's left. Stevenson dutifully notified Pemberton of the move and focused the commanding general's attention yet again to his far left, "which would doubtless be the main point of attack." Within a short time, Stevenson again sent word to

Pemberton that unless reinforced, he could not hold his position against "the heavy and repeated attacks."[42]

Seth Barton promptly pulled his Georgia regiments out of line when he received the order to vacate his Ratliff Road position. "The distance (about 1 ½ miles) was passed at double-quick," reported the brigadier, "and advanced as rapidly as the nature of the ground would admit." Attached to the brigade was Capt. Max Van Den Corput's Cherokee Georgia Artillery, which Barton dispatched the short distance up the Ratliff Road and then west down the Jackson Road. The firing that had for some time merely popped and sputtered across the army's front had finally broken out into a full-blown engagement. Now, these sheets of thunder enveloped the thin, long-faced brigadier as he hurried his men along their way.

Seth Maxwell Barton was a long way from his hometown of Fredericksburg, Virginia. The 33-year old had graduated in the bottom half of the 1849 class at West Point, which he had entered at the young age of 15. Alfred Cumming was one of his classmates. If it could be summed up in a single word, Barton's prewar military career would be labeled "unexceptional." Service in New York was followed by a long decade in the southwestern heat of New Mexico and Texas, where he toiled as regimental adjutant from 1853-1857 for the 1st Infantry and on at least one occasion, fought Comanche. When he resigned after riding to Fort Leavenworth, effective June 11, 1861, Barton was given a captain's

Brigadier General
Seth Barton

National Archives

commission in the Confederate army. Later, as a lieutenant colonel with the 3rd Arkansas, he experienced a variety of early Civil War adventures including participation in the West Virginia skirmishes and a stint during the war's first winter as Stonewall Jackson's chief engineer. A brigadier general's commission in the third month of 1862 was accompanied by a transfer west to Edmund Kirby Smith's Department of East Tennessee. Barton's tenure as a brigade commander was marked with neither highs nor lows until his transfer to Mississippi late that autumn. Blessed with prepared high ground and a wonderful field of fire, Barton's regiments played a prominent role in the repulse of Sherman's Chickasaw Bayou assault at the end of December where, according to a recent biographer, his men stood firm in the face of "three days of rifle and artillery firing and five attempted assaults."

As Barton hurried his regiments cross-country, the fighting around the high ground north of the crossroads seemed to be shifting farther west along Stephen Lee's front. Would he reach the trouble spot in time?

Almost exactly one year after Champion Hill, at New Bern, North Carolina, Barton would lead into battle the remains of the fallen Lewis Armistead's Virginia brigade, and be censured by Maj. Gen. George Pickett for failing to cooperate. More drastic punishment would arrive later that month, meted out by another general for a similar offense, much to the dismay of Barton's regimental officers who would petition unsuccessfully for his return. But late on the morning of May 16, 1863, Barton was demonstrating promptness and a cool head as his men hustled forward to an uncertain future waiting just minutes ahead of them.[43]

* * *

Barton's men were just beginning their difficult cross-country journey when the sporadic skirmishing on Stephen Lee's front wound down and a heavier patter of musketry, accented by the lower, sonorous tones of artillery, took center stage. Directly confronting his Alabama regiments were the brigades of Mortimer Leggett and John Smith. Once the initial probing attack by Logan's heavy skirmish line had been decisively repulsed, Lee glimpsed an opportunity for action and decided on a rather audacious spoiling offensive against a specific part of Logan's line. His goal was to silence or drive off Capt. Henry A. Rogers's four 24-pound Howitzers of Company D, 1st Illinois Light Artillery, which had unlimbered on a small ridge well in advance of Smith's right flank next to a stand of timber. For much of the past hour De Golyer's Michigan pieces had been shelling Lee's men with a "well-directed fire," reported McPherson, but in reality the damage it was inflicting was minimal at best. Once Rogers's heavier guns galloped up and dropped trail just 400 yards from the ridge, however, the effectiveness of the Federal long-arm changed. These guns, explained McPherson, "poured a destructive enfilading fire" that Lee had to stop before it threatened the integrity of his line.[44]

Following up in the wake of Logan's rebuffed advance, Lee decided to move some of his men forward to destroy or drive off Rogers's artillery. The task fell on the unit opposite the battery—Col. Franklin King Beck's 23rd Alabama. With a shout, the Wilcox County Georgian led his regiment forward out of the trees and toward the fence bordering the open sloping field beyond. They had no idea they were heading into a slaughter pen. Once out in the open, De Golyer's Wolverines quickly found the range and yanked their lanyards just as the enemy infantry crossed the fence line. The pieces jumped off the ground and shot flames, smoke and hot metal from their mouths. Osborn Oldroyd observed the effects of the firing with awe:

> Soon we got orders to rise up, and in an instant every man was on his feet. If the former order was well obeyed, the latter was equally so. The enemy charged out of the woods in front of us in a solid line, and as they were climbing the fence between us, which separated the open field from the timber, DeGolier's battery, stationed in our front, opened on them with grape and canister, and completely annihilated men and fence and forced the enemy to fall back. Such terrible execution by a battery I never saw. It seemed as if every shell burst just as it reached the fence, and rails and rebs flew into the air together.[45]

Colonel Beck, however, kept his men moving forward "under a heavy fire" and made directly for Rogers's belching guns.[46]

The surprising attack briefly befuddled the offensive-minded Logan, who would later describe the move as a "spirited resistance." Major Charles J. Stolbrand, Logan's chief of artillery and a Swedish immigrant, was close enough to witness the thrust. He notified General Smith, whose

men were immediately behind in support of the guns. The excited
Stolbrand reported in his thick Scandinavian accent, "Sheneral Schmitt,
dey are sharging you mitt double column . . . dey vant mine guns!"[47]

Smith was well positioned to beat back Colonel Beck's attack, and he
would do so handily with assistance from Col. William Spicely's 24th
Indiana, McGinnis's far right regiment. Two of Smith's regiments, the
45th Illinois and 23rd Indiana, watched as Beck's Alabama infantry
stormed down the ridge into killing range. Hundreds of "clicks" were
heard as they cocked their muskets and methodically leveled their
weapons. When the command of "Fire!" was yelled, a sheet of smoke
billowed in front of their ranks, obscuring their view for a few moments
until the light breeze that morning cleared the air. The volley killed or
wounded many of Beck's gray- and brown-clad attackers. Colonel
Spicely's enfilade fire closed the jaws of the trap Beck had unwittingly
entered. Spicely was advancing his Hoosiers against Cumming's
position on Champion Hill when he "discovered the enemy in large force
moving to my right, and making an effort, as I supposed, to capture our
batteries, stationed in the field to the right." An experienced soldier with
a record stretching back to the Mexican War, Spicely knew an opportunity when he saw it. "I at once halted my command and poured a

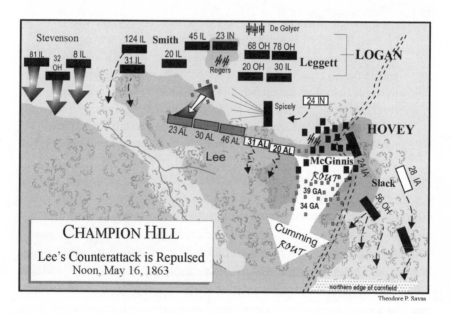

Theodore P. Savas

Colonel William Spicely
24th Indiana Infantry

National Archives

galling oblique fire into his [Lee's] flank." The volley, continued Spicely, though delivered from quite a distance, "[coupled] with the destructive fire of the artillery, checked . . . their advance." Hit in flank and front, Beck ordered a retreat and his survivors raced uphill for the safety of the timber, leaving behind many of their dead and wounded comrades. Beck's worse days remained ahead of him. A kick from a horse would badly break his leg on the retreat to Vicksburg, and a bullet absorbed during an insignificant skirmish near Resaca in October 1864 would end his life.[48]

Having already been bloodily rebuffed himself (the enemy, observed Logan, met our "forward movement with great obstinacy") and now having returned the favor, Logan more fully appreciated the strength of Lee's position. With John Stevenson moving westward toward the creek's bottomland, he settled in Leggett and Smith for a frontal slugfest. The Federal brigades exchanged volleys of lead as the "engagement became general along the entire line." Smith, in particular, continued pushing his line against Lee's center and left, easing his way forward up the ridge. "We had not proceeded over half the distance . . . when poor George Freel [Friel] was shot in the breast and killed instantly," recalled his friend William Clemans. Corporal Friel had only a short time earlier given away his personal effects because of his haunting premonition of an early demise. He was the only member of his company killed or wounded at Champion Hill. "Johnny Vennun stopped and pinned a paper bearing his name, regiment, and his home address on his breast," remembered Clemans. "He now rests in the National Cemetery on the banks of the Mississippi River at Vicksburg, where all our dead were removed." This phase of the intense fighting, recalled Illinois soldier William Crummer, left the 45th's colors "riddled with bullets and our color guards were all killed and wounded."[49]

The lively exchange of musketry continued unabated as Hovey's division on the far side of the field began driving Cumming's Georgians off Champion Hill. The temporary stalemate across Logan's two-brigade front worked to Logan's advantage. His men had Lee firmly pinned in front and Stevenson's brigade was picking and clawing its way west and south toward the ridge upon which the enemy line was ensconced. Soon he would be in a position to turn Lee's flank and sweep the enemy from the ridge. Logan's hard right hook was about to fall.

Stephen Lee is Enveloped

John Stevenson's Union brigade was moving south a few hundred yards beyond Lee's exposed left flank, Smith's brigade was pressing heavily against Lee's center and left, and Barton's Georgians were moving across the Jackson Road through fields and wood lots toward the Confederate left, when disaster struck from an unexpected direction. Lee was directing affairs from behind his threatened left and center, more than satisfied with his brigade's performance thus far given the odds he faced, when a "heavy fire" broke out on his right flank. He quickly galloped his horse in that direction. What he discovered there must have chilled his blood. "I found that Cumming's brigade had been driven back by the enemy," he wrote after the battle, "and the Twentieth and Thirty-first Alabama Regiments, of my brigade, had been compelled to retire, their right flank having become exposed and the enemy having gained their rear." Not only had the Georgia brigade on his right been swept from the field, but his own line was beginning to crumble.[50]

The 20th and 31st Alabama regiments had been battling and holding back Leggett's infantry to their front when Spicely's 24th Indiana, together with Col. Charles R. Gill's 29th Wisconsin, both of McGinnis's brigade, drove through the gap left by Cumming's fleeing troops. Once on the hill crest, the regiments turned to engage and enfilade Lee's position. No troops can stand enfilade fire for long. After braving the deadly storm for some minutes, the regiments trailed rearward in disorder and reformed about 400 yards to the rear on a small ridge north of the Jackson Road. Only the 23rd, 30th, and 46th Alabama regiments remained to man Lee's defensive position. The brigadier guided his horse into the thick of the fight to assess the damage and determine how best to rectify the deteriorating situation. Lee grabbed a battle standard and attempted to rally retreating Alabamans without success. Three horses were shot out from under him this day, and likely one of them fell during this part of the engagement. As his biographer wrote, "several balls tore through his clothing" before one slammed into his right shoulder. Luckily for Lee, the well traveled slug did not have the velocity to break the skin, though it turned his arm black and purple from the elbow to his shoulder joint. Refusing to be relieved, Lee did what he could to keep his remaining three regiments in place. What he did not know was that catastrophe in the form of Stevenson's Federal brigade was already striking from the opposite direction.[51]

The gathering Federals moving stealthily southward under John Stevenson's watchful eye were formed in line three regiments abreast

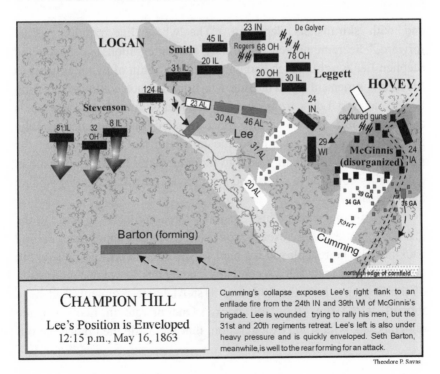

CHAMPION HILL

Lee's Position is Enveloped
12:15 p.m., May 16, 1863

Cumming's collapse exposes Lee's right flank to an enfilade fire from the 24th IN and 39th WI of McGinnis's brigade. Lee is wounded trying to rally his men, but the 31st and 20th regiments retreat. Lee's left is also under heavy pressure and is quickly enveloped. Seth Barton, meanwhile, is well to the rear forming for an attack.

Theodore P. Savas

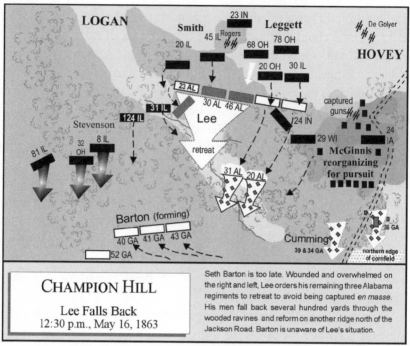

CHAMPION HILL

Lee Falls Back
12:30 p.m., May 16, 1863

Seth Barton is too late. Wounded and overwhelmed on the right and left, Lee orders his remaining three Alabama regiments to retreat to avoid being captured *en masse*. His men fall back several hundred yards through the wooded ravines and reform on another ridge north of the Jackson Road. Barton is unaware of Lee's situation.

Theodore P. Savas

and with skirmishers deployed. "The whole line rapidly pushed forward," he remembered. Cumming's disintegration had uncovered Stephen Lee's right, which had unraveled the width of two regiments as McGinnis's men enfiladed the line. Mortimer Leggett continued pressing heavily against Lee's front. Smith's regiments pinned and held Lee's center and left. It was at this time, recalled Lee, the enemy (John Stevenson) had worked around the left "and had almost gained the Edwards Depot road, half a mile to the rear of my line." No brigade in either army could have withstood such envelopment. Lee's line was no longer tenable.[51]

The brigadier ordered his remaining three regiments to retire to the rear just minutes before escape would have become impossible. Falling back rapidly, he redeployed his men on the next defensible ridge about 600 yards in his rear. "This second line," he reported, "was a continuation of the line on which the 20th and 31st Alabama regiments had been formed at the time they fell back." One private in Lee's brigade remembered, with some exaggeration, that the battle then raged "in our camp ground." A short distance behind the new Alabama position ran the Jackson Road.[52]

Barton Attacks on the Left

Barton was too late, only he did not yet realize it. The Virginian at the head of the Georgia brigade had been picking his way through the fields and thickets from the southeast as fast as possible while Cumming was being crushed and Lee enveloped. The exhausted Georgians crossed the Jackson Road and, perhaps with the use of a courier, located Lee's left flank on the wooded ridge north of the road. "The position was not a good one; the country much broken and covered in most part with dense woods," lamented the Virginian. Barton speedily unraveled his regiments into battle formation on a line angling just south of west in the direction of the bridge, with his left "resting on [the road] and my right on Lee's left." His left stretched to within 600 yards of the Bakers Creek bridge. There were simply not enough men to anchor the army's left on the fast-flowing creek. The brigade's regiments were aligned, from left to right, as follows: 40th, 41st, and 43rd. The 52nd Georgia under Col. Charles D. Phillips was placed in reserve to watch his vulnerable left and support artillery batteries coming up to support him.[53]

Problems plagued Barton's outfit. Though cheered by the company of Col. Abda Johnson, the men of the 40th Georgia would benefit little from his presence for he was seriously ill and unable to lead them. Johnson had ridden out to boost the morale of his men; Lt. Col. Robert M. Young would lead the regiment in his place. Worse yet was the absence of the 42nd Georgia and Lt. Allen M. Sharkey's section of Capt. Samuel J. Ridley's Company A, 1st Mississippi Light Artillery, which had moved earlier in the day to hold the bridge over Bakers Creek. They were too far to render direct assistance, and could not be called up without leaving the bridge uncovered. Like Cumming and Lee, Barton was also going into battle under strength on unfamiliar terrain. Worse, his hastily deployed line of battle was already overlapped on the left by Stevenson's still unseen advancing Federals, who were bearing down on him from the north and west. Barton was about to reprise Lee's unfortunate role.[54]

While the Georgians were falling into line, Barton ordered Captain Corput to unlimber his four 10-pounder Parrott rifles on his far left "near the road," where a reasonable field of fire allowed the gunners to strengthen the brigade's flank and defend the stream crossing. Corput's gunners galloped down the road and onto another piece of property owned by a Roberts family, where they unlimbered on a small ridge west of the house. A section of guns from Captain Ridley's Company A, 1st Mississippi Light Artillery arrived a short time later and deployed on Corput's left in front of a stand of timber. Ridley had originally deployed at Pemberton's headquarters near the Roberts' house south of the crossroads on the Ratliff Road before being ordered to shift north and west to support Lee's Alabamans. When the threat to the army's left loomed large, new orders sent his men thundering in that direction to lend support to Barton. Neither battery was initially supported by infantry. The position was considered so critical that Carter Stevenson dispatched his chief of artillery, Major Anderson, to oversee their operation.[55]

After Ridley's battery rolled into a position and dropped trail, Jim Moore, a member of the battery, was ordered to the rear to look after the battery's forge wagon. Unwilling to miss the fight, Moore protested loudly and refused, but he had a change of heart when threatened with arrest. Begrudgingly, Moore made his way to the rear. Once he heard the guns open fire shortly thereafter, however, he put the forge wagon in charge of "our negro Caleb" and borrowed his brother's horse. Somewhere along the line he was designated for use as a courier, and would spend the remainder of what would be a very trying day carrying dispatches for several generals.[56]

Barton was unaware of the extent of the threat posed by Stevenson's approach. While his men formed, his attention was riveted not on his left flank but on his front, where Smith's regiments (and perhaps elements of Stevenson's left), reported Barton, "having turned Lee's left flank, were already in the timber, pressing vigorously forward." A lack of sleep and exhaustion compounded the Georgians' problems, for they had barely slept the night before after an excruciatingly tiring march, and had just double-quicked across one and one-half miles of rough terrain. Should he remain on the defensive or assume the offensive? Barton was not experienced in making such choices. He chose the latter.[57]

The brigadier ordered his trio of regiments forward, and "with impetuous gallantry . . . [they] dashed upon the enemy's line." Barton's attack probably struck the 20th and 31st (and perhaps the 124th) Illinois regiments of Smith's brigade, and the 20th Ohio of Leggett's brigade,

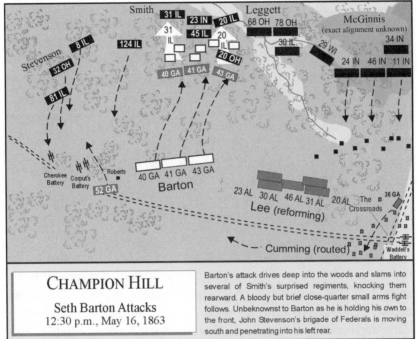

CHAMPION HILL

Seth Barton Attacks
12:30 p.m., May 16, 1863

Barton's attack drives deep into the woods and slams into several of Smith's surprised regiments, knocking them rearward. A bloody but brief close-quarter small arms fight follows. Unbeknownst to Barton as he is holding his own to the front, John Stevenson's brigade of Federals is moving south and penetrating into his left rear.

Theodore P. Savas

stopping them in their tracks and even driving them back a few hundred yards through the timber and underbrush. Colonel Manning Force of the 20th Ohio wrote a friend that the troops all around his regiment retreated, but "the 20th fixed bayonets, stood like a solid wall, and the enemy fell back." Osborn Oldroyd, a member of the same Ohio regiment, agreed, noting in his journal that the Rebels "succeeded in driving

Colonel Manning Force
20th Ohio Infantry

National Archives

[us] a short distance, but their success was only for a moment, for our boys rallied, and with reinforcements drove them in turn."[58]

Against Oldroyd and his companions rushed Col. Skidmore Harris and his 43rd Georgia. "Boys, never give up the conflict!" yelled Harris. "If I am shot down, press on and gain the victory!" The redoubtable Colonel Force ordered his Ohioans to level their weapons. They delivered a hail of fire that swept through the Georgia ranks. "We slaughtered" that regiment, boasted Force. Among the fallen was Colonel Harris, who was mortally struck and captured by the enemy. He died later that evening. Barton's temporary success, however, was also his undoing, for the minor triumph wedged most of his Georgians tightly into a bulging cul-de-sac, the circumference of which was lined with Federals closing in around them. "We now charged into the woods and drove them a little ways, and as we charged over the spot so lately occupied by the foe, we saw the destruction caused by our battery, the ground being covered thickly with rebel grey," remembered Oldroyd. "When we reached the woods we were exposed to a galling fire, and were at one time nearly surrounded but we fought there hard until our ammunition was exhausted, when we fixed bayonets and prepared to hold our ground. A fresh supply of ammunition soon came up, when we felt all was well with us again." Like Force's Ohioans, Smith's men quickly found their footing and, reinforced by the 45th Illinois and 23rd Indiana from the second line, "checked" Barton's counterattack. The two sides settled down for a brief shooting match at close range.[59]

John Stevenson's Attack

The rolling terrain Stevenson's Union brigade negotiated was very difficult, remembered Lt. Col. Franklin Campbell of the 81st Illinois, whose regiment held the right front of Stevenson's line. "We marched through fields and over ditches, fences, through woods, until we met the enemy." Another soldier described encountering "an almost impassable hollow," through which the ranks scrambled and reformed on the far side. Heavy musketry fire a few hundred yards east of their position, the result of triggers pulled by men serving with Barton, Leggett, Smith, and Lee, filled the air as the Illini and Buckeyes passed through the final skirt of timber to "the base of a considerable hill, in possession of the enemy, and upon which they had a battery planted." Unscathed until now, Stevenson's men began taking "discharges of grape and shell," but pushed steadily forward.[60]

The six guns that opened on Stevenson from the high ground belonged to Corput's Cherokee Battery and, on its left, Captain Ridley's 1st Mississippi Light Artillery. Unfortunately for the Southern gunners, only the enervated 52nd Georgia had been detailed to support them, and the approaching Federal line overlapped their position on both sides. Together, these half-dozen pieces and one regiment were tasked with supporting the far left of Pemberton's combat line. They would not be nearly enough.

Stevenson now realized the full extent and success of his turning movement that had carried him into the enemy's rear and bore down on the Southern guns. Joining him on his left was the "Bully One Hundred and Two Dozen," officially known as Col. Thomas J. Sloan's 124th Illinois of Smith's brigade. Shocked at the threat approaching from his left and rear, 27-year-old Colonel Phillips ordered his 52nd Georgia to attack Stevenson's Federals. Barton makes it clear in his report that his other three regiments were fighting Smith's men when disaster in the form of Stevenson's Midwesterners struck from the left. "I had reserved the Fifty-Second Georgia on the left to protect that flank," he explained. "It now moved up rapidly, and in handsome style engaged a brigade that was turning the left."

Stevenson's front stretched well beyond the Rebel guns and was several times wider than the thin regiment that confronted him. Phillips's brave Georgians did not stand a chance. Union muskets by the hundreds leveled, took aim, and shot down the charging Southerners. Several rounds found Phillips, who was struck in left arm, right leg and knee. Another piece of lead tore into his cheek. The officer was lost during the regiment's pell-mell retreat from the field. He was reported missing after the battle, but had been captured by the Federals. The charge failed to impress Stevenson, who casually referred to the 52nd Georgia as the "support" for the guns, which was "soon driven from the field." With the thundering prize now within his grasp, Stevenson's line regiments closed rapidly on the vulnerable artillery.[61]

On the right were the 81st Illinois and 32nd Ohio, which drove the attack home against Captain Ridley's 1st Mississippi Light Artillery. Through no fault of its commanders or men, the entire 32nd Ohio had fallen captive at Harpers Ferry in September 1862, and wished for nothing more than to burnish its stained honor. "Go in, Harper's Ferry cowards!" could be heard as they ran toward the smoking guns. Shell and then canister ripped through their ranks, cutting open wide holes that were quickly filled by other screaming soldiers. As they approached, the Federals leveled their muskets and fired into the packed mass of guns, men, and horses, killing and wounding a number of men and slaughtering the animals where they stood. The man holding his gunners in place was Samuel Jones Ridley, a tall 41-year-old native Tennessean and successful planter from Madison County, Mississippi. "He was a splendid specimen of manhood, a typical Southern planter and gentleman," recalled a soldier who served with him.[62]

Frank Johnston was in command of a section of Napoleons from Battery A, 1st Mississippi Light Artillery that terrible morning. Long after that war, he recalled that "all of the artillery and officers' horses, about forty in number, were killed, and thirty-three out of the forty men were killed or wounded." Once Johnston's own horse was killed, he moved forward to work a gun, determined to fight on. It was about this time Carter Stevenson's chief of artillery, Major Joseph W. Anderson, was shot and killed displaying "extraordinary courage and with a desperate purpose to try to hold the left of the line for the coming reinforcements." Captain Ridley was behind Frank Johnston, riding his horse along the gun line and calling upon his few survivors to "get away if possible." The captain "turned his own horse, as if to ride off, and at that moment was killed, as was his horse." Ridley's corpse, noted Carter Stevenson in his report, was riddled with six shots. Because the guns fell into enemy hands, none of his comrades were able to determine what became of his body.[63]

Ridley's tragic demise did not end the fight for the battery. The blue wave flowed into, around, and in some cases, over the battery pieces. Although a few decided enough was enough and managed to make it to the tree line unscathed, other Confederates refused to relinquish their weapons and continued their forlorn struggle, stuffing their tubes with double canister with a grim determination and bravery that astounded even the Federals. One Northerner recalled how one of Ridley's cannoneers, even with the Federal line a scant handful of yards distant, calmly finished his task, stepped aside, and jerked the lanyard, discharging his piece one final time. Fortunately for the Federals, the tube elevation was askew and the deadly charge passed harmlessly overhead. The Rebel was not so fortunate and fell to the ground, his body riddled with lead balls. "It was the most deadly fight I ever saw," wrote a member of the battery in a Vicksburg paper decades later. "We went there with 82 men and came out with eight."

The scenes of human agony were enough to tear at one's soul. One young gunner painfully shot through the abdomen begged an officer with the 81st Illinois to put his pistol to his head and end his suffering. When the captain declined he asked for the gun so he could do it himself. A Confederate battery member bitterly complained his battery had been "ambuscaded," for it had only been in position a short time before the attack. Charles A. Smith was proud of what his 32nd Ohio accomplished that day. The regiment, he later penned in his diary, "did a noble part charging over hills and ravines and onto the battery, driving the enemy before them and killing a large number. The Rebel prisoners began to come back by hundreds." Stevenson's "brilliant movement, and the glorious results which followed it," wrote Logan after the battle, "speak volumes for the commanding general and his men. Too much credit cannot be awarded for such an exhibition of gallantry."[64]

Corput's Cherokee Georgia Artillery suffered a similarly unpleasant fate. While Stevenson's pair of regiments was overrunning Ridley's battery, Smith's 124th Illinois was slaughtering Corput's gunners in much the same fashion. The Ilini killing volley was delivered at close range. Corpses littered the ground around the Parrott Rifles, but the survivors continued to brave the metal storm, double-shotting their guns to sell the guns as dearly as possible. The Federals raised their bayonet-tipped muskets and with one collective and inhuman scream braved the final few yards to the muzzles. According to one Illinois soldier, "we were ordered to charge and take if possible a battery in our front about two hundred yards. We at once made the charge firing as we went and when they saw we were after their guns they began to hitch the horses to them and retreat but we shot the horses and so we got the entire battery." They also helped capture scores of the enemy, leaving 63 of their own killed and wounded on the field. "Corput's battery . . . was beautifully served," wrote Barton. When there were no longer enough horses to haul away the guns, they fought them to the last "and abandoned them only when they could no longer be used."[65]

The Rebel guns were being overrun while Smith's remaining regiments, and probably the right elements of Leggett's brigade, were smothering Barton's front with a withering fire. Stevenson continued pressing behind Barton's advanced position into his deep left rear. When he discovered he had completely outflanked the Confederate line, reported Stevenson, "I pressed my whole command upon them, gaining possession of the only road and the bridge of Baker's Creek, and capturing a large number of prisoners, together with several abandoned caissons and guns." Barton was too deep into the pocket created by his rapid advance to either maneuver into a new defensive arrangement or quickly and safely withdraw from the closing enemy jaws. To the extent he saw it coming, Barton earlier ordered up the 42nd Georgia from the stream crossing, "having vainly endeavored to cover the left." The regiment did not arrive in time to influence the outcome of events.[66]

Barton's paltry few regiments were exposed to mortal danger from virtually every direction. "The troops on the right now gave way, and my right flank was soon turned and overwhelmed," was how he described the event in his report. "The left was in like manner enveloped and a heavy

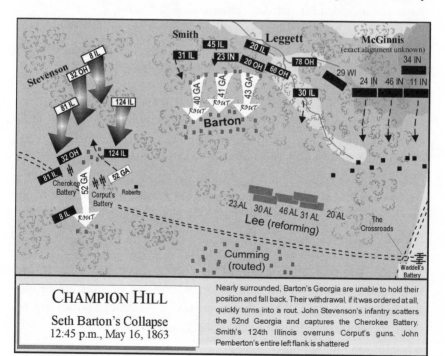

CHAMPION HILL

Seth Barton's Collapse
12:45 p.m., May 16, 1863

Nearly surrounded, Barton's Georgia are unable to hold their position and fall back. Their withdrawal, if it was ordered at all, quickly turns into a rout. John Stevenson's infantry scatters the 52nd Georgia and captures the Cherokee Battery. Smith's 124th Illinois overruns Corput's guns. John Pemberton's entire left flank is shattered

Theodore P. Savas

fire poured in from the rear. . . . [and] I was compelled to fall back." Stevenson and Smith "had so nearly surrounded the whole brigade," he admitted, "that this movement was necessarily accompanied with some confusion." As they retreated, the Southerners heard shouts of "Halt there, you D-N rebels!" Some did and were scooped up as prisoners, while others, mostly the younger men, recalled one member of the brigade, tried to form another line to the rear to no avail. Somehow the 40th Georgia escaped the trap with only moderate losses, and the 42nd Georgia, scampering toward the action from the bridge, seemed to have missed much of the fight. Both claimed Barton "came out with unbroken ranks."[67]

The remaining regiments were not as fortunate. Though no casualty breakdown exists for Barton's separate regiments, he later calculated his losses at 42% (killed, wounded, and missing). The real total was probably higher since the 42nd Georgia, which seems to have been included in this calculation, did not see combat. "The heavy loss of the brigade is the best evidence I can give of the good behavior of the men," wrote Barton with some pride. His plight was recorded in General Smith's report of the fight, which notes the Georgians "fled in the greatest disorder, leaving about 1,100 prisoners and a battery of six guns in our possession." First Lieutenant George S. Durfee of Company A, 8th Illinois Infantry, John Stevenson's brigade, wrote home that they had driven "the enemy like sheep, capturing a battery and lots of prisoners. Our regt. sent about twice their number to the rear." Though overstated, the large number of Southern prisoners is a good indication of the magnitude of the disaster that had befallen Barton.[68]

Many of Barton's shattered companies ran as fast as they could to escape the killing zone. The Southern brigade leader, together with a few hundred men, was carried south across the Jackson Road and then west below John Stevenson's Federal roadblock. The Georgians eventually gained the road again, moved west, and spilled across the stream. "I retired across Baker's Creek," was how Barton later phrased it, "posting the few troops remaining so as to command the bridge."[69]

Stevenson's seething mass of Federal soldiers, meanwhile, had reached the Jackson Road and cut that important Southern logistical artery. Logan's attack severed Pemberton's primary route of escape across Bakers Creek. Grant, who had spent most of the morning around the Champion house "near Hovey, where we were the most heavily pressed," moved with a few members of his staff to the right in search of Logan, whom he found on the Jackson Road. The confusing wrinkled and folded landscape, crisscrossed with creek branches and roads that meandered in several directions made it difficult to fully grasp what they had just accomplished. "Neither Logan nor I knew that we had cut off the retreat of the enemy," Grant candidly wrote after the war. Stevenson had carried one of only two major thoroughfares leading away from Pemberton's rear to Edwards.

What Grant fully appreciated, however, was that victory was lingering in the May air of Mississippi. Logan had completely shattered Pemberton's left flank and Hovey had driven south to the crossroads. His army—or at least a large part of it—was now well positioned to continue rolling up Pemberton's battered divisions away from their Vicksburg base.[70]

Chapter 9

Counterattack

"In the most gallant, dashing, fearless manner, officers and men with loud cheers threw
themselves forward at the run against the enemy's hitherto victorious lines."

— Colonel Francis Cockrell, C.S.A.

THE HEAVY STORM THAT HAD WASHED UP AND OVER HIS ARMY
from the north, rinsing his legions from the high ground like flotsam on a
relentless tide, struck home for Pemberton as the hour passed noon and
approached 1:00 p.m. For two hours too long, the Confederate general
had been overly concerned about his center and right wings—despite
warnings that had evolved into plaintive pleas for assistance from Carter
Stevenson. Only when the trickles of walking wounded approaching his
Roberts house headquarters turned into a flood of unwounded (and in
many cases unarmed) men did Pemberton finally step in a decisive
direction.

After the battle and subsequent fall of Vicksburg, when
recriminations abounded about the conduct of the Southern high
command at Champion Hill, Pemberton queried various couriers and
members of his staff regarding orders he had sent during the battle
seeking reinforcements to bolster his northern flank. One who responded
was staff officer C. McRae Selph, who explained how he "always wrote
the orders I delivered in my book as soon as they were delivered, and

cannot be mistaken either as to the time of their delivery or the language of the orders." According to Selph, it was "about 2 o'clock" when Pemberton sent him riding for Generals Loring and Bowen in search of reinforcements. The order read as follows: "Tell General Bowen to move up at once to assist Stevenson, and tell Loring to move his division—leaving Colonels [T. M.] Scott and Adams' cavalry at the ford—also to the assistance of Stevenson, and crush the enemy."[1]

Selph quickly found both officers, but the news he received was not good. Bowen, the Georgian-turned-Missourian always itching for a fight, told Selph that a heavy enemy force was in his front. Loring's response was along similar lines. Selph rode back to Pemberton with the discouraging news and later recalled that by this time "the enemy were driving back General Stevenson." The troops spotted by Bowen and Loring were elements of Peter Osterhaus's division stretching south in an effort to connect with Smith and Blair on the Raymond Road, and visa versa. In an effort to free up Bowen and Loring to move to support the embattled left flank, Pemberton directed both generals to "move forward and crush the enemy in his front," and then to hurry to the support of Stevenson. Bowen was nearby when he received the order and announced his readiness to "execute his part of the movement" as soon as Loring began his advance.[2]

Lieutenant William Drennan, Featherston's staff officer, had just finished moving Featherston's ordnance train when he sat down beneath a tree close to Generals Loring, Tilghman, and Featherston. The trio were "engaged in quite an animated conversation the principal topic being General Pemberton—and the affairs of the Country generally," the young lieutenant wrote to his wife. "They all said harsh, ill natured things, and made ill-natured jests in regard to Gen. Pemberton." It was then that Pemberton's courier reached Loring with the order to move out and strike the enemy and then move to the army's left to support Stevenson. "The courier who brought it was not out of hearing," continued Drennan, "before they would make light of it [the order] and ridicule the plans he proposed." To Pemberton's dismay, Loring refused to budge. He informed the army commander that "he was threatened by a cavalry force in front and that if he moved, the Enemy would flank him on the right," explained Drennan. "And so he remained in the same place." As Loring later explained it, the enemy was too strongly posted to be attacked, "but that he would seize the first opportunity to assault, if one should offer." In one fell swoop Loring both ignored Pemberton's direct order to attack and modified it so that he could do as he pleased, when he chose. The flouting of Pemberton's directive was not a good omen for the army, and Drennan's keen firsthand observations confirm that obedience to orders and a willingness to cooperate with Pemberton were not present with the cadre of generals holding the right flank of his army.[3]

The back and forth between headquarters and two of the army's division leaders continued when Selph returned yet again with orders from Pemberton to Bowen to send one of his brigades immediately to the left and the other as soon as he was able, and for Loring to stretch north to cover the gap and "not to let the enemy come in." Throughout this exchange, news from the left flank seeping into headquarters grew grimmer with each passing minute. The battle was creeping closer to the Roberts's property and the steady stream of men melting away from the front was a sure sign matters were not going well. Pemberton, remembered one artilleryman, was so agitated by the course of events "that his aide had to assist him to mount his horse."[4]

Bowen Comes Up

If anyone could turn the tide of battle it was John Bowen. His 4,500 stalwart veterans—the best combat troops in Pemberton's army—had spent the morning in line along the Ratliff Road. Except for the early burst of artillery action (one officer remembered the guns had "quite a lively time exchanging complements") nothing but lackadaisical skirmishing had befallen them. However, they were deployed a mile to the south along the Ratliff Road, and so were not well situated to relieve Carter Stevenson. If they were going to make a difference in the battle, they would have to move a long way in a short time. Pemberton, however, could not wait to determine whether Bowen would comply with this order. With his left on the verge of collapse, he sent word directly to Bowen's closest brigade, the Missourians under Francis Cockrell, to move immediately and reinforce Stevenson's left flank.[5]

*   *   *

Colonel
Francis Marion Cockrell

Alabama Department of
Archives and History

Twenty-nine year old Francis Marion Cockrell was a massive 200 lb. six-foot colossus always eager for a fight. He was also a giant among combat leaders, and would end the war with one of the finest fighting records on either side of the Mason-Dixon Line. A prewar lawyer from Warrensburg, Missouri, Cockrell raised a company of militia for the Missouri State Guard and fought with it in the early battles at Carthage and Wilson's Creek. After transferring into the Confederate Army, Cockrell saw heavy combat at Pea Ridge, crossed the Mississippi River as colonel of the 2nd Missouri Infantry, and fought at Corinth, where he distinguished himself at Hatchie Bridge. Although his flank attack had failed at Port Gibson, it was his first combat command as a brigade leader, and the effort clearly demonstrated his mastery of handling large numbers of men under trying circumstances.

Without waiting for additional confirmation, Cockrell ordered his brigade up and marched it "at the quick and double-quick" into a young field of corn and jogged his men cross-country toward the far left flank. Artillery bumped along behind them. One man remembered moving through the fields at "a full run." By this time Bowen seems to have finally grasped the army's left was indeed being turned and his entire division was sorely needed. With Cockrell already on the move, Bowen ordered Martin Green to follow with his regiments as closely as possible on the heels of the Missourians. Private A.H. Reynolds summoned up his recollection of the receipt of this order long after the war when a courier "racing for life" galloped into view. Colonel Dockery, "cool as an iceberg, gave the command: Attention! Load at will. Load!" Dockery, joked Reynolds, "got a job without volunteering." The colonel's words stirred the infantryman: "My heart got right in my mouth, and I believe every other fellow was in like condition; but not a word was spoken by anyone." A Missourian concurred. Moving toward the enemy was a "thrill that stirred our blood and fired our hearts."[6]

Cockrell, meanwhile, sent word to Lt. Col. Findley Hubbell to bring in his five companies of skirmishers and do his best to follow the brigade to the point of danger. Hubbell's command was hurrying to catch up when they spotted Pemberton as they moved past the Isaac Roberts's buildings. A loud cheer was offered as they passed. "His manner seemed to be somewhat excited," remembered the 2nd Missouri's Ephraim Anderson, who watched as the general and a few of his staffers "vainly endeavored to rally some stragglers, who had already left their command." The shaken infantry were members of the 56th and 57th Georgia, whose regiments were even then fighting gallantly in defense of the crossroads against Slack's Federal brigade.

"What command?" inquired Pemberton of Hubbell's trotting column.

"Cockrell's Missourians!" came the reply.

"Hurry on and join the brigade!" shouted the general. "It will be in action in a few minutes!"[7]

After passing Pemberton, the Missourians beheld another novel sight. A group of women had gathered in front of the Roberts house "very nearly within the line of engagement." They were singing "Dixie" to cheer the men onward. "The boys shouted zealously, and I could not refrain from hallooing just once," admitted Anderson. The men hurried on, the brigade now several hundred yards ahead of them.[8]

As Cockrell's regiments continued north, the heavy roll of musketry and rumble of artillery grew louder with each step. Before long, fugitives were seen streaming in their direction. Pemberton initially intended to throw Cockrell in Barton's and Lee's direction, but the sudden collapse of the thin crossroads defensive line and appearance of Slack's Federals there, preceded by a wave of retreating Georgians from Cumming's Brigade, changed Pemberton's mind. Cockrell's new orders were to shift direction and move to Stevenson's right flank—the crossroads. The Missourian complied and was moving "by the file right" a few hundred

yards southwest of the intersection when enemy small arms fire began
zipping overhead like angry spring bees. Worse, the beaten Rebels
making for the rear were beginning to interfere with the movement.
These men, noted one observer, were "thoroughly routed soldiers." It
was time for Cockrell to deploy into line of battle.[9]

The Missourians were now just yards below the Jackson Road with
their right flank just south of the intersection. Sergeant I. V. Smith,
Company E, 3rd Missouri Infantry, remembered long after the war how
the Missourians marched to the support of a Georgia brigade "that had
been driven off the field." When his unit reached the scene of action, the
order "'on the left by file into line!'" was shouted out. Cockrell reported
that he "formed the brigade in line of battle under a heavy fire." On his
right was what remained of Cumming's shattered Georgia brigade,

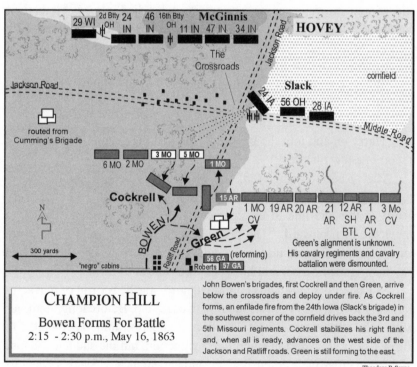

CHAMPION HILL

Bowen Forms For Battle
2:15 - 2:30 p.m., May 16, 1863

John Bowen's brigades, first Cockrell and then Green, arrive
below the crossroads and deploy under fire. As Cockrell
forms, an enfilade fire from the 24th Iowa (Slack's brigade) in
the southwest corner of the cornfield drives back the 3rd and
5th Missouri regiments. Cockrell stabilizes his right flank
and, when all is ready, advances on the west side of the
Jackson and Ratliff roads. Green is still forming to the east.

Theodore P. Savas

several hundred men sheltered in a cut behind the Middle Road east of the intersection. The 56th and 57th Georgia regiments were not with them, for they had run deep into the rear and were in the process of being reorganized by Pemberton himself. Other Georgians were drifting west below the Jackson Road. Hovey's attack had collapsed Cumming's angle on Champion Hill and was now bearing down on the crossroads. Parts of McGinnis's brigade emerged from the distant trees and began firing at the gathering Southerners. If any of them realized time was of the essence it was Francis Cockrell. He ordered Col. James McCown to form his 5th Missouri on the left of the nearest Georgia regiment. The 3rd Missouri was falling into line on the left of the 5th when a satisfied Cockrell turned his horse and rode westward to form the 2nd Missouri.

The fluid state of the battle drilled itself home when Cockrell was notified just a few minutes later that the right side of his brigade was falling back. The general set his spurs only to discover the Georgians "had almost wholly disappeared, and that the enemy had captured Captain Waddell's battery." The result was a heavy enfilade fire against his right from the victorious Hawkeyes, Hoosiers, and Ilini of Slack's brigade. Cockrell would have none of that. He pulled up before his Missourians of the 3rd and 5th regiments and "ordered them to regain their first line, which was quickly done." Private John D. Dale of the 5th Missouri was one of those who had fled backward some distance when bullets began whizzing down the length of the line. When Cockrell ordered the men forward, Dale led the way in a brave one-man charge back to the original line. Other members of the regiment, inspired by Dale's heroism, leaped over an intervening fence and joined him. The 1st Missouri arrived last and took up a position on the far right. Fully formed except for Hubbell's errant skirmish patrol, Cockrell's Missouri regiments were aligned from right to left as follows: 1st, 5th, 3rd, 2nd, and 6th.[10]

Sergeant Smith of the 3rd Missouri marveled at how well the brigade deployed while under fire and within shouting distance of the gathering Federals: "If a good drill master had taken the men one at a time and placed them into line, they would not have been more in their respective places than they were, when we were all in line. It put me in mind of taking a rope by one end and holding to one end and making it straighten out in the road before you." It was a difficult deployment because men were falling from enemy lead without the ability to return fire. "There

were five men wounded in our company before we were all in line,"
recalled Smith. The line formed in a wide lane bounded by a rail fence on
each side. When it looked as though the fire was too heavy and the attack
might be delayed, the men were ordered back over the southern fence and
ordered to lie down. The infantry finished the maneuver only to be
ordered back on their feet and back into the recently abandoned lane.
Black servants who had bravely accompanied the brigade to the battle
line expecting to take part in the attack had to be physically forced out of
line.[11]

A rich thunder was about to be added to the cacophony of killing
sounds reverberating off the high ground and coursing through the
ravines and bottomland: Bowen's artillery was preparing for action.
Landis's Missouri Battery, under the leadership of Lt. John M. Langan,
was rumbling northward up the Ratliff Road and would soon go into
action near the crossroads, where it would vigorously engage the enemy.
Only two of the battery's four guns were available, however, because two
had been disabled during their duel with guns belonging to A. J. Smith's
Union division in the Raymond Road fighting.[12]

When all was ready, Colonel Cockrell "rode down the lines,"
remembered Ephraim Anderson. "In one hand he held the reigns and a
large magnolia flower, while with the other he waved his sword, and gave
the order to charge."

With a shout of defiance and with "gleaming bayonets and banners
pointing to the front," the long line of troops sporting every hue of brown
and gray stepped forward to wrest the vital crossroads back from the
Federals. "I ordered the brigade to charge the heavy, strong lines of the
enemy [who were] rapidly advancing and cheering, flushed with their
success and the capture of our [Waddell's] guns," wrote Cockrell. With a
shout the Missourians stepped off "in the most gallant, dashing, fearless
manner, officers and men with loud cheers threw themselves forward at
the run against the enemy's hitherto victorious lines." According to one
member of the brigade in a letter after the war written to *Confederate
Veteran* magazine, an officer watching the advance turned and asked a
nearby general (perhaps Alfred Cumming) what command he saw
moving to the front. "They are Missourians going to their death," he
replied.[13]

Cockrell was advancing when the four guns of Capt. Schuyler
Lowe's Missouri Battery galloped up and took position on Cockrell's

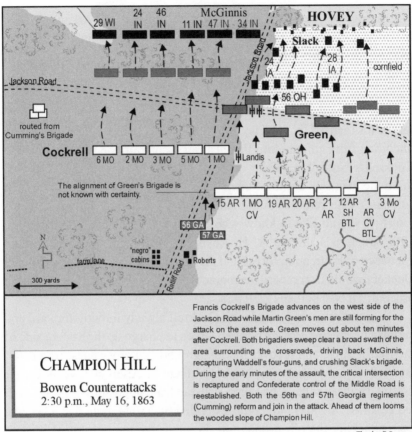

CHAMPION HILL

Bowen Counterattacks
2:30 p.m., May 16, 1863

Francis Cockrell's Brigade advances on the west side of the Jackson Road while Martin Green's men are still forming for the attack on the east side. Green moves out about ten minutes after Cockrell. Both brigadiers sweep clear a broad swath of the area surrounding the crossroads, driving back McGinnis, recapturing Waddell's four-guns, and crushing Slack's brigade. During the early minutes of the assault, the critical intersection is recaptured and Confederate control of the Middle Road is reestablished. Both the 56th and 57th Georgia regiments (Cumming) reform and join in the attack. Ahead of them looms the wooded slope of Champion Hill.

Theodore P. Savas

right. Exactly where they unlimbered is not known with certainty. The gunners leaped from their limbers and caissons and went to work cutting down several small trees in order to open a line of fire through which they were able to shell the fleeing Federals. Private Henry M. Cheavens, a member of Lowe's Battery, remembered the battery managed but one salvo before Green's tramping and cheering infantry moved in front. Unable to safely fire to the front, Cheavens and his comrades trained their guns east down the Middle Road against McClernand's Federal skirmishers. The gunners worked their pieces so rapidly that swab buckets ran dry. A runner was sent to fetch water from a nearby hog wallow, remembered Cheavens, but the thirsty gunners drank the water instead of using it to swab the scalding hot tubes. Somehow Cheavens found time to eat a few sweet potatoes he had gathered that morning.[14]

Riding in the rear with Green's brigade of Arkansans and Missourians was John Bowen. Cockrell's men were forming and Bowen was urging Green's infantry forward, knowing well the consequences of failure. Bowen had complete trust in the capable Cockrell, but he also appreciated the striking power two veteran brigades could deliver opposed to a piecemeal attack dispensed one brigade at a time. Green turned his men off the road north of the Roberts house, where they began uncoiling from column into line near an orchard to the right and behind Cockrell's battle line. Their order of alignment is unknown. The first thing the men saw ahead of them "was a regiment of thoroughly routed soldiers," who refused to stop and poured southward through Green's ranks. "I should like to know who they were," grumbled the disgusted 19th Arkansas's Private A. H. Reynolds. The battle line was formed "between our retreating forces and the advancing foe," was how Colonel Dockery would later record the moment. "Fix bayonets and hold fire until ordered!" It was perhaps 2:30 p.m.[15]

When all was ready, and with Cockrell already moving forward and taking a heavy fire, Bowen ordered Green to charge up the eastern side of the Ratliff Road and recover the lost ground and crossroads. Ironically, Bowen's counterattack was a mirror image of Alvin's Hovey's earlier assault. Both assaulted Champion Hill, but from opposite directions; both led a pair of brigades into combat divided by a road; both had a brigade each attacking the hill proper and the other the terrain east of it; both would capture enemy artillery pieces. Hovey's earlier attack was one of the most successful small division offensives of the entire war. The outcome of Bowen's counterattack had yet to be determined.[16]

*   *   *

By about 1:00 p.m., General Grant had heavily engaged five brigades numbering roughly 10,000 men (McGinnis and Slack of Hovey's division, and Leggett, Smith, and Stevenson of Logan's division) against Carter Stevenson's Division of three brigades (Cumming, Lee, and Barton), perhaps 6,500 effectives. Bowen's pair of large fresh brigades (Cockrell and Green) jumped Southern numbers to something approaching parity—and then some. Grant's brigades had been in heavy action for almost two hours, were winded, and to one degree or another, disorganized. But the Union commander had something near at hand his

Brigadier General
Marcellus Crocker

National Archives

opponent did not: rein-
forcements. While John
Bowen was moving his
brigades in preparation for a
counterattack to drive back
Hovey and recapture the
crucial crossroads, Marcellus
Crocker's Federal division
was arriving on the north side
of Champion Hill.

Crocker's Division Reaches the Field

Although he is typically associated with Iowa troops, Marcellus
Monroe Crocker was a native of Indiana, born in 1830 in the small town
of Franklin. Midway through his studies at West Point, he dropped out to
pursue a career in the law, opening a practice in Des Moines, Iowa. The
lure of military life flowed in his veins, however, and when war broke
out, he enlisted as a captain in the 2nd Iowa and worked his way up
through the ranks. By December, Crocker was the colonel of the 13th
regiment. Until then he had done nothing but guard railroads in Missouri.
His worth as a leader of men, however, became evident by the way he
handled the 13th Iowa in the thick of the fighting at Shiloh as part of
McClernand's division. By the end of the action, 172 of its men had been
killed and wounded. His field acumen did not pass unnoticed by his
superiors, who entrusted him with the "Iowa Brigade" which he led well
at Corinth six months later. His reward was a promotion to brigadier
general, to date from November 29, 1862. It was Crocker's luck and

Quinby's misfortune when the latter took ill in early May. The full bearded and rather grim looking "Iowan," however, was himself lean, frail, and sick. He was suffering from tuberculosis, and would a year hence be relieved of command because of it. Four months after the close of the war he would be dead.[17]

Crocker's brigades were up early on May 16. They broke camp at daylight and marched all morning in the wake of Logan's division. While Hovey and Logan exhausted the morning's middle and later hours developing and then attacking Pemberton's line, Crocker was marching to their succor. Their battle was clearly audible to his infantry, who listened to the shapeless rumble that, step by step, assumed definition as they put more distance behind them. They were three tested brigades each led by a colonel: John B. Sanborn, George B. Boomer, and Samuel A. Holmes. The first two were well up. Holmes, however, had passed the night above Clinton and was trailing some miles behind, guarding the division's wagon train. "Heavy firing was heard," Holmes reported. He was sitting on his horse thirteen miles distant from Champion Hill.[18]

"By ten o'clock the sound of the cannon fell thundering on our ears, and we hurried all we could, as riders came back saying the battle had already begun," remembered Adjutant S.H.M. Byers of the 5th Iowa. The march was hard on Byers, who as a quartermaster sergeant for the past few months "had ridden a horse and had had things easy." The adjutant was determined to stay in the ranks. "I had gone into the army for adventure as well as for patriotism, and I was forever trying to get into the lines where

Colonel
John Sanborn

National Archives

the real adventures were going on." As we approached the field, he continued, "the sound of great salvos of musketry told us the hour had surely come. The sound was indeed terrible." So was the stifling Mississippi heat, which Byers described as "fearfully hot." Water was in short supply. "At the left of the road we passed a pond of dirty water. All who could broke ranks and filled canteens, knowing that in the heat of the fight we would need the water terribly. I not only filled canteen, I filled my stomach with the yellow fluid, in order to save that in the canteen for a critical moment." The filthy water was bad enough, but now other signs heralding matters best not pondered too deeply became too obvious to ignore. Wounded men limped past Boomer's marching regiments. "Little sheds built of branches [and] doctors and their aides [who] had their sleeves rolled up and knives in their hands" were spotted as the infantry approached within sight of the hill. "We knew very well what it all meant," wrote Byers.[19]

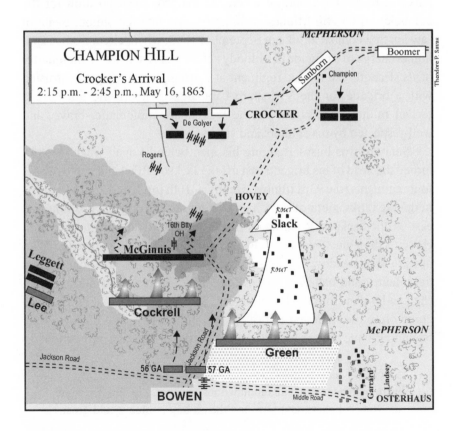

CHAMPION HILL

Crocker's Arrival

2:15 p.m. - 2:45 p.m., May 16, 1863

Crocker's leading brigade under Col. John Sanborn arrived near the Champion house "about the time the engagement became general." McPherson ordered Crocker to send the colonel's brigade to the right to form a reserve for Logan, who was already driving Stephen Lee's Alabamans off the distant timber-clad ridge. "I formed, as ordered, under cover of woods, at the right of De Golyer's battery, and about 400 yards distant," wrote Sanborn. A light smattering of artillery shell fire and errant small arms fire dropped among his men while they were forming, killing and wounding several.

John Benjamin Sanborn was a native of New Hampshire who saw the inside of Dartmouth College for perhaps one year before dropping out for reasons that remain obscure. He must have studied law, for he was admitted to the bar in 1854, the same year he moved west to St. Paul, Minnesota. When the war began, Sanborn was serving as the state's quartermaster general, and soon thereafter became its adjutant general. Anxious to get the front, he leveraged his prominent position for the colonelcy of the 4th Minnesota Infantry. Too late for Shiloh, Sanborn saw his first combat at Iuka in September 1862, where circumstances put him in charge of a brigade in a bloody action that cost it about one-quarter of its strength. He led his regiment at Corinth, but was again entrusted with a brigade for the Vicksburg campaign. Sanborn did not have a formal military education, but he was smart, diplomatic, brave, and well-respected by his soldiers and superiors.[20]

Sanborn was busy arranging his men behind Logan when Boomer turned the head of his brigade east off the Jackson Road and deployed his four regiments (the 93rd Illinois, 5th Iowa, 10th Iowa, and 26th Missouri) in double ranks south of the Champion home. His original position was east of the Jackson Road at the northern foot of the hill to backstop Hovey's division. "We were wheeled into line of battle at the edge of an open field or meadow that sloped up to the wooded hills and ridges where the infantry and batteries of the Rebel army were posted hurling shot, shell and bullets into the Union lines," Sam Byers wrote. "Fighting was going on to the right and left of us, and bullets flew into our own line, wounding some of us as we stood there waiting." The men, he continued,

> Stood still for a while in terrible suspense, not knowing why we
> were put under fire without directions to shoot. Zip, zip, zip came
> the Rebels bullets, and now and then a boy in blue would groan,

strike his hand to a wounded limb or arm, drop his gun and step to the rear; or perhaps he fell in his tracks dead, without uttering a word. We too, who saw it, uttered no word, but watched steadily, anxiously, at the front.[21]

Crocker's third and last brigade under Samuel Holmes, meanwhile, received orders to halt about three miles away from Champion Hill on the Jackson Road near a plantation belonging to Martha Boll. Holmes was to hold the trains in the rear, cover them with one regiment, and bring his other pair to the field as quickly as possible. Grant did not want the wagons anywhere near the field of battle, but it looked as though the infantry would be sorely needed—and soon. Holmes complied, leaving behind the 80th Ohio to guard the vehicles and hurrying forward with the 17th Iowa in the lead and the 10th Missouri trotting behind it. "It was a hurry-up march," remembered the 10th's Capt. Joel W. Strong. Many reasoned they would not enter the battle because they were so far to the rear. Some even gloated over the possibility of having their regiment inscribed in the record as "taking part," without having to fire a shot. Others joked, "Old Grant don't want us to do *all* the fightin.'" When it became obvious they would indeed fight that day, some hid their nervousness with anger. "The men quarreled and snarled at one another when jostled or pushed against," remembered a private in the 10th Missouri. Others hooted at stragglers and wounded who reported masses of Confederates to the front. "I think it is a fact that our expressed vaunting was but a 'bluff,' for I believe most of us were fairly appalled at the serious prospect before us," was how one candid Missourian later explained it.[22]

Boomer was dressing his ranks east of the Jackson Road when General Grant reined in his horse and dismounted behind the lines. "He was so close to the spot where I stood I could have heard his voice," wrote one Iowan. Grant leaned against his "little bay horse, had the inevitable cigar in his mouth, and was as calm as a statue." Knowing how nervous he was himself, Byers remembered thinking that smoking may have "tranquilized the nerves a little and aided in producing calmness." Grant, he concluded, "was calm everywhere, but he also smoked everywhere." The adjutant recalled the general's reaction when a badly wounded man was carried to the rear on a stretcher past him: "He gave a pitying glance at the man I thought—I was not twenty feet away—but he neither spoke nor stirred."[23]

Several Iowans in the 5th regiment "expressed dissatisfaction that the commander of an army in battle should expose himself as General Grant was doing at that moment," Byers would one day write. They watched as staff officers and couriers rode up to him and he gave them orders in low tones they could not make out. "One of them, listening to him, glanced over our heads toward the Rebels awhile, looked very grave, and gave some mysterious nods." When Colonel Boomer rode up to Grant, Byers paid particularly close attention. "He, too, listened, looked, and gave some mysterious nods." Although he could not hear the conversations, Byers did hear five words that further served to chill his blood when an officer shouted down the lines for everyone to get ready: "We are going to charge!" Suddenly it all made sense to Byers. "Something was about to happen . . . . The Commander-in Chief was there to witness our assault." The young adjutant from the rich farm country of central Iowa would see much of war. Before the end of the year he would be a prisoner, make a daring escape more than a year later, and end the conflict serving on William T. Sherman's staff. But on May 16, 1863, he was just a frightened young man standing with hundreds of other frightened young men looking up the slope of Champion Hill in an effort to stare down random death.[24]

*   *   *

At the very front, meanwhile, Hovey's victorious Federals had reached the end of their human tethers. Unfortunately for them, it was at exactly the same moment Bowen's elite division raised the Rebel Yell and drove forward against their extended and not well organized lines. Cockrell's Missouri brigade struck first; Green's regiments swept forward perhaps ten minutes thereafter on Cockrell's right. "Cheers announced the coming up of Green's Brigade," a Missourian serving with Cockrell would later write. Alvin Hovey, who was present with the advance elements of his victorious but disorganized division, remembered how the attack "poured down the road in great numbers upon the position occupied by my forces." The experienced Hovey had a good eye for terrain, and knew what was about to befall his command. "Seeing from the character of the ground that my division was likely to be severely pressed, as the enemy would not dare advance on the open ground before General McPherson, who had handled them roughly on the right," he explained, "I ordered our captured guns to be sent down the hill." He was also enough of a veteran to know reinforcements, if they ever arrived, would be a long time coming.[25]

Francis Cockrell's opening thrust drove northward just west of the intersection, his right initially hugging the Ratliff Road and, beyond the crossroads as he climbed the hill, the Jackson Road. The Missouri Brigade trotted forward, knocking down small undergrowth and tearing down the rail fence in its front. "We seized the lower rails of the fence, gave a lift and a heave, and sent it sprawling," reminisced a member of the 6th Missouri. A comrade in the 3rd Missouri remembered a similar event, explaining, "Our boys took hold of the bottom rail of the fence in front of them and lifted it clear of the ground and threw it twenty or thirty feet, and away we went across a little field and into the edge of a woods."[26]

*   *   *

A few hundred yards away from atop Champion Hill, Bowen's assault was being watched in stunned amazement by General McGinnis. His men had just crushed the Confederate line and ripped it wide open. If the brigadier had a philosophical bent, he may have realized the alarm he was experiencing was the same Alfred Cumming suffered just two hours earlier. "The rebels were driven about 600 yards" from their original line, McGinnis reported, "when, being strongly re-enforced, they turned upon us and made a most determined stand." At the time McGinnis's men were reorganizing in a belt of timber on the hill's south slope. They were about to be overrun. The brigadier yelled out orders to couriers who rode north down the Jackson Road to notify his superiors of the rolling Confederate attack. Reinforcements, he announced, were desperately required.[27]

While McGinnis watched with deep interest, down in the low ground to the south tramped Cockrell's heavy wave of infantry. The first of his regiment to feel the serious sting of enemy fire was the last to have arrived—Col. Amos C. Riley's 1st Missouri, stationed on Cockrell's right flank. Riley's men "most gallantly charged a very superior enemy immediately in their front," Cockrell reported, "at the same time being exposed to such a destructive raking fire from the enemy on their right—all the troops on the right having fallen back." The Missourians were paying a high price for advancing before Martin Green's brigade was up, and it was Slack's men who were doing the collecting. Riley coolly turned two of his companies to absorb and return fire while the balance of the regiment pushed forward with the rest of the brigade. The threat from the right eased substantially a few minutes later when Green's charging brigade struck Slack from the front. It was about this time when Lieutenant Colonel Hubbell's five-company skirmish patrol, exhausted but ready for action, came up behind the center of Cockrell's advance line of battle and "most cheerfully joined in the charge," recalled the brigade commander.[28]

The first reinforcements to reach the embattled McGinnis on Champion Hill were two guns from the 16th Battery, Ohio Light Artillery, under Capt. James A. Mitchell, which unlimbered on the left of Thomas H. Bringhurst's exhausted and bloodied 46th Indiana. Guns belonging to the Lt. Augustus Beach's 2nd Battery, Ohio Light Artillery, may also have arrived just in time to unlimber farther west on the right flank of the 24th Indiana. Henry Watts of the 24th remembered

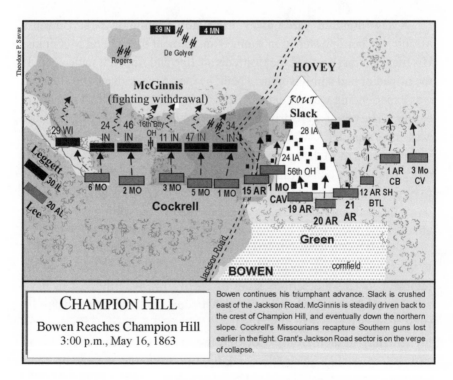

CHAMPION HILL

Bowen Reaches Champion Hill
3:00 p.m., May 16, 1863

Bowen continues his triumphant advance. Slack is crushed east of the Jackson Road. McGinnis is steadily driven back to the crest of Champion Hill, and eventually down the northern slope. Cockrell's Missourians recapture Southern guns lost earlier in the fight. Grant's Jackson Road sector is on the verge of collapse.

Colonel Thomas H. Bringhurst
46th Indiana Infantry

Courtesy of Craig Dunn, Civilwarindiana.com

advancing down the hill to a ravine
and fighting there with his comrades
when the Federal pieces dropped trail.
Cockrell's Missourians were so close
the gunners had to use canister rather
than shell. The captured Confederate guns, still hot to the touch, probably
had not yet been removed from the hill top.[29]

The troops in front of the 3rd Missouri, remembered Sergeant Smith,
had "just formed in line of battle and with empty guns. They ran at the
first volley." Smith remembered watching as a Federal captain implored
his comrades to hold the line. "He was knocked down with a musket by
one of his own men, and we captured him." The Missourians swept past
thin lines of advanced Federals and "met a line of Ohio and Indiana
troops [and] then we had an awfully hard fight," explained Smith.
McGinnis agreed. "At this point occurred one of the most obstinate and
murderous conflicts of the war. For half an hour each side took their turn
in driving and being driven." Alvin Hovey agreed with this assessment.
"Most of the fighting . . . was done at short range, being only from 50 to
75 yards apart and several times not more than fifteen or twenty yards."
Colonel William Spicely, whose Hoosiers of the 24th Indiana had so
handsomely helped drive back Stephen Lee's right flank earlier in the
charge up the north slope of Champion Hill, noted the heavy enemy
reinforcements in his report and explained that after a brief lull, "the
struggle commenced, the most desperate and destructive of the day."

Captain Mitchell's Ohio guns only managed to get off sixteen rounds
before "he saw his pieces were in danger of being captured should he
remain longer in that position," reported McGinnis. Mitchell yelled out
the command "Limber to the rear!" The guns hitched up and made safely
for the rear, but Mitchell did not ride out with them. He had just finished
yelling out the order to withdraw when a minie ball tore through his body.
He died a few hours later. "He fell at his post, nobly and gallantly

performing his duty," lamented McGinnis. Lieutenant George Murdock assumed command of the section "and deserves praise for his coolness and bravery," reported division commander Hovey. Foreseeing the loss of Champion Hill, McGinnis ordered the captured guns hauled away. He only had enough horseflesh to remove two of them. His men spiked the others as they fell back.[30]

In his official report of the battle, General Hovey had nothing but praise for all of the commands in his division. In a lengthy unpublished manuscript penned after the war, however, he was less charitable. The retreat, he wrote for private consumption, was "owing to some mismanagement in the 34th [Indiana], our left flank was left without support, and the rebs turned our flank, giving us a raking fire which caused our right to fall back on a new line, when we again fought them our men falling thick and fast." The excitable McGinnis would call for help three times, but Hovey had none to send him. The division leader could only solicit McPherson and Grant for reinforcements.[31]

Another artilleryman, this one in Confederate gray, fell across the embattled divide, though the victim of a terrible accident rather than a battle wound. A sponger with Guibor's Battery was working in sync with the rhythm of loading and firing his gun when the field piece next to him discharged. In the smoke and noise of battle he mistook the blast as having originated with his own gun, and stepped toward the muzzle to reload the piece. As the unnamed crewman inserted his sponge another red leg yanked the lanyard. The blast disintegrated the tool and drove sharp splinters of wood and metal into the sponger's body, simultaneously breaking both arms and both legs. The tragic accident made those religious or superstitious sit up and take notice, for the man had refused the services of a Catholic chaplain just the night before.[32]

McGinnis's brigade, meanwhile, continued to absorb a terrible pounding of shells and small arms fire on the southern slope of the hill. After shifting slightly to the left, Spicely's men "contested against superior numbers for nearly an hour, under the most galling fire I ever witnessed." His initial fight must have seemed an hour to those experiencing it, but reality was something closer to fifteen or twenty minutes. Cockrell kept up the pressure against what he described as "stubborn resistance," his blood red flags flying high and pressing forward yard by bloody yard. Choking smoke burned lungs and stung the eyes of powder-begrimed men on both sides. "Masses of the enemy threw their whole weight upon the right and center of my line," wrote Spicely the next day while the action was still fresh in his mind. "My men fell by the scores, but yet with determined bravery held the enemy in check." Unable to hold out any longer, he screamed out for his men to withdraw to a new line about 75 yards up the hillside, where they stopped to deliver another volley into the approaching Missourians. By now the smoke was hanging like a heavy shroud over the field and visibility was greatly reduced. The opposing lines were perhaps 50 yards away from one another, loading and firing as fast as humanly possible under grotesquely inhumane conditions. Unable to withstand the surging gray tide, the Iowans fell back again, stopping yet a second time to throw back an enemy that Spicely estimated was "ten times our number."[33]

When word was received that the left of the division had fallen back and the troops on his right were likewise caving in, Colonel Spicely called out for another withdrawal. It was too late. Screaming Missourians were already beginning to infiltrate the entire front of McGinnis's thinning line of defense. It was at this time the 24th Indiana suffered a serious loss. "Here our colors fell," was how Spicely glumly recorded the event. The regiment's Lt. Col. Richard Fulton Barter mistakenly believed the 24th's color-bearer had been wounded and was about to fall. Barter rushed forward and grabbed the staff, waving the banner and cheering "in the very face of the enemy." The staff was severed by minie balls, one of which shattered Barter's hand in a bloody and painful wound. The flag was never recovered and fell into enemy hands. By this time, the brave and well-led men from Indiana were "entirely out of ammunition and overwhelmed in front, my command fell back nearly 300 yards" and formed a new line with the survivors of the 11th Indiana, who had just experienced a similarly terrifying attack. The breathless and bleeding Hoosiers finally had a few moments to regroup and fill their empty cartridge boxes. Colonel Daniel Macauley was not among them. The commander of the 11th Indiana had fallen with two serious wounds, one in each thigh.[34]

On the other side of the battle line was Sgt. James Payne of the 6th Missouri, who left a very similar account of his harrowing experience at Champion Hill. The enemy shots, he recalled, were buzzing all around him as he and his comrades pressed on up the hillside. One finally hit him squarely in the body. The sergeant escaped a serious wound or death only because the slug had hit the blanket he had carried since the battle of Pea

Colonel Daniel Macauley
11th Indiana Infantry

Courtesy of Craig Dunn, Civilwarindiana.com

Ridge the previous year. Dazed and bruised, Payne looked about for another Federal to kill when "another Yank got me in the side." This wound was more serious, and an officer recommended he make his way to the rear.[35]

*   *   *

On the left side of Hovey's division was James Slack's brigade. After its hard-charging effort against the 56th and 57th Georgia and Waddell's guns, Slack had but little time to straighten out his jumbled line just north of the Middle Road and east of the crossroads. His front had been tossed roughly about, and the state of its organization is unclear. Generally, speaking, the 24th Iowa held the right near the intersection, with the 56th Ohio on its left and the 28th Iowa, having just come up, extending the line east. (Colonel John McLaughlin's 47th Indiana, it will be recalled, had moved by the right flank earlier in the attack and was fighting west of the Jackson Road.) It was upon these three regiments that the full fury of Martin Green's attack would fall.[36]

Elements of the brigade had driven perhaps 50 yards beyond Waddell's guns to the rail fence, explained Slack, "when a new rebel line, which had not been in action, appeared in treble our force." Slack was speaking of Green's pending attack from below the Middle Road, which was being directly supervised by General Bowen. Lieutenant Williams watched with his comrades of the 56th Ohio while lying behind the wooden fence. "From our position we could see the enemy forming to attack us, the woods in our front being open with a gradual slope toward them. With their skirmishers well advanced, the main force in two heavy lines of battle moved on our position." Williams never forgot what may have been his best firsthand view of Confederate skirmishers at work.

"The open timber in our front gave us a good view of them as they came on. Their skirmishers sprang from tree to tree until some of them were just across the road from us, and one had dropped behind a rail-cut that I could reach with my gun." The right side of the Ohio line stitched a ragged volley at the approaching infantry. "You had better stop, boys! They may be our men," shouted a captain.

"Captain, take a look at them!" replied Cpl. David Evans.

The captain peered more closely over the fence. "His view was satisfactory," Lieutenant Williams dryly recalled, and prompted the alarmed captain to yell out, "Up boys and give them hell!"

When the order was given, "the whole regiment [opened] the hottest kind of a fire." One eyewitness claimed the "withering" small arms fire forced the first line of Green's advance to "veer off to the right and left" in an attempt to avoid the killing hail of lead rounds.[37]

On the 56th Ohio's left was Col. John Connell's 28th Iowa. The enemy, he later reported, "appeared to be largely re-enforced." Even with the 56th on his right flank, the uneven arrangement of the front allowed some of Green's infantry to shoot down Connell's line. The leaden fire tore into soft flesh, the dull thuds accented by the sickening and sharper sounds of bullets biting into bone. "We were compelled to fall back on account of the murderous flanking fire on our right, to which we were at this time exposed," reported Connell. The "murderous" fire killed and wounded a large number of Iowans as they fell back across the open ground. Company A's Capt. John A. Staley was overrun by Green's Confederates and captured as he headed for the timber.[38]

Iowa Private John Myers had the experience of several lifetimes in his move up and back to the Middle (or what he called the Raymond) Road. The fire Colonel Connell referred to in his report, Myers explained in a letter to his wife, "just naturaly cut us all to peases and scatred our Regiment." Myers was fortunate to escape with his life. "I hat my bick toe shot off and was struck with a spand [spent] grape shot on the rite nea [right knee] and left elbow." Another shot struck him on his left ankle, "witch was a glansing shot." The metal ripped through his trousers and left a high and painful welt across his lower leg. "The other 2 shots," he assured her, "did not penetrate the flesh but lamed me consiterable." Still loading and firing, Myers was shocked to discover that his comrades had abandoned him. Looking around, he noticed that "our men was falling thick and fast." Hobbling to the rear, he fell into a low ditch from which

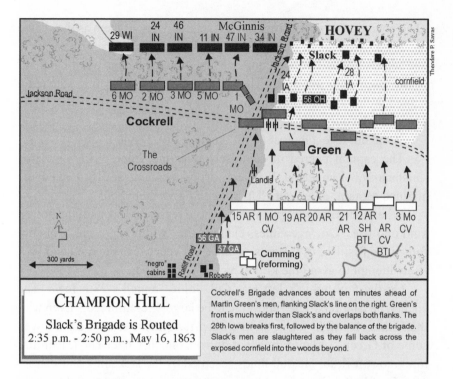

CHAMPION HILL

Slack's Brigade is Routed
2:35 p.m. - 2:50 p.m., May 16, 1863

Cockrell's Brigade advances about ten minutes ahead of Martin Green's men, flanking Slack's line on the right. Green's front is much wider than Slack's and overlaps both flanks. The 28th Iowa breaks first, followed by the balance of the brigade. Slack's men are slaughtered as they fall back across the exposed cornfield into the woods beyond.

several of his friends were loading and firing for all they were worth. The wounded private lifted his musket and fired a few rounds at the approaching enemy when many of the men around him leaped up and ran away. "A few," he remembered, "was hunking [hugging] the ground as clost as posable to avoid beaing hit and the Rebels were coming on the run about 100 yarts off." Lame or not, the determined private "took to heels and run and the balls whisteled around me like hale." Myers could see his regimental line falling back ahead of him when . . .

> Samuel Hamitt [Hammitt] was wounded. He was hit in 2 plases once thro the right breast and once thro the right thi[gh] and he begged for me to cary him off from the field. I piced him up and ran for the nearest plase of shelder and laid him in the shade of a large tree where he was out of danger. I took my canteen and gave him drink and wet his fase and by that time the rebels hat got between me and our regiment, and I took my old gun and left them hav the contants a few times and then ran again not nowing wher I was going to. . . . I felt my way as carfall as posabel thro the thick brush and treas.

The wounded Myers demonstrated remarkable presence of mind, but was utterly lost and "dit not find the regiment til 9 oclock at night."[39]

The Iowans of the 24th regiment, meanwhile, holding the opposite flank (or right side) of Slack's line, had it even worse than their comrades in the 28th Iowa. Heavy lines advanced against them, including Col. Elijah Gates of the 1st Missouri Cavalry, which had been dismounted since before the Battle of Corinth. These tough Missouri fighters were on the left side of Green's Brigade line. Gates was just about to move out to the attack to straighten out Bowen's uneven front when Colonel Cockrell "met me with his saber in hand, and exclaimed he was very glad to see me, for he had been under a desperate fire." Without a target in their front, the Iowans had been firing obliquely into Colonel Riley's 1st Missouri on the far side of the intersection. A brief conference followed, after which Gates "immediately ordered a charge, which my men obeyed as promptly as I ever saw troops in my life."[40]

The dismounted Missouri infantry advanced to within 100 yards of the Iowans when they stopped to pour forth "a most murderous fire upon our lines," reported Slack. The Hawkeyes of the 24th regiment bore the brunt of the fire. The enemy halted, wrote Sergeant Longley, and their fire from the regiment's right flank enfiladed the Hawkeyes. It was the type of "fire that patters in the dust like the big drops of a summer shower and makes the wounded wretches lying there writhe again in impotent agony and terror." The Iowans were deployed just south of Waddell's abandoned guns, which they had recently captured "at the point of the bayonet." Without horses they could not limber them to the rear. The silent bronze sentinels sat just inside the Federal line, the corpses of their former owners collapsed in hideous positions around them. The 24th's Israel Ritter remembered forever how Green's front lapped around their shorter line. "We were soon outflanked on right & left [and] fell back in no great haste." Lieutenant Williams of the 56th Ohio, watching from a short distance to the east, confirmed Ritter's recollection about the length of the line—"The enemy's line overlapped ours, as far as I could see on our left"—but offered a different reason why the Hawkeyes fell back. The 24th Iowa, he observed, "being in open timber, was pushed back after the most desperate hand-to-hand fighting." Slack reported the Iowans of the 24th stood under a withering fire with "unflinching and determined [bravery] . . . for fifteen minutes, but, because of the overwhelming force brought to bear upon them, reluctantly retired from the battery, but kept the rebel re-enforcements at bay by their incessant fire and stubborn resistance."[41]

Regardless of why they retreated, retreat they did. Ritter and an officer tried to carry and drag a wounded man with them, but the speed of the enemy pursuit "compelled [us] to leave him to escape." Another wounded comrade, Thomas E. Langden of Company D cried out for Ritter to help him, but "I left but it was folly to remain. We were badly cut up, lost 8 killed 19 wounded in our Company." For us, recalled Longley, the battle of Champion Hill had ended, "so far as one regiment, as a military organization, is concerned. It is true that many brave souls halt at the very first shadow of an opportunity, and single, in squads, or with other regiments, they still do valiant deeds—do all that man has ever done—lay down their lives," he continued, "but the regiment, as such, is there no more."[42]

The sudden withdrawal of the 24th Iowa, with the earlier retreat of the 28th Iowa, left the 56th Ohio without protection on either flank. "Our right being uncovered, and having no support on our left, our regiment was forced to leave the fence, for which the enemy made a rush," explained Williams. "In a moment we were under the most scorching fire from two or three sides. Under this fire our men fell thick and fast." As the Buckeyes did their best to stem the Southern attack, Williams "witnessed the instant death of two of our gallant young officers, Lt. George W. Manring, of Company A, and Lt. Augustus S. Chute, of Company D." The Ohioans loaded and fired as they fell back, disgusted with their plight, explained Williams, "it being the first time for the Fifty-sixth Ohio to turn their backs to the enemy." The men stopped "at every favorable opportunity . . . [to] give them a few rounds." One opportunity arrived from behind a stump. Both Williams and Pvt. Richard T. Davis were using it for protection. When Williams stood to fire Davis chastised him for needlessly exposing himself. A second later the private fell without a word across the lieutenant's feet, his heart pierced by a minie ball.[43]

*   *   *

The fight from the other side of the field looked about the same: bitter, bloody, and tilting in the favor of the Confederates. Green's Arkansans and Missourians, together with some of Cockrell's men, lapped around and through Slack's regiments, inundating Waddell's silent guns with gray and brown uniforms. Recapturing the pieces provided the men with a tremendous shot of morale and adrenalin. Waddell himself had moved forward with the initial assault and took charge of his recovered battery. "This gallant, fearless officer," remembered Cockrell, "with the assistance of one or two men, opened his battery on the fleeing enemy" like demons possessed, as if in retaliation for their temporary humiliation at losing them in the first place. The shells, fired into the heavily timbered terrain, crashed through the tree tops and sent branches and metal raining down on the withdrawing Federals. "Shells fell bursting in our midst, with the falling branches from the trees, and flying brush that was being mowed down. It seems strange that any of us escaped," remembered a Federal officer who suffered under Waddell's fire.[44]

"The fighting now became desperate," remembered Colonel Dockery of the 19th Arkansas, Green's brigade. A private with the 19th Arkansas identified only as "Purdie" caught Dockery's attention by his "pre-eminently gallant conduct . . . who, during the entire engagement, although frequently recalled by his company commander . . . kept at least 20 or 30 yards in advance of his regiment, using his gun with good effect." After perhaps a quarter-hour of some of the hardest fighting of the day, "the enemy finally gave way," reported the 19th's commander. A. H. Reynolds of the same regiment thought they had been handed a gift: "We had caught the enemy with empty guns, and they gave way easily." Slack's men did give way, but their guns were not empty and they were not easily driven. Aurelius Lyman Voorhis of the 46th Indiana, writing while the battle was still more clearly etched in his mind, put it another way. The earlier attack had disorganized the lines and Green pounced upon them suddenly and heavily. "We got so mixed up," he remembered, "that it was impossible to reform in the face of the enemy."[45]

Lieutenant Williams, meanwhile, left his friend's corpse next to the tree stump and made for the timber bordering the northern edge of the cornfield. "As we neared the fence on our retreat, the fire was terrific. As I turned to fire, my musket being at prime, a bullet from the enemy struck the barrel of my gun, the ball exploding." Four pieces of lead buried themselves in the back of his hand and several larger chunks thudded into the stock of his musket. "My Enfield was in the right place to save me from the fate of my fallen comrades," he wrote with relief many years later. Other comrades experienced similar near-misses as a Missouri battery stationed near the intersection lobbed shells into the timber and blasted canister across the bloody, trampled field. Just after Williams was wounded "one of our boys had the top of his cap shot off his head; another had his canteen and haversack shot off, and another had the side of his pants below the knee cut off, all by pieces of shells bursting among us."[46]

The color guard for the 56th Ohio had not yet made it out of the cornfield when some hard-charging Rebels spotted the flag and decided to make a run for it. "Captain John Yochum [Jochem], with a lot of the boys, came to the rescue," explained Williams, "and the enemy were repulsed." The captain—described by one of his men as "a thorough and polished soldier"—had served in the German army and was a stickler for discipline. The Ohioans were nearing the tree line when Cpl. Thomas S. Jones was shot through the leg and fell to the ground. The corporal pleaded with the passing Williams to help him, and the lieutenant dragged him into the brush. When some of Green's Arkansans spotted the effort they "made a rush for me, but I escaped," forced to leave Jones to his fate. [47]

Another unable to fall back was the 56th's Capt. George Wilhelm. The gallant officer was shouting encouragement to his men when a minie ball struck him in the left breast. Unable to withdraw, he was taken prisoner and hauled several miles from the field. When the not-so-bright soldier tasked with guarding him carelessly "laid down his gun," reported General Slack, the wounded Wilhelm snatched it up, took him prisoner, "marched him into camp, and delivered him [to] the provost-marshal." [48]

The fighting, already severe and deadly, intensified as Slack's men battled the counterattack as best they could in an effort to preserve some semblance of an orderly withdrawal. "How we contested for those little ridges!" remembered Williams. "How we clung to every tree, stump and log." If a man straggled he was killed, wounded, or taken prisoner. Once safely inside the tree line, Lieutenant Colonel Raynor did his best to form a line of battle. Williams marveled at the bravery around him: "It could be seen in the determined face of every comrade the resolve, that if mortal men could hold that line of battle, they were there to do it." It was not to be, or at least, not yet. The non-stop Confederate shells crashing through the trees, coupled with hundreds of minie balls crisscrossing the field, made it impossible for Slack's outnumbered men to hold the line. One of these shells exploded next to Captain Jochem and knocked him to ground, though the shrapnel miraculously missed him entirely. Corporal David Evans was not so fortunate. Evans was the same man who only minutes earlier had convinced his superior the approaching battle lines were the enemy. Two weeks before he had captured the colors of the 23rd Alabama at Port Gibson. At Champion Hill his luck ran out when shards of hot metal from a shell "tore a terrible gash in [his] side." Evans "had been my closest friend for years," remembered Williams sadly. He expired without speaking. The deadly barrage also claimed the lives of William Crabtree and Henry Lewis, both of whom were slain close to Williams. And so, yard by yard, ravine by ravine, and tree by tree, Slack's men fell back under the sledgehammer blows of John Bowen's relentless counterattack, first from the fence along the Middle Road, then across the cornfield, into the trees, and finally north through the woods toward their original line.[49]

Onward Green's Confederates charged across the well-trampled cornfield, into the woods, and across the underbrush-strewn maze of ridges, ravines, and hills toward what was beginning to smell like victory. Now it was their turn to discover just how difficult it was to pursue a beaten enemy over this slice of the Champion family property. "The formation of the country was such that the troops could scarcely advance faster than a walk, and many of the hills were ascended with great difficulty," lamented Dockery. "Notwithstanding, the command pushed impetuously forward, driving back [the enemy] with great confusion."[50]

Carter Stevenson's Division Regroups

Bowen's counterattack was augmented somewhat when Southern troops defeated earlier in the day reorganized and were fed into the attack. After Cockrell and Green crashed forward against Hovey's attenuated front, Pemberton managed to rally Cumming's 56th and 57th Georgia regiments near the Roberts's property. These reinvigorated Southerners went back into the battle near the Ratliff Road and moved north toward the intersection, lending support to the center of Bowen's line. How effective they were and how far they advanced remains in doubt, for we hear nothing more of them.[51]

The left flank of Bowen's attack stretched along the western leg of the Jackson Road and was supported by units from Carter Stevenson's thrashed division. After being swept off the ridge by Logan's attack, Alfred Cumming and Stephen Lee had spent the better part of the next hour trying to organize their men into a cohesive line of battle north of the road. Cumming had thus far been unable to rally his men above the Jackson Road, but "another and more successful effort was made . . . when we reached the road," though by this time Cumming's mass of humanity had drifted many hundreds of yards west in the direction of the Bakers Creek bridge. The new Confederate line in this sector ran roughly parallel to and just north of the Jackson Road about 600 yards below the original position on the wooded ridge overlooking the Champion fields.[52]

"[I] finally assembled a considerable but altogether miscellaneous force without organization," Cumming candidly admitted long after the war to Lee. The milling throng consisted of "the greater part of my Brigade, and I had supposed portions of yours—I had even thought of Barton's also." The Augustan had, by sheer force of will, drawn together perhaps several hundred Georgians from the 34th, 36th, and 39th regiments, though nothing even approximating the "greater part" of his brigade. "While engaged in forming this line we were not pressed by the enemy, who must have been similarly occupied," recalled the grateful brigadier. It was at this time in the battle—Cumming estimated the hour at "between 1 and 2 o'cloc,"—that he saw Stephen Lee for the first time that day. "You appeared in person at some distance on my right. I had no word with you then or later in the day."

And then Bowen's Division came up on the right. The Georgians watched as Cockrell's Brigade "went in on the ground previously occupied by the extreme right of my brigade," said Cumming. Trailing after them later were the reorganized elements of the 56th and 57th Georgia of his own brigade, a fact that must have soothed somewhat the hurt pride Cumming felt that day. With the brigade on his left moving forward—Cumming believed it was Barton's and he was almost certainly correct—he ordered his own regiments to prepare to reenter the fight.[53]

On Cumming's immediate right was Stephen Lee, who enjoyed somewhat better success. The order of his Alabama regiments during this stage of the battle is unknown, though it was probably the same or similar to his earlier alignment. The entire westbound leg of the Jackson Road was "filled with stragglers," observed Lee, many from his own brigade and many more from the completely shattered brigades of Barton and Cumming. Making them once again battle-ready was quite a task. Newly mounted, the brigadier rode into his throng of milling soldiers. His reins were held in his left hand, his right arm and shoulder stiff and unmoving from the pain of his earlier wound. A Mississippi artilleryman who had fallen back from Ridley's battery looked on while Lee attempted what the gunner believed was impossible. "For God's sake rally, men! Rally and drive the enemy back!" When Lee learned Bowen's Division had moved in on his right and was attacking the hill and crossroads, he communicated it to his men and pointed out Cockrell's grand sweeping attack. The Alabamans, remembered the artillerist, formed their lines "as if by magic." It was a "magnificent scene" he remembered in a letter to a former Mississippi artillery captain, "Lee appealing to his men and the Missourians to the rescue."[54]

With "Bowen moving forward and Barton's brigade . . . going on my left," Lee determined to stand tall and drive back the enemy. Whether division leader Carter Stevenson was directly involved in the planning or advance is uncertain. Cumming remembered seeing Lee "take up a color and leading the way to move forward into the woods towards the enemy." This movement, continued Cumming, "was taken up all along the line from right to left, and all together we went in." The move "seemed to me to be somewhat premature owing to the disorganized condition of the line, but your judgment was probably more correct," Cumming later confessed to Lee. His Georgians went up against Mortimer Leggett's stalwarts and were stopped cold after a "sharp and severe" contest, "but [one] of short duration." Thereafter, recalled Cumming, "No strenuous conflict, I would say ensued." Lee's bloodied but still battle-worthy Alabama regiments moved out against Leggett's center and right flank, firing from inside a tree line. Advancing with Lee on the left flank of Col. Charles M. Shelly's 30th Alabama were about 400 stragglers, most of them from Barton's 34th Georgia.[55]

From his position astride the western leg of the Jackson Road on the far right of Grant's line of battle, Brig. Gen. John Stevenson watched as Carter Stevenson's remnants under Lee, Cumming, and Barton launched their counterattack against the left flank of Logan's division. "At this

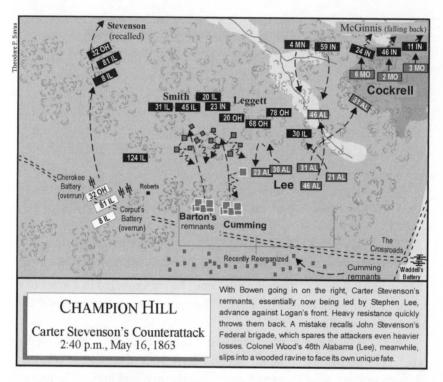

Theodore P. Savas

Stevenson (recalled)

32 OH
81 IL
8 IL

McGinnis (falling back)

4 MN | 59 IN | 24 IN | 46 IN | 11 IN

6 MO | 2 MO | 3 MO

Smith 20 IL **Leggett** **Cockrell**
31 IL | 45 IL | 23 IN
20 OH | 78 OH | 31 AL
68 OH | 46 AL

30 IL

124 IL

Cherokee Battery (overrun) 32 OH   Roberts

81 IL
8 IL   Corput's Battery (overrun)

23 AL | 30 AL | 31 AL | 21 AL
Lee 46 AL

Barton's remnants **Cumming**

Recently Reorganized

The Crossroads

Cumming remnants   Waddell's Battery

CHAMPION HILL

Carter Stevenson's Counterattack
2:40 p.m., May 16, 1863

With Bowen going in on the right, Carter Stevenson's remnants, essentially now being led by Stephen Lee, advance against Logan's front. Heavy resistance quickly throws them back. A mistake recalls John Stevenson's Federal brigade, which spares the attackers even heavier losses. Colonel Wood's 46th Alabama (Lee), meanwhile, slips into a wooded ravine to face its own unique fate.

time I could see large bodies of the enemy moving across my front, out of range, to the support of the attack on our left," reported Stevenson. "I sent twice for a battery to the commanding general," he continued, "but, failing to get it, was powerless to impede their advance."[56]

As Stevenson watched helplessly from a distance, Lee's ragged line jumped fitfully forward out of the timber that had shielded it and up and over a once stout but now broken and scattered rail fence. My men charged ahead, wrote Lee, and "the enemy were broken in some confusion." General Logan remembered the attack somewhat differently. Leggett's brigade maintained itself on Hovey's right flank and held its position there firmly, "although repeated efforts were made by the enemy to break through." His front, continued Logan, "was selected by the enemy for a grand attack. The coolness and unflinching bravery evinced by this brigade . . . cannot be too highly applauded." Stymied against Leggett's right, Lee's left elements, including particularly the 46th Alabama under Col. Michael L. Woods, found a soft spot in the confused Federal defensive alignment "and made a most gallant charge," remembered Lee, driving "almost to his original position in the line of battle." Gallant though the 46th's charge may have been, Lee's Alabamans were in no condition to launch a serious counterattack—as the outcome would eventually prove. Unbeknownst to them, two fresh regiments from Sanborn's brigade were even then moving into a position that would result in the regiment's almost complete destruction.[57]

With little more than a few ad hoc exhausted Rebel regiments pinpricking his line, Logan had little to worry about. The same was not true to the east however, where Cockrell and Green were sweeping everything before them. Indeed, Hovey's division was on the verge of being routed from the field, and Grant's entire line was on the brink of breaking wide open. "The tide of battle," admitted General McPherson, who was watching the disaster unfold from near the Champion homestead, "was turning against us."[58]

* * *

Exactly how and when Grant learned of Bowen's serious counter-thrust is not known for certain—he fails to even directly mention Bowen's massive counterattack in his memoirs—but it might have been a war correspondent who informed him. Sylvanus Cadwallader had trailed Hovey's division during its attack up Champion Hill and then rode hard and fast back down again in the face of the onslaught. Unlike Hovey, however, Cadwallader did not stop and fight. Instead, he continued to the foot of Champion Hill, where he later claimed he found Grant and told him about the threat to his line. Crocker's fresh troops were the only men available to stem the tide of defeat that was obviously coursing through the left flank of the Jackson Road front.[59]

The normally calm Grant, who had by this time moved back near the Champion house, was at first visibly anxious about the deteriorating state of affairs. He paced the yard and asked for information from anyone standing within earshot. When he spotted the recently arrived Colonel Sanborn, he corralled the officer and inquired, "Have we no [more] reserves?" A few minutes later Sanborn heard him mutter, "Where can McClernand be?" Grant was no stranger to sticky situations. At both Fort Donelson and Shiloh, when tactical setbacks brought battlefield defeat within view, he regained his composure and dealt firmly with the situation. Champion Hill fit that mold exactly. A spate of anxious minutes was followed by a calm assessment of the situation and then decisive action. With his ever-present cigar hanging from his mouth, he calmly began hunting up reinforcements and ordering them into action. "When things were going poorly, he acted as if that was exactly how he expected them to go, and sent new men in to make them go better," was how one of Grant's modern biographers summed up the battlefield character of the general.[60]

Crocker's Brigades Join the Battle

Colonel George Boardman Boomer's opportunity to shine in a military capacity arrived on the middle of the afternoon of May 16 in the form of an urgent message delivered by Col. Clark Lagow of Grant's staff. The 30-year old Massachusetts native and son of a Baptist minister had to listen carefully to hear the message above the rolling wave of gunfire just a few hundred yards ahead and beyond the crest of the hill. As a young man, Boomer had benefitted from a classical education at some of the state's finest schools before acute eye strain made further serious study both difficult and painful. Unable to finish his education, the 19-year old made his way to St. Louis to help manage his older brother's bridge-building operation. A refined gentleman, Boomer studied piano in his spare time and learned to speak French so he could move more freely in the upper circles of the city's elite. His entrepreneurial nature and intelligence made him

Colonel
George Boomer

National Archives

popular and earned him powerful friends. When the war broke out, he raised the 26th Missouri Infantry in a state with a sharply divided population and lost many friends as a result. He led the regiment in a series of minor skirmishes inside Missouri before being wounded at the battle of Iuka in September 1862. Thus far in the campaign, his only engagement of note had been in the fight outside Jackson just forty-eight hours earlier, where his brigade lost but one killed and ten wounded. Evaluating him on such a thin record would be unfair. Much of how history would come to judge him, when he is considered at all, is based upon his reaction to Colonel Lagow's anxious message from the commanding general: Hovey's division had broken and Boomer's men were to move "instantly" and save the line.[61]

Hovey, meanwhile, was trying to stem the wholesale retreat of his battered and exhausted division. Even before Boomer completed the initial alignment of his brigade, Hovey knew his "only hope of support was from other commands." When he learned Boomer was up, Hovey dispatched messengers to both Boomer and other officers within Crocker's division pleading for assistance, "but being unknown to the officers of that command," explained Hovey, "considerable delay (not less than half an hour) ensued, and I was compelled to resort to Major General Grant to procure the order for their aid." When proper orders arrived, however, Hovey looked on with pride and hope as the fresh troops "came gallantly up the hill."[62]

The thirty minutes that elapsed from when Hovey sought assistance and Lagow delivered his historic order to Boomer were used by that colonel to finish his deployment and move south in the earlier footsteps made by Slack's brigade along the eastern side of the Jackson Road. "We moved steadily forward in two lines about 700 yards, when orders were received to halt," remembered Col. Holden Putnam of the 93rd Illinois. McPherson wanted Boomer to move by the right flank to connect with Leggett's left. The necessary commands were issued and the mixed brigade of Midwesterners moved by the right across the Jackson Road. The brigade had traveled perhaps half the distance to Leggett's position "when the orders were again countermanded," remembered Putnam, and "Colonel Lagow, of Major-General Grant's staff, brought orders . . . for us to move instantly to the support of General Hovey's division, then being forced back by a superior force of the enemy."[63]

Colonel Holden Putnam
93rd Illinois Infantry

National Archives

Boomer quickly stopped his rightward move toward Leggett and ordered his brigade to change front. About this time an excited General Crocker rode up, perhaps unaware the colonel was endeavoring to plug the gap in the line. "Colonel Boomer," yelled the general, "for god's sake, put this brigade into the fight!" Boomer was doing just that. The French-speaking native of Massachusetts and former bridge-building supervisor rode his horse along the front of the line until he reached Lt. Col. Ezekiel S. Sampson's 5th Iowa, when he reined in the beast and pointed at Adjutant Byers. "I want you to act as Sergeant-Major of the regiment in this battle," he instructed. "Hurry to the left. Order the men to fix bayonets—quick!" Surprised but pleased by the nod of responsibility, Byers saluted and ran down the line screaming at the top of his voice, "Fix bayonets! Fix bayonets!" He had not yet reached the end of the line when he heard other officers shouting, "Forward, quick, double quick, forward!" The stunned adjutant watched as the line lurched forward, "already on the run towards the rebels." When Byers realized the mistake, he continued shouting for the men to fix their bayonets, leaving the Hawkeye infantrymen with no choice but to run uphill into Confederate fire trying to lock their bayonets into place on the end of their muzzles. Clinking loose bayonets notwithstanding, the attack was made "in a most gallant style, ascending a hill, entering a wood, and taking position in front of an enemy of three times his force," observed a proud Marcellus Crocker.[64]

The brigade was moving by the left flank up the uneven and well-traveled slope at the double-quick into the very heart of the combat. In one of his many letters home, Colonel Boomer told his wife that when ordered to move into the hottest spot on the field, "I did it manfully, though [Hovey's] force was completely routed by the time I got on the ground." Colonel Putnam's 93rd Illinois held the vanguard, followed by the 10th Iowa, 26th Missouri, and 5th Iowa. Seeing streams of routed men walking singly and in groups in their direction as they hot-footed it to the crest was disheartening. Stepping over and around the scores of killed and pitifully wounded Federals just below the original Confederate line of battle did not make the task any easier. "There was terrible danger of panic among my men for a moment," admitted Boomer, and for good

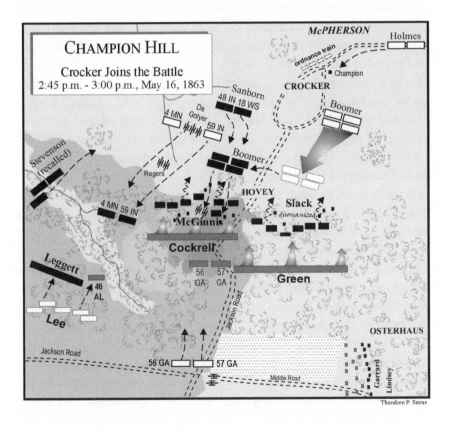

Theodore P. Savas

reason: Cockrell's Missourians and drifting elements of Green's Brigade were fast approaching.

The ragged enemy line of combat veterans with the taste of decisive victory in their mouths was coming over the top of Champion Hill, remembered Private A. H. Reynolds of the 19th Arkansas , when "we met another long line of blues climbing the steep hill. They were within eighty feet of us when we gained the top of the hill, and without orders it seemed as if every man in our ranks fired at once." Out sputtered a deadly volley. "Never before or since have I ever witnessed such a sight," wrote the Arkansan. This "scorching fire," remembered Illinois Colonel Putnam, screamed through the lines and added to the hillside's dead and dying. Private Reynolds agreed, though with some exaggeration of the volley's effectiveness: "The whole [enemy] line seemed to fall and tumble headlong to the bottom of the hill."[65]

Despite the heavy enemy fire and growing crop of corpses, Boomer was going to keep his men in place and plug the gap in the line. "Almost whole companies of wounded, defeated men from the other division [Hovey's] hurried by us," recorded Byers. "They held up their bleeding and mangled hands to show us they had not been cowards." Some of Hovey's men were laughing, which Byers thought exceedingly peculiar given the situation. "Wade in and give them hell!" yelled another bloodied comrade. After allowing McGinnis's thinned and scattered remains to slip past, reported Boomer, "I swung my lines into position under a terrible fire and drove them back," he said matter-of-factly, as if he had performed the maneuver many times over. Putnam recalled being ordered to push forward "until the whole line was on the summit of the ridge," shifting right a short distance, and opening fire, "which was done steadily." His Illinois infantry, together with the Hawkeyes of the 10th Iowa, slid their way down into the hollow that ran behind the original Confederate gun line. The level of combat, already greater than most men would experience at any time during the war, intensified. At times the lines were so close Missourians yelled at members of the 5th Iowa to surrender to save their lives. "They seemed little over a hundred yards away," wrote an Iowan. "There was no charging further by our line. We halted, stood still . . . and killed each other as fast as we could." Two who were killed quickly were Maj. Charles F. Brown, the commander of the 26th Missouri (Union) Infantry, and one of his captains, John Welker of Company B.[66]

Ephraim Anderson, a Confederate Missourian, recalled the bloody passion of the struggle waged that afternoon as Cockrell's Brigade pushed McGinnis's men up and over the crest and into Boomer's arriving infantry:

> The battle here raged fearfully—one unbroken, deafening roar of musketry was all that could be heard. The opposing lines were so much in the woods and so contiguous, that artillery could not be used. The ground was fought over three times, and, as the wave of battle rolled to and fro, the scene became bloody and terrific—the actors self-reliant and determined; 'do or die' seemed to be the feeling of our men, and right manfully and nobly did they stand up to their work.

Anderson was enough of a veteran to know that the firepower he and his comrades were facing was being delivered by fresh troops. The infantry in their front, he explained, delivered those perfect and simultaneous volleys "that can only come from battalions just brought into action." Cockrell also remembered the moment Crocker's men took the field. "Fresh troops of the enemy were rapidly thrown in front of our lines, and were immediately engaged and repulsed. This fearful strife was kept up uninterruptedly for [what seemed like] two and a half hours."[67]

Hovey's division was falling back in nearly useless pieces and Boomer's brigade was being roughly handled. Grant, McPherson, and Crocker desperately sought more fresh troops to throw against the lunging Confederates threatening to break all the way through the center of Grant's line. Colonel Sanborn's brigade, which has sped to the right to support Logan's line, was tapped to prop up Boomer's counterattack. Two of Sanborn's regiments, the 48th Indiana and 18th Wisconsin, were shoved into action on Boomer's right to protect his flank, stem Cockrell's advance, and offer a tenuous connection with Mortimer Leggett's left flank. The effort might have been better served had they been used to reinforce Boomer's left, but no one had a crystal ball to spot the trouble brewing there. We "form[ed] 1st on the right after which we had to double quick to the left, which almost tired us down, as the weather was very warm," remembered Sgt. Samuel E. Snure of the 48th Indiana. Fearful of a Confederate breakthrough but unwilling to remove the desperately-needed artillery belching and jumping behind the lines,

Crocker ordered Sanborn's other pair of regiments to support De Golyer's Michigan battery, which would soon be ordered limbered and drawn to the far right to support John Stevenson's brigade. The 59th Indiana hustled to a position on its left flank, and the 4th Minnesota found a spot on its right.[68]

Like many men in the ranks on both sides, Sam Byers of the 5th Iowa had gone off to war with patriotic ideas about glory. The 23-year-old Iowan had "foolishly wanted to see men killed in battle, and to take a real chance of being killed myself," he admitted candidly after the war. But when real bullets began to pass his head and men around him began to be torn open by the hot bits of metal, his ideas quickly changed. The indiscriminate carnage shocked him. "I might be killed there at any moment, I thought, and I confess to having been nervous and alarmed. Every man in the line near me was looking serious, though determined. We had no reckless fools near us whooping for blood." The dread of death only increased, he recalled, because "my time has probably come now . . . and the suspense, the anxiety, were indeed becoming fearfully intense."[69]

As time passed and the intervening years dimmed memories, soldiers forgot most of the tiny details of their life-changing experience at Champion Hill, but the one thing Byers never forgot was the clamor generated by thousands of men and artillery firing simultaneously. "The noise was simply appalling," was the only way he could describe it. Byers added to the cacophony by lifting his rifled-musket to his shoulder and squeezing the trigger. "The first shot I fired seemed to take all my fear away and gave me courage enough to calmly load my musket and fire it forty times." Others, he noted, fired more than their allotted forty rounds by taking ammunition from the boxes of the dead and wounded. Men began to fall at an alarming rate. Byers, who had "foolishly wanted to see men killed in battle," got his wish fulfilled—over and over again. He watched in horror as Samuel B. Lindsey, a 22-year old captain in Company G, threw his arms in the air "and fell dead in his tracks," the victim of a Missouri minie ball. Corporal William McCulley was loading and firing as fast as he could when a shell fragment clipped him in the face. "The blood covered him all over," remembered Byers, "but he kept on firing." Jerome Darling was a second lieutenant in Company K when death found him in on the northern slope of Champion Hill. Although he believed Darling was killed outright, the 23-year old who had grown up with Byers in tiny Newton, Iowa, lingered with his painful wound before expiring the next day.

These men, explained Byers, were those he actually saw hit or killed, for "I could not see far to the left or right; the smoke of battle was covering everything." By this time even the enemy was invisible and the men simply loaded and fired in their general direction "by guess," though occasionally "the blaze of their guns showed exactly where they stood." "I saw bodies of our men lying near me without knowing who they were, though some of them were my messmates in the morning." Smothered in noise, screams, blood, and smoke, Byers was in torment. The only question in his mind was whether there was any escape from it.[70]

At one time it looked as though Byers would never leave the field. Like so many men, the adjutant worried he would not perform well in action and tried to remain "cool" and fire at specific targets. The fighting had been raging furiously for some time when he spotted a mounted Southern officer. He carefully leveled his rifle and pulled the trigger. A miss. He loaded, leveled, and the stock bucked into his shoulder a second time. Another miss. Eighteen more attempts were expended against the unnamed and now unknowable fortunate rider, who finally turned his mount and left the area. Frustrated, Byers was loading his rifle when a bullet slammed into his chest, knocking his breath out and almost knocking him down. "I am dead, now," he said to himself. He remembered the hit felt as though someone had struck him with a heavy club. The Hawkeye stepped back a few paces "and sat down on a log to finish up with the world. Other wounded men were there covered with blood, and some were lying by me dead. I spoke to no one. It would have been useless; thunder could scarcely have been heard at that moment." All Byers could think was that "It is honorable to die so." Thoughts of friends, family, home or religion did not enter his mind. When he did not die, however, he searched his body and happily discovered "the obliquely fired bullet had struck the heavy leather of my cartridge belt, and glanced away. He grabbed his musket and stepped back into the line of battle and almost immediately a second bullet passed through his hand. Though it bled profusely "the wound did not hurt; I was too excited for that," Byers confessed. He turned his excitement back to the enemy, loading and firing blindly into the mass of smoke-shrouded Confederates.[71]

Boomer's brigade seemed to be holding its own. One at a time each Midwesterner bit off the end of his paper cartridge, poured the powder and ball down his hot barrel, tamped away with his ramrod, seated a percussion cap in place, raised his weapon, and pulled the trigger. Their mouths were filled with bits of gunpowder that made their tongues swell and turn black. Most canteens were either empty or lost. The thirst, remembered one of them, "was intolerable." Byers glanced around him, unable for a time to take his eyes off the features of his comrades. "Every soldier's face was black as a negro's and, with some, blood from wounds trickled down over the blackness, giving them a horrible look."[72]

Perhaps the most emotionally exhausted Federal officer on the front lines on the middle of that hot May afternoon was George McGinnis. The adrenaline rush of victory that had coursed through his body just an hour earlier had been immediately replaced with the sudden shock of pending catastrophic defeat when Bowen struck. McGinnis had almost given up any hope of victory when Crocker's brigades finally marched forward up the slope of Champion Hill. "As we neared the ground upon which the batteries had been captured, and from which the enemy had been driven in the morning, just as it appeared to everyone that the guns [on Champion Hill] would again fall into the hands of the rebels, we were greeted by the shouts of the long promised re-enforcements," McGinnis remembered. Cockrell's Missourians were "momentarily checked," he continued, "but they came down upon us in such immense numbers that in a short time, re-enforcements and all, were compelled to give ground." It was a candid and accurate assessment, and confirmed in the official report of the man who was forcing the bluecoats back. Corporal Theodore D. Fisher of the 2nd Missouri Infantry remembered much the same when he wrote in his diary, "We succeeded in driving them back some distance." His subsequent scrawl was less sanguine: "My friend and townsman, James M. Thomas, is among the killed."[73]

Though George Boomer did not admit it as unequivocally as McGinnis, his men did indeed take back and then give up again large swaths of precious Mississippi real estate. Scores of his men had been shot down, his line was beginning to sag as the wounded, tired, and frightened began leaking to the rear. The enemy was showing no signs of letting up. Evidence of the intense nature of Boomer's action was found in the regimental flag of Holden Putnam's 93rd Illinois, which had been pierced by more than two dozen rounds, its staff splintered four or five times by lead balls. Boomer's situation took a turn for the worse when bullets began enfilading his regiments from the east. The brigade commander, at least after the action was over and he could think about his experience, saw his predicament clearly: "They reinforced again and came up, at the same time endeavoring to flank me on the left. I swung my left back again, and held them until I received two regiments from Holmes's brigade," he carefully explained in a letter to his wife. Hovey remembered the Rebel surge as well when he wrote, "The enemy had massed his forces and slowly pressed our whole line with re-enforcements backward to a point near the brow of the hill." McGinnis and Boomer had been pushed back farther north than even that and were well down the hill by this time. In fact, part of Boomer's brigade was in danger of being routed from the field.[74]

Sam Byers left the best description of what the turning of Boomer's left flank looked like from the firing line. The battle was raging not far below the crest when a young teenager from the left part of the line ran up to Byers and cried out, "My regiment is gone! What shall I do?" Byers shoved him to a hole in the line. "Blaze away right here!" And then the chilling words every soldier fears echoed up and down the front: "My God, they're flanking us!" The regiment on the left had given way and Rebels were pouring through the gap in the line, yelling out for Byers and his Iowa comrades to surrender. "In a moment we would be surrounded," remembered the adjutant. "I ran like a racehorse—so did the left of the regiment amidst a storm of bullets and yells and curses." Though most of the men managed somehow to hold onto their muskets, their collapse was sudden and serious. The race downhill for the rear "with bullets and cannon balls plowing the field behind me will never be forgotten," wrote Byers many years later. "My lungs seemed to be burning up."

As the Iowans fell back, one of them spotted the regiment's flag lying by a log, its former color-bearer dead or wounded. "It is a shame the Fifth Iowa is running!" yelled out one of the men to the equally fleet of foot Cpl. Duncan Teter. In a gallant disregard for his own safety, the corporal grabbed the banner and "with a great oath dared me to stop and defend it." Few others heeded their cries. One participant later wrote, "We might as well have yelled to a Kansas cyclone." When Capt. John Tait reached the spot, he recognized Teter's bravey for what it was and "promoted him on the spot," wrote a bemused Sam Byers. Promotion or no, "the oncoming storm was irresistible and, carrying the flag, we all again hurried rearwards." When Byers and his exhausted comrades reached a point well down the hill, a line of Federal artillery, "loaded to the muzzle with grape shot and canister, opened on the howling mob that was pursuing us." It was then Byers realized they had fallen all the way back near where Grant had sat his horse to watch their advance.[76]

Despite the rout of one of Boomer's regiments, much of the battle was being waged well up the hill's northern slope. Boomer's center and right were still holding, Sanborn was pushing forward two of his regiments farther west, and Holmes was approaching the field. Grant, however, remained on edge. Were Crocker's two engaged brigades enough to save the day? Would Holmes make it to the firing line in time? His two regiments were all Grant had left to call upon.

That the commanding general fully appreciated the seriousness of the Southern attack was amply demonstrated when he sent an order to McPherson to recall John Stevenson's brigade from the army's distant right flank. Stevenson had by this time cut the Jackson Road escape route over Bakers Creek, a fact Grant did not comprehend until after the battle ended. "I received an order . . . to send to the support of the left one of my regiments," reported Stevenson, who sent the 32nd Ohio double-quicking back toward the point of danger under the guidance of one of McPherson's aides. Another order arrived a few minutes later calling back the balance of Stevenson's brigade. The general moved his regiments north across the western leg of the Jackson Road and into the woods through which they had successfully attacked. Stevenson "halted in rear of our batteries," where he availed himself of the opportunity of refilling his cartridge boxes. He was joined there by his 7th Missouri regiment, which had been performing guard duty with the trains. Stevenson's temporary withdrawal reopened the road to the enemy. Luckily for the Federals, the Confederate troops in that sector were so used up they were unable to exploit what might have otherwise been a grievous misstep by the Federal army commander.[77]

Crocker, who was paying close attention to his troops, recognized quickly Boomer would not be able to maintain his position without additional reinforcements. "Colonel Boomer," reported the division leader, "by the most desperate fighting, and with wonderful courage and obstinacy, held his position in spite of the continued and furious assaults of the enraged and baffled enemy. But it was apparent that he sorely needed assistance, and, unless speedily assisted, his position was in danger." It was at this time, "this critical moment," continued Crocker, "when Colonel Holmes arrived in the field with two regiments of the Second Brigade."[78]

The men reached the Champion property just in the nick of time. The 10th Missouri made it without their haversacks and knapsacks, which were dropped along the road from the Boll plantation; the 17th Iowa kept theirs on for the entire march. Holmes's Iowans and Missourians were exhausted, their 13-mile hike under a canopy of roaring battle having taken a toll both mental and physical. Holmes's first view of the battlefield harkened back to what other men similarly situated had already seen. "The enemy occupied a strong position upon a steep, wooded hill, over which the road ran, flanked by deep ravines," Holmes wrote. It was as if Alfred Cumming's original line of Georgians was still waiting on top of Champion Hill, and Holmes was playing the part of McGinnis or Slack. But Cumming's Brigade had already been chewed to pieces by Hovey's division, which had in turn had been ground into disorganized fragments by Bowen, and most of the Federals within eyesight were falling back.[79]

Informed of the unfolding situation in his front by both his own eyes and Marcellus Crocker, Holmes ordered his regiments to prepare for action. Bullets fired a half-mile distant were buzzing past Col. David B. Hillis's vanguard 17th Iowa as it marched quickly up the Jackson Road past the Champion house and its out buildings. Behind the Iowans were Lt. Col. Leonidas Horney and his 10th Missouri infantrymen. "We arrived in the vicinity of the hills on which the

Colonel
Samuel A. Holmes

National Archives

battle was being fought about 2 p.m., and without having time to rest my men (who had that day marched 12 miles through dust and a burning sun with knapsacks on their backs) was ordered forward at a double-quick," reported Colonel Hillis. His regiment had been thinned in the fighting at Jackson two days earlier. One company had been left behind there. Only 228 men were available for battle on May 16.[80]

Hillis double-quicked them about half way up the sloping ground and filed left off the road and into line of battle, his right "resting on the left of the Vicksburg [Jackson] road." By this time most of Boomer's regiments had been pushed halfway down the slope. In front of the arriving Iowans was Colonel Putnam's fighting 93rd Illinois, which had been steadily withdrawing under heavy and relentless pressure northeast toward and then across the Jackson Road, at which time Hillis's Iowans of the 17th arrived and formed behind them. "In doing this," recalled Hillis, "my men suffered from the fire intended for the Ninety-third."[81]

Hillis was forming the 17th when Holmes's 10th Missouri regiment under Colonel Horney filed east off the Jackson Road and formed a line of battle on the left of the 17th Iowa. Like the Iowa regiment, Horney's outfit was under strength and went into the action with perhaps 325 men. Two days earlier, the same regiment fielded 430 bayonets at the Jackson fight. The battle for one of the 325 soldiers in the 10th Missouri ended before it began. "As we were deployed in line preparatory to advancing," wrote Capt. Joel W. Strong of Company I long after the war, "a bullet struck me on the point of the shoulder, paralyzing my arm." The direct shot "felt and sounded like a club," he recalled. Standing near him was Sgt. George W. Hewitt.

"George," groaned Strong through the terrible pain. "Raise my arm and work it around."

Hewitt did as he was asked, moving the limb gently back and forth and around in circles. "When I could feel no bones grate or find no evidence of serious injury," remembered a relieved Strong, he blurted out "That was lucky!" and stooped over to pick up his sword, which had dropped to the ground. "Suddenly, everything seemed to get dark, and the next thing I remember I was with the wounded being brought to the rear! It seems I had fainted." The captain was "all right a while later, but had to carry that arm in a sling for quite a while. It got black and blue down to the elbow and down my shoulder blade onto my back! It was several years before I could throw a stone or snowball."[82]

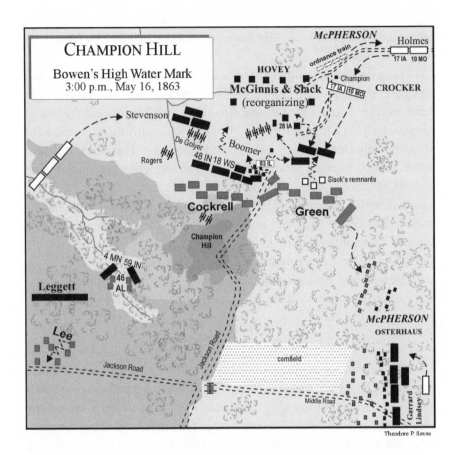

CHAMPION HILL

Bowen's High Water Mark
3:00 p.m., May 16, 1863

Theodore P. Savas

The men were forming when Holmes was removed from command. As he was leading his men into position, he took a swig of liquor from a small flask. A passing staff officer spotted the bottle and reported to General McPherson that Holmes was fighting under the influence. The corps leader immediately relieved Holmes. Fortunately for the colonel, John Sanborn arrived at just that moment with orders from Grant for Holmes to move forward. A distraught Holmes told Sanborn of the incident, pleading, "but what do you think, Sanborn! After all the service I have done on this campaign with my brigade, an order has been made by Gen. McPherson removing me from its command and appointing to command it one of those d—d Washington brigadiers." An empathetic Sanborn wheeled his mount and rode to report the situation to Grant, who wisely rescinded the order. "Say to Col. Holmes that that order is revoked," Grant shot back. "He can retain the command of his brigade as long as he desires."[83]

The order was rescinded just in time, for as soon as Hillis had his line formed Colonel Putnam pulled his bloodied regiment out by the right flank and ran it across the Jackson Road and withdrew toward the rear to reorganize. This left the 17th Iowa "fronting the enemy direct, some 40 or 50 yards only intervening," noted its commander. "This position I held under a well-directed fire, which my gallant fellows returned with interest, for about fifteen minutes, when I ordered an advance, which was executed with a heroism that I am proud of." The 28th Iowa from Slack's brigade had fallen back and was reforming in the vicinity of the 17th Iowa. "Our regiment fell in, in good order . . . and rallied around the old flag at the first call," remembered Lt. Joseph G. Strong.

The back and forth seesaw battle of May 16 would, eventually, tip in favor of the Federals with the arrival of Holmes's 553 bayonets.[84]

*   *   *

John Bowen's stunning removal of first McGinnis's brigade and then Boomer and Sanborn from the Champion Hill heights and lower grounds to the east was not cheaply obtained. Hundreds of men paved the Mississippi ground. One Missouri captain fell at the head of his company when his body was pierced with a minie ball. According to comrade, the mortally wounded officer's last words were, "I guess I'll take supper with Stonewall Jackson tonight." Not every wounded and dying soldier had the time to contemplate his fate. Private William Nichols was torn to pieces by a Federal artillery shell fired by the 16th Ohio Battery from atop the Champion heights. His body was so badly mangled even his close friends could not identity him until they found pictures of his family on his corpse. A more noteworthy casualty occurred on the upper slope of the hill. After hustling his five companies of skirmishers back to their respective regiments, Lieutenant Colonel Hubbell moved forward with the rest of the Missourians and took a bullet in the arm. He would live long enough to learn the outcome of the battle before dying six days later of complications at Coffeeville, Mississippi.[85]

The high Southern casualty rate, coupled with the timely feeding of Holmes's regiments into the mix, helped Boomer not only hold his last position, but prevent the complete tactical turning of his left flank. Martin

Green's men had shattered Slack's brigade, crossed the trampled and bloody cornfield, and penetrated deeply into the woods beyond. They continued grinding forward, driving Slack's disorganized bits and pieces all the way back to their jump-off line, flanking Boomer's left in the process. The momentum of Bowen's thousands of advancing infantry had nearly broken Grant's center wide open. The Rebel line was now fighting within sight of the Champion place and its outbuildings. With Slack's troops no longer waging organized defensive warfare, Green's Arkansas and Missouri infantry were in a perfect position after their deep lodgment to engulf Boomer's vulnerable flank. If Green could swing around to the west, he might roll Boomer and company off the northern slope of the hill. If Cockrell participated in the movement, Grant's entire left wing might be rolled up and destroyed in the bottomland along Bakers Creek. Boomer knew it as well.[86]

Fresh Federals troops, well-handled artillery, and a noteworthy Confederate mistake finally stopped Bowen's forward progress. Colonel Elijah Gates of the 1st Missouri Cavalry (dismounted), part of Green's Brigade, remembered that within about one hour of fighting his men had driven "the enemy about one-half or three-quarters of a mile [from the crossroads] through a corn-field and across some deep ravines before they brought us to a stand . . . [with a] desperate fire." The warriors were separated by a very short distance. "They occupied one ridge and I another," explained Gates, with a deep, narrow ravine between us." Three times the Missouri regiment left its ridge to dislodge and rout Holmes's Iowans and Missourians, and

Colonel Elijah Gates

1st Missouri Cavalry
(dismounted)

Confederates Veteran

three times they were driven back, "unable to ascend the hill on which the enemy was formed." Gates's Missourians could drive no farther. "My loss here was upward of 100 men," he wrote. Gates was encouraging his men to press on during one of the many attempts to dislodge the enemy when several balls smacked into his horse. The beast, he recalled, "lay[ed] down and died like a soldier."[87]

Northern artillery also played a significant role in beating back Bowen's counterattack and preventing his flanking movement, and its effectiveness was largely due to Alvin Hovey's cool head under fire. "The irregularity of our line of battle had previously prevented me from using artillery in enfilading the enemy's line," reported the division leader, "but as our forces were compelled to fall slowly back, the lines became marked and distinct, and about 2:30 p.m. I could easily perceive by the sound of fire-arms through the woods, the position of the respective armies." Hovey promptly went to work, accumulating sixteen artillery pieces west of the Jackson Road—six each from Company A, 1st Missouri Light Artillery and the 6th Wisconsin Battery, and four tubes from the 16th Ohio Battery. As bits and pieces of the Southern line emerged from the woods or popped out of ravines and hollows on either side of the road to charge the guns, the artillery opened on them with everything they had in their ammunition chests, blowing the attackers back again into the timber.

These mini-assaults were especially hard on Green's lieutenant colonels. William H. Dismukes, 19th Arkansas, was leading his men forward when a shell fragment ripped into his body. He was helped off the field and eventually made it to Vicksburg, where he lingered for eight terrible days before dying. H. G. Robertson, another lieutenant colonel from the 20th Arkansas, was killed instantly trying to capture Hovey's roaring artillery. "Through the rebel ranks these batteries hurled an incessant shower of shot and shell, entirely enfilading the rebel columns," Hovey later wrote with satisfaction. General McGinnis witnessed the same thing on the other side of the Jackson Road when crowds of Cockrell's men occasionally oozed forward out of the trees and ravines and into the cleared Champion fields. "Our artillery stationed on the right opened an enfilading fire upon the rebel masses," he reported, almost certainly referring to De Goyler's well-served Michigan guns. The fire "effectively checked their progress."[88]

A Costly Southern Mistake

It is difficult to embellish what Bowen and his 4,500 men accomplished in such a short time. Within perhaps ninety minutes of hard fighting, their unstoppable surge had swept across the Jackson and Middle roads, seized the vital crossroads, and recaptured Waddell's lost battery. They had moved steadily, yard by yard, up the southern slope of Champion Hill and then over its crest—all in the face of an enemy determined to stop their attack. Near the top, remembered Cockrell, "A battery of the enemy attempted to check the impetuous advance" without success. The 5th Missouri charged and overran the ground where a short time earlier the Ohio artillery had been firing. The balance of the line drove the remnants of McGinnis's regiments back into Crocker's reinforcements under George Boomer. At least two (and perhaps all four) of the guns lost earlier that morning (two each from the Botetourt Virginia Artillery and Waddell's Battery) were recaptured. None could be moved, however, "on account of the horses being killed." The Confederate attack did not stop at the gun line, but continued washing more than halfway down the hill's northern side, pushing ahead of it McGinnis's shattered remnants and, after a sharp stand up fight of about thirty minutes duration, Boomer's and Sanborn's as well. Exhaustion slowed them down, and well-handled Federal artillery stood in their way, but a single Southern command decision may well have decided the outcome of Bowen's magnificent counterattack.

Almost all of the participants who left a record of the relentless afternoon combat at Champion Hill described its "uninterrupted" nature. The continual fighting expended ammunition by the wagonload, and the logistics necessary to support such a powerful and prolonged counterattack as that launched by John Bowen began to loom large over the field. Many had worked hard to make sure enough ammunition was on hand to support the effort—and someone else unwittingly impeded the attempt.

Bowen's infantry went into battle with cartridge boxes carrying 40 rounds of ammunition, which was exhausted within an hour. The Rebels were not about to fall back on the cusp of victory, so they scrounged up whatever they could, rummaging through the boxes of their fallen comrades for anything they could fire. Cockrell recalled how his Missouri infantry "even stripped the slain and wounded of the enemy, with whom the ground was thickly strewn, of all their cartridges." Many men fired something closer to 75 or as many as 90 rounds. Rifle-muskets, notes one historian, "kicked like mules," which left the arms and shoulders of many of the survivors black and blue—and very stiff and sore.[89]

When he realized during the early stages of the attack that the battle would be a long one, Cockrell sent two of his staff officers in search of the division's ammunition train. They were unable to locate it. One of his regimental commanders did the same, with similar results. Where were the wagons? When Colonel Dockery of the 19th Arkansas notified General Green that his ammunition was about exhausted, Green informed the horrified colonel that "the ordnance train had been ordered from the field, and it would be impossible to refill the cartridge boxes." The enemy, Green instructed, "must be driven as long as it is possible to advance the lines, if it had to be done with empty guns." Dockery's men, like all their comrades, would strip the dead and wounded. Elijah Gates had a similar experience with his dismounted Missourians. While his men were fighting back and forth in the battle for the ridges east of the Jackson Road, his adjutant bent his ear several times asking, "what we were to do for ammunition?" The disgusted Gates already knew someone at a high level had made a serious blunder. "I told him," relayed Gates, "to take the ammunition from the dead and wounded that lay on the field."[90]

The mystery of what had happened to Bowen's ordnance wagons was solved when the 1st Missouri's Col. Amos C. Riley filed his official report. According to Riley, his ordnance sergeant was on the way to the 1st Missouri, "but was ordered across Baker's Creek by General [Carter] Stevenson." Not a word about the ammunition train or his decision to order it off the field at the height of the battle found its way into Stevenson's report, but the fact that it cropped up in several places without rebuttal lends credence to the charge. Stevenson never explained his decision to order the precious ammunition that belonged to a different division off the field. Nor did he rebut it. We will likely never know why he made what appears, even without hindsight, to have been a mistake of breathtaking proportion.[91]

*   *   *

Francis Cockrell knew he had spent his bolt. Now well down Champion Hill, his Missourians were under pressure from enfilading Union artillery and heavy fire from the front, and were confronted by large numbers of fresh enemy troops. On his left, infantry from Carter Stevenson's Division (Cumming and Lee) had not kept pace with his advance and had been thrown back rather quickly. A threat from that quarter was now beginning to develop. Cockrell was also out of ammunition. Much to his dismay, his men were within sight of a Federal ordnance train parked north of the Champion house. The wagons, remembered Ephraim Anderson, fearful of being captured, "were being turned and driven back under whip." Alas, the prize was beyond their grasp. Unable to advance, Cockrell determined to hold on as long as he could. Perhaps reinforcements would arrived to take advantage of his success. He had yet to learn of a far greater Federal threat approaching from the east.[92]

Martin Green's regiments, meanwhile, were settling into position on Cockrell's right. Green's uneven line ran off the hill and down into the rippled and wooded terrain in the deep northern portion of the nearly 90-degree angle formed by the intersection of the Jackson and Middle roads. As Elijah Gates and his bloodied 1st Missourians discovered, they could not move forward another yard, but they were not about to voluntarily withdraw, either. With his lines holding firm, Bowen sought reinforcements to finish the job he had begun. Runners continued to scour the dead and the wounded for ammunition, and those in the front kept up a desultory fire on Holmes's two regiments and the rest of the enemy reorganizing beyond. For a few minutes the battle waned, as if two great wounded animals had stopped for a well deserved breather.[93]

The killing was not yet at an end, but the Southern tide had reached its highwater mark.

Chapter 10

Procrastination

"General Pemberton desires you to come immediately and with all dispatch to the left, to the support of General Stevenson, whatever may be in your front."

— Maj. Jacob Thompson

THE PERFORMANCE OF JOHN A. MCCLERNAND ON THE MIDDLE Road is one of the nagging issues haunting the battle of Champion Hill.

Two full battle divisions under Peter Osterhaus and Eugene Carr were with McClernand that day as he moved steadily forward during the morning's early hours. Contact was made with Confederate skirmishers about one mile from the crossroads. A rumbling meeting engagement broke out to the south between the divisions of A. J. Smith and William Loring on the Raymond Road. Alvin Hovey, whose division was part of McClernand's XIII Corps, sent word that reached McClernand about 9:30 a.m. of his discovery of the enemy posted on Champion Hill. What should he do, he inquired? McClernand pondered the question, discovered Grant was riding for Champion Hill, and deferred the matter to him in a dispatch of 9:45 a.m. "Shall I hold or bring on an engagement?" he asked. The corps leader had not been getting along with Grant and knew his movements and responses were being strictly scrutinized. He had been cautioned by Grant to move slowly, and so he would. McClernand sent similar word to A. J. Smith, whose division was feeling out Loring's defensive position on Coker house ridge. They would wait for further orders. The normally aggressive McClernand pulled in his horns.[1]

More than two hours would pass before Grant received McClernand's message. During that time Grant arrived at the Champion house and ordered Hovey and Logan to deploy and attack. They did, crushing Carter Stevenson's Division, severing the Jackson Road, overrunning the crossroads, and threatening to collapse the entire left wing of Pemberton's army. McClernand, meanwhile, deployed Osterhaus and cautioned him to await further orders. Although McClernand and his generals believed "the main forces of the enemy were concentrated against [Hovey's] and my [Osterhaus's] positions," it was not so. In fact, the enemy facing McClernand consisted of a handful of skirmish companies left behind after Alfred Cumming's brief sojourn defending the intersection. The main line of defense behind the picket line consisted of only the 56th and 57th Georgia regiments and Waddell's four guns. "The artillery played heavily on us," reported Osterhaus, "but without any injury to the troops, the very broken ground and thick timber exposing them only to very short range of infantry."[2]

By the time noon came and went, however, the Georgia regiments had been crushed and the artillery captured by James Slack's late-morning attack—all within one-half and three-quarters of a mile from McClernand's line. Once they were swept away, the heavy line of skirmishers holding up the two divisions on the Middle Road was the only thing standing between McClernand and an artery leading into the deep rear of Pemberton's entire army. It is ironic that the same rough terrain that rendered the Southern long-arm ineffective shielded this paucity of numbers from probing Federal eyes. A golden opportunity to destroy Pemberton beckoned. Why did McClernand not move aggressively forward?

When he learned less than three (very congested) miles separated McClernand from Champion Hill, Grant at 12:35 p.m. sent him an order. As McClernand put it in his official report, Grant told me to "throw forward skirmishers as soon as my forces were in hand; to feel and attack the enemy in force, if opportunity occurred." Almost certainly Grant believed the order would reach McClernand quickly. It did not. In fact, it was about 2:00 p.m. before the Illinois political general set eyes on the dispatch. By this time John Bowen was moving north to position his two Confederates brigades for their counterattack. "Instantly upon receipt of Major-General Grant's order to attack, I hastened to do so, ordering Generals Smith and Osterhaus to 'attack the enemy vigorously and press for victory,' General Blair to support the former and General Carr the latter, holding Lawler's brigade in reserve," wrote McClernand.[3]

Osterhaus's division had been uncoiled in line of battle for hours, skirmishing heavily with the enemy deployed perhaps 600 or 800 yards east of the crossroads. Positioned astride the Middle Road was Brig. Gen. Theophilus T. Garrard's brigade. On Garrard's left, two regiments of Col. Daniel W. Lindsey's brigade stretched Osterhaus's line southward into the more open rolling country falling away toward the Raymond Road. Lindsey's short line, however, was not long enough to connect with the right flank of Col. Giles Smith's brigade of Frank Blair's division, which was operating on the Raymond Road. Brigadier General Michael Lawler's brigade from Eugene Carr's division was ordered up from the rear of the column and given "instructions . . . to open communication with General Smith, keep it open during the engagement, and to anticipate any movement the enemy might make with a view to turn our left," remembered Lawler. His line was also too short, forcing him to fill the gap with a line of skirmishers.

Skirmishing in front near the road and on McClernand's left "was quite brisk," remembered the corps leader. Every Federal backed up or deployed in the Middle Road sector could hear Hovey's engagement loud and clear. They could see some of it, too. Osterhaus had advanced far enough to discover the Middle Road intersected with "the road on which General Hovey was advancing . . . and here the enemy made a most desperate attempt to prevent the junction of the divisions. We could see his columns advancing in great numbers, and I considered it prudent to straighten [and reinforce] my line." It was about 2:30 p.m. Osterhaus was preparing his lines for battle and watching Green's Brigade of John Bowen's Division slamming into the crossroads area and sweeping Slack's exhausted brigade from the field. McClernand's men were aligned perpendicular to Bowen's right flank. But not a soldier stepped forcefully forward to crush the attack. According to McClernand, the extension of Lindsey and Smith's brigades, together with other measures, were taken "in part . . . in compliance with Major-General Grant's order, based on information, of which he had advised me, that the enemy was in greatest strength in front of my center and left, and might turn my left flank and gain my rear." Earlier operations seems to confirm this in McClernand's mind, for he believed Loring's Confederates had been moving to flank him but had been thwarted by the appearance of A. J. Smith's division on the Raymond Road. Osterhaus spotted Loring's brigades—"large numbers of them (infantry and artillery) massed on a commanding ridge." Large numbers of the enemy were moving against Hovey, the strength of the enemy behind his aggressive line of skirmishers was unknown, and a strong force was posted with artillery off his left flank across generally open terrain. McClernand would move forward, but he would do so, at least initially, with caution.[4]

McClernand's handling of his divisions on the Middle Road, while in general accordance with Grant's orders, was not understood by the men in the ranks. A soldier of Brig. Gen. William P. Benton's brigade, Carr's division, could scarcely determine the reason for delay. "For four hours we stood there listening, waiting and wondering why we were not put into the fight," seethed the 33rd Illinois's Pvt. Edward H. Ingraham. As a sergeant in the 69th Indiana, Garrard's brigade, Osterhaus's division, Samuel P. Harrington was closer to the action than Ingraham. "[We were] so anxious and ready but was not ordered up," he scribbled in his diary.[5]

*   *   *

One-armed William Wing Loring, the Confederate version of John McClernand but with more vitriol in his veins, seemed intent on making trouble for his superior. Like McClernand and Grant on the other side of the field, the relationship between Loring and Pemberton was deeply strained. Loring neither liked nor respected his army commander, and the frequent run-ins between the headstrong Mexican War veteran and the indecisive (and in Loring's eyes, less able) bureaucrat had bruised the egos of both men. The feud that had been festering since Loring's repulse of the Federals at Fort Pemberton during Grant's Yazoo Pass Expedition two months earlier erupted into open loathing in mid-May. In camp, personal feuds can be handled without endangering lives; in the field in the face of an aggressive foe, mutual distrust and even hatred has a way of developing into disrespect, followed by a lack of cooperation. Such was the case on this day.[6]

Major General
William Wing Loring

Museum of the Confederacy

Earlier in the day, Carter Stevenson's many pleas for assistance had procured help in the form of John Bowen's Division. His two brigades would not be enough. The enemy, General Pemberton later wrote, "continued to move troops from his left to his right, increasing his vastly superior forces against Stevenson's and Bowen's divisions." Pemberton's observation is simply wrong. Logan and Hovey (and eventually Crocker, when he arrived) did not "vastly" outnumber Stevenson and Bowen, and Grant was not shifting troops from the Raymond or Middle Roads to reinforce McPherson on the Jackson Road. The situation on the Confederate left, however, was indeed critical to the army's survival. Orders to Loring had thus far produced excuses as to why he could not move north. It was time for decisive leadership. Convinced (incorrectly) that Grant had stripped his left to feed his right, and that "there was no important force" confronting Loring, Pemberton sent several couriers, one after the other, with direct orders to march his two nearest brigades (Abraham Buford and Winfield Featherston) to the left, leaving behind Lloyd Tilghman's Brigade to defend the Raymond Road and protect the bridge (then under construction) and ford in his rear. Pemberton reported the time as about 2:00 p.m. Bowen was preparing to attack and drive Hovey from the crossroads. Pemberton was finally attempting to decisively deal with the threat against his left.[7]

Loring refused to budge. A reply to the first courier told Pemberton a large force was confronting Loring, and that a column was endeavoring to flank him. Loring later claimed Bowen believed the same thing (that the Federals were attempting to move around the army's southern flank), and that he faced a deployed enemy corps with a strong skirmish line that could go over to the offensive at a moment's notice. Loring was right. He did face a strong enemy in the divisions of A. J. Smith and Frank Blair, but orders to move were orders to move. Pemberton knew what was happening on the left flank—and Loring did not (his report described the heavy combat around Champion Hill as "desultory firing.") Other than an occasional artillery discharge and scattered skirmish fire, Loring's front was quiet. Pemberton angrily fired off another message. The army's assistant inspector general and former U. S. Secretary of the Interior under James Buchanan, Maj. Jacob Thompson, carried the order "at the full speed of my horse."

Thompson reined in his mount before Loring, saluted, and exclaimed, "General Pemberton desires you to come immediately and with all dispatch to the left, to the support of General Stevenson, whatever may be in your front."

"Does General Pemberton know the enemy is in great force in my front?" asked Loring.

Thompson stuck to his guns. "I do not know whether General Pemberton knows that or not," he shot back before reiterating the order word for word. "If you do not comply, the responsibility will be yours, General, not mine."[8]

Thompson's earnest delivery of the order, followed up by one more that explained the crumbling strategic situation to Loring, finally stirred the recalcitrant division leader to action. Loring ordered his entire division northward out of line. "I was ordered . . . to proceed without delay," remembered Abraham Buford, who put his mixed-state regiments "at once into motion by the left flank and at the double-quick." Winfield Featherston did likewise, noting later "this order was promptly obeyed; General Loring and myself rode at the held of the column."

Private John V. Grief of Company D, 3rd Kentucky Mounted Infantry, was one of these double-quicking for the left that afternoon with Buford. "We passed through a terrific artillery fire," he remembered. One of the shots tore off a large tree limb and fell on top of J. G. Brooks of the same company, pinning him to the ground. Brooks, recalled Grief, "was captured before he could extricate himself, but was recaptured after being a prisoner a half hour."[9]

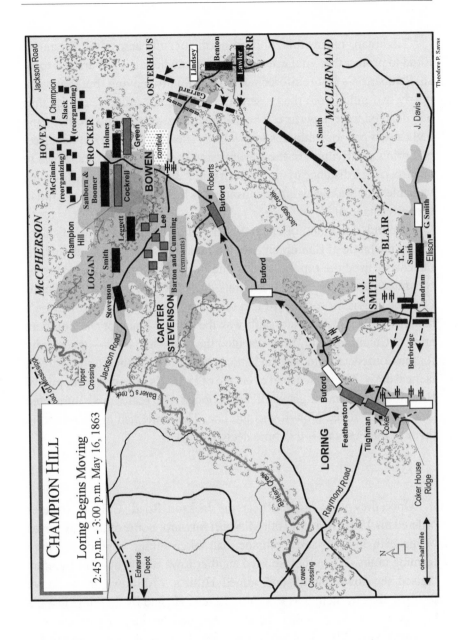

CHAMPION HILL

Loring Begins Moving
2:45 p.m. - 3:00 p.m. May 16, 1863

Theodore P. Savas

Tilghman, meanwhile, shifted north (or left) across the Raymond Road to protect that vital artery or move elsewhere if word arrived to do so. Pemberton's last reinforcements were finally moving, but they were nearly two miles from the crossroads sector, and Loring's petty qualms had delayed their departure. The different messages to and from Loring had caused precious minutes to tick away. Pemberton realized the effect of Loring's dallying. "In the transmission of these various messages to and fro, over a distance of more than a mile," Pemberton reported, "much valuable time was necessarily consumed, which the enemy did not fail to take advantage of."[10]

The indecisive and often confused Pemberton made many mistakes during the battle of Champion Hill, but he was exactly correct about how the enemy used the time wasted trying to get Loring to move where he was most needed. While the generals dueled, Grant pumped Marcellus Crocker's division southward in a counterattack that stemmed Bowen's hammer stroke. Bowen's assault was the critical hour for the Southern army at Champion Hill. It represented the best—and only—opportunity for the Confederates to win the battle outright or fight their opponent to a tactical draw. The presence of even one of Loring's brigades in support of Bowen's attackers might well have tipped the scales and unraveled Grant's right flank. Now it was too late. The battle had again turned in favor of the Federals—this time decisively so.[11]

*   *   *

Once they were aligned near the Jackson Road, Colonel Holmes ordered his 17th Iowa and 10th Missouri forward. Some of the Hawkeyes of the 28th Iowa, Slack's brigade, had taken refuge behind Holmes's forming ranks. When they spotted another Iowa regiment close by, they "raised the Iowa shout" and joined Hillis's 17th Iowa in its move forward. One of them was Pvt. John Myers. He had by this time lost his big toe and suffered other wounds, and had no idea where his own regiment was. When Holmes's men went forward, he explained to his wife, "I went in with them and got them [the Southerners] compleatly confused and then we mate a bayonet charge on them and took 2,000 prisoners." The homespun Hawkeye "helped to take them to a convenient plase for safe keeping and then went in a hunt of my own Regiment but did not succeed in finting it." The 10th Missouri's Major Francis C.

Deimling recalled the advance. "We charged up the hill over ground of the roughest character, meeting and checking the enemy who was driving back in disorder and confusion the troops in our advance," he penned in his report. My two regiments, Holmes added, "gallantly and heroically rushed with their commands into the conflict."

The Confederates opposing them tried to reform behind a fence but failed. Holmes's Iowans and Missourians had found a soft spot in the line, perhaps near the joint where Cockrell's right and Green's left came together—or was supposed to. There they charged at an oblique angle up the eastern skirt of Champion Hill, driving steadily before them whatever opposition stood in their path. The Confederates were paying dearly for the mishandling of Bowen's ordnance train.[12]

Except for Colonel Holmes's third regiment (the 80th Ohio, in the rear guarding the trains), all three of Marcellus Crocker's brigades were on the field and counterattacking to save the center-right of Grant's army. Their move into combat, wrote correspondent Cadwallader, was "when the real battle began." Hovey's and Logan's men would have vehemently disagreed with that mistaken (and even hurtful) observation. The bloodied remains of the former commander's division fell back behind Crocker's men into the fields and timber beyond the Champion house to regroup and refill their empty cartridge boxes. "Gen. Hovey's division was then formed back in the woods, what was left of us," remembered Aurelius Lyman Voorhis of the 46th Indiana, part of McGinnis's brigade. Hovey was proud of his men. "I never saw fighting like this," he penned in his official report. Nearly one-third of his soldiers had been killed, wounded, or captured. Everyone of them would have disagreed with Cadwallader's characterization.[13]

Crocker struck Bowen's assault at its climax and sapped its strength as the Federals fell back before the onslaught of Southern fire and steel, yielding yard by yard and giving as good as they got. Hovey's troops, however, performed the lion's share of bloody work this day, as one of Crocker's brigade commanders soon learned to his embarrassment. What was left of James Slack's hard-fought brigade was falling back through the lines of Colonel Holmes's newly-arrived brigade when that colonel rode up, looked about, and turned to an officer standing near Lieutenant Williams of the 56th Ohio.

"Have these stragglers fall in on the left of my brigade," he ordered.

The unnamed and utterly offended officer from Slack's command raised his voice in response. "These are the men who have fought this battle; there are no stragglers here."

Chastised, Holmes looked again at the men milling about and saw for the first time their "powered, blackened faces" and the dazed bloodied appearance of men who had just endured horrific combat. The colonel removed his hat, noted one observer, and apologized profusely. "I beg your pardon," Holmes replied. "True enough, there are no stragglers on this line."[14]

Grant himself arrived about this time and "found the troops that had been so gallantly engaged for so many hours withdrawn from their advanced position." Hovey's survivors were filling their cartridge boxes and hunting up water for their empty canteens. "I directed them to use all dispatch, and push forward as soon as possible," remembered Grant, explaining to them "the position of Logan's division" and how he had worked his way beyond the enemy's left flank.[15]

*   *   *

With Boomer, Sanborn, and now two of Holmes's three regiments thrown into the fight, the whole supported with heavy concentrations of Federal artillery, Bowen's counterattack reached its anti-climactic end. The Confederates had driven the enemy as far as they could, were completely exhausted after a night with but little rest, and were now out of ammunition and facing a strong thrust by fresh troops supported by more than two dozen pieces of well-handled artillery. The static firefight that erupted for perhaps a quarter-hour at the end of the long Southern tether ended with the Southerners being pushed slowly, but irresistibly, backward. About this time additional Southern batteries arrived near the crossroads to take up positions to support the failing counter-offensive. Guibor's four-gun Missouri Battery under Lt. William Corkery unlimbered somewhere behind the left side of Cockrell's line, where it "did effective service in saving the left of the brigade from being flanked," wrote the appreciative general. Lieutenant Richard C. Walsh and the six guns of Wade's Missouri Battery, in conjunction with Landis's pieces, would do "good service on the right of the brigade." Later, when these cannoneers began falling in the service of their guns, Father John Bannon, chaplain of the Missouri brigade, heroically volunteered and helped work one of them. The additional guns would not be enough to stem the withdrawal. Samuel Lockett, Pemberton's engineer, summed up John Bowen's counterattack and slow retreat with a concise word-picture. "Bowen's division sustained its reputation by making one of its grand old charges," he explained after the war, "in which it bored a hole through the Federal army, and finding itself unsupported turned around and bored its way back again." Private William L. Cotton, Company F, 5th Iowa, Boomer's brigade, said the same thing a bit more succinctly when he wrote home eleven days later, "the veterans of Quinby brought them to."[16]

Bowen's battered brigades might have found a line and held their ground until Loring's Division reached them except for the discovery of the threat closing in from the east. With orders now in hand to attack, McClernand's once-creeping divisions on the Middle Road were pressing aggressively westward and had come into view. "About this time the enemy began to flank us on the right," was how Colonel Dockery of the 19th Arkansas recalled the appearance of McClernand's men. Some of Waddell's guns opened upon them, but strong reinforcements were required if the field was to be held. The flanking enemy seen dribbling out of the eastern skirt of woods and thickets comprised the advancing skirmish line fronting Peter Osterhaus's division. Behind it tramped regiments from Garrard's and Lindsey's brigades. Behind that was Eugene Carr's division. Blocking them was what was left from the orphan skirmishers of Cumming's brigade and a handful of other gallant souls. Sergeant Robert H. G. Gaines, Company K, 23rd Alabama, had fallen back far enough to reach one of Waddell's unoccupied 12-pound howitzers. "Unassisted, [he] used [it] with good effect," wrote Dockery. "The sergeant alone fired about 12 or 15 rounds, when, being noticed by General Green, 4 volunteers were obtained . . . who gallantly assisted . . . in working the piece, causing the enemy to stop their advance on that particular point." The volunteers, "whose names I have not been able to learn, deserve great credit for their bravery."[17]

*   *   *

General Grant knew what snatching victory from the jaws of defeat felt like. He had seen and smelled it at Fort Donelson, and then again two months later at Shiloh. The same scent mingled with the heavy clouds of powder smoke and lingered in the hot afternoon air. The same sight of his earlier victories greeted his eyes: fresh troops taking the field and an exhausted enemy falling back. It was time to close out the day.

Small but significant Federal victories were won ravine by ravine, hollow by hollow, fence line by fence line. One of the most spectacular of these mini-victories took place soon after Crocker committed his division to battle.

After spending a short time in support of De Golyer's Michigan battery, the 59th Indiana and 4th Minnesota of Sanborn's brigade "were ordered to hasten forward and assist the right [left] of General Logan's division, which was reported to be hard pressed," remembered the 4th Minnesota's Col. John E. Tourtellotte. The Hoosiers stormed ahead with them on the left. Other elements from Logan's division were already several hundred yards ahead, seeping their way south across the Jackson Road. "The men threw their knapsacks and blankets from their shoulders and dashed forward in the direction indicated at the double-quick step up the hill, into the woods, and upon a body of the enemy," Tourtellotte wrote in his report. The enemy was Col. Michael L. Woods's advancing 46th Alabama, part of Stephen Lee's attempt at a counterattack north of the Jackson Road. Organized at Loachapoka, Alabama, in May of 1862, these soldiers from the Deep South had hit a soft spot in Logan's divisional line and driven too far north—alone.

The 4th Minnesota found Woods and his men in a ravine at a most inopportune moment. The 59th Indiana, about 100 yards farther east hit the same ravine at an oblique at almost the same time. The double misfortune was too much for Woods and his men. Within a few minutes, 118 of them were on their way to a Federal prison pen, their one-way tickets stamped by the 4th Minnesota. Sergeant John Ford, Company C, 59th Indiana, grabbed the colors from the 46th's color-bearer, and the Hoosiers added "many prisoners" to the pool of captured. General Lee saw the disaster unfolding and tried to extract the regiment without success. "The enemy having advanced very rapidly upon the right, the Forty-sixth Alabama could not be reached, and I regret to say that this excellent regiment, under its gallant field officers . . . was captured." The 30th Alabama was more fortunate. It had attacked north with Woods and his regiment, but received Lee's order to fall back just in time and narrowly avoided a similar fate. Several contingents from Alfred Cumming's Brigade had also advanced with Lee's men, with the same

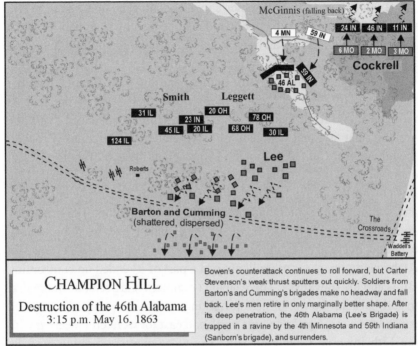

McGinnis (falling back)

4 MN 59 IN 24 IN 46 IN 11 IN

6 MO 2 MO 3 MO

Cockrell

59 IN

46 AL

Smith   Leggett

31 IL   20 OH
          23 IN   78 OH
          45 IL 20 IL   68 OH   30 IL
124 IL

Lee

Roberts

Barton and Cumming
(shattered, dispersed)

The
Crossroads,

Waddell's
Battery

CHAMPION HILL

Destruction of the 46th Alabama
3:15 p.m. May 16, 1863

Bowen's counterattack continues to roll forward, but Carter Stevenson's weak thrust sputters out quickly. Soldiers from Barton's and Cumming's brigades make no headway and fall back. Lee's men retire in only marginally better shape. After its deep penetration, the 46th Alabama (Lee's Brigade) is trapped in a ravine by the 4th Minnesota and 59th Indiana (Sanborn's brigade), and surrenders.

Theodore P. Savas

result. "The enemy, flushed with his previous success," he explained, "and in number much superior to ours, drove our men apparently along the whole division front; slowly at first, afterwards more rapidly."[18]

Sanborn's remaining regiments, the 48th Indiana and 18th Wisconsin, went in on the left of the 59th Indiana, "in support of what seemed to be General Hovey's right," reported an unsure but correct Sanborn. The 48th advanced "into a most galling fire of musketry." Sanborn thought these men held their position "at least three hours," though in reality it was closer to a single hour. The regiment "stood like a wall of adamant [men] wherever it was placed till the close of the engagement," boasted the proud colonel. The 18th Wisconsin played the orphan's role, moving "from right to left and back two or three times" as circumstances demanded. The Badgers "moved with great promptness, and held every position firmly until removed by orders," observed Sanborn. The 18th led a charmed existence at Champion Hill and somehow managed to avoid suffering a single loss running up and down just behind heavily engaged lines.[19]

By this time, George Boomer's men had attacked up Champion Hill to its crest, been driven back down the slope step by step, had formed a line and fought hard for an hour around the Champion outbuildings, and had run out of ammunition. When Samuel Holmes's 17th Iowa and 10th Missouri slipped into line, Col. Putnam and his 93rd Illinois, together with some of Boomer's other men, eased their way to the rear to reorganize and refill their cartridge boxes. Holmes advanced "with the greatest alacrity and enthusiasm," remembered Marcellus Crocker, though against Confederates who had reached the end of their physical endurance and the bottoms of their cartridge boxes. Colonel Hillis's 17th Iowa drove the enemy before them "in confusion . . . completely routing and scattering his center, and capturing a stand of colors, 175 prisoners, and recapturing four pieces of artillery which had been previously captured, but retaken by the enemy." Somehow Stephen Lee's errant 31st Alabama regiment (or more likely just a part of it) ended up confronting Hillis and his Hawkeyes. The Alabama regiment had been one of the first to fall back in the initial heavy fighting. After it regrouped, its attack carried it several hundred yards north and east for its fateful meeting with the 17th Iowa on Champion Hill. The close-quarters fighting cost the Alabamans their flag and color bearer, which Sgt. Evan C. Swearngin of Company F and Pvt. Albert Trussel of Company G, captured.

Holmes's second regiment, the 10th Missouri under Lt. Col. Leonidas Horney, moved forward on the left of the Jackson Road "over the hills and ravines, fighting the enemy, who contested the ground closely," remembered the 10th's Major Deimling. The Confederates opposing him belonged to Green's Brigade, but without ammunition and being threatened from the right by McClernand's advancing Federals, they were more than willing to give up their Mississippi real estate for a chance to escape POW status. "We finally found ourselves overpowered," was how one dazed Southerner remembered the dismal aftermath of their whirlwind victory on Champion Hill. Colonel Elijah Gates, whose men of the 1st Missouri Cavalry (dismounted) were waging a fighting retreat back across the Middle Road, estimated the time as "about 3 o'clock." General Green rode up and informed Gates for the first time the withdrawal was not just to a new position but from the field entirely. "Orders were to fall back beyond Baker's Creek, below the bridge over which we had crossed in going out the night before," recorded Gates. With the enemy blocking the western leg of the Jackson Road, there was no other way off the field.[20]

As the division fell back before Lieutenant Colonel Horney's advancing 10th Missouri and other Federal reinforcements, Green's officers detailed skirmishers to cover the withdrawal. "About twenty of us, mostly from my company, were left to cover the retreat, being sharpshooters," remembered Archable H. Reynolds of the 19th Arkansas, Green's Brigade. Reynolds and his comrades remained well behind the withdrawing regiment and made good use of the hills and hollows as they grudgingly gave ground. "We stopped in a hollow that headed up near the Bolton [Jackson] road," continued Reynolds. They waited for several minutes until the 19th Arkansas was out of sight before six of the men climbed up and looked toward the enemy. "A regiment of Federal infantry was just filing out of the big road to our right and about eighty yards away and advancing at trail arms." Reynolds was watching Missourians flying the Stars and Stripes. Only minutes earlier they had arrived at a fence with the well bloodied and thoroughly trampled cornfield on its opposite side. The 19th Arkansas, noted the 10th Missouri's Major Deimling, fell back "and they made no further appearance in this direction." After a timely reorganization, the 10th Missouri moved by the right up the eastern flank of Champion Hill across "the Vicksburg road" to the support of the embattled 17th Iowa.[21]

Reynolds and his 19 comrades watched as the Missourians, in perfect order, moved within killing distance. A Federal officer rode in front of the lines. James Larry was an Irish private in Horney's 10th Missouri. "He was an old time Irishman," recalled one of his comrades. When asked after the bloody hard-fought fight at Raymond what he thought of the battle, Larry had replied, "I've seen worse difficulties than that in the Old Country with sticks and bricks, but not so many got kilted!" Anxious to seek out the enemy, the irrepressible Private Larry ran forward and found Reynolds and his comrades sheltered in the ravine. He looked down at them and yelled, "Come on! Here they are!" swinging his hat wildly in the air. Horney, spurred his horse forward. "Billy Watts knelt beside a little oak tree and fired, when the officer fell as if dead or mortally wounded," remembered Reynolds. Each of the men aimed at an individual enemy and pulled their triggers.

The 10th Missouri's Capt. Joel W. Strong watched the unfolding drama with horror. The Southerners, first Billy Watts and then others,

rose and fired at his commanding officer, ignoring Private Larry—
"apparently the little Irishman was too small game for them," he recalled.
The cascade of bullets riddled Horney and his horse, killing both
instantly. Major Deimling, the regiment's surviving senior officer,
assumed command and opened fire with the left of the line, "checking
and driving them back." The angry Missourians stormed the ravine.
"Those who survived the rush surrendered," remembered Strong.[22]

Archable Reynolds recalled the same event from his own
infantryman's perspective of combat:

> Immediately I primed my gun, a Springfield rifle, and was
> loading it and watching for another shot and walking backward
> down the hill, dragging my gun butt on the ground, intending to get
> my man when they came over the hill, and had just rammed the ball
> home when my foot came in contact with a root of a huckleberry
> bush that had been rotted up and I fell sprawling with my head down
> hill, and before I could recover they were upon us.
>
> They fired a volley just as I fell, and I have always felt that the fall
> saved my life. The next instant they were at us with bayonets. I
> raised up on my right elbow just as a big fellow was in the act of
> thrusting his bayonet through me and fired. The muzzle of my gun
> was within four feet of his breast and loaded with a Springfield rifle
> ball and a steel ramrod.

Reynolds had fallen within a few feet of the hollow where he had
been fighting. He picked up his story from that point:

> With what strength I had left I sprang over the precipice of the
> cave; but before I could scramble down the lifeless corpse of my
> antagonist preceded me with a heavy thud into the slush below. In
> the next minute we were prisoners of war and passed by where Billy
> Watts had killed the officer just as they were conveying him off. I
> noticed then that it was not over forty yards from where he fell to the
> public road leading to Bolton.[23]

* * *

Peter Osterhaus had orders to attack, but found it difficult to move his
brigades forward in anything resembling a coordinated assault. The right

of his divisional line was held by Theophilus Garrard above the Middle Road, and the left by a pair of David Lindsey's regiments. Both men had orders to advance. Although blunted by the aggressive Southern skirmish line and Waddell's guns along the road proper, Osterhaus extended his right flank north and slowly worked it through woods and hills closer to the vital vicinity of the crossroads. Martin Green watched the movement on his right with rising alarm. His brigade was many hundreds of yards north of the Middle Road, fighting for its life. Pinned in front by Hovey's remnants and Crocker's fresh reinforcements, it was about to be engulfed from the flank and rear by Osterhaus. The brigadier dispatched Capt. William Pittman, the 12th Arkansas Sharpshooter Battalion's assistant adjutant-general and a member of Green's staff, to find Pemberton and notify him of the movement and "seek reinforcements to check it, and also to strengthen the right of the brigade."[24]

Pemberton was also alarmed, and had been in a high state of anxiety for the last several hours. He had been waiting impatiently at his Roberts house headquarters for Loring to arrive when he learned that McClernand's approach along the Middle Road had evolved into a heavy and more aggressive display of force. "Where is Loring!" he groaned with worry, sending staffers galloping off to look for him. Riding west a bit, Pemberton saw that Carter Stevenson's Division was almost completely shattered and on the verge of losing what little cohesion it had left. He located Stevenson somewhere along the Jackson Road.

"General, I have repeatedly ordered two brigades of General Loring's division to your assistance, and expect them momentarily. Can you hold your position?" asked the army commander. Large numbers of hatless and unarmed men were streaming past the two generals, "deserting their comrades, who in this moment of greatest trial stood manfully at their posts," reported Pemberton.

"I cannot hold much longer," replied Stevenson adamantly. His next observation emphasized just how inexperienced he was as a combat leader: "I am fighting 60,000 to 80,000 men."

If not before, Pemberton now learned with certainty that Federals (John Stevenson's brigade) had cut off access down the Jackson Road to the Bakers Creek bridge. Shouting above the din of combat raging just a hundred yards north of them, Pemberton answered Stevenson. "I will find Loring myself and hasten him up!"[25]

With that the embattled commanding general rode east toward the crossroads and south along the Ratliff Road in search of his errant division. He had not progressed too far south when he spotted the head of an infantry column. Loring's Division—or at least one brigade of it—was finally up.

Loring Arrives at the Crossroads

When Loring at long last gave him marching orders, Abraham Buford acted promptly. His men had spent most of the day in line on the Ratliff Road far to the south. Now, finally, they were moving by the left flank for the embattled crossroads. Running behind the mounted, beefy faced Kentuckian, was his unusually large brigade of 3,000 effectives comprised of eight regiments—four from Alabama, two from Kentucky, and one each from Arkansas and Louisiana. Their brigadier was 34 years old, six feet tall, and at 300 (and often heavier) pounds offered an "imposing physique with a dominating will and forceful personality." Other than his girth and thick dark wavy hair, mustache, and chin whiskers, his most salient feature was his eyes, which drooped heavily and gave him the appearance of a sleepy hound dog recently aroused. His performance at West Point was distinguished only by his lack of academic ability: he graduated in 1841 just one slot above dead last. Buford performed well in Mexico, however, and earned a brevet advancement to captain and

Brigadier General
Abraham Buford

Alabama Department of
Archives and History

the permanent rank six years later. When Buford grew tired of military life, he returned to his scenic Kentucky plantation to raise thoroughbred horses and short-horn cattle. For a time he served as president of the Richmond & Danville Railroad.

Although a staunch advocate of state rights, Buford did not eagerly embrace the Southern Confederacy. After all, he had a comfortable life in Kentucky—how long would that last if he threw in his lot with the South? When Rebel forces invaded in the fall of 1862, however, he shed the clothes of a gentleman and donned the gray, accepting a brigadier's appointment in November. He led cavalry for a time before a transfer sent him to Pemberton, who in turn shuttled the general to Franklin Gardner's post at Port Hudson, where a brigade was created for Buford to command. After a difficult railroad journey east to Tennessee that never fully managed to reach its destination, Buford's Brigade was shuttled back to Pemberton when Federal boats passed the Vicksburg batteries. On May 16 he was in charge of one Loring's three brigades, jogging his 3,000 infantrymen toward the cauldron of battle near the crossroads south of Champion Hill. The stress to reach the threatened sector in time was palpable, but not as intense as the financial disasters that would over take him twenty years later, strip away his plantation, and induce him to take his own life.[26]

"My command double-quicked the distance (about 2 miles) under a scorching sun, through corn and rye fields, in about half an hour," reported Buford, who moved up both sides of the Ratliff Road a short distance before cutting across country near "the negro cabins" to head northeast to aid Green. Colonel Alpheus Baker may have been the first man in the brigade wounded that day. The column was "near the negro cabins" when a rifle round found the commander of the 54th Alabama, penetrating his boot and breaking one of the bones of his instep. After inspecting the painful wound, Baker climbed back in the saddle and led his regiment "until exhausted." Buford believed he was somewhere behind Green's right rear, "which was falling back in disorder before an overpowering force of the enemy," when Pemberton found him. In reality, he was behind the center of Bowen's command. By this time, the army leader was wisely formulating an exit strategy from the shrinking battlefield. Buford would play a key role in making the departure possible. Pemberton ordered him to move west beyond the intersection to

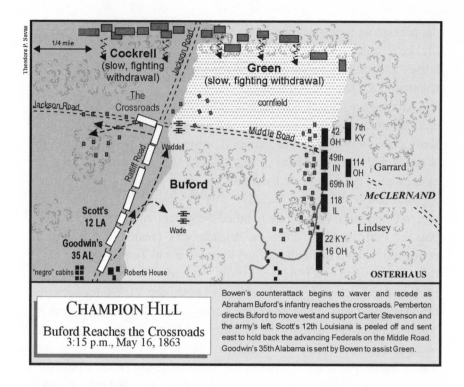

CHAMPION HILL

Buford Reaches the Crossroads
3:15 p.m., May 16, 1863

Bowen's counterattack begins to waver and recede as Abraham Buford's infantry reaches the crossroads. Pemberton directs Buford to move west and support Carter Stevenson and the army's left. Scott's 12th Louisiana is peeled off and sent east to hold back the advancing Federals on the Middle Road. Goodwin's 35th Alabama is sent by Bowen to assist Green.

"hold the road immediately in rear of General Lee's brigade about one-half mile west of the crossroads."[27]

Like so many of Pemberton's brigades that day, Buford's would also fight in pieces—much to his vexation. The idea to use part of Buford's command to satisfy Francis Cockrell's earlier pleas for help crossed Pemberton's mind after he gave Buford orders to proceed west and after Buford was long gone. Riding near the end of the long column of troops, Pemberton spotted the 12th Louisiana under Col. Thomas Scott. He ordered the Louisianans to Cockrell's support, but changed his mind soon thereafter and sent them instead "to the right of General Green's brigade (then engaged) [to] attack a Federal force then attempting to turn General Green's right flank." Shortly before or after Scott was pulled from Buford's column, Bowen did the same thing, peeling away Col. Edward Goodwin's 35th Alabama and directing it toward the crossroads. Buford did not notice the pilfering of his two rear regiments until he was well west of the crossroads and forming his brigade south of the Jackson Road under the cover of a patch of timber.[28]

Buford's trek west exposed how roughly Carter Stevenson's Division had been handled. "Across this road our men were hastening in wild disorder and in consternation before a very heavy fire of the enemy," reported Buford. The retreating Confederates pressed against and "continually" broke through the brigadier's column, "rushing pell-mell from the scene of action and resisting all attempts made to rally them." Many of the men disrupting Buford's marching order belonged to Stephen D. Lee and Alfred Cumming, the survivors of the recent unsuccessful attack north of the Jackson Road. Both officers toiled hard to form some semblance of order below the Jackson Road. It was difficult work. "The horses of my adjutant and myself were struck by shots delivered from the right of that road in plain view, and at a very short range," Cumming later remembered.[29]

Cumming had virtually no success. Once his men had been driven south of the Jackson Road, he reported, "the flight became precipitate. On this occasion scattered bands of [the enemy] crossed the road in close pursuit of the fugitives. After this it became impossible to rally them again, though strenuous efforts to do so were made several hundred yards from the road." Cumming's battle was over, and he could do nothing more but follow his "fugitives" cross country toward the lower ford.[30]

Lee's "fugitives" were more experienced than Cumming's men and so better equipped to weather the trauma inflicted upon them. Unlike Cumming, Lee managed to gather the core of his brigade around him, even though the 46th Alabama was gone entirely and much of the 31st Alabama was no where to be found. Huddled with these stalwarts, Lee conceded defeat. "Boys, there are not enough of you," remembered one who watched and listened as the general spoke. "If there were, we would redeem the day yet; as it is, you might as well go on with the rest." With that the Rebels fell back but "rallied about half a mile [south] of the Edwards Depot [Jackson] Road and in the rear of Buford's brigade, Loring's division, which had just arrived on the field at about 3:30 p.m.," Lee reported officially after the battle. The brigadier, however, according to one source who learned it from a soldier on the field, remained well to the front until the foot soldiers had departed. Private Joseph Bogle of Company I, 34th Georgia, Cumming's Brigade, remembered watching as Lee scanned his dangerous surroundings alone, "the last man on the field ... the bullets falling in a shower around him." Captain William Elliott, Lee's assistant adjutant-general, demonstrated "conspicuous gallantry," remembered Lee, when "he bore the colors of the Thirty-fourth Georgia, which he brought out of the action, the gallant color-bearer having been killed."[31]

With the remnants of Carter Stevenson's Division falling back through his lines, Abraham Buford was exposed to what was pressing up behind them. Following the beaten soldiers was a line of the enemy composed of regiments from the brigades of Mortimer Leggett (Logan) and Sanborn (Crocker). These men opened "a most galling fire . . . and their line, some 200 yards distant, posted in a heavy thicket of timber and undergrowth, unexposed to view," remembered Buford. The proximity of a strong Federal force meant, for all intents and purposes, "the enemy held possession of the road, and that I must retake it in order to comply with the command of General Pemberton." The Kentuckian realized quickly it would have been "a wanton destruction of life to have formed a line of battle with my brigade in its then position . . . exposed, too, to an enfilading fire from a battery which had been established by the enemy on a commanding eminence at short range." He changed the direction of the head of the column to the left, moved quickly 150 yards "from the crest of the rise in the road occupied by the enemy, to a covered position, and formed the brigade."

It was at this point Buford discovered his brigade was light two complete regiments: the 35th Alabama and 12th Louisiana were nowhere to be found. The sudden realization they had been snatched away without notice or permission enraged him. "Two of my strongest regiments were detached from the rear of my brigade. . . . The strength of my brigade at this critical moment was thus unceremoniously and materially reduced, this being done without my knowledge, and without any report being made to me of the fact by the generals who gave the orders." The words were penned exactly one month after the battle. Buford was still seething with anger over the (understandable) lack of protocol.[32]

Even while the 35th Alabama and 12th Louisiana regiments were moving toward their assigned positions, and Buford's six remaining regiments were forming into line to support Stevenson's drooping front, Pemberton realized these few reinforcements would not be enough to retrieve the day's fortunes. The game was up, or as he later reported, "Finding that the enemy's vastly superior numbers were pressing all my forces engaged steadily back into old fields, where all advantages of position would be in his favor, I felt it to be too late to save the day, even should . . . Featherston's brigade, of General Loring's division, come up immediately."[33]

On Bowen's right, Martin Green's line was steadily giving ground, falling back southward across the chewed up and littered landscape now being crossed by infantry a third time. Bowen found Pemberton at his Roberts house headquarters and gave him the latest news, all of it distressing. The two regiments from Buford (12th Louisiana and 35th Alabama) might help hold back the enemy from the east, but neither Green nor Cockrell could hold their positions much longer without ammunition. None was to be had. Pemberton ordered Bowen to withdraw his command slowly from the field. It was time to escape the closing Federal arms threatening to squeeze his army into oblivion.[34]

*   *   *

Francis Cockrell was troubled by the order to retire. The directive was delivered by Arkansan Capt. William Pittman, the ubiquitous assistant adjutant-general who had spent much of the day carrying orders for Green. "There is an order to retire," he told the Missouri brigadier. Cockrell later admitted he delayed communicating the order to his regimental leaders in the hope "that Major-General Loring's division might still arrive in time to push forward the successes and advantages so gallantly and dearly won." Pemberton had told Cockrell there were no reinforcements except Loring's men, who were on the way. By this time, however, it was too late. Green was falling back slowly on his right, and the wooded and ravine-cut ground north of the cornfield was being filled with Crocker's advancing men "in order of battle almost perpendicular to our own," remembered Cockrell. "I was thus forced to withdraw, which was done in good order." Ephraim Anderson, of Cockrell's Brigade, also wrote of the "hostile columns . . . closing in on our flank. . . . . At the end of all this hard and desperate fighting—this gallant and triumphant advance, it seemed to become necessary to fall back."[35]

Although the front was collapsing rapidly, neither Cockrell nor Green could have pulled off their magnificent fighting withdrawals had it not been for the timely arrival of Scott's 12th Louisiana and Goodwin's 35th Alabama—the two filched regiments from Abraham Buford's Brigade. Their gallant accomplishments on the field of Champion Hill have for too long been overshadowed by more prominent—if less important—events.[36]

"What regiment are you?" Bowen had shouted when he had earlier set his eyes on Goodwin's command.

"The 35th Alabama, Buford's Brigade!" yelled back Colonel Goodwin.

"Come with me!" ordered Bowen.

Not in the habit of arguing with generals, Goodwin complied. Pemberton had done much the same with Scott's 12th Louisiana just minutes earlier.

Under the guidance of one of Bowen's aides, Edward Goodwin marched his Alabamans out of the procession and was conducted "directly to the front" for 100 yards and instructed to "move straight forward until [you] meet the foe." Goodwin stopped long enough to form a strong line of battle and fix bayonets.

"Forward!"

Goodwin's solid wall of Alabamans tramped slowly up the Ratliff Road, picking their way through drifting powder smoke beneath high-flying minie balls. They had marched but a short distance when the energetic Martin Green rode like a specter out of the smoke and informed Goodwin he was sorely needed elsewhere. As Goodwin later reported, Green ordered him to "move to the right to the support of the First Missouri (Wade's) Battery, which was in great danger." Goodwin faced his line east and moved off the Ratliff Road in the direction indicated, and after a short distance came upon four unmanned Missouri guns, which their crew had just seconds earlier abandoned. Goodwin deployed behind the bronze pieces in a small protective swale. "The battery men, being reassured by the appearance of the regiment, rushed with enthusiasm to their guns and for an hour worked them with a celerity and a daring that I believe never has been surpassed during this war," Goodwin later reported to his superiors. "The enemy poured volley after volley of shot, shell, grape, and canister upon us, but owing to a fortunate position I lost only 1 man." The unlucky "1 man" was Lt. George C. Hubbard, who was visiting the regiment and assigned to serve with Company F by the request of its captain.[37]

The view from the other side of the field looked much different through Col. Daniel Lindsey's eyes. Little is known of this officer except that he was a Kentucky native and a prominent officer in the state's

Colonel
Daniel Lindsey

National Archives

militia. Like many brigades on both sides, Lindsey's also fought in dribs and drabs at Champion Hill. Earlier in the day, soon after contact had been made with Confederate skirmishers on the Middle Road, four companies from his 114th Ohio had been siphoned off to assist Garrard's brigade. A short time later, the balance of the 114th regiment, together with the 42nd Ohio, was also shuttled north to fight above the Middle Road on Garrard's right. That left Lindsey with two under strength regiments, the 22nd Kentucky and 16th Ohio, both of which had shed some companies to lend support to Osterhaus's artillery.

When word arrived to move forward with them, Lindsey advanced "to take the woods to our right and front, which had the appearance of being a point at which the enemy were rallying and reforming such of his broken columns as had been driven back on the right." In other words, Lindsey was moving west toward the milling mass of Green's disorganized regiments. A "very large drain" broke up the order of Lindsey's regiments, which only served to intensify the fire delivered by Goodwin's 35th Alabama and some of Green's Arkansans and Missourians in Lindsey's direction. The flying lead was so "severe," reported the colonel, that once they had crossed the drain he ordered his men to move rapidly forward without taking the time to reorganize his lines.

The decision proved unfortunate. The 16th Ohio drifted to the left, leaving the 22nd Kentucky to enter the woods alone, where it lost more than a dozen men to wounds and fell back behind the brow of a small hill. Lieutenant Colonel George W. Monroe rallied his command and the

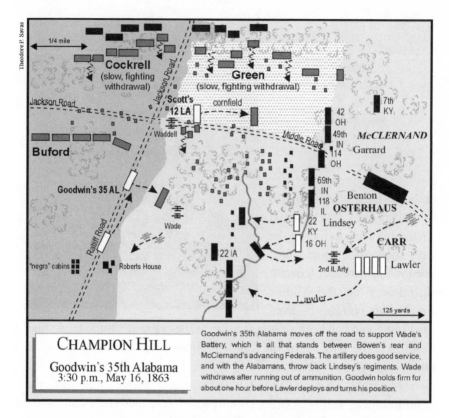

CHAMPION HILL

Goodwin's 35th Alabama
3:30 p.m., May 16, 1863

Goodwin's 35th Alabama moves off the road to support Wade's Battery, which is all that stands between Bowen's rear and McClernand's advancing Federals. The artillery does good service, and with the Alabamans, throw back Lindsey's regiments. Wade withdraws after running out of ammunition. Goodwin holds firm for about one hour before Lawler deploys and turns his position.

Kentuckians stood fast. The Ohioans sidled back and took up a position to their right, and the pair of regiments advanced a second time. The men held the skirt of the woods for about thirty minutes, estimated Lindsey, when a battery supported by infantry opened on them. These same Kentuckians and Buckeyes had suffered heavily at Chickasaw Bayou. Up to this point, only one man had been killed and 19 wounded, and both outfits were jumpy. Possibly they were ill-served by their officers. Whatever the cause, they broke and ran. "I regarded my advance as an important one, and regret exceedingly my inability to maintain it," wrote a candid Lindsey. He was carried a couple hundred yards to the rear with his men, and there worked hard to reorganize the regiments.[38]

General McClernand, meanwhile, was riding up and down his line in an effort to keep his advance moving. He was an offensive-minded general, and was more than ready to take the fight to the enemy. The "sharp skirmish" that had been going on for hours erupted into a hot contest, recalled the corps leader, the battle "raging all along my center and right." The direction of Bowen's retreat carried his men across the left front and flank of Garrard's line—"rather unexpectedly to both parties," observed Osterhaus, who had already sent word to Garrard that the enemy were retreating and not forming for an attack. The presence of the enemy on his flank, together with the enervated remnants of Cumming's skirmish companies and Scott's 12th Louisiana, stalled "for some time" Garrard's advance. Private William L. Rand, a soldier in Company B, 118th Illinois, wrote to his parents after the battle that he and his comrades waited for the enemy to advance, but "Mr. reb did not attack." The lines in the woods did drift close now and again, however, and Rand recalled how at one point a Confederate officer shouted out orders for the Federals to throw down their guns and surrender, promising not to fire upon them. John G. Fonda, the colonel of the 118th Illinois, remembered Rand, "told him to go to [Hell] and poured a volley into them."[39]

To add weight to Garrard's push, McClernand called upon Brig. Gen. William P. Benton's brigade of Carr's division. Picking forward through the clogged road and choking terrain, however, took considerable time. Private William Murray of the 33rd Illinois was surprised at the number of dead on this part of the field where only heavy skirmishing had taken place. "One could walk for many rods by stepping alternately upon the dead body of a Union soldier and then upon that of a Confederate," was how his diary would read by day's end.[40]

A couple hundred yards to the south, Lindsey's sputtering advance against Wade's guns and Goodwin's

Brigadier General
William P. Benton

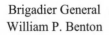

National Archives

Brigadier General
Michael Kelly Lawler

National Archives

35th Alabama convinced McClernand to order up Carr's second and last brigade under the command of Brig. Gen. Michael Kelly Lawler. Lindsey's pair of regiments, believed Lawler incorrectly, "had been sent out as skirmishers in advance of my brigade." The 48-year old native of Ireland was an experienced Mexican War militia commander and just the man to steady Lindsey's men. Lawler was an aggressive brawler, a proclivity aided by his fat frame and 250 pounds. Earlier in the war he had been acquitted of charges that he pummeled insubordinate soldiers with his fists and threatened to do the same to his superiors. Wounded at Fort Donelson, he had been promoted to brigadier in November of 1862 and displayed much ability at Port Gibson. Lawler was a fighter in every sense of the word, and would prove it soon enough before the ramparts at Vicksburg. Noted one observer, the general was "as brave as a lion, and has about as much brains." Still, he held the esteem of many of his men, as one Badger State warrior concluded simply, "he will do."[41]

The Irish general moved his command rapidly to Lindsey's assistance "to support these regiments and to check the enemy's advance." The 22nd Iowa was dispatched ahead "to annoy the enemy and attract his attention while the remainder of the brigade was getting into position." Aquilla Standifird of the 23rd Iowa scribbled his thoughts into his diary as the racket filled his heart with both confidence and trepidation. "We could but think what would be the result—who would be the victors," he wrote. The brigade was organized and moved forward through an area filled with deep ravines choked with "cane brakes," recalled one soldier. In the ensuing chaos of bringing forward reinforcements, friendly fire claimed two soldiers of the 33rd Illinois.[42]

Despite these and other problems, Lawler's line moved out in tolerably good order and was taken under fire by the same artillery and infantry that had forced back Lindsey's men. After emerging unscathed through several shell bursts, the provoked Irishman ordered up the four guns of Company A, 2nd Illinois Light Artillery. The "Peoria battery," he proudly recalled, galloped into position on a small rise in the field, unlimbered, and opened on the Confederates, silencing the guns and forcing their withdrawal from the field. In reality, Wade's Missouri gunners had emptied their caissons and withdrawn voluntarily. By this time Lindsey had his men under control and advancing yet a third time. Lawler's brigade joined them, but "the rebel's broke and fled, pressed by the brigade as rapidly and closely as a proper precaution and the conformation of the ground would permit." The Confederates were not followed up as closely as Lawler would have liked. Lindsey recalled the same enemy withdrawal, which was so swift his skirmishers were only able to get in "an occasional shot."[43]

The enemy retreat experienced by Lawler and Lindsey was not as precipitous as they reported. After an outstanding display of gunnery that slowed down considerably the advancing Federals, Wade's men limbered the guns and made for the rear after emptying their ammunition chests. The battery had no sooner departed than Lawler's advancing brigade, his line extended by Lindsey's pair of regiments, outflanked the 35th Alabama on the left and opened an enfilading fire that forced Goodwin to adjust his lines accordingly and seek out Green for further orders. By this time, Green's front was collapsing rapidly from all sides. "Our friends gave way and came rushing to the rear panic- stricken," remembered Goodwin. The Alabama colonel rushed among the fleeing men and ordered them to stop and face the enemy, "but they heeded neither my orders nor those of their commanders." Shocked and angered by their inability to stand, Goodwin "brought my regiment to the charge bayonets, but even this could not check them in their flight." Three stands of regimental colors ran through the unyielding line of the 35th Alabama Infantry. "Both the officers and the men, undismayed, united with me in trying to cause them to rally. We collared them begged them, and abused them in vain," complained Goodwin.

The recently arrived colonel had no way of knowing what Green's men had just experienced, but Green fully appreciated the extent of their recent ordeal. They would never hold and he knew it. They had also been ordered to withdraw off the field. The brigadier told the gallant Goodwin to pull back his regiment and follow Wade's battery to the rear. He did as ordered and fell in behind Thomas Scott's 12th Louisiana, which was withdrawing from its own hair-raising fight north of the Middle Road, several hundred yards east of the crossroads. Green permitted Goodwin—"at my urgent solicitation," noted the Alabaman—to seek out and rejoin Buford's Brigade, which was aligned just a short distance to the west on the other side of the Ratliff Road. The Alabamans, Loring would later write, "had distinguished themselves." Indeed they had.[44]

*   *   *

After being cleaved from Buford's column by Pemberton, Col. Thomas Moore Scott's 12th Louisiana had scurried north to the intersection and then east down the Middle Road toward Osterhaus's Federals. The 34-year old Scott was about to demonstrate why a year later he would be a dependable brigadier general upon whom superiors would call in times of trouble. "Upon arriving on the ground," he wrote, "I found General Green's brigade (or at least the right of it) retiring from

the field in great confusion." Scott called a halt and formed into a line of battle "at right angles to the line occupied by Green's forces, and ordered my men forward." Green's men were facing north and falling slowly

Colonel Thomas M. Scott
12th Louisiana Infantry

National Archives

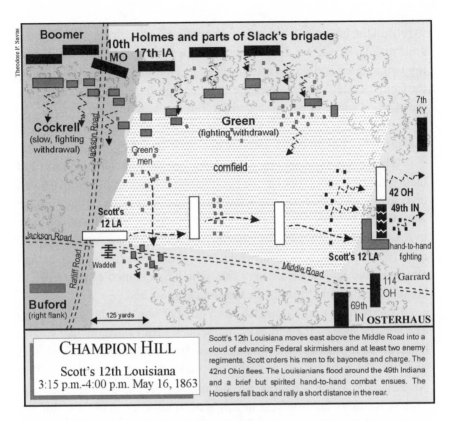

CHAMPION HILL

Scott's 12th Louisiana
3:15 p.m.-4:00 p.m. May 16, 1863

Scott's 12th Louisiana moves east above the Middle Road into a cloud of advancing Federal skirmishers and at least two enemy regiments. Scott orders his men to fix bayonets and charge. The 42nd Ohio flees. The Louisianians flood around the 49th Indiana and a brief but spirited hand-to-hand combat ensues. The Hoosiers fall back and rally a short distance in the rear.

back southward, and Scott's Louisianans were facing east. Exactly where Scott formed his line is unclear, but it was likely in the undulating ground north of the Middle Road in the cornfield. When a "heavy fire" tore through Scott's lines he called a halt and "returned [it] with spirit." Ordering his men to advance and fire at will, the Louisianans moved steadily east with, what Scott later claimed, was "great steadiness and precision." Ahead about 50 yards away, Scott could see at least two enemy regiments (probably Col. James Keigwin's 49th Indiana, Garrard's brigade, and Maj. Frederick A. Williams's 42nd Ohio, Lindsey's brigade) advancing west on the north side of the Middle Road. Scott's spirited fire dispersed the Federal skirmish line. From Scott's perspective, it now appeared as though he was facing three regiments "on a strong position on the crest of the hill."[45]

The heavy Federal fire slicing above and through his lines convinced Scott he could not maintain his position. "I determined to try cold steel," was his melodramatic but apparently accurate description of his decision to rely on the bayonet. Scott ordered his men to cease firing, fix bayonets, and "make a steady advance in line without yelling, that they might hear my commands; and never was an order more implicitly obeyed." When the Confederates "commenced the attack," reported a disgusted Keigwin, the 42nd Ohio troops on his right fell back with some speed. To Keigwin's dismay, his left flank was exposed because whatever regiment was tasked to hold the position had not come up.

"The enemy came down on it and charged into the flank, and some of them got to my rear," the Hoosier colonel later reported. "My men stood up bravely, and, after passing a few blows with the butts of their pieces, were forced to retire." Scott simply noted his shock tactics "caused them to flee in great confusion," and that he remained in his advanced position until recalled. Keigwin, meanwhile, rallied his 49th Indiana on a small elevation and laid down a heavy fire, which he claimed caused Scott to break and fall back "faster than they had approached."

Exactly how the regimental-sized combat was fought is irrelevant. The significance of the action is that Scott's 12th Louisiana had single-handedly held back at least two and possibly three Federal regiments that were in the process of driving into Green's rear. Goodwin's 35th Alabama and Wade's Battery had done much the same thing below the Middle Road by holding up Lindsey's tepid advance, and then slowing down Lawler's more aggressive thrust.[46]

*   *   *

On both sides of the Ratliff Road, well to the west of the giants standing tall in Louisiana and Alabama gray, gathered the disorganized, exhausted, and bloodied remains of Bowen's outstanding division. They had reached their original jump-off position and were now falling back farther south and west, some down the Ratliff Road and others across the fields and wood lots toward the lower crossing. What was left of Carter Stevenson's even more hard-hit division was gathered west of them, clumps and knots of milling men stretching away into the smoky distance on the next ridge south of the Jackson Road. Lee's men had just suffered their second bloody set back north of the road and much of the 46th Alabama was heading toward captivity after its demise in a Mississippi ravine. Abraham Buford's Brigade offered the only rock-solid anchor on this part of the field.

Once he arrived and deployed, remembered Abraham Buford, "I awaited the approach of the enemy, who must advance through an open, clear space. The enemy, however, halted in the road and established a battery. To have charged him from my position, with my brigade reduced in strength and over an open space of several hundred yards, would have cost it half its numbers." Instead, the Kentuckian moved his brigade by the right flank into some timber to find another means to get at the enemy in his front. "I had not completed the disposition of my command when I discovered that the enemy were rapidly turning both the right and left flanks of the position I held, as well as that occupied by him, against which I proposed to move," Buford fumed. "Why bother attacking the enemy in my front?" he wrote in rhetorical fashion. Buford continued:

> In all probability I might have taken the position at a great sacrifice, but it would be untenable, and I would have been forced to have given it up almost immediately, besides running the risk of having my entire brigade captured, as I was entirely without support, my strength reduced nearly one-third by the regiments being detached, and as all the troops of our center and of the left wing were leaving the field in great disorder. I therefore threw my brigade back about a quarter of mile from the negro cabins, and in the direction of Edwards Depot, on a commanding position, where I joined you with General Featherston's brigade.

The "you" to whom Buford referred was his division commander, William Loring. The general himself had finally arrived, though far too late to do anything other than slow down the enemy and cover the retreat of a broken army. J. V. Greif of Buford's 3rd Kentucky Mounted Infantry remembered falling back and taking up a position "on a ridge near our hospital—a double log house, where we were joined by our skirmishers and the Thirty-Fifth Alabama and Twelfth Louisiana Regiments."[47]

* * *

After he had ordered Buford to support Stephen Lee's line and plucked Scott's 12th Louisiana out of the marching column and kicked it east down the Middle Road, Pemberton had ridden south down the Ratliff Road in search of Loring. He expected to meet him quickly, but the road behind Buford was empty. The perplexed and angry commander returned to his headquarters and ordered several staff officers to hunt up Loring. He also met with Bowen at this time, learned the front could no longer hold, and ordered the army's withdrawal. It was only after this sequence of events that Pemberton discovered William Loring had finally arrived behind Carter Stevenson's front. But how did he get there without being seen?[48]

Other than recording in his report that his command arrived sooner than expected to save some artillery pieces, Loring conspicuously avoided discussing the details of his march to the army's left. Pemberton's staffer E. H. Bryan, however, wrote about the march in a letter to Pemberton three months after the event. Loring had left his Raymond Road position perhaps thirty minutes after Buford, but for reasons still unclear did not follow Buford north up the Ratliff Road. Instead, wrote Bryan, "[Loring] had followed a fence in a westerly direction and at right angles to [the Ratliff Road]." Featherston reported he had employed a guide to show him "the nearest way." The small road was unknown to Pemberton and his staff, and apparently not well known by Featherston's guide because the route was a winding indirect course to the army's left flank. When Bryan learned the direction Loring and Featherston took, he galloped a half mile before overtaking the column of Mississippi troops. Loring was found riding at its head.

"What road is this?" inquired Loring.

"I don't know, general," replied Bryan, "but you are on the wrong road and are heading in the wrong direction." When a surprised look crossed Loring's face, Bryan added, "Instead of heading north, general, you are marching west."

"Well, then you will lead the way and I will follow," Loring replied.

Bryan answered quickly. "I am unacquainted with the roads, general, except for the one over which I just traveled." To his amazement, Loring gave the order "forward!" and continued his march "in a northwesterly course."[49]

Luckily for Loring and the army, the country lane eventually veered north toward the retreating left flank of the army, though the route was "considerably longer than the direct route," chastised Pemberton in his report. The news of Loring's route dumbfounded Pemberton, who entertained bitter thoughts of Loring: "Had the movement in support of the left been promptly made when first ordered, it is not improbable that I might have maintained my position." By the time Loring arrived, the

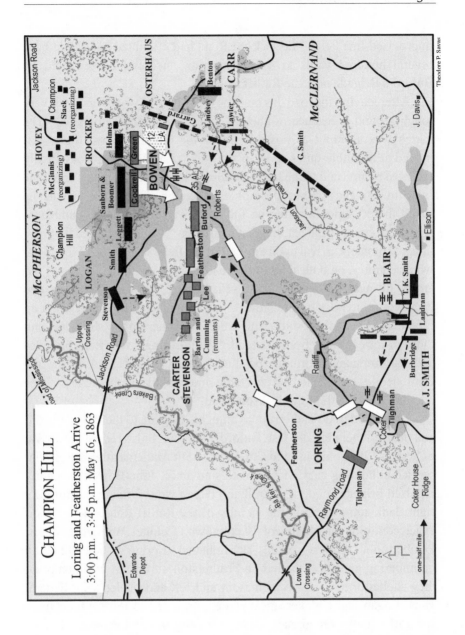

CHAMPION HILL

Loring and Featherston Arrive
3:00 p.m. - 3:45 p.m. May 16, 1863

McPHERSON

HOVEY

Jackson Road

Champion
Slack
(reorganizing)

McGinnis
(reorganizing)

CROCKER

Holmes

Sanborn &
Boomer

Champion
Hill

Smith   Leggett

LOGAN

Stevenson

Upper
Crossing

Road of Mississippi

Jackson Road

Bakers Creek

Edwards
Depot

Bakers Creek

Lower
Crossing

CARTER
STEVENSON

Barton and
Cumming
(remnants)

Lee

Featherston

Buford

Roberts

35 AL

Green

12
LA

BOWEN

Cockrell

OSTERHAUS

Garrard

Benton

Lindsey   Lawler

CARR

G. Smith

Jackson Creek

McCLERNAND

J. Davis

Ellison

BLAIR

T. K. Smith

Landram

Burbridge

Ratliff

A. J. SMITH

Featherston

LORING

Tilghman

Coker   Tilghman

Coker House
Ridge

Raymond Road

Tilghman

N

one-half mile

Theodore P. Savas

improvised line below the Jackson Road had crumbled and fallen back several hundred yards to a new position anchored on the right by Buford's Brigade near the Ratliff Road.[50]

After leaving the road, his men moved through "woods and over very rough ground a distance of about 2 miles," recalled Featherston. "The march was as rapid as possible under the circumstances; the troops moved at a double-quick most of the way." The Mississippians finally emerged behind and to the left of Buford, who was arriving just about the same time to take up a new position. Featherston was shocked by what he found there: "Upon arriving on the field, we found a large number of stragglers going to the rear in great confusion." Loring reported the same thing. "Upon my arrival upon this part of the field," he wrote, "I found the whole country, on both sides of the road, covered with the fleeing of our army, in many cases in large squads, and, as there was no one endeavoring to rally or direct them, I at once placed my escort under an efficient officer of my staff, with orders to gather up the stragglers and those in retreat away from the road." With Loring's two fresh brigades and the remnants forming on their flanks and behind them, the Confederates established a respectable line of battle on the ridge perhaps one-half mile south of the Jackson Road.[51]

Loring ordered Featherston to align his brigade to the left of Buford and ordered them to hold fast. Buford's line was bolstered by the arrival of Scott's 12th Louisiana and Goodwin's 35th Alabama after their stellar service in holding back McClernand's advance. John Bowen's recently repulsed brigades under Cockrell and Green were forming on Buford's right flank somewhere in the vicinity of the Ratliff Road, though their exact condition or alignment is unknown. Colonel William Withers, Pemberton's artillery chief, strengthened Loring's new line by unlimbering guns near the left on Featherston's front, from which point they shelled the woods to their front and left and dueled with Federal guns. Logan and Crocker, meanwhile, continued to reform their men, some of whom were already slowly pressing forward against this line, edging near Featherston's spongy and as yet still unformed and unanchored flanks—especially his left. The Mississippians had some difficulty determining what direction to face. Lieutenant Colonel Marcus D. L. Stephens, 31st regiment, for example, could not figure out how to align his men. When General Lee rode past, Stephens "asked him to direct me where to form a line." Lee pointed out a position, "and I found that the enemy was on my left, my right, and in front," remembered Stephens. Dismayed, he sought out Featherston and inquired which way he should face in forming. "It makes no difference," Featherston replied. "Face any way and go to fighting." Lee had been riding up and down the line in an unsuccessful search for Carter Stevenson. When he spotted Loring, Lee "reported to him for orders." The few hundred weary Alabamans he had with him were directed to take up a position on Featherston's left.[52]

Lieutenant William Drennan, Winfield Featherston's staff officer, had not made the winding march north with the column. He had been busy overseeing the movement of the division's ordnance trains to the army's left so Loring's men would have ready access to ammunition. When he finished, Drennan rode up the Ratliff Road and then cut across a rye field heading northwest in search of the division. "I had not gone far, before I met bodies of men—some without hats—their guns thrown away—and looking as if they had just escaped from the Lunatic Asylum," he wrote in a letter home to his wife. The sight of the army falling to pieces around him was a distressing experience:

> On my urging them for God's sake, not to fly the field in that manner—would invariably reply that "they were all that was left of their company." I exhorted and plead with numbers to return—that by their efforts united with those who had gone to their assistance [Loring], that the day would yet be ours and the tide of battle turned—but nothing but a drawn saber or presented bayonet will halt men fleeing from the battle field.
>
> As I rode on further, I saw large numbers wounded—and in every conceivable manner. The earth in some places red with blood—and here and there a mangled soldier who had ceased to feel either the pain of his wound or the sting of defeat, and was sleeping the sleep that knows no waking.

Drennan galloped on and met Col. William Withers, Pemberton's artillery commander. The state of the Southern long-arm, Withers informed Drennan, was just as bad as the deteriorating state of the infantry. Many guns had been captured and the enemy was heading right in their direction. "I turned around," wrote Drennan, and the pair rode out of harm's way. "[I] learned that Stevenson and Bowen had been badly repulsed and that on Loring now depended the fortunes of the day." Withers had just left Loring and directed Drennan to him. He arrived about the same time as Captain Taylor of Pemberton's staff, who informed Loring of Pemberton's orders to withdraw. Once again Loring and Featherston openly questioned the commanding general's authority by taking steps to disobey a direct order. On this occasion, even Colonel Withers and Stephen Lee drank from the same poisoned well.

In his official report, Loring claimed Taylor's order did not reach him until after he planned an attack against the enemy, which was only partially true: "It was . . . determined that under these circumstances it was necessary, in order to save large numbers of men and guns, as well as to be able, in case the emergency should arise, to retire the army in safety and good order to the ford over Baker's Creek, along the only road open to it, that a vigorous and well-directed attack should be made upon the enemy." Stephen Lee and Colonel Withers, continued Loring, informed him that "an attack upon the enemy's right during the panic which had befallen his center . . . could overwhelm it, retrieve the day, certainly cut him off from the bridge on our extreme left (of which it was highly important we should hold possession), and save our scattered forces. Dispositions were at once made for the attack, in which General Lee lent a cordial and able assistance." While contemplating this move, continued Loring, "I received an order for the forces to fall back, and my assistant adjutant-general, who had been dispatched to General Pemberton for orders, returned stating that the general said that the movement must not be made; that I must order a retreat and bring up the rear. Officers were immediately sent to advise those not yet informed to retire, and as rapidly as possible, in the direction of the ford, that being the only road left open."

In reality, Loring did not "immediately" order a withdrawal. Lieutenant Drennan—the most keen and objective observer to leave a record on the Southern side—was present with Loring at this time. His letter to his wife was never intended to be made public, which makes his observations even more convincing and reliable. His recollection does not agree with Loring's version of events. "We arrived at the head of the Div. just as Gen'l Loring had received an order from Gen'l Pemberton 'to retreat in the direction we came,'" recalled the staff officer. "Loring thought, as did Featherston & Withers, that the day was not lost and Loring, after hesitating a moment, ordered a 'forward'—when Capt.

Taylor of Pemberton's staff, rode up and pre-emptorily ordered a retreat."[53]

*   *   *

Loring and his generals were planning how to affect their withdrawal while Grant was guiding his horse south down the littered slope of Champion Hill on his way to the crossroads. The steady advance of Crocker's division and the defeat of Lee's counterattack by Logan's brigades and Sanborn's regiments had straightened out and filled in the Federal line on the army's left. Sanborn's troops had pushed forward to the Jackson Road (and in many places beyond it) and were now in touch with Mortimer Leggett's left flank, which comprised the left flank of Logan's well advanced division. With that link, the Union soldiers had reconstructed the line they occupied before Bowen's attack. For a short time, the opposing legions were where they had been just before Bowen struck. On the other side of the line, Crocker's left wing infantrymen under Samuel Holmes finally came into contact with McClernand's corps. It was a breathtaking moment, and Grant arrived north of the crossroads to witness it. The connection between McPherson and McClernand was a bit tenuous at this point, but together they formed a giant sickle ready to harvest the hollow stalks of Pemberton's wavering army. And Grant sensed it immediately:

> I saw on my left and on the next ridge a column of troops, which proved to be Carr's division, and McClernand with it in person; and to the left of Carr, Osterhaus' division soon afterward appeared, with his skirmishers well in advance. I sent word to Osterhaus that the enemy was in full retreat, and to push up with all haste. The situation was soon explained, and after which I ordered Carr to pursue with all speed to Black River, and across it if he could, and to Osterhaus to follow.

Grant now had a solid line containing portions of five divisions. Some Federal officers shouted orders for their men to stop firing at the helpless and defeated enemy, fearing the combat had degenerated into something akin to murder. Grant would have none of that. McClernand was acting on earlier orders to press home his attack, as he was now doing so well. Fresh orders were sent to continue doing so. Crocker would do the same. Logan's far right under Stevenson was already advancing, turning the enemy away from the upper crossing of Bakers Creek. As far as Grant was concerned, it was time to close the jaws of the trap. Launching a coordinated attack at this time, however, even with a single division against a beaten enemy, proved to be quite a difficult feat.[54]

John Logan agreed it was time to knock out the enemy, and was planning to make life as difficult as possible for Carter Stevenson and William Loring. The enemy pressing against the front and left of Loring's new line of battle belonged to John Stevenson's brigade. After being ordered to abandon the Jackson Road and return closer to the Champion house to oppose Bowen's threatening counterattack, Stevenson discovered his brigade was not needed as earlier believed to knock back the charging Confederates. McPherson ordered him instead to move his brigade back to my "old ground and press the enemy." When he arrived and once again severed the western leg of the Jackson Road and blocked access to the Bakers Creek crossing, Stevenson aligned his regiments and advanced cautiously through the timber, up and down through the gullies in a slow but steady move southward. De Golyer's Michigan battery had been sent to support Stevenson's efforts. The 8th Illinois led the way. Well ahead on the other side of the timber were the men Stephen Lee had gathered and deployed on Featherston's left flank.[55]

*   *   *

Lieutenant Drennan was not present to witness John Stevenson's probing thrust against the left of Loring's new divisional line. Featherston had ordered the staffer to put the ordnance train in motion for the lower crossing. Drennan found it a half-mile to the rear heading in the wrong direction, "with the sergeants all badly frightened as they had been ordered by some strolling cavalry, to burn the wagons." The lieutenant had no sooner turned the train around when General Pemberton and his escort arrived on scene.

"Where in the Hell are those wagons going?" the commanding general snapped at a very surprised Drennan.

"I have been ordered to remove them," he replied. "There is no other way to get them off the field, General. The enemy is advancing in our rear, and we can only retreat by way of the ford on Bakers Creek."[56]

To Drennan's relief, Stephen Lee arrived at that exact moment and confirmed to Pemberton what Drennan had just relayed, together with information about Loring's deteriorating position one-half mile north of where they now sat their horses. Drennan watched as Pemberton, without speaking another word, "turned his horses's head and with his staff and escort rode rapidly away in the direction he had just come."[57]

Chapter 11

Retreat

"It was my conviction at the time, confirmed by all I have learned since, that, properly
supported by General Blair's division, we could have captured the whole rebel
force opposed to us, and reached Edwards Station before sunset."

— Brig. Gen. Stephen Burbridge

GIVEN BOTH THE ROUGH MANNER IN WHICH TWO OF HIS THREE
divisions had been handled and the loss of the Jackson Road and upper
crossing over Bakers Creek, Pemberton's retreat from the Champion Hill
battlefield unfolded remarkably well. Loring's calm handling of Buford
and Featherston in the midst of a chaotic situation helped settle anxious
nerves and provide a foundation behind which the withdrawal could
proceed.

Not every aspect of the retreat was smooth, however—especially
among some of the rolling vehicles. Some of the wagons belonging to
Carter Stevenson's Division, remembered Capt. George E. Brewer of the
46th Alabama, were involved in a "stampede." Fearing capture or worse
(rumors were rampant the enemy had seized both crossings over the
creek) in the ensuing chaos, teamsters cut horses from harnesses and
artillerists spiked several guns. There was good reason for the men in the
ranks to worry, for if they were ever to reach Edwards Depot and cross
behind the Big Black River, they had to make it south to the Raymond

Road and then west across Bakers Creek from that point. Pemberton had sent Samuel Lockett and his engineers early that morning to bridge the creek at its southern crossing because the high waters prevented its fording. By 2:00 p.m., Lockett had cut the banks down and erected a workable bridge. By the time the bridge was ready to use, however, the creek had fallen sufficiently for the infantry and wagons to wade and roll across.[1]

The teamsters may have panicked during the withdrawal, but much of the infantry did not. Pemberton asked Loring to cover the retrograde movement with his division. One brigade would be left behind to hold back Federal pursuers so the rest of the army could cross over the creek. Loring gave the nod to Featherston.

Winfield Scott Featherston saw about as much combat at the head of a brigade (and occasionally in divisional command) as most generals would during the Civil War. The tall and trim native Tennessean was 42 years old during the spring of 1863. He was not a military man but an attorney and politician, and one whose states rights ardor lost him his congressional seat in 1850. When war broke out, Featherston raised a company of Mississippi infantry and was quickly elected colonel of the 17th regiment. His experience as a combat leader was wholly obtained during his tenure in Virginia, where he saw action at Blackburn's Ford, First Manassas, and Ball's Bluff, where he first gained the attention of his superiors for handling his men well under

Brigadier General
Winfield S. Featherston

*Alabama Department of
Archives and History*

fire. "Old Swet," as he was called, performed solidly during the Peninsula Campaign and Seven Days' Battles (where he was seriously wounded in the shoulder) and earned acclamation from James Longstreet for his "gallantry and skill." His star, in Virginia at least, had reached its apex. Featherston's performance at Second Manassas was so poor he did not warrant mention in Longstreet's report. Ill during much of this period, he missed the Maryland Campaign and thus the opportunity to fall back into favor with Robert E. Lee, who wanted to replace him with another officer. Featherston was enough of a politician to know his opportunities in Virginia were limited and after the battle of Fredericksburg requested service in the Gulf States. Lee promptly granted the request. Featherston assumed command of a Mississippi brigade in February 1863 and was assigned to a division led by another outcast from Virginia—William Loring. Other than the Steele's Bayou affair, Champion Hill represented Featherston's first real prospect to demonstrate his ability to his new army. Alas, his opportunities on May 16 were of small magnitude, but he intended to make the most of the few cards dealt his way.[2]

The withdrawal began with Carter Stevenson's men. "I received orders from [Pemberton] to withdraw the troops in order to Big Black Bridge," Stevenson reported. What was left of Lee's hardy brigade (and there was not much) pulled out first from the far left of Loring's line, followed by all manner of stragglers and broken units. Stevenson's survivors fell back cross country until they struck the country road Loring had taken to reach the field. Turning right, or southwest, they marched largely in silence directly for the lower crossing almost two miles distant. "General Lee was ordered to move with his brigade as rapidly as practicable to the ford on Baker's Creek, where the road from Raymond to the depot crosses it," recalled Featherston. Abraham Buford's large brigade was the next to leave. On Buford's right was Bowen's Division, which pulled out of line and retreated south along the Ratliff Road about one-half mile before turning right (southwest) toward the southern crossing on the country road behind Buford's men.[3]

By this time or shortly thereafter, John Stevenson learned the tide had turned for good. He had just sent the 8th Illinois south to press and test the left of Loring's line when a courier rode up to inform him the enemy was retiring from the field across the lower crossings of Bakers Creek. The general ordered De Golyer's battery to move with the 7th

Missouri and 81st Illinois regiments west down the Jackson Road to the upper river crossing. If Stevenson crossed over promptly, he might be able to interrupt the Southern withdrawal over the lower ford.[4]

Winfield Featherston's Confederate brigade was left largely alone on the field. Featherston recalled being "ordered soon after to place my brigade in line of battle, so as to hold the enemy in check, and to hold my position until our troops had all passed me in the direction of the depot." It was a tall order and one that in the face of an aggressive enemy could well have spelled his destruction. The native Tennessean promptly obeyed, aligning his regiments "so as to cover the different avenues of approach." Behind him on a piece of high ground were three guns from Capt. Alcide Bouanchaud's Company A, Pointe Coupee Louisiana Artillery, which "kept playing upon the enemy, who were cautiously advancing in our rear as well as on our right and left flanks," remembered Featherston, perhaps with some exaggeration. The gunners, he added, demonstrated "both skill and courage" in the face of a determined enemy, an observation utterly devoid of embellishment. The brigadier actually advanced his brigade at least once a short distance to occupy better ground before falling back while covering the army's retreat. "In our last position the enemy advanced on our rear, as well as on our right and left flanks, and a brisk skirmish ensured, in which they were held completely in check until the brigade and artillery were withdrawn slowly and in good order," he reported.[5]

Marcus Stephens of the 31st Mississippi recalled these same defensive efforts, if in more descriptive terms. The enemy "formed in the valley or hollow below us and commenced advancing when all of the cannon opened on them with grape and canister, which soon drove them back to the foot of the hill. They reformed and charged again," Stephens continued, "and again were driven back in great disorder. They failed to come again, so we cut down the gun wagons, spiked the guns, and silently moved [across] a little creek."[6]

Featherston's deft choice of positions, which were successively taken up with guns from the Pointe Coupee Artillery, parried every threat and successfully held the enemy at bay well north of the Raymond Road. Remarkably, his losses during this operation would total just a single missing soldier. Unfortunately, the same cannot be said for Bouanchaud's gallant Louisiana artillerymen. Featherston's report notwithstanding, at some point during the early stages of the withdrawal

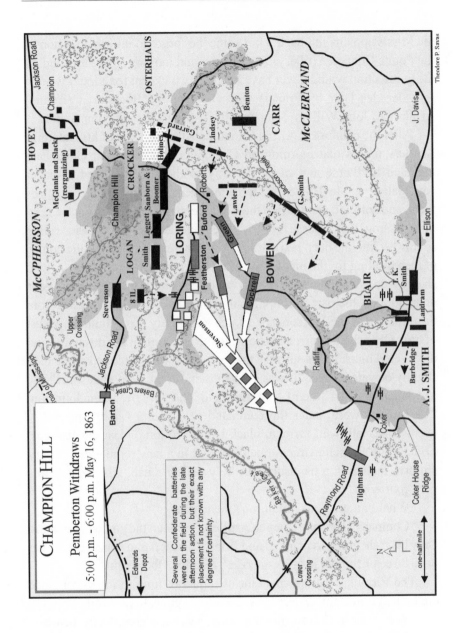

CHAMPION HILL

Pemberton Withdraws

5:00 p.m. - 6:00 p.m. May 16, 1863

Several Confederate batteries were on the field during the late afternoon action, but their exact placement is not known with any degree of certainty.

Theodore P. Savas

the Mississippians fell back—but someone forgot to inform a section of the Pointe Coupee Artillery. The blunder and moving story surrounding the gun section would never have been known except for a letter written four decades later by Francis Obenchain of the Botetourt (Virginia) Artillery to John William Johnston, the battery's former commander.[7]

After the collapse of Alfred Cumming's line and loss of his Botetourt Artillery pieces that morning on Champion Hill, Sergeant Obenchain mounted his horse and made his way to the rear, watched in eager anticipation while Bowen's Division swept forward and recaptured them, and suffered anew when the Confederates were driven back a final time, losing the pieces forever. The dejected soldier began riding southwest into the deep rear of the army, apparently following the course of men heading for the lower ford. With him rode Captain Johnston, who shared a chunk of ham with the ravished sergeant. For a reason that goes unmentioned, the pair split up. Small arms fire could still be heard from the direction of the Jackson Road when an artillery piece thundered west of him. Obenchain spurred his horse in the direction of the discharge and discovered much to his surprise that two guns were deployed alone on a slightly elevated ridge. "It was evident to me at the time, that somebody had failed to order [them] from the field," he wrote Captain Johnston. "These guns were under the command of a young Lieut., apparently twenty-one, tall, well formed, black hair worn long, clear cut features, evidently of French extraction and dressed in a new regulation artillery uniform including a handsome artillery officer's cap. His manner was very courteous."[8]

"What unit are you?" inquired Obenchain.

"Company C, Pointe Coupee Artillery," replied the young lieutenant. Only his right gun was manned and firing. "The left gun was silent. There were three or four dead at its muzzle," recalled Obenchain.[9]

The Virginia sergeant spent the next quarter-hour trying to convince the French Louisiana officer to withdraw his guns, to no avail.

"You must withdraw for the army has been completely beaten," explained Obenchain. "It is withdrawing from the field and you have no support!" The lieutenant refused. His orders were to unlimber and hold back the enemy, and that is what he was going to do.

By this time, Federals from Logan's division were approaching from the north "in plain view. The enemy's line was broken as the men were taking advantage of the gullies [for protection]," Obenchain explained to

Captain Johnston. To Obenchain's dismay, there was not a single Confederate infantryman within sight "except for the dead and wounded. I knew positively there were none of our troops anywhere near the section." Determined to save himself, Obenchain wished the lieutenant well and turned his horse's head and road west toward the creek. He realized then someone blundered, and it haunted the fellow artilleryman to his grave.[10]

After riding but a short distance, the sergeant came across the ill Abda Johnson, colonel of the 40th Georgia, Barton's Brigade. Johnson had been too ill to command his men, but had insisted on being with them for the fight. Now he was wandering in a confused state behind the lines without a clue as to where his regiment was located. Obenchain knew he was sick and inquired as to both his health and his command.

"Colonel, where is your regiment?"

Johnson pointed northwest toward some woods in the direction of the upper ford. "Over there, I believe. The 40th Georgia."

"Colonel, do you not know we have been completely defeated and are retreating off the field?" inquire Obenchain.

"No, I did not know this," was Johnson's anemic reply.

"I do not think your troops are in those woods, sir. The last men to have held them were from Stevenson's Division, and they have already fallen back." As Obenchain would later learn, what was left of the 40th Georgia was on the west side of Bakers Creek opposite the upper crossing with General Barton.[11]

Obenchain explained to Colonel Johnson the plight facing the section of guns belonging to the Pointe Coupee Artillery. "Colonel, would you please go back and order the Lieut. to leave the field." As the sergeant explained to his correspondent, the gunner would have obeyed Johnson because he was a superior officer. Whether Johnson answered directly is unclear. Obenchain merely wrote that "he showed no inclination to go to him."

Discouraged by the colonel's attitude, the sergeant advised him to leave. "You should get away from here if you don't want to be captured."

"How are you going?" asked Johnson, meaning what direction was the gunner without a command going to take.

"I am making for the bridge," he replied, pointing toward the upper crossing. If Obenchain had originally intended to cross at the lower ford, he had by this time changed his mind.

"We'll be killed sure if we go that way," answered Colonel Johnson.

Nothing more was said and the men started on their way, Obenchain disgusted at his inability to help the nameless lieutenant, and Johnson too sick and exhausted to refuse to follow what he believed a suicidal route to safety. "How we got out I don't know," Obenchain wrote to Captain Johnston in 1903. The pair made it to the creek just ahead of Stevenson's Federals and slipped up and over the crossing point. On the far side was General Barton with several hundred men from his command. Obenchain rode immediately up to Barton and explained the Louisiana artillery's predicament.

"General, if you will give me a written order, I will carry it back to the Lieut.," he said.

Barton was contemplating the request when Obenchain added a sentence he forever after regretted. "As I was heading this way I noticed the enemy is planning to plant a battery over there," he said, turning and pointing across the creek. Obenchain was referring to Captain De Golyer's Michigan guns, which he must have seen moving to unlimber (under John Stevenson's watchful eye) to knock back Barton's men and open up the crossing point.

"They will enfilade some of my brigade!" replied an excited Barton, who without another word turned his horse's head and rode off to alter the alignment of his men—the plight of the Pointe Coupee Artillery forgotten. Shortly thereafter, Barton voluntarily withdrew his men from the upper crossing.[12]

And there the story of the lieutenant and section ends, though not for Obenchain. "Several times since the war I have met men who claim to have been members of the Federal regiment that confronted the two guns and they told me they captured the guns and that the Lieut. was killed," he wrote to Captain Johnston. "Ever since the occurrence the young Lieutenant's face has haunted me, and I was distressed no little when told, in after years, his sad fate. True, I might have lost my life going back to him," he continued, "but I was not only willing but was anxious to save him and his guns. Bravery like his ought to be made known."

Obenchain implored Johnston to help him discover the identity of the lieutenant. "[I have] no other object than to let the world know something of a man who was not only brave, but maybe sacrificed his life in the performance of what he thought to be his duty. If he believed what I told him then, language cannot describe such courage—such soul," wrote Obenchain. He concluded with these words:

> As a rule, those who meet defeat do not like to talk about it, but when they know they did all that was possible for them to do, I do not understand why they should feel ashamed of defeat. There are thousands of men in our armies who proved themselves to belong to the heroic, and yet there is record in writing, of but a few of them. If for no other reason, the young Lieut. may have sisters and brothers still living and a story of his last minutes may be solacing to them. 'He was killed' is all that has been said of, alas, too many.[13]

Because of the confused (and often cursory) nature of the reports regarding this stage of the battle, exactly what happened to these guns is not known with any degree of certainty. The 8th Illinois of Stevenson's brigade was reported to have attacked about this time and in this vicinity and captured one gun and 500 prisoners (largely infantry). Whether the piece belonged to this forlorn French lieutenant history has yet to identify will probably never be known.[14]

*   *   *

A dark cloud lingered over the entire withdrawal operation. Two divisions of fresh Federal infantry under A. J. Smith and Frank Blair had been stationary much of the day on the Raymond Road opposite Pemberton's right wing. They began to awaken late that afternoon.

One mile directly west of their position was the southern crossing over Bakers Creek. It was now approaching 5:00 p.m. and Pemberton had at least seven and possibly eight of his nine brigades moving southwest on a country road for the same crossing. Only one brigade under Lloyd Tilghman was blocking the Raymond Road to keep Smith and Blair away from the lower crossing. Heavy artillery and small arms fire was now clearly audible from Tilghman's position on Coker house ridge. Was the battle creeping westward, or were the acoustics playing tricks on Southern ears? Buford and Featherston had reported threats to the rear from approaching Federals.

Was Tilghman still blocking the Raymond Road? Was the lower crossing still in friendly hands?

*   *   *

It was indeed a fortuitous meeting. The sun was past its zenith when Lloyd Tilghman and his brigade, together with two batteries of artillery, abandoned their blocking position on the Raymond Road and set out for the army's distant left flank. The extraordinary move conducted in the face of two Federal divisions was in response to an order he had received from General Pemberton to join the balance of Loring's Division, which had marched to the far left about one hour earlier. Unlike his division leader, Tilghman had moved immediately to execute Pemberton's directive. It was the right response, but his promptness brought the army within a cat's whisker of annihilation.

Lloyd Tilghman was a native Marylander and 46 years old at Champion Hill. A soldier by training, he had graduated in 1836 from West Point after a less than laudable academic performance that dropped him into the bottom quartile of his class. He resigned from the service almost immediately to become a railroad engineer, but volunteered and served well as an aide for Gen. David Twiggs during the war with

Mexico. Tilghman resigned a second time with the rank of captain and crossed back into his chosen vocation, building lines for iron horses in the South, across Panama, and in Kentucky, where he settled down in the 1850s and became active in the state's militia service.

Brigadier General
Lloyd Tilghman

National Archives

A new conflict—this time between the various states of the Union—beckoned Tilghman back into the service at the head of the 3rd Kentucky Infantry. Although he had no experience leading combat troops, he was sporting a collar with three stars enveloped by a brigadier general's wreath by the war's first autumn. When he raised noisy but accurate concerns about the appalling state of the river defenses in Tennessee, Gen. Albert S. Johnston placed Tilghman in charge of their development. It was an unfortunate choice for both men, and especially for Tilghman. Despite his ardent pleas for men and materiel, neither arrived in sufficient quantity to alter the course of events in February 1862, when U. S. Grant's combined expedition smothered Forts Henry and Donelson. Tilghman demonstrated sound judgment by sending away most of his garrison, and personal bravery by remaining behind to defend the indefensible Fort Henry. But his name is forever linked to the flooded bastion's capitulation and his captor's subsequent account of Tilghman's hand-wringing supplications that his reputation might emerge unscathed from such an embarrassing event. It would not.

Six months as a prisoner of war followed before Tilghman was exchanged. He rejoined the army in northern Mississippi, where he was given a brigade under William Loring. In early December, he assumed temporary charge of a division and acted as the army's rearguard as it fell back south. The assignment resulted in a small but sharp skirmish at Coffeeville against pursuing Federals. The next month, he was given command of William Baldwin's Brigade. Now he stood with it at Champion Hill. Tilghman was a capable engineer and a stickler for military discipline. He was also an inexperienced combat leader, and on May 16, 1863, happenstance had tossed him into an awesome position of responsibility along the Raymond Road.[15]

When Major General Loring had finally moved north in response to Pemberton's urgent pleas for assistance, he left Tilghman behind with orders to block the Raymond Road and, as Col. Arthur E. Reynolds of the 26th Mississippi Infantry later reported, "prevent a flank movement of the enemy down it on our right." He was also instructed to "hold himself in readiness to move up to the support of the other brigades of the division should it become necessary." As a precaution, Loring sent a guide to point out Tilghman's route. When the order to move arrived, Tilghman withdrew his five regiments (1st Confederate Infantry Battalion, and the 6th, 15th, 23rd, and 26th Mississippi regiments), and his 10 guns (four

Colonel
Arthur E. Reynolds

*Alabama Department of
Archives and History*

from McClendon's (Lt. J. Culbertson's) Company C, 14th Mississippi Artillery Battalion and six from Company G, 1st Mississippi Light Artillery under Capt. John J. Cowan) and moved out. The exact route he traveled is uncertain, but it was quickly "found to be impracticable for artillery." Without hesitation, Tilghman countermarched his brigade and moved west a short distance before turning north on a different country road another guide assured him "communicated with our left flank." After but a few hundred yards, a surprised General Pemberton and his escort approached from the opposite direction.

"General Tilghman, why are you moving your brigade?" inquired the army commander.

"I received an order from you to move to the left flank, General Pemberton," replied the perplexed brigadier.

"That order was countermanded almost an hour ago with instructions for you to hold your position!" shot back the commanding general. "You must move your brigade back to the Raymond Road and prevent the enemy from moving up it and seizing the crossing over Bakers Creek!"

Earlier, Stephen Lee had ridden upon a similar scene and rescued Lieutenant Drennan from a tongue-lashing by Pemberton. Now, to Tilghman's relief, the army's chief engineer reined in his horse and saluted the generals. Samuel Lockett carried with him the order rescinding Tilghman's move to the far left. "I'm sorry, general," Lockett apologized to both men. "My horse broke down and I was unable to obtain another until a short time ago." Tilghman had never seen the order rescinding the move.[16]

Luckily, Tilghman's 1,500 men had only moved a short distance. The Marylander countermarched again and threw a new line across the Raymond Road several hundred yards behind the Coker house ridge and well west of its intersection with the Ratliff Road. Within a few minutes he had a strong line studded with artillery pieces. This line, however, like so many others formed that day, was missing almost half a regiment. Earlier in the day, before Tilghman had slid north to cover the Raymond Road when Loring marched for the left flank, he had spotted the enemy moving a line of battle out of the woods around the Ellison house. Colonel Robert Lowry of the 6th Mississippi, trailing at the end of Tilghman's column, was thrown forward with half his regiment to form a heavy skirmish line and shield the movement. The 23rd Wisconsin's Griffin Jones watched the Mississippians fan out and move east. "These rebs," he would later write, "came forward with their sleeves rolled up like butchers." Lowry's involvement sucked him into a sharp action. Like Alfred Cumming's skirmishers, Lowry was unable to easily detach his five companies when Tilghman mistakenly marched the brigade toward the left. Lowry did his best to keep up, sidling north under fire. Unbeknownst to the colonel, however, Tilghman met up with Pemberton, countermarched, and redeployed astride the Raymond Road. Lowry, meanwhile, marched all the way up the Ratliff Road, moved cross-country, and finally fell in with the left wing of the army. As Tilghman formed for battle, Lowry was moving his Mississippians southwest with the detritus of Stevenson's and Bowen's divisions, shuffling along the small country road heading southwest for the Bakers Creek crossing.[17]

* * *

While Tilghman was moving hither and yon in an effort to follow orders, Brig. Gen. Stephen Burbridge was chomping at the bit placed in his mouth, much as a race horse stamps its hooves while penned inside the starting gate. Holding the reins of the pompous hero of Arkansas Post was A. J. Smith, and Burbridge could do little other than wait for the order to move forward. The heavy battle raging for several hours to the north was audible to every man on the Raymond Road (Frank Blair remembered it as "a severe engagement"), but the hot Mississippi day along the Raymond Road was broken only by skirmish and artillery fire.[18]

The early morning had begun with great promise when Smith's division discovered Confederate skirmishers as far east as the Davis farm. Burbridge's quickly-formed line of battle had moved them back westward. Six 10-pound Parrott rifles belonging to Capt. Ambrose A. Blount's 17th Independent Battery, Ohio Light Artillery, assisted in speeding them on their way. When the young Kentucky general saw a heavy body of enemy retreating in the distance, his elation turned to apprehension that "they might avail themselves of some prominent hills, from which they could sweep the plain we were in." He pushed briskly forward and within a few minutes, the opposing skirmishers fanned out to begin their individual death duels. "As we rose to the crest of the hill [I] had abundant reason to congratulate myself upon my speed," bragged Burbridge, "as the enemy had rallied and planted their battery on the second hill, not having had time to form on the first." Burbridge was watching William Loring deploy his three brigades on the Coker house ridge position. The heavy pattering of small arms fire and roaring Rebel artillery pieces gave him pause, and he pulled back behind the gentle ridge and called for reinforcements to attack the enemy before him. What Burbridge did not know was that other than a sharp artillery duel, nothing of substance would occur along the Raymond Road for some six hours.[19]

It was not for a want of effort. Burbridge sent "repeated application[s] to General Smith for re-enforcements, both of infantry and artillery." What he did not know was Smith and Blair were under orders from McClernand to not bring on a general engagement until further orders arrived. The three arms of Grant's army were stepping carefully forward along three separate and widely-separated roads seeking out Pemberton's divisions. Only Smith's southern wing had made full contact. In an effort to bolster his front and make a strong showing, Smith eventually sent Burbridge the 19th Kentucky and 77th Illinois from Col. William Jennings Landram's trailing brigade. These regiments, Burbridge recalled, "were ready and impatiently awaiting orders to move forward." Private Merrick J. Wald, Company C, 77th Illinois, wrote in his diary that his regiment was "called up this morning at 3:00 a.m. and started before the sun was up. [We] went eight miles then the fighting

Colonel
William Landram

National Archives

commenced, run us from one hill to another until I was pretty near gone up the spout." A section of 3-inch ordnance rifles, under the capable leadership of Capt. Patrick H. White of the Chicago Mercantile Battery, was unlimbered north of the road, as were the additional Ohio pieces, all of which opened with shell on the strong Confederate position on Coker house ridge. Burbridge, however, was an infantry commander and not an artilleryman. He wanted to engage his foot soldiers, and what he believed was a good opportunity to do so was slipping away. "It was my conviction at the time, confirmed by all I have learned since," he later penned in his report, "that, properly supported by General Blair's division, we could have captured the whole rebel force opposed to us, and reached Edwards Station before sunset." Such, however, was not to be.[20]

Well before noon, the strains of the battle raging around Champion Hill far to the north reached the ears of those waiting for orders on the Raymond Road. So little small arms fighting took place there that one private's diary reflects the fact that he believed Smith's division was held in reserve. The artillery duel, however, broke the monotony for the men and thrilled many onlookers. The noisy, colorful, but largely innocuous exchange of metal "beat anything I ever saw," remembered Cpl. Carlos W. Colby of Company G, 97th Illinois, part of Landram's brigade. Captain White of the Chicago Mercantile Battery was more personally involved in the duel than was Corporal Colby. It was "one of the hottest artillery fights I was ever in," recalled the captain. "I was deaf and dazed from the bursting shells; I could hardly hear myself give an order and one of my ears bled." The artilleryman used "alternatively shell and canister, in order to disable them by killing their horses."

The Confederates did the same thing, of course, and one of their shell fragments crushed the skull of Sgt. Ernest Warden, Company F, 83rd Ohio (Burbridge's brigade). Warden, reported Col. Frederick W. Moore, "was a brave, intelligent, and faithful soldier . . . whose loss is much to be deplored." Another enemy artillery round "came very near killing [Lt. Col. [Lysander] Webb," wrote Merrick Wald of the 77th Illinois. "Liet. Of Co K was [also] wounded this evening." Private Henry N. Faulkenberry of Company D, 31st Mississippi, wrote in his journal that the "artillery was very heavy, the muskets a constant volley." Faulkenberry would soon be transferred to the division's wagon train, which would carry him behind the Big Black and into the Vicksburg fortifications. His superior, Lt. Col. Marcus Stephens, remembered the low intensity but constant fighting as Smith's division poked and prodded against the Coker house line. "We were threatened in our front all day, the enemy shot . . . shell into our line all the time but we were held in reserve and directed to hold our position in front of the enemy," explained Stephens. "We were from time to time changing our position to confront the threatened advance." Frustrated by remaining quiescent under this fire, Burbridge had "drawn up in line of battle to charge on a battery," wrote Wald, "but they were thought to be too many for us."[21]

It was not until Loring's languid move north with two of his three brigades in the middle of the afternoon, followed a short time later by Lloyd Tilghman's interrupted march north to join him, that A. J. Smith gave the nod to Burbridge to brush aside Colonel Lowry's 6th Mississippi skirmishers and occupy the abandoned Coker house position. By the time Burbridge reached the ridge and deployed his brigade and two batteries of artillery, complete with skirmishers well to the front, Tilghman was back in position blocking the Raymond Road about 350 yards west of the ridge. From this new position Burbridge continued his hours-long duel with the Confederates. As the guns re-opened, Sgt. Thomas B. Marshall of Company K, 83rd Ohio Infantry, seized an opportunity to examine the Coker house. "One cannon shot went straight through the house," he wrote long after the war in his regiment's official history. "In the room nearest the battery was a piano, standing diagonally across the room, with the corner just in the right place in the path of the ball. Of course, it was knocked off, but the tones were all left. . . .

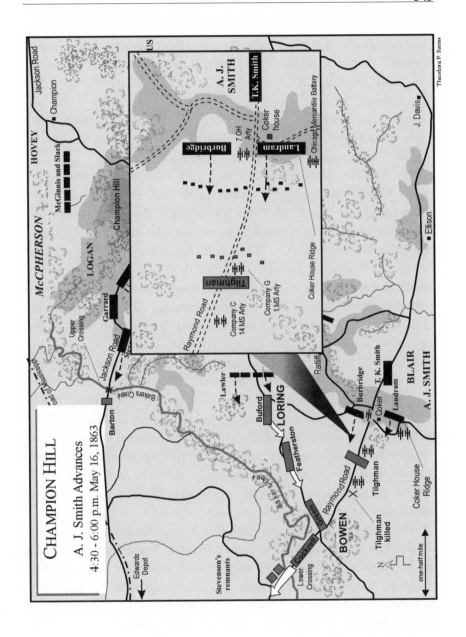

CHAMPION HILL

A. J. Smith Advances

4:30 - 6:00 p.m. May 16, 1863

Theodore P. Savas

Sergeant [David B.] Snow took the occasion to try the piano, and it furnished very good music as his fingers flew over the keys." The result was most incongruous. Skirmish fire cracked in the distance and deep-throated artillery pieces roared and smoked nearby while soft melodies from a damaged piano in an abandoned home in the middle of a battle drifted through walls punctured by shell fire. It is not known whether the impatient Burbridge heard the music.[22]

By 3:00 p.m. (and perhaps earlier), Col. Giles A. Smith's brigade, Frank Blair's division, had moved north and connected with the outstretched left flank of Peter Osterhaus's division, which was advancing toward the crossroads in the Middle Road sector. Blair's remaining brigade under Col. Thomas K. Smith remained in support of A. J. Smith's division. Finally, a solid (if thin) contact had been firmly established with Smith on the Raymond Road. Grant's line was now a giant crescent stretching from the upper crossing of Bakers Creek east past the crossroads, and then south just beyond the Ratliff Road all the way down to the Coker house ridge position. McClernand was doing what he could to move the two divisions with him forward and probably assumed Smith was aggressively doing the same. He was not.

The corps leader had earlier sent a message to Smith ordering him to "attack the enemy vigorously, and press for victory." Messages were routinely exchanged all morning and afternoon between the Middle and Raymond roads. It is possible Smith did not receive this particular order. If he did, he did not obey it as heartily as he should have. Heavy knots of Federal skirmishers were slipping aggressively forward and had moved deep into the Confederate rear, as had Company C of the 4th Indiana Cavalry, which was even now exploring behind the Confederate front. What Smith seems not to have known was that Pemberton's army was leaving the field, flooding its way toward the lower Bakers Creek crossing. Neither did he realize the heavy division he had been exchanging lead and iron with for much of the day now consisted only of Lloyd Tilghman's lone brigade, which had hurried back in position to block Smith's advance.[23]

* * *

Lieutenant Drennan was not as thrilled about the Federal shell fire as Corporal Colby of the 97th Illinois. After his run-in and dressing down by General Pemberton, Drennan had "urged the wagons on," and within a short time was near (and just north of) the Raymond Road on a country path unmarked on any map. He was unaware the Coker house ridge had been abandoned and that the enemy now occupied it. As the surprised officer wrote his wife, "I found that I would be between the fire of our own and the Enemy's guns, so I made a detour to the right—and by dint of careful driving and making a hundred men throw rails for a quarter of an hour in an ugly slough, I succeeded in reaching the road to Edwards, as the shot and shell of the enemy came rattling down it."[24]

While Drennan was building his own corduroy road to save the division's ordnance wagons, Buford's Brigade, followed by the slower moving rear guard under Featherston, arrived in the vicinity of Tilghman's left flank. According to Col. Arthur Reynolds, who filed the report for Tilghman's Brigade at Champion Hill, Loring "formed them immediately on the left," though other reports do not specifically mention this deployment. What is certain is that their withdrawal from the left wing had been thus far successful, but it had not been easy, and the brunt of the stress had fallen upon Scott's 12th Louisiana.[25]

After rejoining the brigade, Buford allowed Scott's Louisianans a rest of "some fifteen or twenty minutes," after which Scott led Buford's column, with flankers deployed, on its southwesterly journey toward Bakers Creek. The colonel remembered marching about three-quarters of a mile when fighting broke out in the rear. Buford, who was riding close to Scott, ordered him "to form a line at right angles to the road." The position was "excellent," recalled Scott, and as his men deployed, the balance of the brigade "retired to the rear of my line." Two guns from the Pointe Coupee Artillery dropped their carriages to strengthen the line. The tail of Buford's column hurried through the gathering infantry, "hotly pressed by a force of the enemy's cavalry, preceded by dismounted skirmishers." Ever resourceful, Scott concealed his men behind a crest of a hill "and allowed them to come within range, when I fired by rank upon them with great effect, causing them to retire precipitately." Private J. V. Greif of the 3rd Kentucky Mounted Infantry confirmed the episode after the war: "The enemy swept around a point of woods, in close range, [and] these Louisianans raised up and gave them a volley which settled the matter." Loring praised Scott's actions throughout the afternoon fighting, correctly branding him both "able and daring." Buford also recorded the event, noting, "The enemy charged

Major General
Frank P. Blair

National Archives

forward, but were met by the fire of the Twelfth Louisiana and the artillery, which effectually checked the ardor of his pursuit, and caused him to follow our immediate rear with great caution."[26]

In addition to the Federal cavalry and infantry pressing toward Buford's right rear, strong bodies of infantry were now filtering across the Ratliff Road from the east, including Michael Lawler's brigade from Carr's division and, farther south, Giles Smith's brigade from Blair's division. General Blair watched the drama unfold from high ground running north along the Ratliff Road. He could make out bits and pieces of Loring's distant withdrawal. "A portion of his flying columns endeavored to make good their retreat by crossing my front and that of General A. J. Smith," reported Blair, "the rear guard making a stand at different points to check our advance and enable the main body to escape with the artillery, ammunition, and baggage." Giles Smith's brigade "moved rapidly in line of battle," continued Blair, "driving the enemy's skirmishers through the thick forests and over very broken and difficult ground."[27]

General Lawler remembered ordering up the redoubtable Peoria Battery—Company A, 2nd Illinois Light Artillery—a second time to drive back the stubborn rear guard. Lieutenant John Yoist and his fellow gunners with the Pointe Coupee Artillery won rave reviews for their work, but the pressure from the advancing Federal infantry and deadly accurate counter-battery fire quickly took its toll. The long-arm Illini, wrote Lawler, opened a fire on the Louisiana artillery that "was so accurate and severe that it silenced them, killing the horses of one piece, and as our advance was close upon them, they were compelled to abandon it." Giles Smith, meanwhile, sent two companies of the 8th Missouri Infantry, under the command of Maj. Dennis T. Kirby, "to make a detour to the left and endeavor to flank the enemy's battery." The movement, lamented Blair, "was soon discovered." Scott pulled his 12th Louisiana out of line and retired, as did Yoist's section of artillery. In their wake were several abandoned caissons, wagons of ammunition, and at least one gun. As luck would have it, the 8th Illinois from Stevenson's brigade was driving south and arrived just in time to capture the abandoned piece.[28]

Once his brigades reached the Raymond Road, Loring informed Tilghman the army was in full retreat to the Big Black, and that Pemberton "had directed him to maintain his position at all hazards until sundown." The artillery and small arms firing at this time, remembered Colonel Reynolds of the 26th Mississippi, was "continuous [and] kept up until dusk." Loring agreed. Tilghman, he reported, "was carrying on a deadly and most gallant fight. With less than 1,500 effectives he was attacked by from 6,000 to 8,000 of the enemy with a fine park of artillery; but being advantageously posted, he not only held him in check, but repulsed him on several occasions, and thus kept open the only line of retreat left to the army." Loring's portrayal of the intensity of Smith's "attack" was exaggerated—the losses for Smith's entire division were only 22 wounded men—but the "fine park of artillery" description was right on the money, as the unfortunate Tilghman was about to discover.[29]

The ubiquitous Lieutenant Drennan saw and heard many things during the battle of Champion Hill, but one event in particular remained with him for the rest of his life. After figuring out he had led the ammunition trains between the opposing lines, Drennan turned southwest and eventually struck the Raymond Road. He was galloping forward to check what was in his front, he explained to his wife,

> when I saw four men with a litter, bearing off the body of Gen'l Tilghman—who was mortally wounded and died in ten minutes. The shell that killed him must have passed over the road for three hundred yards and it was full of men, wagons, artillery, and everything—and still did not explode until near him. Poor Tilghman—three hours before I had sat and listend to him talking

and jesting, full of life an gaiety—and then 'he was gone to that course from whence no traveler returns.'

As Drennan learned from the litter bearers, the general had been "shot in the upper part of the stomach with a small piece of a shell, while sighting a piece of McLendin's [Capt. J. M. McLendon] Battery." The shot probably originated from one of the Chicago Mercantile Battery tubes.[30]

Colonel Reynolds, upon whose shoulders command of the brigade fell because of his senior colonel status, recalled the demise of Tilghman in his report, noting the time as 5:20 p.m. "At the time he was struck down he was standing in the rear of a battery, directing a change in the elevation of one of the guns." Reynolds continued:

> I cannot here refrain from paying a slight tribute to the memory of my late commander. As a man, a soldier, and a general, he had few if any superiors. Always at his post, he devoted himself day and night to the interests of his command. Upon the battle-field cool, collected, and observant, he commanded the entire respect and confidence of every officer and soldier under him, and the only censure ever cast upon him was that he always exposed himself too recklessly.[31]

Loring was a friend of Tilghman's and lamented his passing in his official report of the battle. After noting his combat acumen, Loring wrote, "The bold stand of this brigade under the lamented hero saved a large portion of the army." Loring had many faults and shaved the truth on several occasions, but his assessment of Tilghman's courageous stand on the Raymond Road was precisely correct.[32]

Lieutenant F. W. Merrin was a member of McClendon's 14th Mississippi Artillery Battalion (Lt. J. Culbertson commanding). Many years after the battle, Merrin wrote a detailed account of Tilghman's final minutes for *Confederate Veteran* magazine. As he recalled it, the Federal skirmishers had taken up residence in a series of "plantation cabins" and were "picking our men off rapidly." Tilghman, who was watching the battle near McClendon's guns, "dismounted from his horse and gave some directions about sighting the gun. While this was being done a shell from one of the enemys guns on the line exploded about fifty feet to the front. A ragged fragment of this shell struck the General in the breast, passing entirely through him and killing the horse of his Adjutant a little farther to the rear. His death occurred, of course, very soon, and his remains were carried to the rear." The general's body was transported to the Yeiser house, situated south of the Raymond Road between two Magnolia trees near the lower crossing on Bakers Creek. Surgeons there pronounced Tilghman dead on arrival. "That night [the corpse] was started to Vicksburg, accompanied by his personal staff and his son, Lloyd Tilghman, Jr.," continued Merrin, "and the next evening they were buried in the city cemetery in Vicksburg."[33]

Reynolds assumed command after Tilghman's death. To his dismay, he discovered his batteries were scraping the bottom of their ammunition chests. They would have to withdraw within a few minutes. Lieutenant Drennan also made a disturbing discovery. After viewing Tilghman's corpse, he rode west and crossed Bakers Creek. He finally felt safe—"as far as pursuit of the Enemy was concerned"—but the day's events suddenly sunk in. "Now, for the first, time," he told his wife, "I could realize a battle had been fought and that we have been sadly defeated." It was as if blinders had been lifted from his observant, but not fully comprehending, eyes. "When I saw scores and hundreds of men coming wildly along with no regard to order, with Artillery men who had lost their guns, riding frantically along, Officers without commands vainly inquiring where such and such a regiment was—men without hats or guns rushing at full speed—poor wounded men hobbling along, and asking for a surgeon—teamsters shouting and swearing at their mules, with the distant roar of an occasional shot from the battery on the hill—all made it look like what I have read of Bull-run and thought of a rapid retreat."[34]

Once on the western side of the stream, Drennan watched in admiration as John Bowen "endeavored to rally the Army as it came along." The staff officer might have gone back east of the creek in search of the division and escaped the hardships of the forthcoming siege at Vicksburg had not Pemberton's chief of ordnance ordered him to ride with the trains across the Big Black River. "It was slow progress until we arrived at the Big Black—as it was covered with Artillery, the trains of the Army—straggling and wounded men—and every conceivable conveyance with women and children fleeing their homes and abandoning them to the Yankees," remembered the lieutenant. Drennan did not cross the river until an hour before midnight. When he finally bedded down for the night, he could not sleep because his friends had gone missing. "My system was greatly fatigued, but such was my anxiety for the command—and intense desire to know what had become of it, that I could not sleep," he confided to his wife. "After nature was exhausted, and I was overcome," he continued, "I had frightful dreams caused by what I had seen during the day. God grant that I may never be so situated, to see what I saw that day. Such sights harden the soul to think of, and it is painful to recollect anything of them."[35]

Many of the troops Bowen tried to rally without success belonged to Carter Stevenson's Division, which was by this time a division in name only. The head of the retreating Confederate column was well over the creek and had either reached Edwards or soon would. Pemberton fully appreciated the importance of holding both the upper and lower crossing points. He had ridden across the stream with Bowen and ordered that general to deploy his two brigades and hold the crossing open for Loring's Division. Who was available to secure the upper crossing? Alfred Cumming's Georgians traversed the bridge and ford not as a brigade but as a horde. "The brigade was indeed badly shaken on that disastrous day," he would write Lee just a few weeks before the turn of the next century. Pemberton later used the collapse of the Georgians to help explain the devastating May 16 loss. Those of Barton's regiments that used the lower ford could be described with similar adjectives. Cumming, together with a few staff officers and artillerists, crossed the creek between the bridges and made for the Big Black. Order amongst these Georgians was not restored until they reached Edwards. Many did not rejoin the ranks until well on the way to Vicksburg. "A large number of men had shamefully abandoned their commands," scolded Pemberton, "and were making their way to the rear."[36]

Only Stephen Lee's hard-hit command of Stevenson's Division retained some semblance of order—a testament to Lee's character and leadership abilities. Pemberton ordered Lee to march his men cross-country to support Adams's cavalry, which Pemberton supposed were watching the upper bridge. Lee did as he was ordered, but when he found "the enemy already held the bridge with a large force," he wisely moved by the left flank toward the Big Black Bridge, which he reached about 10:00 p.m. that evening. Satisfied Bowen had the situation well in hand at the lower crossing, Pemberton, meanwhile, rode for the Big

Black Bridge to oversee the important crossing operation that was about to commence there.[37]

Lee was probably not too surprised to discover a large force of Federals on the western side of the stream. After all, he had been fighting along the Jackson Road all day and knew that important logistical artery had been in Federal hands for many hours. However, the ease with which the enemy managed to cross was because of a mistake committed by Seth Barton.

The upper and lower crossings on Bakers Creek were held, respectively, by remnants of Seth Barton's command and John Bowen's brigades. If the upper crossing point was captured by the Federals, Grant would be able to flank the lower crossing and sever Pemberton's direct route to Edwards and the Big Black River bridge crossing. Barton may not have fully realized this—although he should have. Once his brigade

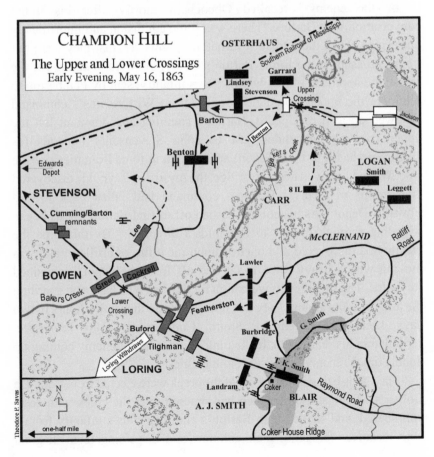

was broken up and routed early that afternoon, Barton crossed the creek on the upper span with a portion of his command and sent a dispatch to Col. Alexander W. Reynolds, the same man who had hours earlier overseen the removal of the army's wagon train to Edwards. Alerting him of the disaster, Barton urged him to send the large wagon train on the far side of the Big Black and reinforce him as soon as possible. "I immediately put the train in motion, leaving two regiments and a section of artillery to protect it, and moved rapidly with the remainder of my force to the support of General Barton," reported Reynolds. It looked as though Barton was going to vigorously defend the upper crossing.[38]

Late that afternoon artillerist Sgt. Francis Obenchain—the same sergeant who was so concerned with saving the section of Pointe Coupee guns—crossed the bridge and met up with Barton. "Some troops were seen marching from the woods some distance south of us, which all took to be the enemy," recalled Obenchain shortly after his initial conversation with Barton. "There was some confusion and immediately our troops began the retreat. It turned out, however, that they were our troops crossing at the ford." Barton's Georgians were breaking for the rear at the approach of Stephen D. Lee's infantry, sent by Pemberton to reinforce the upper crossing. Troopers from Wirt Adams's command followed up as a rear guard. Barton's stunning abandonment left the upper crossing unattended just as John Stevenson's Federals (as Obenchain had informed Barton) approached in force from the opposite side. When he arrived near the bridge, the mystified Reynolds discovered "the troops of General Barton's command had fallen back toward Edwards Depot." As his courier dashed off to find Barton, shells began whistling through the air in Reynolds's direction. "By this time the enemy had discovered and opened upon me a fire of artillery, and was moving with a heavy force to cut me off from the depot," explained Reynolds. The stress levels were high for the men who had been guarding the army's 400 wagons. They had not slept more than a few hours in two days. Lieutenant Calvin M. Smith, Company D, 31st Tennessee, scribbled in his diary as he looked into the distance: "enemy coming up double quick, enemy before us, double quick. . ."[39]

The shells being lobbed west of the creek were ejected from Capt. De Golyer's Michigan guns, which had crossed over the creek with ease, unlimbered, and shelled both Barton's and Reynolds's infantry from a long distance, "breaking their columns and dispersing them in great disorder through the woods," remembered Brig. Gen. John Stevenson. With them were the 7th Missouri and 81st Illinois. Grant was now west of Bakers Creek in strength. John Logan lauded his brigadier's efforts, noting that he advanced his men "at the double-quick on the main road leading to the Big Black River." The pursuit covered two miles and spread "great consternation in his ranks," wrote the pleased Logan.[40]

The quick-thinking Reynolds, meanwhile, grasped the significance of the passage of the creek and realized his entire force was in danger of being cut off and captured. The enemy, he reported, was "moving with a heavy force to cut me off from the depot. . . . The enemy (about one division) had already crossed the bridge and had gained a point nearer the depot than my troops had succeeded in reaching. My safety now depended in out-maneuvering him." With that, Reynolds's Tennesseans began what had to be one of the most unusual marches of war:

> I marched in parallel lines with him for at least half of a mile. Taking advantage of a dense wood, I changed my direction to the right, and by a rapid movement joined the other troops of my command, and made for Bridge-port—a point on the Big Black 1½ miles above the bridge—where our main army had crossed. At Bridgeport I found a light pontoon bridge, over which I passed two regiments and one piece of artillery. In attempting to throw over a caisson, the bridge gave way, carrying down the caisson. I extricated myself from this dilemma by cutting out one of the boats forming the bridge, and by it I crossed my entire command by 3 o'clock on the morning of the 17th.[41]

The rapid approach of nightfall ended John Stevenson's pursuit of Reynolds, with the advance elements of Logan's division within three miles of the Big Black.[42]

Reynolds's ordeal in crossing the river on the Bridgeport pontoon bridge included a sharp rear guard action. The Tennesseans were in the act of crossing when Col. Clark Wright of the 6th Missouri (U.S.) Cavalry appeared out of the morning darkness. Clark exaggerated the episode by claiming he attacked Reynolds and "his lines broke and he fled precipitately toward this place [Bridgeport], when I came up and fought him three hours. . ." Reynolds did not report a single man killed or wounded, so the engagement could not have been as dramatic as Wright recorded. However, he did claim to have rounded up "some 160 prisoners, two wagons and teams with provisions," which coincides with Reynolds's official tabulation of 143 men "missing." Undoubtedly the bulk of these men were broken stragglers, picked up along the road after their exhausting ordeal.[43]

At the same time Stevenson was moving west and north after Reynolds, John McClernand was riding with Eugene Carr's fresh division west down the Jackson Road and over Bakers Creek. McClernand was rubbing his hands in anticipation of making up for lost time, and a good opportunity had presented itself for doing just that. The general ordered Brig. Gen. William P. Benton's brigade to march south. With any luck, he would disrupt or even cut off the Confederate withdrawal across the lower ford. Osterhaus's brigades, trailing behind Benton, were ordered by McClernand to bear down on Edwards.[44]

* * *

As Stephen Lee had learned soon after crossing Bakers Creek, "General Loring had not followed my brigade, but had halted on the opposite side." The gallant brigadier would not learn until much later that Loring would never cross over to the western side of the stream.

With the sun dropping low on the western horizon, Loring knew he could not hold out much longer east of the stream. Federals were pressing down from the north and against his front from the east. Loring had earlier sent two couriers to find Pemberton and inquire how the retreat was progressing, but they were unable to locate the commanding general. One of the staff officers returned from the far side of the creek, however, bearing a message from General Bowen, whose men were holding the ford on Pemberton's orders so that Loring could safely cross. "For God's sake, hold your position until sundown and save the army," was Bowen's message to Loring as elements of Stevenson's Division were still crossing. Bowen also told the courier Loring should not worry because he could hold the crossing point, which was Loring's only viable exit from the field to Edwards Depot.[45]

And then matters took a significant turn for the worse. Within minutes of learning the bridge crossing was in Bowen's safe hands, a written message from that general reached Loring: the enemy had crossed the upper bridge and had outflanked Bowen, who had fallen back toward the Big Black Bridge. The note ended with these ominous words: "Do your best to save your division."

Bowen's tenure as protector of the lower crossing had been cut short by the appearance of William Benton's brigade of McClernand's corps. Francis Cockrell memorialized the moment in his report: "While delaying here, the enemy, having crossed the creek above us, advanced and placed a battery in position to command the road from this crossing to Edwards Depot, and immediately a brisk fire was opened from this battery." The six Federal guns belonged to Capt. Martin Klauss and his 1st Battery, Indiana Light Artillery. Thankfully they were overshooting their targets in the growing darkness. The situation at the lower bridge grew even more confusing when Cockrell heard men shouting at the crossing, ordering the men to turn around and countermarch east. Spurring his horse to the stream, he found Carter Stevenson and his staff, together with Colonel Scott's 12th Louisiana, turning about in the belief the Federals had cut the road ahead of them. The towering Missourian assured them such was not the case, but that they were threatening from the north and thus had better be quick about crossing.[46]

Once the Louisianans had passed by, Cockrell rode to the crossing and peered through the gathering shadows of the early evening. "No other troops were coming to cross (not even stragglers)," he recalled. Where was Loring? With the enemy slipping down against his vulnerable left and moving to cut him off, "and believing that the enemy probably [already] occupied the road to Edward's Depot," Cockrell moved west overland, keeping the road on his right. My men, he explained, marched "under cover of darkness through plantations [and] along and across ravines." Martin Green's men followed suit, even though replenished with ammunition. They were exhausted and had had enough fight for one day. Their long and bloody travail ended about midnight, when the straggling division reached the Big Black River.[47]

Bowen's withdrawal left Loring to his own devices. "We at once made a movement toward the ford, there being no other road of retreat," he formally reported more than two months later. The only guide Loring knew of had accompanied General Pemberton "to direct him to Big Black Bridge." With his limited options narrowing rapidly, Loring determined to withdraw and force his way, if necessary, across Bakers Creek. With Featherston and Buford trailing behind him, Loring ordered Reynolds to withdraw Tilghman's Brigade from its blocking position on the

Raymond Road. Kentucky Pvt. J. V. Greif remembers "putting fifty rounds of cartridges in our haversacks from an abandoned ordnance wagon" before marching to support the withdrawal. While Reynolds pulled the regiments west, others prepared to make the withdrawal. "I mounted all the wounded of our Reg't. that I could on artillery horses and we were soon ordered to move forward and follow the moving columns, and not to speak a word above a whisper," recalled Lieutenant Colonel Stephens of the 31st Mississippi. The division would make for the creek. Darkness was arriving when the one-armed division leader reached the crossing well ahead of his shuffling column. Two important facts were discerned by his reconnaissance: no organized body of Southern troops held the ford, and heavy concentrations of enemy troops "occupied the commanding ridge across the creek, his artillery playing upon the crossing." The realization that he was now boxed in on three sides must have been a most unsettling discovery.[48]

Salvation appeared in the form of Dr. W. B. Williamson, located by Buford and described by Loring as "a highly respectable gentleman of Edwards Depot, who said he knew the whole country, and thought he could take me to a ford on Baker's Creek, 3 or 4 miles below." From that point, explained the doctor, Loring could march cross country and reach either Edwards or the Big Black River. Low on viable options, he snapped up the idea. Buford sent a courier over the creek to locate and bring back Scott's 12th Louisiana. Scott hustled his men back from nearly one mile west of the creek while enemy "skirmishers commenced firing" upon his rear and artillery shells rained down through the early evening darkness. "My regiment was the last command to cross Baker's Creek," he wrote in his report, "and no other could have crossed without heavy fighting under disadvantages." The dismounted Missourians of the 3rd Cavalry, separated from Bowen's command, also slipped back east of the stream to augment Loring's caravan.[49]

And so began Loring's controversial journey. The difficult affair was conducted in pitch darkness, thousands of men stumbling through the muddy bottomland and cursing at their bad luck as they moved toward the creek. "By a well-concerted movement we eluded the enemy upon three sides," boasted Loring, "and to his astonishment made our flank march from between his forces [Smith to the east and north, McClernand to the north and on the far side of the creek] across the fields to a given point in the woods skirting Baker's Creek." The night was too dark and trail to poor, however, to hug the creek and move far south. At Dr. Williamson's suggestion, the column was reversed and moved east to reach another road. The Confederates were now moving *toward* A. J. Smith's and Frank Blair's divisions, "upon the ground where the battle was fought," wrote Loring. "It became necessary to move with great caution," remembered Buford, and only over neighborhood roads and paths long unused."

Men stumbled their way through fields to reach the ill-kept plantation roads, which were little more than hardscrabble, mud-covered footpaths running south off the Raymond Road perhaps 1,000 yards east of the stream. It was indeed a bold maneuver, and one the plucky Loring somehow managed to pull off. His Rebels trod within a few hundred yards of thousands of Smith's camping Federals. Loring remembered seeing their campfires, "and at times our small parties were near enough to hear them." Marcus Stephens remembered the same thing. "We moved silently on, pressing through the lines of the enemy, who were all busy building fires to cook supper," he wrote. "They would ask whose command, but not a word was said by us." A terrible scare coursed through the Mississippians when a "loud clear shot put us all on lookout," continued Stephens. "A poor soldier had fallen down in a rocky branch and his gun fired. All was silent again and we moved on through the Camp of the enemy . . . who all seemed cheerful and happy." Another Confederate remembered marching "all night [and] passing by and even through some Federal bivouacs without molestation." Some sleepy Union soldiers asked their identity, whereupon a wily man in the ranks would answer, "ours," "go to Sheol," or "99th Rhode Island." Keeping cool and having the courage and strength to continue, wrote an Alabama private, was attributable to sheer "grit."[50]

As Stephens's recollection makes clear, infantry could barely navigate the trails; artillery—as the men quickly discovered—absolutely could not. "The unused plantation roads upon which we moved were in such bad condition as to render it impossible to carry our artillery over them," explained Loring, "and we were obliged to destroy that which we had with our commands, bringing the horses and harness with us, the balance having gone with the army into Vicksburg." We tried "all possible means of saving them, which the retreat, nature of the ground, and presence of the enemy permitted," explained Buford. A dozen guns and seven wagonloads of artillery and small arms ammunition—perhaps the same wagons Lieutenant Drennan had guided so carefully throughout much of the day—were destroyed, "rendering them useless to the enemy." Blair's Federals would discover them the following morning. The difficult but thus far successful escape took a turn for the worse when the head of the column reached a lower ford opposite Mount Moriah. The northwest horizon was lit up as if the sun was about to rise in that unexpected quadrant of the sky: Edwards Depot was burning.[51]

Loring decided to continue on to Whitaker Ford on Fourteenmile Creek. He had been told it was just a few miles ahead. Once there, he would locate a road leading to the bridge over the Big Black River. The journey proved closer to ten or more miles and at midnight he called a halt. Doctor Williamson was not familiar with this part of the county, but introduced Loring to a local planter named Andrew J. Vaughn, who was better informed about the lay of the land. Vaughn, however, proved to be no help at all. "He declared that it was impossible," reported Loring, "as all the lower fords over Baker's Creek were swimming, and that to Big Black Bridge he could not take us without moving through the enemy's lines at Edwards Depot. He also informed us that a large force of the enemy had that day passed by his house."

"Our men were somewhat demoralized," admitted Buford, "our artillery abandoned, the troops intensely fatigued, we had but a few rounds of ammunition, the great part of which would be ruined by swimming the river, as we had no means to build a bridge or boat." Under these terrible conditions, Loring and his subordinates huddled to discuss the deteriorating situation. Loring summed up the meeting in his report:

> It was known that the enemy had troops at all ferries over Big Black below the mouth of Baker's Creek, and that the river was a deep and difficult stream to cross. The condition of the command was also taken into consideration, being without artillery, with but few rounds of cartridges; having no implements for immediate construction of a bridge or ferry; our entire train having gone into Vicksburg, and being without supplies of any kind; also the distance to the river was so great that it would have been impossible to have reached it until late next day, when the enemy was sure to have been posted to prevent crossing. After a full consultation with my brigadiers, all of us were of the opinion that it was impossible to attempt the passage of Big Black at any point, and in doing so the entire division would certainly be lost. Subsequent events have

fully shown that we were right in this determination. It was then determined to force the rear of the enemy between Raymond and Utica.

It was settled. Loring would march his command on May 17 southeast to Crystal Springs, a village on the New Orleans, Jackson & Great Northern Railroad some 22 miles south of Jackson. "We kept up our weary march all night and all the next day without food or water," wrote Stephens. "As we approached the good people would remove the buckets, ropes, and Pumps from their wells or cisterns and no water could be had [except] from ponds or creeks that we chanced to cross." As might be expected, "many of the men fell sick from the poor water." On the second day of the march, Stephens sent out three men from each company to find something to eat. "We camped near the Pearl River, had a good supper & rations for the next day," he recalled. The next effort at foraging was not as successful. "Nothing but Corn meal for support & we had to make 'ash cakes' or cook the meal in a corn shuck."

Two days later, on May 19, Loring and his brigades reached Jackson, where he reported his arrival to Gen. Joseph Johnston. The division's remarkable odyssey was at an end. Loring's decision to move east instead of attempting to cross Bakers Creek, however, would have far-reaching effects he could never have foreseen.[52]

Chapter 12

Tally

"There they lay, the blue and the gray intermingled; the same rich, young American blood flowing out in little rivulets of crimson; each thinking he was in the right; the one conscious of it today, the other admitting now it were best the Union should be maintained one and inseparable."

—William F. Crummer of the 45th Illinois,

WITH THE BATTLE WON AND DARKNESS RAPIDLY APPROACHING, Grant's soldiers dropped to the ground in exhaustion. Most spent the evening on the battlefield or close to it, utterly worn out by the day's horrific events. "When we camped that night we had quite a few that would never answer to roll call again this side of eternity," remembered the 20th Illinois's William Clemans. What Clemans and his comrades discovered that night, and especially when the sun rose the following morning to allow them to view their handiwork, was a shocking scene of suffering and death.[1]

"Sutch a site that I witnestt there I hope I may never hav to witness again," were the words John Myers of the 28th Iowa scribbled home to his wife. "The deat men and wouted layed as thick on the field as sheap in a paster." Charles Hobbs of the 99th Illinois, Benton's brigade, recalled that "The Battlefield was awful to look upon." Alvin Hovey agreed. "It was . . . literally the hill of death; men, horses, cannon, and the *debris* of an army lay scattered in wild confusion. Hundreds of the gallant Twelfth Division were cold in death or writhing in pain, with large numbers of Quinby's [Crocker's] gallant boys, lay dead, dying, or wounded, intermixed with our fallen foe. . . . [O]ur heroes slept upon the field with the dead and dying around them." The general was proud of his division's efforts and of the army's victory. "The loss to the Rebs was immense. We took about 3,000 prisoners, 27 pieces of artillery, and 10,000 stand of small arms." My division, he wrote in his unpublished memoir, "having suffered the most, was left behind to bury the Dead and care for the wounded and gather up small arms, which lasted two days."[2]

A Missourian who had helped throw back Hovey's hard-charging division remembered the same grim picture. "Men lay in heaps," he wrote. "A little swag was in the ground here and the blood ran in a stream, as water would have done, after a hard rain." While the blood was running in red ribbons on the Mississippi soil, the screams and cries of the wounded and amputees filled the gullies that had so recently reverberated with the sounds of artillery and small arms fire, remembered another.[3]

In his published recollections of service under Grant at Fort Donelson, Shiloh, and Vicksburg, William F. Crummer of the 45th Illinois, Smith's brigade, did his best to impress upon readers what the field at Champion Hill looked like once the firing stopped. "I would like to portray the scene that we gazed upon," he began.

> It was a horrible picture and one that I carry with me to this day. All around us lay the dead and dying, amid the groans and cries of the wounded. Our surgeons came up quickly and, taking possession of a farm house, converted it into a hospital, and we began to carry ours and the enemy's wounded to the surgeons. There they lay, the blue and the gray intermingled; the same rich, young American blood flowing out in little rivulets of crimson; each thinking he was in the right; the one conscious of it today, the other admitting now it were best the Union should be maintained one and inseparable.
>
> The surgeons made no preference as to which should be first treated; the blue and the gray took their turn before the surgeon's knife. What heroes some of those fellows were; . . . with no anesthetic to sooth the agony, but gritting their teeth, they bore the pain of the knife and saw, while arms and legs were being severed from their bodies.

These wounded, according to one Union witness, were "in Every corner of the fence and behind Every log." An officer from the 124th Illinois discovered the same thing. "I could hardly keep my horse from stepping on dead or wounded soldiers," wrote Lt. Richard L. Howard. "Several clung to my horse and to my feet, and begged me . . . to give them water." Too tired and hungry any longer to care, Ira Blanchard of the 20th Illinois found what he described as "a clean looking 'Reb'" among the dead, dug through the Confederate's haversack, and ate his supper.[4]

Even before the bullets stopped flying, orderlies, comrades, and even prisoners were busy transporting the unfortunates to the nearest house, outbuilding, cabin, barn, or lean-to. Every structure on the field was soon overflowing with bullet- and shell-torn men from both armies. The soldiers were through butchering and it was time for a more humane variety of bloodletting to begin. Generally speaking, the battlefield hospitals were run by Federal surgeons since most of their Confederate counterparts had already moved across Bakers Creek. A few Southern doctors established facilities on the battlefield, where surgeons and chaplains such as Fr. John Bannon aided the wounded as best they could. Others hospitals were established at Edwards and other points along the route of retreat. At times the work was even dangerous to the doctors. The fluid nature of the fighting endangered their lives when the ebb and flow of the action lapped too close for comfort to some of the makeshift hospitals. In a facility below Champion Hill, for example, Dr. Thomas W. C. Williamson of Colonel Spicely's 24th Indiana was struck and severely wounded operating on a patient. The work was bloody, exhausting, and stressful. Surgeon Eugene B. Harrison of the 68th Ohio, Leggett's brigade, was busy tending to torn bodies from about noon until 2:00 a.m. on May 17, when he finally collapsed from exhaustion and slipped away for a few hours of rest. He was back at work by 5:00 a.m. and operated round the clock until 9:00 p.m. that night. "I had never worked harder" at any point during the war, he later recalled.[5]

The surgeons had far too many wounded to attend to waste time with hardheaded soldiers. Sergeant Abraham Newland of 124th Illinois, Smith's brigade, was one such example. The attending surgeon was ready to work on the sergeant's ghastly head wound and ordered up a healthy dose of brandy. Newland refused. When the doctor told him he would die if he did not partake, Newland nodded his understanding.

Unable to speak, he scribbled out a message that read: "If I die, I will die sober." The surgeon turned away and muttered, "Die, then." Newland defied the doctor's last order.[6]

Another difficult patient was recalled by William Crummer, who wrote about "a fine-looking officer and Colonel of some Louisiana regiment" who had been shot through the leg "and was making a great ado about it." Edward D. Kittoe's examination of the wound prompted the following conversation:

"Your leg must be amputated," concluded the 45th Illinois's surgeon.

"Oh, I can never go home to my wife on one leg!" cried out the officer. "Oh, oh, it must not be!"

"Well, that, or not go home at all," he replied gruffly. The Confederate officer thought for a few moments and finally agreed with the doctor. The limb would have to be removed.

"Within a few minutes," wrote Crummer, "he was in a condition (if he got well) to wear a wooden leg when he went home to his wife."[7]

While surgeons and orderlies toiled endlessly with what seemed to them to be an infinite number of wounded men, others tried to cope with the massive number of Confederate prisoners that threatened to overwhelm the Federal army. Union soldiers spent the night rounding up even more stragglers, with whom many generous Federals shared what little food they carried with them. The 48th Ohio and 108th Illinois, both of Landram's brigade, were selected to guard the captured Confederates.[8]

Amid the carnage, acts of compassion abounded. On the torn heights of Champion Hill, James Llewellyn of the 11th Indiana discovered a wounded Georgian named J. T. Pritchard of Company F, 36th Georgia. Llewellyn offered the Southerner a canteen of water taken from a dead soldier and made sure the stretcher bearers carried him to a hospital. Many years later Llewellyn moved to Arkansas, where he became friends with a Confederate veteran. The two discussed the war and discovered both had been at Champion Hill. It was then that Pritchard recognized his new friend was the man who had saved his life.[9]

Pritchard was one of the lucky ones who reached medical care. Many more lay where they fell for days. "Is there a Mason among you?" croaked a wounded Confederate who had remained on the field through the night and much of the following day before two officers on Grant's staff found him. Another begged some officers to end his life. "Kill me!

Will some one kill me?" The grotesquely injured infantryman had been shot through the head, and the course of the bullet had clipped both optical nerves, blinding him. He died before dawn.[10]

Charles Longley of the 24th Iowa, Slack's brigade, felt the pain that courses through a survivor's veins when small groups of men from his broken regiment "slowly, oh, too slowly," reassembled at day's end around the colors. "How each new arrival is welcomed and each missing one mourned. The report of those present finally cuts off the hope that any more will come that night, and the roll is called. Name after name is called to which there is no response save the saddened look with which each one marks and emphasizes the silence," he wrote. Captain James W. Martin, Company I, organized a prayer service following roll call, "the reverent attention testified the fitness of remembering God when Death is near." By this time, remembered Longley, the sun was rapidly sinking beneath the horizon, "the fading tints of twilight touch pitifully the features drawn with pain, and makes more ghastly the upturned faces of the dead—for the words of General Grant in his *Personal Memoirs*, 'Hovey's division' (meaning us the living, the wounded, and the dead) 'remained on the field where they had fought so bravely and bled so freely."[11]

The men of Holden Putnam's hard-hit 93rd Illinois, George Boomer's brigade, endured a similar experience in their bivouac—as did virtually every outfit that had been bloodied in the battle. When the Illini formed for the first time since the fighting ended on the morning of May 17, it was a shocking sight. "Then tears came, unbidden, to the eyes of brave men," reads the outfit's regimental history. "The fearful losses of the previous day had not until then been fully realized. That short line told all."[12]

Champion Hill was no different than any other combat. In its wake were an enormous number of corpses waiting to be buried. The dead could not be left above ground for long because the stifling Mississippi weather would quickly decompose the lifeless flesh. Colonel Holmes's brigade, Crocker's division, and George McGinnis's brigade, Hovey's division, were ordered to oversee the odious task of collection and interment. Most of the graves were dug by captured Confederates and slaves. McGinnis ranked Holmes, and so assumed command of the operation. The men from the two brigades buried the dead from both sides in shallow trenches. Little effort was made to identify individual victims, who were gathered together near where they fell and pulled into the graves with ropes and belts. The loathsome task was finally completed late Sunday, May 17. Hundreds of individual mounds and overturned piles of dirt atop narrow trenches crisscrossed the once lovely Champion Hill.[13]

Finding missing and dead friends became a priority for many of the survivors. "In every direction could be seen the lights carried by those in search of the wounded, as they moved among the trees," recalled Lt. Richard Howard of the 124th Illinois. Some of them may have been from the 56th Ohio of Slack's brigade, which lost heavily that day with 20 killed, 90 wounded, and another 28 missing. The 56th's Lt. Benjamin Roberts took a squad of men to find every dead Buckeye and give him a proper burial. With torches high above their heads, the men scoured ground. "We . . . saw some of the awful sights of a battlefield," remembered Lieutenant Thomas Williams. "One, always remembered, was a very large rebel, sitting with his back against a large stump, with more than a deathly pallor, having bled to death; and so many others, lying dead as they fell, friend and foe, now at peace." And then the Ohioans began to find their dead friends. "We soon found our slain comrades, and having prepared a place, side by side we placed our gallant comrades, shrouded in their rubber blankets." The sights witnessed "on that bloody field can never be forgotten," wrote the young lieutenant. "Where our brigade stormed the enemy's battery [Waddell's] at the junction of the roads, the dead men and horses were in piles."[14]

The men of the 124th Illinois buried two Confederate officers, Maj. Joseph W. Anderson (Carter Stevenson's chief of artillery), and Col. Skidmore Harris of the 43rd Georgia, Barton's Brigade. The officers were buried on the hill close to where Anderson's guns had stood. Another artillery commander was buried just a short distance away without any fanfare and few witnesses. What was left of Capt. Samuel Jones Ridley's body was tucked carefully under the soil by his personal servant, who gathered his personal effects to carry home.[15]

Coincident with the burial of the dead was the gathering of the thousands of stands of small arms and equipment scattered over the field from north of the Champion house miles south to the lower crossing of the creek—and beyond. This, too, was left to the Federals serving with Holmes and McGinnis. Cavalry scouts scouring the field's perimeter located several abandoned (and mostly spiked) artillery pieces left by the retreating Confederates. To Capt. Daniel W. Ballou of the 10th Missouri Cavalry was credited the honor of capturing eleven of the twelve guns Loring left behind the night before.[16]

As he made his way to the front amidst his victorious troops, Grant witnessed firsthand the breadth and depth of the carnage wrought by the battle. He initially rode toward Edwards but turned around and headed back for the crossroads. Without tents or wagons, he trotted south on the Ratliff Road and drew up his horse at the Isaac Roberts house— Pemberton's former headquarters. The place was now a Confederate field hospital, so there was no room for the general and his entourage. As exhausted as his men, Grant threw down a blanket and spent what had to have been a fitful night out on the porch. Always compassionate toward the enemy, Grant ordered his surgeons to "be sure to treat the Confederate wounded just as if they were our own wounded."[17]

Grant's son Fred made his own rounds over the battlefield. Instead of turning back, he had continued on until reaching a Confederate hospital. He dismounted and walked among the wounded, soaking in the scene around him. "They were not feeling very friendly toward the Yankees, and they threatened to kill me," the younger Grant remembered long after the war. After dodging a party of Federal skirmishers who tried to capture him, Fred eventually found his way back to the crossroads and south to his father's porch on the front of the Roberts place.[18]

Assistant Secretary of War Charles Dana was riding about the field even before the firing had completely died out. The Confederates were rapidly retreating and dusk was approaching when Dana found General Logan on the army's right flank. According to Dana, Logan shared none of the thrill of victory coursing through the army. Indeed, Logan appeared despondent. "He declared the day was lost, and that he would soon be swept from his position," remembered Dana. When he tried to convince him of the complete victory, Logan would not hear of it. He tried to convince Dana that the North had lost the battle. The intense combat leader never could quite shake the pessimistic streak that engulfed him at the end of nearly every battle.[19]

General Hovey, whose division had borne the brunt of the fighting, also rode the field. He reined in his mount when he reached the position of his old regiment, the 24th Indiana. The general was astonished at the sight of its thinned ranks. "Where are the rest of my boys?" he cried out. Someone gave Hovey a tour of the hillside and hollow through which the regiment had fought. The sight of so many dead and wounded comrades caused the hardened veteran to turn away, mount his horse, and ride away weeping.[20]

The heavy sadness that pervades the aftermath of every battle was lifted, if only for a short while, when around sundown a mail shipment arrived and was distributed to the various Northern regiments. "The fierce struggle through which we had just passed was forgotten as we read the news from home," wrote one fortunate soldier in the 20th Ohio. "As the excitement [of receiving mail] passed," wrote another in the 124th Illinois, we discovered "we greatly needed rest." Sleep, however, was hard to come by with the day's awful events firmly etched in their minds. The steady tramp of passing troops and the groans and cries of the wounded were not melodies with which one easily falls asleep.[21]

Despair and sorrow pervaded the defeated Confederate army in an even deeper and more meaningful way. "The battle was over, and we had lost," anguished a Missouri Confederate who had earlier experienced the exhilaration of victory with Cockrell. "I had gone into that day's battle with six men in my mess, and I was the only one that was left. I felt very lonesome that night I can tell you." The lack of blankets, supplies, and food, wrote another, only made matters that much worse.[22]

The major houses on the field, including the Champion residence, as well as the Coker, Roberts, and Yeiser houses, were all damaged to one degree or another by flying metal before being overrun with wounded men. A Federal examining the field witnessed the dramatic effects of the combat the following morning when he passed by a house around which the fighting had raged. "[It was] a solitary house," he wrote, "with all its surroundings swept away clear as if a cyclone had passed that way." On the porch were several women crying over their loss. They had remained in the house throughout the battle—a terrifying ordeal.[23]

Captain Sidney S. Champion of Company I, 28th Mississippi Cavalry, was not directly involved in the fighting on May 16. His outfit had been conducting scouting operations near the Big Black River. Champion knew a major engagement had been fought near his home, and that night saw "a large fire" burning brightly from that direction. Two days later, he wrote his wife to tell her he was safe inside the Vicksburg defenses, and to inquire about her and the children. "I am fearful our home is nearly destroyed—probably the house burned . . . but I have no regrets on that score—I have ceased to regret about property." As for the battle itself, he wrote, "that there was a great mismanagement is evident—if not serious blunders." After the war, a Federal physician told a Champion descendant that, "while performing amputations on her dining room table, the blood would get so deep on the floor that a soldier had to take an ax and cut a hole in the floor so the blood could run out under the house." Sid and Matilda Champion's picturesque plantation home still stood, but the property had been turned into a slaughter-house.[24]

One of the men who fought within musket range of the Champion homestead was a member of 3rd Missouri Infantry, Cockrell's Brigade. His mother opened a letter about eight weeks later written in an unfamiliar hand and signed over the name Sarah F. Bigelow. "On May 16, a battle was fought at Champion Hill . . . in which your son, Robert Hyde Woodson, was engaged," wrote Mrs. Bigelow. "He was among the wounded, his left leg being so badly injured that amputation above the knee was necessary." Corporal Woodson and four other wounded Southern soldiers were being cared for in the Masonic Lodge at Bovina, Mississippi. After explaining the Confederate defeat, Bigelow relived Robert's final hours:

> I was one of several ladies who visited the hospital daily to render what service we could to our pour wounded soldier; and all that we could do was done to make them comfortable. Mrs. Col. Dockery [Col. Thomas Dockery's wife] and myself assisted in the care of [your son]. . . . His manly qualities, his patience, gentleness and submission won the respect and admiration of all who met him.
>
> It was thought he was doing very well for three weeks, but toward the last he failed rapidly, till finally, nature gave way and, quietly and peacefully, he expired at 10 a.m., June 14, 1863.
>
> When it was thought he could not survive (it being impossible to send for a clergyman), I inquired of him if he was a member of the church, to which he replied that he was not but that he had seriously thought of becoming so; and when asked if he knew he had but little time left on earth, he replied, 'his trust was in Jesus.' He appeared to be perfectly conscious at the time, but too weak to converse much.
>
> I asked him if I should write to you, of whom he had frequently spoken, and what I should say; he could not speak but made an affirmative motion, and several times seemed trying to speak but

> could not, excepting to say, after I had read some of the prayers for
> the visitation of the sick, 'They are good prayers.'
>
> Tearful and sorrowing hearts surrounded his dying bed, and all
> regretted that one so young and gifted must so soon be a martyr for
> his country's cause.

Robert Hyde Woodson was buried in the Bovina Episcopal churchyard.[25]

*   *   *

Grant threaded slightly more than 29,000 men onto the field of battle
and lost 410 killed, 1,844 wounded, and 187 missing, or 2,441 men. This
equates to 8.4 percent of those engaged or on the field available to fight.
Conversely, John Pemberton had available perhaps 24,000 men. Total
reported losses for the Confederates come in at 381 killed, 1,018
wounded, and 2,441 missing (mostly captured), or 3,840. This equates to
16 percent of those engaged or on the field and available to fight.

For those seeking clarity and meaning in these numbers, however, it
is better to narrow the lens a bit and focus on those actually engaged. On
the Federal side, the three divisions under Hovey, Logan, and Crocker
shouldered the vast majority of the fighting. These Federal divisions
totaled 15,380 men and made up 53 percent of Grant's army on the field.
Of these, 2,260 were killed, wounded, or captured, which equates to 14.7
percent of those engaged. A more telling statistic is that those three
divisions suffered 92.6 percent of the Federal losses on May 16.

On the Confederate side, the two divisions of Carter Stevenson and
John Bowen, a total of 16,313 men, bore the brunt of the fighting. They
accounted for 68 percent of Pemberton's army at Champion Hill. Of this
total, 3,721 were killed, wounded, or captured, which equates to 22.8
percent of those engaged. These two divisions suffered 97 percent of the
total Southern losses on May 16. Confederate losses appear dramatically
higher if Alexander W. Reynolds's Tennessee brigade is not counted as
part of Stevenson's total (it was not in action at Champion Hill, but it was
lightly engaged later that night while crossing Big Black River), and
Loring's entire division is counted among the missing (it was, after all,
permanently lost to Pemberton just as surely as if it had been captured *en
masse.*) Regardless of how the numbers are tallied, Grant's army won a
decisive strategic and tactical victory at Champion Hill.[26]

*   *   *

U. S. Grant's army was as exhausted and bloodied as its opponent, but not as disorganized and dispersed. Victory, then as now, is a remarkable tonic for an ailing effort, and the decisive engagement of May 16 energized the Federal campaign. Months of failure and disappointment had been washed away in just a few hours. The campaign was not over by any means, but there was a sense in the ranks that something had changed—that the decisive battle in Mississippi had been waged and won. The army's final movements before sunset on May 16 helped dictate what would follow on the morrow.

Grant's overall performance must be ranked as outstanding. After turning west from Jackson, he drove his corps forward quickly, fanned out on the confusing network of roads, and brought his enemy to battle. This bold move seized the initiative and caught his opponent by surprise. Although neither McClernand nor A. J. Smith moved as aggressively forward as Grant might have liked (or at least later claimed), their heavy presence pinned Pemberton's right and center in place, which in turn allowed the Confederate left wing to be turned and crushed. If there was still doubt about the fate of Vicksburg, Grant's vigorous pursuit to and through Edwards and across the Big Black River put the matter to rest.

After finally pushing through to the crossroads and then moving rapidly down the Jackson Road and across Bakers Creek, the vanguard of John McClernand's XIII Corps, in the form of Eugene Carr's division, arrived in Edwards about 8:00 p.m., "where the flames were consuming a train of cars and a quantity of stores which the enemy had fired," reported the corps leader. Barton's men had set the fire before evacuating west over the Big Black. "Both, to a considerable extent, were saved by the activity of the men." Loring's exhausted command watched these same flames light the northwest horizon on their march to Jackson. The Illinois political general's role at Champion Hill is cloaked by controversy— some of it justified, much of it unfounded. Overlooked by many casual students is a sentence Grant wrote in his report that all but excuses his corps commander's "tardiness": "The delay in the advance of the troops immediately with McClernand was caused, no doubt, by the enemy presenting a front of artillery and infantry where it was impossible, from the nature of the ground and density of the forest, to discover his numbers." By the time he penned his report a month after the battle,

McClernand was fully aware his "delay" in engaging the enemy aggressively had raised eyebrows and set lips to moving. "The loss sustained by my corps attests to the severity of this memorable battle," he wrote. It is justifiable praise aimed primarily in the direction of Alvin Hovey and his redoubtable division—the only one of McClernand's four division that suffered heavily in the battle. Individual praise for the overall performance of Peter Osterhaus, Eugene Carr, and A. J. Smith will not be found in McClernand's official report.[27]

During the pursuit of the beaten enemy, noted Carr, "many prisoners were taken, who were simply ordered to the rear. I made it a rule, whenever I was in front, to dispose of prisoners in that way, thus saving my own men for more important duties, and being satisfied that some one in the rear would pick up and secure the prisoners." Carr's honest admission of how he handled captured soldiers probably accounts for the gross exaggeration between the number of men initially reported as having been taken prisoner, and the actual number transported to points north. Many of these Confederates simply melted away into the night rather than wait around for a provost guard to pack them aboard trains and boats for a free trip to Camp Morton or Point Delaware.

Of McClernand's divisions, Carr's losses were the lightest. After shelling and threatening Bowen's command near the lower crossing, William Benton had marched his men north and was the first of Carr's brigades to reach the rail depot. He reported one man wounded and two killed. Michael Lawler, the brawling Irishman whose fine use of artillery had helped open up large chunks of the Confederate line, pursued Loring's retreating columns toward the lower crossing before abandoning the effort and marching to Edwards. "Although my brigade was not permitted to take a very prominent part in the battle of Champion Hill," wrote Lawler, "still, enough was done to enable me to prove my men and satisfy myself thoroughly of their valor and soldierly qualities." Lawler lost not a single man.[28]

Peter Osterhaus's division arrived in Edwards later that evening. Like Carr, Osterhaus also claimed to have captured large numbers of men. "Thousands of the enemy were found scattered everywhere, and fell into our hands as prisoners of war. In one instance," he continued, "Colonel Lindsey, with the Sixteenth Ohio and Twenty-second Kentucky Infantry alone, took more prisoners than the whole number of his brigade combined; also a number of cannon and small-arms became ours." Only a fraction of these "thousands" ended up in Union hands.[29]

After his lackluster performance against the stalwart Edward Goodwin and his 35th Alabama, Colonel Lindsey had driven forward through unoccupied woods almost the entire distance to Bakers Creek before moving on to Edwards Depot as ordered. He arrived there about midnight. "[That] My entire command, both officers and men, have exhibited an alacrity and promptness in the execution of all duties assigned them [is] truly gratifying to me," were the misleading words Lindsey used to close out his report. The bulk of his losses—six killed, 41 wounded, and 13 missing—were suffered by the regiments that served with other commanders in heavier fighting. Lindsey's total was increased by one wounded man when G Company's Capt. Evan D. Thomas of the 22nd Kentucky was severely burned trying to destroy a wagonload of captured ammunition.[30]

Theophilus Garrard's brigade followed up across the upper crossing after Barton, Reynolds, and the rest of the Confederates in that area. Garrard's casualties totaled 11 killed, 44 wounded, and 13 missing. His report has never been located, and little more can be added to his story.[31]

A. J. Smith's division dropped for the night where darkness found it, spread out between the Coker house ridge and Bakers Creek, or as McClernand put it, "some 3 miles southeast of Edwards Station." Frank Blair's division, the only one of William T. Sherman's XV Corps division that fought on May 16, camped in the same vicinity as Smith. It did not suffer any losses.

As Stephen Burbridge of Smith's division reported, "The night after the battle the men lay upon their arms, hourly expecting an attack" that never arrived. The men formed into a line of battle at dawn and advanced west fully expecting to renew the battle. Instead they discovered, much to their delight, that the field was solidly in Federal hands and the enemy was long gone. Burbridge reported his losses as 16 wounded. Smith's second brigade under William Landram had spent most of the day in reserve. Its losses were six wounded.[32]

Alvin Hovey's division's losses were horrific. It was the first to be heavily engaged, and one out of every three men was left on the field when Bowen's counterattack swept them off Champion Hill. "I cannot think of this bloody hill without sadness and pride," reads his official report. "Sadness for the great loss of my true and gallant men; pride for the heroic bravery they displayed." James Slack agreed with his commander's assessment. "In point of terrific fierceness and stubborn persistency, [the battle] finds but few parallels in the history of civilized warfare. For two long hours my brigade held in check fully three times their number," he continued, "and I hesitate not in saying, had they not so gallantly and determinedly resisted, the fortunes of the day might have been greatly damaged, if not our glorious triumph turned into a defeat." His conclusion is difficult to argue with. Lieutenant Colonel John McLaughlin of the 47th Indiana summed it up pretty well when he observed, "Taking into consideration the length of time we were engaged, the overwhelming numbers to contend with, and the loss sustained, is satisfactory evidence of the gallantry and courage shown by the officers and men under my command. They did their whole duty." They did indeed. Slack also noted the large number of prisoners his brigade captured, all of whom "were handed over to the provost-marshal without any account being taken of them." The brigade spent the night on the field and marched for Edwards the next morning. Slack went into battle with 1,809 men and lost 108 killed, 363 wounded, and 93 missing, or 31 percent of those engaged.[33]

George McGinnis's brigade also suffered heavy losses. "Were I to attempt to do justice to the daring, endurance, and gallant conduct of the officers and men of the First Brigade, I should fail. Their actions speak for them; in proof of which let facts be submitted." The numbers do indeed speak for themselves. Out of 2,371 men engaged, 90 were killed outright, 506 were wounded, and 23 went missing, or 26 percent. McGinnis's men slept on the field and remained there to care for the wounded and bury the dead.[34]

"This, by far the hardest fought battle of all since crossing at Bruinsburg, and the most decided victory for us, was not won without the loss of many brave men, who heroically periled their lives for their country's honor," wrote James McPherson, commander of XVII Corps. "Their determined spirit still animates their living comrades, who feel that the blood poured out on Champion's Hill was not spilt in vain. Every man of Logan's and Crocker's divisions was engaged in the battle." McPherson's observation was certainly true. His own role in the battle once the firing began, however, is unclear: Although he was in tactical command of the attack, McPherson seems to have spent most of the day observing the action instead of dictating its direction.

John Logan had nothing but praise for his brigade commanders, and rightly so. Each had proven worthy of command. "To my brigade commanders, upon all of whom weighty responsibilities were imposed, the fidelity with which their various duties were discharged contributed to the success which has attended our arms," reported Logan. "All of them gave me repeated indications of the coolness, firmness, and decision of character so essential in time of action." Logan himself had been active and aggressive from the beginning of the battle to its conclusion.[35]

Mortimer Leggett, whose report for Champion Hill has yet to surface, lost 21 killed and 189 wounded. His brigade did not move around much once the serious fighting began, but it did suffer the division's heaviest losses, which amply demonstrates the intensity of the largely static small arms engagement between his Midwesterners and the Alabamans of Stephen Lee's Brigade. Leggett's men spent the night on the field and headed for the Big Black River the following morning.[36]

Near the close of the fighting, John Smith was ordered to keep his brigade astride "the road to Edwards Station [Jackson Road]," which he did. "Where all did so well it would be hard to discriminate," he wrote. "All was done that bravery could accomplish." His regiments moved west a bit and bivouacked near the creek before moving with the rest of the division to the Big Black River on May 17. Smith's losses were 22 killed, 104 wounded, and nine missing.[37]

John Stevenson's men had the division's hardest job on May 16, and they executed it flawlessly. The brigade's turning movement was one of the keys to winning the battle as decisively as it was won. After taking Captain De Golyer's battery and pursuing the Confederates toward Edwards, Stevenson camped his brigade about three miles northwest of the upper crossing. "This was unquestionably the great battle of the campaign," he wrote on July 7, 1863, "and I am proud that the officers and soldiers of the command conducted themselves throughout the day with the utmost valor and determination." Given all that was done, it is rather surprising Stevenson's losses were not heavier than eight killed, 35 wounded, and 18 missing.[38]

At the head of General Quinby's division, Marcellus Crocker had arrived in a timely fashion on the field at exactly where he was most required. "Of the conduct of the officers and men of the division I cannot speak too highly," he penned nine days later. "Their charge at Jackson, seldom if ever excelled in any campaign, has been the theme of universal praise; the stubbornness and courage with which they fought at Jackson and Champion's Hill have won for them the admiration of the army." His division camped on the field of battle. It left the next day, without Holmes, and reached the Big Black River about noon.[39]

"The conduct of all the officers and men of my command during the entire campaign has been more than satisfactory," wrote Col. John Sanborn. "It has been most gallant and praiseworthy. There has been no shirking and no desire to shirk on the part of either officers or men, and I have not found or even heard of a man out of his position in battle or on the march. I know not how soldiers could do more." His support of the artillery, coupled with the well-timed attack that wiped virtually an entire regiment out of the Confederate order of battle, contributed substantially to holding back the Confederate counterattacks. For these accomplishments, four men gave their lives and 46 others their blood.[40]

Like Sanborn, Samuel Holmes's two thin regiments had also played a significant role in bringing the Southern counterassault to a halt. His regimental commanders, he wrote in his report, "have rendered distinguished service in the operations of the brigade." All mourned the loss of the ambushed Leonidas Horney, "truly a capable and valiant soldier." Holmes lost 12 killed, 87 wounded, and four missing. After the fight, he was ordered to remain on the field to help McGinnis collect the wounded and bury the dead.[41]

Of Crocker's three brigades, George Boomer's played the most prominent role, driving straight up Champion Hill, battling the enemy at close range, and then falling back with appalling losses—more than three times the other two brigades of the division combined. He left no official report of his actions on this field because he was killed but a short time later. His detailed letters home to his beloved wife Mary, however, serve the purpose almost as well. "The victory was great and decisive, but, oh! at how dear a cost to me!" he penned the morning after the battle. "Five hundred and fifty-one of my brave men were killed or wounded! I cannot bear to think of it—the way they fought and fell." Boomer was especially troubled by the death of his "dear friend" Major Charles Brown, 26th Missouri Infantry. "He was as noble and gallant as he was pure and true, and his spirit will never die. He handled the regiment he commanded during that hot fight as though it were pastime, and his praise is on every tongue. Captain [John] Welker was also killed, and we buried him with

Lieutenant-Colonel [Leonidas] Horney, of the Tenth Missouri, and my dear friend Brown, this morning, side by side, in rude coffins, with a description of the locality, that will identify their graves if the rude mementos we placed at their heads are lost." The "rude" mementos were not lost, though Boomer did not live long enough to learn it. Leonidas Horney moldered in Mississippi soil for almost two years until his remains were located and shipped home. On February 15, 1865, they were interred with military honors in his family's burial plot, Row 2, Tomb 6, at Thompson Cemetery, Littleton Township, Schuyler County, Illinois.[42]

Despite the long and often heavy exchange of iron rounds, the Federal artillery suffered but few casualties. On the far left wing on the Raymond Road, the Chicago Mercantile Exchange Battery lost three wounded, while its companion 7th Battery, Ohio Light Artillery, lost not a single man. The batteries that fought closer to Champion Hill suffered only slightly heavier losses. The 16th Battery, Ohio Light Artillery, lost one killed and one wounded, while Company A, 1st Missouri Light Artillery sent two wounded to the hospital. Despite all the gallant fighting and galloping action endured by Captain De Golyer's battery, the Michigan red legs suffered but a single battle death. The artillery accompanying Crocker's division, specifically the 6th Battery, Wisconsin Light Artillery, lost two wounded.[43]

Cavalry losses were even lighter. Captain John L Campbell's 3rd Illinois, which had screened the advance of Osterhaus's division as it moved west down the Middle Road, lost one wounded trooper. Colonel Clark Wright's 6th Missouri Cavalry lost two killed and one wounded in its evening pursuit of Alexander Reynolds's Tennesseans near the Big Black River. None of the other cavalry organizations that served in the Champion Hill operations suffered casualties.[44]

*   *   *

"Had the movement in support of the left been promptly made when first ordered, it is not improbable that I might have maintained my position, and it is possible the enemy might have been driven back, though his vastly superior and constantly increasing numbers would have rendered it necessary to withdraw during the night to save my communications with Vicksburg." With those words, Pemberton opened a salvo against William Loring that still echoes today. The victors largely basked in the soft light of victory and congratulated themselves for a job well done; Pemberton and other Southern generals, Loring included, sought out scapegoats to rationalize what had transpired along swift-flowing Bakers Creek as a means of escaping from the harsh light of history's judgment. Many mistakes were made at Champion Hill, and there is blame enough to go around. There were also remarkable demonstrations of bravery, intelligent leadership, and sacrifice. Many good men dressed in Confederate grays and browns died there.[45]

As the commanding officer of the army, the blame for the defeat must begin and end at Pemberton's doorstep. His march from Edwards on May 15 was poorly planned and carried the exhausted army within reach of the Federals. Pemberton's reconnaissance information was woefully inadequate for field work. Pemberton and his staff had to have known of the existence of the Jackson Road, running west below the railroad before turning south and looping up and over Champion Hill. Why was it not heavily patrolled? The nasty surprise marching on that route landed a devastating right hook against the Confederate army, a punch from which it was unable to recover. Once the battle began and warnings from Carter Stevenson arrived of the threat to his left, Pemberton hesitated to act until it was too late. None of the generals or primary sources mention seeing him riding along the left flank to judge the situation for himself. The initiative—which is so important in military actions—was lost to the Southerners early that morning and only for a short time, during Bowen's attack, was it gained back, only to be lost again quickly thereafter. The indecision about where to employ Cockrell's Missouri brigade when it arrived near the crossroads wasted valuable time. When Bowen finally attacked, it was brilliantly delivered. What more might have been achieved had Pemberton taken with him one or even both of the infantry divisions (John Forney and Martin Smith) left behind in Vicksburg? While his small army battled superior forces, thousands of soldiers marked time in the rear.

Still, all of this begs the question of why Pemberton was entrusted with such an important field command in the first place. He was a bureaucrat—a clerk. His tenure in South Carolina reinforced these facts. He had absolutely no experience leading an army in the field—especially against a general as skilled in the military arts as U. S. Grant. Pemberton was way over his head, as the result abundantly demonstrated.

Carter Stevenson's best day of the war was not at Champion Hill. Many of his troops were as inexperienced as he was, but they were not leading the largest division in the army. To his credit, Stevenson avoided casting direct blame on others—perhaps because he knew much of the blame for the bloody fiasco on the left began and ended with him. He did not assume the mantle of responsibility comfortably, however. Ten weeks later, on July 29—long after the smoke of battle cleared and even Vicksburg had been lost to the enemy—Stevenson penned two sentences into his official report in an effort to explain how it was the enemy pierced his front so easily at Champion Hill: "My line, as will thus appear, was necessarily single, irregular, divided, and without reserves. Under the supposition that the army was to move forward in pursuance of the instructions given in the morning, this ground was not reconnoitered with a view to taking up a position for battle until we were on the move facing the enemy." All true. However, Stevenson studiously avoided mentioning uncomfortable issues that undercut this explanation. How was it that a division commander did not see fit to run a strong skirmish force north on the Jackson Road as soon as its existence became known? Why did he not solve his problem of a "single" line of battle "without reserves" by recalling all or at least a large part of Col. Alexander Reynolds's large brigade as soon as it became obvious the Federals were deploying to attack his position? (It took Seth Barton, of all people, to request assistance from Reynolds and then only after it was too late to retrieve the day's fortunes.) The baffling decision to send away Bowen's ammunition train still awaits explanation.[46]

Alexander Reynolds's men rightfully grumbled about marching a full day without rest and then being ordered to spend the next day escorting the wagons back off the field—but the complaining stopped when they learned how different their fate would have been had they not been with the wagons. As it was, they avoided the battle entirely and were only caught up at the tail end of the miserable affair while crossing the Big Black River in search of safety on its far bank. Reynolds lost not a man killed or wounded, though he did leave behind 143 stragglers and/or prisoners. "I beg leave to say that in the arduous marches and perilous positions in which my troops have been placed they performed all their duties with cheerfulness and courage," he reported ten weeks later. "All the officers and men behaved well." By the time the brigade stumbled into Vicksburg on May 17, the men had seen some combat and been on their feet for some sixty hours.[47]

Alfred Cumming wrote similar praise about his own regimental commanders—and he probably even believed it. Theirs was an unfortunate set of circumstances, for Cumming was a good general. At Champion Hill, however, he was the beneficiary of extraordinarily bad luck. Nothing was in his (or their) favor—not the terrain, numbers, alignment, or his opponent (Hovey). Even the command he was tapped to lead was ill-fated, for these 2,500 Georgians had never been in serious combat and he knew them not at all. There was not a brigade on the field that could have held fast under the same dreadful conditions Cumming was thrown into—not even Cockrell's famed Missouri brigade. "The regimental commanders and field officers, though their efforts were unsuccessful," Cumming explained, "without an exception acted with great courage and judgment, as did also, as a general thing, the company officers." The brigade's dead totaled 142, the wounded 314, and the captured or missing 539. The numbers speak for themselves; the men held out as long as humanly possible.[48]

Seth Barton's disastrous outing was also mostly attributable to bad luck, bad timing, and bad terrain. His was a roller coaster of highs and lows that day. When called to the left flank, he responded with alacrity, as if possessed with a soul for combat on a par with Francis Cockrell or Stephen Lee. If one is inclined to find fault with the handling of his brigade east of the creek, a complaint might be raised about his impetuous drive deep into a woods knowing full well no friendly troops were protecting his left flank. It was brave, it was reckless, and it was fatal to many of his men. Once he found himself on the far side of Bakers Creek, however, Barton demonstrated the presence of mind to send an urgent plea to Reynolds for assistance; Reynolds had the presence of mind to heed it. It was another high point in a day boasting too few of them. But then Barton stumbled badly. Depending on which source you believe, he either lost complete control of his men when Lee's infantry moved north toward him (which almost certainly seems to have been the case), or he simply ordered his men to uncover the upper bridge in the face of the approaching enemy while the army was negotiating the lower ford. If the move was indeed voluntary, it demonstrated an uncooperative streak in his character—the same charge that would result in his removal from command in Virginia the following year. Either way, the result was the same: Barton's evacuation left Bowen to be turned out of his position to the south, which in turn meant that Loring was unable to cross his division and move toward the Big Black River. In a removed sense, Barton's failure at a critical hour funneled Pemberton toward his fateful decision at the Big Black Bridge. "The heavy loss of the brigade (over 42 per cent.) is the best evidence I can give of the good behavior of the men," Barton wrote in his report. In all, 58 were killed, 106 were wounded, and 737 were captured or missing. Francis Obenchain of the Botetourt Artillery, in a letter written long after the war, criticized Barton's report and called it "very misleading." As for which parts were disingenuous, Obenchain did not directly say. What is not in doubt is that these Georgians did all they could do; it was leadership they were lacking.[49]

Of Stephen Dill Lee at Champion Hill, only kind things can be written. He was diligent, observant, and maneuvered his men quickly and well under pressure—the exact attributes so sorely lacking that day in his division commander. It was his patrol under Lt. Col. Edmund Pettus that spotting the Federals approaching from the north, his choice of the terrain upon which the army would fight its battle on the left flank. Lee defended his first position to the last possible moment before falling back, and then reorganized and took to the offensive—actions that helped stave off an even more serious defeat. When Stevenson's Division poured like the mob it was across Bakers Creek at the end of the day, only Lee's Brigade was in some semblance of order. That he had control of his men when others did not was demonstrated by Pemberton's request that he move across country to help guard the upper crossing. It was his movement that sent Barton's men tumbling for the rear. Ill-luck did not easily leave this army. Lee's Alabamans reached the Big Black that night at 10:00 p.m. As might be expected from his experiences on the field, Lee's casualties were also heavy: 44 killed, 142 wounded, and 604 captured or taken prisoner.[50]

Stephen Lee was the shining example of a Southern brigade commander at Champion Hill; John Bowen was the hero of the hour at divisional command. Although he delayed complying with Pemberton's first call for assistance (a curious lapse yet unexplained satisfactorily), he responded quickly thereafter with enthusiasm, energy, and sage judgment. His counterattack was one of the most successful of the war, and had it been properly supported—even by a single brigade from Loring's Division—there is no telling what calamity might have befallen

Grant's thinly spread and well bloodied divisions. It was a near-run affair as it was. When his men were finally forced back, visions of the Federal ordnance trains sitting like ripe fruit waiting to be plucked from low-hanging branches filled their lustful eyes. Alas, without ammunition or reinforcements, they would forever remain out of reach. Bowen died before filing a report of his division's conduct.

He would end the war as one of the best combat brigadiers on either side, but the accolade was small comfort after Champion Hill. Francis Cockrell would never forget how close he came to victory on May 16, 1863. The propinquity of success was especially bitter given what the Missourians experienced the following day inside the Big Black bridgehead. Almost a month after the fall of Vicksburg, Cockrell was rightly swollen with pride about his brigade's role at Champion Hill:

> I cannot speak with too much praise of the gallantry, coolness, and dashing, fearless, and even reckless impetuosity shown by the officers and soldiers of this brigade in forming their line of battle under heavy fire, with the troops on their right and left falling back past them in disorder and confusion, and an enemy greatly outnumbering them rapidly advancing, cheering and flushed with their hitherto successful charges and their capture of the guns, and then, in the midst of these, in throwing themselves into the breach with continued cheers, and driving the enemy back 500 to 600 yards, and recapturing Captain Waddell's battery and a battery of the enemy.

The gallant effort cost Cockrell's Missouri brigade 65 killed, 293 wounded, and 242 captured or taken prisoner. The Missourian may have held some bitterness at Pemberton's decision to stay and fight rather than retreat quickly behind Bakers Creek once the proximity of the enemy was discovered. "I would say that, in my opinion, our whole army could safely have crossed back over Baker's Creek after the cannonading between the cavalry referred to and even after the engagement between my batteries and the enemy referred to," he wrote in November 1863 in a response to questions concerning his observations of the battle. "After crossing Baker's Creek, there could have been, in my opinion, no trouble in reaching Edwards Depot (only a short distance), and with Baker's

Creek then between us and the enemy." Might-have-beens lingered within Cockrell.[51]

Martin Green delivered his best performance of the war on May 16, though his death shortly thereafter left the task of writing the brigade's report on Thomas Dockery's able shoulders. Unlike virtually every other after-action report, Dockery's contained exceptional detail without flowery praise. The accomplishments spoke for themselves. The brigade did not suffer as heavily as Cockrell's, but with 66 killed, 137 wounded, and 65 missing, it suffered enough. Without the gallant stands of Scott's 12th Louisiana and Goodwin's 35th Alabama, Green's regiments would not have exited the field. Standing shoulder-to-shoulder with Cockrell's troops, Green and his men would endure more bloodletting inside the entrenchments at the Big Black.[52]

"Of Generals Featherston and Buford and Col. A. E. Reynolds, commanding brigades . . . too much cannot be said in commendation," lauded William Wing Loring in his report. "The rapidity and skill with which they executed their orders, and the boldness which their gallant commands met and successfully repulsed the powerful attacks of the enemy, delaying the Yankee army and securing a safe retreat to that of ours across the ford, entitles them to the highest praise." Unfortunately, the same thing cannot be written of the man who penned those words.

Loring did not execute Pemberton's orders with "rapidity and skill," and if Lieutenant Drennan's observations are accurate, Loring and other generals of his command actively undermined the commanding general's authority by talking in negative terms about him and laughing openly at him in front of subordinates. Loring's resume already contained an entry marked "unmanageable subordinate" for behavior during the war's early months in Virginia where his disdain for military discipline almost cost the Confederacy the service of Thomas J. "Stonewall" Jackson. Loring was jealous of his rank and equally resentful of professional soldiers. Would the course of the battle at Champion Hill have changed if Loring had immediately responded and arrived on the field earlier? It is impossible to say, and it is not the right question to ask. The real issue is whether Loring was slow in responding to Pemberton's repeated requests and made excuses for not executing his orders with "rapidly and skill." The jury is not out on that question.[53]

On the positive side of the ledger must be tabulated his good use of ground and disposition of his first two brigades, the steadiness he brought to what was otherwise a chaotic field, and his withdrawal in the face of the enemy. Whether he could have crossed Bakers Creek safely will never be known, but the fact that Buford was able to call back the 12th Louisiana from some distance without much difficulty seems to indicate the feat would have been easier than the fate to which Loring consigned it thereafter in its wandering odyssey to Jackson. His large division entered the Mississippi capital city with about 3,000 fewer men than it began the battle with—stragglers all.[54]

Winfield Featherston turned in a good performance and showed some talent in the way he handled his brigade. He marched it quickly, deployed it swiftly, and maneuvered it with authority—attributes he had not demonstrated since the bloodletting at Glendale in Virginia one year earlier. During the day's skirmishes, wrote Featherston, "and, in fact, the entire day, my brigade behaved well. All orders were promptly obeyed, and an eagerness to meet the enemy was manifested during the engagement by the whole command." Featherston did all that was asked of him, but the losses suffered by his brigade speak to the intensity of the action he faced. Loring could write of "successfully repuls[ing] the powerful attacks," but powerful attacks inflict casualties. The entire day extracted but one dead, one wounded, and one missing, and the first two of these were inflicted during the early morning bombardment on the Raymond Road. In the final analysis, one must at least marvel at the luck so many Mississippians enjoyed in ducking Northern lead.[55]

If the performances turned in by Winfield Featherston and Abraham Buford could be traced separately on a piece of paper and then overlaid, the coordinates would match almost perfectly. Buford, too, moved forward quickly when Loring finally released him, put his men into line smartly, and led them from the field in an orderly manner. He knew Tom Scott was his best regimental leader, and he deftly utilized his tactical skills to parry what could otherwise have been a dangerous rear guard pursuit. After praising both Scott and Edward Goodwin of the 35th Alabama, Buford noted, "The other regiments were directly under my immediate observation during the whole day, and I was more than gratified at the gallant bearing of the commanding officers, as well as that of the other field and company officers. To say that I am proud to command the brigade evinces but slightly the high regard and estimation I have for the troops. Their quickness of motion, their ardor, powers of endurance, and steadiness exhibited during the engagement of Saturday and on the retreat are worthy of mention." Buford's losses were 11 killed and 49 wounded. Two-thirds of these (five killed, 34 wounded) were suffered by Scott during his engagement against Osterhaus on the Middle Road. Despite his hearty engagement against Lindsey and Lawler, Goodwin lost only one man killed. That means the balance of Buford's losses sustained were five killed and 15 wounded.[56]

If Lloyd Tilghman resides today in the Valhalla described by Alfred Cumming in his letter to Stephen Lee, he is likely still wringing his hands in the hope that, one day, his reputation will emerge from beneath the Civil War record he carved out for himself. Tilghman suffered the misfortune of dying too quickly without ever having established himself as an able combat leader. He was brave to a fault, and he proved it at both Fort Henry and Champion Hill when he dismounted in the middle of an artillery barrage to sight a gun. But blocking a road far from the major scene of combat against the tepid pressing delivered by A. J. Smith is not likely to resuscitate Tilghman's reputation anytime soon. His losses were five killed, 10 wounded, and 42 missing—30 of which (one killed, two wounded, and 27 missing) were the result of the difficult skirmishing assignment handed to Robert Lowry's 6th Mississippi.[57]

Unlike the Northern long-arm, Southern artillery suffered one of its worse days of the war at Champion Hill. The returns for Carter Stevenson's Division (Ridley's Company A, 1st Mississippi Light Artillery, Johnston's Botetourt (Virginia) Artillery, Van Den Corput's Cherokee Georgia Artillery), are incomplete, but casualties were very heavy across the board. Captain Waddell's Alabama Battery, for which returns are available, show nine killed, 10 wounded, and five missing. Returns for Bowen's artillery are more complete. For the batteries attached to Cockrell's Brigade, Wade lost two wounded and two missing, Landis four killed and one wounded, and Guibor two missing. There are no breakdowns for the batteries that served with Green. Twenty-seven pieces of artillery were lost.[58]

Casualties for Wirt Adams's Mississippi cavalry and Brown's 20th Mississippi Mounted Infantry were not reported. Adams, too, made good his escape from the field at Champion Hill. Rather than follow the army behind the Big Black River and into the Vicksburg defenses, he led his troops in a roundabout journey and joined Joe Johnston around Jackson. Adams turned in a solid performance and did all that was asked of him. Of Brown's performance virtually nothing is known. [59]

*　　*　　*

"I think it due to myself, in bringing this portion of my report to a conclusion, to state emphatically that the advance movement of the army from Edwards Depot on the afternoon of May 15 was made against my judgment, in opposition to my previously expressed intentions, and to the subversion of my matured plans." This was how Pemberton phrased his effort to avoid the responsibilities of his actions in his report submitted in August 1863.

One is hard pressed to find more pitiable words from a *commanding general's* pen.[60]

Chapter 13

Aftermath

"Under these circumstances nothing remained but to retire the
army within the defenses of Vicksburg."

— Lt. Gen. John C. Pemberton

SOLDIERS FROM BOTH ARMIES REMEMBERED THAT MAY 17, THE
third Sunday of the month, dawned just as bright and beautiful as the day
before. Before the sun would set, another critical battle in the campaign
to capture Vicksburg would be fought.[1]

After Champion Hill, events in the Vicksburg theater of operations
moved at a dizzying pace. Grant was now in an ideal position to maintain
his strategic initiative by closely following his demoralized enemy and
inflicting a killing blow. If he could drive his Army of the Tennessee west
quickly and decisively, he might catch and destroy Pemberton outside
Vicksburg's heavy defenses and avoid what might otherwise be a long
and difficult siege.

Grant authorized the divisions of Carr and Osterhaus to continue
driving toward Edwards on the Jackson Road. A. J. Smith moved his
division across Bakers Creek and also turned toward Edwards. By early
May 17, the balance of William T. Sherman's XV Corps had arrived

from Jackson. Grant ordered Sherman to march his troops northward to Bridgeport, where Reynolds had crossed his Confederate brigade the night before. Grant also ordered Blair's division to reunite with Sherman at Bridgeport. Spirits were high in the Federal ranks. Everyone knew they had scored a hard-fought victory on May 16, and Grant was the man to follow it up. Their spirits were also lifted by rumors that Pemberton had been killed in the fighting.[2]

Those units most heavily engaged at Champion Hill were given a brief respite. Crocker, Logan, and Hovey formed the second wave of Union divisions heading toward Edwards and the Big Black River. One of these outfits was under new management. Marcellus Crocker had for some time been fighting off the onset of tuberculosis, and by May 17 he was no longer able to command in the field. Fortunately, Isaac Quinby was available to step in and reassume command of his old division.[3]

With Pemberton falling back in disorder, Grant knew the only impediment between his army and Vicksburg was the Big Black River. If the Confederates made a stand, that would be the place to make it.

*   *   *

May 17 did not dawn as bright for the Confederates. Pemberton's army had been routed and its losses, though not yet calculated, had been heavy. Worse still was that a significant portion of his army under Loring had simply disappeared, and nothing had yet been heard from Reynolds' Brigade and the army's four hundred wagons. May 16 had indeed been a difficult and perhaps decisive day.

Despair pervaded Vicksburg. News of the defeat reached the hill city within hours. "My pen almost refuses to tell of our terrible disaster of yesterday," diarist Emma Balfour wrote with a heavy heart. "From 6 o'clock in the morning until five in the evening the battle raged furiously. We are defeated—our army in confusion and the carnage, awful! Whole batteries and brigades taken prisoners—awful! awful!" Balfour was also suffering under the false information that her close friend Stephen D. Lee had fallen in the action. Young Annie Broidrick, another of Vicksburg's citizens, had also listened to the battle. To her, the fighting sounded like "a vast cane break on fire." Although many miles away, "windows and mirrors in the house . . . were broken and shattered." The news for Vicksburg's citizens was about to get much worse.[4]

Pemberton wanted to march directly for Vicksburg and its powerful ring of defenses, but was burdened by knowledge that Loring had not yet rejoined the army. As a result, Pemberton decided to hold open a bridgehead for Loring to cross the Big Black River, unaware he had in fact been cut off by Grant's Federals and was making for Jackson. In an effort to keep his army together, Pemberton sent John Bowen's bloodied division into a line of fortifications east of the river with orders to hold the position until Loring reached the west bank. A small brigade of Tennesseans under Brig. Gen. John C. Vaughn bolstered Bowen's position.[5]

The Confederate defenses in front of the bridge stretched across a large bend in the river. Pemberton later described the position as "somewhat in the shape of a horseshoe." Across the narrowest portion of the horseshoe was the mile-long Confederate line of earthworks, in front of which ran a small bayou. That obstruction, together with the parapets constructed earlier by Pemberton's engineers, provided the Southern infantry with what appeared to be a good defensive position. The ground in front of the works south of the railroad was mostly open and provided a good field of fire. On the left or northern sector of the line, however, was a copse of wood that offered protection to any force approaching from that quarter.[6]

Bowen's exhausted division filed into "our ditches," as one Southerner described the fortifications, early on the morning of May 17. Cockrell held the right of the line and Green the left. Vaughn's Tennessee brigade was holding the center of the line and was already in position when Bowen's men arrived. The Tennesseans had yet to be involved in any serious fighting. Most of the men had been conscripted from east Tennessee, a region openly hostile to the Confederacy. Pemberton did not believe Vaughn's front would be attacked. The 4th Mississippi Infantry took position amid the Tennesseans to add to their strength and morale. Some twenty pieces of artillery studded the line, mostly south of the railroad where the fields of fire were better suited to artillery.[7]

Pemberton later wrote of his confidence that Bowen and his men could hold the line: "I knew that the Missouri [and Arkansas] troops, under their gallant leaders, could be depended upon." The position was risky, however, for the men were hemmed in by the curve of the river. If the fortifications were captured, most of the Confederates fighting on the east bank would be stranded. Little cover existed between the defenses and the river, and the position was not deep enough to construct a second line of defensive works. If a sudden retreat became necessary, the only viable means of escape were across the railroad bridge and the steamer *Dot,* which had been transformed into a floating bridge. A collapse of the front, therefore, would likely create a bottleneck of chaos. Bowen would indeed have to hold his position—at least until Loring arrived.[8]

* * *

Loring never arrived, but Grant did. The Union commander had his men up early on May 17 marching toward Vicksburg. "[T]he unwelcome sound of the bugle greeted our ears [at 2:00 a.m.]," remembered one member of Carr's division. Rations quickly went out, and the soldiers sleepily downed a "pint of corn meal and a slice of bacon."[9]

John McClernand had been driving his XIII Corps vigorously forward and arrived near the river before the sun brightened the eastern sky. Carr's division led the advance and deployed in line on McClernand's right, along the northern section of the Confederate fortifications. Lawler's brigade formed with its right on the river, with Benton's brigade positioned near the Jackson Road. Osterhaus, next in line, formed his division along the middle and left of the Federal corps line. Lindsey's brigade formed the right and Garrard's men took position on the left. A gap remained south of the line, but Burbridge's brigade of A. J. Smith's division arrived and filled it. Artillery was unlimbered. The scent of renewed combat was again in the morning air.[10]

Soon after the line was formed, McClernand opened with his guns and a spirited artillery duel ensued. Bowen's exhausted soldiers huddled behind their breastworks during the bombardment, keeping an open eye for Loring and praying for his arrival so they could withdraw to safety. Except for the trees north of the railroad, the Federal soldiers did not have any cover of note and could only lay on the ground and hope the Confederate gunners missed their mark. An enemy shell hit and exploded a Union limber. The blast sent shrapnel flying in every direction, some of which embedded itself in General Osterhaus's leg. The wound was severe enough to force him from the field. Brigadier General Albert Lee assumed command of the division.[11]

General Lawler saw clearly the desperate plight of his men and determined to remedy the situation. The fighting Irishman led his brigade into cover on the extreme right of the Union line. He used the copse of trees and even a meander scar to shield his movement. Despite a continuous blistering fire from Confederate artillery and small arms, the soldiers reached the trees without sustaining serious casualties. The bold move changed the course of the battle: Lawler was now close enough to assault the Southern works. He ordered his men to fix bayonets. By an odd geographic quirk, Lawler's regiments faced south looking down the front of the Southern line of entrenchments, with the river directly behind them.[12]

With a shout, Lawler's brigade burst forth from the dry lowland and took Green's Confederates completely by surprise. Before the stunned enemy knew it, the Federals were within shouting distance of the earthworks. Instead of striking the Missourians and Arkansans directly, however, the Union regiments charged south across their front before angling in toward the center of the Confederate line about midway between the river and the railroad. Green's men managed one ragged volley that did not seem to have any appreciable effect. Lawler, however, stopped his brigade long enough to deliver a volley at Vaughn's Tennesseans before ordering his Hawkeyes and Badgers to launch a bayonet attack. The Federals slashed and sloshed across the small bayou and up the reddish clay earthworks. Although they were some of the freshest men in the entire Confederate army, the Tennesseans could not hold their position. Vaughn's brigade melted away and within a few seconds, a large mob of men were stampeding for the railroad bridge 1,400 yards behind them.[13]

Panic is contagious, and like an electric shock, it coursed through the remainder of the Southerners manning the Big Black River bridgehead. Green's men had watched with disbelieving eyes as the Federals poured across their front. Now they were watching with mouths agape as the enemy spilled through a couple hundred yards of suddenly abandoned front. "Our troops were completely surprised and were really surrounded before they knew it," Sgt. W. L. Foster of Company E, 21st Arkansas Infantry, wrote to his wife. Green's men were veterans and knew that if they remained behind their entrenchments, they would be trapped against the river and cut off from their only route of escape. By the hundreds they fell back, fleeing for their lives. Cockrell's Missourians, manning the far right (or southern) wing of the bridgehead were equally amazed at Vaughn's sudden collapse. "I watched this disorderly falling back [the

Tennesseans] a few minutes, when I saw that the enemy had possession of the trenches . . . and were rapidly advancing toward the bridge," Cockrell reported in disbelief. He, too, knew the import of the collapse and ordered his men to the rear. In only a few minutes, Lawler had shattered the Confederate line and driven an entire division (Bowen) and another brigade (Vaughn) back in confusion. McClernand's other brigades followed Lawler's example and launched attacks of their own, but by this time there was no one left to fight. The Confederates manning the bridgehead had vanished. For all they cared, Loring could fend for himself.[14]

Few Confederate casualties were suffered during the initial charge. The primary Southern losses occurred during the retreat to escape across the bridge or the steamer *Dot*. During the predictable bottleneck that quickly developed, some 1,750 Confederates fell into Union hands. One Southerner called the region between the river and defenses the "Jeff Davis Slaughter pen." Many of those unable to cross the bridge jumped into the river to swim across to the west bank. Many of these drowned or were shot during the attempt. Others simply threw down their weapons rather than try to run the gauntlet of Union fire or risk the muddy waters of the Big Black River. "Our Brigade captured the 60th Tenn. Reg. every single one, the Colonel and all," wrote an elated member of the 23rd Wisconsin, Burbridge's brigade. In addition to the infantry, eighteen pieces of artillery also fell into Federal hands. This disaster, Pemberton tried to later explain, was because of a mysterious order to move the battery horses across the river.[15]

As the victorious Federals were mopping up on the eastern bank, several struck up conversations with their prisoners. One Northerner recalled that a Confederate, when asked what he thought of the Federals, responded that "they could go where they pleased." The same Federal marveled at the sight of the Southern soldiers. "None of them have uniforms," he wrote in disbelief. "They have all kinds of clothing—they are hard looking critters."[16]

The sudden and disastrous loss of the Big Black River defenses and more than 1,750 soldiers convinced Pemberton his effort to connect with Loring had gone badly awry. For all he knew, the Federals had captured or destroyed Loring's Division. The preservation of his army and Vicksburg were now Pemberton's primary concern. Loring, if his division was still in existence, would have to fend for himself. "Under these circumstances nothing remained but to retire the army within the defenses of Vicksburg," wrote Pemberton.[17]

Many soldiers had already begun their retreat into the city. As one artilleryman scribbled in his diary, "the retreat of our army may be properly denominated a rout." By that evening, the entire Confederate army was marching westward for all it was worth. Pemberton rode ahead of his men to prepare Vicksburg for the arrival of Grant and his legions. The divisions operating on Vicksburg's flanks under Martin L. Smith and John H. Forney were directed to march for the city. John Bowen's and Carter Stevenson's men also filed into the trenches.[18]

One can only wonder what was going through Pemberton's mind as he made his way toward Vicksburg. He had lost two battles in as many days, and nearly half his mobile army. His worse fear—and that voiced earlier and often by Joseph E. Johnston—was on the verge of coming true. If he entered the entrenchments around the city, his army would be trapped against the Mississippi River with no reasonable means of escape. He still had the opportunity to evacuate the city to the north (as Johnston would later instruct him to do) and escape. But as far as Pemberton was concerned, Vicksburg was his charge, and he would do everything he could to protect the city. The general calmly summed up his appalling situation when he confided to an accompanying officer, "Just thirty years ago I began my military career by receiving my appointment to a cadetship at the U.S. Military Academy, and to-day—the same date—that career is ended in disaster and disgrace."[19]

The Confederates at the bridge, meanwhile, did their best to fight back and escape. Major Samuel Lockett, Pemberton's engineer, ordered the soldiers to destroy the bridge and the *Dot* to halt Grant long enough for Pemberton to pull back his disorganized masses to safer ground. Lockett covered the bridge with turpentine and burned it down; the *Dot* and other steamboats in the vicinity suffered the same fate. Two Confederate brigades remained behind to annoy the Federals and delay any bridge building effort.[20]

Southern sharpshooters also helped blunt the Federal advance. Grant's 12-year old son Fred, who made a habit of riding close to the point of danger, enjoyed himself as he pursued the retreating Confederates to the river. He was close enough to the action to watch while some swam to the west bank. Fred's enthusiasm was quickly dampened when a Confederate sharpshooter drew a bead on him. The shot hit him in the leg. Thinking he was mortally wounded, the young Grant called out to a nearby staff officer, "I am killed!" "Move your toes," shot back the officer. When he discovered his toes wiggled just fine, he was greatly relieved. Grant later wrote that the wound "was slight but very painful." The officer "recommended our hasty retreat," remembered Grant. "This we accomplished in good order."[21]

The appearance of the defeated Confederate army stumbling into Vicksburg was demoralizing for both soldier and civilian alike. Stories of defeat and rumors of treachery abounded. Rumors had it that Pemberton sold Vicksburg for $100,000. An Alabama cavalry private described the army as "all dejected." A member of Pemberton's staff admitted the same thing, writing that the "army [was] shockingly demoralized." "If an attack is made tomorrow, we are lost," prophesied Pvt. James E. Payne of Company K, 43rd Georgia Infantry, Barton's Brigade. "I have never been low spirited, but things look too dark for even me to be hopeful."[22]

The soldiers were tired and beaten, but the civilians were horrified. The two fresh divisions under Smith and Forney presented a façade of calm and organization, but when the bloodied veterans of Champion Hill and Big Black River bridge arrived, anguish coursed through those who watched them. "I hope never to witness again such a scene as the return of our routed army," wrote a distraught Emma Balfour. "From twelve o'clock until late in the night the streets and roads were jammed with wagons, cannons, horses, men, mules, stock, sheep, everything you can imagine that appertains to an army—being brought hurriedly within the intrenchment. Nothing like order prevailed, of course, as divisions, brigades, and regiments were broken and separated." Shocked they might have been, but the people of Vicksburg turned out in force to aid the troops. Many opened their pantries; others carried water to the street corners for the exhausted men. Balfour looked on with desperation, however. "Poor fellows," she wailed, "it made my heart ache to see them." Thomas C. Skinner, a Kentuckian serving with a mounted infantry outfit, summed it up when he said simply, May 17 was "one long day."[23]

*   *   *

As one might expect, the exact opposite feeling prevailed in the Union ranks. Grant's vigorous pursuit had reaped such huge dividends he felt he could in good faith disregard an order from Washington directing him to support Nathaniel Banks at Port Hudson. Grant's punch at the bridgehead had routed and driven Pemberton into the box that was Vicksburg and captured 1,750 prisoners at a cost of 279 killed, wounded, and missing. Grant was not about to stop. After months of trying and dying, Vicksburg was now firmly within his grasp. Instead of collecting himself east of the river, he ordered his three corps across the Big Black River. Vicksburg was doomed.[24]

*   *   *

Engineers had spent months digging nearly ten miles of entrenchments studded with forts, redans, and redoubts to protect Vicksburg from a land-based attack. They did their work well, for the siege that was about to begin lasted for 47 days. When Johnston learned of the defeat at Champion Hill, he advised Pemberton to abandon the city and save the army. Pemberton called another council of war and the decision was made to defend the city. Johnston, clearly the wrong man to attempt to raise the siege, notified Richmond that Pemberton's army was as good as lost.

Grant launched two major assaults against the Vicksburg defenses, one each on May 19 and May 22. His rationale for doing so was that the enemy had been routinely beaten and was demoralized. A quick victory would avoid the necessity of a protracted siege. The Confederates had indeed been beaten, but they could still fight. Grant's efforts were high-profile and bloody failures. Thereafter, he opted to press and starve the garrison into submission. His engineers encircled the city in a 12-mile ring of Federal works anchored above and below the city on the Mississippi River. They roughly paralleled the enemy entrenchments. By the end of May, Grant's army had increased to some 50,000; by the end of June, more than 20,000 additional men had joined the effort.

The trapped Confederates soon ran short of food and good water. When beef and pork stocks ran out, they slaughtered mules. The civilians suffered as well from the lack of supplies and daily artillery bombardments. Too weak and demoralized to take the offensive, Pemberton polled his senior officers and decided to surrender his army. On July 3, he met with Grant and agreed to discuss capitulation terms.

The following day, after an exchange of notes, Pemberton agreed to surrender.

Union soldiers saw white flags fluttering above the Confederate works that morning. "The rebels that was in the sitty surenderd them selves up to our commanding general Grant," wrote one Union soldier. Grant's Army of the Tennessee, led by the 81st Illinois, 45th Illinois, and 4th Minnesota, marched victoriously into the hill city. After nine months, Vicksburg—one of the most sought-after cities in the Confederacy—had fallen. "The long struggle is over," wrote a relieved General Logan to his wife.[25]

The Federals quickly took control of the city. Soldiers raised the United States flag above the Warren County Courthouse while Confederates "looked on in amazement." The Federals viewed the symbol with pride. "The glorious old Stars and Stripes float over the Court House," one Northerner wrote home. The 20th and 45th Illinois were assigned to act as the city's provost guards while the Confederates—described by one as "hardly able to move"—marched out and formally surrendered. The capture netted some 29,000 Confederates and 172 artillery pieces, together with all the miscellaneous items used by armies. Because there were not enough steamboats to carry them north, the garrison was paroled rather than imprisoned.[26]

The loss was a stunning blow to Southern morale and led to the surrender of Port Hudson five days later—the final Confederate bastion along the river. No one in the country was happier than President Lincoln, who noted that "the Father of Waters again goes unvexed to the sea."[27]

* * *

The monumental and historic Vicksburg campaign was over. Grant had his prize, Lincoln had his key, and the South had another decisive defeat to deal with. The victory spun the war in an entirely different direction. Vicksburg threw both Grant and Sherman into the national spotlight. The former would win big again at Chattanooga, be put in charge of all the armies, and move east to battle Robert E. Lee; the other would carry out Grant's operational plan to split the South again by driving a wedge south below Chattanooga to Atlanta, and then march from that city eastward to the sea.

Based upon the numbers involved and blood expended, Champion Hill was but a pale imitation of Shiloh, Antietam, Fredericksburg, and Chancellorsville. The generals who led the divisions, corps, and armies east of Bakers Creek were either largely unknown, like John Pemberton, Carter Stevenson, or John McClernand, or laboring under the burden of a tarnished record, like U. S. Grant. Not a single popular icon of the day was to be found on the order of battle. The fighting was waged in a region many considered to be the "backwater" of the war, and certainly far removed from major media centers like Washington and Richmond. Coverage of the battle was skimpy and brief. To the best of our knowledge, no photographers arrived to record for posterity the stiffening corpses, torn landscape, and freshly dug graves of those who gave their lives on that warm Mississippi day. For these and for other reasons, few then or thereafter gave much thought to the battle; almost no one recognized the significant consequences of its outcome. The land remained in private hands, the field remained largely unmarked. History threw a shadow on Champion Hill.

Hindsight and the ability to sift through official reports, letters, diaries, and other items of historical interest paints a different portrait than the one perused by those fighting the war. Today, it is easy to understand and accept that the fighting on May 16, 1863, was the decisive battle of the entire Vicksburg campaign. Grant's crossing of the Mississippi River was an important event, and Joe Johnston's rapid and premature abandonment of Jackson helped make the Union victory possible, but the combat at Champion Hill crushed the spirit of the Vicksburg army in the field and compelled its general to hasten within the city's fortifications. The battle's outcome, however, was anything but preordained. Had Pemberton scored a victory that day, Grant's army would have been in a very difficult situation, and possibly cut off from its riverine base of supplies. He did not yet enjoy a significant advantage in numbers, and Pemberton had behind him another two large divisions upon which to call. Given all that had occurred up to that point in the war, a sound defeat for Grant in May might well have ended his career.

The result of the fighting had long lasting repercussions on the course of the war. The victory ended Pemberton's career and launched Grant's in an entirely different direction. His victory outside Vicksburg tossed him up into the country's first tier of generals. He was no longer considered the bumbling drunk general from Illinois cutting canals across nameless swamps and crafting crazy schemes to open the Mississippi River. His future victories both in Tennessee and Virginia would one day lead to his election as president of the United Sates. Grant's growing military and political power redounded to William Sherman's benefit as well and left him in charge of the major Federal operation in the Western Theater when Grant moved east to conquer Virginia.

None of this would have unfolded as it did without a few hours of desperate fighting around an insignificant country crossroads and on the slopes of a rugged rise called Champion Hill.[28]

Thereafter

After flanking John Bowen's men away from the lower crossing with his brigade, **William P. Benton** fought through the remainder of the Vicksburg campaign as well as at Mobile during the last months of the war. He returned to his law practice and became a government agent. He died of yellow fever in New Orleans in 1867.

Though his role at Champion Hill was limited, **Frank P. Blair's** service throughout the war was one of solid accomplishment. He rose from division to corps command in the Army of the Tennessee and closed out the conflict fighting with his friend William T. Sherman in the Carolinas. After the war, Blair ran unsuccessfully for vice-president in 1868. He served two years in the United States Senate from Missouri before retiring due to ill health. He died in 1875.

After skillfully leading his brigade in the battle-saving counterattack up Champion Hill, **George B. Boomer** was killed leading his troops in the unsuccessful assault on the Vicksburg earthworks on May 22, 1863.

After Vicksburg, **Stephen G. Burbridge** commanded the District of Kentucky, chasing after John S. Mosby and making many enemies in the political process. Burbridge was ostracized in his home state because of his wartime actions. He died in 1894.

Eugene A. Carr continued to command division-size forces throughout the war, first in Arkansas and then at Mobile. After the war, Carr returned to the 5th United States Cavalry and fought Indians for nearly three decades. The old soldier died in 1910.

After serving in the rest of the Vicksburg campaign and some minor operations thereafter, **Marcellus M. Crocker** was relieved of command because of his poor health. Tuberculosis ended his life in 1865. Crocker ranks high among Union division commanders.

Manning F. Force, the vibrant leader of the 20th Ohio, took command of a brigade at Vicksburg. He was wounded in the face in the Atlanta campaign and awarded the Congressional Medal of Honor for his heroism. After the war, Force resumed his law practice and began his career as a writer of history. He died in 1899.

After his unspectacular performance on the Middle Road, **Theophilus T. Garrard** held only minor garrison positions after Vicksburg and was mustered out in 1864. He farmed and ran a salt works in his native Kentucky and died in 1902.

Ulysses S. Grant defeated Pemberton at Champion Hill and again the following day at the Big Black River, besieged Vicksburg, and accepted its surrender on July 4, 1863. The victorious general scored a stunning victory in the battles around Chattanooga that fall and was elevated in March 1864 to commanding general of the Federal armies. Grant moved east and located his headquarters with the Army of the Potomac. His bloody battles against Robert E. Lee in 1864-1865 eventually led to the fall of Richmond and the end of the war in Virginia when Lee surrendered at Appomattox. Grant went on to become the eighteenth president of the United States. He died of throat cancer in 1885, just after completing his memoirs.

David B. Hillis resigned as colonel of the 17th Iowa (Holmes's brigade) but still managed to attain a brevet brigadier general's commission. He returned to his medical practice and some fame in the scientific community. He died in 1900.

After his division fought much of the battle at Champion Hill, **Alvin P. Hovey** spent his post-Vicksburg days mostly in recruitment work in his native Indiana. He returned to his law practice after the war and held many political positions, including Minister to Peru, congressman, and governor. He died in office in 1891.

Of **Samuel A. Holmes** but little is known. After Vicksburg he remained in the army and led the 40th Missouri Infantry at Nashville. How he spent his postwar years and when they ended has not been determined.

James Keigwin of the 49th Indiana (Garrard's brigade) took over command of the brigade during the early stages of the Vicksburg siege and led it well. He resigned his command after the surrender because of a lingering and painful back injury sustained a year earlier. Keigwin was unable to work because of it, and spent much of the next four decades living off a pension. He died in 1904.

William J. Landram participated in the May 22nd assault on the Vicksburg defenses, where his brigade suffered heavy losses. He was promoted to brevet brigadier general in 1865 and mustered out in February 1865. He died in 1895.

Michael K. Lawler performed well during the balance of the fighting at Vicksburg and went on to command his brigade and division in the trans-Mississippi theater of operations. He was brevetted a major general on March 13, 1865. After the war, Lawler became a horse trader until he retired to a farm in Illinois. The brash Irishman died in 1882.

Mortimer D. Leggett continued to command brigade, division, and corps-sized units. His defense of what is now known as "Leggett's Hill" at the battle of Atlanta won him lasting fame. The New York native participated in the March to the Sea and returned to private life after the war. He served for a few years as a Commissioner of Patents and formed a company that eventually became a part of General Electric. Leggett died in Ohio in 1896.

After the fall of Vicksburg, **Daniel W. Lindsey** became adjutant general for his home state of Kentucky. He later resumed his law practice and lived a long life before dying in 1917.

John A. Logan was awarded the Congressional Medal of Honor for his service at Vicksburg, and went on to fight in many of the war's most important Western Theater battles. He led the Army of the Tennessee for a short time after James B. McPherson was killed outside Atlanta in July 1864, but lost it to a "West Point" general—a perceived slight he never forgot or forgave. After the war, Logan worked on behalf of veterans and was an unsuccessful candidate for vice president in 1884. He was elected as a United States Senator from Illinois and was holding that position when he died in 1886.

After his good service and wounding at Champion Hill, **Daniel Macauley** of the 11th Indiana (McGinnis's brigade) won a brevet brigadier general's commission for his outstanding service at the 1864 battle of Cedar Creek in Virginia. He died in 1894.

After Vicksburg's surrender, the 47th Indiana's **John McLaughlin** (McGinnis's brigade) was assigned to the XIX Army Corps and took part in the Red River campaign with Nathaniel Banks. He rose to the rank of colonel and closed out the war in the fighting around Mobile. McLaughlin moved to Kansas and worked as a gunsmith. He had seven children and was still alive as of 1883.

After leading his corps through much of the fighting in the Vicksburg campaign, **John A. McClernand** was relieved of command by Grant following the May 22nd assault and McClernand's claims thereafter regarding the role of his men in the effort. He regained his command the following year, but by that time it had been dispersed across Louisiana and Texas—far from the active theater of operations. McClernand resigned in disgust in 1864 and returned to Springfield, Illinois, and Democratic politics. He was later instrumental in establishing the national military park at Shiloh. The fighting political general died in 1900.

George F. McGinnis proved at Champion Hill he could handle a brigade, but held only small commands after Vicksburg. He served in a variety of political positions after the war, and was postmaster of Indianapolis when he died in 1910.

James B. McPherson led his corps through the Vicksburg, Meridian, and Chattanooga campaigns. He let slip through his fingers a golden opportunity to cut off and disperse Joseph E. Johnston's army at Snake Creek Gap during the early stages of the Atlanta campaign. McPherson was killed in the Battle of Atlanta on July 22, 1864. Although he was supported and liked by Grant and Sherman, McPherson never lived up to his reputation as a competent field commander.

After missing much of the Champion Hill fighting, the Prussian-born **Peter J. Osterhaus** was wounded the following day at Big Black River. Osterhaus continued leading his men in many of the Army of the Tennessee's battles. He quarreled with Sherman over a leave of absence issue, but his performance was never in doubt. After the war, Osterhaus served as a United States consul before dying in 1917.

Like his brigade commander at Champion Hill, **Holden Putnam**'s time on this earth was coming to an end. He led his 93rd Illinois (Boomer's brigade) gallantly during the balance of the campaign, and was killed at Missionary Ridge on November 25, 1863.

John B. Sanborn had the honor of leading the Federals into Vicksburg after the surrender. He spent the remainder of the war in the trans-Mississippi Theater. After the war, Sanborn worked as an Indian agent and was elected to the United States House of Representatives and Senate. He died in 1904.

After missing Champion Hill, **William T. Sherman** led his corps through the Vicksburg campaign and took over the Army of the Tennessee when Grant became head of the Federal armies. Sherman conducted the Meridian campaign, where he first implemented his total warfare policy. He went on to capture Atlanta, and thereafter conducted his infamous March to the Sea and into the Carolinas, though by this stage of the war there was no serious opposition confronting him. The war effectively ended with Joe Johnston's surrender to Sherman. Sherman later served as commander-in-chief of the army. He died in 1891.

After heavy fighting at Champion Hill, **James R. Slack** fought with his brigade in the Red River campaign and in the operations around Mobile, Alabama. He served as a judge after the war and died in 1881.

Andrew J. Smith led his division and then a corps in many of the major Western operations, including the Red River campaign, Tupelo, Nashville, and Mobile. After the war, he served as commander of the famous 7th United States Cavalry before becoming city auditor for St. Louis. He died in 1897.

Giles A. Smith did not have much of an opportunity to stand out at Champion Hill. He made up for it thereafter and rose to division command. After sustaining a serious wound at Missionary Ridge in November of 1863, he led his brigade throughout the Atlanta campaign and March to the Sea. After the war, Smith was a political appointee of President Grant. He died in 1876.

After leading a brigade at Vicksburg, **John E. Smith** went on to lead a division and fought in most of the battles in the Western Theater. After the war, he became colonel of the 27th United States Infantry. He retired in 1881 and died sixteen years later.

T. Kilby Smith served through the Vicksburg campaign and led his men up the Red River in 1864. When the war ended, he became a consul in Central America, but returned to the United States for his retirement. He died in 1887.

William T. Spicely (McGinnis's brigade) continued leading his 24th Indiana after his outstanding tactical accomplishments at Champion Hill. He received a brevet brigadier general's commission for his action at Mobile at the end of the war. Spicely died in 1884.

John Stevenson held a series of small commands after Vicksburg. His flanking attack at Champion Hill was the highlight of his military career. He remained in the army after the war and became a colonel in the Regular Army at the head of the 30th United States Infantry. Stevenson eventually retired to his law practice in St. Louis and expired in 1897.

John E. Tourtellotte (Sanborn's brigade) commanded the 4th Minnesota throughout the war and rendered distinguished service at the battle of Allatoona in 1864. Tourtellotte remained in the Regular Army, rising to the rank of major in the 7th Cavalry before retiring in 1885. He died six years later.

*   *   *

After escaping from Champion Hill, **Wirt Adams** harassed Grant's army around Jackson and went on to lead his cavalry under Nathan Bedford Forrest for the balance of the war. He spent his remaining years in Vicksburg and Jackson as a state revenue agent and postmaster. Adams was killed on a Jackson city street in 1888 by a pistol-wielding irate newspaper editor.

Seth Barton surrendered with his brigade in Vicksburg. He was later transferred east and given command of Lewis Armistead's former brigade, which had been part of George Pickett's Division during the bloodletting at Gettysburg. Pickett relieved him of command—ostensibly because of his judgment in the field—in the spring of 1864 during the Bermuda Hundred fighting. Barton's subordinate officers petitioned for his reinstatement, to no avail. During the fall of 1864, Barton was given command of a brigade of infantry and artillery to help defend Richmond. He was captured at Sailor's Creek, returned to his native Fredericksburg, and died there in 1900.

The perfectly delivered counterattack at Champion Hill was **John S. Bowen's** crowning wartime achievement. After withdrawing into the Vicksburg entrenchments, he contracted dysentery. Captured, paroled, and exchanged, the general died only a few days later—ironically, on a farm near the Champion Hill battlefield. His remains were eventually buried in the Vicksburg city cemetery.

After the Vicksburg campaign, **Abraham Buford** transferred to the cavalry and served well with Nathan Bedford Forrest. Buford returned to Kentucky after the war ended and became engaged in various profit-making schemes, including horse racing. He also served in his state's legislature. His money-making efforts were not successful, and he lost most of his fortune before taking his own life in 1884.

Though the hard-fighting **Francis M. Cockrell** surrendered at Vicksburg, he went on to lead his famous Missouri brigade through many of the Western Theater's major battles. Like so many other Southern comrades, enemy lead found him on the field of Franklin. After recovering from his severe wound he returned to duty at Fort Blakely to defend Mobile's land side. He was captured there as the war wound its way to conclusion. Cockrell returned to Missouri and was elected to the United States Senate, where he served for thirty years. The remarkable civilian general is widely recognized as one of the war's finest combat leaders. He died in 1915.

Alfred Cumming surrendered in Vicksburg. After he was paroled, he led a brigade through the Atlanta campaign, where he displayed time and again his competence as a leader of men in combat. Without doubt, Champion Hill was an aberration in an otherwise outstanding career. Cumming was severely wounded at Jonesboro and unable thereafter to take the field. He retired and spent his remaining years farming in Georgia until his death in 1910.

Thomas P. Dockery (Green's Brigade) continued to lead his 19th Arkansas until he was promoted to brigadier general and given command of an Arkansas brigade in the trans-Mississippi Theater. After the war, he became a civil engineer in Texas. He died in 1898.

Winfield S. Featherston continued to command his brigade as part of Loring's Division. His record during the Atlanta and Tennessee campaigns is one of solid, and occasionally outstanding, service. He surrendered with the army in North Carolina in 1865. After the war, Featherston made a name for himself in Mississippi politics before dying in 1891.

After taking command of Edward Tracy's Brigade, **Isham W. Garrott** retreated with the army into Vicksburg and commanded his 20th Alabama until he was killed during a skirmish on June 17, 1863. His appointment to brigadier general, dated May 28, arrived at Vicksburg after his death.

Elijah Gates (Green's Brigade) was captured the day after Champion Hill in the disaster at Big Black River Bridge, but escaped a few days later. He lost an arm in the fighting at Franklin and was captured, but again escaped only to be captured yet a third time at Fort Blakely at Mobile. Gates farmed after the war, served as a sheriff, and was elected state treasurer. "The grand old man" of St. Joseph, Missouri, died at the ripe old age of 88.

Edward Goodwin (Buford's Brigade) of the 35th Alabama, whose gallant service holding back McClernand's advance along the Middle Road helped Martin Green's men fall safely back, died in the fall of 1863. Some records show him in command in 1864, but these are apparently incorrect. The cause of his death is unknown.

Martin E. Green escaped the collapse of the Big Black River bridgehead and slipped into Vicksburg. He was slightly wounded on June 25, but killed two days later when a Federal sharpshooter's bullet pierced his head as he peered over the earthworks. He was buried in Vicksburg, but the exact site of his grave has been lost.

Joseph E. Johnston's failure to rescue Vicksburg was merely one example of a passive style of generalship he would continue to display through the Atlanta campaign. Because of his failure to stop Sherman in Georgia and his running quarrel with President Jefferson Davis, the president removed Johnston from command in July 1864. Robert E. Lee reinstated Johnston during the war's final weeks in an effort to stop Sherman's march through the Carolinas, but his was an impossible task. He surrendered to Sherman in North Carolina. Ironically, Johnston's outstanding offensive action of the war took place at Bentonville in March 1865, where he fell upon and nearly crushed one wing of the Federal army. By that late date, however, any success he might have earned was too little, too late. After the war, Johnston served as a congressman and railroad commissioner before dying in 1891 when he contracted a cold standing bareheaded in the rain at William T. Sherman's funeral.

After his stellar conduct at Champion Hill, **Stephen D. Lee** went on to become the youngest lieutenant general in the Confederacy. He eventually led a corps during the Atlanta campaign with mixed success. After the war, Lee continued his spectacular career, first as president of Mississippi Agricultural and Mechanical College (now Mississippi State University), as commander of the United Confederate Veterans, and finally as a commissioner on the Vicksburg National Military Park Commission. He died in 1908.

After his heroic work in rebuilding the bridge over Bakers Creek, **Samuel H. Lockett** continued as an engineering officer until the end of the war. He later served as a military engineer in Egypt, Chile, and Columbia. He died in 1891.

After escaping from the Champion Hill battlefield, **William W. Loring** and his division joined Joseph E. Johnston at Jackson and took part in the feeble efforts to raise the siege of Vicksburg. He later defended the state against Sherman's Meridian campaign, led a division in the Atlanta campaign and Hood's Tennessee campaign, and surrendered with the army in North Carolina. Loring joined the forces of the Khedive in Egypt, where he won decorations for his service. He returned to the United States and died in 1886. He never changed his opinion of John Pemberton.

Robert Lowry led his 6th Mississippi through most of the rest of the war and saw hard fighting in the Atlanta campaign and again during Hood's disastrous raid into Tennessee. Lowry assumed command of the brigade when its commander, John Adams, was killed at Franklin. He was appointed brigadier general in February 1865 and ended the war fighting in North Carolina. He was elected governor of Mississippi in 1881. Lowry died in Jackson in 1910.

After the debacle at Champion Hill, **John C. Pemberton** withdrew into Vicksburg, which he surrendered on July 4, 1863. Rumors abounded that he purposefully surrendered the city on Independence Day. Paroled and exchanged, Pemberton was left without a command. When he reported for duty and met Joe Johnston, Pemberton refused to shake his hand. He resigned and took an appointment as a lieutenant colonel of artillery. After the war, Pemberton moved to Virginia and Pennsylvania. The stigma of being a Northerner and a loser in the field rested heavily on his shoulders until his death 18 years later. Justified or not, he will be forever linked with the defensive fiasco at Vicksburg.

Private **James Franklin Pierce**, Company D, 3rd Mississippi Infantry (Featherston's Brigade), survived Champion Hill and went on to have a daughter, who had a son, who had a son, who had the author. Pierce's family stories of the fighting at "Baker's Creek" were passed down through the generations, and planted the seed that germinated into the book you are now reading.

After his miserable and exhausting experience at Champion Hill (where he was with the wagons and missed the fighting), **Alexander W. Reynolds** went on to surrender at Vicksburg, command a brigade in Carter Stevenson's Division, and be wounded at New Hope Church in Georgia during the Atlanta campaign. After the war, he fought in Egypt with William W. Loring, died there in 1876, and was buried in Alexandria.

After taking command of Tilghman's Brigade, **Arthur E. Reynolds** escaped with Loring to Jackson. He was later transferred to Virginia, where he fought in the Petersburg campaign and was wounded. He entered Mississippi politics after the war and died in 1880.

Thomas M. Scott's outstanding performance at the head of the 12th Louisiana (Buford's Brigade) held back several enemy regiments along the Middle Road. During the retreat he deftly extracted his command from the jaws of capture on the night of May 16 by returning to the east bank of Bakers Creek. Scott served in Mississippi until the forces defending that state were sent east to fight in the Atlanta campaign. Scott was promoted to brigadier general to date from May 1864, and capably led his brigade during that long and bloody effort. He fell severely wounded at Franklin. Scott returned to Louisiana after the war and farmed until his death in 1876.

Champion Hill was **Carter L. Stevenson's** first real battlefield experience, and it was not a good one. Many more followed, however, and he improved as a commander. He took part in every one of the Army of Tennessee's combats except Franklin, and surrendered with Joe

Johnston in North Carolina in 1865. After the war, Stevenson returned to Virginia, where he worked as an engineer until his death in 1888.

After he was mortally wounded, **Lloyd Tilghman** was taken to the Yeiser house, where he was pronounced dead. His remains were eventually transported and buried in New York City. Tilghman is memorialized by a statue in Vicksburg National Military Park. Though the description of his death is inaccurate, it nevertheless honors the memory of the highest-ranking officer killed during the campaign. His sons returned to the Champion Hill battlefield in 1907 and placed a monument at the site of their father's death.

* * *

Matilda Champion returned to her home after the battle, happy to discover the lovely structure was still standing. It was burned to the ground about six months later by a Union soldier. When her husband died in 1867, Matilda resorted to manual labor with the children and worked hard to educate them. She lived a long life before dying on December 10, 1907.

After Pemberton surrendered Vicksburg, **Sid Champion** was imprisoned and later exchanged. He remained with the cavalry and was seriously wounded during Hood's Tennessee campaign during the fighting at Franklin. He ended the war as a lieutenant colonel. Sid returned home and built another home across the road from where the other had stood, this one facing the railroad. His health was not good, however, because he never fully recovered from his wound. Sid died in 1867, leaving his beloved Matilda with four young children.

Order of Battle

Confederates

Army of Vicksburg

Lieutenant General John C. Pemberton

Loring's Division
Major General William W. Loring

First Brigade
Brigadier General Lloyd Tilghman (k)
Colonel Arthur E. Reynolds

1st Confederate Infantry Battalion: Lieutenant Colonel G. H. Forney
6th Mississippi: Colonel Robert Lowry
15th Mississippi: Colonel Michael Farrell
23rd Mississippi: Colonel Joseph M. Wells
26th Mississippi: Colonel Arthur E. Reynolds, Major Tully F. Parker
Culberson's Mississippi Battery: Lieutenant J. Culberson
Cowan's Mississippi Battery: Captain James J. Cowan

Second Brigade
Brigadier General Abraham Buford

27th Alabama: Colonel James Jackson
35th Alabama: Colonel Edward Goodwin

54th Alabama: Colonel Alpheus Baker (w)
55th Alabama: Colonel John Snodgrass
9th Arkansas: Colonel Isaac L. Dunlop
3rd Kentucky: Major J.H. Bowman
7th Kentucky: Colonel Ed Crossland
12th Louisiana: Colonel Thomas M. Scott
Bouanchaud's Pointe Coupee LA Artillery: Captain Alcide Bouanchaud

Third Brigade
Brigadier General Winfield S. Featherston

3rd Mississippi: Colonel Thomas A. Mellon
22nd Mississippi: Colonel Frank Schaller
31st Mississippi: Colonel John A. Orr
33rd Mississippi: Colonel David W. Hurst
1st Mississippi Sharpshooter Battalion: Major William A. Rayburn
Wofford's Mississippi: Captain Jefferson L. Wofford

Stevenson's Division
Major General Carter L. Stevenson

First Brigade
Brigadier General Seth Barton

40th Georgia: Lieutenant Colonel Robert M. Young
41st Georgia: Colonel William E. Curtis
42nd Georgia: Colonel Robert J. Henderson
43rd Georgia: Colonel Skidmore Harris (k)
Captain Mathadeus M. Grantham
52nd Georgia: Colonel Charles D. Phillips (c)
Major John J. Moore
Corput's Cherokee Georgia Artillery: Captain Max Van Den Corput

Second Brigade
Brigadier General Stephen D. Lee (w)

20th Alabama: Colonel Isham W. Garrott
23rd Alabama: Colonel Franklin K. Beck
30th Alabama: Colonel Charles M. Shelley

31st Alabama: Lieutenant Colonel Thomas M. Arrington
46th Alabama: Colonel Michael L. Woods (c)
Captain George E. Brewer
Waddell's Alabama Battery: Captain James F. Waddell

Third Brigade
Brigadier General Alfred Cumming

34th Georgia: Colonel James A. W. Johnson
36th Georgia: Colonel Jesse A. Glenn
39th Georgia: Colonel Joseph T. McConnell (w)
Lt. Col. J. F. B. Jackson
56th Georgia: Colonel Elihu P. Watkins (w)
Lt. Col. John T. Slaughter
57th Georgia: Colonel William Barkuloo

Fourth Brigade
Colonel Alexander W. Reynolds

3rd Tennessee: Colonel Newton J. Lillard
31st Tennessee: Colonel William M. Bradford
43rd Tennessee: Colonel James W. Gillespie
59th Tennessee: Colonel William L. Eakin
Claiborne's Maryland Battery: Captain Fred O. Claiborne

Artillery
Major Joseph W. Anderson (k)

Botetourt Virginia Battery: Capt. John W. Johnston
Ridley's Mississippi Battery: Captain Samuel J. Ridley (k)
Captain William T. Ratliff

Bowen's Division
Major General John S. Bowen

First Brigade
Colonel Francis M. Cockrell

1st Missouri: Colonel Amos C. Riley

2nd Missouri: Lieutenant Colonel Pembroke S. Senteny
3rd Missouri: Colonel William R. Gause
5th Missouri: Colonel James McCown
6th Missouri: Major S. Cooper
Wade's Missouri Battery: Lieutenant Richard C. Walsh
Landis' Missouri Battery: Lieutenant John M. Langan
Guibor's Missouri Battery: Lieutenant William Corkery

Second Brigade
Brigadier General Martin E. Green

15th Arkansas: Lieutenant Colonel William W. Reynolds
19th Arkansas: Colonel Thomas P. Dockery
20th Arkansas: Colonel D. W. Jones
21st Arkansas: Colonel Jordan E. Cravens
12th Arkansas Sharpshooter Battalion: Lieutenant John S. Bell
1st Arkansas Cavalry Battalion (dismounted): Captain W. S. Catterson
1st Missouri Cavalry (dismounted): Colonel Elijah Gates
3rd Missouri Cavalry (dismounted): Lieutenant Colonel D. Todd Samuels
Dawson's Missouri Battery: Captain William E. Dawson
Lowe's Missouri Battery: Captain Schyler Lowe

Cavalry

Wirt Adam's Mississippi Cavalry: Colonel Wirt Adams
20th Mississippi Mounted Cavalry: Lieutenant Colonel W.N. Brown

---

Federals

Army of the Tennessee

Major General Ulysses S. Grant

XIII Army Corps
Major General John A. McClernand

Ninth Division
Brigadier General Peter J. Osterhaus

First Brigade
Brigadier General Theophilus T. Garrard

118th Illinois: Colonel John G. Fonda
49th Indiana: Colonel James Keigwin
69th Indiana: Colonel Thomas W. Bennett
7th Kentucky: Lieutenant Colonel John Lucas

Second Brigade
Colonel Daniel W. Lindsey

22nd Kentucky: Lieutenant Colonel George W. Monroe
16th Ohio: Captain Eli W. Botsford
42nd Ohio: Major William H. Williams
114th Ohio: Colonel John Cradlebaugh

Artillery
7th Michigan Artillery: Captain Charles H. Lanphere
1st Wisconsin Artillery: Captain Jacob T. Foster

Cavalry
3rd Illinois Cavalry, Companies A, E, and K: Captain John L. Campbell

Tenth Division
Brigadier General Andrew J. Smith

First Brigade
Brigadier General Stephen G. Burbridge

16th Indiana: Colonel Thomas J. Lucas
67th Indiana: Lieutenant Colonel Theodore E. Buehler
83rd Ohio: Colonel Frederick W. Moore
23rd Wisconsin: Colonel Joshua J. Guppey

Second Brigade
Colonel William J. Landram

77th Illinois: Colonel David P. Grier
97th Illinois: Colonel Friend S. Rutherford
108th Illinois: Lieutenant Colonel C. Turner
130th Illinois: Colonel N. Niles
19th Kentucky: Lieutenant Colonel John Cowan
48th Ohio: Colonel Peter J. Sullivan

Artillery
Chicago Mercantile Battery: Captain Patrick H. White
17th Ohio Battery: Captain Ambrose A. Blount

Cavalry

4th Indiana Cavalry, Company C: Captain Andrew P. Gallagher

Twelfth Division
Brigadier General Alvin P. Hovey

First Brigade
Brigadier General George F. McGinnis

11th Indiana: Colonel Daniel Macauley (w)
Lieutenant Colonel William W. Darnell
24th Indiana: Colonel William T. Spicely
34th Indiana: Major Robert A. Jones
46th Indiana: Colonel Thomas H. Bringhurst
29th Wisconsin: Colonel Charles R. Gill

Second Brigade
Colonel James R. Slack

47th Indiana: Lieutenant Colonel John A. McLaughlin
24th Iowa: Colonel Eber C. Byam
28th Iowa: Colonel John Connell
56th Ohio: Lieutenant Colonel William H. Raynor

Artillery

2nd Ohio Battery: Lieutenant Augustus Beach
16th Ohio Battery: Captain James A. Mitchell (k)
Lieutenant Russell P. Twist
Company A, 1st Missouri Light Artillery: Captain George W. Schofield

Cavalry

1st Indiana Cavalry, Company C: Lieutenant James L. Carey

Fourteenth Division

Brigadier General Eugene A. Carr

First Brigade

Brigadier General William P. Benton

33rd Illinois: Colonel Charles E. Lippencott
99th Illinois: Colonel George W.K. Bailey
8th Indiana: Colonel David Shunk
18th Indiana: Colonel Henry D. Washburn

Second Brigade

Brigadier General Michael K. Lawler

21st Iowa: Colonel Samuel Merrill
22nd Iowa: Colonel William M. Stone
23rd Iowa: Colonel William H. Kinsman
11th Wisconsin: Colonel Charles L. Harris

Artillery

Company A, 2nd Illinois Light Artillery: Lieutenant Frank B. Fenton
1st Indiana Artillery: Captain Martin Klauss

Unattached

2nd Illinois Cavalry, 7 companies: Lieutenant Colonel D. B. Bush
6th Missouri Cavalry, 7 companies: Colonel C. Wright
Kentucky Company of Engineers and Mechanics: Capt. William F. Patterson

XV Army Corps
Major General William T. Sherman

Second Division
Major General Frank P. Blair

First Brigade
Colonel Giles A. Smith

113th Illinois: Colonel George B. Hoge
116th Illinois: Colonel Nathan W. Tupper
6th Missouri: Lieutenant Colonel Ira Boutell
8th Missouri: Lieutenant Colonel David C. Coleman
13th U.S. Infantry, 1st Battalion: Captain Edward Washington

Second Brigade
Colonel T. Kilby Smith

55th Illinois: Colonel Oscar Malmborg
127th Illinois: Colonel Hamilton N. Eldridge
83rd Indiana: Colonel Benjamin J. Spooner
54th Ohio: Colonel Cyrus W. Fisher
57th Ohio: Colonel Americus V. Rice

Artillery
Company A, 1st Illinois Light Artillery: Captain Peter P. Wood
Company B, 1st Illinois Light Artillery: Captain Samuel E. Barrett

XVII Army Corps
Major General James B. McPherson

Third Division
Major General John A. Logan

First Brigade
Brigadier General John E. Smith

20th Illinois: Major Daniel Bradley

31st Illinois: Lieutenant Colonel John D. Rees
45th Illinois: Colonel Jasper A. Maltby
124th Illinois: Colonel Thomas J. Sloan
23rd Indiana: Lieutenant Colonel William P. Davis

Second Brigade
Brigadier General Mortimer D. Leggett

30th Illinois: Lieutenant Colonel Warren Shedd
20th Ohio: Colonel Manning F. Force
68th Ohio: Lieutenant Colonel John S. Snook
78th Ohio: Lieutenant Colonel Zackariah M. Chandler

Third Brigade
Brigadier General John Stevenson

8th Illinois: Lieutenant Colonel Robert H. Sturgess
81st Illinois: Colonel John J. Dollins
7th Missouri: Captain Robert Buchanan
32nd Ohio: Colonel Benjamin F. Potts

Artillery
Company D, 1st Illinois Light Artillery: Captain Henry A. Rogers
Company L, 2nd Illinois Light Artillery: Captain William H. Bolton
8th Michigan Artillery: Captain Samuel De Golyer
3rd Ohio Artillery: Captain William S. Williams

Seventh Division
Brigadier General Marcellus M. Crocker

First Brigade
Colonel John B. Sanborn

48th Indiana: Colonel Norman Eddy
59th Indiana: Colonel Jesse I. Alexander
4th Minnesota: Lieutenant Colonel John E. Tourtellotte
18th Wisconsin: Colonel Gabriel Bouck

Second Brigade
Colonel Samuel A. Holmes

17th Iowa: Colonel David B. Hillis
10th Missouri: Lieutenant Colonel Leonidas Horney (k)
Major Francis C. Deimling
24th Missouri, Company E: Lieutenant V. Chalefoux
80th Ohio: Colonel Matthias H. Bartilson

Third Brigade
Colonel George B. Boomer

93rd Illinois: Colonel Holden Putnam
5th Iowa: Lieutenant Colonel Ezekial S. Sampson
10th Iowa: Colonel William E. Small
26th Missouri: Major C. F. Brown

Artillery
Company M, 1st Missouri Light Artillery: Lieutenant Junius W. MacMurray
11th Ohio Battery: Lieutenant Fletcher E. Armstrong
6th Wisconsin Battery: Captain Henry Dillon
12th Wisconsin Battery: Captain William Zickerick

Cavalry Division
Captain John S. Foster

2nd Illinois Cavalry, Companies A and B: Lieutenant W. B. Cummins
4th Missouri Cavalry, Company F: Lieutenant Alexander Mueller
4th Independent Company Ohio Cavalry: Captain J. S. Foster

Notes

Chapter 1

1. Earl S. Miers, *The Web of Victory: Grant at Vicksburg* (Baton Rouge: Louisiana State University Press, 1955), 279.

2. Samuel Carter III, *The Final Fortress: The Campaign for Vicksburg, 1862-1863* (New York: St. Martin's Press, 1980), 12.

3. Carter, *Final Fortress*, 12-14.

4. Carter, *Final Fortress*, 18, 21.

5. Herman Hattaway and Archer Jones, *How the North Won: A Military History of the Civil War* (Urbana: University of Illinois Press, 1983), 35.

6. For more information Forts Henry and Donelson, see Benjamin F. Cooling, *Forts Henry and Donelson: The Key to the Confederate Heartland* (Knoxville: University of Tennessee Press, 1987). For Shiloh, see Larry Daniel, *Shiloh: The Battle That Changed the Civil War* (New York: Simon and Shuster, 1997).

7. New Madrid and Island Number Ten information can be found in Larry Daniel and Riley Bock, *Island No. 10: Struggle for the Mississippi Valley* (Tuscaloosa: The University of Alabama Press, 1996).

8. Surprisingly little has been written on the fall of New Orleans. For more information, see Chester G. Hearn, *The Capture of New Orleans, 1862* (Baton Rouge: Louisiana State University Press, 1995).

9. After Shiloh, the war in the West merged into a single theater. Three major Federal armies converged on Corinth, forcing the Confederates to concentrate in a similar manner. The Federal armies were again divided once Corinth fell. One army moved east toward Chattanooga, which compelled the Confederates to follow suit with part of their army.

10. *War of the Rebellion: The Official Records of the Union and Confederate Armies*, 128 vols (Washington, D.C., 1890-1901), Series I, volume 10, part 1, 671, hereafter cited as *OR*. All references are to Series I unless otherwise states. For more

information on Iuka and Corinth, see Peter Cozzens, *The Darkest Days of the War: The Battles of Iuka and Corinth* (Chapel Hill: The University of North Carolina Press, 1997).

11. James Field to his cousin, November 16, 1862, James Field Letter, OHS.

12. W. L. Foster to his wife, June 20, 1863, Civil War Papers, MDAH; William Thomas Daniel to his wife, March 31, 1863, William Thomas Daniel Letters, GDAH; Howard Stevens to his uncle, July 21, 1863, Howard and Victor H. Stevens Letters, Gregory A. Cocco Collection, Harrisburg Civil War Roundtable Collection, USAMHI; Alman Phillips to his brother and sister, May 7, 1863, George Thornton Fowler Letters and Papers, GDAH; John Fiske, *The Mississippi Valley in the Civil War* (New York: Houghton, Mifflin and Company, 1900), 241; Terrence J. Winschel, *Vicksburg: Fall of the Confederate Gibraltar* (Abilene: McWhiney Foundation Press, 1999), 20.

13. *OR* 17, pt. 1, 465-525.

14. *OR* 17, pt. 2, 463.

15. *OR* 17, pt. 1, 599-697.

16. John F. Marszalek, *Sherman: A Soldier's Passion for Order* (New York: Free Press, 1993), 207. Earlier in the war, during his tenure in Kentucky, Sherman declared the war would be long, bloody, and would require large numbers of men to win it. The angry public response, coupled with his exhausted mental and physical state, triggered something approaching a nervous breakdown (or what some at the time termed "insanity"). Sherman, of course, was correct.

17. *OR* 17, pt. 1, 613.

18. *OR* 17, 371-421.

19. Milton W. Shaw to Alf, March 10, 1863, Milton W. Shaw Letter, McCain Library and Archives, University Libraries, USM; Charles A. McCutchan to "Mattie," June 10, 1863, Charles A. McCutchan Letters, IHS.

20. *OR* 24, pt. 1, 430-467; Ulysses S. Grant, *Personal Memoirs of Ulysses S. Grant*, 2 vols. (New York: Charles L. Webster and Co., 1885-1886), 1: 268.

21. *OR* 24, pt. 3, 12; pt. 1, 23; Marszalek, *Sherman*, 214. The river changed course in 1876 near the line Grant had been working thirteen years earlier. The course change left Vicksburg high and dry except for backwater that filled the old river bed.

22. *OR* 24, pt. 1, 16; *OR* 24, pt. 3, 32.

23. Grant, *Personal Memoirs*, 1: 269.

24. Louis Trefftzs to W. P. Trefftzs, March 14, 1863, Louis Trefftzs Papers, ISHL; J. A. Turley to his brother, nd, J. A. Turley Letters, TSLA. One Federal at Lake Providence, Louisiana, noted that the itch "is popular here."

25. James K. Worthington to "Lizzie," April 23, 1863, James K. Worthington Letters, *Civil War Times Illustrated* Collection, USAMHI; *OR* 24, pt. 1, 517-518, 564-570. One transport and six barges were lost on the second attempt.

Chapter 2

1. *OR* 24, pt. 1, 251-252.

2. Lawrence Hewitt, "John Clifford Pemberton," in William C. Davis, ed., *The Confederate General*, 6 vols. (Harrisburg: National Historical Society, 1991), vol. 5, 8; Michael B. Ballard, *Pemberton: A Biography* Jackson (University Press of Mississippi, 1991), 40-41, 64; Foote, *The Civil War*, 2: 368.

3. *OR* 17, pt. 2, 717; Ballard, *Pemberton*, 114-115.

4. Ballard, *Pemberton*, 120.

5. Ballard, *Pemberton*, 117.

6. Ezra J. Warner, *Generals in Gray: Lives of the Confederate Generals* (Baton Rouge: Louisiana State University Press, 1959), 282-283.

7. John S. Kountz, *Record of the Organizations Engaged in the Campaign, Siege, and Defense of Vicksburg* (Washington, DC: Government Printing Office, 1901), 54-56; Warren E. Grabau, *Ninety-Eight Days: A Geographer's View of the Vicksburg Campaign* (Knoxville: The University of Tennessee Press, 2000), 605-608.

8. Warner, *Generals in Gray*, 90-91.

9. Kountz, *Record of the Organizations Engaged in the Campaign, Siege, and Defense of Vicksburg*, 52-54; Grabau, *Ninety-Eight Days*, 605-608.

10. *OR* 24, pt. 1, 250; Warner, *Generals in Gray*, 29-30.

11. Kountz, *Record of the Organizations Engaged in the Campaign, Siege, and Defense of Vicksburg*, 56-59; Grabau, *Ninety-Eight Days*, 605-608.

12. Warner, *Generals in Gray*, 193-194.

13. Winfield S. Featherston Biographical File, J. F. H. Claiborne Papers, UNC; Kountz, *Record of the Organizations Engaged in the Campaign, Siege, and Defense of Vicksburg*, 67-68; Grabau, *Ninety-Eight Days*, 605-608. Featherston was a U.S. Representative before the war.

14. *OR* 24, pt. 1, 251; Warner, *Generals in Gray*, 292-293; Kountz, *Record of the Organizations Engaged in the Campaign, Siege, and Defense of Vicksburg*, 48-52; Grabau, *Ninety-Eight Days*, 605-608.

15. E. W. Pettus, "Colonel Franklin K. Beck—A Sketch," Edmond W. Pettus Papers, ADAH, 1; Kountz, *Record of the Organizations Engaged in the Campaign, Siege, and Defense of Vicksburg*, 48-52; Grabau, *Ninety-Eight Days*, 605-608. Tracy fell at Port Gibson on May 1. Stephen D. Lee assumed command and led the brigade at Champion Hill.

16. Kountz, *Record of the Organizations Engaged in the Campaign, Siege, and Defense of Vicksburg*, 59-61; Grabau, *Ninety-Eight Days*, 605-608.

17. Marszalek, *Sherman*, 217.

18. *OR* 24, pt. 1, 48; Fiske, *The Mississippi Valley*, 228.

19. *OR* 24, pt. 1, 48; Fiske, *The Mississippi Valley*, 228.

20. Bearss, *Vicksburg*, 2: 129-140. Bearss is one of the first historians to make the strong case that Streight's raid played a significant part in confusing Pemberton as to Grant's true intentions.

21. *OR* 24, pt. 1, 501-511; *OR* 23, pt. 1, 280-295.

22. *OR* 24, pt. 1, 49; Marszalek, *Sherman*, 220; William Terry Moore Reminiscences, UM.

23. Bearss, *Vicksburg*, 2: 129; Francis Vinton Greene, *The Mississippi* (New York: Charles Scribner's Sons, 1882), 145.

24. Natchez *Daily Courier*, May 12, 1863; New Orleans *The Era*, May 5, 1863. Many Southern newspapers followed the raid with extensive press coverage.

25. Catton, *Grant Moves South*, 371.

26. Warner, *Generals in Blue*, 183-184. The latest and best biography on Grant is Brooks D. Simpson, *Ulysses S. Grant: Triumph over Adversity, 1822-1865* (Boston: Houghton Mifflin Co., 2000).

27. Ezra J. Warner, *Generals in Blue: Lives of the Union Commanders* (Baton Rouge: Louisiana State University Press, 1964), 184

28. Warner, *Generals in Blue*, 184-185.

29. *OR* 7, 679, 680.

30. Warner, *Generals in Blue*, 185.

31. Warner, *Generals in Blue*, 185.

32. Catton, *Grant Moves South*, 437-438.

33. For more information on McClernand, see Richard L. Kiper, *Major General John Alexander McClernand: Politician in Uniform* (Kent: The Kent State University Press, 1999).

34. Warner, *Generals in Blue*, 293.

35. *OR* 24, pt. 3, 249-251.

36. Warner, *Generals in Blue*, 307.

37. Warner, *Generals in Blue*, 307.

38. *OR* 24, pt. 3, 249, 257-259; John B. Sanborn, *The Crisis at Champion's Hill: The Decisive Battle of the Civil War* (St. Paul: np, 1903), 9. The division commanded by Crocker was originally led by Brigadier General Isaac F. Quinby until he left the army on medical leave. Command of the division passed to Col. John B. Sanborn until Crocker took over after the division crossed the Mississippi River. Crocker is listed here as being in command for simplicity's sake, as he led the division at Champion Hill.

39. Marszalek, *Sherman*, 218.

40. Warner, *Generals in Blue*, 441-442.

41. Warner, *Generals in Blue*, 441-442.

42. Marszalek, *Sherman*, 216-217.

43. *OR* 24, pt. 3, 249, 252-253.

44. *OR* 24, pt. 1, 643; "History of the 24th Indiana," 48, Alvin Hovey Collection, IU, 48; Grant, *Personal Memoirs*, 1: 285, 288.

45. Charles Calvin Enslow to his wife, April 6 and 17, 1863, Charles Calvin Enslow Papers, LC; *OR* 24, pt. 1, 48; Grant, *Personal Memoirs*, 1: 284.46. Ira Payne to his parents, May 4, 1863, Edwin W. and Ira A. Payne Letters, ISHL; Grant, *Personal Memoirs*, 1: 285.

47. OR 24, pt. 1, 143; Grant, *Personal Memoirs*, 1: 285.

48. *OR* 24, pt. 1, 575, 576.

49. *OR* 24, pt. 1, 576; Bearss, *Vicksburg*, 2:347.

50. W. W. Loring to R. W. Meminger, May 10, 1863, John C. Pemberton Papers, NA; *OR* 24, pt. 1, 257; *OR* 24, pt. 3, 792-793. For Pemberton's perception on the lack of

cavalry, see the long and unfinished John C. Pemberton Letter, John C. Pemberton Papers, LC. Other copies of this letter exist. One is in the United States Army Military History Institute in the John C. Pemberton Papers. Apparently, he began writing the letter soon after the campaign ended, but never finished it. See Thomas L. Connelly to Benjamin Cooling, April 5, 1971, John C. Pemberton Papers, USAMHI. Pemberton's letter has been reprinted in Janet B. Hewett, Bryce A. Suderow, and Noah Andre Trudeau, eds, *Supplement to the Official Records of the Union and Confederate Armies* (Wilmington: Broadfoot Publishing Company, 1995), Part 1, Volume 4, no. 4, 307-343. Loring also complained of the lack of cavalry.

51. Winschel, *Triumph & Defeat*, 57-62, provides good information on the development of the Port Gibson battle.

52. M. Ellis to his uncle, June 2, 1863, Hubbard Trowbridge Thomas Letters, IHS; *OR* 24, pt. 1, 48; History of the 24th Indiana, Alvin Hovey Collection, IU, 49; Grant, *Personal Memoirs*, 1: 285-286.

53. *New York Tribune*, May 19, 1863.

54. Edwin C. Bearss, "Martin Edwin Green," *The Confederate General*, 3: 30-31.

55. Arthur W. Bergeron, Jr., "Edward Dorr Tracy," *The Confederate General*, 6: 55.

56. Bearss, *Vicksburg*, 2: 356-358.

57. Warner, *Generals in Blue*, 70-71; *OR* 24, pt. 1, 625-626.

58. Warner, *Generals in Blue*, 352-353; Winschel, *Triumph & Defeat*, 68.

59. *OR* 24, pt. 1, 49, 581-683; M. Ellis to his uncle, June 2, 1863, Hubbard Trowbridge Thomas Letters, IHS.

60. Bearss, *Vicksburg*, 2: 361-364; Winschel, *Triumph & Defeat*, 68; *OR* 24, pt. 1, 679.

61. Winschel, *Triumph & Defeat*, 67-68.

62. Warner, *Generals in Blue*, 235.

63. Winschel, *Triumph & Defeat*, 72-73; *OR* 24, pt. 1, 674, 675.

64. *OR* 24, pt. 1, 603, 617.

65. *OR* 24, pt. 1, 677-678.

66. *OR* 24, pt. 1, 673. The 6th Missouri Infantry launched an aggressive spoiling attack. Colonel Eugene Erwin left a detailed official report on his regiment's role at Port Hudson. *OR 24, pt. 1, 670-671.*

67. Bearss, *Vicksburg*, 2: 366-367, 402, 404; *OR* 24, pt. 1, 671, 673-674. Green's losses are reported elsewhere. His losses on the Bruinsburg front, if any, are unknown but were probably very light.

68. *OR* 24, pt. 1, 659, 660.

69. Bearss, *Vicksburg*, 2: 386-389; "History of the 24th Indiana," Alvin Hovey Collection, IU, 49.

70. *OR* 24, pt. 1, 659, 660.

71. *OR* 24, pt. 1, 611, 613, 669. Slack mistakenly reported that Cockrell's flanking attack included a Louisiana regiment. Baldwin had two Louisiana regiments in his brigade (the17th and 31st), but neither joined Cockrell's effort. They did, however, launch a brief afternoon probing attack after Cockrell's repulse. The Federals also

mistakenly estimated the length of their engagement with Cockrell as "two hours." *OR* 24, pt. 1, 676-677; Winschel, *Triumph & Defeat*, 83-84.

72. *OR* 24, pt. 1, 660, 676.

73. *OR* 24, pt. 1, 660, 676; Bearss, *Vicksburg*, 2: 406-407. There is some discrepancy as to the size of Bowen's command at Port Gibson. According to Bearss, it numbered about 6,800 (including Tracy), plus 16 artillery pieces.

74. John A. Logan to his wife, May 4, 1863, John A. Logan Papers, LC. Federal Ira Payne wrote home that at Port Gibson, he had finally witnessed "a real battlefield." Ira Payne to his parents, May 4, 1863, Edwin W. and Ira A. Payne Letters, ISHL.

75. *OR* 24, pt. 1, 49; John A. McClernand to his commanders, May 2, 1863, Letters Sent, 13th Army Corps, Army of the Tennessee, NA; John E. Smith Report of Port Gibson, May 5, 1863, J. W. Miller Papers, ISHL; Grant, *Personal Memoirs*, 1: 287. Many Federals referred to the Battle of Port Gibson as Thompson's Hill.

76. *OR* 24, pt. 3, 807.

77. *OR* 24, pt. 1, 666.

78. *OR* pt. 24, pt. 1, 49; John V. Boucher to "Woman," May 6, 1863, Boucher Family Letters, Civil War Miscellaneous Collection, USAMHI.

79. Natchez *Weekly Courier*, May 6, 1863.

Chapter 3

1. *OR* 24, pt. 1, 35.

2. *OR* 24 pt. 1, 752-753, 759.

3. *OR* 24, pt. 3, 284-285; Bearss, *Vicksburg*, 2: 431-438, 464, offers a chapter on the Grant-Banks correspondence that helped determine Grant's ultimate course of action.

4. Bearss, *Vicksburg*, 2: 451-452.

5. Grant, *Personal Memoirs*, 1: 290, 291; Bearss, *Vicksburg*, 2: 452.

6. Bearss, *Vicksburg*, 2: 452; John A. McClernand to E. A. Carr, May 6, 1863, Letters Sent—13th Army Corps, Army of the Tennessee, NA; Edward P. Stanfield to his father, May 26, 1863, Edward P. Stanfield Letters, IHS; Greene, *The Mississippi*, 140; Grant, *Personal Memoirs*, 1: 293; Jim Giauque to his parents, May 15, 1863, Giauque Family Papers, MHS; "Lon" to his parents, May 14, 1863, and "Swain" to "Friends at home," May 29, 1863, both in Thomas Marshall Letters, IHS.

7. J. P. Lesslie to his wife, May 13, 1863, J. P. Lesslie Letters, Co.C, 4th Indiana Cavalry Regimental File, VNMP; John A. McClernand to E. A. Carr, May 6, 1863, Letters Sent—13th Army Corps, Army of the Tennessee, NA; Edward P. Stanfield to his father, May 26, 1863, Edward P. Stanfield Letters, IHS; Greene, *The Mississippi*, 140; Fiske, *The Mississippi Valley*, 233; Grant, *Personal Memoirs*, 1: 293; General Orders No. 35, Letters Sent—Medical Department, 17th Army Corps, Army of the Tennessee, NA; Jim Giauque to his parents, May 15, 1863, Giauque Family Papers, MHS; "Lon" to his parents, May 14, 1863, and "Swain" to "Friends at home," May 29, 1863, both in Thomas Marshall Letters, IHS. See "History of the 24th Indiana," in the Alvin Hovey Collection, IU, for detailed examples of foraging. Although McPherson left "Primary Depots" south

of Vicksburg "for temporary relief," McClernand's Corps carried its wounded with it toward Jackson. There were also hospitals located at Grand Gulf and, later, at Raymond. One wounded Federal did not think much of the Grand Gulf hospital: "It is pretty warm here and we are poorly cared for" he wrote home.

8. *OR* 24, pt. 3, 807, 821; Samuel H. Lockett to his wife, May 3, 1863, Samuel H. Lockett Papers, UNC.

9. For a detailed essay on the most significant effort from the Trans-Mississippi Theater to help Pemberton, see Terry Winschel, "To Rescue Gibraltar: John Walker's Texas Division and its Expedition to Relieve Fortress Vicksburg," in *Civil War Regiments: A Journal of the American Civil War* (1993), Vol. 3, No., 3, 33-58.

10. *OR* 24, pt. 1, 257, 259; Samuel H. Lockett to his wife, May 8, 1863, Samuel H. Lockett Papers, UNC.

11. Ballard, *Pemberton*, 147-148.

12. Bearss, *Vicksburg*, 2: 475; Ballard, *Pemberton*, 148.

13. W. W. Loring to John C. Pemberton, May 14, 1863, John C. Pemberton Papers, NA; *OR* 24, pt. 1, 261; S. M. Thornton to his wife, May 15, 1863, Gardner Collection, MSU; "History of the 24th Indiana," in the Alvin Hovey Collection, IU, 55; I. V. Smith Personal Memoirs, Western Historical Manuscript Collection, UMC, 28; S. H. Lockett, "The Defense of Vicksburg," in Clarence Buel and Robert Johnson, eds., *Battles and Leaders of the Civil War*, 4 vols. (New York: Thomas Yoseloff, 1956), 3: 487; Bearss, *Vicksburg*, 2: 561.

14. *OR* 24, pt. 1, 261; Bearss, *Vicksburg*, 2: 641-642.

15. Bearss, *Vicksburg*, 2: 488-490; *OR* 24, pt. 3, 297.

16. *OR* 24, pt. 1, 637; Mary Amelia (Boomer) Stone, *Memoir of George Boardman Boomer* (Boston: Press of Geo. C. Rand & Avery, 1864), 250.

17. *OR* 24, pt. 1, 637; Diary, H. S. Keene, 6th Wisconsin Battery, VNMP.

18. Warner, *Generals in Gray*, 118-119; *OR* 7, 376.

19. *OR* 24, pt. 1, 736-737.

20. Bearss, *Vicksburg*, 2: 491-492; *OR* 24, pt. 1, 645, 704.

21. Warner, *Generals in Blue*, 281-282.

22. Bearss, *Vicksburg*, 2: 493, 496.

23. *OR* 24, pt. 1, 737-738.

24. Warner, *Generals in Blue*, 118. Dennis's Vicksburg report has not been located.

25. As related in Bearss, *Vicksburg*, 2: 495; *OR* 24, pt. 1, 646.

26. Warner, *Generals in Blue*, 459.

27. *OR* 24, pt. 1, 707-708; 738.

28. *OR* 24, pt. 1, 716.

29. Bearss, *Vicksburg*, 2: 497.

30. Bearss, *Vicksburg*, 2: 497-498; *OR* 24, pt. 1, 744. Gregg later stated that Colonel Beaumont did indeed notify him of the large force in his front, which prevented him from going forward with his attack. *OR* 24, pt. 1, 738.

31. *OR* 24, pt. 1, 646.

32. Bearss, *Vicksburg*, 2: 500-501; *OR* 24, pt. 1, 646. The report left by Col. Manning Force of the 20th Ohio claiming 30 dead Texans stands at odds with the regiment's reported 22 killed. *OR* 24, pt. 1, 715.

33. Warner, *Generals in Blue*, 102.

34. *OR* 24, pt. 1, 723. Crocker skipped some details, for after Sanborn was deployed his two left-most regiments (48th and 59th Indiana) were sent east of the road, where they were told they were not needed.

35. *OR* 24, pt. 1, 744.

36. *OR* 24, pt. 1, 745-746.

37. Bearss, *Vicksburg*, 2: 507-508; *OR* 24, pt. 1, 745-746.

38. *OR* 24, pt. 1, 746.

39. *OR* 24, pt. 1, 704, 716-717, 738-739; Bearss, *Vicksburg*, 2: 510; Edward P. Stanfield to his father, May 26, 1863, Edward P. Stanfield Letters, IHS; Letters Sent—17th Army Corps, Army of the Tennessee, NA.

40. *OR* 24, pt. 1, 646; Charles F. Vogel Diary, May 17, 1863, MDAH; Henry O. Dwight, "A Soldier's Story," Henry O. Dwight Papers, Civil War Miscellaneous Collection, USAMHI; New York *Daily Tribune*, November 21, 1886.

41. *OR* 24, pt. 1, 704-705.

42. *OR* 24, pt. 1, 738-739; Bearss, *Vicksburg*, 2: 511.

43. *OR* 24, pt. 1, 50; pt. 3, 300; Bearss, *Vicksburg*, 2: 513-514; Alfred Theodore Goodloe, *Confederate Echoes: A Voice From the South in the Days of Secession and of the Southern Confederacy* (Nashville: Publishing House of the M.E. Church, 1907), 274.

44. Isaac H. Elliot, *History of the Thirty-Third Regiment Illinois Veteran Volunteer Infantry in the Civil War: 22nd August, 1861, to 7th December, 1865* (Gibson City, IL: The Association, 1902), 39; Thomas B. Jones, *Complete History of the 46th Regiment of Illinois Volunteer Infantry* (Freeport, IL: W. H. Wagner and Sons Printers, 1907), 195.

Chapter 4

1. There are few good biographies on Johnston. The latest pure biography is Craig L. Symonds, *Joseph E. Johnston: A Civil War Biography* (New York: W.W. Norton & Co., 1992). For a thoughtful and revisionist study on Johnston's tenure in Virginia, see Steven Newton, *Joseph E. Johnston and the Defense of Richmond* (Lawrence: University Press of Kansas, 1998). Historian Richard McMurry offers a contrary view to Newton in "Ole Joe in Virginia: Gen. Joseph E. Johnston's 1861-1862 Period of Command in the East," by Richard M. McMurry, in Steven E. Woodworth, ed., *Leadership and Command in the American Civil War* (Savas Woodbury, 1996), 1-28.

2. McMurry, in "Ole Joe in Virginia: Gen. Joseph E. Johnston's 1861-1862 Period of Command in the East," 1-28, offers a substantial analysis and discussion on this point.

3. For an outstanding study of the war in the West and Davis's relationship with his other generals, see Steven E. Woodworth, *Jefferson Davis and His Generals: The Failure of Confederate Command in the West* (Lawrence: University Press of Kansas, 1990).

4. *OR* 24, pt. 1, 215; *OR* 24, pt. 3, 870; Joseph E. Johnston, *Narrative of Military Operations, Directed During the Late War Between the States, by Joseph E. Johnston, General, C.S.A.* (New York: D. Appleton and Co., 1874), 172-173; Ballard, *Pemberton*, 142-143; Symonds, *Joseph E. Johnston*, 209-210. Ballard attributes the trouble between Johnston and Pemberton to ideological differences. Ballard also cites the command trouble between Johnston, Davis, and Pemberton as more proof of the Confederacy's unworkable departmental system. According to Symonds, Pemberton was fixated on defending geographic features, while Johnston desired a war of maneuver.

5. *OR* 24, pt. 1, 50.

6. *OR* 24, pt. 1, 50; Israel M. Piper Diary, May 13, 1863, 99th Illinois Regimental File, VNMP.

7. Jim Stanbery, "A Failure of Command: The Confederate Loss of Vicksburg," in *Civil War Regiments: A Journal of the American Civil War* (1992), Vol. 2, No., 1, 54.

8. *OR* 24, pt. 1, 785.

9. Bearss, *Vicksburg*, vol.2, 530-531, 554-555.

10. *OR* 24, pt. 1, 786.

11. *OR* 24, pt. 1, 753, 759, 786; Bearss, *Vicksburg*, 2: 531-533.

12. Sanborn, "The Campaign Against Vicksburg," MOLLUS-Minnesota, 2: 130; *OR* 24, pt. 1, 638.

13. Frank Johnston, "The Vicksburg Campaign," *Publications of the Mississippi Historical Society* (Oxford: Mississippi Historical Society, 1909), 10: 77; *OR* 24, pt. 1, 749-787.

14. *OR* 24, pt. 1, 753.

15. *OR* 24, pt. 1, 729, 775, 777, 782, 786.

16. *OR* 24, pt. 1, 723; Diary, H. S. Keene, 6th Wisconsin Battery, VNMP.

17. Edwin C. Bearss and Warren Grabau, *The Battle of Jackson, May 14, 1863* (Baltimore: Gateway Press, 1981), 24-25. This slim book contains invaluable research and observations by two of the campaign's outstanding historians. *OR* 24, pt. 1, 723.

18. Bearss, *Vicksburg*, 2: 557-558; *OR* 24, pt. 1, 51.

19. *OR*, 24, pt. 1, 749-787; Sanborn, *Crisis*, 9; Symonds, *Joseph E. Johnston*, 208. Grant dispersed Johnston's army. Many were captured immediately while others retreated in various directions. Troops riding the rails to Jackson were stalled, and hundreds more milled about until captured. One Federal remarked, "we found a good many rebels scattered through the woods." Edward P. Stanfield to his father, May 26, 1863, Edward P. Stanfield Letters, IHS.

20. *OR* 24, pt. 1, 51; Grant, *Personal Memoirs*, 1: 298-299.

21. *OR* 24, pt. 1, 261; Foote, *The Civil War*, 2: 367.

22. *OR* 24, pt. 1, 261; Winfield S. Featherston Report, November 10, 1867, Featherston Collection, UM. According to Featherston, Pemberton's officers were called together to a meeting. Alfred Cumming to Stephen D. Lee, November 3, 1899, Letters and Papers Covering Organizations: Miscellaneous—Georgia, Massachusetts, New Hampshire, and Rhode Island, Memorial, Monument and Exposition Commission Records, MDAH. All subsequent references refer to this letter and collection.

23. *OR* 24, pt. 1, 261; Fiske, *The Mississippi Valley*, 237; Greene, *The Mississippi*, 149; Bearss, *Vicksburg*, 2: 565.

24. *OR* 24, pt. 1, 261; Ballard, *Pemberton*, 156.

25. *OR* 24, pt. 3, 808, 815.

26. *OR* 24, pt. 3, 842.

27. *OR* 24, pt. 1, 261; Foote, The Civil War, 2: 367.

28. Ballard, *Pemberton*, 155-157, offers an insightful discussion of this aspect of the campaign. *OR* 24, pt. 3, 876.

29. Johnston, *Narrative of Military Operations*, 181.

30. Edwin May Diary, May 2-May 20, 1863, Edwin May Papers, ISHL; David C. Turnbull to his friend, May 29, 1863, David C. Turnbull Papers, ISL; Mortimer D. Leggett to "Morilla," May 10, 1863, Mortimer D. Leggett Papers, LMS; Copies of the Leggett papers concerning Vicksburg are in the Leggett Papers, VNMP. Many reported on the fast marches, punctuated by the fighting, which is supported by the drop off in available letters during this period. Once the marching campaign ended, letters explain that the failure to write was because of a lack of time to do so; diaries kept by the soldiers often contain empty pages or very short entries for the dates between May 1 and May 20.

Chapter 5

1. "The War Between the States," Isaac E. Hirsh Papers, MSU, 28; W. T. Rigby to his brother, May 15, 1863, Rigby Family Papers, UI.

2. *OR* 24, pt. 1, 50-51; pt. 2, 12, 31; "The War Between the States," Isaac E. Hirsh Papers, MSU, 28; W. T. Rigby to his brother, May 15, 1863, Rigby Family Papers, UI.

3. *OR* 24, pt. 1, 148; pt. 2, 13-14; Henry Clay Warmoth, "The Vicksburg Diary of Henry Clay Warmoth: Part II (April 28, 1863-May 26, 1863)," Paul H. Hass, ed., *Journal of Mississippi History,* 32, no. 1 (February 1970), 70.

4. *OR* 24, pt. 1, 148.

5. *OR* 24, pt. 2, 13; Thomas S. Hawley to his parents, May 18, 1863, Thomas S. Hawley Papers, MHS.

6. *OR* 24, pt. 1, 148, 616; *OR* 24, pt. 2, 31, 134.

7. *OR* 24, pt. 1, 148; *OR* 24, pt. 2, 41; T. J. Williams, "The Battle of Champion's Hill," *MOLLUS-Ohio* (Cincinnati: The Robert Clarke Company, 1903), 5: 204.

8. OR 24, pt. 1, 639, 646-647; R. L. Howard, *History of the 124th Regiment Illinois Infantry Volunteers, Otherwise Known as the "Hundred and Two Dozen," From August, 1862, to August, 1865* (Springfield: H.W. Rokker, 1880), 95; Osborn H. Oldroyd, *A Soldier's Story of the Siege of Vicksburg From the Diary of Osborn H. Oldroyd* (Springfield: self published, 1885), 22; George W. Modil Diaries, May 15, 1863, MDAH.

9. *OR* 24, pt. 1, 639, 724, 730, 775-776, 783; *OR* 24, pt. 2, 65; William A. Russ, ed., "The Vicksburg Campaign as Viewed by an Indiana Soldier," *Journal of Mississippi History*, 19 (January-October 1957), 268.

10. *OR* 24, pt. 1, 754; Marszalek, *Sherman*, 222.

11. John P. Davis Diary, May 15, 1863, John P. Davis Papers, ISHL; S. S. Farwell Letter, May 15, 1863, Sewall S. Farwell Papers, SHSI; *OR* 24, pt. 1, 754. The troops at Jackson read reports printed in Southern newspapers of Joseph Hooker's defeat at Chancellorsville earlier in the month.

12. *OR* 24, pt. 1, 754.

13. *OR* 24, pt. 3, 315; *OR* 24, pt. 1, 754; Marszalek, *Sherman*, 222.

14. *OR* 24, pt. 1, 754.

15. *OR* 24, pt. 1, 754; Marszalek, *Sherman*, 222.

16. *OR* 24, pt. 1, 51, 148; Bearss, *Vicksburg*, 2: 571.

17. *OR* 24, pt. 2, 13.

18. Francis A. Dawes Diary, May 15, 1863, *Civil War Times Illustrated* Collection, USAMHI; Fiske, *The Mississippi Valley*, 235; S. E. Sneier to "Sir," June 21, 1863, Samuel E. Sneier Letter, IHS; Aquilla Standifird Diary, May 14 and 15, 1863, Western Historical Manuscript Collection, UMR; T. H. Yeatman to James B. McPherson, May 15, 1863, James B. McPherson Papers, LC; Charles L. Longley, "Champion's Hill," *MOLLUS-Iowa* (Des Moines: Press of P. C. Kenyon, 1893), 1: 210-211. The Federals also took an abundance of cotton, which caused some concern about the correct procedure in dealing with owners of agricultural produce.

19. *OR* 24, pt. 1, 262; *OR* 24, pt. 2, 74; S. M. Thornton to his wife, May 15, 1863, Gardner Collection, MSU; William A. Drennan to his wife, May 30, 1863, William A. Drennan Papers, MDAH.

20. *OR* 24, pt. 1, 262; *OR* 24, pt. 2, 74; S. M. Thornton to his wife, May 15, 1863, Gardner Collection, MSU; William A. Drennan to his wife, May 30, 1863, William A. Drennan Papers, MDAH.

21. *OR* 24, pt. 1, 262; Bearss, *Vicksburg*, 2: 573-574; Ballard, *Pemberton*, 158; S. M. Thornton to his wife, May 15, 1863, Gardner Collection, MSU.

22. William A. Drennan to his wife, May 30, 1863, William A. Drennan Papers, MDAH; Almon Phillips to his brother and sister, May 7, 1863, George Thornton Fowler Letters and Papers, GDAH.

23. *OR* 24, pt. 1, 262; *OR* 24, pt. 2, 74; Ballard, *Pemberton*, 158; Jim Giauque to his parents, May 15, 1863, Giauque Family Papers, UI; William A. Ruyle Memoir, Harrisburg Civil War Roundtable Collection, USAMHI, 14; *OR* 24, pt. 1, 262; John Cowdery Taylor Diary, May 14-16, 1863, Taylor Family Papers, UV; Bearss, *Vicksburg*, 2: 575; Ballard, *Pemberton*, 158. John Taylor, one of Pemberton's staff officers, wrote the following in his diary for the May 14 entry: "Bakers Creek reported swimming on the Raymond road." This implies that Pemberton knew as early as May 14 of the creek's condition. Pemberton, however, would not have marched his army toward the ford if he knew he could not cross over it. This and other examples confirm Taylor's entries were written after the fact. For example, his account for May 16 discusses Loring's march to Jackson following the Battle of Champion Hill. Loring, however, did not reach Jackson until May 19. In addition, members of Pemberton's army, with which Taylor traveled, were still discussing the mystery of Loring's whereabouts well *after* May 16. Taylor learned of the flooded Bakers Creek on May 15 with everyone else, but did not have time to write his diary until much later.

24. *OR* 24, pt. 1, 262; *OR* 24, pt. 2, 74-75.

25. Lloyd Tilghman to R. W. Memminger, May 15, 1863, and Lloyd Tilghman to J. Thompson, May 15, 1863, both in John C. Pemberton Papers, NA; F. W. M., "Career and Fate of Gen. Lloyd Tilghman," *Confederate Veteran*, Vol. 1, No. 9 (September 1893), 275. Bowen had by this time been nominated for major general, but had not been confirmed by the Confederate Senate.

26. William A. Drennan to his wife, May 30, 1863, William A. Drennan Papers, MDAH. Drennan was referring to fellow staffer Capt. William R. Barksdale.

27. *OR* 24, pt. 1, 262; *OR* 24, pt. 2, 75, 90; Ballard, *Pemberton*, 159.

28. *OR* 24, pt. 2, 110, 114, 116, 118; Henry Martyn Cheavens, "A Missouri Confederate in the Civil War: The Journal of Henry Martyn Cheavens, 1862-1863," ed. James G. Moss, *Missouri Historical Review*, 57, no. 1 (October 1962), 38; I. V. Smith Personal Memoirs, Western Historical Manuscript Collection, UMC, 28. In all likelihood, the enemy campfires were signs of roving bands of skirmishers or cavalry. No major Federal units were in sight of the Confederate line of battle on the night of May 15.

29. *OR* 24, pt. 2, 93, 101, 103, 107, 108; John Cowdery Taylor Diary, May 14, 1863, Taylor Family Papers, UV; Alfred Cumming to Stephen D. Lee, November 3, 1899, MDAH.

30. *OR* 24, pt. 2, 75, 87. The plantation was owned by a "Jefferson Davis," but not the same Jefferson Davis who was serving as the Confederacy's president.

31. Lawrence L. Hewitt, "William Wirt Adams," in *The Confederate General*, 1: 7-8.

32. *OR* 24, pt. 1, 263; John Cowdery Taylor Diary, May 14, 1863, Taylor Family Papers, UV.

33. *OR* 24, pt. 3, 881-884; Ballard, *Pemberton*, 158; Clifford Dowdey, *The Seven Days: The Emergence of Lee* (Boston: Little, Brown and Co., 1964), 143.

34. *OR* 24, pt. 1, 263; Ballard, *Pemberton*, 157.

Chapter 6

1. Only two monuments and one tablet mark the battlefield.

2. For a geographical study of the campaign and battle, see Grabau, *Ninety-Eight Days*. Much of the topographical descriptions that follow are taken from this book and personal observation of the field.

3. James F. Brieger, *Hometown Mississippi* (np: np: 1980), 178.

4. *OR* 24, pt. 2, 42.

5. For more on the Champion family, see the Sydney S. Champion Papers, DU.

6. Louis W. Knobe Diary, May 16, 1863, ISL; Emma Balfour Diary, May 16, 1863, MDAH; Winfield S. Featherston Report, November 10, 1867, Featherston Collection, UM; I. V. Smith Personal Memoir, Western Historical Manuscript Collection, UMC, 28; Harvey M. Trimble, *History of the Ninety-Third Regiment Illinois Volunteer Infantry From Organization to Muster Out* (Chicago: The Blakely Printing Co., 1898), 26; Cheavens, "A Missouri Confederate," 38.

7. Partial Letter, n.d., James S. Fogle Letters, ISL; D. L. Roush to his wife, nd, Daniel Levi Roush Letters, 99th Illinois Regimental File, VNMP; S. E. Sneier to "Sir," June 21, 1863, Samuel E. Sneier Letters, IHS; Philip Roesch Diary, TSLA, 6; "National Register of Historic Places Nomination Form," Champion Hill Battlefield Foundation, Inc. Subject File, MDAH; S.H.M. Byers, "Some Recollections of Grant," *The Annals of the Civil War*, ed. Alexander Kelley McClure (New York: Da Capo Press, 1994), 343; Oldroyd, *A Soldier's Story*, 25. One Federal referred to the battle as "Magnolia Hill," a name usually given to Port Gibson. Many Federals were fascinated with alligators, an animal few if any had ever seen before. Many remarked on the sightings in their letters home or diaries. One reported "the curiossity of seeing 2 alligators," and another later remembered many soldiers made rings of alligator bones.

8. Charles F. Shedd Letter, May 15, 1863, Shedd Family Papers, SHSI; Owen Johnston Hopkins, *Under the Flag of the Nation: Diaries and Letters of a Yankee Volunteer in the Civil War*, Otto F. Bond, ed. (Columbus: Ohio State University Press, 1961), 60; S. H. M. Byers, "How Men Feel in Battle; Recollections of a Private at Champion Hills," *Annals of Iowa* 2, no. 6 (July 1896), 439.

9. James E. Payne, "Missouri Troops in the Vicksburg Campaign," *Confederate Veteran* 36, no. 9 (September 1928), 340; Sanborn, *Crisis*, 8; Terrence J. Winschel, "Champion Hill: A Battlefield Guide," brochure printed in 1989; L. B. Northrop, "A Hill of Death," *Civil War Times Illustrated*, 30, no. 2 (May-June 1991), 31; "Descendant Clarifies Champion Hill History," Jackson *Daily News*, May 24, 1984.

10. *OR* 24, pt. 1, 51-52; Bearss, *Vicksburg*, 2: 579.

11. *OR* 24, pt. 1, 51-52, 736. In his report, Foster listed the officer as a member of the 20th Georgia Mounted Rifles and included a question mark after it. There was no such outfit with Pemberton, but the 20th Mississippi Mounted Infantry was operating with Wirt Adams that morning on the Raymond Road.

12. James H. Wilson Journal, May 16, 1863, James H. Wilson Papers, LC; *OR*, 24, pt. 1, 51-52, 736; James Patterson Diary, May 16, 1863, SHSI; Special Orders No. 137, May 15, 1863, Special Orders Received—13th Army Corps, Army of the Tennessee, NA. James Harrison Wilson reported the two employees as William Hennessey and Peter McCardle. McClernand claimed orders were issued the previous night for his divisions to move forward the morning of May 16. *OR* 24, pt. 1, 148.

13. *OR* 24, pt. 3, 319.

14. A. Lee to A. J. Smith, May 15, 1863, Letters Sent—13th Army Corps, Army of the Tennessee, NA; *OR* 24, pt. 1, 148-149.

15. Warner, *Generals in Blue*, 454. The participants on both sides, as is common with most engagements, offered widely varying estimates of when particular events occurred. The times used in this book represent estimates based upon the best evidence possible, and are offered so that the reader may follow the unfolding of events in some sequential manner that makes sense.

16. Warner, *Generals in Blue*, 54-55; *OR* 17, pt. 1, 726; Bearss, *Vicksburg*, vol. 1, 415.

17. *OR* 24, pt. 2, 32.

18. *OR* 24, pt. 2, 87-88; Bearss, *Vicksburg*, 2: 581; Ben Patteson, "The Yellow Hammer Flag," *Confederate Veteran*, 8, no. 5 (May 1900), 240; "The War Between the States," Isaac E. Hirsh Papers, MSU, 29; Thomas O. Hall, "The Key to Vicksburg," *The Southern Bivouac*, 2, no. 9 (May 1884), 393; R. S. Bevier, *History of the First and Second Missouri Confederate Brigades 1861-1865 and From Wakarusa to Appomattox, A Military Anagraph* (St. Louis: Bryan, Brand and Company, 1879), 186; Greif, "Baker's Creek and Champion Hill," 350.

19. "The War Between the States," Isaac E. Hirsh Papers, MSU, 29; Thomas O. Hall, "The Key to Vicksburg," *The Southern Bivouac*, 2, no. 9 (May 1884), 393; R. S. Bevier, *History of the First and Second Missouri Confederate Brigades 1861-1865 and From Wakarusa to Appomattox, A Military Anagraph* (St. Louis: Bryan, Brand and Company, 1879), 186; Greif, "Baker's Creek and Champion Hill," 350.

20. J. P. Cannon, "History of the 27th Reg. Alabama Volunteer Infantry C.S.A.," 27th Alabama Papers, ADAH, 38; James Dinkins, "Witticisms of Soldiers," *Confederate Veteran*, 3, no. 9 (September 1895), 270.

21. *OR* 24, pt. 1, 263.

22. William A. Drennan to his wife, May 30, 1863, William A. Drennan Papers, MDAH.

23. *OR* 24, pt. 1, 263; William A. Drennan to his wife, May 30, 1863, William A. Drennan Papers, MDAH.

24. *OR* 24, pt. 1, 263; pt. 2, 93; Calvin Smith, "We Can Hold Our Ground," F.G. Carnes, ed., *Civil War Times Illustrated*, 24, no. 2 (April 1985), 28.

25. *OR* 24, pt. 2, 94; Lee, "The Campaign of Vicksburg," 37; Bearss, *Vicksburg*, 2: 587; E. W. Pettus, "Colonel Franklin K. Beck—A Sketch," Edmond W. Pettus Papers, ADAH, 1; John McKee Gould, "History of Company E," 20th Alabama Papers, ADAH.

26. *OR* 24, pt. 1, 263, 265; *OR* 24, pt. 3, 884; J. V. Greif, "Baker's Creek and Champion Hill: What Abe Buford's brigade and Others Did There," *Confederate Veteran*, 4, no. 10 (October 1896), 351.

27. Alfred Cumming to Stephen D. Lee, November 3, 1899; *OR* 24, pt. 1, 70.

28. *OR* 24, pt. 1, 263; *OR* 24, pt. 2, 82; Winfield S. Featherston Report, November 10, 1867, Featherston Collection, UM. Featherston wrote two reports of Champion Hill. The Federals captured his original report in September 1864, at Jonesboro, Georgia. Nevertheless, it still managed to find its way into the *Official Records*. In November 1867, Featherston wrote a second report from memory for Joseph E. Johnston; William A. Drennan to his wife, May 30, 1863, William A. Drennan Papers, MDAH; James R. Binford, "Recollections of the Fifteenth Mississippi Infantry, C.S.A.," Patrick Henry Papers, MDAH, 41; J. P. Cannon, "History of the 27th Reg. Alabama Volunteer Infantry C.S.A.," 27th Alabama Papers, ADAH, 38. James R. Arnold, *Grant Wins the War: Decision at Vicksburg* (New York: John Wiley & Sons, Inc., 1997), 150, reasons that Loring recommended deploying the army out of hate for Pemberton, hoping such a move would trigger a battle that Pemberton would lose. While Loring had serious differences with Pemberton, many of which will become obvious in this study, I have found no evidence Loring placed the army in danger. Arnold's study should be used with caution.

29. *OR* 24, pt. 2, 75.

30. *OR* 24, pt. 2, 82-83.

31. William A. Drennan to his wife, May 30, 1863, William A. Drennan Papers, MDAH.

32. *OR* 24, pt. 1, 263; pt. 2, 75, 94; William A. Drennan to his wife, May 30, 1863, William A. Drennan Papers, MDAH.

33. *OR* 24, pt. 1, 148-149.

34. *OR* 24, pt. 1, 76, 88, 91; James Adams to "Kate," December 22, 1863, Israel L. Adams Family Papers, LSU; Binford, "Recollections," Patrick Henry Papers, MDAH, 41; Bearss *Vicksburg*, 2: 589. The only casualties suffered by the 22nd Mississippi Infantry on May 16 were John McCrossen, Company D, who was mortally wounded, and John Berry, Company F, who was slightly wounded. Exactly when they fell is unknown, but given the movements of Featherston's Brigade, to which they belonged, it is likely they were injured during the initial artillery barrage. If so, John McCrossen may well hold the unenviable distinction of being the first man killed on the field at Champion Hill. Dunbar Roland, *Military History of Mississippi, 1803-1898* (Spartanburg, 1988), 247.

35. *OR* 24, pt. 2, 32, 91, 255; *OR* 24, pt. 1, 148.

36. William A. Drennan to his wife, May 30, 1863, William A. Drennan Papers, MDAH.

37. *OR* 24, 2, 83, 116, 118. The report for Martin Green's Brigade at Champion Hill was penned by Col. Thomas P. Dockery of the 19th Arkansas Infantry. Green was killed in late June during the siege of Vicksburg before he could complete his report of the fighting for May 16, 1863.

38. *OR* 24, pt. 2, 110.

39. Ephraim McDowell Anderson and Edwin C. Bearss, *Memoirs: Historical and Personal; Including the Campaigns of the First Missouri Confederate Brigade* (Dayton, OH, 1988), 310.

40. Anderson, *First Missouri Brigade*, 310.

41. A. H. Reynolds, "Vivid Experiences at Champion Hill, Miss.," *Confederate Veteran*, 18, no. 1 (January 1910), 21.

42. Anderson, *First Missouri Brigade*, 310-311; *OR* 24, pt. 2, 32.

43. Stephen Lee's Brigade was originally led by Brig. Gen. Edward D. Tracy, who was killed in the fighting at Port Gibson on May 1. Colonel Isham W. Garrott assumed temporary command after Tracy fell until Lee arrived and assumed command near Warrenton.

44. *OR* 24, pt. 1, 263; *OR* 24, pt. 2, 94, 108.

45. Arthur W. Bergeron, Jr., "Alexander Welch Reynolds," *The Confederate General*, 5: 82-83.

46. *OR* 24, pt. 2, 14, 101, 108. Stevenson later reported Lee relieved Reynolds "about 9 a.m.," but Reynolds was almost certainly relieved earlier. *OR* 24, pt. 2, 94.

47. *OR* 24, pt. 2, 108.

48. McClernand to Hay, May 15, 1863, Letters Sent—13th Army Corps, Army of the Tennessee, NA; *OR* 24, pt. 2, 13-14. Theophilus Toulmin Garrard was promoted to brigadier general after Champion Hill, to date from November 29, 1862.

49. W. A. Rorer to his cousin, June 13, 1863, Lionel Baxter Collection, *Civil War Times Illustrated* Collection, USAMHI; Charles Dana to Edwin M. Stanton, July 12, 1863, Charles A. Dana Papers, LC; *OR* 24, pt. 2, 13, 104, 134; General Orders No. 25, Robert H. Carnahan Papers, USAMHI; Thomas B. Sykes to James Sykes, June 5, 1863, Rufus Ward Collection, MSU; Charles A. Dana, *Recollections of the Civil War: With the Leaders at Washington and in the Field in the Sixties* (New York: D. Appleton and Co., 1898), 64; Clay Sharkey, "Battles are Often Won or Lost by Errors of the Head," H. Clay Sharkey Papers, MDAH, 5; Francis Marion Baxter to "Ret," Thursday the 23rd, [?], Francis Marion Baxter Papers, MDAH; J. M. Love Diary, May 4, 1863, UM. The actions of the 20th Mississippi Mounted Infantry are difficult to document as virtually nothing exists concerning its actions. The unit was definitely present at Champion Hill. Thomas Sykes writes of members of the regiment acting "very gallantly at Bakers Creek," but gives no specifics. W. A. Rorer of the 20th Mississippi remembered the regiment, though mounted, had "done more fighting in six weeks than most of the cavalry in this state have done since the war commenced."

50. *OR* 24, pt. 2, p. 14.

51. Warner, *Generals in Blue*, 168.

52. *OR* 24, pt. 2, 14.

53. *OR* 24, pt. 1, 149; pt. 2, 14, 29.

54. *OR* 24, pt. 2, 108.

Chapter 7

1. *OR* 24, pt. 2, 41, 48; *OR* 24, pt. 1, 639. As noted earlier elsewhere, the time at which particular events were reported to have taken place varied widely, something that is true for almost every Civil War battle. I have endeavored to synchronize the activities in such a way that they make chronological sense. Occasionally, this means the narrative will treat a particular event, and then return and discuss a different event on another part of the field that was taking place simultaneously to the one previously described.

2. *OR* 24, pt. 2, 41; Warner, *Generals in Blue*, 235; http://www.Statelib.Lib.in.us/www/ihb/govportraits/hovey.html.

3. *OR* 24, pt. 2, 41.

4. *OR* 24, pt. 1, 149; *OR* 24, pt. 3, 316-317.

5. *OR* 24, pt. 2, 49.

6. Francis Obenchain to James Johnston, November 27, 1903, Francis G. Obenchain Letters—Botetourt Virginia Artillery File, VNMP; Francis G. Obenchain to William T. Rigby, June 27, 1903, Letters and Papers Covering Organizations: Virginia (Botetourt Artillery), Memorial, Monument and Exposition Commission Records, MDAH; Francis G. Obenchain to John W. Johnston, January 8, 1903, Botetourt Artillery Regimental File, VNMP; Mary Johnston, "Dedication of a Bronze Tablet in Honor of Botetourt Battery," *Southern Historical Society Papers* 35 (January-December 1907), 43.

7. Terrence J. Winschel, "The Guns at Champion Hill (Part II)," *Journal of Confederate History*, 6 (1990), 97-98; Jerald H. Markham, *The Botetourt Artillery*

(Lynchburg: H.E. Howard, 1986), 37-38. Although this study contains many serious errors of fact, it has a substantial amount of information on this battery not readily found elsewhere.

8. Winschel, "The Guns at Champion Hill (Part II)," 98; Markham, *Botetourt Artillery*, 38.

9. *OR* 24, pt. 2, 101.

10. Herman Hattaway, "Stephen D. Lee," *The Confederate General*, 4: 59, 63; Warner, *Generals in Gray*, 183.

11. Stephen D. Lee, "The Campaign of Vicksburg, Mississippi, in 1863—From April 15 to and Including the Battle of Champion Hills, or Baker's Creek, May 16, 1863," *Publications of the Mississippi Historical Society* (Oxford: Mississippi Historical Society, 1900), vol. 3, 37, 38, 42. After the surrender of Vicksburg, what was left of Waddell's Battery was reorganized into three batteries under Capt. Winslow D. Emery, Battery A; Capt. Richard H. Bellamy, Battery B; and Capt. T. J. Key, Battery C. Waddell's Battery Papers, ADAH.

12. *OR* 24, pt. 2, 101.

13. *OR* 24, pt. 2, 101, 104.

14. *OR* 24, pt. 2, 41, 49.

15. *OR* 24, pt. 2, 41, 48, 57; Williams, "Battle of Champion's Hill," 205. The order of alignment of Slack's regiments is difficult to determine. According to Lt. Joseph Strong of the 28th Iowa, *OR* 24, pt. 2, 58-59, his regiment was originally posted on the left of the 47th Indiana, which Slack confirms. The report filed by Lt. Colonel John McLaughlin for the 47th Indiana is not helpful on this subject, and the reports for the 56th Ohio and 24th Iowa have not been located. Slack records that he formed his brigade in two distinct lines of battle, and that the Ohioans and Iowans provided skirmishers. He does not definitively place their parent regiments, however.

16. *OR* 24, pt. 2, 41, 48, 57; Charles L. Longley, "Champion's Hill," 208. Historian Edwin C. Bearss, *Vicksburg*, 2: 594, claims the 47th Indiana and 56th Ohio were in the front line, but the sources he cites do not confirm this alignment. Williams, "The Battle of Champion's Hill," 205, states definitively the right flank of the 56th Ohio was formed "on the road." Until more evidences surfaces, it is impossible to confirm the order Slack's regiments went into battle.

17. Markham, *Botetourt Artillery*, 39.

18. *OR* 24, pt. 1, 52; *OR* 24, pt. 2, 42; Bearss, *Vicksburg*, 2: 594-595.

19. John P. Davis Diary, May 16, 1863, ISHL; *OR* 24, pt. 1, 52, 639; Sylvanus Cadwallader, *Three Years With Grant: As Recalled by War Correspondent Sylvanus Cadwallader*, ed. Benjamin P. Thomas (New York: Alfred A. Knopf, 1955), 77; Howard, History of the 124th Regiment, 95; John B. Sanborn, "The Campaign Against Vicksburg," 2: 131; Manning F. Force, "Personal Recollections of the Vicksburg Campaign," 1: 301.

20. *OR* 24, pt. 1, 647; Manning Force, "Personal Recollections of the Vicksburg Campaign," 1: 302.

21. Force, "Personal Recollections," 302; Dana, *Recollection of the Civil War*, 68; Oldroyd, *A Soldier's Story*, 25.

22. *OR* 24, pt. 1, 52, 647, 709, 715; Henry O. Dwight, "A Soldier's Story," Henry O. Dwight Papers, Civil War Miscellaneous Collection, USAMHI; New York *Daily Tribune*, November 21, 1886; Ira Blanchard, "Recollections of the Civil War Service in the 20th Illinois Infantry, Co. H.," Ira Blanchard Papers, ISHL, 83.

23. Henry Watts Civil War Reminiscences, ISL, 79; "History of the 24th Indiana," Alvin Hovey Collection, IU, 56.

24. "Descendant Clarifies Champion Hill History," Jackson *Daily News*, May 24, 1984. The lives of the Champion family members would never be the same again. Matilda and her children spent the next few months at her father's residence in Madison County.

25. Byers, "How Men Feel in Battle," 439; *OR* 24, pt. 1, 639, 647; *OR* 24, pt. 2, 42, 60.

26. Byers, "How Men Feel in Battle," 440.

27. *OR* 24, pt. 1, 639-640.

28. OR 24, pt. 1, 101; Lee, "The Campaign of Vicksburg," 43.

29. W. L. Ritter, "Sketch of the Third Battery of Maryland Artillery," *SHSP*, 10, no. 8-9 (August -September 1882), 392-401; *OR* 24, pt. 2, 94.

30. *OR* 24, pt. 2, 104; Alfred Cumming to Stephen D. Lee, November 3, 1899, MDAH.

31. Edwin C. Bearss, "Alfred Cumming," *The Confederate General*, 2: 44-45.

32. *OR* 24, pt. 2, 104.

33. OR 24, pt. 2, 104-105; Alfred Cumming to Stephen D. Lee, November 3, 1899; *OR* 24, pt. 2, 104.

34. Markham, *Botetourt Artillery*, 40. The conversations outlined here are based upon and reconstructed from Obenchain's very specific recollection of events.

35. *OR* 24, pt. 2, 104-105; Cumming to Lee, November 3, 1899, November 3, 1899, MDAH.

36. *OR* 24, pt. 2, 104; Bearss, *Vicksburg*, 2: 596-597. There is some discrepancy as to whether Lee moved on his own initiative, as he claimed in his official report, or whether Carter Stevenson was present after the initial move to Champion Hill and ordered him to extend his line northwest along the ridge to correspond to Federal movements. Stevenson's report, *OR* 24, pt. 2, 94, is equivocal on this point; Lee's is not. Lee was engaged directly in the events described and, at least initially, Stevenson was well to the south with Cumming's Brigade.

37. *OR* 24, pt. 2, 101. Lee insisted he moved on his own initiative. See note 36 above.

38. John Myers, "'Dear and Mutch Loved One'–An Iowan's Vicksburg Letters," Edward G. Longacre, ed., *Annals of Iowa* 43, no. 1 (Summer 1975), 53; *OR* 24, 1, 52, 640. Frederick D. Grant, "A Boy's Experience at Vicksburg," *MOLLUS-New York* (New York: D.D. Putnam's Sons, 1907), 3: 94. Like all good generals, Grant avoided whenever possible making piecemeal attacks. He worked hard to synchronize and remain in close contact with James McPherson who, like William T. Sherman, was one of Grant's favorite subordinates. However, he seems to have maintained a less vigorous level of communication with John McClernand, whom Grant despised. At this time, McClernand was riding with division leader Peter Osterhaus on the Middle Road. McClernand tried

hard to keep in contact with the divisions operating on his flanks (the Raymond and Jackson roads) and keep Grant informed of what was transpiring on his own front. McClernand notified Grant of the early action on A. J. Smith's Raymond Road sector and forwarded immediately Alvin Hovey's query about bringing on the Jackson Road battle. In his official report, Grant claims to have maintained close coordination with McClernand, but the facts indicate the "coordination" was not as adamant, often, or clear as Grant has led us to believe.

Chapter 8

1. *OR* 24, pt. 1, 53.

2. Lee, *The Campaign of Vicksburg*, 39.

3. Charles Dana to Edwin M. Stanton, July 12, 1863, Charles A. Dana Papers, LC; *OR* 24, pt. 2, 42.

4. Warner, *Generals in Blue*, 299; *OR* 24, pt. 2, 49, 101.

5. *OR* 24, pt. 2, 49.

6. Williams, "Champion's Hill," 205.

7. Williams, "Champion's Hill," 206.

8. *OR* 24, pt. 2, 55. For a discussion on the relative placement of Slack's regiments, see note 14, Chapter 7.

9. *OR* 24, pt. 2, 42, 58; W. T. Rigby to his brother, May 18, 1863, Rigby Family Papers, UI; Grant, *Personal Memoirs*, 1: 303. James H. Wilson Journal, May 16, 1863, James H. Wilson Papers, LC. Wilson's journal offers what appears to be a reasonably accurate (and very interesting) account of the time various events transpired on the Champion Hill field. However, as noted elsewhere, the exact hour at which events occurred, as reported by participants, varies widely and they can only be plotted with a reasonable degree of accuracy, but nothing approaching certainty.

10. Francis G. Obenchain to William T. Rigby, June 27, 1903, Letters and Papers Covering Organizations: Virginia (Botetourt Artillery), Memorial, Monument and Exposition Commission Records, MDAH; Francis G. Obenchain to John W. Johnston, January 8, 1903, Botetourt Artillery Regimental File, VNMP; Markham, *Botetourt Artillery*, 40. Cumming, *OR* 24, pt. 2, 105, mistakenly claimed Waddell supplied only a single gun to reinforce Johnston's pair of pieces, but eyewitness accounts (previously cited) clearly state that two guns unlimbered next to the Virginia section.

11. *OR* 24, pt. 2, 55, 205; Alfred Cumming to Stephen D. Lee, November 3, 1899, MDAH. Cumming claims his men returned fire, but this does not seem to have been the case.

12. *OR* 24, pt. 2, 55, 205; Williams, "The Battle of Champion's Hill." Cumming mistakenly attributed the first wave of McGinnis's attack to "the Seventh and Eleventh Illinois," when his front line was in fact composed of the 11th Indiana as his left flank regiment, and the 29th Wisconsin and 24th Indiana.

13. Henry Watts Civil War Reminiscences, ISL, 80; *OR* 24, pt. 2, 55; Longley, "Champion's Hill," 212-213; Williams, "Champion's Hill," 206.

14. *OR* 24, pt. 2, 55, 105; Alfred Cumming to Stephen D. Lee, November 3, 1899, MDAH.

15. *OR* 24, pt. 2, 55, 58.

16. *OR* 24, pt. 2, 55, 58.

17. OR 24, pt. 2, 42, 54-55, 59, 104-105; Williams, "The Battle of Champion's Hill," 206.

18. *OR* 24, pt. 2, 49, 105; William Brotherton to Levy Brotherton, May 18, 1863, William Brotherton Papers, EU; J.R. Horn to his wife and children, June 6, 1863, James Russell Horn Letters, GDAH.

19. Markham, *Botetourt Artillery*, 40; *OR* 24, pt. 2, 105; Joseph Bogle Reminiscences, 10.

20. Markham, *Botetourt Artillery*, 40; Alfred Cumming to Stephen D. Lee, November 3, 1899, MDAH.

21. *OR* 24, pt. 2, 49, 105; J. R. Horn to his wife and children, June 6, 1863, James Russell Horn Letters, GDAH; Aurelius Lyman Voorhis Journal, May 16, 1863, IHS; Augustus Sinks, "Four Years in Dixie," Augustus Sinks Journal, ISL, 37; *OR* 24, pt. 2, 42, 49; Winschel, "The Guns at Champion Hill," 102; Alfred Cumming to Stephen D. Lee, November 3, 1899, MDAH.

22. William Brotherton to Levy Brotherton, May 18, 1863, William Brotherton Papers, EU.

23. Markham, *Botetourt Artillery*, 41.

24. *Ibid.*, 40; Francis G. Obenchain to William T. Rigby, June 27, 1903, Letters and Papers Covering Organizations: Virginia (Botetourt Artillery), Memorial, Monument and Exposition Commission Records, MDAH; Francis G. Obenchain to John W. Johnston, January 8, 1903, Botetourt Artillery Regimental File, VNMP.

25. *OR* 24, pt. 2, 105.

26. Lee, "The Campaign of Vicksburg," 45; Longley, "Champion's Hill," 212-213.

27. Lee, "The Campaign of Vicksburg," 45; Williams, "The Battle of Champion's Hill," 206.

28. Longley, "Champion's Hill," 212; Williams, "Champion's Hill," 205-206. The captain died six days later.

29. Longley, "Champion's Hill," 213; Williams, "Champion's Hill," 205-206.

30. *OR* 24, pt. 2, 42, 55, 105; J. M. Kulgar Reminiscences, GDAH, 37; Samuel R. Mackrill Diary, May 16, 1863, SHSI; Longley, "Champion's Hill," 213; Israel M. Ritter Diary, May 16, 1863, Civil War Miscellaneous Collection, USAMHI; *OR* 24, pt. 2, 42, 55.

31. *OR* 24, pt. 2, 55.

32. *OR* 24, pt. 2, 55, 105.

33. *OR* 24, pt. 2, 105-106; "National Register of Historic Places Nomination Form," Champion Hill Battlefield Foundation, Inc. Subject File, MDAH.

34. Williams, "Champion's Hill," 206-207.

35. Williams, "Champion's Hill," 206-207; Longley, "Champion's Hill," 213. Officially, Lt. Col. John Wilds does not appear to have been wounded at Champion Hill.

However, many men who were wounded tended to themselves and did not report their injuries.

36. Ulysses S. Grant, "The Vicksburg Campaign," *Battles and Leaders of the Civil War*, Clarence Buel and Robert Johnson, ed., 4 vols. (New York: Thomas Yoseloff, 1956), vol. 3, 511.

37. William F. Crummer, *With Grant at Fort Donelson, Shiloh, and Vicksburg* (Oak Park, IL, 1915), 103.

38. Ira Blanchard, "Recollections of the Civil war Service in the 20th Illinois Infantry, Co. H.," Ira Blanchard Papers, ISHL, 84; James Pickett Jones, *"Blackjack: John A. Logan and Southern Illinois in the Civil War Era* (Carbondale: Southern Illinois University Press, 1995), 166.

39. William Clemans Memoirs, UIL, 9.

40. *OR* 24, pt. 2, 101-102; *OR* 24, pt. 1, 644; Oldroyd, *A Soldier's Story*, 22.

41. *OR* 24, pt. 1, 719; E. Z. Hays, ed., *History of the Thirty-Second Regiment Ohio Veteran Volunteer Infantry* (Columbus, OH: Cott & Evans, Printers, 1896), 44-45. Shelby Foote, in *The Civil War, A Narrative. Fredericksburg to Meridian* (New York: Random House, 1963), 373, relates an unattributed and almost certainly apocryphal story about an unnamed Federal private who approached General Logan to inform him that Pemberton's left flank was "up in the air" and could be turned: "I've been over the rise yonder," he said, pointing to the right, "and its my idea that if you'll put a regiment or two over there you'll get on their flank and lick 'em easy." Logan, wrote Foote, discovered the report was true and acted accordingly. There is no evidence to support this story.

42. *OR* 24, pt. 1, 264; *OR* 24, pt. 2, 94.

43. *OR* 24, pt. 2, 100; Archie McDonald, "Seth Maxwell Barton," *The Confederate General*,1: 67; Warner, *Generals in Gray*, 18-19.

44. *OR* 24, pt. 1, 640.

45. Oldroyd, *A Soldier's Story*, 23.

46. *OR* 24, pt. 2, 102.

47. Ira Blanchard, "Recollections of the Civil War Service in the 20th Illinois Infantry, Co. H.," Ira Blanchard Papers, ISHL, 84; Jones, *Blackjack*, 166.

48. *OR* 24, pt. 2, 45, 53; *OR* 45, pt. 1, 693; Oldroyd, *A Soldier's Story*, 23. No report has been located for the 23rd Alabama's service at Champion Hill, and Lee's report does not break down casualties by regiment. Therefore, it is unknown how many men fell in this attack. Given the nature of the open terrain and large numbers of Federal infantry within a few hundred yards, Beck's losses were probably substantial.

49. OR 24, pt. 1, 646-647; William Clemans Memoirs, UIL, 9; Crummer, *With Grant at Fort Donelson, Shiloh, and Vicksburg*, 104. Friel was among the identified dead.

50. *OR* pt. 2, 101-102.

51. *OR* 24, pt. 1, 717; *OR* 24, pt. 2, 98, 102; J. D. Howell to Thomas M. Owen, n.d., 20th Alabama Papers, ADAH; Jack D. Welsh, *Medical Histories of Confederate Generals* (Kent: The Kent State University Press, 1995), 137; Lee, "The Campaign of Vicksburg," 45; William Milner Kelley, "A History of the Thirtieth Alabama Volunteers (Infantry) Confederate States Army," *Alabama Historical Quarterly* 9, no. 1 (Spring 1947), 140; *Jacksonville* (Alabama) *Republican*, August 15, 1863.

52. *OR* 24, pt. 1, 717; *OR* 24, pt. 2, 102; "Lieutenant General S. D. Lee," *Confederate Veteran*, 2, no. 3 (March 1894), 70; "General Stephen D. Lee, Commander in Chief U.C.V., Successor to Gen. John B. Gordon," *Confederate Veteran*, 12, no. 2 (February 1904), 54; Hattaway, *Lee*, 87; Lee, "The Campaign of Vicksburg," 44.

53. *OR* 24, pt. 2, 100.

54. *OR* 24, pt. 2, 100.

55. *OR* 24, pt. 2, 100; William Terry Moore Reminiscences, UM. In his official report, *OR* 24, pt. 2, 95, Carter Stevenson claimed that Barton's left rested "on Bakers Creek, near the bridge." Barton's line could not have stretched as far as the bridge, so this is incorrect. Barton's own report, *OR* 24, pt. 2, 100, is somewhat confusing. It can be read with his left anchored either on the Jackson Road (the technically correct reading) or on the creek, but it certainly did not stretch to the bridge. Either way it was probably slightly refused off Lee's left flank. His men later advanced to strike the attacking Federals as the enemy was making "an attempt to turn Lee's flank," so Barton's line of infantry was probably angled south of west before he ordered it forward.

56. William Terry Moore Reminiscences, UM.

57. *OR* 24, pt. 2, 100.

58. Manning Force to "Miss Perkins," May 21, 1863, Manning F. Force Papers, LC; The original Force Papers are in UW. *OR* 24, pt. 1, 640, 712; Oldroyd, *A Soldier's Story*, 22.

59. *OR* 24, pt. 1, 640, 712; *OR* 24, pt. 2, 100; Manning Force to "Miss Perkins," May 21, 1863; Oldroyd, *A Soldier's Story*, 22; Warren H. Campbell Reminiscences, Bible Records, Military Rosters and Reminiscences of Confederate Soldiers, GDAH, 254.

60. *OR* 24, pt. 1, 648, 717, 721; John A. Logan Report, May 26, 1863, Letters Sent—Logan's Division, Army of the Tennessee, NA; *OR* 24, pt. 1, 648; Hays, *History of the Thirty-Second Regiment*, 43. Colonel James J. Dollins was in command of the 81st Illinois, Stevenson's brigade, but was killed at Vicksburg during the May 22, 1863, attack on the works; Lt. Col. Franklin Campbell assumed command.

61. William A. Lorimer, *History of Mercer County, With Biographical Sketches* (Chicago: Munsell Pub. Co., 1903), 69; *OR* 24, pt. 1, 718; *OR* 24, pt. 2, 100. After Phillips fell, Maj. John Jay Moore assumed command of the 52nd Georgia. Phillips survived but his combat life was over. He was paroled at Johnson's Island and forwarded to City Point, Virginia, on February 24, 1865. He ended the war in Georgia on recruiting service.

62. "The Brave and True Capt. S. J. Ridley," *Confederate Veteran* 2, no. 11 (November 1894), 343; Hays, *History of the Thirty-Second Regiment*, 43.

63. "The Brave and True Capt. S. J. Ridley," 343; Frank Johnston, in "How Major Joseph W. Anderson Was Killed," *Confederate Veteran* 20, no. 10 (October 1912), 466, offers several very specific and credible eyewitness details about Major Anderson, but Johnston's recollection of how the battle unfolded, and especially the timing of the major events involved, cannot be reconciled with other more credible accounts and are not to be trusted.

64. W. O. Connor to Francis G. Obenchain, February 23, 1904, W. O. Connor Letters, Cherokee Georgia Artillery Regimental File, VNMP; Ira Batterton to his sister, May 27, 1863, Ira A. Batterton Papers, ISHL; Arthur P. McCullogh Diary, May 16, 1863,

ISHL; *OR* 24, pt. 2, 95, 100; *OR* 24, pt. 1, 640, 648, 721; Hays, *History of the Thirty-Second Regiment*, 43; William Terry Moore Reminiscences, UM; M. N. Twiss Statement, July 9, 1863, Joseph Forrest Papers, ISHL; John Logan Power Diary, May 16, 1863, MDAH; W. P. Gault, *Ohio at Vicksburg: Report of the Ohio Vicksburg Battlefield Commission* (np: np, 1906), 68; Bearss, *Vicksburg*, 2: 604, 605n. One member of the 8th Illinois was a steamboat pilot, and had earlier piloted a transport in the April 22 passage of Vicksburg and the April 29 action at Grand Gulf. General Logan turned the captured Mississippi guns over to Company F of the 32nd Ohio.

65. John A. Logan Report, May 26, 1863, Letters Sent - Logan's Division, Army of the Tennessee, NA; *OR* 24, pt. 1, 648, 718; *OR* 24, pt. 2, 100, 102; Hays, *History of the Thirty-Second Regiment*, 43; Ira Blanchard, "Recollections of the Civil War Service in the 20th Illinois Infantry, Co. H.," Ira Blanchard Papers, ISHL, 85; William Clemans Memoirs, UIL, 9; W. O. Connor to William T. Rigby, February 24, 1904 and W. O. Connor to Francis G. Obenchain, February 23, 1904, W.O. Connor Letters, Cherokee Georgia Artillery Regimental File, VNMP.

66. *OR* 24, pt. 1, 718; *OR* 24, pt. 2, 100.

67. *OR* 24, pt. 2, 100; Joseph Bogle Reminiscences, GDAH, 9; George S. Durfee to his uncle, May 21, 1863. There is some confusion concerning whether Lee or Barton was the first Confederate brigade to break. It seems clear from all the reports that Lee fell back first as Barton was coming up to support him, and then Barton attacked, was surrounded, and almost destroyed. Bearss, *Vicksburg*, 2: 604, holds this view. Lee's official report can be read to mean he held with a portion of his command (three regiments) while both Cumming and Barton were driven back, and that John Stevenson's Federals had nearly or already reached the Jackson Road before he fell back. His use of the description "Barton was going," can be read to imply Barton was falling back instead of advancing, especially since he uses the word "re-enforcing" in the same sentence to describe the beginning of Bowen's counterattack. *OR* 24, pt. 2, 102. Barton's report states Lee's men fell back first: "the troops on the right now gave way." *OR* 24, pt. 2, 100. Long after the war, when Lee was a park commissioner at Vicksburg, he wrote an article explaining how Barton arrived and was forming only to discover Stevenson "had already turned Lee's left, and was virtually between Lee and the bridge." Lee, "The Campaign of Vicksburg," 40. (Lee wrote in the third person.) It is interesting to note that Lee did not say his men were or had retreated, but merely that Stevenson had driven onto the ridge and into the woods west and south of Lee's left flank. In fact, Lee remained unconvinced to the end of his days as to who was driven back first. This is demonstrated by a letter he wrote to Alfred Cumming asking as much. Cumming, however, fought on Lee's right flank and was thus unable to shed any light on the issue—and he was honest enough to say so. Alfred Cumming to Stephen D. Lee, November 3, 1899, MDAH. My research demonstrates to my satisfaction that the only way all the reports and movements can be fully explained and understood is if Cumming broke first on the right (of which there is no dispute), followed by Lee's two right regiments (of which there seems to be no serious doubt). Thereafter, it appears Lee's remaining three regiments were enveloped and fell (or were ordered) back several hundred yards to a second line north of the Jackson Road. Barton was at this time

forming in Lee's left-rear, advanced, drove back the enemy some distance, was himself nearly surrounded, and was then effectively routed from the field.

68. *OR* 24, pt. 1, 709; *OR* 24, pt. 2, 100; George S. Durfee Correspondence, UIL. Smith's claim to have captured six guns is difficult to reconcile with other equally credible claims by Stevenson's regiments, though George Durfee made the same claim in a letter home just five days after the fight. Smith also notes the 41st Alabama and 31st Georgia "were captured nearly entire." Neither unit existed in Pemberton's army. In all likelihood he mixed up the numbers and state designations when referring to Barton's 41st Georgia and Lee's 31st Alabama, both of which suffered heavily in the battle.

69. *OR* 24, pt. 2, 100.

70. *OR* 24, pt. 2, 100; *OR* 24, pt. 1, 53, 640, 721; Grant, *Personal Memoirs*, 1: 303-304.

Chapter 9

1. *OR* 24, pt. 2, 121. C. MacRae Selph may have recorded the time as "about 2 o'clock," but it was certainly much closer to 1:00 p.m. or perhaps even a bit earlier. This is another good example of how the watches on any Civil War battlefield often differed widely.

2. *OR* 24, pt. 2, 121.

3. *OR* 24, pt. 2, 121; William A. Drennan to his wife, May 30, 1863, William A. Drennan Papers, MDAH.

4. William T. Moore to Capt. W. T. Ratliff, October 5, 1902, VNMP; *OR* 24, pt. 2, 121; William A. Drennan to his wife, May 30, 1863, William A. Drennan Papers, MDAH.

5. *OR* 24 pt. 2, 110, 116, 121-122; Bevier, *History of the First and Second Missouri Confederate Brigades*, 193; Sanborn, *Crisis*, 20; A. C. Riley, "Confederate Col. A. C. Riley, His Reports and Letters, Part II," Riley Bock, ed., *Missouri Historical Review*, 85, no. 3 (April 1991), 276.

6. *OR* 24 pt. 2, 110, 123; Reynolds, "Vivid Experiences at Champion Hill, Miss.," 21; Payne, "Missouri Troops," 341; Anderson, *First Missouri Brigade*, 310-311; Phillip Thomas Tucker, *The Forgotten Stonewall of the West: Major General John Stevens Bowen* (Macon: Mercer University Press, 1997), 276. Tucker, Bowen's modern biographer, accuses Pemberton of delaying his response to the crisis on Stevenson's front, yet completely exonerates Bowen for refusing to come the first time he was called to support Carter Stevenson. As far as I am aware, it is one the only recorded instance of Bowen's refusal to act quickly and decisively on the field of battle when ordered by a superior to do so.

7. *OR* 24 pt. 2, 110, 123; Reynolds, "Vivid Experiences at Champion Hill, Miss.," 21; Payne, "Missouri Troops," 341; Anderson, *First Missouri Brigade*, 310-311.

8. Anderson, *First Missouri Brigade*, 311-312; Bevier, *History of the First and Second Missouri Confederate Brigades*, 188. Both Anderson and Bevier later wrote these women were at the Champion house, but that was of course impossible, as that structure

was on the far side of the high ground and in enemy hands. They mistook the Champion house for the Roberts house, Pemberton's headquarters.

9. *OR* 24 pt. 2, 110.

10. *OR* 24, pt. 2, 110-111; Anderson, *First Missouri Brigade*, 312; Reynolds, "Vivid Experiences at Champion Hill, Miss.," 21; Phillip Thomas Tucker, *The South's Finest: The First Missouri Confederate Brigade From Pea Ridge to Vicksburg* (Shippensburg: White Mane Publishing Company, Inc., 1993), 161, 163; Tucker, *Westerners in Gray: The Men and Missions of the Elite Fifth Missouri Infantry Regiment* (Jefferson, NC: McFarland & Company, Inc., Publishers, 1995), 184-185; Riley, "Confederate Col. A. C. Riley," 276. James Arnold, *Grant Wins the War*, 172-174, claims McGinnis' brigade never moved south from the crest of Champion Hill. Firsthand accounts from members of this brigade, however, prove otherwise. See, for example, Augustus Sinks, "Four Years in Dixie," Augustus Sinks Journal, ISL, 37, and Henry Watts Civil War Reminiscences, ISL, 80, for just two examples of the depth of McGinnis's advance.

11. *OR* 24, pt. 2, 111, 119; I. V. Smith, "Personal Memoirs," 29; Bevier, *History of the First and Second Missouri Confederate Brigades*, 188; Payne, "Missouri Troops," 341; Tucker, *Westerners in Gray*, 187.

12. *OR* 24, pt. 2, 111; Phillip Thomas Tucker, *The Confederacy's Fighting Chaplain: Father John B. Bannon* (Tuscaloosa: The University of Alabama Press, 1982), 128; See also John Bannon Diary, May 16, 1863, USC.

13. *OR* 24 pt. 2, 110; Anderson, *First Missouri Brigade*, 312; Bevier, *History of the First and Second Missouri Confederate Brigades*, 188; Phillip Thomas Tucker, *Westerners in Gray*, 179; T. B. Sproul, "Letter," *Confederate Veteran*, 2, no. 7 (July 1894), 199.

14. Cheavens, "A Missouri Confederate," 38-39.

15. *OR* 21, pt. 2, 116; Anderson, *First Missouri Brigade*, 312; Reynolds, "Vivid Experiences at Champion Hill, Miss.," 21; Tucker, *The Confederacy's Fighting Chaplain*, 128; See also John Bannon Diary, May 16, 1863, USC.

16. *OR* 21, pt. 2, 116; Anderson, *First Missouri Brigade*, 312; Reynolds, "Vivid Experiences at Champion Hill, Miss.," 21.

17. Warner, *Generals in Blue*, 102.

18. *OR* 24 pt. 1, 724, 730; Edward P. Stanfield to his father, May 26, 1863, Edward P. Stanfield Letters, IHS.

19. Byers, "How Men Feel in Battle," 441; S. H. M. Byers, *With Fire and Sword* (New York: The Neale Publishing Company, 1911), 73.

20. *OR* 24, pt. 1, 730, 731; *OR* 24, pt. 2, 65; Warner, *Generals in Blue*, 418-419.

21. *OR* 24, pt. 1, 730, 731; *OR* 24, pt. 2, 65, 66. Colonel Putnam of the 93rd Illinois thought the brigade deployed south of the road, which is another indication of how difficult it was for the men to figure out the compass direction in the confusing terrain. Byers, "How Men Feel in Battle," 441; Byers, *With Fire and Sword*, 73.

22. *OR* 24, pt. 1, 724, 730, 776; Joel W. Strong Reminiscences, 12, MHS; Sanborn, *Crisis*, 26.

23. Byers, "How Men Feel in Battle," 441.

24. Byers, "How Men Feel in Battle," 442; Bevier, *History of the First and Second Missouri Confederate Brigades*, 188.

25. John Griffin Jones to his parents, June 20, 1863, John Griffin Jones Papers, LC; *OR* 24 pt. 2, 42. Bearss, *Vicksburg*, 2: 611n, claims two guns were removed. Other sources claim all four remained on the hill.

26. Bevier, *History of the First and Second Missouri Confederate Brigades*, 188; Payne, "Missouri Troops," 341; Tucker, *Westerners in Gray*, 187; I. V. Smith, "Personal Memoirs," 28.

27. *OR* 24, pt. 2, 49. The alignment of McGinnis's regiments at this point in the battle is not known with any precision. If one was to hazard a rough guess by piecing together the thin available evidence, the 34th Indiana ended up near the Jackson Road on the far left, with the 47th Indiana (Slack's regiment) next or intermingled with the 11th Indiana and 46th Indiana, followed by the 24th Indiana and 29th Wisconsin extending the line on the hillside westward toward the left flank Leggett's brigade. Hovey Unpublished Memoir, 57, IU; *OR* 24, pt. 2, 49, 53, 55, 57.

28. *OR* 24 pt. 2, 111, 119; I. V. Smith Personal Memoir, Western Historical Manuscript Collection, UMC, 29; Reynolds, "Vivid Experiences at Champion Hill, Miss.," 21; Bevier, *History of the First and Second Missouri Confederate Brigades*, 188; Payne, "Missouri Troops," 341; Tucker, *Westerners in Gray*, 187.

29. *OR* 24, pt. 2, 49; *History of the 46th Indiana*, 59-60; Bearss, *Vicksburg*, 2: 610-611n. Bearss is the only source for the deployment of the 2nd Ohio Battery, and he reiterates that two of the four captured Rebel guns had been removed by this time. Henry Watts Civil War Reminiscences, ISL, 80.

30. Smith, "Personal Memoirs," 28-29; *OR* 24, pt. 2, 49-50, 53-54; Hovey Unpublished Memoir, 75, IU; Dana, *Recollections of the Civil War*, 64. Though written long after the event, Smith's memoir is remarkably accurate in most respects. However, he claimed at the beginning of Cockrell's attack that his regiment struck "the 13th U. S. Regulars." This was not possible, as the 1st Battalion, 13th U.S. Infantry was part of Col. Giles A. Smith's brigade, Blair's division, Sherman's Corps. Blair was trailing behind A. J. Smith's division on the far Union left along the Raymond Road, and was nowhere near Bowen's attack.

31. *OR* 24, pt. 2, 49-50, 53-54; Dana, *Recollections of the Civil War*, 64.

32. Tucker, *The Confederacy's Fighting Chaplain*, 124.

33. *OR* 24, pt. 2, 53-54; Williams, "Champion's Hill," 207.

34. *OR* 24, pt. 2, 45, 54.

35. Payne, "Missouri Troops," 341.

36. *OR* 24, pt. 2, 55-59.

37. Williams, "The Battle of Champion Hill," 207.

38. *OR* 24, pt. 2, 59.

39. Williams, "The Battle of Champion Hill," 207; *OR* 24, pt. 2, 59; Myers, "'Dear and Mutch Loved One,'" 53.

40. *OR* 24, pt. 2, 118-119.

41. *OR* 24, pt. 2, 55; Williams, "The Battle of Champion Hill," 207; Israel M. Ritter Diary, May 16, 1863.

42. *OR* 24, pt. 2, 55; Williams, "The Battle of Champion Hill," 207; Longley, "Champion's Hill," 214; Israel M. Ritter Diary, May 16, 1863. Colonel John Connell's report for the 28th Iowa claims his regiment fell back.

43. Williams, "The Battle of Champion Hill," 208.

44. *OR* 24 pt. 2, 111; Williams, "The Battle of Champion Hill," 209.

45. *OR* 24 pt. 2, 116; Reynolds, "Vivid Experiences at Champion Hill, Miss.," 21; Aurelius Lyman Voorhis, *The Life and Times of Aurelius Lyman Voorhis*, ed. Jerry Voorhis (New York: Vantage Press, 1976), 123. Arnold, *Grant Wins the War*, 182, claims some of Slack's units never retreated. Substantial evidence wholly contradicts this patently incorrect claim. Slack's own report, *OR* 24 pt. 2, 55, explains how he "directed the whole command to retire gradually." He also reported his order was carried out. I was unable to more fully identify "Purdie," the soldier identified in Dockery's official report, *OR* 24, pt. 2, 117.

46. Williams, "The Battle of Champion Hill," 208-209.

47. Williams, "The Battle of Champion Hill," 209.

48. *OR* 24, pt. 2, 56.

49. Williams, "The Battle of Champion Hill," 209-210.

50. *OR* 24, pt. 2, 59; Williams, "The Battle of Champion Hill," 207.

51. *OR* 24, pt. 2, 106.

52. Alfred Cumming to Stephen D. Lee, November 3, 1899, MDAH.

53. *OR* 24, pt. 2, 106. It is understandable that Cumming would confuse the men on his left. Everyone was exhausted, the commands were intermingled, and several hundred of Barton's men advanced with Lee's reformed line.

54. *OR* 24, pt. 2, 102; W. T. Moore to W. T. Ratliff, 1902, Letter Files, VNMP.

55. *OR* 24, pt. 2, 102.

56. *OR* 24, pt. 1, 718.

57. *OR* 24, pt. 1, 648; *OR* 24, pt. 2, 102. Lee later wrote that, after Cumming's line broke and his own brigade thereafter was driven back by frontal and enfilade fire, the 20th and 31st Alabama regiments (the pair that had held the right front of Lee's first line of battle looking north and facing Logan's division) "fought gallantly against the two brigades of McGinnis and Slack." Lee, "The Campaign of Vicksburg," 45. These regiments, however, were not in a position to have battled Slack generally, because except for McLaughlin's 47th Indiana, Slack's entire brigade fought on the east side of the Jackson Road.

58. *OR* 24 pt. 1, 640, 724.

59. Cadwallader, *Three Years With Grant*, 79.

60. Sanborn, *Crisis*, 13; William S. McFeely, *Grant: A Biography* (New York: W. W. Norton & Company, 1981), 131.

61. *OR* 24, pt. 2, 66; Stone, *Memoir of George Boardman Boomer*, 252; Bearss, *Vicksburg*, 2: 614.

62. *OR* 24, pt. 2, 43-44.

63. *OR* 24, pt. 2, 66; *OR* 24, pt. 1, 724, 730; Byers, "Some Recollections of Grant," 344-345; Trimble, *History of the Ninety-Third Regiment*, 30; Byers, "How Men Feel in Battle," 441; Cadwallader, *Three Years with Grant*, 79.

64. Stone, *Memoir of George Boardman Boomer*, 252; *OR* 24, pt. 2, 66; *OR* 24, pt. 1, 724; Byers, "How Men Feel in Battle," 443.

65. Stone, *Memoir of George Boardman Boomer*, 252; *OR* 24, pt. 2, 66; *OR* 24, pt. 1, 724; Henry G. Hicks, "The Campaign and Capture of Vicksburg," *MOLLUS-Minnesota*, 100; Reynolds, "Vivid Experiences at Champion Hill, Miss.," 21.

66. *OR* 24, pt. 2, 66; Byers, "How Men Feel in Battle," 443; Stone, *Memoir of George Boardman Boomer*, 252.

67. Anderson, *First Missouri Brigade*, 313; *OR* 24, pt. 2, 111.

68. *OR* 24, pt. 1, 730. Samuel E. Sneier letter, June 21, 1863, IHS. Colonel Sanborn noted in his report that the Confederate left (i.e., Lee and Barton) fell back after he was ordered to move forward and support Boomer, who was counterattacking and slowing down John Bowen's own counterattack. We know for certain, however, that Bowen's attack and Hovey's collapse occurred after Lee's and Barton's brigades gave way. The events were not at all simultaneous. Sanborn may have been referring to Lee's second anemic attack launched from just above the Jackson Road.

69. Byers, "How Men Feel in Battle," 443.

70. Byers, "How Men Feel in Battle," 444.

71. Byers, "How Men Feel in Battle," 444.

72. Byers, "How Men Feel in Battle," 444.

73. *OR* 24, pt. 2, 50; Theodore D. Fisher Diary, MHS.

74. Nicholas C. Buswell to Richard Yates, n.d., Nicholas C. Buswell Papers, ISHL; Byers, "Some Recollections of Grant," 345; Byers, "How Men Feel in Battle," 444. Stone, *Memoir of George Boardman Boomer*, 252; *OR* 24, pt. 2, 44. The 93rd Illinois retired its flag because it was shredded beyond repair. It was sent home and housed in the state archives.

75. *OR* 24, pt. 2, 50, 66; Byers, "Some Recollections of Grant," 346; Byers, "How Men Feel in Battle," 445.

76. Byers, "How Men Feel in Battle," 444-445.

77. *OR* 24, pt. 1, 718, 724, 730.

78. *OR* 24, pt. 1, 724.

79. *OR* 24, pt. 1, 776.

80. *OR* 24, pt. 2, 63-64.

81. *OR* 24, pt. 2, 63. Colonel Putnam's report for the 93rd Illinois, *OR* 24, pt. 2, 66, does not specifically discuss being driven back across the road. However, Hillis is very specific about where his troops aligned for battle, and his report is credible.

82. Joel W. Strong Reminiscences, Alphabetical Files, MHS, 12.

83. *OR* 24, pt. 1, 724, 779; *OR* 24, pt. 2, 63, 112, 117; Sanborn, *Crisis*, 14, 32; Joel W. Strong Reminiscences, Alphabetical Files, MHS, 12.

84. *OR* 24, pt. 1, 776, 779, 783; *OR* 24, pt. 2, 59; Trimble, *History of the Ninety-Third Regiment*, 30-31.

85. Finley L. Hubbell, "Diary of Lieut. Col. Hubbell, of 3d Regiment Missouri Infantry, C.S.A.," *The Land We Love* 6, no. 2 (December 1868), 105; Tucker, *The South's Finest*, 166, 168.

86. *OR* 24 pt. 2, 44, 111; Stone, *Memoir of George Boardman Boomer*, 252; Tucker, *Westerners in Gray*, 195.

87. *OR* 24, pt. 2, 44, 119.

88. *OR* 24, pt. 2, 44, 46, 50, 117. There were two large groups of guns operating at this time: De Goyler's Michigan pieces (with Rogers and perhaps others) behind Logan's center and left, which moved up as the battle progressed, and the 16 pieces Hovey gathered and put in to action to stem Bowen's counterattack. But where did he put them? Bearss, *Vicksburg*, 2: 615, claims the guns were placed southeast of the Champion home on the east side of the Jackson Road. However, from this point the terrain would have made it nearly impossible to enfilade the Confederate lines. Hovey makes it clear in both his report and map, *OR* 24, pt. 2, 43-44, that these 16 pieces were deployed somewhere west of the road, and I believe his report and accompanying map are credible.

89. *OR* 24, pt. 2, 111; Bearss, *Vicksburg*, 2: 611.

90. *OR* 24, pt. 2, 116, 119.

91. *OR* 24, pt. 2, 111. Colonel Riley's report, which has not been located, is referenced inside Cockrell's after-action report.

92. Anderson, *First Missouri Brigade*, 313.

93. *OR* 24 pt. 2, 63, 111, 117-118; Anderson, *Memoirs*, 312-313; S. C. Trigg, "Fighting Around Vicksburg," *Confederate Veteran*, 12, no. 3 (March 1904), 120; Trigg mentions that Bowen's men destroyed several of the Union wagons. Tucker, *The Forgotten Stonewall of the West*, Bowen's biographer, mentions that a handful of Missourians reaching the wagons, but cites no credible supporting evidence. No corroborative evidence has been found for such an assertion.

Chapter 10

1. *OR* 24, pt. 1, 52, 149.

2. *OR* 24, pt. 2, 15.

3. *OR* 24, pt. 1, 52, 149; *OR* 24, pt. 3, 316-317.

4. *OR* 24, pt. 2, 15, 134; Richard L. Kiper, *Major General John Alexander McClernand: Politician in Uniform* (Kent: Kent State University Press, 1999), 246-247. McClernand's biographer cites the difficult terrain and extensive amount of time needed for the delivery of orders, but still faults the general for not pressing his attack as hard as he might have. For a more sympathetic view of McClernand, see Terrence J. Winschel, "Fighting Politician: John A. McClernand" in *Grant's Lieutenants: From Cairo to Vicksburg*, ed. Steven E. Woodworth (Lawrence: University Press of Kansas, 2001), 139.

5. Edward H. Ingraham to his aunt, May 21, 1863, D. G. and E. H. Ingraham Letters, ISHL; Samuel P. Harrington Diary, May 15, 1863, Rudolph Haerle Collection, USAMHI; Elliot, *History of the Thirty-Third Regiment*, 40. A soldier in Eugene Carr's division wrote home after the battle that Champion Hill caused "no great loss to us," an opinion that illustrates well how little combat Carr's division experienced.

6. William A. Drennan to his wife, May 30, 1863, William A. Drennan Papers, MDAH; Ballard, *Pemberton*, 133; James W. Raab, *W. W. Loring: Florida's Forgotten General* (Manhattan, KS: Sunflower University Press, 1996), 12.

7. *OR* 24, pt. 1, 264; H. J. Reid, "The 22nd Mississippi Regiment," J. F. H. Claiborne Papers, UNC. Pemberton's recollection of the when specific events transpired on the battlefield varies widely from other participants. For example, he noted that Carter Stevenson's rout took place about 4:00 p.m., which is probably at least two hours later than it actually transpired.

8. *OR* 24, pt. 1, 264; *OR* 24, pt. 2, 70, 126; Ballard, *Pemberton*, 162.

9. *OR* 24, pt. 2, 83; J. V. Greif, Baker's Creek and Champion Hill: What Abe Buford's Brigade and Others Did There," 351. Buford believed the order to move north was delivered "about 3 p.m." Featherston reported it as "2 or 3 o'clock in the evening." Colonel Arthur E. Reynolds, who wrote the report for Tilghman's Brigade, reported the movement to the left began about noon. As should be obvious by now, the time events transpired was wholly unsynchronized, and trying to decipher events based upon when something was done, time-wise, is simply impossible.

10. *OR* 24, pt. 1, 264; *OR* 24, pt. 2, 76, 79, 83, 91, 126; Ballard, *Pemberton*, 162.

11. *OR* 24, pt. 1, 264.

12. John Whitten Diary, Inside Front Cover, LC; *OR* 24, pt. 1, 776, 783; *OR* 24, pt. 2, 64, 66; Myers, "'Dear and Mutch Loved One,'" 54.

13. Voorhis, *The Life and Times of Aurelius Lyman Voorhis*, 123; *OR* 24, pt. 2, 44.

14. *OR* 24, pt. 2, 53; Grant, *Personal Memoirs*, 1: 304; Cadwallader, *Three Years With Grant*, 79; Williams, "Champion's Hill," 210.

15. *OR* 24, pt. 1, 53.

16. *OR* 24, pt. 2, 120; Lockett, "The Defense of Vicksburg," 3: 487; William Cotton Letter, May 27, 1863, William L. Cotton Letters, SHSI.

17. *OR* 24 pt. 2, 116-117; Tucker, *The Confederacy's Fighting Chaplain*, 128. See also John Bannon Diary, May 16, 1863, USC.

18. *OR* 24, pt. 1, 730-731; *OR* 24, pt. 2, 62; 102, 106.

19. *OR* 24, pt. 1, 731; *OR* 24, pt. 2, 62, 102; Henry C. Adams, *Indiana at Vicksburg* (Indianapolis: William B. Bradford, 1911), 274. The 34th Indiana also claimed to capture the colors of the 46th Alabama, with its field officers and 127 men.

20. *OR* 24, pt. 2, 119.

21. *OR* 24, pt. 1, 783.

22. *OR* 24, pt. 1, 783; Strong, Reminiscences, 12.

23. Reynolds, "Vivid Experiences at Champion Hill, Miss.," 21. For Reynolds and many of his comrades, the war was over—at least for a while. Reynolds was transported to Camp Morton, Indiana, on to Fort Delaware, Delaware, and finally to Point Lookout, Maryland. He was exchanged in December 1863. Many others were not so fortunate. Private W. F. Almond of Company H reached Fort Delaware on August 30,1863, and died there on June 18, 1864. He is buried on the Jersey shore.

24. *OR* 24, pt. 2, 117.

25. *OR* 24, pt. 1, 264-265. Carter Stevenson's report, *OR* 24, pt. 2, 96, is remarkably similar and agrees in all aspects with Pemberton's version of these events.

26. "Abraham Buford," by Lawrence Hewitt, *The Confederate General*, 1: 145-146.

27. *OR* 24, pt. 2, 84, 86; Welsh, *Medical Histories of Confederate Generals*, 12. Baker's wound was a serious one, and on May 21, he requested thirty days' leave to allow his foot to heal.

28. *OR* 24, pt. 2, 84.

29. *OR* 24, pt. 2, 106; Alfred Cumming to Stephen D. Lee, November 3, 1899, MDAH.

30. *OR* 24, pt. 2, 106.

31. *OR* 24, pt. 2, 102-103; Emma Balfour Diary, May 17, 1863; Joseph Bogle Reminiscences, GDAH, 9-10.

32. *OR* 24, pt. 2, 84.

33. *OR* 24, pt. 1, 265.

34. *OR* 24, pt. 1, 265.

35. *OR* 24, pt. 2, 112, 117.

36. *OR* 24, pt. 2, 119.

37. *OR* 24, pt. 2, 88; Anderson, *First Missouri*, 313. One historian of the battle places Goodwin's troops in the cornfield northeast of the crossroads fighting an indistinct enemy. Bearss, *Vicksburg*, 2: 621. This, however, must be incorrect for several reasons—in addition to the fact that the sources cited do not specifically support that conclusion. The situation was indeed highly volatile and confused, but if we are to make sense of Goodwin's battle experience at Champion Hill, we must resolve with some degree of certainty where he fought and who opposed him. According to his report, Goodwin was collared by Bowen "near the negro cabins," along the Ratliff Road on the Roberts farm property (Pemberton's headquarters) about 600 yards south of the crossroads. Goodwin was guided a short distance (100 yards) toward what he called "the front," and ordered to move forward until he met the enemy. His exact direction is not stated, but logic would tell us he was moving north up the Ratliff Road. Goodwin then met up with Martin Green, who ordered him to "move to the right" to support Wade's Battery. Moving to the "right" meant Goodwin marched his regiment east off the Ratliff Road—directly toward the left front of Peter Osterhaus's division. Goodwin never mentions reaching or seeing the crossroads, nor does he specifically state how far he marched, though he strongly implies the distance to Wade's guns was very short. If he was supporting Wade's artillery above the crossroads, he would have described his march to that place in much different terms. He also would have been hundreds of yards west of Scott's 12th Louisiana and well behind Green's men—which does not make much sense given the fighting Goodwin went on to describe. So where was he and who was he fighting when he supported Wade' Battery for more than one hour under a rain of artillery fire and musketry? There is only one logical answer: Green caught Goodwin a couple hundred yards below the crossroads on the Ratliff Road and ordered him to move east off the road and deploy there. In that position, Goodwin held back the left flank elements of Peter Osterhaus's advancing division. A simple process of elimination forces us to reach this conclusion. Goodwin's regiment was the only large body of organized Confederates available to oppose Daniel Lindsey's (and later, Michael Lawler's) advance. Green's men were clearly ending their fight above the Middle Road at this time and retiring in a

disorganized state below it, as several Federal reports (and Goodwin himself) clearly state. They were also out of ammunition, and Osterhaus specifically notified Garrard they were retreating and not reforming for an attack. *OR* 24, pt. 2, 15. Further, Green's withdrawal through Goodwin's lines was only *after* Goodwin spent an estimated one hour under fire. Lindsey's report specifically notes being shelled by a battery that was supported by a strong infantry (i.e., organized) force, and then falling back in a small rout, which was confirmed by Goodwin; Cockrell complimented Walsh's (Wade's) battery for "its good service on the right of the brigade in checking the enemy in his attempt to gain the rear of our right flank." *OR* 24, pt. 2, 26, 88, 111. The Peoria Battery, brought up thereafter by Lawler, aggressively shelled the Alabamans in return. There were no other organized regiments available in this sector other than Goodwin's 35th Alabama. Until evidence surfaces to contradict this conclusion, there is no other reasonable interpretation of the sources and no way to account for Goodwin's meticulously recorded activities. Coupled with the wonderful performance of Col. Thomas Scott's 12th Louisiana north of the Middle Road, it also goes a long way toward explaining what held up McClernand's advance that afternoon.

38. *OR* 24, pt. 2, 26. It is difficult to discern what was happening on Theophilus Garrard's front, for his report of Champion Hill has not been located.

39. W. L. Rand to his parents, May 25, 1863, Rand Family Papers, ISHL.

40. *OR* 24, pt. 2, 15; William M. Murray Diary, May 16, 1863, Letters and Diaries File, VNMP.

41. Warner, *Generals in Blue*, 276; Dana, *Recollections of the Civil War*, 65; George W. Gordon Diary, May 24, 1863, George W. Gordon Papers, USAMHI.

42. *OR* 24, pt. 2, 15, 134; *OR* 24, pt. 1, 151; G. H. Fifer letter, May 30, 1863, Joseph Wilson Fifer Papers, ISHL; Elliot, *History of the Thirty-Third Regiment*, 40; Cadwallader, *Three Years With Grant*, 83.

43. *OR* 24, pt. 2, 26, 135; Aquilla Standifird Diary, May 16, 1863, Western Historical Manuscript Collection, UMR.

44. *OR* 24, pt. 2, 77, 88.

45. *OR* 24, pt. 2, 89.

46. *OR* 24, pt. 2, 15, 22, 89.

47. *OR* 24, pt. 2, 84; Greif, "Baker's Creek and Champion Hill," 351.

48. *OR* 24, pt.1, 265.

49. *OR* 24, pt. 2, 120-121.

50. *OR* 24, pt. 1, 265; *OR* 24, pt. 2, 121; H. Grady Howell, *To Live and Die in Dixie: A History of the Third Mississippi Infantry, C.S.A.* (Jackson: Chickasaw Bayou Press, 1991), 202. There is no evidence Buford's line straddled the Ratliff Road.

51. *OR* 24, pt. 2, 76, 84, 91; Weldon Hudson, "William Spencer Hudson in the Civil War," T. M. Weldon Hudson Papers, UM, 8. General Buford, in his report in *OR* 24, pt. 2, 84, makes it clear he retreated "about a quarter of a mile" south of a line originally taken up near the "negro cabins," which was in the vicinity of Pemberton's headquarters on the Roberts's place, which in turn was some 600 yards south of the crossroads.

52. M. D. L. Stephens Recollections, 31st Mississippi Papers, MDAH, 17-18.

53. *OR* 24, pt. 2, 76; William A. Drennan to his wife, May 30, 1863, William A. Drennan Papers, MDAH. That Loring had been planning an attack before receiving Pemberton's first withdrawal order is confirmed by Abraham Buford's report. "I was ordered to move my brigade into position, so as to move against the enemy's right and pierce his line, and thus, by a vigorous and well-directed attack, force him to abandon the field, it having been reported that his center was falling back, and thus retrieve the day. I was joined here by the Twelfth Louisiana and Thirty-fifth Alabama Regiments, and moved rapidly forward, and was forming in position, when I was informed by one of my staff officers that you had received positive orders to withdraw the forces from the field, and had commenced retiring." *OR* 24, pt. 2, 86.

54. *OR* 24, pt. 1, 53, 776; *OR* 24, pt. 2, 15, 44, 50, 62; Grant, *Personal Memoirs*, 1: 304; Sanborn, *Crisis*, 15.

55. *OR* 24, pt. 1, 718.

56. William A. Drennan to his wife, May 30, 1863, William A. Drennan Papers, MDAH. Drennan's reference to the enemy advancing "in our rear" is almost certainly a reference to the Federals under A. J. Smith and Frank Blair, who were pressuring Lloyd Tilghman's Brigade along the Raymond Road, which will be covered in detail in the next chapter.

57. William A. Drennan to his wife, May 30, 1863, William A. Drennan Papers, MDAH. Stephen Lee's arrival in the deep rear at this time makes perfect sense because the hundreds of men from the several commands he had gathered and deployed on Featherston's left flank had been attacked and routed by the advancing 8th Illinois of John Stevenson's brigade, and by this time Lee had been ordered to move for the lower crossing. (This event is discussed in the next chapter.) Lee, however, does not mention this humiliating incident in his report, or in Lee, "The Campaign of Vicksburg." However, John Stevenson left a very precise report; Lee, by his own words, held the far left of the army's new line; and Featherston's Brigade suffered only one man missing during this stage of the fighting. Therefore, the attack by the 8th Illinois and prisoners they took had to have come from Lee's amalgamated organization, together with the large knots of stragglers who were wandering the battlefield at this time. There is no other plausible explanation.

Chapter 11

1. George E. Brewer, "Reminiscences of George E. Brewer," 46th Alabama Papers, ADAH; J.W. Harmon, "A Recollection From an Old Confederate," 35th Alabama Papers, ADAH, 17; *OR* 24, pt. 1, 70, 265.

2. Edwin C. Bearss, "Winfield Scott Featherston," *The Confederate General*, 2:119-120. Stephen Lee, in "The Campaign of Vicksburg," 48-49, claimed Carter Stevenson's Division had orders to retreat before Loring's arrival.

3. *OR* 24, pt. 2, 76-77, 84, 91-92.

4. *OR* 24, pt. 1, 718.

5. *OR* 24, pt. 2, 92.

6. *OR* 24, pt. 2, 92; Stephens, Recollections, 18-19.

7. Featherston's total losses for the entire battle were but one killed, one wounded, and one missing. These losses were all suffered by the 22nd Mississippi Infantry during the early morning artillery exchange on the Raymond Road.

8. Francis Obenchain to John Johnston, November 27, 1903, VNMP.

9. Francis Obenchain to John Johnston, November 27, 1903, VNMP. Obenchain wrote that he "believed he told me that his section was a part of the Pointe Coupee battery, but of this I am not so sure that I am right." The Point Coupee artillery had two companies (A and C, each with four guns) engaged at Champion Hill, both attached to Abraham Buford. *OR* 24, pt. 2, 82. Both companies were under the command of Capt. Alcide Bouanchaud, who seemed to be personally directing Company A at this time of the fighting. Company C's record is less clear, though it seems Lt. John Yoist was in command of one section of Company C's guns. The fact that Obenchain believed the lieutenant was French, the location of the meeting, and the sequence of events, leads me to conclude Obenchain was correct, and that he had stumbled on the other section from Company C. The mystery deepened when Arthur W. Bergeron, Jr., Louisiana's premier historian, was asked about this story, of which he was not aware. He responded as follows: "I can't claim that my notes are absolutely complete, but I cannot find any lieutenants of Company A or Company C who died at Champion Hill. In fact, I think I have accounted for all of them through the end of the siege. The only death I have found in the battalion was that of Lieut. Oscar M. D'Aubigne of Company B, who was killed on May 29, 1863." E-mail dated April 11, 2004

10. Francis Obenchain to John Johnston, November 27, 1903, VNMP. The conversation is constructed as accurately as possible from the specific information provided by Obenchain in his letter.

11. Francis Obenchain to John Johnston, November 27, 1903, VNMP. Obenchain wrote that "Green's and Cockrell's were out of those woods" by that time, but if Johnson pointed northwest, Obenchain could only have meant Carter Stevenson's command. If, however, Johnson pointed to the northeast, and Obenchain was mistaken as to the direction, the reference to Green and Cockrell would have been correct.

12. Francis Obenchain to John Johnston, November 27, 1903, VNMP.

13. Francis Obenchain to John Johnston, November 27, 1903, VNMP.

14. *OR* 24, pt. 1, 718.

15. Editor, "Gen. Lloyd Tilghman," *Confederate Veteran* (1918), 18: 318; Terry L. Jones, "Lloyd Tilghman," in *The Confederate General*, 6: 48-49.

16. *OR* 24, pt. 2, 79-80. The conversation presented herein is constructed as accurately as possible from the very specific comments contained in Col. Alexander Reynolds's report, which was filed for Tilghman's Brigade after that officer was killed. Reynolds estimated the time as "about 1 o'clock" and that the second line was formed "at 1:30 o'clock," demonstrating once again the wide variance of the recollections of when specific events transpired at Champion Hill. In reality, it was closer to 4:00 p.m. Pemberton does not mention the incident with Tilghman in his report, perhaps because the general was dead and there was no need to raise an issue that might be misinterpreted by others.

17. *OR* 24, pt. 2, 80; John Griffin Jones to his parents, June 20, 1863, John Griffin Jones Papers, LC. Colonel Lowry's losses in the skirmish action were one killed, two wounded, and 27 missing.

18. *OR* 24, pt. 2, 255.

19. *OR* 24, pt. 2, 32. The exact alignment of Burbridge's brigade is not known. Only two of his four regimental reports have been published. Similarly, A. J. Smith's Champion Hill report has not been found.

20. *OR* 24, pt. 2, 32. Merrick J. Wald Diary, transcription in Illinois files, Theodore P. Savas Collection. For more on the Chicago Mercantile Battery, see George Troop Letters, Thomas R. Stone Collection, USAMHI and George Perry Letters, Squire and Chester Tuttle Collection, USAMHI.

21. J. W. Egleston Diary, May 16, 1863, IHS; Isaac Jackson, *Some of the Boys . . . : The Civil War Letters of Isaac Jackson: 1862-1865*, Joseph Orville Jackson, ed. (Carbondale: Southern Illinois University Press, 1960), 93; Carlos W. Colby, "Bullets, Hardtack and Mud: A Soldier's View of the Vicksburg Campaign," ed. John S. Painter, *Journal of the West*, 4, no. 2 (April 1965), 151; Rick Williams, *Chicago's Battery Boys: The Chicago Mercantile Battery in the American Civil War* (New York: Savas Beatie, 2004), material from which was taken prior to publication, courtesy of the author and publisher. *OR* 24, pt. 2, 37; Merrick J. Wald Diary, Savas Collection. No lieutenant of Company K is listed as a casualty. Stephens, Recollections, 16; Faulkenberry, Diary, May 16, 1863.

22. *OR* 24, pt. 2, 32; Thomas B. Marshall, *History of the Eighty-Third Volunteer Infantry* (Cincinnati, 1912), 80.

23. *OR* 24, pt. 2, 32, 255; *OR* 24, pt. 3, 318; Dana, *Recollections of the Civil War*, 66.

24. William A. Drennan to his wife, May 30, 1863, William A. Drennan Papers, MDAH.

25. *OR* 24, pt. 2, 80.

26. *OR* 24, pt. 2, 77, 86, 89; Greif, "Baker's Creek and Champion Hill," 351. Buford mentioned Scott's deployment, but not the interval involving the march southwest.

27. *OR* 24, pt. 2, 256.

28. *OR* 24, pt. 2, 84, 135, 255-256; Featherston's Brigade Report and Buford's Brigade Report of Bakers Creek, Confederate States Army Casualties: Lists and Narrative Reports 1861-1865, NA; Winschel, "The Guns at Champion Hill," 104; *OR* 24, pt. 2, 84, 135, 256; "The War Between the States," Isaac E. Hirsh Papers, MSU, 31.

29. *OR* 24, pt. 2, 77, 80.

30. William A. Drennan to his wife, May 30, 1863, William A. Drennan Papers, MDAH.

31. *OR* 24, pt. 2, 80.

32. *OR* 24, pt. 2, 77.

33. F. W. Merrin, "Career and Fate of Gen. Lloyd Tilghman," *Confederate Veteran* (1893), 1: 275. It is interesting to note how Lieutenant Drennan's letter, written for his wife's consumption just a short time after the battle, and Merrin's article written three decades later, agree on all major points—which further confirms Drennan's veracity as a keen and truthful observer. In 1907, General Tilghman's sons located the spot on which

their father had fallen and erected a boulder with a bronze tablet affixed to it. Bearss, *Vicksburg*, 2: 627.

34. William A. Drennan to his wife, May 30, 1863, William A. Drennan Papers, MDAH.

35. William A. Drennan to his wife, May 30, 1863, William A. Drennan Papers, MDAH.

36. *OR* 24, pt. 2, 102-103, 106; *OR* 24, pt. 1, 265; Alfred Cumming to Stephen D. Lee. "I have of course ever been aware, My Dear General," Cumming wrote to Stephen Lee, "that Pemberton in his report of that disastrous campaign, 'reflects' upon the conduct of the Georgia Brigade. Needing every possible excuse that he could bring to bear to shield himself; that he should have done so, has ever seemed to me, from his standpoint, natural and to have been expected. If in that Valhalla to which he [has] long since taken his departure, and where as Dick Taylor [General Richard Taylor, CSA] tells us, the souls of Heroes commune together—if he shall there have derived any satisfaction there from, let him have it."

37. *OR* 24, pt. 2, 102-103, 106; *OR* 24, pt. 1, 265.

38. *OR* 24, pt. 2, 108.

39. *OR* 24, pt. 2, 100, 108; F. G. Carnes, ed., "We Can Hold Our Ground: Calvin Smith's Diary," *Civil War Times, Illustrated* (April 1985), 28. Bearss, *Vicksburg*, 2: 630, claimed Barton ordered his men to fall back and abandon the crossing once he learned the rest of Pemberton's army was crossing Bakers Creek at the lower crossing. This is what Barton wrote in his report, and what Bearss cites as support for his observation. *OR* 24, pt. 2, 100. However, this cannot have been the case. Bowen was still waiting at the lower bridge for Loring's Division to cross. He was only forced away when McClernand's men moved west of the creek and then William Benton's brigade marched south to flank the lower ford. Therefore, if Barton was already gone by the time John Stevenson's Federals reached and crossed the upper bridge ahead of McClernand (as Obenchain and Reynolds both clearly claim), Barton's report on this point is a fabrication at worse, or a glaring error, at best. Either way, it is not true.

40. *OR* 24, pt. 1, 648.

41. *OR* 24, pt. 2, 108. The caisson and its limber that fell into the river belonged to the 3rd Maryland Artillery. They were recovered in 1964, together with 150 rounds of ammunition in three ammunition chests. Bearss, *Vicksburg*, 2: 631n.

42. *OR* 24, pt. 1, 648; *OR* 24, pt. 2, 108.

43. *OR* 24, pt. 2, 108, 143. The 6th Missouri Cavalry had been operating north of the railroad during the Champion Hill fight.

44. *OR* 24, pt. 1, 151, 718; *OR* 24, pt. 2, 16, 24, 108.

45. *OR* 24, pt. 2, 77.

46. *OR* 24, pt. 2, 112; Bearss, *Vicksburg*, 2: 631.

47. *OR* 24, pt. 2, 112, 117.

48. *OR* 24, pt. 2, 77; Greif, "Baker's Creek and Champion Hill," 351; Stephens, Recollections. Although the 31st Mississippi did not report any casualties, this does not mean the regiment did not suffer any wounded. It was common during the Civil War for men who were lightly injured to remain with their commands and not be reported as

wounded, and it is probable that these are exactly the sort of men to whom Lieutenant Colonel Stephens referred.

49. *OR* 24, pt. 2, 77, 90. A long-standing myth has been widely circulated and accepted by many to the effect that General Loring's decision to march down Bakers Creek and then, ultimately, to Jackson, Mississippi, was voluntary. In other words, he could have easily crossed over to the west side of the creek, but chose not to do so to spite Pemberton and get away from his command. One veteran claimed Loring said, "you can tell General Pemberton to go to hell and that I am going through to General Johnston." I have been unable to locate any reliable contemporary evidence to support such a claim that Loring's decision to march to Jackson was insubordinate in any respect. Indeed, it looks as though he labored long and hard to find a way to reach the Big Black, but was unable to do so.

50. *OR* 24, pt. 2, 77; Stephens, Recollections, 19; J.P. Cannon, "History of the 27th Reg. Alabama Volunteer Infantry C.S.A.," 27th Alabama Papers, ADAH, 41.

51. *OR*, pt. 2, 77, 85-86.

52. *OR* 24, pt. 2, 78; Stephens Recollections, 19-20. Winfield S. Featherston Report, November 10, 1867, Featherston Collection, UM. Featherston called Andrew Vaughan "Mr. Harvey" in his official report.

Chapter 12

1. William Clemans Memoirs, UIL.

2. Myers, "'Dear and Mutch Loved One,'" 54; Charles Hobbs, "Our May Party," Hobbs Letters, 99th IL Regimental File, VNMP; *OR* 24 pt. 2, 44; Hovey Manuscript, IU, 58.

3. I. V. Smith Personal Memoir, WHMC, UMC, 29.

4. Crummer, *With Grant at Fort Donelson, Shiloh, and Vicksburg*, 104-106; Ira Blanchard, "Recollections of the Civil War Service in the 20th Illinois Infantry, Co. H," Ira Blanchard Papers, ISHL, 86; Howard, *History of the 124th Regiment*, 100-101.

5. *OR* 24, pt. 2, 46, 117; David Dudley Carlton Diary, May 16, 1863; Eugene B. Harrison Diary, May 16, 1863, Civil War Miscellaneous Collection, USAMHI; Tucker, *The Confederacy's Fighting Chaplain*, 125.

6. Howard, *History of the 124th Regiment*, 98-99.

7. Crummer, *With Grant at Fort Donelson, Shiloh, and Vicksburg*, 104-106. The only Louisiana infantry at Champion Hill were in Colonel Scott's 12th regiment, and he was its only full colonel. The 45th Illinois was also on another part of the field. It is likely Crummer is mistaken as to their identity, though the story was clearly etched in his mind.

8. Albert C. Boals Diary, May 17, 1863, ISHL; Charles F. Vogel Diary, May 17, 1863, MDAH.

9. Noah Beecher Sharp Papers, IHS, 2; John Llewellyn, "Battle of Champion Hill, Miss.," *Confederate Veteran* 14, no. 8 (April 1906), 363. T. I. Pritchard was probably Corporal J. T. Pritchard of Company F, 36th Georgia.

10. Dana, *Recollections of the Civil War*, 54-55.

11. Longley, "Champion's Hill," 214.

12. Trimble, *History of the Ninety-Third Regiment*, 34-35.

13. *OR* 24, pt. 1, 776, 784; *OR* 24, pt. 2, 46; Voorhis, *The Life and Times*, 123.

14. Howard, *History of the 124th Regiment*, 101; William's, "The Battle of Champion's Hill," 210-211.

15. Augustus Sinks, "Four Years in Dixie," Augustus Sinks Journal, ISL, 37; Ira A. Batterton to his sister, May 27, 1863, Ira A. Batterton Papers, ISHL; Howard, *History of the 124th Regiment*, 97.

16. *OR* 24, pt. 2, 256.

17. William S. Forbes, "Recollections of General Grant During the Siege of Vicksburg," *MOLLUS-Pennsylvania* (np: nd), 2: 23; Winschel, "Champion Hill;" Grant, *Personal Memoirs*, 1: 306; Badeau, *Military History*, 273.

18. Grant, "A Boy's Experience," 94.

19. Dana, *Recollections of the Civil War*, 53-54.

20. Adams, *Indiana at Vicksburg*, 262-263.

21. Oldroyd, *A Soldier's Story*, 23; Howard, *History of the 124th Regiment*, 99; Voorhis, *The Life and Times*, 123.

22. Personal Memoirs of I. V. Smith, UMC, 29; A.G. Fraser to his sisters, November 14, 1863, A. G. Fraser Papers, MDAH.

23. William Clemans Memoirs, UIL, 9; William L. B. Jenney, "Personal Recollections of Vicksburg," *MOLLUS-Illinois* (Chicago: The Dial Press, 1899), 3: 260.

24. Sid Champion to his wife, May 18, 1863, Sydney S. Champion Papers, DU; Binford, "Recollections," Patrick H. Papers, MDAH, 42. These papers are also at the Kennesaw Mountain National Battlefield in Georgia. Ironically, the home survived the battle and subsequent occupation, only to be destroyed by fire later in the war.

25. Sarah F. Bigelow to Mrs. Woodson, June 16, 1863, Western Historical Manuscript Collection, UMC.

26. *OR* 24, pt. 2, 7-10; Livermore, *Numbers and Losses in the Civil War*, 99-100; Kountz, *Record of the Organizations Engaged in the Campaign, Siege, and Defense of Vicksburg*, 8-9, 12, 15-16, 18, 33-34, 39, 51, 58, 68; Bearss, *Vicksburg*, 2: 642-645.

27. *OR* 24, pt. 1, 53, 150-151. It is interesting to compare Grant's official report with his much more strident and anti-McClernand coverage in his memoirs.

28. *OR* 24, pt. 1, 151, 616; *OR* 24, pt. 2, 26. Losses are based upon official records and, when those are not available, the tables supplied in Bearss, *Vicksburg*, 2: 642-651.

29. *OR* 24, pt. 2, 16.

30. *OR* 24, pt. 2, 28.

31. *OR* 24, pt. 2, 16.

32. *OR* 24, pt. 2, 32, 37.

33. *OR* 24, pt. 2, 44-45, 46, 56, 37, 58.

34. *OR* 24, pt. 2, 50-51.

35. *OR* 24, pt. 1, 648-649.

36. *OR* 24, pt. 1, 648-649.

37. *OR* 24, pt. 1, 709.

38. *OR* 24, pt. 1, 718.

39. *OR* 24, pt. 1, 724-725.

40. *OR* 24, pt. 1, 733.

41. *OR* 24, pt. 1, 777.

42. Stone, *Memoir of George Boardman Boomer*, 252; http://www.rootsweb.com/~Ilschulyl/rosters/rosters10thMissouri.html.

43. Bearss, *Vicksburg*, 2: 646-651, and associated official records reports.

44. Bearss, *Vicksburg*, 2: 646, 648.

45. *OR* 24, pt. 1, 265.

46. *OR* 24, pt. 1, 94-95, 99-100; Lee, "The Campaign of Vicksburg," 45; Winschel, "The Guns at Champion Hill," 100.

47. *OR* 24, pt. 2, 109.

48. *OR* 24, pt. 2, 106-107.

49. *OR* 24, pt. 2, 100; Francis G. Obenchain to William T. Rigby, June 27, 1903, Letters and Papers Covering Organizations: Virginia (Botetourt Artillery), Memorial, Monument and Exposition Commission Records, MDAH.

50. *OR* 24, pt. 2, 103.

51. *OR* 24, pt. 2, 113, 115.

52. *OR* 24, pt. 2, 117.

53. *OR* 24, pt. 2, 78-79.

54. *OR* 24, pt. 2, pt. 3, 917.

55. *OR* 24, pt. 2, pt. 2, 92.

56. *OR* 24, pt. 2, 86, 88, 89.

57. Bearss, *Vicksburg*, 2: 643.

58. *OR* 24, pt. 2, 642-645, and associated official records reports.

59. Vicksburg *Evening Post*, March 19, 1936, Adams Mississippi Cavalry Regimental File, VNMP. A postwar newspaper reported Pemberton ordered Adams into Vicksburg, but he contacted Johnston who rescinded the order. This is doubtful because these communications could not have taken place within such a short span of time.

60. *OR* 24, pt. 1, 269.

Chapter 13

1. William Clemans Memoirs, UIL, 9; William L.B. Jenney, "Personal Recollections of Vicksburg," *MOLLUS-Illinois* (Chicago: The Dial Press, 1899), 3: 260.

2. James Wilson Journal, May 16, 1863, James Wilson Papers, LC; *OR* 24, pt. 1, 53.

3. *OR* 24, pt. 2, 60; Trimble, *History of the Ninety-Third Regiment*, 34.

4. Emma Balfour Diary, May 17, 1863, MDAH; Annie Louise Harris Broidrick, "A Recollection of Thirty Years Ago," Annie Louise Harris Broidrick Collection, UNC, 15.

5. *OR* 24, pt. 1, 266; Raab, *W. W. Loring*, 120; Winschel, *Triumph and Defeat*, 111.

6. *OR* 24, pt. 1, 266-267.

7. George R. Elliott Diaries, May 17, 1863, TSLA; *OR* 24, pt. 1, 266-267.

8. *OR* 24, pt. 1, 266-267. The Confederates had removed the *Dot*'s machinery.

9. Robert S. Shuey to his brother, May 18, 1863, John C. Pemberton Papers, NA.

10. *OR* 24, pt. 1, 53-54. The west bank was higher than the east bank.

11. *OR* 24, pt. 2, 132, 136; Bearss, *Vicksburg*, 2: 666.

12. *OR* 24, pt. 2, 136-137; Charles Boarman Cleveland, "With the Third Missouri Regiment," *Confederate Veteran*, 31, no. 1 (January 1923), 19.

13. *OR* 24, pt. 2, 128-143; pt. 1, 267.

14. George W. Gordon Diary, May 24, 1863, George Gordon Papers, USAMHI; *OR* 24, pt. 1, 267-268; Foster to his wife, June 20, 1863, Civil War Papers MDAH; Tucker, *Stonewall of the West*, 286.

15. John Jones to his parents, May 29, 1863, John Jones Papers, LC; *OR* 24, pt. 1, 267-268; Colby, "Bullets, Hardtack and Mud," 151; Winschel, "Champion Hill," 105.

16. Robert S. Shuey to his brother, May 18, 1863, John C. Pemberton Papers, NA.

17. *OR* 24, pt. 1, 268-269.

18. John Power Logan Diary, May 17, 1863, MDAH; *OR* 24, pt. 1, 268-269.

19. Lockett, "The Defense of Vicksburg," 488; J. T. Hogane, "Reminiscences of the Siege of Vicksburg," *SHSP*, 2, no. 4-5 (April-May 1883), 223.

20. *OR* 24, pt. 2, 73; Jasper N. Whiphers Diary, May 17, 1863, Alexander Roberts Papers, ISHL; William Clemans Paper, UIL, 9; Fiske, *The Mississippi Valley*, 240.

21. Grant, "A Boy's Experience," 94-95.

22. J. M. Love Diary, May 16, 1863, UM; Joseph Dill Alison Diary, May 17, 1863, UNC; John C. Taylor Diary, May 17, 1863, Taylor Family Papers, UV; James E. Payne, "General Pemberton and Vicksburg," *Confederate Veteran*, 36, no. 7 (July 1928), 247.

23. Emma Balfour Diary, May 17, 1863, MDAH; Thomas C. Skinner to "Hannah," May 20, 1863, U.S. Grant Papers, LC.

24. Charles A. Dana to Edwin Stanton, May 23, 1863, Charles A. Dana Papers, LC.

25. John Logan to his wife, July 5, 1863, John A. Logan Papers, LC; John Ford to his father, July 4, 1863, John Ford Letters, USAMHI; Charles Vanamburg to his father, July 4, 1863, Charles Vanamburg Papers, USAMHI; Logan H. Roots to "Mr. Hewett Kind Sir," July 24, 1863, Edwin C. Hewett Correspondence, UIL.

26. Howard Stevens to his uncle, July 21, 1863, Howard and Victor H. Stevens Letters, Gregory A. Cocco Collection, Harrisburg Civil War Roundtable Collection, USAMHI; C. J. Gill to his wife, July 4, 1863, C. J. Gill Letters, Letters and Diaries File, VNMP; William F. Schlag to D. C. Smith, July 10, 1863, D. C. Smith Papers, ISHL; S. H. M. Byers, *What I Saw in Dixie: Or Sixteen Months in Rebel Prisons* (Donsville, NY: Robbins and Poore, Printers, Express Printing House, 1868), 1.

27. Henry Steele Commager, ed., *The Blue and the Gray: The Story of the Civil War as Told by Participants*, 2 vols. (New York: Meridian, 1994), 2: 677.

28. Logan H. Roots to "Mr. Hewett Kind Sir," July 24, 1863, Edwin C. Hewett Correspondence, UIL.

Modern Photographic Gallery

All photos courtesy of the author

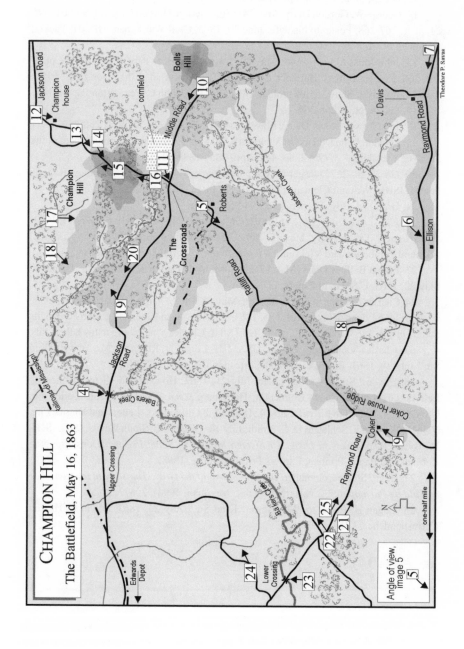

CHAMPION HILL
The Battlefield, May 16, 1863

1. *Port Gibson: The Shaiffer House* (see map, page 49). John Bowen's Confederates tried to stop U.S. Grant's advance into Mississippi near Port Gibson. The house is the only surviving structure on the battlefield. The Port Gibson fighting erupted here and swept past this point toward Magnolia Church on May 1, 1863.

2. *Port Gibson: Bruinsburg Road* (see map, page 56). Confederate Brig. Gen. Edward D. Tracy deployed his brigade on each side of the road pictured above. Peter Osterhaus's Federal division drove back the Southerners and killed Edward D. Tracy near this point.

3. *Battle of Raymond.* (see map, page 74). Federals of James McPherson's XVII Corps met the John Gregg's Confederate brigade south of Raymond along Fourteenmile Creek. The Federals established artillery positions on the ridge in the foreground of this photo (which looks north) while the battle raged in the creek bottomland below.

4. *Upper Bakers Creek Crossing.* This view looks south. The bridge stood where the mass of logs now rests. Pemberton crossed the creek here on May 15 on his way to Champion Hill. At the end of the battle, the Federals drove Seth Barton's men away from this area and cut off the Confederates from this escape route.

5. *The Ratliff Road.* This view looks south below the Roberts house, which Pemberton used as his headquarters during the battle. Bowen's Division held the high ground along the left before it was called north to the crossroads, where Bowen launched his dramatic counterattack. After he was defeated, many Confederates retreated along this route and then southwest along a country road to the lower crossing.

6. *The Ellison Property.* During the night of May 15, Pemberton made his headquarters along this road in the Ellison house. This view looks south across the road to where the house once stood. Pemberton's cavalry leader, Wirt Adams, advised Pemberton that the Federals were advancing west along the Raymond Road.

7. *The Raymond Road.* Two Federal divisions under A. J. Smith and Frank Blair marched along this stretch of the Raymond Road during their early morning advance to find Pemberton's army. This view looks west toward the J. Davis property. The original road has obviously been long out of use.

8. *The Raymond Road at Jackson Creek*. William. W. Loring's Division manned the ridge in the foreground to block the Federal advance across Jackson Creek. This view looks south toward the modern bridge across the creek, which is visible in the left distance. Loring eventually moved west to the Coker house ridge.

9. *The Coker House*. This deteriorating home, complete with cannonball holes, sits atop a commanding ridge that cuts across the old Raymond Road. Loring's infantry and artillery manned the ridge for much of the day. Federals from Smith's and Blair's divisions occupied it late in the day when Lloyd Tilghman mistakenly moved off it. He was killed by artillery firing from near this position. Standing on the south side of the house is Vicksburg National Military Park historian Terry Winschel (left), the park's Natural Resources Program Manager Kurt Foote (center), and the author (right).

10. *McClernand's Approach.* This view of the Middle Road and surrounding terrain was taken about one-half mile east of the vital crossroads. Except for the pavement, it is very similar to its 1863 appearance. Confederate skirmishers deployed here to delay John McClernand's two divisions under Peter Osterhaus and Eugene Carr.

11. *The Crossroads.* This view looks southwest across the Middle Road to the crossroads from what was the southwest corner of the cornfield. The Ratliff Road is visible in the upper left, running south. The Jackson Road entered in the foreground and turned sharply west, or to the right. This area changed hands three times during the fighting and was the key to the battlefield.

12. *Site of the Champion House.* This view looks southwest to where the Champion house once stood. U.S. Grant used the house as his headquarters during the battle. Surgeons also used it as a hospital. Federals formed in this vicinity to assault Champion Hill. Matilda Champion planted the large oak tree on right. Standing in what would have been the front walk are (from left to right), Vicksburg National Military Park Natural Resources Program Manager Kurt Foote, the author, and the park's historian, Terry Winschel.

13. *The Jackson Road looking south and climbing toward Champion Hill.* Federals of Hovey's division deployed astride this road between the Champion house and the hill. The highwater mark of Bowen's counterattack reached this area, where it was thrown back by Union reinforcements from Marcellus Crocker's division.

14. *Champion Hill*. Graveling rights to Champion Hill were sold during the 1930s. As a result, some thirty feet of the crest of the historic hill was quarried and used for constructing roads. The apex of Alfred Cumming's Confederate line was formed in this area. This photo, which looks southwest, shows the evidence of the excavation, as well as the present day crest of the hill.

15. *The crest of Champion Hill*. The modern day crest is some thirty feet lower than the original hill. This view looks north from behind Cumming's line of battle. Vicksburg National Military Park historian Terry Winschel (left), the author (middle), and the park's Natural Resources Program Manager, Kurt Foote (right), are seen here discussing the alignment of the right shank of Alfred Cumming's Confederate line just before the Federals attacked it.

16. *The Jackson Road between the crossroads and Champion Hill.* This view looks north toward Champion Hill. The crossroads is behind the photographer. The road climbs slowly up the southern slope of the hill. The Alabamans and Georgians under Stephen Lee and Alfred Cumming raced up this road to deploy on the crest to prevent the Federals from turning Pemberton's left flank. The "cornfield," through which both Slack and Green attacked, is now overgrown and on the right side of this image.

17. *Logan's assault, looking south.* John Logan's division attacked across this valley against Stephen Lee's Confederate brigade (Carter Stevenson's Division), which held the wooded ridge in the distance. The strength of Lee's defensive position is evident. The attack of Colonel Beck's 23rd Alabama against Rogers's artillery battery took place on the ground in the right center distance.

18. *John Stevenson's approach, looking southwest.* Stevenson's Federal brigade moved in this direction beyond the Confederate army's left flank. (There was no road here in 1863.) The flank attack cut off Pemberton's army from the upper crossing of Bakers Creek. Seth Barton's Georgians attacked toward the camera through the woods on the left hand side of the photograph.

19. *The Roberts cemetery on the Jackson road, facing northeast.* This cemetery holds graves that pre-dated the battle, but no participants mentioned the graveyard in their reports or letters. It was in this vicinty that Barton's artillery was overrun by Federals belonging to John Logan's division.

20. *The Jackson Road, facing west toward the upper crossing of Bakers Creek.* Carter Stevenson's defeated brigades fell back across this stretch of the road after being driven off the wooded ridge to the right. Abandoned long ago, the Jackson Road was a critical logistical artery for Pemberton's army. On the morning of the battle, his wagon train rolled over this route on its way back across the stream.

21. *The Coker House ridge from Cotton Hill, looking east.* Confederate batteries and Tilghman's infantry brigade manned Cotton Hill (foreground) to block a Federal advance along the Raymond Road and keep open the lower crossing of Bakers Creek—Pemberton's last route of escape. The roof of the Coker house can be seen in the clump of trees in the center distance.

22. *The lower Bridge Road cut, facing north from the Raymond Road.* Most of Pemberton's army made its escape on the evening of May 16 marching on this route (toward the camera) while elements of Loring's Divison held out as a rear guard a short distance to the east (Tilghman) and northeast (Featherston and Buford).

23. *The lower Bakers Creek crossing, looking north.* With the upper crossing in Federal hands, Pemberton's only route of escape was at this point. Tilghman's Brigade held back the enemy on the Raymond Road while most the balance of the army (except Loring's Division) crossed here on a new bridge and at the ford.

24. *West of Bakers Creek, looking northeast.* The Confederates were escaping west toward Vicksburg via the lower crossing of Bakers Creek when Federals flooded over the upper crossing. Stephen Lee's infantry moved in the direction you are looking, only to discover William Benton's brigade had turned south and was moving to cut the Raymond Road to Edwards Depot. This ultimately prevented Loring's Division from crossing and reuniting with Pemberton's army.

Big Black River Bridge. (This image is not keyed to a map.) Pemberton established a bridgehead on the east bank of the Big Black River, which Grant promptly attacked on May 17, driving its defenders into Vicksburg. Michael Lawler's brigade assaulted across the far right of this field and broke the Confederate front, which was located in the distant tree line. The railroad leading to the bridge is about one-quarter mile to the left on the far side of Highway 80, which can be seen on the left.

25. *Lloyd Tilghman monument on Cotton Hill, facing east.* Tilghman was directing artillery fire from this spot when a piece of shrapnel, fired from an artillery piece on the Coker House ridge, struck him in the chest. "He fell to the earth a corpse," remembered one eyewitness. Tilghman's sons dedicated the monument in 1907.

Blood stains and gravestones. Blood can still be seen on and under the Champion family dining table (top and middle images). Surgeons transformed the Champion house into a makeshift hospital, and operated on wounded men on Matilda Champion's dining room table. Sid Champion V kneels at Sid Champion I's grave. Matilda's husband survived the war but died within a few years. The family still owns much of the battlefield.

Bibliography

Abbreviations

Alabama Department of Archives and History—ADAH
Brown County Historical Society—BCHS
Cornell University—CU
Duke University—DU
Emory University—EU
Georgia Department of Archives and History—GDAH
Illinois State Historical Library—ISHL
University of Illinois—UIL
Indiana Historical Society—IHS
Indiana University—IU
Indiana State Library—ISL
State Historical Society of Iowa—SHSI
University of Iowa—UI
Kennesaw Mountain National Battlefield Park—KMNBP
Library of Congress—LC
Lincoln Memorial Shrine—LMS
Louisiana State University—LSU
University of Mississippi—UM
Mississippi Department of Archives and History—MDAH
Mississippi State University—MSU
University of Missouri-Columbia—UMC
University of Missouri-Rolla—UMR
Missouri Historical Society—MHS
Military Order of the Loyal Legion of the United States—MOLLUS
National Archives—NA
University of North Carolina—UNC
Ohio Historical Society—OHS
University of Southern Mississippi—USM
University of South Carolina—USC
Tennessee State Library and Archives—TSLA
United States Army Military History Institute—USAMHI
University of Virginia—UV
Vicksburg National Military Park—VNMP
University of Washington—UW

Official Publications

The War of the Rebellion: A Compilation of the Official Records of the Union and Confederate Armies. 128 vols. Washington D.C.: Government Printing Office, 1880-1901.

Manuscript Collections

Alabama Department of Archives and History, Montgomery
    F. K. Beck Papers
    Forty-sixth Alabama Infantry Papers
    Edmond W. Pettus Papers
    Thirtieth Alabama Infantry Papers
    Thirty-fifth Alabama Infantry Papers
    Twentieth Alabama Infantry Papers
    Twenty-seventh Alabama Infantry Papers
    Twenty-third Alabama Infantry Papers
    Waddell Battery Papers
    M.L. Woods Papers
Brown County Historical Society, New Ulm
    August Schilling Diary
Cornell University, Rare and Manuscript Collections, Ithaca
    Asa Fitch Papers
Duke University, Special Collections Library, Durham
    Sydney S. Champion Papers
    George Hoke Forney Papers
Emory University, Robert W. Woodruff Library, Atlanta
    William Brotherton Papers
Georgia Department of Archives and History, Atlanta
    Bible Records, Military Rosters and Reminiscences of Confederate Soldiers
    Warren H. Campbell Reminiscences
    W. H. H. Rogers, "The Flint Hill Grays"
    Joseph Bogle Reminiscences
    J. B. Childs Reminiscences
    William Thomas Daniel Letters
    George Thornton Fowler Letters and Papers
    James Russell Horn Letters
    J. M. Kulgar Reminiscences
Illinois State Historical Library, Springfield
    Ira A. Batterton Papers
    Ira Blanchard Papers
    Albert C. Boals Diary
    Nicholas C. Buswell Papers
    John P. Davis Papers
    John C. Dinsmore Papers
    Joseph Wilson Fifer Papers
    Joseph Forrest Papers
    D. G. and E. H. Ingraham Letters
    Edwin May Papers
    Arthur P. McCullough Diary
    J. W. Miller Papers
    Edwin W. and Ira A. Payne Letters
    David W. Poak Papers
    Rand Family Papers
    Alexander Roberts Papers
    D. C. Smith Papers
    Louis Trefftzs Papers
    Wallace-Dickey Family Papers

Indiana University, Lilly Library, Bloomington
    Alvin Hovey Collection
Indiana State Library, Indiana Division, Manuscripts Section, Indianapolis
    James S. Fogle Letters
    Louis W. Knobe Diary
    Daniel Roberts Letters
    Augustus Sinks Journal
    David C. Turnbull Papers
    Henry Watts Civil War Reminiscences
State Historical Society of Iowa, Iowa City
    William L. Cotton Letters
    Sewall S. Farwell Papers
    Samuel R. Mackrill Diary
    James Patterson Diary
    Shedd Family Papers
Kennesaw Mountain National Battlefield Park, Marietta
    Sydney S. Champion Papers
Library of Congress, Manuscripts Division, Washington D.C.
    Charles A. Dana Papers
    Charles Calvin Enslow Papers
    Manning F. Force Papers
    U.S. Grant Papers
    John Griffin Jones Papers
    John A. Logan Papers
    James M. McClintock Papers
    James B. McPherson Papers
    William F. Patterson Papers
    John C. Pemberton Papers
    Edwin M. Stanton Papers
    John Whitten Diary
    James H. Wilson Papers
Lincoln Memorial Shrine, A.K. Smiley Public Library, Redlands, CA
    Mortimer D. Leggett Papers
Louisiana State University, Special Collections Department, Baton Rouge
    Israel L. Adams Family Papers
    University of Mississippi, Archives and Special Collections, Oxford
    Lionel Baxter Collection
    Champion Hill Map
    Featherston Collection
    J. M. Love Diary
    William Terry Moore Reminiscences
    T. M. Weldon Hudson Papers
Mississippi Department of Archives and History, Jackson
    Record Group 9—Confederate Records
      31st Mississippi Records
      M. D. L. Stevens Recollections
      Withers Artillery Papers
    Record Group 12—Memorial, Monument and Exposition Commission Records
      Letters and Papers Covering Organizations: Miscellaneous—Georgia,
    Massachusetts, New Hampshire, and Rhode Island
      Letters and Papers Covering Organizations: Virginia (Botetourt Artillery)
      Emma Balfour Diary

Francis Marion Baxter Papers
Champion Hill Subject File
Champion Hill Battlefield Foundation, Inc. Subject File
Civil War Papers
William A. Drennan Papers
A. G. Fraser Papers
Patrick Henry Papers
George W. Modil Diaries
John Logan Power Diary
H. Clay Sharkey Papers
Charles F. Vogel Diary
Mississippi State University, Special Collections Department, Starkville
Gardner Collection
Isaac E. Hirsh Papers
Rufus Ward Papers
Missouri Historical Society, St. Louis
Alphabetical Files
Joel Strong Reminiscences
Civil War Collection
Theodore D. Fisher Diary
Thomas S. Hawley Papers
National Archives and Records Administration, Washington D.C.
Record Group 109
Confederate States Army Casualties: Lists and Narrative Reports 1861-1865
John C. Pemberton Papers
Carter L. Stevenson Papers
Record Group 393
General Orders Issued—13th Army Corps, Army of the Tennessee
Letters Sent—Logan's Division, 17th Army Corps, Army of the Tennessee
Letters Sent—13th Army Corps, Army of the Tennessee
Letters Sent—17th Army Corps, Army of the Tennessee
Letters Sent—Medical Department, 17th Army Corps, Army of the Tennessee
Special Orders Received—13th Army Corps, Army of the Tennessee
Ohio Historical Society, Columbus
James Field Letter
James H. Smith Letters
Theodore P. Savas Collection, El Dorado Hills, CA
Merrick J. Wald Diary
Tennessee State Library and Archives, Nashville
Brigham Family Papers
George R. Elliott Diaries
J. W. Harmon Memoirs
Robert Robb Diaries and Memoirs
Philip Roesch Diary
J. A. Turley Letters
United States Army Military History Institute, Manuscripts Department, Carlisle Barracks
Robert H. Carnahan Papers
Eugene A. Carr Papers
Civil War Miscellaneous Collection
Boucher Family Letters
Henry O. Dwight Papers
Winfield S. Featherston Papers

Eugene B. Harrison Diary
Israel M. Ritter Diary
Civil War Times Illustrated Collection
Lionel Baxter Collection
L. B. Claiborne Memoirs
Francis A. Dawes Diary
Robert M. Dihel Letters
John W. Ford Letters
Marcus O. Frost Letters
James K. Worthington Letters
George W. Gordon Papers
Harrisburg Civil War Roundtable Collection
Gregory A. Coco Collection
Howard and Victor H. Stevens Letters
William A. Ruyle Memoir
Rudolph Haerle Collection
Samuel P. Harrington Diary
Thomas R. Stone Collection
George Troop Letters
Squire and Chester Tuttle Collection
George Perry Letters
John C. Pemberton Papers
Charles Vanamburg Papers
University of Illinois, Illinois Historical Survey, Urbana-Champaign
David C. Carlton Diary
William Clemans Memoirs
George S. Durfee Correspondence
Edwin C. Hewett Correspondence
Edwin May Papers
Edward McGlynn Letters
Indiana Historical Society, Indianapolis
J. W. Egleston Diary
Richard Emerson Blair Letters
Gilbert H. Denny Letters
William Harper Letters
Thomas Marshall Letters
Charles A. McCutchan Letters
Ross-Kidwell Papers
Noah Beecher Sharp Papers
David Shockley Letters
Samuel E. Sneier Letter
Edward P. Stanfield Letters
Hubbard Trowbridge Thomas Letters
Aurelius Lyman Voorhis Journal
University of Iowa, Special Collections, Iowa City
Giauque Family Papers
Rigby Family Papers
University of Missouri-Columbia, Western Historical Manuscript Collection, Columbia,
Samuel Bassett Hamacher Letters
William F. Jones Papers
I. V. Smith Personal Memoirs
University of Missouri-Rolla, Western Historical Manuscript Collection, Rolla

Aquilla Standifird Diary
University of North Carolina, Southern Historical Collection, Chapel Hill
    Joseph Dill Alison Diary
    Annie Louise Harris Broidrick Collection
    J. F. H. Claiborne Papers
    Winfield S. Featherston Biographical File
    H. J. Reid, "The 22nd Mississippi Regiment"
    Clyde Hughes Papers
    Taylor Family Letters
    Samuel H. Lockett Papers
    Edward D. Seghers Account Book
University of South Carolina, The South Caroliniana Library, Columbia
    John Bannon Diary
University of Southern Mississippi, McCain Library and Archives, Hattiesburg
    Gore Civil War History Collection
    Milton W. Shaw Letter
University of Virginia, Special Collections Department, Alderman Library, Charlottesville
    Taylor Family Papers
University of Washington, University Libraries, Seattle
    Manning F. Force Papers
Vicksburg National Military Park, Vicksburg
    Letters and Diaries File
        C. J. Gill Letters
        W. M. Murray Diary
        Mortimer D. Leggett Papers
    Regimental Files
        Adams Mississippi Cavalry File
        W. O. Connor Letters—Cherokee Georgia Artillery File
        Charles A. Hobbs Letters and Diary - 99th Illinois File
        J. P. Lesslie Letters—Co. C, 4th Indiana Cavalry File
        George Nester Letters—1st Indiana Artillery File
        Francis G. Obenchain Letters—Botetourt Virginia Artillery File
        Israel M. Piper Diary—99th Illinois File
        Daniel Levi Roush Letters—99th Illinois File
        Lyman J. Shaw Diary—99th Illinois File

Newspapers

Cincinnati *Daily Gazette*, June 5, 1863
Jackson *Daily News*, May 24, 1984
Jacksonville (Alabama) *Republican*, August 15, 1863
Natchez *Daily Courier*, May 12, 1863
Natchez *Weekly Courier*, May 6, 1863
New Orleans *The Era*, May 5, 1863
New York *Daily Tribune*, November 21, 1886
New York *Herald*, July 29, 1863
New-York *Tribune*, May 19, 1863
St. Louis *Republican*, July 25, 1863
Vicksburg *Evening Post*, March 19, 1936

Printed Primary Sources

Adams, Henry C. *Indiana at Vicksburg*. Indianapolis: William B. Bradford, 1911.

Anderson, Ephraim McD. *Memoirs: Historical and Personal Including the Campaigns of the First Missouri Confederate Brigade*. St. Louis: Times Publishing Co., 1868.

Bevier, R. S. *History of the First and Second Missouri Confederate Brigades 1861-1865 and From Wakaruse to Appomattox, A Military Anagraph*. St. Louis: Bryan, Brand and Company, 1879.

"The Brave and True Capt. S. J. Ridley." *Confederate Veteran*, 2, no. 11 (November 1894): 343.

Brewer, George E. "The Defender of Vicksburg." *Confederate Veteran*, 22, no. 10 (October 1914): 457-459.

Byers, S. H. M. *What I Saw in Dixie: Or Sixteen Months in Rebel Prisons*. Donsville, NY: Robbins and Poore, Printers, Express Printing House, 1868.

———. "How Men Feel in Battle; Recollections of a Private at Champion Hills." *Annals of Iowa* 2, no. 6 (July 1896): 438-449.

———. *With Fire and Sword*. New York: The Neale Publishing Company, 1911.

———. "Some Recollections of Grant." *The Annals of the Civil War*. ed. Alexander Kelley McClure. New York: Da Capo Press, 1994.

Cadwallader, Sylvanus. *Three Years With Grant: As Recalled by War Correspondent Sylvanus Cadwallader*. ed. Benjamin P. Thomas. New York: Alfred A. Knopf, 1955.

Cheavens, Henry Martyn. "A Missouri Confederate in the Civil War: The Journal of Henry Martyn Cheavens, 1862-1863." ed. James G. Moss. *Missouri Historical Review*, 57, no. 1 (October 1962): 16-52.

Cleveland, Charles Boarman. "With the Third Missouri Regiment." *Confederate Veteran*, 31, no. 1 (January 1923): 18-20.

Colby, Carlos W. "Bulletts, Hardtack and Mud: A Soldier's View of the Vicksburg Campaign." ed. John S. Painter. *Journal of the West*, 4, no. 2 (April 1965): 129-168.

Commager, Henry Steele. *The Blue and the Gray: The Story of the Civil War As Told By Participants*. 2 vols. New York: Meridian, 1994.

Crummer, Wilbur F. *With Grant at Fort Donelson, Shiloh and Vicksburg: And an Appreciation of General U.S. Grant*. Oak Park: E.C. Crummer and Co., 1915.

Dana, Charles A. *Recollections of the Civil War: With the Leaders at Washington and in the Field in the Sixties*. New York: D. Appleton and Co., 1898.

Dinkins, James. "Witticisms of Soldiers." *Confederate Veteran*, 3, no. 9 (September 1895): 270-271.

Eggleston, E. T. "Scenes Where General Tilghman was Killed." *Confederate Veteran*, 1, no. 10 (October 1893): 296.

Elliott, Isaac H. *History of the Thirty-Third Regiment Illinois Veteran Volunteer Infantry in the Civil War, 22nd August, 1861, to 7th December, 1865*. Gibson City, IL: The Association, 1902.

Force, Manning F. "Personal Recollections of the Vicksburg Campaign." *MOLLUS-Ohio*. Cincinnati: Robert Clarke Company, 1888. 1: 293-309.

Foster, Tom. "Reminiscences of Vicksburg." *Confederate Veteran* 2, no. 8 (August 1894): 244.

Fremantle, James Arthur Lyon. *The Fremantle Diary: Being the Journal of Lieutenant Colonel James Arthur Lyon Fremantle, Coldstream Guards, on His Three Months in the Southern States*. ed. Walter Lord. Boston: Little, Brown and Company, 1954.

F. W. M. "Career and Fate of Gen. Lloyd Tilghman." *Confederate Veteran*, 1, no. 9 (September 1893): 274-275.

Gault, W. P. *Ohio at Vicksburg: Report of the Ohio Vicksburg Battlefield Commission*. n.p., 1906.

"General Lloyd Tilghman." *Confederate Veteran,* 18, no. 7 (July 1910): 318-319.

"General Stephen D. Lee, Commander in Chief U.C.V., Successor to Gen. John B. Gordon." *Confederate Veteran,* 12, no. 2 (February 1904): 53-54.

Goodloe, Alfred Theodore. *Confederate Echoes: A Voice From the South in the Days of Secession and of the Southern Confederacy.* Nashville: Publishing House of the M. E. Church, 1907.

Grant, Frederick D. "A Boy's Experience at Vicksburg." *MOLLUS-New York.* New York: D. D. Putnam's Sons, 1907. 3: 86-103.

Grant, Ulysses S. *The Personal Memoirs of Ulysses S. Grant.* 2 vols. New York: Charles L. Webster and Co., 1885-1886.

——. "The Vicksburg Campaign." *Battles and Leaders of the Civil War.* 4 vols. New York: Thomas Yoseloff, 1956. 3: 493-539.

Greif, J.V. "Baker's Creek and Champion Hill: What Abe Buford's Brigade and Others Did There." *Confederate Veteran,* 4, no. 10 (October 1896): 350-352.

Hall, Thomas O. "The Key to Vicksburg." *The Southern Bivouac,* 2, no. 9 (May 1884): 393-396.

Hays, E. Z., ed. *History of the Thirty-Second Regiment Ohio Veteran Volunteer Infantry.* Columbus, OH: Cott & Evans, Printers, 1896.

Hewett, Janet B., Suderow, Bryce A., and Trudeau, Noah Andre. *Supplement to the Official Records of the Union and Confederate Armies.* Wilmington: Broadfoot Publishing Company, 1994-.

Hicks, Henry G. "The Campaign and Capture of Vicksburg." *MOLLUS-Minnesota.* Minneapolis: Aug. Davis, Publisher, 1909. 6: 82-107.

Hogane, J.T. "Reminiscences of the Siege of Vicksburg." *Southern Historical Society Papers* 2, no. 4-5 (April-May 1883): 223-227.

Hopkins, Owen Johnston. *Under the Flag of the Nation: Diaries and Letters of a Yankee Volunteer in the Civil War,* ed. Otto F. Bond. Columbus: Ohio State University Press, 1961.

Howard, R.L. *History of the 124th Regiment Illinois Infantry Volunteers, Otherwise Known as the "Hundred and Two Dozen," From August, 1862, to August, 1865.* Springfield: H. W. Rokker, 1880.

Hubbell, Finley L. "Diary of Lieut. Col. Hubbell, of 3d Regiment Missouri Infantry, C.S.A." *The Land We Love,* 6, no. 2 (December 1868): 97-105.

Irwin, Samuel S. "Excerpts From the Diary of Samuel S. Irwin: July 5, 1863 - July 17, 1863." *Journal of Mississippi History,* 37 (February-November 1965): 390-394.

Jackson, Isaac. *Some of the Boys: The Civil War Letters of Isaac Jackson: 1862-1865.* ed. Joseph Orville Jackson. Carbondale: Southern Illinois University Press, 1960.

Jenney, William Lebanon. "With Sherman and Grant From Memphis to Chattanooga - A Reminisce." *MOLLUS-Illinois.* Chicago: Cozzens and Beaten Company, 1907. 4: 247-265.

Jenney, William L. B. "Personal Recollections of Vicksburg." *MOLLUS-Illinois.* Chicago: The Dial Press, 1899. 3: 247-265.

Johnston, Frank. "How Major Joseph W. Anderson was Killed." *Confederate Veteran,* 20, no. 10 (October 1912): 466.

Johnston, Joseph E. *Narrative of Military Operations, Directed During the Late War Between the States, by Joseph E. Johnston, General, C.S.A.* New York: D. Appleton and Co., 1874.

Johnston, Mary. "Dedication of a Bronze Tablet in Honor of Botetourt Battery." *Southern Historical Society Papers,* 35 (January-December 1907): 29-49.

Jones, Thomas B. *Complete History of the 46th Regiment Illinois Volunteer Infantry.* Freeport, IL: W. H. Wagner and Sons, 1907.

Lee, Stephen D. "The Campaign of Vicksburg, Mississippi, in 1863—From April 15 to

and Including the Battle of Champion Hills, or Baker's Creek, May 16, 1863."
Publications of the Mississippi Historical Society (Oxford: Mississippi Historical
Society, 1900), 3: 21-53.

"Lieutenant General S.D. Lee." *Confederate Veteran*, 2, no. 3 (March 1894): 70.

Llewellyn, James. "Battle of Champion Hill, Miss." *Confederate Veteran*, 14, no. 8 (April
1906: 363.

Lockett, S. H. "The Defense of Vicksburg." *Battles and Leaders of the Civil War*. 4 vols.
New York: Thomas Yoseloff, 1956, 3: 482-492.

Longley, Charles L. "Champion's Hill." *MOLLUS-Iowa*. Des Moines: Press of P.C.
Kenyon, 1893. 1: 208-214.

Manahan, T.A. "Letters From Veterans." *Confederate Veteran*, 2, no. 8 (August 1894):
227.

Memminger, R.W. "The Surrender of Vicksburg—A Defense of General Pemberton."
Southern Historical Society Papers, 12, nos. 7,8,9 (July-September 1884):
352-360.

Myers, John. "'Dear and Mutch Loved One'—An Iowan's Vicksburg Letters." ed. Edward
G. Longacre. *Annals of Iowa*, 43, no. 1 (Summer 1975): 49-61.

Oldroyd, Osborn H. *A Soldier's Story of the Siege of Vicksburg From the Diary of
Osborn H. Oldroyd*. Springfield: privately published, 1885.

Patteson, Ben. "The Yellow Hammer Flag." *Confederate Veteran*, 8, no. 5 (May 1900):
240-A.

Payne, James E. "General Pemberton and Vicksburg." *Confederate Veteran*, 36, no. 7
(July 1928): 247.

——. "Missouri Troops in the Vicksburg Campaign." *Confederate Veteran* 36, no. 9
(September 1928): 340-341.

Porter, David D. *Incidents and Anecdotes of the Civil War*. New York: F. Appleton and
Co., 1885.

Reynolds, A. H. "Vivid Experiences at Champion Hill, Miss." *Confederate Veteran*, 18,
no. 1 (January 1910): 21-22.

Riley, A. C. "Confederate Col. A.C. Riley, His Reports and Letters, Part II." ed. Riley
Bock. *Missouri Historical Review*, 85, no. 3 (April 1991): 264-287.

Ritter, W. L. "Sketch of the Third Battery of Maryland Artillery." *Southern Historical
Society Papers*, 10, no. 8-9 (August-September 1882): 392-401.

Russ, William A., ed. "The Vicksburg Campaign as Viewed by an Indiana Soldier."
Journal of Mississippi History, 19 (January-October 1957): 263-269.

Sanborn, John B. "The Campaign Against Vicksburg." *MOLLUS-Minnesota*. St. Paul:
St. Paul Book and Stationary Company, 1890. 2: 114-145.

——. *The Crisis at Champion's Hill: The Decisive Battle of the Civil War*. St. Paul: np, 1903.

Shelton, A. H. Letter to Editor. *Confederate Veteran*, 24, no. 6 (June 1916): 286.

Smith, Calvin. "We Can Hold Our Ground." ed. F.G. Carnes. *Civil War Times Illustrated*, 24,
no. 2 (April 1985): 24-31.

Sproul, T. B. "Letter." *Confederate Veteran* 2, no. 7 (July 1894): 199.

Stephenson, Jon. "Literal Hill of Death." *America's Civil War*, 4, no. 4 (November 1991):
23-29.

Stockwell, Elisha. *Private Elisha Stockwell, Jr. Sees the Civil War*. ed., Byron R. Abernathy.
Norman: University of Oklahoma Press, 1958.

Stone, Mary Amelia (Boomer), *Memoir of George Boardman Boomer*. Boston: Press of Geo.
C. Rand & Avery, 1864.

Strode, E. W. "Recollections of an Artilleryman." *Confederate Veteran*, 2, no. 12 (December
1894): 379.

Trigg, S. C. "Fighting Around Vicksburg." *Confederate Veteran*, 12, no. 3 (March 1904):
120.

Trimble, Harvey M. *History of the Ninety-Third Regiment Illinois Volunteer Infantry From Organization to Muster Out.* Chicago: The Blakely Printing Co., 1898.

Voorhis, Aurelius Lyman. *The Life and Times of Aurelius Lyman Voorhis.* ed. Jerry Voorhis. New York: Vantage Press, 1976.

Warmoth, Henry Clay. "The Vicksburg Diary of Henry Clay Warmoth: Part II (April 28, 1863-May 26, 1863)." ed. Paul H. Hass. *Journal of Mississippi History* 32, no. 1 (February 1970): 60-74.

Wells, W. Calvin. "Gen. John S. Bowen." *Confederate Veteran* 21, no. 12 (December 1913): 564.

Williams, T. J. "The Battle of Champion's Hill." *MOLLUS-Ohio.* Cincinnati: The Robert Clarke Company, 1903. 5: 204-212.

Secondary Sources

Allardice, Bruce S. *More Generals in Gray.* Baton Rouge: Louisiana State University Press, 1995.

Arnold, James R. *Grant Wins the War: Decision at Vicksburg.* New York: John Wiley & Sons, Inc., 1997.

Badeau, Adam. *Military History of Ulysses S. Grant, From April, 1861, to April, 1865.* 3 vols. New York: D. Appleton and Company, 1868-1881.

Ballard, Michael B. *Pemberton: A Biography.* Jackson: University Press of Mississippi, 1991.

Bearss, Edwin C. *The Vicksburg Campaign.* 3 vols. Dayton: Morningside House, Inc., 1985.

——, and Warren Grabau, *The Battle of Jackson, May 14, 1863* (Baltimore: Gateway Press, Inc., 1981).

Brieger, James F. *Hometown Mississippi.* np: np, 1980.

Carter, Samuel III. *The Final Fortress: The Campaign for Vicksburg, 1862-1863.* New York: St. Martin's Press, 1980.

Catton, Bruce. *Grant Moves South.* Boston: Little, Brown and Company, 1960.

Cole, Donald B. *The Presidency of Andrew Jackson.* Lawrence: University Press of Kansas, 1993.

Cooling, Benjamin F. *Forts Henry and Donelson: The Key to the Confederate Heartland.* Knoxville: University of Tennessee Press, 1987.

Cozzens, Peter. *The Darkest Days of the War: The Battles of Iuka and Corinth.* Chapel Hill: The University of North Carolina Press, 1997.

Daniel, Larry. *Shiloh: The Battle That Changed the War.* New York: Simon and Shuster, 1997.

——, and Bock, Riley. *Island No. 10: Struggle For the Mississippi Valley.* Tuscaloosa: The University of Alabama Press, 1996.

Davis, William C. *Jefferson Davis: The Man and His Hour: A Biography.* New York: Harper Collins, 1991.

——. *The Confederate General.* 6 vols. Harrisburg: National Historical Society, 1991.

Dowdey, Clifford. *The Seven Days: The Emergence of Lee* (Boston: Little, Brown and Co., 1964.

Dubay, Robert W. *John Jones Pettus: Mississippi Fire-Eater: His Life and Times 1813-1867.* Jackson: University Press of Mississippi, 1975.

Fiske, John. *The Mississippi Valley in the Civil War.* New York: Houghton, Mifflin and Company, 1900.

Foote, Shelby. *The Civil War: A Narrative.* New York: Random House, 1958-1974.

Fuller, J.F.C. *The Generalship of Ulysses S. Grant.* Bloomington: Indiana University

Press, 1958.

Grabau, Warren E. *Ninety-Eight Days: A Geographer's View of the Vicksburg Campaign*. Knoxville: The University of Tennessee Press, 2000.

Greene, Francis V. *The Mississippi*. New York: Charles Scribner's Sons, 1882.

Hattaway, Herman. *General Stephen D. Lee*. Jackson: University Press of Mississippi, 1976.

———, and Jones, Archer. *How the North Won: A Military History of the   Civil War*. Urbana: University of Illinois Press, 1983.

Hearn, Chester G. *The Capture of New Orleans, 1862*. Baton Rouge: Louisiana State University Press, 1995.

Hess, Earl J. *Pickett's Charge: The Last Attack at Gettysburg*. Chapel Hill: The University of North Carolina Press, 2001.

Hewitt, Lawrence L. *Port Hudson: Confederate Bastion on the Mississippi*. Baton Rouge: Louisiana State University Press, 1987.

Howell, H. Grady. *Going to Meet the Yankees: A History of the "Bloody Sixth" Mississippi Infantry, C.S.A*. Jackson: Chickasaw Bayou Press, 1981.

———. *To Live and Die in Dixie: A History of the Third Mississippi Infantry, C.S.A*. Jackson: Chickasaw Bayou Press, 1991.

Johnston, Frank. "The Vicksburg Campaign." *Publications of the Mississippi Historical Society* (Oxford: Mississippi Historical Society, 1909), 10: 63-90.

Jones, Archer. *Confederate Strategy From Shiloh to Vicksburg*. Baton Rouge: Louisiana State University Press, 1991.

Jones, James Pickett. *Blackjack: John A. Logan and Southern Illinois in the Civil War Era*. Carbondale: Southern Illinois University Press, 1995.

Kelley, William Milner. "A History of the Thirtieth Alabama Volunteers (Infantry) Confederate States Army." *Alabama Historical Quarterly*, 9, no. 1 (Spring 1947): 115-167.

Kiper, Richard L. *Major General John Alexander McClernand: Politician in Uniform*. Kent: The Kent State University Press, 1999.

Kountz, John S. *Record of the Organizations Engaged in the Campaign, Siege, and Defense of Vicksburg*. Washington, DC: Government Printing Office, 1901.

Livermore, Thomas L. *Numbers & Losses in the Civil War in America: 1861-65*. Millwood: Kraus Reprint Co., 1977.

Lorimer, William A. *History of Mercer County, With Biographical Sketches*. Chicago: Munsell Pub. Co., 1903.

Markham, Jerald H. *The Botetourt Artillery*. Lynchburg: H.E. Howard, 1986.

Marszalek, John F. *Sherman: A Soldier's Passion for Order*. New York: Free Press, 1993.

McFeely, William S. *Grant: A Biography*. New York: W.W. Norton & Company, 1981.

McPherson, James M. *Crossroads of Freedom: Antietam: The Battle that Changed the Course of the Civil War*. New York: Oxford University Press, 2002.

Miers, Earl S. *The Web of Victory: Grant at Vicksburg*. Baton Rouge: Louisiana State University Press, 1955.

Newton, Steven. *Joseph E. Johnston and the Defense of Richmond*. Lawrence: University Press of Kansas, 1998.

Northrop, L.B. "A Hill of Death." *Civil War Times Illustrated* 30, no. 2 (May/June 1991): 24-26, 28-33, 62-67.

Parrish, William E. *Frank Blair: Lincoln's Conservative*. Columbia: University of Missouri Press, 1998.

Pemberton, John C. *Pemberton: Defender of Vicksburg*. Chapel Hill: The University of North Carolina Press, 1942.

Raab, James W. *W.W. Loring: Florida's Forgotten General*. Manhattan, KS: Sunflower

University Press, 1996.

Rhea, Gordon. *Cold Harbor: Grant and Lee, May 26-June 3, 1864*. Baton Rouge: Louisiana State University Press, 2002.

Roland, Dunbar. *Military History of Mississippi, 1803-1898* (Spartanburg: The Reprint Company, 1988.

Shea, William L. *Vicksburg Is the Key: The Struggle for the Mississippi River*, with Terrence J. Winschel. Lincoln: University of Nebraska Press, 2003.

Simpson, Brooks D. *Ulysses S. Grant: Triumph over Adversity, 1822-1865*. Boston: Houghton Mifflin Co., 2000.

Stanbery, Jim. "A Failure of Command: The Confederate Loss of Vicksburg." *Civil War Regiments: A Journal of the American Civil War* 2, no., 1 (1992): 36-68.

Stanchak, John E. "A Mississippi Home Stands, A Silent Witness to a Battle." *Civil War Times Illustrated*, 30, no. 2 (May/June 1991): 19-19, 21, 60-61.

Symonds, Craig L. *Joseph E. Johnston: A Civil War Biography*. New York: W.W. Norton and Co., 1992.

Tucker, Phillip Thomas. *The Confederacy's Fighting Chaplain: Father John B. Bannon*. Tuscaloosa: The University of Alabama Press, 1982.

——. *The South's Finest: The First Missouri Confederate Brigade From Pea Ridge to Vicksburg*. Shippenburg: White Mane Publishing Company, Inc, 1993.

——. *Westerners in Gray: The Men and Missions of the Elite Fifth Missouri Infantry Regiment*. Jefferson, NC: McFarland & Company, Inc., Publishers, 1995.

——. *The Forgotten Stonewall of the West: Major General John Stevens Bowen*. Macon: Mercer University Press, 1997.

Warner, Ezra J. *Generals in Blue: Lives of the Union Commanders*. Baton Rouge: Louisiana State University Press, 1964.

Welsh, Jack D. *Medical Histories of Confederate Generals*. Kent: Kent State University Press, 1995.

Williams, Rick. *Chicago's Battery Boys: The Chicago Mercantile Battery in the American Civil War*. New York: Savas Beatie, 2004.

Winschel, Terrence J. "Champion Hill: A Battlefield Guide." Tour Guide Brochure, 1989.

——. "The Guns at Champion Hill (Part II)." *Journal of Confederate History,* 6 (1990): 94-105.

——. "To Rescue Gibraltar: John Walker's Texas Division and Its Expedition to Relieve Fortress Vicksburg." *Civil War Regiments: A Journal of the American Civil War*, 3, no., 3 (1993): 33-58.

——. *Vicksburg: Fall of the Confederate Gibraltar*. Abilene: McWhiney Foundation Press, 1999.

——. *Vicksburg Is the Key: The Struggle for the Mississippi River*, with William L. Shea. Lincoln: University of Nebraska Press, 2003.

——. *Triumph and Defeat: The Vicksburg Campaign*. Mason City: Savas Publishing Company, 1999; Savas Beatie LLC, 2004.

——. "Fighting Politician: John A. McClernand." In *Grant's Lieutenants: From Cairo to Vicksburg*, ed. Steven E. Woodworth, 129-150. Lawrence: University Press of Kansas, 2001.

Woodworth, Stephen E. *Jefferson Davis and His Generals: The Failure of Confederate Command in the West*. Lawrence: University Press of Kansas, 1990.

——, ed. *Leadership and Command in the American Civil War* (Campbell: Savas Woodbury, 1996.

——, ed. *Grant's Lieutenants: From Cairo to Vicksburg*. Lawrence: University Press of Kansas, 2001.

INDEX